Answering Kennedy's Call

Pioneering the Peace Corps in the Philippines

EDITORS: PARKER W. BORG, MAUREEN J. CARROLL,
PATRICIA MACDERMOT KASDAN, STEPHEN W. WELLS

A PEACE CORPS WRITERS BOOK

An imprint of Peace Corps Worldwide.

A PEACE CORPS WRITERS BOOK

An imprint of Peace Corps Worldwide.

PEACE CORPS WRITERS EDITION, MARCH 2011

Copyright © 2011 by Parker W. Borg, Maureen J. Carroll, Patricia MacDermott Kasdan, and Stephen W. Wells. All rights reserved. Printed in the United States of America by Peace Corps Writers of Oakland, California, a component of PeaceCorpsWorldwide.org. No part of this book may be used or reproduced in any manner whatsoever without written permission except in the case of brief quotations contained in critical articles or reviews.

Library of Congress Control Number: 2010943323.

John Halloran's Essay, "A Wedding in Samar" is an excerpt from his posthumous book by the same name, published in 2011 by Puzzlebook Press.

Ravelo Argamaso's essay, "Lipoma of the Hand—a Story of Candelaria," is excerpted from an article by the same name from the *International Journal for Plastic and Reconstructive Surgery*, 1984.

Edited by Parker W. Borg, Maureen J. Carroll, Patricia MacDermott Kasdan, and Stephen W. Wells.

For more information, contact peacecorpsworldwide@gmail.com.

Peace Corps Writers and the Peace Corps Writers colophon are trademarks of PeaceCorpsWorldwide.org.

ISBN 978-1-935925-01-9

1. United States—Foreign Relations—1961–1963, 2. Peace Corps, 3. Philippines.

First edition

Maps by Parker W. Borg
Cover classroom photo by H.A. Figueras, Black Star.
All other photos in the book were provided by essay writers from their personal collections.

We dedicate this book to the Filipinos who welcomed us into their workplaces, homes and hearts and who taught us many important life lessons. We also honor the memory of our fellow volunteers who did not live long enough to celebrate this remarkable milestone of the 50th anniversary of the Peace Corps and of our service.

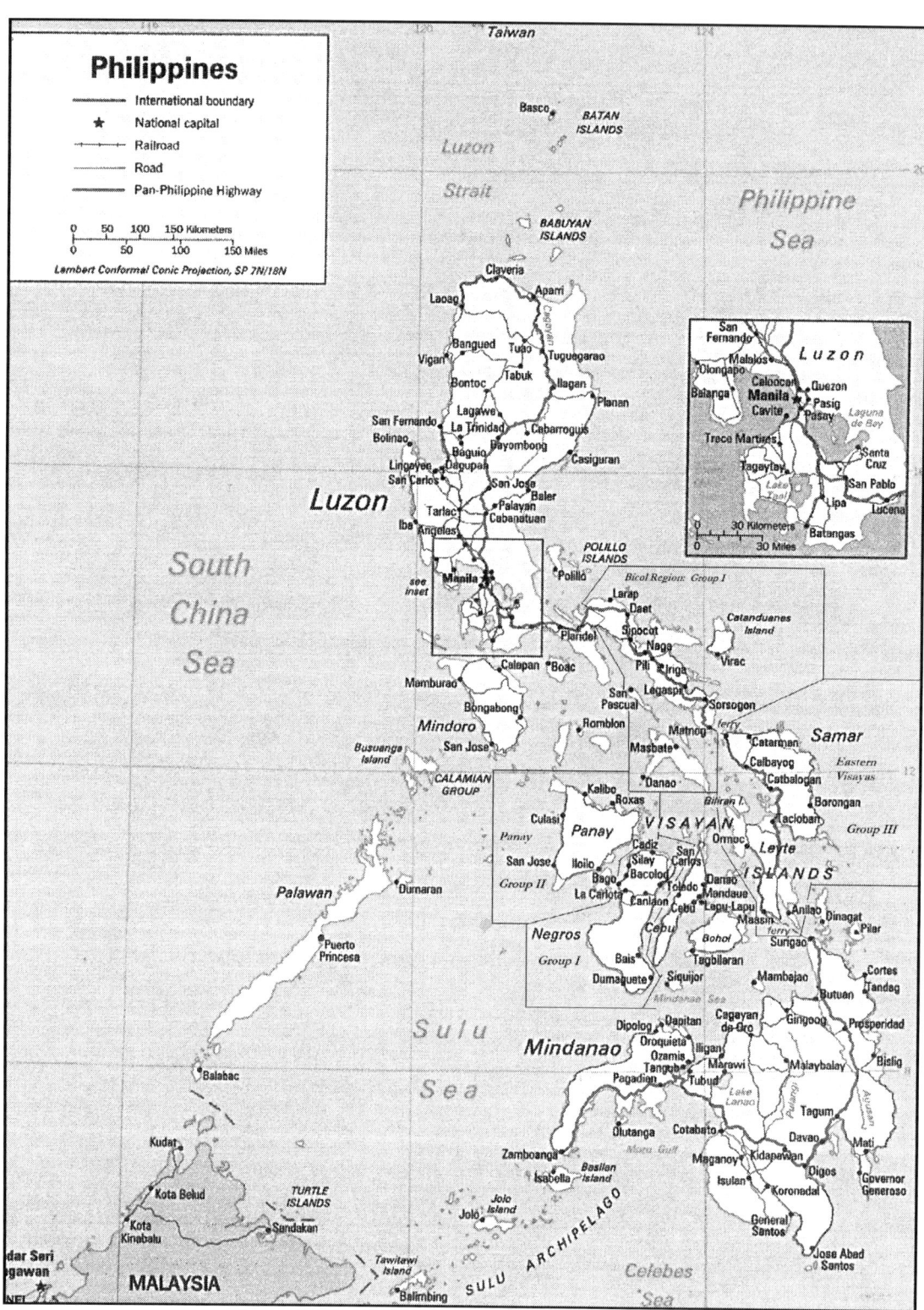

Table of Contents

Introduction 1

The Beginnings of the Peace Corps in the Philippines 4

Philippines I

Emery Bontrager, *The Accidental Volunteer*. 15
Parker Borg, *Images of Revolution and Reality* 19
Bruce Campbell, *A Place of Being* 29
Tom Carlton, *Son of a Kwan* 36
Maureen J. Carroll, *Not for Girls Like You: A Jersey Girl's Journey* 39
Leonel "Lone" Castillo, *An Hispanic American in the Philippines* 49
Don Cecchi, *Rosemary Clooney, Bing Crosby, the Philippines and Me* 52
Judith Cridler Claire, *Final Score* 63
Marjorie Donnelly Clarke, *A Paradoxical Experience* 65
Kathryn "Judy" Conway, *From Indifference to Commitment* 68
Margo Heineman Daniels and Pera Daniels, *Once Upon a Time in a Land so Far Away* 72
Dolores Ducommun, *My One and Only True Home* 81
Mike Forman, *Volunteer and See What Happens* 85
Richard Gilbert, *The World's Worst Peace Corps Volunteer* 95
Marianne Gould, *Life at The End of the Road...and Beyond* 100
Hans C. Groot, *Returning "Home"* 104
Martha Allshouse Hull, *Belafonte to the Rescue* 108
Martin Hurwitz, *Undeterred* 113
Ellen Brindle Jeronimo, *Fifty Years—Are You Kidding?* 118
Mary Baker Johnson, *A Life Changing Experience* 120
Pat Joslyn Johnson, *Scholarships, Seminars and Salingogon* 125
Dave King, *Adjusting to Peace Corps Life* 129
Rayna Larson, *Life of a Wife—Volunteer Style* 133
Stan Mazaroff, *Roads Worth Taking; Risks Worth Remembering* 144
Sally Pierce McCandless, *Letters Home* 150
Ray McEachern, *The Time of My Life* 153
Barbara Bassett McIver, *Some Old, Old Memories* 158
Warren McNeely, *What I Took Away from San Jose* 162
Ray Meyer, *On Becoming a Peace Corpz* 164
Jerry Mullins, *A Grand Adventure: A Peace Corps Memoir* 166
Pat Nash, *Mission Sunday* 170
Phil Nicholas, *Languages and Love: My Peace Corps Experience* 174
Lee Ann Justice Pelea, *An American Life in the Albay Town of Tiwi* 176
Ron Peters, *Taking My Uncle's Advice* 183
Dave Pierson, *Delayed Contribution* 190
Beth Sorenson Plummer, *Sketches from the Philippines* 192
Karen Long Santos, *A Lifelong Adventure Launched by the Peace Corps* 198

Nancy Jeffers Schmidt, *An Unforgettable Journey* ... 207
Brenda Brown Schoonover, *On Being an American* ... 214
Clair Whiting Sharpless, *On Being a Teacher's Aide in a Rural Barrio* ... 219
Tom Sharpless, *Teaching Science in the Philippines* ... 224
Claire Horan Smith, *Remembering Gini* ... 228
Ann Snuggs, *Joining the Peace Corps Twice* ... 232
John Stickler, *The PCV Who Wasn't There* ... 237
Charlotte Hough Stocek, *Remembering Life in a Small Filipino Village* ... 241
Stu Taylor, *Finding A Role in Rural Albay* ... 246
Ralph Thomas, *Reflections on a Peace Corps Life in the Visayas and Mindanao* ... 250
Anne Wilson, *Fifty Years of Hindsight* ... 255
Evelyn Mittman Wrin, *Milaor Memories* ... 263
Deane Wylie, *Life Beyond California* ... 267
Duncan Yaggy, *Innocents Abroad* ... 270

Philippines II
Joan Aragone, *Thank You, President Kennedy* ... 279
William Austin, *Carabao Bill* ... 284
Phyllis Smith Baer, *Precious Time Warp* ... 286
Linda Cover Bigelow, *The Adventure Continues* ... 291
Marthlu Bledsoe, *Lessons* ... 294
Philip Bloom, *As I Remember—Days in the Peace Corps* ... 298
Sylvia Boecker, *Peace Corps Is Powerful* ... 300
Al Bradford, *Peace Corps Stories* ... 304
Nancy Dunetz, *Colossal Chutzpah* ... 308
Lila Gardner, *The Onwacan (The Awakening)* ... 311
Phyllis Clemensen Halton, *Engaging the World* ... 315
Richard Holtzman, *My Peace Corps Journey* ... 320
Patricia MacDermot Kasdan, *Tasting Rice* ... 323
Tom Kincaid, *A Philippine Journey Renewed* ... 329
Hazel Land, *Immersion* ... 334
Owen Maher, *Reaching Out* ... 337
Lenny Mirin, *Notes on a Few Days in Sara, Iloilo and Washington, D.C.* ... 339
Harvey (Zvi) November, *Abing November Remembers* ... 343
Anne LaBarre O'Connor, *A Charmed Life* ... 345
Linda Henry Perron, *What the Peace Corps Meant to Me* ... 347
Eric Peterson, *Diin ka makadto?* ... 349
Jerry Poznak, *Three Filipinos and Me* ... 352
Eliot Putnam, *A Guest in Another Culture* ... 357
Janet Everett Putnam, *Just What the Doctor Ordered* ... 362
Nick Royal, *The Peace Corps and Me* ... 365
Frances McDonald Santos de Dios, *Memories of Rural Life on Panay* ... 368
John Schweitzer, *Did My Peace Corps Experience Make a Difference?* ... 371
Martha Spencer, *Double the Challenge* ... 374
Susan Thompson, *Ah, Memories...* ... 376

Patricia Toalson, *Peace Corps Philippines: Important and Hard* 379
Bob Tyler, *The Nipa People* 382
Carl Valentine, *Peace Corps Reflections* 384
David Ziegenhagen, *David's Peace Corps Adventure* 386

Philippines III
Steve Wells, *Outward Bound* 391
Jonathan Epstein, *Ordinary Happiness* 399
Douglas Foley, *The Good Old PC Days and a Life Well Spent* 401
Sunshine Gibbs, *The Human Connection* 406
Wayne Guise, *Why Can't We Be More Like Them?* 408
John Halloran, *Samar Memories* 411
Fred Knoth, *Peace Corps English Fluency Projects in the Philippines: Then and Now* 417
Kathy Hannan Rohan, *A Day in the Life of a Peace Corps Volunteer* 423
Ruth Kesselring Royal, *Two Peace Corps Vignettes* 424
Charles Terry, *Proud to Be a (Lower Case) "Peace Corps Pioneer"* 428
Steve Wells, *"I Thought You Were One of Us"—Achieving Fluency in the Language* 433
Alexandra York, *Little Charlie Joins the Peace Corps* 438

Staff
Larry Fuchs, *The Peace Corps Philippines: Big Ideals and Big Adjustments* 446
Bill and Jay Warren, *The Magical Years* 453
Lawrence C. Howard, *A Sense of Belonging* 456
Harvey Pressman, *Winging It for Peace?* 459
Charles Dey, *An Unintended Consequence* 463
Aniceto "Annie" Gison Bontrager, *The Job of My Life* 465
Bert Pumento, *A Priceless Opportunity* 468

Filipinos' Perspectives
Vladimir Velasco, *Looking Back to a Life Changing Month* 472
Susan Carlton, *The Paracaleño Perspective* 475
Gloria Rada, *Memories from Camarines Sur 1961-63* 477
Emma Perfecto, *Letter to a Volunteer's Mother* 479
Remedios Sierra, *Excerpts from Letters* 482
Freddy Hernandez, *Tribute to an American Peace Corps Volunteer* 483
Ravelo V. Armagaso, *Lipoma of the Hand—A Story of Candalaria* 486

Supporting Material
Map of the Philippines vi
Map of the Bicol Provinces 12
Map of the Island of Negros Provinces 14
Map of the Panay Provinces 278
Map of the Eastern Visayas 390
Glossary 489
Volunteer Name Lists 493

THE WHITE HOUSE
WASHINGTON

May 22, 1961

Dear Peace Corps Volunteer:

    I want to congratulate you for being among the first to volunteer for service in the Peace Corps. As you know, you are now eligible to take the Peace Corps Entrance Examination on May 27 or June 5.

    Nations in Latin America, Southeast Asia and Africa have already indicated their interest in having Peace Corps Volunteers serve with them. In the months ahead agreements with these nations will be concluded and Peace Corps projects announced. Once you qualify as a Volunteer you will be eligible for these undertakings.

    I was gratified to learn of the many capable people who have applied to serve in the Peace Corps and of the wide range of skills you represent. I hope that those of you who are chosen will carry your mission to these lands in such a way as to demonstrate the desire of Americans from all walks of life to be of service. The success or failure of the Peace Corps may well be determined by how well our first Volunteers live up to these high ideals.

    I wish you the best of good fortune in your Peace Corps tests.

Sincerely,

John Kennedy

Introduction

Now the trumpet summons us again—not as a call to bear arms, though arms we need; not as a call to battle, though embattled we are—but a call to bear the burden of a long twilight struggle, year in and year out, "rejoicing in hope, patient in tribulation"—a struggle against the common enemies of man: tyranny, poverty, disease, and war itself.

Can we forge against these enemies a grand and global alliance, North and South, East and West, that can assure a more fruitful life for all mankind? Will you join in that historic effort?

In the long history of the world, only a few generations have been granted the role of defending freedom in its hour of maximum danger. I do not shrink from this responsibility—I welcome it. I do not believe that any of us would exchange places with any other people or any other generation. The energy, the faith, the devotion which we bring to this endeavor will light our country and all who serve it—and the glow from that fire can truly light the world.

And so, my fellow Americans: ask not what your country can do for you—ask what you can do for your country."

—JOHN F. KENNEDY, January 20, 1961

To this day, the above excerpt from John F. Kennedy's inaugural address stirs the imagination of Americans and moves many to action. Within six weeks of the speech the new President signed an Executive Order founding the Peace Corps—an agency whose staff and volunteers took to heart his call to ask what they could do for their country to battle the "enemies of man"—particularly the enemies of poverty and disease. Thousands of Americans volunteered for the Peace Corps. The writers and editors of this book were among the first to be selected for service in the Philippines, the first Peace Corps country in Asia and one of the initial 13 countries that invited Peace Corps volunteers. This book is a collection of their stories about being among the first in what has turned out to be one of President Kennedy's greatest legacies.

Three factors set the program in the Philippines apart from others during the first years of the Peace Corps' existence. First, it was the largest program in the world, absorbing 25 percent of all volunteers at the beginning. Second, all volunteers in the first years were assigned to be "teacher's aides." After training and arriving at their posts, it became clear that neither the volunteers nor the local school officials had a clear or consistent understanding what that role meant. This made it all the more challenging for volunteers in their work and for staff in their administration and evaluation, prompting Larry Fuchs, the first director of the program, later to call the position a "non-job."[1] And third, the Philippine program occurred in a nation that only 15 years earlier had become independent of the United States, which had acquired the Philippines in 1898 in its single effort at establishing an imperialist colonial empire. This gave the program a distinctly different political and social dynamic from that in the other early Peace Corps countries.

---

[1] "The 'non-job'" is the title of Chapter II of his book about the early days of the Peace Corps in the Philippines. See Lawrence Fuchs, *Those Peculiar Americans*, (New York, Meredith Press, 1967).

As the fiftieth anniversary of the establishment of the Peace Corps approached, the editors of this volume speculated that the recollections of their fellow pioneer volunteers in the Philippines would not only be interesting to share with each other and their families after so many years, but could also serve as an archival record of the Peace Corps during its first years.

The editors attempted to contact all former volunteers, who had joined the Peace Corps for the Philippines project in 1961—all members of Philippines Groups I, II, and III. Each was invited to submit an essay which explained their motivation for joining the Peace Corps; their thoughts about the training programs, their interpretation of the job as an educational aide; their life and interactions in the communities of their assignment; their impressions of the Philippines in the 1960s; their continuing connections with their communities, Filipinos, and the Peace Corps; and the impact of the Peace Corps experience on their lives. This list of topics was intended as suggestions for topics that might be covered rather than an outline that everyone had to follow.

Of the 233 volunteers who entered the program in 1961, the organizers were able to establish contact with 170 people, a reasonably high percentage given deaths and lost addresses over the intervening years. Of this number ninety-five submitted essays. In addition, this volume includes the reminiscences of seven former members of the staff of Peace Corps/Philippines from these first years plus statements from about a half dozen Filipinos who had become acquainted with the early volunteers and recorded their observations, in some cases many years ago.

In messages covering their submissions, some former volunteers wrote about approaching the task enthusiastically; others about becoming energized after old letters, photos, and diaries jogged their memories about events they hadn't considered for decades. Of those who declined to participate one or two wrote that they had tried to craft an essay, but found the process too emotional to finish; several claimed they were too busy with life's other business to take the time; and the others ignored the invitation for unknown reasons.

Each essay tells a unique story and shows the diversity of experiences that most of us did not realize about each other at the time because we assumed that others were coping in the same ways that we were. Despite the different approach taken by each volunteer, many common themes come through the essays.

When President Kennedy proclaimed a "New Frontier" and talked of passing the torch to a new generation, it's important to recall that we were living in a different America, one emerging from the social patterns of the 1950s. On the domestic front, these had been the "Leave It to Beaver" years of stay-at-home moms, limited career opportunities for women, the first years of school desegregation, the growing civil rights movement, and the ubiquitous draft as a key feature in the life of all males after the age of eighteen. Internationally, we were seized by the global communist threat, the decolonization in Africa and Asia, and the negative image of Americans abroad popularized by *The Ugly American*.[2] When the Peace Corps began in 1961, the big issues that defined the decade—the sexual revolution, the widespread use of hallucinatory drugs, the first appearance of the Beatles in the US, the protests against the Vietnam War, and the Civil Rights Act—were still a few years off.

The essays invariably cite the importance of Kennedy's words as a primary inspiration for joining the Peace Corps, but frequently noted other factors—seeking adventure and foreign travel, escaping from unexciting jobs, moving beyond the patterns of segregated America, and hoping for an alternative to military service. The essays further illustrate how Peace Corps ser-

---

[2]William J. Lederer and Eugene Burdick, *The Ugly American* (New York: W.W. Norton, 1958).

vice forever changed the lives of many former volunteers, providing them a new outlook on other cultures and pushing them into careers that they might never have previously contemplated—particularly in the public sector.

The prospective volunteers who arrived at the training programs for the Philippines represented a broad cross section of America. They came from big cities, small towns and farms from across the country; they included a rainbow of ethnic and religious backgrounds; they represented the range of American higher educational institutions and held degrees in a wide array of subjects beyond education; and they claimed political outlooks that were both liberal and conservative. For many of the volunteers, this was their first interaction with anybody outside the narrow community where they had grown up or gone to college. Many of the essays comment on these positive first encounters with their fellow Americans of different backgrounds. By the end of the tours in the Philippines the essays give the sense that the bonding that occurred through the common Peace Corps experience was stronger than all the factors that previously separated the group.

Upon arriving in the Philippines and taking up their jobs in their communities, the volunteers came face-to-face with the reality of life in the rural Philippines. While Peace Corps volunteers all over the world faced cultures and customs different from those at home, several features were uniquely Filipino: the rural customs and culture that had been shaped more significantly by the 400 years of Spanish colonial rule than by the more recent and relatively short forty-five years of American rule after 1901; the harsh memories of the Japanese occupation during WWII that were alive after 15 years; and the contrastingly fond recollections that Filipinos had for the Americans as liberators, permitting the volunteers prolonged celebrity status.

The goodwill towards Americans was sufficiently strong in most rural Filipino communities that it mattered little what the volunteers might be doing. The combination of the vague "education aide" job title, the local goodwill, and the overwhelming Filipino hospitality presented a challenge to volunteers. They could relax and enjoy themselves or they could try to find something to do. It was a question of "being" vs. "doing." Rural Filipinos were often content with the volunteers merely being present at functions, while most of the volunteers felt they had to be doing something, building something, or achieving some objective. Many volunteers learned to combine their achievement focus with the patience needed to sit through endless speeches, take *merienda* (snacks) several times during a morning or an afternoon, or practice folk dances endlessly during school hours in preparation for an upcoming fiesta. Sorting out "what to do" provides a common theme for many of the essays.

Most of the volunteers were single and in their early to mid-twenties, prime years for finding mates and settling into married life. While rural Filipino custom required chaperones whenever males and females might find themselves alone and females to travel with companions anytime they ventured away from their homes, romance was not uncommon among the volunteers or between volunteers and Filipinos. Many of the essays tell the stories of cross cultural courtships and weddings that blended American and Filipino customs.

Reflecting back after nearly fifty years, many of the essays discuss the former volunteers continuing connections to the Philippines, the ways the Peace Corps service influenced their lives, and the lessons learned they learned as volunteers and applied in subsequent years.

The Editors
October 14, 2010

The Beginnings of the Peace Corps in the Philippines

Taking on a Towering Task

"We're going to be 'education aides,' not teachers! What does that mean?" This was the first question many of us asked as we were getting ready to join the Peace Corps and go to the Philippines in 1961. Since none of the training staff at Penn State that summer seemed to have a much better idea about what we might be doing, they provided the group the basics of elementary education. No sooner had the first group of these future 'aides' finished their training than a second group of prospective volunteers arrived to take their places. By January 1962, the first two groups had both arrived in the Philippines and a third group of some 50 volunteers had begun similar training. By June 20, 1962, four groups of volunteers were on the job in the Philippines as education aides and training had begun for Groups V and VI. What was going on? Why was the US flooding the Philippines with so many volunteers before it was clear what an 'educational aide' might be and whether this was a viable activity?

***

Excitement about the idea of the Peace Corps had filled the air in the weeks before and after John F. Kennedy's 1961 inauguration. The press, student groups, labor unions, voluntary organizations and foundations all had responded enthusiastically to the initial proposal. Despite his speeches and pronouncements, the President, however, is said to have had doubts about this new form of national service. As a way to flesh out and get a handle on the vision that was capturing popular opinion, the President asked his brother-in-law and close advisor, Sargent Shriver, to develop a plan for what might come next.[1]

Among the many ideas to emerge about the Peace Corps during these early days was one put forward by Warren Wiggins, an official with the International Cooperation Administration (the predecessor of the Agency for International Development). On February 1, 1961, two weeks after the inauguration, Wiggins circulated a paper titled *A Towering Task*, with an aim to "stimulate thought" about the proposal. The question in Wiggins' mind was not whether the Peace Corps should be established, but its scope and timing. He pointed out that most proposals argued for small pilot projects that could be gradually expanded if they were successful. These proposals argued for a safe approach: a few initial projects, a small number of volunteers, and no great expectations about results, but with the advantage that such an approach would avoid "a fiasco" during the early days when success would be important for political reasons.

Wiggins argued that a slow and steady approach would be a mistake: a small program could fail as easily as a big one, a small program would make little difference in the world at large or on American society, and a small program would be an inadequate response to the growing demand for service opportunities among American youth. Rather than starting with a program of one or two thousand volunteers in the first year, Wiggins proposed a "quantum

---

[1] Karen Schwarz, *What You Can Do for Your Country*. (New York: William Morrow and Company, 1991), pp. 30-1.

jump" in the first 12-18 months to 5-10,000 volunteers with a plan to grow in a few years to 30,000 volunteers and possibly higher. The question for him then became how could the Peace Corps implement such a massive program in a short period of time?[2]

As an illustration of how a "5,000-youth, one-country program" might work, Wiggins picked English teaching in the Philippines as his single example. He argued that large numbers of American volunteers could teach English because the volunteers would all possess a common level of skill and would be recognized from the beginning for their competence. The Philippines would be a good target country because English was "not only the medium of instruction in the public schools but also the official language of government, trade and commerce." Wiggins concluded his argument for a large program in the Philippines by noting that the country's history, the existing rudimentary English skills, the demand for English, and the institutional capacity of the educational system would permit the absorption of large numbers of American youth.[3]

Four days after Wiggins issued his paper, Sargent Shriver read it in the middle of the night. Shriver dispatched a wire on February 5, which Wiggins received at 3 am, telling him to bring 15 copies to a planning meeting the following morning at 10 am. At the end of the meeting, the planners were in agreement that Wiggins' paper should be the basis for the plan to launch the Peace Corps on a bold scale.[4] Thus, *A Towering Task* was the "pivotal founding" document in the establishment of the Peace Corps.[5] At Shriver's request, Wiggins dropped everything and began working for him full time. Shriver reported back to the President that contrary to the views of some of his advisors, the Peace Corps "should be of significant size and launched immediately."[6] The President signed the Executive Order creating the Peace Corps on March 1, 1961 and shortly thereafter named Shriver the first Director.

Many factors, some not specifically cited by Wiggins, made the Philippines an ideal target for a large Peace Corps presence. Most Filipinos were aware of the story about an early boatload of American teachers known as Thomasites who had arrived at the beginning of the Twentieth Century to launch the country's English based educational system. Filipinos throughout the country had many positive recent experiences with Americans. They remembered that General Douglas MacArthur had kept his promise and returned to liberate the country from the Japanese in 1944, independence from the US had been achieved in 1946 without armed struggle, and the US had assisted in the repression of the Communist movement in the early 1950s. Although some nationalists occasionally displayed hostility toward the US because of its military bases at Subic Bay, Cavite, and Clark Field, the historic good will plus a large economic assistance program and a favorable quota for the import of Philippine sugar ensured that relations between the two nations remained strong.

---

[2]Warren Wiggins. "A Towering Task," Draft Paper of February 1, 1961. (Peace Corps Digital Archives—Collection of Speeches, Essays, and Letters, 34 pages). See pp. 1-11. William Josephson is also credited with writing this paper and becoming one of the founding leaders of the early Peace Corps, but only Wiggins' name appears on the version in the Archives.

[3]Warren Wiggins, pp. 12-25.

[4]"Who's Who in Washington: Profile of Warren Wiggins," *The Volunteer* (Vol. 1, No. 5, May 1962), p. 4.

[5]As noted in the Peace Corps Digital Library, where Wiggin's "A Towering Task" can be accessed.

[6]Schwarz, p. 30.

The first discussions with Philippine officials about a Peace Corps program led to the early realization that while the Philippines would welcome English language support, the country already had an excess number of teachers. The original concept had to be modified. While Wiggin's document spelled out how American volunteers might work in six classes a day, it also "made absolutely clear that *no* Philippine teacher will be made unemployed as a consequence of this program."[7] As a result, the concept of the "education aide" evolved.

The project profile for the Philippines Peace Corps program, which circulated before the training program began, stated:

> PROJECT DESCRIPTION: To improve the quality of the English spoken in the rural areas of the Philippines, to help Filipino teachers of rural elementary schools learn to speak better English and gain greater understanding of scientific principles, to raise teaching standards in both English and science, Peace Corps volunteers will be assigned as educational aides on Filipino teaching staffs in rural elementary schools in four major regions of the Philippines. Educational aides will supplement, not replace, Filipino teachers.[8]

Dr. Lawrence Fuchs, the Dean of Faculty at Brandeis University, was named the first Director of Peace Corps Philippines (officially known as the Peace Corps Representative) in August 1961. On September 26, after he'd been in the Philippines for three weeks, he addressed an open letter to all the trainees at Penn State about the warm welcome he had received from Filipino officials and his first days with fellow staff members Bill Warren and Paul Hare who were also on duty. Noting that some Philippine leaders were critical that the project was not adequately focused on promoting economic and technical growth, he explained that accordingly "the Volunteers will be available in the schools to help with science and math as much as English and that Volunteers will also be free to participate in a wide range of community projects…"[9] Science and math were now on an equal footing with English and the door was open for community development.

The Philippine program became one of the early Peace Corps projects, but it was not the first to enter training or arrive overseas. The programs for Ghana, Tanganyika and Colombia had begun their training activities two to three weeks before the first group of Philippine volunteers arrived at Penn State on July 29, 1961. Training for Philippines I ended on September 14, 1961, the day of one of the key votes in the Congress on the Peace Corps legislation and one week before the President signed it into law. When the first 128 Philippines volunteers arrived at Manila Airport on October 12, volunteers had already arrived

---

[7] Wiggins, p. 23. The report envisioned a five-year program for volunteers to be teaching English. Concurrently, US economic assistance was intended to provide training in the US for the upgrading of the English language skills among Filipino teachers so that the Peace Corps program could be phased out. While the AID mission never established this massive teacher training program, the Peace Corps began shifting out of the elementary schools and into the teacher training institutes in the Philippines in the mid-1960s.

[8] "Project Profile III. The Philippines." (Undated handout from Peace Corps Washington from the summer of 1961). This was probably sent as a descriptive document to all volunteers selected for training for the Philippine project. A follow-up "Peace Corps Profiles," by Peace Corps/Washington, outlining the first nine global Peace Corps projects and issued 1 November 1961 described the Philippines program in almost identical words.

[9] Fuchs, Lawrence H. Letter sent to all Penn State Trainees on September 26, 1961.

in five other countries. Though not the earliest program, Peace Corps Philippines quickly established itself as the largest program. By June 20, 1962, there were 1051 volunteers on the ground in 18 countries: 272 of them (or 25 % of the total number) were in the Philippines. Another 1838 prospective volunteers were in training for 28 countries. Among this group, 282 (of 15 % of the total) were slated to go to the Philippines.[10]

After his two years as Director, Larry Fuchs wrote that the most striking feature of the Philippine program was its size. By the middle of 1963, nine waves of volunteers had begun their jobs, about 600 of whom were education aides and 22 community development workers. He continued, "For nearly a year, about a quarter of all Peace Corps Volunteers were serving in the Philippines." Fuchs noted three other striking features about the program: first, volunteers by the end of 1962 were scattered in 400 locations throughout the archipelago, some more than 12 hours by bus from the nearest other Peace Corps household; second, most of the volunteers were assigned as educational aides, "jobs which had not previously existed;" and third, the Philippines long and extensive history with the United States set it apart from other countries where volunteers were serving.[11] While the total numbers of volunteers in the Philippines never reached the level suggested by Wiggins in his report, the project in the Philippines was large and based from the beginning on his English teaching proposal.

Over the years more than 200,000 Americans have become Peace Corps volunteers, serving in 139 countries. The Peace Corps Website states that 8,000 volunteers have served in the Philippines since 1961. Peace Corps suspended the Philippine program in 1990 because of the threat from Communist rebels, but started it up again in 1992. The activities of Peace Corps Philippines have changed over the years, but education remains a prominent part of the program. In the middle of 2010 there were 130-140 volunteers in the education project with plans to add another 100 in 2011.[12] The project is described on the website in terms that are not too different from the project in 1961:

> Volunteers are assigned to primary and secondary schools as resource teachers for English, math, science, Information and Communication Technology (ICT), and special education. They help Filipino teachers improve English language fluency and introduce new teaching methods. At universities, Volunteers teach classes and work with student teachers and staff to prepare new teachers. Volunteers help improve the quality of learning by enhancing school libraries and developing low-cost instructional materials. They organize teacher-training programs to provide professional development for Filipino teachers.[13]

---

[10] *Peace Corps 1st Annual Report to Congress* for the Fiscal Year Ended June 30, 1962. According to this report, the first volunteers arrived overseas in the following order: Ghana (51 PCVs on 08/30/61); Santa Lucia (15 PCVs on 09/08/61); Colombia (about 50 PCVs on 09/08/61); Nigeria (39 PCVs on 09/26/61); and Tanganyika (35 PCV's on 09/30/61). This report listed incorrectly, however, the beginning of the training dates for the Philippine program as July 13 and therefore may be erroneous for the dates of some of the other listed programs.

[11] Lawrence H. Fuchs, "Philippines," *Peace Corps Volunteer* (Vol. I, No. 8, June 1963), pp. 10-13.

[12] According to a message from the current Director Peace Corps Philippines to Maureen Carroll in the summer of 2010.

[13] The Peace Corps Website [http://www.peacecorps.gov/index.fm?shell=learn.wherepc.asia.philippines]. Other projects in the Philippines include youth, the environment, and business development.

The Training in 1961 to Become Education Aides

The core training for the first Philippine groups took place far from the reality of Southeast Asia at Penn State in the mountains of central Pennsylvania. Group I began its program there in late July 1961 with six days of classes per week from 8 am in the morning until 8:20 in the evenings with breaks for lunch and dinner. Each day was broken up classroom-style into 75-minute sessions for courses in American studies, Philippine studies, English, science, math, and Peace Corps orientation. Afternoon sessions included discussion groups and cultural activities, including square dancing, both so that we could better represent America. Psychological evaluations of each volunteer's suitability for service were important parts of the initial training, but it was never explained what might be the criteria for the selection of volunteers. Group II was also told that an important selection measure would be the questionnaire in which volunteers noted the names of fellow volunteers they would like as housemates—the more mentions, the greater suitability.

The topics for discussion groups at Penn State included such subjects as "Communism: what's its appeal" and "Is co-existence with communism possible?"[14] While such topics were explained as essential components of the training so that volunteers could discuss American foreign policy with the leftists they might encounter overseas, this political training was equally importantly as a sop to conservatives in the Congress and around the country who were concerned that left leaning radicals were the joining the new organization in large numbers.

One member of Philippines Group I became a particular target of conservative concern. When it became known that 23-year-old Charles Kamen, a trainee from Miami, Florida, had dared to laugh out loud during a Rotary Club presentation in December 1960 of the anti-Communist film, *Operation Abolition* (produced by the House Un-American Affairs Committee or HUAC about student protests against a session they held in San Francisco), several members of Congress protested to Sargent Shriver, noting that leftists and beatniks were becoming part of the new organization; they demanded that Kamen be terminated. While Kamen was permitted to complete his training, he ultimately did not receive an invitation to go to the Philippines, much to the consternation of his fellow trainees in Group I. In addition to the anti-communism training, an added result of the Kamen incident was the requirement that all volunteers were required to take a "loyalty oath."[15]

Most of the males in Group II began their training by attending a special Outward Bound School that had been set up in Puerto Rico for the Peace Corps. Afterwards they joined the females from their group at Penn State for a program similar to that of the Group I volunteers. By December 1961, when Group III began training, it had been determined that all Philippine volunteers, males and females, should be graduates of the Outward Bound program before they arrived at Penn State.

---

[14] As listed on a handout for discussion during the week of September 4-10, 1961.

[15] There is a good discussion of the Kamen incident in Gerard T. Rice, *The Bold Experiment: JFK's Peace Corps* (University of Notre Dame Press, Notre Dame, Indiana, 1985) pp. 85-89.

Following a short leave in the US, each group of volunteers arrived in the Philippines for in-country training. Groups I and II headed for the University of the Philippines (UP) College of Agriculture at Los Baños for six weeks of orientation. This training program consisted of Tagalog language instruction for a few hours every morning, followed by demonstrations on the teaching of English and science; lectures on Philippine history; sociology, and culture; and visits to schools and communities in the area. Group III did its in-country training at the UP Main Campus in Diliman, Quezon City. Group III also spent part of their training time gaining classroom experience by doing student teaching at a nearby elementary school under the supervision of UP trainer/educators.

One central message that emerged early in the training program and stuck with most of the volunteers was the importance of "rolling with the punches." The term originated in the training at Penn State, but it became the byword for what do in cases of adversity. As many essays note, there were frequent opportunities to follow this guidance, even though the expression was not always verbalized.

Going into the Provinces

Each of the first three groups of volunteers went to a separate region in the central part of the Philippines. None of these first volunteers was assigned initially to the greater Manila area, to communities near US military bases, to the remote mountainous areas of the north, or to the conflicted Muslim/Christian areas in the south. During the course of the first two years, some volunteers transferred to these areas, either because of changes in assignment or to serve as Volunteer Leaders planning for and working with subsequent Peace Corps groups. At the beginning, however, all volunteers in the first three groups had the distinction of being the first Peace Corps volunteer in a particular community, almost all of which were smaller towns and barrios in the Catholic heartland of the country.

Groups I, II, and III were assigned to 15 provinces in four areas—the Bicol, Negros, Panay, and the Eastern Visayas—each of which boasted distinct regional characteristics. About three quarters of the volunteers from Group I went to the Bicol Region (which consisted of the southeastern end of the island of Luzon and several nearby islands), an area characterized by occasional volcanoes, rolling hills, and numerous broad valleys, where the economy was based on small scale rice farming and ocean fishing. The Bicol also produced small quantities of coconuts for the commercial production of copra and abaca for Manila hemp. The other 25 percent of the Group I volunteers went to the island of Negros, the nation's most important sugar cane producing region, where large haciendas and sugar centrals were fixtures of the landscape and the distinctions between the wealthy class of planters and large communities of laborers were fixtures of social life. All but three of the volunteers from Group II[16] were assigned to the island of Panay, which has been the second most important rice producing area in the country and is also major source of fish from both the ocean and fishponds. The volunteers in group III were all assigned to the two Eastern Visayan islands of Leyte and Samar, both of which can be characterized as hilly (except for one valley in northeast Leyte), thickly forested and relatively lightly populated with economies based on rice farming and some commercial production of abaca and coconuts.

---

[16] The three volunteers from Group II were assigned to the island of Negros.

Finding a Role as Education Aides

While Sargent Shriver may have selected the model of *A Towering Task* to launch Peace Corps quickly and on a massive scale, all volunteers in the Philippines faced a daunting task of their own as outsiders trying to find a role for themselves in small towns and barrios where neither they nor their hosts knew what they were supposed to be doing. Some might have characterized this search as a personal "towering task,"—if they had known about the history of the program.

As the essays explain, the role as an education aide presented a challenge to almost everyone. Although the Bureau of Public Schools issued a document with dozens of suggested general and specific activities for volunteers as educational aides,[17] it was never clear how widely it circulated, especially among the more remote schools in the region. The PC Manila staff was stretched so thin that there was little time to supervise everyone's daily activities. Leaders selected from among the volunteers theoretically were supposed to guide others in their regions, but they were usually too busy with their own schools, future planning, or administrative details to offer much supervision.

In response to an inquiry from Sargent Shriver in 2002 about the Peace Corps in the Philippines during the 1961-63 years, Larry Fuchs wrote in May of that year:

> Because our project was misconceived in the first place, it was saved only by the remarkable ingenuity of volunteers. I could not answer the question (about the role) put to me on July 5, 1962 in a letter… We were stuck with the concept of a volunteer aide. … How, in the end, (the letter had asked) would we be able to speak of an accomplishment, since there was no specific accomplishment being planned? … So, there was a need for improvisation which, in a way, fit with the overall administration of the Peace Corps. Sarge Shriver was one of the great improvisational and inspirational leaders of our time. One had the feeling that as Peace Corps director (we called it "representative" in those days) one could stumble, but in the end, Sarge would back creative, improvisational leadership where it was necessary—and it certainly was in Peace Corps Philippines…[18]

During the summer months of school vacation, April and May, all volunteers were required to find summer projects. These projects included camps, health projects, community development activities, radio programming, and training for newly arrived volunteers. Some found projects in areas near their places of assignment, but most found them elsewhere in the country. More than a few volunteers changed their assignments at the end of the summer holiday either to schools in other parts of the country or to associated non-educational projects. This gave their essays two distinct sections in the essays they wrote: before and after the summer break. Whatever happened at the end of the holiday, most volunteers viewed the summer experience favorably—and some recalled these summer activities to the exclusion of what they had done during the previous school year.

---

[17]Bureau of Public Schools, Department of Education, Republic of the Philippines, "Administration and Supervision of the Peace Corps Volunteers in the Philippines." An undated document that circulated in about November 1961 included 12 general functions and 24 possible specific duties.

[18]Fuchs, Larry. "Thoughts on the Peace Corps in the Philippines: Notes Sent to Sarge Shriver, May 2002." Unpublished letter.

Reflections

Did the program in the Philippines succeed? The Peace Corps Act of 1961 specified a purpose and three goals: which direct the agency to this day:

To promote world peace and friendship by
1. Helping the peoples of interested countries to meet their needs for trained manpower;
2. Helping to promote a better understanding of the American people on the part of the peoples served;
3. Helping to promote a better understanding of other peoples on the part of the American people.[19]

When reflecting on their personal experiences, most of the volunteers focused on the first objective, meeting Philippine needs for trained manpower. Since there were no specific objectives and no measurable guidelines for the job as teacher's aides, many concluded that this would be impossible to determine, but most were skeptical. Some wrote in their essays about individual cases where they thought they'd achieved a breakthrough, but nobody sang praises of the education aide program as conceived. The more common reaction was that service in the Philippines had achieved it greatest success in providing a new image of Americans to rural Filipinos and making the individual volunteer a better citizen of the world—the second and third goals of the Peace Corps, but ones that some may have forgotten, if in fact they ever knew about the three objectives.

Some volunteers extended for a third year either as volunteers or volunteer leaders. Others married Filipinos and remained in the Philippines for a period of years. Of the volunteers who returned to the US, many went immediately into graduate school. When choosing jobs either immediately after returning or after additional schooling, most selected work in the public sector—teaching, medicine, social work, and diplomacy. In almost every case, the Peace Corps experience in the Philippines had a profound impact on the way they subsequently interacted with the world.

Fifty years later many of the volunteers have retained their strong connections with the Philippines. A few have made the Philippines their residence. Several make visits almost every year or so to stay connected with family members. Others have returned once or twice over the years. Whatever the current connection with the Philippines might be, a large number of the former volunteers have found that the cross cultural communication skills they picked up in the Philippines have permitted them to interact with greater ease with other cultures elsewhere in the world and similarly within the US.

The bottom line is that each of the stories tells of a unique experience by a young American following a vague job outline and interacting with a Filipino community during the idealistic early days of the Kennedy Presidency. While these Americans generally worked hard to succeed in the roles they envisioned for themselves, equal credit is probably due to those Filipinos in each community who provided the welcoming acceptance and patience that permitted this undefined program to become a successful people-to-people exchange.

Parker W. Borg
October 14, 2010

---

[19] Peace Corps Act of 1961 (PL 87-293 of September 22, 1961).

Philippines I

July 29, 1961—Arrival at Penn State for training

October 12, 1961—Arrival in the Philippines for training at Los Baños

December 1961—Arrival in Bicol & Negros

June 1963—Completion of Peace Corps service

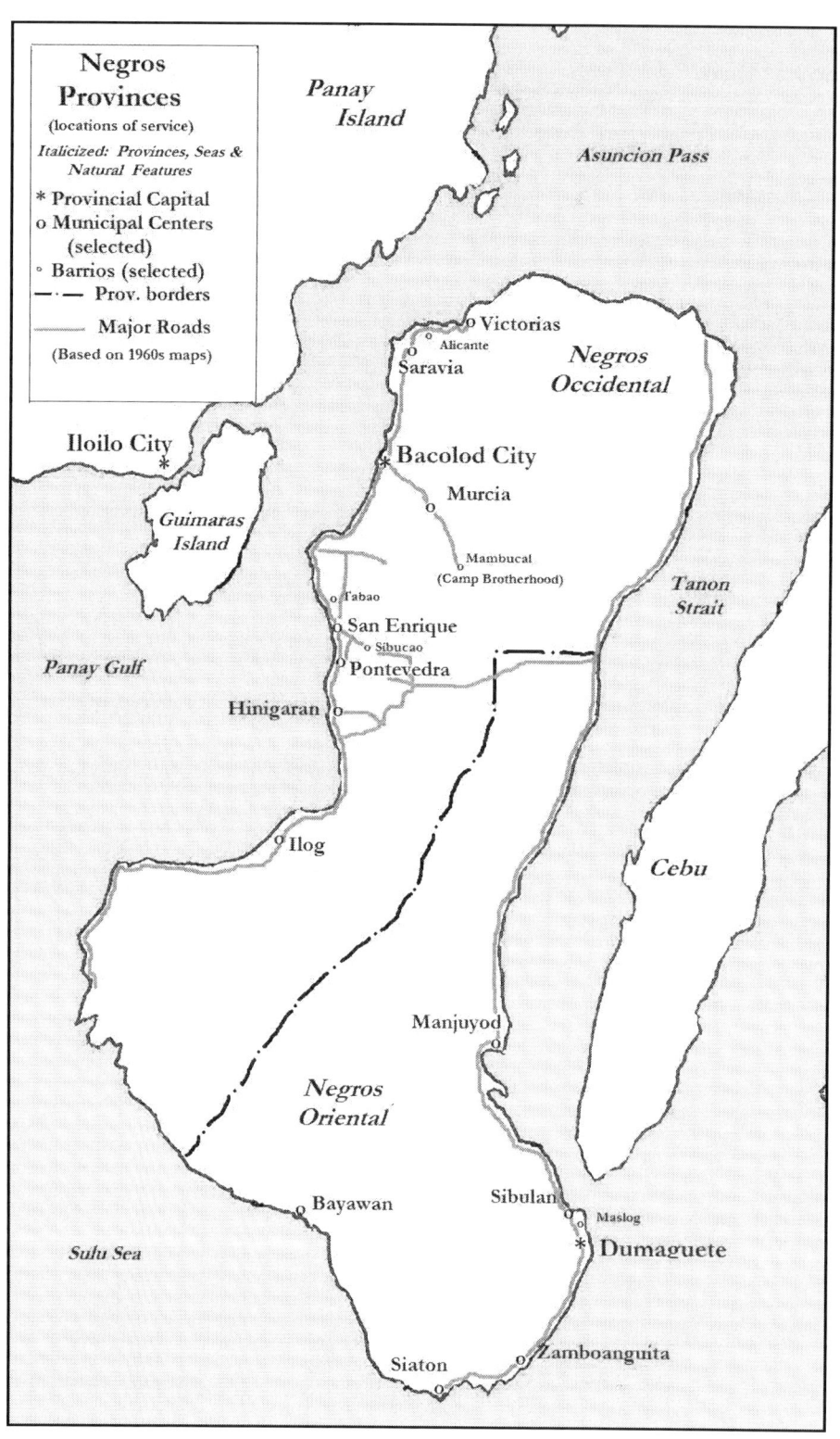

Emery Bontrager
The Accidental Volunteer

In January 1961, my college roommate Kenny and I watched JFK's inaugural address on TV. We thought it was a great speech and were both very impressed with the part about "Ask not, etc." After the speech, I told Kenny that I would really like to join this new agency and see the world. In the latter part of April that year, I received a letter from Washington D.C., thanking me for expressing my interest in the Peace Corps and telling me to report in May to the local Post Office on a Saturday morning at 9:00 am to take a qualifying test and complete an application for the Peace Corps. When Kenny got back to our apartment, I showed him my letter. It was exactly like his letter. I asked him how this happened and he said "Oh, I forgot to tell you that I saw this sign-up notice on the Student Union Bulletin Board for all people interested in joining the Peace Corps. So I signed us up." Kenny woke me up very early on a Saturday saying, "This is the day we take the Peace Corps test." I said, "Let me sleep, its Saturday." He insisted that I go with him. I thought it would be a waste of time because I'd never qualify with my academic record.

Two very worrisome events were about to occur in my life—first, I was facing graduation from Kansas University in June; second, as soon as I graduated, my local Draft Board was going to draft me into the Army. I had received six deferments from them already and they hated to give deferments. Two weeks after graduating that June, I received my "Dear Emery" draft notice. I reported to the Kansas City Army Induction Center for my physical exam. I volunteered to take a battery of tests and promised to enlist so that I would have some choices in my service duties. At the end of a very exhausting day, I was interviewed. I was told that I qualified for Officers Training School. I could be inducted into the Army tonight and be on the bus in the morning to basic training. I also qualified for assignment to the Counter-Intelligence Corps (CIC). The interviewer explained that the disadvantage if I selected the CIC was that I could not be inducted that day because they would have to run a background check on me and this would take about two months. I immediately selected the CIC.

That night I called home to tell my parents I'd be returning the next day. Mom said, "You got a telegram from something called the Peace Corps and you have been selected for the Philippines Project." I was aware that by joining the Peace Corps one would be given a deferment from the draft. I called some college friends and we celebrated my good fortune.

Upon returning home, I took the telegram to my Selective Service Board Office and asked for another deferment. The Executive Secretary was extremely upset, said she knew nothing about the Peace Corps and as far as she was concerned, I was not eligible for another deferment. To appeal this decision, I would have to travel to the Regional Draft Board Headquarters in Dodge City, Kansas (a three-hour drive). There, they knew about the new Peace Corps and I was granted another deferment. I was destined to be in the Peace Corps. An accident can be defined as "an unforeseen incident," "lack of intention," or "unplanned." And that is how I got into the Peace Corps.

Following seven weeks of training at Penn State, we boarded an old military transport for the Philippines. After flying for 37 hours, we arrived at Manila International Airport. When we got off the plane, we all went through the welcoming reception line. I was tired. Even though the Director and Staff of the Philippines Project, the Secretary of Education, and many staff from that Department were in the reception line, nothing impressed me until I got toward the end of this line when I stepped in front of the most beautiful young lady I had ever seen. I thought if even a small percentage of the girls in the Philippines were half as beautiful as this lady, I was really going to enjoy the next two years. Actually, I have really enjoyed the last 45 years because I married that very lady that I met in the reception line: Annie Gison Bontrager.

Following another seven weeks of training at Los Baños, I was assigned to Paracale, Camarines Norte. The most valuable thing I got from all the training was three lifetime friends. Let me explain. Throughout months of training, we all had to line up in alphabetical order for everything like immunization shots, physical exams, etc. Roommate assignments at training sites were done alphabetically. As a result, **B**ontrager, Parker **B**org, Tom **C**arlton, and Don **C**ecchi always stood near each other in line, participated in the same small group sessions, and roomed in nearby dorm rooms during training. We each selected the others as housemates when the house grouping assignments/selection process was made. As a result, the four of us lived for the two years together in our house in Paracale. I consider the three as friends for life.

I was assigned to Tawig Elementary School, a small school with three rooms in the Barrio of Tawig. Each of the three teachers taught two grades. The school classrooms were all in one building which was set back about 100 yards from the only road to Paracale. Tawig was about six kilometers from town and I could catch the bus about a block from our house for the ride which took about 20 minutes. The principal in our school was Miss Villarosa, who taught the third and fourth grades. I was assigned to teach English as a second language and basic science in Mr. Ely Zenarosa's fifth and sixth grades. Ely and I became good friends in a short time; Ely loved to visit and I learned a lot from him.

During the second week of my assignment to teach at Tawig, I noticed a tarp covered pile of building material. I accidently asked Ely what that was. He said that the Congressman from this district, who had been running for reelection this past November, sent the building material as part of a campaign promise to build a home economics building for our school. The problem was that he sent only 1/3 of the materials; two other barrios (not in our school district) received the other parts of the building. Ely concluded his explanation saying "that's practically the way of politics in the Philippines." I remarked that it would be a real waste to let that material rot away. The next morning, Ely told me that our Principal, Miss Villarosa, wanted the two of us to talk to the Barrio Capitan to see if the community would be able to help in building a home economics building for our school using the materials and getting the rest of the material from private sources. The next day, Ely and I visited with the Barrio Capitan and a couple of his friends. I mainly listened and acted like I understood what was going on. We didn't hear anything further about the building project, although I noticed several different men looking over the pile of materials during the next couple of weeks.

Time passed. The end of the school year was nearing when one day after school, our Volunteer Leader, Jim Gilbreth, came by the house. He asked me what my project was all about. I told him that I didn't have a project. He said that he was contacted by the School Superintendent from Daet, the Provincial Capital, and from Peace Corps Headquarters in Manila saying they were interested in the Peace Corps project that I was working on. He explained that it was something about a home economics building for Tawig School. I told him what little I knew and he instructed me to be at Tawig School the following Saturday. I went to see Ely who didn't know any more than I did. We went to Miss Villarosa's house to find out what was happening. She only knew that the District Superintendent was going to be there on Saturday and we were to be there also.

When Saturday arrived, I was at the school at ten o'clock along with maybe 25 people from the barrio and staff people from Daet. The men from the barrio were outlining the dimensions of a building foundation. About an hour later, the Secretary of Education, Dr. Roces, and several of his staff members from Manila arrived. Shortly thereafter, Dr. Larry Fuchs, the Peace Corps Director for the Philippines, drove into the school yard in a car. After a short *merienda*, everybody went out to the building site. Dr. Fuchs and Dr. Roces and a couple of other men all got shovels and while each broke ground, a photographer from the provincial newspaper took pictures.

After the ground-breaking ceremony, Dr. Fuchs asked me to join him in his car because he wanted to talk to me. In the car we visited briefly about my work and then he said, "Emery, you are doing a really great job here." Then he said he had to leave to catch a flight back to Manila. I was greatly relieved, and I thought this Peace Corps job is really great! I like it when I don't do anything and get congratulated for doing a good job. When we left Paracale one and a half years later, the building was still not finished. Thankfully, when Parker Borg and I visited 35 years later, the building had been finished, was still there and had been in full use for more years than anyone there could remember.

When the summer vacation arrived, we all went to Manila for meetings. While there, Doug Watts and I were offered a change of job assignment to "pretest" Peace Corps participation in a new community development project in conjunction with the Philippine agency Presidential Assistant for Community Development (PACD). I believe that the "Tawig Project" was the reason I was offered this new assignment. And, I was to do this pretest project assignment in the barrios of the Paracale Municipality. I really liked this new assignment—everything but the bed bugs. (But that's another story). I felt that community development had the potential to be a very worthwhile program. I never really believed in the 'English as a Second Language Project."

After my two-year Peace Corps term was over, I took my $75.00 per month readjustment allowance in the Philippines and spent the next year living in Manila. Annie and I were "going steady," but we were having problems with her father. Dr. Gison did not want his daughter to marry a foreigner.

He'd spent four years in the United States and felt that divorce was too easy; he did not want his daughter to suffer that fate. So I stayed in Manila and every Sunday after Mass (I'm not even Catholic) I visited Annie's family. In the old traditions of the Philippines, I chopped wood and carried water for the family and thus proved that I was worthy to earn the right to the hand of my wife.

When I look back and ask myself what did I give to the Peace Corps, the Philippines, or to our country, I have to admit that I gave very little when compared to what I received. Most important of all, I gained a wonderful wife. The second thing I gained was a group of lifelong friends—Returned Peace Corps Volunteers and Filipinos both in the Philippines and here in the United States. Finally, I realized that, even though one can set goals in life, many "accidents" happen along the way that lead to something better than anything I could have planned. I learned that it really is better to "roll with the punches."

Upon leaving the Philippines in July of 1964, Emery stayed with his Paracale housemate Tom Carlton in Los Angeles, where he found a job with an insurance investigating company, obtaining a Private Investigator's (PI) License. After 18 months, he felt sufficiently readjusted to his own culture that he needed a job with some meaning. In September 1966, Emery went to work for the Los Angeles County Department of Probation, working with juveniles. His first (and last assignment) with Probation was supervising youth in the Juvenile Hall, where all doors were locked and he soon grew weary of carrying around a heavy key ring.

Tom Carlton was working at the time for the Los Angeles Department of Public Social Services and encouraged Emery to apply. He did and was assigned to the Aid to Families with Dependent Children (AFDC). After a year he was accepted into their new program, Community Protective Services, which provided protection for neglected and abused children of families that were not on welfare. A consultant for this project from USC's School of Social work encouraged him to get his master's degree in Social Work. With the help of a state scholarship and his wife, Emery obtained his master's degree from USC in 1970.

When Emery returned to work, he first supervised a unit of Protective Services and Foster Care Workers; then a unit providing Foster Parent training and support services, and finally a two-year stint directing a section of social service auditors. He became the Executive Assistant to the Director of the New Department of Children's Services, where his major work was to serve as liaison between his Department and the Los Angeles County Board of Supervisors. The five "Kings" each represented districts of almost three million residents of the County. This involved working very closely with the Supervisors Staff and keeping them informed of the Department's needs and problems—before the Los Angeles Times *found out about them. Ten years into this assignment, he reached his 30 years with LA County and retired in 1994. Annie retired that year also. In the following years, they have traveled, played golf, bowled, and enjoyed life.*

(Both photos show Emery with his wife Annie; the first in 1966 and the second more recently.)

Parker W. Borg
Images of Revolution and Reality

Naïve Anticipations

Political ferment was everywhere as the 1960s dawned—or so it seemed to me as a freshly minted college graduate. Having majored in international relations, I had studied Castro's takeover in Cuba, the revolts against colonialism in Africa, the continuing confrontation with the Vietcong in Vietnam, etc. In the Philippines, the struggle against the Huks had only ended a few years earlier. As I got ready to begin my Peace Corps service there, I wondered whether talk of revolution against landowners and corrupt officials was a part of the daily conversations in the rural communities. Were there remnant groups of rebels still lurking in the villages and plotting subversion? I wanted to understand this turmoil firsthand.

I felt myself fortunate to be one of the few volunteers assigned to a town where the national language was also the local dialect. I was excited about learning Tagalog, because I visualized sitting on the bus each day and overhearing the revolutionary thoughts I expected to be permeating the region. I imagined a world of anger over presumed injustices at the village level. While I never became as fluent as I would have liked, I learned enough Tagalog to permit me to get the drift of conversations during my daily bus rides. They surprised me. I heard the men talking about their rice fields, broken tools, sports, and women. When I listened to women, I heard about children, prices in the market, and gossip about friends. I never overheard a single revolutionary thought from anybody on the bus.

The rural world of the Philippines was not what I had naïvely anticipated, but I learned many other lessons during these two years about the Philippines and about my own ability to cope in a culturally unfamiliar environment.

Rhetoric and Determination

Like most of my friends, I was turned on by John Kennedy's rhetoric during the 1960 political campaign, but in the end I could not vote for him because of what I considered irresponsible statements about defending a couple of islands off the Chinese coast from Mainland attacks. Beginning with his inaugural statement, however, I increasingly liked his ideas and his words, particularly the "ask not" line.

As a college senior in 1961, with only the vaguest of plans for the immediate future, I went down to the Peace Corps' temporary headquarters in Washington during spring break to inquire about the new organization. I learned from the official who met me that the Peace Corps had no interest in people like me, because I offered no skills. I had two negative strikes: I had studied a useless subject like international relations and had gone to an Ivy League school.

The official explained that the Peace Corps would be interested in experienced teachers, health workers, farmers, and technical specialists, preferably from heartland schools, not generalists like me.

The tentative rejection forced me to reconsider my approach. I became intent on making my way into the Peace Corps, not only because of the opportunity to understand more about a Third World country by working in one, but also to see first hand how this new U.S. program might be launched. I checked into the plans for the first Peace Corps programs and recall that they were going to be located in Tanzania, Ghana, Santa Lucia, and the Philippines. All were of a technical nature, except the Philippine program, which was to be in the field of education. Since I had focused my undergraduate attention on Asia, the Philippines sounded like a perfect fit. When I filled out the Peace Corps application, I acknowledged my lack of experience, but wrote that I was interested in teaching and slanted all my answers appropriately without specifying any country of interest.

After graduation I returned home to Minnesota and waited. My parents couldn't believe I had no plans beyond an optimistic assumption that I would be joining the Peace Corps. They told me I needed to get serious, find a job, etc. They reminded me that having paid for my college education, they expected me to do something productive. I shouldn't waste my time and their investment on something like the Peace Corps. In the middle of July, I received an acceptance notification for the Philippines project with a starting date for training in two weeks. My parents' cool reaction warmed after one of the Minneapolis newspapers interviewed me, ran a long story about me as one of the first volunteers from Minnesota, and their friends began complimenting them on my "achievement."

I was happy to have been selected, but as soon as I arrived at the training program at Penn State, I became anxious about the hovering threat of selection-out. From the beginning, we knew some of us would be deemed unsuitable, but the criteria were as vague as the future jobs. Each of us sat for what seemed like a couple of hours with a psychologist, answering questions about our backgrounds, beliefs and motivations. I remember being worried when I was one of the few called back for a second interview. Although I never learned what might have been the concern, I suspected that bells had gone off when I told the psychologist I expected I might learn more from the Filipinos than they would learn from me. My interviewer questioned my idealism and made lots of notes. In the end, I was accepted, but about 25 members of the group washed out at the training stage. It was a traumatic experience for all of us because we had no sense about the selection standards.

Many of us questioned from the beginning what we were doing at Penn State, a school with no apparent connection with any part of Asia. Perhaps, we speculated, Peace Corps headquarters wanted the appearance of training programs at universities with strong technical reputations rather than those "soft" places in warmer locations, because the Peace Corps legislation was still wending its way through Congress. Penn State had one or two faculty members with Philippine experience who assisted with our training, but it was tough for everyone because of the vagueness of our future jobs. The Penn State training provided basic courses in teaching math, science and English at the elementary school level, but with a focus on the latest American techniques rather than the reality of the school environment in the Philippines. For the cultural context, Penn State assembled a group of Filipinos studying at other American institutions, but these students were from elite Filipino families studying at elite American graduate schools. They were smart and congenial, but they provided little knowledge about rural Filipino life.

Finding Myself in Two Mining Towns in Camarines Norte

I was assigned with three other male volunteers to the town of Paracale in Camarines Norte Province at the northern end of the Bicol region of Luzon. It was about a 12-hour bus ride from Manila to Paracale, but only an hour by plane because of the rutted dirt road that passed for the national highway for the last two-thirds of the trip. This town of about 3,800 people was at the confluence of a small river and the Pacific, with three beautiful beaches within easy walking distance. Paracale had been famous for its gold since pre-Spanish times, but the modern version of the industry collapsed in the 1950s, when the underground mines were flooded by nearby dredging, resulting in the loss of many lives and the basis for the local economy. When we arrived, we found there was still a small professional class of doctors, lawyers, and goldsmiths, but most of the people were fishermen, teachers, and government workers. Commercial life was limited to the early morning market and few general stores. It was a town living in a past without much prospect for the future, but for me it was an idyllic place. I couldn't believe that the Peace Corps had assigned us to such a spectacular site, one which I imagined might one day boast an elegant resort hotel or two.

Our house seemed the product of the past prosperity. Set on stilts in a fenced-in compound above a more modest lower house, it had separate bedrooms for each of us, paneled walls, glass windows, a tin roof and an indoor flush toilet. Pooling our money, we hired a teen age boy to handle the marketing and cooking and a teen age girl to do our laundry once a week. Paracale had electricity, but it only operated for four hours in the evenings and regularly blacked out. The town also had a community water system, but the pressure was so weak that people dug holes in the street beneath the underground pipes, rigged up spigots, and carried the water in buckets back to their homes. One member of our household, Emery Bontrager, who had grown up in rural Kansas, put an old oil drum on our roof and a pump in our sink. At night when the water pressure was at its maximum, we could pump enough water into the drum for the needs of the next day. When we demonstrated Emery's achievement to our neighbors, they acknowledged his ingenuity, but showed no interest in trying to duplicate it at their homes. Life was good in Paracale, but we learned from this experience that the innovations of youthful outsiders were of limited interest to the local community.

While the four of us each had assignments to schools in separate communities, we spent most of our free time together in Paracale during the first year. After many months of participating as a group in community activities and socializing with the same people, we were surprised how frequently we were called by the wrong name. When we queried our new friends about the confusion, we were told, "All you Americans look the same." We were stunned because even though none of us was unusually tall or short, thin or fat, we thought we all looked quite different from the other. Emery was probably the tallest and thinnest with sharp features and sandy, brown hair. Tom Carlton from Los Angeles was shorter with wavy, blond hair, Don Cecchi from New York City had jet black hair, and my hair was reddish-brown. We didn't think we looked anything alike, but realized that just as we had trouble distinguishing Filipinos from each other at the beginning, they had similar problems with us. Identifying characteristics were culturally determined. In addition to size and shape, we had grown up using the colors of hair and eyes as distinguishing features. In Paracale, by contrast, where almost everyone had more or less the same dark hair and dark eyes, it seemed that skin tones (shades of brown) and nose shapes were the important factors; thus, by local standards, we all had very light skin and very sharp noses—no distinguishing characteristics.

My school was in Jose Panganiban, a separate municipality about fifteen miles away, which required I catch a bus each morning, ride for about 20 minutes, and transfer to another bus for the final 20 minute ride to my school. I was initially pleased to have the long commute because the buses were noisy with conversations and I would be able to learn what was on the minds of my fellow passengers.

Jose Panganiban, named after a local figure from the independence movement, was larger than Paracale. It had about 5000 residents and supported two to three times that population in surrounding rural barrios. Although the economy of most towns in the Bicol region was based on farming or fishing (or both), Jose Panganiban, like Paracale, had originally been a gold mining center, but after the gold ran out in about the 1920s, it had become the support center for the largest iron mine in the Philippines at Larap, a company town of about 9000 people eight miles down the road. Whereas Paracale was a grid of nearly rectangular streets with fenced in yards and trees in a picture postcard setting on the ocean, Jose Panganiban was densely packed with tinderbox houses, gritty, and distinctly third world urban. One match and the whole town might disappear.

The town sat on a narrow strip of flat land between a dirty, shallow bay and a steep hillside. The urban area was about one mile long and two streets wide. All of the houses on the bay side stood on stilts above the muddy flats, permitting the tides to carry the daily dumping of garbage out to sea. People commonly kept pigs below the houses that were above the high water mark. The elementary school hugged the hillside; it consisted of some fifteen buildings, each with two or three classrooms, some made of concrete blocks and others of nipa thatch. They were all located at different levels so that each building had a clear view of the town and bay below. Narrow paths, which became muddy and slippery when it rained, wound up the hill connecting the classrooms. The high school was just outside the center of town on reclaimed land at the head of the bay.

Before arriving in our villages, we realized that each of us would have to craft our own roles. While we were formally classified as teachers' aides, the exact meaning was as vague at the end of training as it had been at the beginning. We were supposed to work in the classrooms, but couldn't replace the teachers, presumably because of labor issues. Administrative disorganization at the Peace Corps staff level in Manila permitted loose interpretation of this amorphous concept. If we preferred to work outside the schools on community development, we could. If we didn't want to do anything but goof off, we could get away with this too—and some of us did. The Filipinos were much too polite to complain. At the same time, if we couldn't figure out what to do, there was nobody to help. One of the older volunteers in the province was assigned the task of also being a volunteer leader, but he had his own teaching "job," never visited my school, and never tried to offer more than administrative support. The Peace Corps assigned a staff member to work in the Bicol region, but he lived more than a day's drive away and rarely visited. The Peace Corps staff in Manila was consumed with the training and assignment of several subsequent batches of volunteers shortly after we arrived in the provinces. As far as I was concerned I was on my own.

I stuck with the schools and the idea of trying to define a teaching role. Looking back, I realize this was particularly important for me because of the comments I'd heard in Washington about the unsuitability of liberal arts graduates when I first inquired about Peace Corps. I had to prove to myself—and to anyone who might come to check—that I could do the job.

Rather than working with just one class of students or just one subject area, I eventually worked out an arrangement with the town's elementary and high schools that I would maximize my contact with small groups of students of all ages. The elementary school had about six sections of each grade; the high school was about half the size. A couple times each week I took over different classrooms for about an hour each, working in the elementary school Monday through Thursday and in the High School on Friday. I taught beginning English to first graders, mathematics skills to third graders, science to sixth graders, literature to the first year high school students and current events and history to the fourth year seniors. The teachers seemed pleased with my participation, mostly because it gave them a break in their work day. After school hours, I advised the high school students on the production of the yearbook, directed a school play, coached a speech team and joined the other teachers to learn folk dances for upcoming festivals.

I realized rather quickly that as a teacher I needed to be active and animated to keep the kids' attention. Remembering little about the teaching techniques we learned at Penn State, I kept trying to recall how it had been when I was in elementary and high school; what I liked; and what seemed to work. When teaching science, I tried to think of experiments which would demonstrate scientific principles. This was a new concept for many of the students whose past science classes had relied on rote memorization. In math class, I figured out games to teach concepts like multiplication. I don't think any Peace Corps staff members visited me in my school during the first year. I never learned whether my principal or my Filipino colleagues thought I was doing a good job because they never said anything. I realized such comments were unlikely because 1) that would be impolite, 2) I was an amusing source of local prestige, and 3) I was an American—and Americans presumably knew all the answers.

The kids were a mixture of the smart and not so smart, a few relatively well-off but the majority hard core poor. The kids whose parents had full time jobs at the iron mine had their own elementary and secondary schools in Larap. The kids who attended the schools in Jose Panganiban had parents who might have once worked at the mine or wanted to work there. In addition to a few families of fishermen, municipal officials and teachers, the permanent residents of Jose Panganiban sold things in the market, ran shops and eating stalls, provided legal and medical services, did day labor, and even worked in local whorehouses. A large number of people, however, appeared to be out of work, perhaps the wannabes for jobs at the mines. It was a much poorer and more transitory town than either Larap or Paracale.

By the beginning of the second academic year, I wanted to find a place to stay in Jose Panganiban during the week so that I might participate more easily in after school and evening activities. While several school officials offered me space in their homes, I wanted my own room and my independence. Finding a place was not easy because of the town's overcrowded, ramshackle conditions. It was not until January 1963 that I found a small room (8' x 10') for $3.50 a month above a pharmacy in the home of a woman whose children had moved away. To my surprise, particularly since the room was on the second floor, the bathroom I shared down the hall always had running water. It was one of the nicest bathrooms

I'd seen in the province. I heard that the owner's connections permitted a direct link to the town reservoir, but I never figured out the plumbing or the politics of this luxury. I picked up some bread at the local bakery for breakfast, ate lunch with the principal from the elementary school, and took dinner as a boarder in a home a few doors from my new residence. From that point on, I spent four or five nights a week in Jose Panganiban and returned to Paracale only on weekends or for special events. Despite the town's poverty and general lack of sanitation, I was healthy, enjoying my life and feeling productive in my work.

Given the limited Peace Corps monthly stipend, I travelled extensively in the Philippines. Looking back, I don't know how I might have afforded it. I tried to go to Manila for the weekend once every six weeks or so, usually on the 12-hour overnight bus, but occasionally via the non-stop flight from Larap when I could scrape together the money. On holidays I travelled down to other towns in the Bicol, up to Mountain Province, into the Visayan region and down to Mindanao. During my first summer, I worked at the agricultural college at Los Baños in a program that was training Filipino community development leaders. During my second summer, I got an internship with the Agency for International Development in Manila, where I studied non-American assistance programs. Many of my colleagues found reasons to transfer to other locations, sometimes as a result of these summer travel and work experiences, but I never gave any thought to leaving my school. I wanted to remain in Jose Panganiban and complete the second year with the local community of students and teachers.

Reflections on the Local Education Scene

The ages of the kids in each class in Jose Panganiban ranged over a couple years, particularly in the fifth and sixth grades because of shortcomings in Filipino education. The smaller barrios usually offered schooling until grade three. Schools for grades four to six existed only in larger villages. The only high school in the municipality was in Jose Panganiban (except for the one in Larap operated exclusively for the children of the mine workers). There seemed to be about a 50 percent drop in student population between third grade and fourth grade and again between sixth grade and high school.

In spite of the schooling, the education system was creating functional illiterates. The students began learning English in first grade. By third grade all classes were taught in English. English language education may have been the key to world communications, but it was irrelevant to the average rural resident who might never leave the province. Incentives were minimal in most villages to send children to the next level of schooling in town. While education was free, there were endless school fees, voluntary contributions, and transportation considerations. Even if the kids continued until sixth grade before returning to their village lives, they would quickly forget their English, which meant the math and science they might have studied in English were also gone. In addition, their classes in Tagalog had been rudimentary. This system changed afterward, but at the time the Philippines was attempting to educate large numbers of children who reverted to functional illiteracy within a short time after finishing their education.

As a result of all the flaws in the educational system, many elementary level students in towns like Jose Panganiban were teenagers. Few of them went on to high school, but they were often eager to learn as fifth and sixth graders. This age difference could have its advantages.

One year a group of fifth and sixth graders wanted to have a football team to join the provincial competition, but none of the other males wanted to be their coach. Not having a clue how to play the game I'd always called soccer, I found a book, read up on the rules, and became the football coach. My coaching focused on simple fitness drills, passing the ball rather than hogging it oneself, and discussions about the effects of smoking and drinking. Since the average age of our team was three or four years older than the boys on the other teams—and nearly twice the size, we had an easy time winning the local and provincial championship. I was proud of the team and told them that their success showed what interest and dedication could achieve.

Reflections on My Impact as a Volunteer

Having been one of the youngest and least experienced of the volunteers in the ways of the classroom, I had few expectations about what I might accomplish, but thus did not share the frustrations of some of my better trained colleagues. I put forward a consistent effort for two years and felt at the end that I had acquitted myself adequately.

I have no idea what my impact might have been on the community or on the individuals with whom I worked. Some of the other volunteers became involved in construction projects, largely, I thought at the time, out of frustration with their teaching assignments. When they departed, however, they left behind something concrete and measurable. I left nothing that could be photographed or memorialized.

Several of the teachers said they admired some of my teaching methods and said they would try similar activities, but I have no idea how much of this was polite talk with their American guest. On more than one occasion I made egregious factual errors in classes, shocking the teachers who occasionally observed me. I was always pleased to acknowledge my mistakes and tell the teachers that their vision of infallible Americans was seriously flawed. Americans make mistakes like everyone else. I remained friends with some of the teachers and the principal of my elementary school for many years after my departure.

Did I have an effect on the students? I like to think that I did, particularly on the older ones who seemed to be absorbing more from the classroom and who were better able to communicate their views, but I lost contact with all of them. One of my former students found me some 25 years later and wrote about important impact that I had on his decision to become a journalist in Manila. It was a nice tribute, but I always presumed it to be an isolated episode.

Reflections of the Philippines after 35 Years

Although I had returned in 1965 to visit my two towns in Camarines Norte, little had changed in the two short years. In 1996 on the 35th anniversary of our arrival in the Philippines, a group of us took the opportunity after a Peace Corps reunion conference in Manila to drive south from the capital along the National Highway into the Bicol, stopping for a few days in Paracale and Jose Panganiban before continuing to the southern tip of the peninsula and crossing the San Bernardino Strait to the island of Samar.

First and foremost I was struck by the sheer number of Filipinos. The population had nearly tripled from about 28 million in the early 1960s to more than 70 million in the 1990s. Villages I had known well seemed overwhelmed by a flood of people, but there was little corresponding evidence in Camarines Norte of an increase in jobs or opportunities outside the traditional sectors—farming, fishing, mining and government work. Teachers said they had to cope with as many a fifty students in a classroom. A depressing number of friends said their children had gone off to Manila to study, work, and probably never to return because there were no jobs at home.

Second, poverty was pervasive. The percentage of poor people seemed to have grown larger as the population soared. This was particularly evident in Manila where the gap between the very rich and the very poor was aptly demonstrated by the gated communities of Makati and the surrounding shanty towns. Towns like Paracale and Jose Panganiban were largely collections of run-down concrete buildings, unpainted wooden dwellings and shacks make of scrap material. Residents may have had electricity more regularly and owned television sets, but life for the average Filipino remained difficult.

Third, the road network was still abysmal. The main streets in Manila and other big towns seemed to follow the same routes as 35 years earlier, but were infinitely more congested. The "superhighway" to the south did not extend beyond Laguna Province, the next province to the south of Manila. While the National Highway through the next province, Quezon, was now a two lane ribbon of concrete, the quality deteriorated once it reached Camarines Norte, where the reconstructed road looked like a series of local projects smoothed by hand implements. The road connecting Paracale and Jose Panganiban was "under construction" and took more than twice the travel time it had taken in the 1960s.

Fourth, the forests of tropical hardwoods which had lined the roads in the more remote stretches of Quezon Province and Camarines Norte had all but disappeared. If they'd been replaced by anything, it was the coconut palm, a symbol of times past when Philippine copra was seen as the economic future (rather than the oil palm which had been planted at the same time in former rainforests of Malaysia.)

Having seen the changes that had occurred over the previous 35 years elsewhere in the region, particularly in Malaysia, Thailand, and Indonesia, it was distressing to see the Philippines falling increasingly behind its neighbors.

Lessons Learned

I had gone to the Philippines expecting I would learn more about the country than Filipinos would learn from me. I believe this was the case. While I put in a good faith effort and did as much as I could to be an effective in my undefined role, my Peace Corps years were probably more important for my education than they were for any of my students.

By the end of my first year, I had abandoned any thought that I was going to overhear revolutionary thoughts riding on a bus. This made my decision to relocate to the town of my school the second year much easier. I may not have heard any revolutionary plotting, but I learned a lot about the difficulties of life for the average Filipino in a town like Jose Panganiban. I had trouble living on my equivalent of $55 per month, a salary similar to that of my fellow teachers. All I needed to do with my monthly stipend was take care of myself; they needed to provide for large families, support distant relatives, pay for health care and school fees, put kids through college, and have a reserve for emergencies. And as I reminded myself more than once, the teachers were part of the middle class. Others had it much tougher.

Although I didn't fully realize it as I was getting ready to depart in June 1963, the experiences in the Philippines shaped both my outlook and attitude toward life in general and the rest of the world in profound ways. Looking back with the benefit of hindsight, five lessons stand out.

First, I liked living overseas. I had enjoyed my life in the Philippines and looked forward to living outside the United States again. In subsequent years I've had the opportunity to live in Malaysia, Vietnam, Congo, Mali, Iceland, and Italy. I approached the new life in each country with the same enthusiasm I had felt when I went to the Philippines—though with more preparation and hopefully less naïveté about what I might find. In each, I tried to learn the local language, understand cultural practices, interact with local people, and appreciate the society for what it had to offer. People often asked in recent years what had been my favorite country. I have no answer because I enjoyed each for what it had to offer and never made comparisons. Life in all of them had provided daily adventures in the unknown.

Second, I didn't mind the third world travel and eating experiences. I learned that I could not only reach my destination with less than first class accommodations, but I also enjoyed it because it offered more memorable experiences and more opportunities to meet interesting people. I had also eaten in so many awful restaurants, particularly when travelling on Filipino buses that my stomach seemed fortified for just about anything so long as it was cooked. When I left the Philippines, I did not fly out of Manila like my fellow volunteers, but departed on a smuggling boat plying the waters between the Sulu Archipelago and North Borneo. It was probably stupid, but I didn't worry about it at the time. In subsequent years I've traveled to many remote corners of the world, sometimes under dangerous conditions. Whether driving from the Texas border to the Panama Canal, riding a scooter along the rice paddies of Vietnam during the war, flying in missionary planes to remote villages in the Congo (then Zaire), I've rarely had much concern about failing to reach my destination.

Third, I learned I could develop expertise on issues I'd never formally studied if I applied myself. Figuring out how to become an effective teacher in the Philippine school system had taken time, but having achieved it, I had confidence when asked to accept subsequent challenges in unfamiliar fields. Over the course of my diplomatic career, I have been asked every two of three years to become involved in unfamiliar subjects. Within one ten year period, I moved from working on food security issues in Africa to combating international terrorism, then to dealing with Information Age issues, strengthening American counter narcotics initiatives, and negotiating a base agreement for the Defense Department. I looked upon learning each new issue with varying degrees of enthusiasm, worked hard to master the subject, and believe the changing focus kept me intellectually more alert.

Fourth, statistics may provide important data, but they tell an incomplete part of the story. The Philippines had been my first experience with bureaucracies trying to keep track of numbers and changes—students, ages, textbooks, oral hygiene, etc. I saw that the statistics were only as good as the input, which varied from rigorous to slapdash. Collating these numbers at the provincial and national level may have provided data, but the numbers were often meaningless. In subsequent years, whenever I've read statistical information, particularly from third world environments—and often from the so-called developed world as well, I have been skeptical about their significance.

Fifth, and probably most importantly, change comes at a slower pace than most Americans are prepared to accept. The intense knowledge that I had gained about the tough life Filipinos faced in a small town like Jose Panganiban helped me acquire a better big picture perspective about the gap between big cities and small villages. Visiting rural communities in Vietnam, Congo, and Mali in subsequent years, while living in a capital city, I felt that my Peace Corps experience in the Philippines not only gave me a better sense of the difficulties with rural development, but more importantly why development programs rarely worked as we expected them in these other third world societies. While the Philippines—like every country—is unique, its culture of third world poverty offered many similarities to other places and presented many of the same obstacles to change.

Following his Peace Corps assignment, Parker Borg attended Cornell University on a Ford Foundation Fellowship for former volunteers. After receiving an MPA degree in 1965, he joined the State Department and served more than 30 years as a Foreign Service Officer. He was nominated by three separate Presidents for Ambassadorial positions and held senior jobs at the State Department in the areas of counter-terrorism, narcotics suppression, the international dimensions of information technology, and African Affairs. He was nominated as American Ambassador to Mali, Burma, and Iceland, but never went to Burma because of Senate objection to Burma's human rights problems. When nominated to go to Mali in 1981, the Peace Corps Director at the time, Loret Ruppe,

informed him that he was the first former volunteer to become an Ambassador. Other overseas assignments included embassy assignments in the Congo and Malaysia and as a civilian advisor in Vietnam during the war.

Following his retirement from the State Department, Parker taught courses in diplomacy and foreign policy at the American University of Rome and the American Graduate School of Paris. He and his wife Anna Maria Anderson Borg, who has also spent a career as an American diplomat, are the parents of three daughters.

(The first photo shows Parker carving a lechon (roast pig) during training at Los Baños with Brenda Brown and other volunteers looking on; the second photo shows Parker with his wife Anna.)

Bruce Campbell
A Place for Being

Starting Point

Having graduated from Whitman College in Washington State in 1959 with a degree in Economics and Business Administration, I applied for officer's candidate school with the U.S. Air Force. I was to report to Lackland Air Force Base in Texas for training—when there was an opening. In the interim, I pursued graduate training in secondary education and science at Eastern Oregon University, completed my student teaching, and received a secondary school teaching certification. I had earlier received state certification as a bartender, which provided me with the income I needed to live and to pay for the graduate credits.

Early in 1960, I got in touch with Oregon's congressional delegation to inquire about the "peace corps" that was being legislatively proposed by Senator Hubert H. Humphrey. They kept me informed about its progress as the idea morphed into reality during the first months of the Kennedy Administration. I completed the application and began another waiting period. Because of the repeated delays from the Air Force, I had signed a teaching contract as a high school instructor in a rural community in Eastern Oregon. Some two weeks later, I received a telegram that I was accepted for Peace Corps training for the Philippines at Penn State. The superintendent of the contracted school district was not pleased, but after some persuasion the school board allowed me to be released from my contract. Eventually the Air Force transferred my status to the Air Force Reserve, and I was able to pursue my Peace Corps adventure.

I arrived at Penn State University with my copy of Barry Goldwater's *Conscience of a Conservative*, so my political identity was not exactly consistent with the majority of the other trainees. My roommate actually refused to converse with me because of it. On the other hand, my roommate was not selected to serve, and most other volunteers accepted my position when they learned that Barry Goldwater was a supporter of the Peace Corps and that "conservative values" at that time included the recognition of an individual's responsibility to serve others. My values have not changed over the years, but I have changed my political identity and affiliations. The "conservative party" has forsaken serving others to serving only self.

My knowledge of the Philippines was very limited. An uncle was a colonel in the Air Force, and he and his family were stationed at Clark Air Force Base for a number of years. I had seen frequent news reports of communist rebels in residence in the Islands. Penn State training provided a good introduction to Los Baños, our in-country training site, and Los Baños in turn was a good introduction to life in the barrio, but the real training was eventually provided by the teachers and citizens of our community assignments. One of my vivid memories from Penn State—aside from the 100 percent humidity and my first fire flies—was a remark by Carlos Romulo, the Philippines Ambassador to the United Nations. In comparing his physical size and the influence of the Philippines to the world, he said that he often had to tell others, "I feel like a dime among nickels."

Welcome to San Jose, Camarines Sur

I was assigned to a rural community of about 15,000, located four miles west of the Pacific, in Southern Luzon, in the general geographical area known as the Bicol. Mount Isarog, a quiet volcano, protected San Jose from the west and a coastal range bordered the area to the north and south. The immediate area was surrounded by low flat rice fields, dotted by coconut, abaca (also known as Manila hemp), and banana crops.

In early December 1961, an open-air Alatco bus stopped at the outskirts of San Jose, and four Peace Corps volunteers jumped down from the bus with suitcases, three birds (in two cages) and a monkey, also caged. The luggage was sorted and placed in the care of a local citizen. As the bus passed on, we encountered four somewhat majestic carabaos, washed, polished and appearing to be rather ashamed of their colorful flowered neck wreaths. Leis also landed around the necks of the four Americans—myself, Tim Peterson from Hawaii, Ray McEachern from Florida, and Warren McNeely, from Washington State. Our respective head teachers for our assigned schools put straw hats on each of us and assisted us in mounting each of our carabaos. Once situated, the parade to the municipal square began.

As we caught our first glimpses of this new hometown, the citizens also took the opportunity to inspect these "strange Americans" who they were told, weren't really experts at anything, but were here to live with them, understand them, and to aid their teachers in the instruction of English and science. Their thinking, later revealed in conversations, went along these lines. Americans are, of course, known for enjoying a high standard of living, which is possible in their home states; but these had decided that they wanted to live like people in San Jose. Is that not a bit strange? Why have they come? They aren't technical experts, they don't have any monetary aid to disperse, we have a surplus of educators in our country, most of us are very pro-American, and most of us have some use of the English language. They are the Peace Corps sent by President Kennedy. They are very welcome. We haven't had Americans in our communities since liberation. Why are they here?

The curiosity about our purposes was best illustrated by my co-teacher, Mr. Peñero. He was a sixth grade teacher at Kinalansan Elementary School (four kilometers south of San Jose), and he gave the main address at my formal reception at the school. Likening the Peace Corps to a science experiment, he presented his interpretation of why "we" were there. The following is a copy of his hand-written text.

Welcome Program for P.C.V. at Kinalansan
December 14, 1961
Unit 32 Human Relations, Experiment #1

Major Problem: To prove that white and colored peoples can work harmoniously together in the promotion of friendly relations between their home countries.

Minor Problem: To prove that whites don't consider colored peoples inferior but their equal.

Materials: Peace Corps Volunteer—in our particular case, Mr. Campbell, 10 Filipino teachers, 350 pupils of varying sizes and capabilities and crowded compartments called classrooms.

Procedure: Drop slowly one volunteer into a homelike structure called school and mix him thoroughly with 10 teachers. Gradually add into the mixture 350 pupils with technicolor smell—stirring them once in awhile with a dash of English and Science. Feed the volunteer *gulay* and *bagoong* once in a blue moon to sharpen his longing for the luxuries and comforts back home.

Observations: Observe carefully the following:

If the volunteers have patience to repeat what they say or if their words fail to register on dull ears, like mine.

If the volunteer, after mixing thoroughly, still stands out with an air of superiority or vanishes with the mixture humble and friendly.

Observe carefully how his towering nose twists right and left with his nostrils closing into mere slits when he is given an overdose of that atomic fall-out which we call in Bicol *"ator"* (carabao droppings).

Conclusion: Results, yet unknown.

Anceleto Peñero

Thus was my formal introduction to my new assignment at Kinalansan and the challenge inherent in "serving."

Settling In

Following the grand carabao parade in San Jose, formal presentations by local officials, refreshments, lunches, the announcement of the escape of Tim's monkey—and then of its capture, we went to our new residence.

The house was unpainted concrete and wood with two bedrooms upstairs and a living and dining area, kitchen, and extra storage space downstairs. Thirty feet from the back door was another structure housing a cement, manual flush toilet and a shower area. Running water came from three oil barrels mounted on a frame above our house, supplied from a manual pump. Municipal electricity was available from 6 pm to 6 am. The cooking stove was a kerosene burner. A hedge bordered the yard, which contained cassava plants, a coffee tree, breadfruit tree, papaya trees, a mango tree, orange and lemon trees, pineapple, and one large coconut palm.

Jose Valencia, a 19-year-old boy, was at the house to greet us. The community had selected him to be our cook, helper, friend and counselor. We had not planned on domestic help. We were told that if we were to fulfill our obligations to our schools, we would not have time to be at the markets at 6 am in the nearby town of Goa or to attend the fish market, beef, and pig markets, which occurred at different times and different places in the area. We later learned that there are social obligations, for those that can afford such, to assist those in need. By accepting the service of Jose, we would be providing him the home he needed a well as providing him the opportunity to perfect his use of English. Jose turned out to be necessary not only for daily maintenance of the household, but also as a very valuable resource for local cultural interactions. There were many such "cultural activities" for which the Penn State and Los Baños training didn't provide any guidance—such as the appropriate response when asked in the middle of the night to accompany a neighbor on a serenade vigil to the family of his "beloved."

Our all male household in San Jose was complemented by the all female household of Claire Horan, Betty Jo McMakin, Virginia Hopkins and Sue Johnson in Tigaon, located about 18 kilometers to the southwest. They served as hostesses for some of the social events in San Jose and provided holiday festivities in their home.

Once community relationships were established, our household dispersed to live in the communities in which our schools were located. Tim had a nipa hut built on the beach in Sabang, Ray moved to his nipa hut in Lagonoy, I moved to a nipa hut in Kinalansan and Warren remained in San Jose where he served in the Central School. Prior to the conclusion of the tour, Stan Mazaroff, who had served as a Volunteer Leader, acquired a nipa hut in Telegrafo, on the beach, two kilometers south of Kinalansan.

During the school summer recess, we could pursue other projects. The first summer, I chose to work with the Department of Forestry at the University of the Philippines in Los Baños. The primary objective of the project was to discover ways for Filipinos to develop an appreciation of their national forests, which were suffering from the slash and burn methods of the *kaingiñeros* in the northern provinces. Another volunteer, Lynne Walker, and I developed a program concept in which a young boy would be selected to visit the forest and report what he saw and promote an appreciation that the national forest belonged to all Filipinos and that they should all be concerned about its well-being. Thus *Pepito Visits His National Forest* came to be. A Pepito was selected from an orphanage in Manila. Contacts and travel arrangements were being made, and a book for school children was being formatted. Then the Peace Corps Office in Manila sent word that there had been objections to the project and that it was thereby cancelled. They could not reveal the source of the objections; however those working on the project highly suspected that the ones most likely to object were the foreign lumber companies that subsidized the activities of the Department of Forestry at the College. We knew it could not be the *kaingiñeros*. Fortunately, Smoky the Bear didn't experience the same fate with the U.S. Forest Service as Pepito did in the Philippines.

During the second summer recess, plans stayed local. We organized Camp Oriox, a summer camp for students in the region to learn world geography and perfect their English. The camp was built on a site on Mt. Isorog that also had an irrigation dam that provided for swimming activities. We selected counselors from high school students who applied for the positions. Financing of the camp was all provided through local resources and was a very rewarding experience for all. I learned that one must take caution in rescuing a drowning person. I came across a young man, not associated with the camp, in the swimming area making three attempts to surface, his arm raised above his head. I dove in and when near the victim, found myself submerged by the body of the man. Eventually, we both made it to shore, and after 24 hours of sleep, I was able to continue my responsibilities at the camp.

A Special Person

My Peace Corps experience would not be complete without the mention of the Principal Teacher at Kinalansan, Mrs. Emma Perfecto. Mrs. Perfecto had majored in English, later received a Master's and PhD in English. She and her husband Edmundo, who was also a principal teacher in a barrio school in the district, had two daughters and a son. They resided in San Jose. Some years later, following Mrs. Perfecto's achievement of her PhD in English as a Second Language at the University of Hawaii, Mrs. Perfecto visited me in Oregon. I was able to take her on a tour of Oregon, which included her first visit of "snow" on Mount Hood and the rural experiences of Eastern Oregon. When I returned to the Philippines upon the twenty-fifth anniversary of the Peace Corps, Mrs. Perfecto was serving as the Superintendent of the Bicol education district with offices in Legaspi. She had arranged all of the special activities for me upon my return to the Bicol. A few years later, Mrs. Perfecto had a heart attack, which took her life at an untimely age. One of her daughters is a medical doctor in Manila, the other daughter a nurse in Southern California, and her son is a dentist in Southern California. Her husband was also living with the daughter in California. (For a glimpse into the life of Mrs. Perfecto and her concept of my involvement in the Peace Corps, a copy of a letter she wrote to my parents appears in another section of this book)

Ties that Bind: Old and New

Upon my return to the States, following a brief tour of Hong Kong, Taipei, Tokyo, Kyoto, and Anchorage, I enjoyed a few days of "notoriety": the gift of a can of Haley's hash and a can of Haley's beef stew from a sponsor at a radio station, a television interview, and a number of speaking invitations. I made numerous job applications and accepted a teaching position in Cove, Oregon, instructing high school science, seventh grade science, and business courses. My father, in the early stages of his career, the years around 1935, had been superintendent of the Cove School District, and it was where my parents were living when I was born. I happened to be with a group of students in the gymnasium, when the social science instructor burst into the gym and yelled, "Someone finally shot the son-of-a-bitch." President Kennedy had been assassinated! Thankfully the other faculty and students did not share the sentiment of the social science teacher

Following the school year at Cove, I accepted a position with the Bureau of Indian Affairs, which was the beginning of a long career working in true grassroots development with a number of different tribes in Oregon in education and health projects. The association with Indian Health Service (IHS) led to an opportunity to reconnect with Peace Corps, which had contracted with IHS to provide the training for volunteers headed to Korea as health auxiliaries. I was detailed for five months to serve as Assistant Director of Training at the training site at Ghost Ranch, New Mexico. The training included the development of community health projects to be selected by the trainees. My contingent conducted a rabies vaccination project on the Hopi Reservation. Working with the Hopi Tribal Council, the trainees conducted classes in the schools and the community, and they immunized over 90 percent of the dogs in the communities on the mesas housing the Hopis.

I have maintained communication with principals and teachers at the Kinalansan Elementary School over the last 50 years. Hearing about their progress is still a part of my everyday enjoyments.

In 1986, the twenty-fifth anniversary of the Peace Corps, I returned to Kinalansan, and received a report on the partial results of the 'science experiment' my co-teacher has described twenty-four years earlier. The very same Mr. Peñero gave the following address at a formal ceremony at Kinalansan Elementary:

Fond Memories

Dedicated to Mr. Bruce Campbell
Kinalansan, Oct. 10, 1986

It was once upon a time, some twenty-four years before, Kinalansan had the privilege to have a volunteer form the U.S. Peace Corp. An active & handsome American, a gentleman from Oregon. Mr. Bruce Campbell, ever smiling, cooperative and amiable.

Our school then was just wobbling on its feet. After being completely knocked down by typhoon Harriet. So we had to pick up rubbles and every little bit to be made into a building, which to us was the very best we could do. When it rained we had running water all around serving as a cascading shower during our lesson hours. Our floors were sticky chocolate that gave free boots for our numb feet. Teachers and pupils of the school made it a day to celebrate.

Bruce had to cramp himself in our little Harriet kitchenette. His back against the walls that pricked...pressed by a table that squeaked. Every time he stands he bumps against the starry roof; but that made him very polite. He had to bow without any complaining word.

Yes, those were the days when we were closely nit together. With pretty Mrs. Emma Perfecto, yet our ever humble principal teacher. We were happy, we were all smiles, our hearts were full of cheer.

It is nice to see again, Bruce our American friend. Back to our place after twenty-four years. Now with his friend, Gary Chamberlin, let's give them a hearty cheer...Shout MABUHAY!

May our friendship live longer.

Anceleto Peñero

In December of this past year, I received a letter from a Bryan Jacobs. The return address was San Jose, Camarines Sur, Republic of the Philippines. Bryan, a volunteer in Group #268.[1] He had just arrived in San Jose, the first volunteer to serve there since our original group of four. Bryon's duties in costal resource management include "*maningisda* registration" and solid waste management. He is a recent graduate of the University of Oregon. His first letter concluded:

> I am having a great time here and I'm nothing but optimistic about the next two years. As you know, the Philippines is a wonderful country filled with a culture of caring and welcoming people. As my adventures continue,

---

[1] Editors note: Group CCLXVIII for those used to original group designations.

which I know they will, I will continue to try to stay in touch. Please feel free to write me back with questions, advice, stories or just a supportive word.

We have exchanged a few e-mails since the original letter, and Bryan has made a presentation to the Kinalansan Elementary School and forwarded me stories of my friends.

Did I bring the Peace Corps back home, or did the Peace Corps make me a home, a "place of being in the world"? I believe it has given me "a place in being in this world.," and I thank Bill Moyers' address at the memorial service at the Arlington National Cemetery on the occasion of the 25th Peace Corps Anniversary for giving me that perspective. In my century-old home in the corner of Northeast Oregon, I have a place of being in this world.

Final Words

As I wrote for the *Memory Book* on the occasion of the 25th anniversary of the Peace Corps:

> To some, in 1961, a part of the "American Dream" included a pursuit of understanding of the world's citizens.
>
> There was a sense of the maturing of human emotion that nurtured a respect for difference and thus a sense of understanding that could transcend thinking alike, looking alike, acting alike and worshiping alike. There was the spirit that the world could tolerate difference, if it understood difference and it could understand difference through cultural respect, sensitivity and the sharing of not only technical skills and resources, but also the sharing of human emotion.
>
> The Peace Corps provided a means and symbolized a Nation which was concerned with this philosophy and these ideals. It is with pride and humility that I evaluate my experience. It is with concern that I wish to maintain "our" share of this "American Dream."

With the passage of yet another 25 years from thoughts written in 1986, I find that the same challenges exist to this aspect of my "American Dream;" however, I have been able to integrate the Peace Corps experience in my personal life expanding the two-year tour of duty into a lifetime of commitment and rewards.

Bruce Campbell resides in the small northeastern Oregon town of Milton-Freewater. It is the epicenter of 68 of the 73 years of his life: his birth place being 70 miles to the southeast; his college, 10 miles to the north; his home for 43 years, 30 miles to the south. A part of his heart and being still remains 6,000 miles to the southwest in the barrio of Kinalansan, San Jose, Camarines Sur in the Republic of the Philippines, and with the volunteers with whom he served. The Peace Corps was not just a two-year assignment; it became an integral part of his life experience for the past 50 years.

Tom Carlton

(Written by his son, Chris Carlton)

Son of a Kwan

On this special occasion of the 50th anniversary of the Peace Corps, it is a great honor for me to write on behalf of my late father, Tom Carlton, and to contribute to the reflections of the Group I volunteers who traveled to the Philippines in 1961. My father left this world far too early in 1992. My family and I feel his absence everyday, but we are constantly reminded of the significant impact his Peace Corps service in the Philippines had on his life. His experiences there as a twenty-something kid from Los Angeles shaped the man he would later become—a Doctor of Social Work whose influential career included writing, teaching and administration at Virginia Commonwealth University in Richmond, Virginia, and more importantly, the head of a Filipino-American family of five whose deep Filipino roots were made stronger by his love and passion for the Philippines, its people, and its culture.

Like a lot of teenagers, I didn't show much interest in asking my father to talk about his life before my siblings and I were around. I regret it now, since we lost Dad so early, but I wasn't completely oblivious to the effects his service in the Peace Corps had on his life. I have gained my perspective on his experience through my own life growing up in a Filipino-American family, by seeing the extremely close friendships Dad maintained with the people who shared his experience, and by recently reading the letters he wrote home while he was in the Philippines.

I know that he joined the Peace Corps to be part of its noble effort to spread peace, goodwill, and hope throughout the world in countries and communities that needed the most assistance with basic needs and education. I also believe he was searching, in a way, for inspiration and direction, trying to find out who he was and what he wanted to do in his life. His letters tell the story of how he arrived in a country of other-worldly natural beauty, with his mind open to new experiences, new connections, and a new way of life. They continue through his time in service with stories of overcoming obstacles in his and others' attempts to complete various tasks and projects both in the town of Paracale and in Manila. In addition to the service workload he undertook, he sprinkled in times of social-butterflying around town, eating, drinking, and soaking in the company of his fellow volunteers and townspeople while exploring the town, the province, and beyond.

Though the work was a critical aspect of the PC being there at the time, in his words, Dad described their goal in the following way, "The biggest thing we're doing in the Philippines is getting to know and understand the people and seeing the magnificent beauty of this country. We are doing a good job of it and we are also bringing the Filipinos a better view of America and Americans and this is important." I'm sure the fledgling Peace Corps felt it could get its footing in part by building upon the existing relationship between post-WWII Philippines and the United States.

Dad quickly found that many Filipinos admired and respected him and his fellow PC volunteers seemingly just for being from America. In one early letter, he somewhat jokingly noted, ."..the Peace Corps is the poorest group of Americans ever to hit these islands. Our Filipino friends can't get over how little money we have. They think it's terrible. But this might help dispel the image that all Americans are rich. From one point of view however, we really are rich. Things we take for granted are life-long dreams for most Filipinos—things they dream of and never have." I know in his heart he was there trying to give the people of the Philippines the kind of basic resources they needed to lift themselves and their communities up, but also the knowledge and self-reliance it took for them to continue doing so once the Peace Corps volunteers finished their service there.

In another letter, he included a quote from a friend of his from back home that I think describes the feelings he had for Filipinos as well as the importance of the Peace Corps to them and the other countries in which they worked—"If everyone all over the world could be as cordial and friendly as the Filipinos we wouldn't have to have armies and H bombs. We could have four or five million young people in Peace Corps types of endeavors. It's a hell of a lot better to learn how to help your fellow man than to learn to kill him." Like a lot of his observations in life, Dad's quote on his friend's words were to the point. "Very well said!" he wrote.

On a personal level, reading the letters my father wrote home during this time was like stepping back in time to live through it with him. In a way, the letters are the raw, true impressions of his time there, perhaps even more vivid than he could have told it after time and distance might have changed how he remembered it. Having recently visited the Philippines with my mother and my wife, I found that his descriptions of the country's beautiful people and landscape hit home much more strongly for me. I've walked in his footsteps from Manila to Paracale and the Bicol region. When he wrote of the places he had seen, it was with the same awe and wonder I felt when I saw them with my own eyes, 45 years later. I would have loved to have been there with him to fulfill his pledge to return there someday. He never did make it back. However, his professional life after his Peace Corps service ended was largely influenced by what he learned of himself and of the value of helping others while in the Philippines. He taught English and history on the elementary and high school levels in Paracale, and found out firsthand what a great gift knowledge is for those who pursue it and for those who help others gain it. He continued his education in the field of Social Work, eventually earning his Doctorate from the University of Pennsylvania. His mother called him a career student, and the importance of higher education was no doubt further impressed on him while in the Philippines. As a professor, advisor, and administrator at the VCU School of Social Work, he indeed helped many others along their paths as students and social workers.

While his professional career was certainly distinguished and admirable, it was my father's role in the lives of his family and friends that stands out as his life's best work. So many of the friendships and connections he made in the Peace Corps have been interwoven into the fabric of our family and continue today as we approach this 50th anniversary.

As fate would have it, Paracale is my mother's hometown. Although she was in college in Manila during my father's service in her town, he was well-known by my grandparents and the rest of the Heraldo family there. My uncle was even one of his English students at the school. And when my mother immigrated to California in 1968, my grandfather, out of respect for my dad's character, wrote him a letter asking that he look after her in her new country. After she eventually arrived in Los Angeles, it was through the famous Peace Corps couple, Emery and Annie Bontrager (Tito Emery and Tita Annie to me and my siblings), that the match was made.

My father's friendships with his housemates and other Group I volunteers proved to be life-long, and have endured even beyond his passing. Several attended my brother's wedding in 1999 and mine in 2003, which included a Filipino Barrio Fiesta where the PC contingent danced the Tinikling, drank rum, and sang, just the like the good old days. The love and respect for each other and our family, born out of their shared experience in the Peace Corps, was evident that day, as it has been my whole life. Also in attendance at that Barrio Fiesta was a large group of Filipino-Americans from Richmond. My father strongly supported our involvement with and was very much active in the Filipino community in Richmond. He served as parliamentarian for the Filipino-American Association of Central Virginia, and it seems he was always called on to speak a few words of welcome at events, or to give a toast, or to provide counsel to members, carrying on his service role in the U.S. as he had done in the Philippines.

In closing, I would like to add some of my own impressions of the Peace Corps. I see it as a wonderful organization that provides important, valuable resources and services to countries and people in need. All great organizations are only as great as the people who are associated with them and make them what they are. Peace Corps volunteers are a rare breed of special, good-minded people, who serve others through kindness and great personal sacrifice. Their reward is a better world, a better sense of self, and friendships and memories to last a lifetime and beyond. The Group I volunteers in the Philippines know this from living it. I count myself lucky to have learned it from my father, through his life, his stories, his letters, and his friends and family. *Maraming salamat po sa lahat.*

Chris Carlton is the middle child of Tom and Susan Carlton. He is a proud Filipino-American currently residing in Washington D.C., with his wife Elizabeth and son Tommy. He has been on a leave of absence from the Information Technology industry to be a stay-at-home dad to Tommy for the past year, and could not think of a more important, fulfilling role in his life. He loves playing golf, watching University of Virginia sports, traveling (2 trips to the Philippines!), and spending time with his family. Grandson Tommy recognizes his grandfather Tom in photos and calls him Lolo (grandfather).

(The first photo shows Tom with the bartender at his favorite Manila hangout, the El Bodegon Restaurant; the second photo from December 2009 shows Tom's wife Susan holding their grandson Tommy flanked by son Ricky and his wife Michelle, daughter Elizabeth, and son Chris along with his wife Elizabeth.)

Maureen J. Carroll
Not for Girls like You: A Jersey Girl's Journey

Jersey Girl

Around midnight on a hot summer night in early July 1961, the one telephone in the house rang, awakening me and my parents. I got there first, fearing bad news, and was stunned to hear that it was Western Union calling *me*. I had never had a telegram before. It was from R. Sargent Shriver, inviting me to become a Peace Corps Volunteer in the Philippines—8 weeks training at Penn State University, two weeks at home and then off to the Philippines. I was to be an "aide in the elementary school system assisting rural school teachers in the teaching of English, science and math." I was to report to Penn State in two weeks. My heart raced. I had actually been selected!

I was 23 years old, living at home in Jersey City and working in New York City. I had flown but once—on a spring break trip to Bermuda, which was the extent of my international experience. A graduate of a Catholic women's college in 1959, I had followed a traditional path of English majors by enrolling in a master's degree program in the fall of that year. I dropped out when I began to question my commitment to a career in metaphysical poetry of the 17th century. Although I was certified to teach high school English, it was too late to get a teaching job, so I went to work as a correspondent in Shareowner Communications for AT&T.

My job at AT&T was a cut above the mainly secretarial jobs available to women college graduates at the time. It used my brain, I didn't have to do my own typing, and it paid well. However, I worried that I could turn into a career telephone company employee who accumulated anniversary pins, collected stock, and adopted the conservative values of Ma Bell. Life was good, but it didn't seem to be terribly meaningful. I had inquired about working as a teacher on Indian reservations. I had looked into moving to California. I was definitely ready to "move out," to have an adventure while doing something that was socially redeeming.

I got caught up in John F. Kennedy's campaign for the presidency and even went to Washington D.C. for the inauguration. I took to heart his rhetoric during the campaign that spoke of new frontiers, challenged us to become peacemakers rather than warmongers and declared the passing of the torch to a new generation of Americans. Then came the inaugural address in which the President challenged me to do something for my country, a challenge to ask not what my country could do for me, but what I could do for our country—what "we" could do together for the freedom of man! I was ready! Joining the Peace Corps was the answer to my restlessness.

When I got the invitation to the Philippines, my parents brightened. I had received previous communications from the Peace Corps asking if I would be willing to serve in Nigeria. I was willing to go anywhere, but my parents were hesitant about Africa, steeped as we all were in the stereotypes of "the Dark Continent." On the other hand, who hadn't heard of the Philippines—a former U.S. colony, World War II battles, the return of Douglas MacArthur? And, what's more, it was Catholic!

I had no hesitations about accepting Shriver's invitation even though a favorite uncle of mine, literally on his deathbed at the time, warned me that the Peace Corps was "not for girls like you."

A New Home in Castilla

Following an eleven-hour overnight train trip on hard benches in third class cars, a week of welcomes in various stopover towns on the way to our site, and an in-service program with the teachers of our district, my housemates and I FINALLY arrived at our site—Castilla, Sorsogon. We had completed 15 weeks of academic and somewhat irrelevant training in the United States at Penn State University and in the Philippines at the agricultural college in Los Baños. Two strengths of the training were the excellent cultural training at Los Baños and the advice from our Penn State Training Director to remember to "roll with the punches."

Castilla was the central town of a municipality that comprised 26 roadside, mountain, and coastal barrios in the province of Sorsogon in southern Luzon across the San Bernandino Straits from Samar and about 600 kilometers from Manila. Castilla's location, six kilometers off the National Road, made it less "advanced" than some of its barrios situated on the road. In fact, residents in other towns or barrios called people from Castilla *"camotes,"* a play on the word for sweet potatoes, suggesting slow-wittedness. It was an unfair rap. Most people in Castilla made their subsistence living by small-scale fishing. Unfortunately, when the bay seemed low on supply, they resorted to "dynamite" fishing. Many of our neighbors had stubs for fingers, and many an evening explosions pierced the quiet.

Castilla had been occupied by the Japanese during World War II. As untouched as we had ever been by war, we found it surprising that the war was still so fresh in people's minds. Townspeople referred to the "atrocities" in hushed voices and pointed out to us the site of beheadings near the home economics building of the school. They relished telling us tales of hiding out in the mountains and of the hope that was engendered by U.S. flyovers dropping chocolates marked with the phrase "I shall return" before Douglas MacArthur's landing at Leyte.

Unusual for a town, Castilla didn't have a market or even a market day. Aside from a few *sari-sari* stores that sold canned corned beef, candles, soap, salt and other sundries, there were no other businesses at all. An elementary school, a rural health clinic, and a few municipal offices were the limited evidence of government interest in the approximately 1000 residents, mostly under 15 years of age. No one had a private vehicle. One Alatco bus ran between Castilla and the capital of Sorsogon several times a day. On the other hand, Castilla's location on Sorsogon Bay, overlooking Bulusan Volcano, had the compensations of a yet-to-be-discovered resort—unspoiled beach and pleasing views.

I lived there with several other female Volunteers—Hope Gould, Gloria Paulik, and Anne Wilson—in a small wooden house with a corrugated tin roof, raised on poles above the ground. We had three rooms. A *sala* (living room) was large enough to hold two small bamboo and rattan beds in one corner and it included a built-in space for a shrine. The bedroom held two other beds and two giant dressers built for us by local carpenters. The kitchen had a firewood stove, no refrigerator, and a sink with no running water. We also had a small bathroom that had a cement floor, a water seal toilet, a faucet that didn't run and a shower-head that didn't work. There was no electricity. On a ground level of the house was a small former *sari-sari* store that we converted into a community library. The front fence of the house overflowed with magenta bougainvillea, and the back yard had a papaya tree or two. A ladder-like set of stairs led to the house.

Our landlord, Magno Laban, lived next door in a multi-generational household. Mr. Laban was a retired school teacher and took great pride in his command of the English language. He translated his name as "Great Warrior." Watching the town's reaction to our arrival, he challenged our own command of the language by christening us "cynosures." He delighted that we had to use the dictionary to find out that the word meant "the centers of attention"—which indeed we turned out to be, regardless of our attempts to blend into the community.

Although there were four of us, the community impressed on us the need for single women to have a *kisama* (companion) to maintain a proper image. Our companion was a young woman in her '30s named Caridad Japon, who was called Ca-RING. She cooked the simple daily diet of rice and fish, swept and polished the beautiful real mahogany floors, and protected our belongings when we were out or away—there were no locks on the doors.

The idea of a "servant" was initially anathema to our Peace Corps philosophy of living "like the people," but we soon found out that most teachers—our counterparts—had someone to help around the house. According to our "advisors," we had another very important need to employ Caring. She was an "orphan" with no family of her own who needed a home. As people with supposed means, it was clear that we had a responsibility to contribute to the economic life of the community. We complied with the advice—as we wisely learned to do on other matters over time. Caring slept on a mat on the floor in the kitchen. She turned out to be an extremely delightful companion and an excellent cultural informant until she came down with tuberculosis a year later. We stayed in touch for many years after my service until her untimely death in the late '70s.

As I think back to our living arrangements, I'm struck by how we managed to live in such close quarters for so long. Most of the members of our group were assigned to four-person households, reflecting Peace Corps care to avoid the dire predictions of many in Congress about what could happen to us if sent out alone to live in remote communities. (Today most Volunteers live alone or with families.) Many in our group broke up their households, and each person moved out to neighboring barrios. One of our household members, Anne Wilson, transferred to Manila for better job satisfaction. The three of us remaining stayed intact. Somehow or other, we made it work despite occasional tensions because of personality differences or the degree of frustration each of us may have felt at different times about the meaning of what we were doing. The camaraderie was a valuable asset in dissecting and learning from our experiences and in designing school and community projects.

A Day in the Life

It amazes me that to this day I can close my eyes and conjure up my daily life in Castilla quite vividly.

I wake up at 4:30 in the morning because I have to catch the first bus out of town to a nearby barrio where I work. There won't be another bus until way after the opening of school. I shower by scooping cold water from an empty five-gallon kerosene can that holds water drawn from a nearby pump. I dress in the dark since we don't pump up the kerosene lamps until night-time. I eat rice and a cold fried egg for breakfast before I climb onto the Alatco #166 truck-like bus that stops in front of our house. Mr. Allipio, the driver known as "The Camel," is hunched over the wheel, and Waldo, the effervescent conductor in a crisp khaki uniform, urges passengers to get on "quickly, quickly, quickly." Also on board are some neighbors and a few squealing pigs, clucking chickens and inert sacks of pungent copra stashed in the storage area under the passengers or in the rear of the bus, a space known as the "kitchen." (One day, a very large cow in the kitchen proceeded to urinate a substantial flow, flooding our feet before we could lift our legs.) We all greet each other in the local language, Bikol, which I never master much beyond greetings, small talk, and marketing phrases.

I get off the bus at the intersection of the dirt road out of Castilla and the paved National Road, sit on a hard bench in front of the still-closed corner store, and wait for the sun to rise, signaled by the roosters crowing and nearby residents sleepily going to the water pump for morning baths. I then report to the Milagrosa Elementary School, a short walk away, which has a large sandy campus dotted with whitewashed stones outlining garden and flower plots tended by the children using machetes—all installed before an inspection visit from district school officials. The school has only two small buildings housing six grades in classrooms with hard mud floors, old, broken down desks, and no bathrooms. The classrooms are decorated with Palmer method alphabet cards, photos of national hero Jose Rizal, and homemade teaching aids.

The children, barefoot and wearing faded and sometimes torn clothing, assemble to sing the national anthem before an empty flag pole to start the day. (We later receive a beautiful new flag of the Philippines from an American elementary school class with whom we have become pen-pals.) Many of the children are malnourished but nothing daunts their spirit or their abundant smiles. They often bring me "gifts" of guavas or other fruit they pick on their way to school. Most of them will never go beyond sixth grade and many will drop out after grade 4 to help their families farm meager plots of upland rice or *camotes*.)

During the day I attempt to "co-teach" with the regular teachers, as I'm supposed to do, but they demur and I wind up teaching instead, consoling myself that I am at least demonstrating good technique in second-language teaching. I spend the day going from class to class, teaching the children to distinguish the sounds of "p" and "f," "b" and "v" etc. and to recite English dialogs to gain fluency in a language that will always be secondary in their lives. I am thrilled when Mario is able to recite the nursery rhyme "Peter Piper picked a peck of pickled peppers" with perfect "p" sounds," when Eden can deliver "Fi, Fi, Fo Fum, I smell the blood of an Englishman" with perfect "f's," or when the first grade teacher Mrs. Chavez asks thoughtful questions about reinforcing the lesson. I don't allow myself to think about the disconnect between these accomplishments and the lofty goals of the Peace Corps or my own dreams of making the world a better place.

As the day goes on, I sometimes wilt from the insistent heat and accompanying lassitude that make siestas a welcome practice. On other occasions I shout my language drills above the torrential rains on the leaky tin roof of the school and watch the students pick banana tree leaves to use as umbrellas as they scurry home to help with chores.

Once home again, it's time for *merienda* as each of us returns from our separate schools. A large thermos of hot water for tea sits on the kitchen table, and there is a treat of hot fried *camotes* or fried bananas. We trade stories of the day and read our mail from home. Then it's onto our extra-curricular activities—staffing our library, trying to motivate the youth club we have formed to engage in some community activity, perhaps practicing a folk dance with teachers for the next community program. We might also go down to the black volcanic sand beach and take a swim with neighbor children. Captain Eustacio Lastrella, who owns the property adjacent to the beach, has painted our names and states in large white hearts on the trunks of palm trees. He has christened the beach "Blue Seal Beach" and has painted a large sign saying "Welcome Global Visitors." (Blue seal means first class—taken from the blue colored stamps that seal American cigarette packs.) When we admire his handsome leather jacket, he tells us that he is "smuggled head to foot," and he frequently warns us about the "goddam Chinese."

We get lots of visitors. We are curiosities, and we are status symbols—aspects of our service that we do not enjoy. Among them might be Jun, the Pepsi Cola delivery man with a crush on one of my housemates, the former guerilla who called himself Captain Douglas during the years of the Japanese occupation, or an American reporter based in Manila setting out to find out the truth about the Peace Corps. Innocencia Legaspi, a *lola* (grandmother) who wears traditional dress, often comes by to sing to us as she gets drunk on the bottle of *tuba* (palm wine) that she carries. Pedro, the deaf-mute carpenter, salutes us when he drops by and sits with us in silence. They all come unannounced, and they stay for a while. Except for the American reporter, they don't mind if we have nothing to talk about. They seem to just like being in our house. Occasionally, a young person will drop by and begin to use a coconut husk to polish our floors. Unsolicited favors are usually the first installment in building *utang na loob* (reciprocal debt.)

The final visitors of the day are likely to be the *lavendera* (laundress) Jacinta and a few of her seven children. She comes to pick up laundry that she will wash in the stream outside of town, using rocks to beat the sheets and clothes clean. We often have to ask her to desist from chewing betel nuts when ironing our clothes. The stains are gross. We love Jacinta. Her husband is a drunk, and she is dirt poor, but she is always cheerful. She is so small and wiry that you imagine she will fly away in a tropical wind. We have a deal in which we give her the fish heads from our daily fish—we won't eat them and Filipinos see them as delicacies. Her two little girls, Edna and Norma, 4 and 2, roll around on the laundry bags. Her handsome son, Alfredo (7 or 8) has a grin that lights up the room. He brings his guitar and we sit around singing American classics like *You Are My Sunshine,* a Filipino folk song like *Bahay Kubo,* or the latest popular music hit, *Fly(Ply) Me to the Moon.*

In the evening, we pump up the Petromax kerosene lamps for light, do some homework, discuss how we can have "more impact," write a letter home, or watch the geckos copulate on the ceiling. The town is shut down except for a few late night mahjong players, their tiles clicking away in the silence. The mosquito nets are up and almost everyone is asleep—unless there is a full moon. Then, the light in the streets, otherwise unavailable, brings folks out to stroll around town, get into mischief, or court sweethearts with *haranas* (serenades).

Reflections on the Life

I was happy in the Philippines despite an attack or two of culture shock and intermittent job frustrations. Despite my totally urban background, I really liked living in a very rural setting. I loved the beauty and the scale of the place, and the warm, interdependent relationships among people. I liked "having influence" which accrued to us as Volunteers, but especially as Americans. It meant, for example, that we could get the hospital emergency room service to tend to a very sick child right away instead of letting him wait for hours. I liked discovering how similar we humans all are, regardless of color, height, or culture, and I was intellectually challenged by the conundrums involved in trying to create change in the schools or the community.

The job was always the rub. We had all joined the Peace Corps "to make a difference in the state of the world." We were frustrated by the vagueness and seeming lack of importance attached to the role of an elementary school aide. We couldn't be teachers because we would have been replacing the abundant supply of Filipino teachers. During our in-country training, a Bureau of Public Schools official had alarmed us by suggesting that we could function like tape recorders in the classrooms, demonstrating proper pronunciation of English when called upon by the teachers. In our free time, we were supposed to do community development since it was assumed that by our very presence we would be "agents of change."

We were casualties of the rapid start-up of the Peace Corps. There really was no well-developed program—it was up to us to make our own way. Surprisingly, most of us did. Many left the schools altogether, but some of us, myself included, did carve out a way to contribute to the schools (worked more than one school, ran monthly teacher workshops, traveled to remote barrios to stay for a week and work intensively with teachers) and to launch various community projects (youth clubs, demonstration pig-raising, summer schools and camps).

Nevertheless, the dominant theme of our service was an examination of fundamental questions: What is the role of the Peace Corps Volunteer in the Philippines? Why are we here? What difference can we make? As the discussions ensued with passion but without resolution, Peace Corps kept sending more and more Volunteers. Within a year or two, over 600 Volunteers were all over the islands, most of them still as elementary school aides.

Our Filipino colleagues were as confused and mystified as we were about our purpose, but on the whole, they were happy to have us. After all, we were sent by the great John F. Kennedy, and we were also seen as the reincarnation of the Thomasites—the hardy American teachers who had sailed to the Philippines shortly after the turn of the 20th century on the *S.S. Thomas* and brought a semblance of the American public school system to a country where the Spaniards had refused to provide universal education for Filipinos. Filipinos were happy to have us "go around and enjoy"—and from my re-reading of my intermittent diary entries, I seem to have done a lot of that. We attended fiestas and special events all over the province and beyond, spent a summer working in Manila, and travelled to other parts of the country on vacations or for conferences.

Other frustrations occasionally challenged my basic satisfaction. It was almost impossible for us to overcome "special treatment" by virtue of being American. As single females we could not drink or smoke in public. We could not date without chaperones, and at barrio dances we were the major attraction for men who needed to get drunk to get up the nerve to ask us to dance. The lack of respect for time, the class boundaries, the pomposity and neglect of many politicians, the view that problems or injustices were fate rather than opportunities for change, the frequent requests from strangers for "a little Christmas," and the seemingly intractable poverty all wore thin at times. At the same time, much of what we experienced as frustration taught us viscerally the dire effects of hundreds of years of colonialism upon a native population, whose independence movement we Americans had crushed at the turn of the century.

The plus sides of living in the Philippines, however, definitely outweighed the negatives.

The day I left Castilla in May of 1963 was so gut-wrenching that when I got to Legaspi to overnight before the next day flight to Manila, I got physically ill. Leaving behind such a profound experience and people to whom I had grown so attached, wondering if I would ever see them again, shook me to my core. I cried and threw up all night. I also regretted that I had to leave behind the live chicken, the *pomelos*, and the mangos that had been thrust into the jeep as I left town.

Footprints in the Sand?

On some small scale, even within the fundamentally flawed concept of our program, I believe I made some contributions to the teaching skills of some teachers and to the English language ability of some students. Although we often had late night discussions about the dangers of cultural imperialism, we somewhat unabashedly promoted what we thought were good American or western values—sanitation means good health, success comes from hard work and not just from luck, peaceful action to change conditions is a requirement of democracy, knowledge is power, etc. Perhaps they had some effect on some lives we touched.

At an absolute minimum, we certainly provided a lot of entertainment for towns and barrios without television or movies. We were the hottest show in town. Our every action—from swimming and sunbathing to dancing the twist—was observed with great curiosity and satisfaction

Filipinos were fond of saying, "it is good that you are here" or "we are grateful to President Kennedy for sending us Peace Corpse" or "Peace Corpse is better than the U.S. Ambassador." Their satisfaction with our presence had more to do with the fact that we chose to live with them in their communities as they lived and tried to speak their language rather than from any technical contributions. There was no doubt that we exposed a new image of Americans abroad—not as the military on their bases or the foreign service and business investors locked in gated communities in Manila—but as friends, counterparts, and even, in some cases, as lovers.

What I describe as possible "impact" in the Philippines is ephemeral and a stretch of the imagination. We had no clear sense of purpose other than individual interpretations of the purpose of the Peace Corps, no measureable program objectives, no indicators of success, and no systems to collect data. For which, in some perverse way, I am grateful.

However, we did lay the groundwork for the Peace Corps to be around today—50 years later with close to 200,000 former Volunteers having served in 139 countries. We did prove that young Americans imbued with idealism, openness, a sense of adventure and a willingness to learn could live successfully in villages around the globe and return home as citizens forever changed. And I know that despite our suspicions or conclusions that we Americans gain more than the host countries, the countries continue welcoming Volunteers and asking for more. They seem to see value we miss or underestimate.

Continuing Connections with the Philippines

On April 27, 2010 *The Washington Post* ran a story about upcoming Philippines elections describing the sudden largess political candidates were bestowing on the poor to win votes. It mentioned that the Philippines is the only country in Southeast Asia where the absolute number of poor people has increased since 1990. According to the reporter, "politicians who win election in this former U.S. colony have one of the worst records of Southeast Asia for stiffing the poor, coddling the rich and indulging themselves—bad governance has gone hand in glove with rising crime, a surge in political killing, stagnant foreign investment, and a restless search by tens of thousands of doctors, nurses and other highly skilled Filipinos for opportunities outside their homeland…. A weak central government has also provided an opening for Islamist extremists operating in the southern Philippines…."

It saddens me that the Philippines is seemingly worse off than when I lived there 50 years ago. On my last trip in 2005, I could see the results of the population explosion. While the country's total land area remains the same, 95 million people are now living on it rather than the 28 million in 1961. In Castilla, small houses now abut each other rather than being spread out around the town. I saw how the government revered overseas workers and afforded them privileges on their trips home. I wondered how a country could be proud of having to export its citizens all over the globe to earn a living—until I found out that the economy survives based on the remittances from overseas workers. Unfortunately, many of the skilled workers who go overseas wind up taking menial jobs. Nonetheless, they still earn more than they would at home.

I've been fortunate to have returned to the Philippines five times—twice in the mid-60s, and then in 1974, 1996 and 2005. Each time I have visited Castilla and seen friends, former teachers and students—some of whom are now grandparents.

My most recent visit (2005) was under the auspices of the Peace Corps Alumni Foundation for Philippine Development (PCAFPD). I have been with the organization for more than 20 years and have been the president for many of those years. Founded as a means for former Volunteers to "continue their commitment to Philippine development," PCAFPD is my strongest continuing connection with the country. We grant scholarships to young Filipinos to attend college. We have graduated 127 and now sponsor 50 more. My engagement in the program is my way "paying back" Filipinos for allowing me to spend two years in their country learning how to be a better American and world citizen and for the extraordinary hospitality, friendships, and support they gave me.

The other major continuing connection is with Norma, the youngest daughter of our former *lavendera* Jacinta. Norma is now about 50 years old, single, and with two grown, married daughters. She is as poor as her mother was—and she too now does laundry to earn her living. For the past 40 years I have tried through tuition assistance to get someone in the family, starting with Norma, who was valedictorian of her high school class, to get a college education—the most promising ticket for getting out of the cycle of poverty. Pregnancy-forced marriages derailed higher education for Norma and for each of her daughters. My efforts to help Norma start businesses—e.g. a piggery—have gone nowhere because of typhoons or volcano eruptions, poor decisions, theft or some other calamity that plagues the poor. If I live long enough, I'll probably wind up trying to get Norma's grandchildren to get college degrees!

Continuing Connections to the Peace Corps

I have had a continuing relationship with the Peace Corps that is unusual among my fellow Volunteers. When I moved to Washington in late 1963, I went to work for the Peace Corps. Within a year I had become a program evaluator and for the next four years, I travelled around the world examining Peace Corps programs and reporting about them directly to Sargent Shriver. In the private sector, I worked under contract on two pre-service training programs for Volunteers going to Ethiopia and Ghana. In 1991, after 20 years away, I rejoined Peace Corps as Country Director in Botswana, and in the mid-90s I was the director of the Africa Region for close to three years. I have served on numerous internal committees or task forces examining and revising Peace Corps operations, including a study that recommended a major restructuring of the agency. In my retirement years, I have worked as a consultant training new Country Directors.

In short, I've looked at Peace Corps from all sides over many decades. I can be its fiercest critic as well as its most stalwart defender. I visited hundreds and hundreds of Volunteers at their sites in more than 20 countries during the '60s and again in the '90s. Despite Peace Corps organizational or staff failures, my own included, Peace Corps Volunteers, across generations, continue to "get" the meaning of the Peace Corps and go out and make it happen, just as we did 50 years ago. Whatever their motivations, they still seem to me to represent the "best of America" abroad.

Significance

My uncle was wrong. The Peace Corps was for girls like me—a Jersey girl who needed to spread her wings. The Peace Corps and the Philippines radically changed the direction and the quality of my life for the better. Following my service, I came home "the long way" through Asia, the Middle East, and Europe, arriving home a few days before Martin Luther King's *I have a Dream* Speech at the Lincoln Memorial. Watching it and feeling a bit of a stranger in my hometown and my country, I knew I had to move to Washington D.C. Kennedy was still president, and there were so much more that needed to be done.

Except for a few years living in Africa in the '90s, I have lived in Washington for 47 years. I've travelled widely. I've had a great professional and personal life, totally infused and enriched with the sensibilities developed in my Peace Corps experience. I spent less than half of my career working for Peace Corps, but everything I have done in other jobs was shaped or informed by the experience. For example, the confidence I developed as a Volunteer made me always ready to take on challenging assignments beyond my abilities. I lost all fear or suspicion of "differences" among people. I developed a "global" view before it was fashionable. And, most wonderfully, to this day, my closest friends and the majority of those in my network of friends somehow turn out to have had a Peace Corps connection either as Volunteers or staff throughout the world. They are interesting people with sound, compassionate values, and they are always ready for fun and adventure.

The Peace Corps is a simple and powerful idea—which is why it is so popular abroad and important at home. Americans leave home for two years, live at intimate levels among people very different from themselves, try hard to be useful in their communities, seek nothing in return but understanding and friendship, and come home world-wise and changed forever. Loret Miller Ruppe, Peace Corps Director in the 1980s, frequently pointed out that the Peace Corps budget was less than that of a military marching band. What a bargain!

Following her Peace Corps service and a trip home around the world, Maureen Carroll moved to Washington D.C. where she still resides. During the '60s and the '90s Maureen worked for Peace Corps as a program evaluation officer, a country director in Botswana, and as a director of the Africa Region. Between those two Peace Corps stints, she held management positions with the General Learning Corporation, the Leadership Institute for Community Development, University Research Corporation, and National Public Radio. For nine years she was the Director of the National Center for Alcohol Education. Her last position before retiring in 2003 was as the Africa Regional Director for The Centre for Development and Population Activities (CEDPA). For a number of years, Maureen has been president of The Peace Corps Alumni Foundation for Philippine Development (PCAFPD), a non-profit that finances university education for Filipinos. She has also been active in keeping track of the Group I Kwans and supporting their get-togethers. Her latest volunteer activity is answering phones in the White House Presidential Correspondence Unit. She's happy again with a president whose persona reminds her of the one who sent her off on her Peace Corps adventure nearly 50 years ago.

(The first photo shows Maureen in the classroom at her school in Milagrosa, Sorsogon.)

Leonel "Lone" Castillo

An Hispanic American in the Philippines

Making Connections

At first I thought life in the Philippines would be like going back to an earlier Texas. There were so many similarities; even some words were the same. Like my own ancestors, the culture had an overlay of Spanish thought with many identical notions of culture and courtesy. The Filipinos, like my ancestors, also had to deal with an American incursion into their lives.

Like many Filipinos, I had to first learn another language: Spanish and then English. Later I was able to master English sufficiently that I could be selected to join the Peace Corps as an English teacher.

I was also blessed in my early days by being Catholic. I had learned about Catholicism and its reach into the Philippines and other parts of the world. As a result, learning a little about *Pinoys* (the slang term Filipinos often use to refer to themselves) was like learning about my personal history. I knew from my own early life about habits, rites, marriages, death, funerals and fiestas—and a little about the social life. Later, I learned a little about cemeteries, illnesses, and family ties with the U.S. Army.

About ten of my uncles ("tios") had been on active duty during World War II in posts in Europe and the Pacific. One uncle, my Tio Tony, had been in the Philippines and gone ashore with General MacArthur on the island called Leyte. He had told me a great story about the carnage around Tacloban, Leyte. All of my other "tios" had been in the European theater. Tio Tony told about having to kill a courageous Japanese soldier when he was told to take no prisoners. He said he carried the memory of that Japanese soldier from Tacloban, Leyte to Bloomington, Texas, outside Victoria.

My father, Severino Castillo, stayed home in Texas during the War, first in Victoria, where I was born along with my three siblings: one brother, Eferino, and two sisters, Mary and Anita. Later we moved to Galveston, where he worked as the chief of the docking gang for Todd Shipyards.

During the 1960 Presidential campaign I was impressed with John F. Kennedy. I had also learned to dislike Mr. Nixon. My only political activity was to tear down Nixon signs and replace them with Kennedy signs between 4 and 5 in the morning. Later, I thought I might do some political work after the Peace Corps. I also had learned during the campaign a little about world cultures and ethnic groups, in particular that blacks had much in common with Mexicans or Latinos.

Philippine Postings

After completing the training program at Los Baños I was assigned as a teacher's aide along with Pat Brennan and John Siedensticker to the Municipality of Murcia in Negros Occidental. One of my side projects in Murcia was to promote the raising of pigs through a program called *Livestock for Progress*. Youngsters could acquire pigs which they raised and sold, splitting the proceeds fifty-fifty with the organizations which bought the pigs. The whole program was run by the people of Murcia. My job was getting it started and finding the initial capital.

During my first summer I was asked to run the language program in the Waray and Cebuano dialects for the Group III volunteers who would be going to the Eastern Visayas. This work led to a request from the Peace Corps staff that I become a volunteer leader in the region to help the new volunteers from Group III become adjusted to their work in Leyte and Samar. I went to my new office in Tacloban, Leyte shortly after I was named. Ironically this was not far from the place where MacArthur landed and that my Tio Tony had described in such detail.

In Tacloban we made our Peace Corps regional headquarters at the home of a prominent Filipino family, the Chapmans, whose patriarch had been an American soldier during World War II. My volunteer leader colleagues, Duncan Yaggy, Len Giesecke and I hired one of the Chapman family members to work with us as a staff assistant, a beautiful woman, Evelyn Chapman, who was a great help to us as she knew how to communicate in two languages and also knew many people from the area. She spoke English well and was fluent in her native language, Waray. From her I learned some good *Pinoy* jokes, which played on the different languages, their quirks, and strange sounds.

In a few months Evelyn and I were inseparable. We were married on February 11, 1963. When we met notable American and Filipinos, one problem was that I looked more Filipino and she looked "American." This caused a few problems. Once when I met the Philippine Ambassador to the U.S., he asked for the "American." Since I was a tall dark person with a Spanish surname, he assumed I was a *"Pinoy."*

After the Group III volunteers were settled, I began working on the Group IV volunteers who were going to be assigned to the nearby Visayan Islands of Cebu and Bohol. Once they arrived, Evelyn and I moved to Cebu City to support them. Later I moved to an assignment as a PC staff member in Iloilo, Panay, where our first child, Avalyn, was born about a year later. She became known as Bing as a child and is still known to family and friends as Bing.

After returning from the Peace Corps, Lone earned a Master's of Social Work degree from the University of Pittsburgh and began his career as a political activist in the Houston area, working first with the Galveston-Houston Catholic Diocese and the Mexican-American Education Council. He led a successful boycott of the Houston School system in 1971, which led to the recognition of Mexican-Americans as its own racial group. That same year Lone was elected as Controller of the City of Houston, the first Hispanic ever to hold public office in Houston. He co-founded and became President of Houston International University, a school which targeted Hispanics for degrees in social work and public administration.

In 1974 Lone became Treasurer of the Texas Democratic Party. He resigned from his position as Houston Controller when President Carter asked him in 1977 to become Secretary of the Immigration and Naturalization Service (INS). Upon returning from Washington in 1979, Lone remained active in politics and civic affairs in the Houston area. When asked how it felt after an unsuccessful run for mayor of Houston in 1979, Lone chuckled and said, "I had a big ego and a small brain…that's a part of politics."

Despite several strokes in recent years, Lone continues to work for the community at-large in the Houston area. His latest passion includes renewable energy and the use of solar panels. Evelyn and Lone are the parents of two children, a daughter who is an attorney and a son who is a doctor. They have four grandchildren.

(The first photo shows Lone with a co-teacher at Murcia; the second shows Lone with his wife Evelyn on the left and grandchildren Nicholas, Paul Nathan, Kate and Faith from left to right between them.)

Don Cecchi

Rosemary Clooney, Bing Crosby, the Philippines and Me

The Place: Paracale, Camarines Norte Province, the Philippines
The Date: Sunday, December 8, 1961
The Time: Dawn. The stars have only just begun to fade.

It is my first morning in the town where I am to be stationed for my Peace Corps service. I am asleep, under my mosquito net, in my bamboo frame bed, with a woven rattan "mattress," when suddenly....................

!!!!!!!!!!!!!!!!!!!! C A C O P H O N Y !!!!!!!!!!!!!!!!!!

A metallic screeching, scratching, ear-splitting clamor shreds the humid, tropical air. Through the haze of a very deep sleep, I realize it is the voice of Father Regala, the local Catholic priest, blaring a blessing from the loudspeakers that adorn the crucifix atop the local church, part of a sound system that has survived from before World War II. Given the din, and the audio quality, I'm not sure if he is speaking in Latin or Tagalog. He finishes and a very raspy Rosemary Clooney, more the victim of a well-worn record than laryngitis, sings *Dear Lady of Fatima*, followed by, what else? *White Christmas* by, who else?, Bing Crosby, and then Perry Como's *Lord's Prayer*, (Protestant version), and *Jingle Bells*. I am then serenaded with a medley of rock and roll, followed by a few ballads, including one of my all-time favorites, *One More Chance*. ("One......more CHANCE," da-da-da-dum, "One ....more CHANCE," da-da-da-dum, "All... I ask... is ONE....... MORE........CHANCE," BOOM, "to break my HAR-AR-ART.") The dogs of the town join in mournful chorus—the most enthusiastic are the three or four who live directly below my window. For the first time I am hearing the call to the people of Paracale to attend the *misa de gallo*, the mass of the rooster. I am also experiencing no little cognitive dissonance. Fortunately, I have always been a heavy sleeper. I wake up the second morning but am fast asleep before Father Regala completes his portion of the morning program. The third morning I don't hear it at all. Rosemary and Bing? Rock and roll? I could have been back in New York City.

Soon the exotic become the norm, the unusual the commonplace. My eyes and ears are no longer assaulted by the foreignness of the town and I can begin really to settle in. That slow, easy Filipino pace becomes infectious, I begin to make friends, and they and their way of life become a part of me, not merely for two years, but forever.

A Short Digression

As I begin to write, I hear, in my mind's ear, a song from *The Fantasticks*, one of the most romantic musicals ever written:

> Try to remember the kind of September
> When life was slow and oh, so mellow.
> Try to remember the kind of September
> When grass was green and grain was yellow.
> Try to remember the kind of September
> When you were a tender and callow fellow.
> Try to remember, and if you remember,
>   Then follow.[1]

But I caution myself: when the past is recalled, do not be seduced by the embrace of retrospective romanticism. I change tunes and hear lyrics more cynical, but more on the mark:

> He: We met at nine
> She: We met at eight
> He: I was on time
> She: No, you were late
> He: Ah, yes, I remember it well
>   We dined with friends
> She: We dined alone
> He: A tenor sang
> She: A baritone
> He: Ah, yes, I remember it well[2]

A promise: I hereby disavow romantic retrospection. That done, I can assure the reader of the veracity of the following: the early '60s were a heady time, an exciting time, a time of hope. John F. Kennedy was the first president to have been born in the 20th century and his election presaged the social changes that were about to sweep the land. And we, the very first Peace Corps Volunteers, were part of that change. We had heard Kennedy's call, "Ask not............," and we had followed. Ah, yes, I remember it well.

Motivations to Join

I had campaigned for Kennedy in 1960 and was overjoyed that he won. When the formation of the Peace Corps was announced (in newspapers? the evening news?), I rushed to

---

[1] *The Fantasticks,* music and lyrics by Harvey Schmidt and Tom Jones.
[2] *Gigi,* music and lyrics Alan Jay Lerner and Frederick Lowe.

get an application (by mail? by phone? at the post office? Was there a written test? A physical exam? Ah, yes, I remember it well.) I was doing summer stock in San Juan, Puerto Rico, when the acceptance letter came. The producer released me from my contract, and I flew home. No second thoughts whatsoever. My motivations were clear and several:

• I knew, very definitely, that I would benefit. How else would I have the opportunity to live and work abroad, totally immersed in a foreign culture?

• I hoped that I would make some small contribution; I was never so naïve as to believe that it would be anything grand. The thought also passed through my mind (quickly dismissed) that the very concept of the Peace Corps was somewhat arrogant. What could young people, most newly graduated from college with, like me, a liberal arts degree, no less!, contribute to foreign countries?

• If nothing else, it was an adventure and a risk. It mattered not a whit that no one knew where we were going or what would happen or what we would do. In fact, that was a very large part of the allure. Damn the torpedoes, full speed ahead.

Definitely not at the top of my list of motivations, but in the interests of full disclosure: I had no desire to be in the military. After my Peace Corps stint, my draft board tried, gloatingly, hungrily, fortunately unsuccessfully, to draft me. I'd even received my "greetings" letter. But that's a whole other story.

Adapting to the Philippines

We were told we would be teachers' aides. No one knew quite what that meant, least of all the teachers whom we were supposed to be aiding. That, however, was the least of it. There were days when the culture drove me crazy—the endemic, all pervasive corruption; the fact that the Philippines was rich in natural and human resources, yet mired in poverty; the educational system which did not address the bleak future of the children. Other days, which I describe as "giddy time," I was able just to laugh. Some of the Peace Corps staff and I were not enamored of one another (I was told I was a pessimist; I viewed them as starry-eyed idealists who had little idea of what was really happening in the field. Ultimately, we just ignored one another.) By and large, however, adapting to the culture was incredibly easy and I don't remember having experienced any culture shock. For that, there are multiple reasons:

• **The Philippines' Attitude toward Americans:** The Peace Corps arrived only 16 years after WWII and, with rare exception, Filipinos held the U.S., and Americans generally, in high regard. I, personally, never experienced any "anti-American" sentiments.

• **Knowledge of the Philippines:** When my acceptance arrived, I knew precious little about the Philippines. I was aware of some of what had occurred during WWII, certainly the Bataan Death March, and that the U.S. had occupied it for about 50 years before "we gave them" their independence somewhere in the '40s. Ultimately, my appalling ignorance didn't matter. We lived with Filipinos throughout training, an invaluable experience, and were given excellent courses about the history, politics, language and culture of the country. We also learned that the influence of American pop culture was the least of it. More profound was the colonial impact America had had on the education, language and politics of the Philippines. The U.S. had established a universal system of education, which the Spanish had never done, with English as the medium of instruction, and their constitution and system of government are directly modeled on ours.

- **What I Brought to the Party:** Having worked in theatre, I was prepared to deal with all manner of crises. I was 23 when I joined the Peace Corps and had been a theatre production manager, Off-Broadway and in summer stock, for four years, during and after college. Egos are always alive and well in the theater, and I'd dealt with producers, directors and choreographers, union actors, musicians, and stage hands. And with stars. Some of them were on their way up (then unknown, future Academy and/or Tony Award winners Joel Grey, Estelle Parsons, George Firth, Dick Latessa and George Coe), others on their way down. Red Buttons (difficult, shall we say?); Joan Blondell (not in a good mood, but Mike Todd, a former husband, had died that week), Joan Bennett (a very funny lady and a class act all the way) and Imogene Coca (shy, modest, absolutely delightful, with whom I became friends). I had had a star refuse, for half an hour, to come back on stage for the second act of *West Side Story* (Julius LaRosa, remember him?, who threw a very big Sicilian hissy fit. "Julius, the show must go on." (I actually used that cliché.) In Milwaukee, I'd worked for a New York producer, who, mid-way through the season, was being sought by federal and state authorities (tax evasion), the city police (stolen goods and unpaid bills) and the actors, musicians and stagehands unions (he'd spent the salary bonds). He came to me, at 7:00 am in the hotel, and said: "I'm leaving town. Do what you can," and then he fled to England. I cleaned up the mess as best I could and then raced, exhausted, back to the comfort of New York City. Ain't show biz fun! Having survived theatrical lions', and lionesses', dens, I was prepared for the great unknown and for anything that the Peace Corps might throw my way.
- **Housemates:** Whom one lived with was a key to how well, or not so well, one adapted. I was assigned to live with three other volunteers—Parker Borg, Tom Carlton and Emery Bontrager—all of whom I had listed as people I wanted to be with, and we got along extraordinarily well. (Parker was teaching in a town that was difficult to reach and decided to move to that town, although he visited often.) We lived on the second floor of a very simple, corrugated tin roofed, two-story wooden house which was, by Filipino standards, capacious, i.e. we each had our own cubby hole in which to sleep. We hired an unemployed, 19-year-old young man to be our "houseboy," Nestor David (nesTOR daVEED), the nephew of one of our school principals (ah, political connections!) who had a great sense of humor, quickly learned all the American expletives and became a full member of the household. We had a dog, *Wakas* (the end), a cat whom we just called Cat and, for a time, a monkey we named Natalie. We did, or didn't, do things together, we had our own Filipino friends; the two years sped by. Emery stayed on after our term was over and married a Filipina, Annie Gison. They are living happily ever after. After he got back to the States, Tom met and also married a Filipina, Susan Heraldo, whose family was from Paracale. Tom died some years ago. A Filipino tradition is to take a photograph of the deceased in an open coffin with his family surrounding him. The reader may be appalled by this tradition. I don't care. I treasure the picture that was taken of Emery, Parker and me with Tom in his coffin. What better Filipino farewell could we have given him? I am weeping as I write.

Paracale — A Very Special Place

Paracale is bordered by water on three sides, the Philippine Sea to the north, a wide river to the east, an inlet on the south, its economy based on fishing and rice and copra farming. One can walk, at a leisurely, tropical pace, from one end of town to the other in five, no more than seven, minutes. When Tom, Parker, Emery and I arrive in Paracale, it appears to be no different from most other small provincial towns in the Philippines. There are quite a few clapboard houses, bleached to a dull brown by the climate. Some are two-storied, most just one. The latter sit on pilings and have corrugated metal or nipa palm roofs and small porches with a few chairs or stools and, often, potted plants and flowers. Pigs, chickens and dogs frolic under the house. Many of the fishermen live in huts built totally of nipa, directly over the water, supported by pilings sunk into the river, connected by rickety, wooden bridges 18 inches wide. The farmers also live in nipa huts, but on land. A very few two story cement block homes, occupied by the more prominent families, are scattered about. Three or four general stores, called sari-sari, dot the town and there are tiny stands where anemic produce is sold. Scattered about are riotously colored bougainvillea flowers and frangipani which fill the air with an intoxicating scent. The sun beats down but there are only a few palm and pomelo trees offering shade. Two or three old women wander about, bearing woven baskets, selling fish and tomatoes. Some sell only balut, "ba-LOOOOOOOOOOT, ba-LOOOOOOT," they cry out, fertilized duck eggs which are boiled four or five days before the chicks are due to hatch, and then eaten. They are considered to be a delicacy, in spite of the few soft feathers one finds, and are believed to be an aphrodisiac.

In the central plaza, a playground and the post office adjoin the "earthquake Baroque" Catholic church, the town hall is directly opposite. Hidden in the northwest corner of the town is a tiny, wooden *Iglesia ni Cristo* church, an early 20th century Protestant denomination indigenous to the Philippines. There are only a few congregants, but no one views them as "different," or questions why they aren't Catholic. A central marketplace, nothing more than a cement slab protected by a metal covering, operates, raucously, on Fridays, the local farmers and fishermen are joined by traveling merchants who sell clothing, bolts of fabric, kitchenware, odds and ends. A pig is slaughtered on market day, the only time we can buy pork; fish and chicken are available every day. Posters of American products can be seen throughout the town and the children's sliding pond in the playground is painted with images of Mickey Mouse, Pluto, Charlie Brown and Lucy. No one owns a car, only one resident owns a jitney, and the lumbering wood buses and the jitneys from elsewhere in the province don't come very often. Except for the morning call to the *misa de gallo*, the Angelus in the evening and the occasional battery operated radio, the town is incredibly, blessedly, quiet.

The Gold Boom. Paracale means "ditch diggers," and refers to the people who pan gold. The town has, for millennia, been known to have both surface and subterranean gold. There is an ancient saying: *"ang gintong Paracale? Mawala may di bale,"*—"Paracale gold? Never mind if you lose it, there's always more." In 160 A.D., a Greek mapmaker, Claudius Ptolemy, referred to the gold in Maniolas, an ancient name for the area which would have included Paracale. Spanish documents state that "Paracale could yield as much gold as from any possession in the world." The Muslims, who came to the southernmost areas of the Philippines in the 12th and 13th centuries, raided Paracale for gold in both pre- and post-Christian times, as recently as 1809.

Dredge mining was done, on a very small scale, between 1909 and 1927. In 1933, everything changes. Subterranean mining begins, a gold rush erupts with volcanic force. The economic boom attracts workers from all over the Philippines, and from Europe and the United States. The population surges from 2000 to 35,000. The streets are so crowded that one has to walk sideways to avoid bumping into people. Paracale becomes famous and is known as "Little Manila."

While the rest of the world is drowning in the maelstrom of the Great Depression, Paracale is riding a sunami of prosperity. It is a scene out of a Hollywood movie. In 1939, the town fiesta lasted for four days. The 38 page souvenir program for the event is entitled: *1939 Paracale Town Fiesta and Carnival: Educational, Commercial, Industrial and Agricultural Fair and Exposition.* In it are pictures of the airplane landing strip and a fleet of taxis with liveried drivers. Filipino and American corporations have taken ads, as have hotels, restaurants, ("Best Drinks, Best Chow" claims one, "Peppy Dancing at the Miners Club Grill" boasts another), at least four movie houses (*The Adventures of Marco Polo* with Gary Cooper"), bowling alleys, a tennis club, dress shops for women tailor shops for men. Among the scheduled sporting events are track and field, basketball, indoor (sic) baseball, tennis, badminton, ping pong, handball, marksmanship, boxing, wrestling, swimming, boat races. Each day begins with a religious ceremony, every night there are the ever popular Filipino coronation balls. There are, of course, "cabarets," i.e. brothels, for which there are neither pictures nor advertisements (but see "hotels" above). The boom, and the foreign presence, will affect Paracale far into the future.

During the boom there are a few Japanese stores and Japanese workers, primarily carpenters, who keep to themselves in town. They drive around the province on weekends, everyone assumes to have picnics and see the sights. In the autumn of 1941, they begin, gradually, to depart. Paracaleños notice, but think nothing of it. Besides, it would be impolite to ask why they are leaving and, anyway, the Japanese are strange and have never made an effort to become part of the community. All of them are gone by December 7, 1941. Pearl Harbor is bombed. All becomes clear.

When the Japanese invade the Philippines, many of the same workers return to Paracale as soldiers, with detailed maps of the entire region that they had been creating for several years. So much for picnicking and sightseeing. They occupy Paracale, primarily to guard the no longer operating gold mines. Mr. Daguchi, who had seemed, in the past, to be their natural leader, is now a full Colonel and is accompanied by 60 soldiers. Friends of mine speak, very quietly, very reluctantly, of some of the horrors they had witnessed, beheadings and physical and water torture. A close friend was on the Death March in Bataan, then interned in a concentration camp; another, a woman, had fought in the mountains with the Filipino guerillas. One Paracaleño who had lived through the war, is called upon at parties to do very funny, if perhaps racist, (who can blame them?) caricatures of the Japanese.

In 1946, the mine is reopened, albeit on a much smaller scale. At 10:30 am, on December 15, 1952, there is a cave-in. The official death toll is 56; in fact, it is much higher. Only one Paracale native dies, a young mining engineer. It is his first day on the job. Except for him, Paracaleños always refused to go down into the mines. There were countless jobs aboveground, or they were farmers, fishermen, servants, store owners and workers. They "knew that sooner or later, there would be an accident." Paracale comes to a halt, literally in one day. The boom is over, the mine is closed.

All of the foreigners return to their homes, only a handful of the fisherman who were originally from elsewhere in the Philippines, stay on. By the time we arrive in 1961 everything has been dismantled and removed. The lush, prolific, tropical flora has reclaimed the area. Barely a trace of the mines can be seen. An occasional, crumbling, cement stairwell, in the middle of an empty lot, leads to nowhere and nothing. A collapsing phone booth, with a decal of a 1930s telephone, in a corner of the town hall, is filled with disintegrating government papers. Paracale has become the slow, sleepy Filipino town it has been since the beginning of time, its residents, once again, earning their living by fishing and farming and by doing what people all over the world do to live a subsistent life. "Little Manila" is gone, residents describe Paracale as a ghost town.

Adapting to Paracale. Having lived with foreigners, including Americans, during the boom, Paracaleños had witnessed ways of life other than their own, a rare occurrence for a provincial town. As a result, the four of us are not perceived as objects of curiosity, or "status symbols," as are Volunteers elsewhere. For this, we are extremely grateful. Yes, they make some fuss, there are welcoming parties, but that would happen for any newcomer. We are able to relax immediately and our becoming part of the community is expedited. The ease of the culture (*bahala na*: never mind, what happens happens), and the warm, welcoming nature of Filipinos (being hospitable is one of their highest cultural values), greatly facilitate my transition from New York City to a small, isolated peninsula town (population, including surrounding barrios, 3000) with no running water or telephones and only the slightest trickle of electricity for a few hours a day. It also helps that I, an Italian-American, share many Filipino cultural values: close-knit, extended families, a love of children and food, and having a good time.

Equally important, there is no overwhelming economic divide, as there is in other towns and cities, which would have made living there much more difficult. Most of the people are poor, some grindingly so; a few families are "better off," but no one is rich. Over time I come to realize that Paracale is an incredibly self-contained town with a friendliness that goes well beyond the usual Filipino norm. There is virtually no crime and local gossip, something for which Filipinos are famous, is gentle and passed along, usually, with humor. Everyone does, truly, get along. There is a natural, quiet rhythm to the town. Life goes on.

I become close friends with a number of people, all of whom are in their 30s and 40s—more on them later—which eases my transition into the town. But mention must be made here about two of them: Dr. Bernardo and Mrs. Valeria Formoso.

Dr. Bernardo was a doctor from the north; Mrs. Formosa, a nurse from the central Philippines. They came to work at the mine, met, fell in love, married, and had two children. When the mine is closed they decide that they have come to love Paracale; it has become their home. They stay and have a third child. "Doc" is a jolly man who hums as he walks along, lost in his own world, and he loves a good laugh. He likes everyone and never has a bad word to say about anyone. Mrs. Formoso, too, is quick to laugh, but is more perceptive about people and the ways of the world than he. Never truly judgmental, she does think that people sometimes behave "foolishly."

Interested only in making enough money to send their children to college, they treat patients for just a few pesos, sometimes just for some fish or a hand of bananas. They both advocate birth control, in opposition to the Catholic Church, and distribute condoms whenever they can. The most respected and loved people in town, they become our surrogate parents. We depend on them for many things, including information and advice.

Accomplishments

I was young, the Philippines a foreign culture, all over the world change comes slowly, if at all. Being fully cognizant of that, I knew that I would not accomplish a great deal, let alone bring about world peace and *kumbaya*. In addition, although the volunteers had been told that there were jobs waiting for us, when we arrived in the provinces most of us were greeted by Filipinos with the following question: "So what are you here to do?" It was sink or swim time.

Some volunteers, and staff members, joined the Peace Corps with overly enthusiastic expectations about what they could do and ended up depressed and guilty that they weren't doing more. I began with low expectations about what I could accomplish and decided to go for the small wins. Maybe, if I was very lucky, larger ones would follow. At the very least, I knew that it benefits the U.S. when its citizens live and work within, and come to know, foreign cultures, and for the people of other countries to experience life with "ordinary" Americans. And, in my case at least, gamble, get drunk and carouse with.

I had originally been assigned to teach in an elementary school where I was accomplishing nothing. Then, I realized that the Paracale high school students, particularly the juniors and seniors, needed help with their English and were being taught little of their own literature. In spite of their severely limited English ability, and irrelevance to their lives, they were being taught American lit (*The Gettysburg Address*); European lit (*Beowolf, Canterbury Tales, Merchant of Venice*), remnants of the curriculum that had been established 70 years earlier. There was very little Filipino lit. So I transferred to the high school and, among other things, beefed up the courses in Filipino literature. At least they would be able to read about, and discuss, topics and people that reflected their own lives.

Small Wins. I pushed the students in a way their own teachers didn't and, in certain instances, for cultural reasons, couldn't. One student was a member of a prominent family and could barely read English, or much Tagalog for that matter. I told him, and his family, that I would fail him if he didn't apply himself. As an American, I was not as bound by the cultural constraints their Filipino teachers were, and could be more blunt. Years later, when I returned to Paracale, he happened to be there. He told me: "I'm now a merchant seaman and think of you all the time. If you hadn't forced me to learn to read, I'd be going crazy at night on the ocean." And, just to assure me that he was telling the truth, he rattled off a list of authors and books, mostly mysteries, he had read.

More generally, I believe I did have some affect on all the students. I expected them to, and they did, work harder than they might have otherwise. They learned more of their own literature, their English improved and, as one student told me years later: "You respected us, and gave us confidence in ourselves. The other teachers didn't."

God knows I did push them, sometimes, I'm sure, much too hard. But I would not let them finish what for most would be their last year in school doing nothing more than memorizing names, dates, titles and authors. I made them write essays, multiple choice tests were kept to a minimum, their written English improved. I let them read whatever they wanted to, and didn't care if it was on the "approved" list of books. Since I had expanded the curriculum, some worried about the national exams they would have to take at the end of the year. To assure them they would be fine, and to cover my own ass, I made sure that they were prepared for the tests. Everyone passed.

A Larger Win. Although the schools were closed during the summer, volunteers had to have summer projects. Knowing that I had worked in the theater, the managers of an iron mine elsewhere in the province ask me to create a theater program for the local teens who, I was told, "got into trouble" with nothing to do during the summer. I agreed, thinking that I'd at least take advantage of how talented and musical Filipinos are and produce a variety show. But that didn't seem like much and I wanted more. Why not produce and direct a full production of *The King and I?* It's an ideal show for the Philippines—glorious music, dance, romance, melodrama, many children. And the King has lots of wives, a fantasy for many Filipino men. I had a friend in New York send me the musical score and a script. In for a penny, in for a pound.

Everyone, Filipinos and Americans, told me I was crazy. The teenagers I would be working with had never seen, let along done, a real musical. But we did it. We built the sets and costumes, and rehearsed our asses off. About 100 teenagers, including a local "gang," sang and danced and acted, played in the band and worked as stagehands. We even had a pair of twins for "The March of the Siamese Children." Damn right, we did it! We were sold out for all five performances and the owner of the movie house in the provincial capital asked if we could "take it on the road," and perform in his theatre. To my, and their, great disappointment, we couldn't because school was about to begin.

I must confess, there were times when I began to question my own sanity. During rehearsals, I lost 12 pounds, which I could ill afford, and was a nervous wreck opening night. If we bombed, I was in serious danger of "losing face," a cultural value I had incorporated.

My "face" aside, the effect it had on the kids is what matters. They were ecstatic with what they had accomplished. Also, because it was a mining town with more disposable income than there would have been elsewhere, we charged a few pesos for the tickets. Since I had made sure that the costs of the production were covered, I told the kids that all the receipts would be donated to a recipient of their choice, the local church, which made them proud. Years later, when I returned, they brought out the photos, and relived the experience, their excitement and pride still exuberant.

Big deal accomplishments? Of course not. But I am proud of what I was able to do and would urge everyone to hear Kennedy's (Obama's?) call and do something similar, either overseas or here at home.

The Effects of Peace Corps Service

It is difficult for me to separate the effects that the Peace Corps experience, *per se*, had on me from the time I spent in Paracale after the Peace Corps. In regard to the former, I continue to be proud to have represented the U.S. as a volunteer and, hopefully, to have had some small beneficial effects on the lives of the Filipinos with whom I came in contact, including their perceptions of the U.S. It was also the beginning of my not only learning about a foreign culture but of truly knowing, and becoming a part of that culture. Understanding and respecting the behavior and thought processes of people different from me has certainly had a beneficial effect on both my personal and professional life. It was, quite simply, a seminal event in my life. In January, 1962, I wrote in a letter home: "Less and less do I think of myself as being a part of the Peace Corps and use it only as a nebulous frame of reference, which is all that it is. This is, without a doubt, going to be two of the best years of my life." I believed it then, and believe it still. Even more important, however, was the effect of my return to Paracale to write a book about it.

I vacationed to Paracale for about a month in 1971, just before martial law was declared. Soon after getting back to the States, *The New York Times* published an Op-Ed piece I wrote, "President Marcos: Another Pacific Dictator." As a result of that article, several things happened:

- A publisher called the morning it ran, and made me an offer to write a book. Thinking that that kind of opportunity would never happen again, I decided to leave Lincoln Center, where I was General Counsel, to return to Paracale to do research, interview people and to begin writing a "portrait of a village."

- In the weeks before my return, I was contacted by a number of Filipinos who were either living in or visiting New York. Some telephoned to thank me but, out of fear of reprisals, chose to remain anonymous. Most wanted to meet, including Congressman Salvador "Doy" Laurel, later to become Vice-President during the Aguino administration, with whom I became close friends and with whom I would stay whenever I visited Manila.

- I was told by a number of Filipinos that Marcos wanted to know who this guy was who was saying these terrible things about him, and was having me followed around New York City by, what I suppose might be called, his secret police, always three of them, always recognizable. The theory was that I was a front for anti-Marcos forces and Marcos wanted to discover who they were. My code name was Dan Carlos—couldn't he have called me something with a little class? Like DON Carlos? At his invitation, I had dinner with Carlos Romulo, then the Philippines' delegate to the UN, a Marcos *tuta* (lap dog), a little man, in all senses of that word, in his not so little apartment at the Waldorf Astoria Hotel. I assured him that I was not going back to start the revolution. With a dismissive wave of his hand, Romulo told me: "You're nothing," and that he and Marcos "couldn't care less about who I was or what I wrote." However, not wanting to spend any time in a Philippine jail, and just to be on the safe side, I secured letters from three U.S. Senators and several Congressmen, all wishing me well and asking that I stay in touch with them while I was in the Philippines. For added protection, my agent got me a press card. When I went back to the Philippines I was followed, for a few months, by the military, then left alone.

- (The book, by the way and for a variety of reasons, was never published. Win some, lose some.)

Upon my return to Paracale, I renew my friendships with Noe Rayos, a bus driver; Luciano "Whitey" Morales and his wife "Mamie," Fred Bacuno, a government worker; Peping Era, a copra farmer; and Ricardo Lotik, owner of a few, very small rice fields, father of five sons—Ricardo II, Ricardo III, Ricardo IV, Ricardo V, and Donald. Once again, we "hang out," play cards or mahjong, drink San Miguel beer or Tanduay rum and, as before, gamble, get drunk and carouse. From dusk to dawn, I fish with the fishermen in their small outrigger bankas in the middle of the ocean; plant rice with the farmers; bury the dead; and help Dr. Formoso birth some babies, including one breach birth (slide your hand in, grab a leg, gently, steadily, pull.) I force myself to learn Tagalog, in order to better communicate and understand the culture.

More important, people trust me enough to share their lives and thoughts. They maintain their senses of humor, but few have hopes for a better future for themselves or their children, most suffer fear and disappointments—the woman who fled her home, hundreds of miles away, to escape her husband who beat her, the man who believes he is a failure because he is not financially able to send his children to college, another who tells me what occurred on the Bataan death march and in his concentration camp. Having insisted, during my Peace Corps days, that superstitions are "only for the ignorant," some now speak openly about their beliefs in magical spirits, *mangkukulam* and *aswang* (evil) and *duende* (mischievous, invisible elves). I am allowed to witness pre-Christian rites. None of this would occur had I not returned and become truly a part of the culture and, especially, of Paracale.

In September, 1972, in a plane on my way back to the States, I wrote of the morning I left Paracale: "The Formosos had packed an ice container with fresh fish and two enormous cardboard boxes, tied with rope, full of food for me to take to their children in Manila. There was no room for the rice cakes, still hot from the marketplace, so Mrs. Formoso and I stuffed them in my suitcase. *"Talagang ang provinciano ako,"* I muttered in Tagalog ("I really am a provincial."). What might normally have been a barely humorous one-liner, sent the two of us into peals of nervous laughter. Suddenly, we stood for a minute, silently looking at one another. "Yes," Mrs. Formoso said quietly, "you really have become a provinciano."

I remember it well.

When Don Cecchi returned from Peace Corps service, he went to law school, during which time he was business manager of the New York production of The Fantasticks. *He was active in the anti-Vietnam War movement, became General Counsel of Lincoln Center, then went on to work for Mayor Ed Koch as Assistant Commissioner of Economic Development and then to the American Society of Composers, Authors and Publishers (ASCAP) as Director of Planning and Operations. He co-produced a revival of* The Dairy of Anne Frank, *with Eli Wallach and Anne Jackson, and has sat on the boards of several non-profit arts organizations, and of MBAs4NY, which offered pro bono financial and management consulting to downtown companies that had been devastated by 9/11.*

More recently, drawing upon his own experiences as a primary caregiver for relatives and friends, and as a patient (over an eight year period, seven bouts of five different cancers, with a few benign tumors thrown in for good measure,)he created a management consulting firm which focuses on healthcare and medical projects. He has published a number of articles, and gives lectures and seminars, which address those issues. He is especially proud of having received the National Institutes of Health Director's Award, and the NIH Clinical Center Director's Award for his contributions to the NIH where he sits on a number of committees and is a research subject (medical euphemism for guinea pig.) Now cancer free for ten years, he has been described by NIH doctors as a "medical anomaly" and a "medical miracle." He thoroughly enjoys both appellations.

(The first photo shows Don next to Father Regala and surrounded by Lotik family members when he became their child's godfather in the Paracale barrio of Batobalani in 1962.)

Judith Cridler Claire
Final Score

My life was enriched by my time in the Philippines, especially by my adopted family. It was a time of small successes and amusing failures.

Success: A telegram arrived in San Francisco just one day before I was to fly to the Philippines. It was from my mother, who wrote, "Mist is heavy, grapes are purple, must you go?" I decided to send fifty of the seventy-five dollars of my monthly readjustment allowance to her. She was recently divorced and had just started college.

Success: I was assigned to Catanduanes, the closest island to California according to my barrio neighbors. It was also known as "typhoon island."

Success: I survived a typhoon of 140 mile an hour winds a few days after arriving. The typhoon blew the roof off my barrio school. After that, during the rainy season, the first grade teacher held an umbrella over her head when she wrote on the blackboard.

Success: I soon realized that I needed to move out of the big, strongest house in Bato to be a real participant and neighbor in the barrio of Sibacungan, a move that saved my life. I rented a small, former *sari sari* store across the road from my co-teacher. The school had no books, no real science classes. There were no vegetables or fruits in the barrio. Rice farmers barely raised enough rice. A few chickens and pigs roamed the barrio. Why fence them? If they can scratch out a diet, there is no need to buy feed.

Success: My co-teacher, Mrs. Taperla, taught fourth grade in her home. Mrs. Taperla's mother died when she was five, and her father drowned crossing the river when she was eighteen. He had remarried, and she had three half brothers. She put herself through school and later married and had three children. Her husband worked as a security guard in Manila and came home to visit every two to three months. Mrs. Taperla welcomed any children he fathered in Manila, and when they were older, they visited her.

Success: My friend Petra married and had two children, but she decided to use her version of birth control and left her husband. She took her daughter, and her husband kept the son. Social acceptance is a most highly prized goal in traditional Philippine society. Petra was an outcast, but she did solve the birth control problem. Petra and I cut coconuts and abaca and just plain enjoyed each other's company.

Success: My greatest pleasure on the island was the weekly meetings with my adult education ladies. We met in each other's houses and had a great time. Birth control methods were of great interest, but since I had no experience, I was no help. Petra was the only real example of one way to limit children. Women did die in childbirth, and many children were blind due to malnutrition while others had tuberculosis. I pinned up some pictures from *Life Magazine* in my one room hut. My adult ladies borrowed my magazines. They especially liked the ads for Maidenform bras, "I dreamed I was (insert whatever) in my Maidenform bra." They chose those pictures for their walls.

First Failure: There was only one outhouse in Sibacungan, used by Mrs. Taperla's family and me! Lucky me! Our PCV group decided to build a community outhouse in the middle of the barrio for all to use. We dug away in the hot sun. Onlookers pointed and laughed, seeing another example of "those crazy volunteers." However, no one was interested in or wanted an outhouse. Lime was used to keep the one outhouse somewhat sanitary. Lime was also chewed with betel nuts by the locals. Why waste lime in an outhouse?

Failure: The vegetables we planted in the school garden were always eaten by the pigs. No fence worked. I announced that I was going to poison the pigs. The teachers all laughed.

At night, I listened to Voice of America on my portable radio. Often, several neighbors slept on my floor (unmarried women were not to live alone). The teachers were interested in our civil rights movement. They saw pictures in *Life* of dark skinned people being beaten, hosed, and attacked by dogs. Mrs. Taperla, who had warm, brown skin, black hair and lovely lips, told me how ugly they looked. The science teacher told me that if he ever visited the United States, he would not wear a hat so his straight hair would be noticed, and he would not be considered to be a Negro. As I listened to the radio news, I wondered why we were here when we had so many problems at home.

Getting off the island was quite a task! Once a week, a small plane circled to see if the ground was not too wet. Often, the pilot dipped down and then departed, although he did do a mail drop. The launch, filled with chickens, dried fish, and people was a four-hour trip at night.

The week before I returned to the United States, I was given a party. The food included my chicken Maria Manok—cooked! Maria lived in my house and later in a small "house." attached to the nipa hut. My adult ladies gave me a dozen eggs for my trip home. I donated them to friends in Manila.

Success: Fountain Street Church in Grand Rapids, Michigan agreed to send the children of my co-teacher, Mrs. Taperla and her husband, to college. I have kept in touch with them, and one has visited me here. She met a nice cowboy in Oklahoma and married him.

Upon my return, I got a scholarship to study at Howard University in Washington D.C. and to be part of the Cardozo Peace Corps Project at Cardozo High School in Washington. I arrived in time to join the March on Washington on August 28, 1963. Three months later, JFK was dead. A year later, I was teaching at Shaw Junior High School in Washington. There were no books, broken-out windows, and children who needed better nutrition and eyeglasses. The loss of Malcolm X in 1965 and Martin Luther King, Jr. and Robert Kennedy in 1968 left me with a sadness that I have to this day.

And yet, as I reflect on the experience of being among the first Volunteers, unskilled and not programmed to be of real help, I recall a quote from an article by Norman Cousins in *The Saturday Review* just a few months before I joined the Peace Corps. He wrote, "The key to success abroad is confrontation, not solution. Invest self in the human situation as you find it. A sensitive response is the prime qualification." I think I succeeded at that.

Judith Cridler Claire retired from the Washington D.C. public schools and the Smithsonian Museum of American Art and is now raising vegetables on her patio (no pigs around). She has been creating political art, primarily using collage, from 1963 to the present and is still looking for a good or bad home for it before it hits the dumpster!

Marjorie Donnelly Clarke
A Paradoxical Experience

In Dylan Thomas's poem *A Child's Christmas in Wales*, he plunges his hand into a ball of holidays and out comes Mrs. Prothero and the firemen. When I plunge my hand into memories of the Philippines, all sorts of snippets tumble out but, disappointingly, not a cohesive whole.

I could start with Father Vergara, the town priest in Manjuyod municipality about 30 miles north of Dumaguete City in Negros Oriental. He was young, small, upright and in my memory always dressed in a starched white cassock. Earnest, serious, the best speaker of English in the town, he volunteered to give us Cebuano lessons by conducting bible readings in our house. We declined.

There was also Mr. Kadile, perhaps the oldest teacher at my school, the only one brave enough to volunteer for a science experiment about sound that I was demonstrating. I can still feel my embarrassment and his humiliation as the simple demonstration failed because he was deaf in one ear.

There were the children. Santos, a sweet, undernourished boy whom I remember climbing the tall papaya tree in front of our house when there was, at last, a ripe one. I don't remember if we shared it with him. Lestita was the pretty little girl who lived next door to us. She was the daughter of Tia Bado, the *lavendera*. I remember watching from the window as Lestita took her morning pee, a squatting sleepyhead at the foot of the bamboo ladder that led up to where her family lived.

Of course there were my roommates. Jenny Grant donning a large shower cap with flip-flop in hand to chase and kill the *tapay-tapay*. These were large gray, hairy spiders that would occasionally appear on our ceiling. Gina Cochran with whom I took my first walk in town to get away from the curious people who sat in our living room or peered through our windows. We walked to the beautiful seaside only to discover that we were being followed by a small group of young men. Perhaps they followed us for our protection, perhaps because they were curious, perhaps so we would not be "lonely." That was a concept that was very alien to us. We were after all two very independent young women. I'm appalled to remember that I briefly considered throwing stones to make them go away.

There were the students who came to live with me when we PCVs decided to set up separate households. Rosita, in high school, was calm and had a good sense of humor. I remember trying desperately to get her through her science homework and failing. Milagros was younger. I think her year with me was by far the most secure and stable she had ever experienced. Both girls worked hard to help me work out the puzzles of shopping and cooking and cleaning in the Philippines. In fact they did almost all of it. Milagros grew very dependent and attached to me. I deeply regret not working to provide a new place for her when I left. I don't know where she is now.

There were our leaders. I remember resenting Sargent Shriver's visit to the Philippines. He seemed to be basking in the glow of the success of the Peace Corps. I felt he hadn't a clue and should just go away. I remember Mrs. Fuchs correcting my Tagalog because I did not put a respectful *po* at the end of something I had addressed to her. I remember the warmth and support provided by Larry and Betty Howard when we made trips to Dumaguete City. I also remember being chided by Larry for spending too much time in the kitchen cleaning up when I should be entering into the lively discussion that was going on in the living room. Thinking about that household now, I realize how young the Howards were then too.

There was the food. *Pan de sal* from not very vermin-free flour, wonderful fruit—our town was well known for its mangos which were delicious and plentiful. There was guava jelly, calamansi juice, *bud-bud* (sweet sticky rice cooked in coconut milk and wrapped in banana leaves) and thick bitter-sweet hot chocolate. I would be very happy to find that combination somewhere in the U.S. There was *bibingka*, a steamed rice cake, and the staple—canned Portuguese sardines. Our boiled water was kept in a great clay jug and most food was kept in a moat on the kitchen table to keep it from the ants. We occasionally had good fish from Mr. Sycip's fish ponds.

There were adventures. Boat journeys to Cebu with cots on deck so close together that you could barely get up to go to the bathroom. There was a trip with Gina to Sulu on which the hatch on the small boat was nailed shut over us for the journey. There was a terrifying (for me) trip into a basalt mine in Siquihor. There was a trip to the mountains where I met my first scorpion and where we rode horses into a pond, deep enough that the horses had to swim. Most horrifying of all was a nighttime trip with fishermen in large dugout boats who after setting up lights and nets detonated a dynamite charge and then the stunned or dead fish floated to the surface and were caught.

Whenever I've been asked about my experience in the Peace Corps, I have always said it is the best thing I've done in my life except for having children. However, when I sat down to make an outline for this little essay I found that my chronological list—the list that traced my official Peace Corps experiences—contained a lot of dissatisfaction and failure.

Training was too long, they weren't ready for us. I felt alienated throughout the training both at Penn State and in the Philippines. I hated being told that I had prepared for a dash and that this was a marathon. I was unhappy at the cuts made in our group before we left—I particularly remember someone—Charlie(?) who was bright and energetic and motivated but perhaps too much of a challenge for those in charge. I never did gain facility in the language and was disappointed in my inability to speak Cebuano. I had little tolerance for the lengthy speeches in "Filipino English" when we finally reached the Philippines. I was dismayed at being treated with a kind of respect by Filipino teachers three times my age because I was an American or a guest. I never did find a comfortable ongoing role at my school. I made a questionable choice of housing when I moved to a comfortable bamboo house that belonged to the owner of the sugar plantation in town. This list could continue on much longer.

The puzzle is how I can know that my Peace Corps experience was "the best thing I've done in my life" when my memories of that experience are so mixed.

I believe it is largely because being placed in a culture so foreign from my own provided an amazing "coming of age" opportunity. I am sorry I was not a more effective teacher of English, math or science to the children in my village. I think I was a least a decent representative American in my town. My politics and world view were permanently affected by the experience.

Our country is large and rich and isolated. If the Peace Corps provides only a meaningful international experience for the people who participate in it, it will have done enough. It will have benefit for those individuals and for our country. If, in addition, Peace Corps volunteers can enhance education, build bridges, add sanitation, or help the people in their host nations in other ways, this is icing on the cake.

After traveling home through Asia, Marjorie Donnelly Clarke lived in NYC and worked in publishing as a children's book editor for about 10 years. She married, had a daughter and the family moved to a small mill town in Connecticut where they still live and where their son was born. After doing some free lance editing, Marjorie took a job with IBM and worked in software support at large insurance companies. She now works part time as an Administrative Assistant for a behavioral health clinic. She and her husband have two grown children and three grandchildren.

(First photo shows Marjorie on survival weekend at Penn State with E.V. Dobbins standing behind her; the second photo shows Marjorie with her family.)

Kathryn "Judy" Conway
From Indifference to Commitment

Slow on the Draw

My journey to Peace Corps was not a direct route. I lived in Kansas City at the time. I had worked on Kennedy's election and had learned of his plan to expand U.S. international outreach. He wanted other countries to recognize the U.S. as an honest and involved country willing to share our talent and our resources with those in need, both friends and foes alike. This humanitarian philosophy appealed to me. Kennedy signed the executive order creating the Peace Corps on March 1 of 1961. My roommate at that time wanted to take the tests being administered for Peace Corps and asked me to go along. I went because she didn't want to go alone. I wasn't motivated by altruistic thoughts of being generous and giving without measure. In fact, I suggested leaving after lunch, but my friend wanted to complete the tests. So we did.

A stranger offered us a ride home. Just for conversation to break the silence, I asked this woman if she would actually go to Peace Corps if invited. She very enthusiastically said yes. Later on I told my roommate that I thought this woman was a little carried away and needed to give this experience a lot more thought.

But shortly after that, I was the one who received the telegram stating, "You have been selected as a Peace Corps Volunteer to serve in Chile." As I stood there looking at the telegram and rereading it, I realized I was giving this serious thought. I reflected upon the opportunity this telegram offered me to live in another culture, to know the people and to learn about their customs. My life as a creative designer for Hallmark Greeting Cards could not possibly compete. Fifty years later I am still surprised and stunned by my apparent initial indifference to the idea of being a Peace Corps Volunteer.

I decided to ask my parents what they thought. My mother said that if she were my age she'd do it in a heartbeat. However my father was vehemently opposed. He feared I might get a disease in Chile and die there. Mom suggested I request reassignment to another country. I called a friend in Senator Symington's office, who went over to the new Peace Corps office and requested a reassignment for me. She called me to ask if the Philippines would be okay. It was perfect. My father had served in the Philippines during the Second World War. I knew he would think this country was a safe place. I had been surprised at his reaction to my initial assignment. Yet, I am thankful luck played a role in my decision to join Peace Corps and in my country assignment. I am grateful that I could experience the close and strong friendships our group made with Filipino people and with each other. Many of these friendships have lasted for fifty years. The impact of my Peace Corps experiences, both personally and professionally, is immeasurable, profound and lasting.

On the Ground

Because my father had spent time in the Philippines I had some personal information about the country. He fondly remembered a friendly and welcoming people. Through him I felt a familiarity and bond with the Philippines and its people when I arrived. Understanding the culture, language and history came during our extensive raining sessions at Penn State and Los Baños. The training was intense and comprehensive. We arrived on site as well prepared as one can be when beginning work in an entirely new cultural setting and country.

Despite thorough formal training and insightful information from friends and relatives who knew the country, I was still overwhelmed by our welcome when we arrived in the Philippines. Our reception was similar to one for international dignitaries. People lined the road waving flags in all the villages and towns where our buses passed. *A merienda* awaited us at every stop. Our arrival was the beginning of our fiesta-filled life. For two years there was a fiesta for every occasion. Many events illustrated the contrast in our two cultures. When Eugene Burdick spent the day with me at my barrio elementary school I realized the Filipinos had no idea who he was. None of them had heard of his book *The Ugly American* or the ideas contained in it. Yet in the U.S. everyone was talking about this book. The rote teaching methods and the *hiya* (shame) culture in classrooms were an immediate and ongoing challenge to most volunteers. The classrooms at home focused on individual performance, reasoned responses and some competitive spirit. Teaching methods here were totally foreign to us in every sense of the word.

In Hinigaran, our town, we were welcomed, respected, befriended and often honored with celebrations during our stay. For two years we were the center of attention at any public event. The whole town came to thank us at our *despedida* when we finished our service. The Philippine people appreciated our service and generously expressed their gratitude.

An expression of Philippine support was demonstrated in the financial support they provided for Camp Brotherhood, a project developed and run by the volunteers in Negros Occidental. Peace Corps volunteers from other islands who joined our project were a significant factor in its success. Those very long days were fun days; teaching every morning at LaSalle College in Bacolod City and hurrying back up the mountain to take on our duties as camp counselors.

Our remote little barrio was not quite like Manila, the city my father had experienced and described. Our cinder block house was on the shore of the Sulu Sea, an exotic location. We had indoor plumbing and electricity part time. Our house was primitive by comparison to U.S. homes. However, it was much more upscale than the nipa huts of our students who lived in more remote barrios. Often stagnant water stood beneath these homes breeding disease. Teachers' homes were usually slightly better than the students.

Our schools were also nipa with dirt floors. These flimsy structures were dangerous places during the severe weather conditions so common there. We were assigned as teacher aides but most of us became the teacher. Schools had morning and afternoon breaks including one break with coconut milk and cookies. Students went home for lunch. The curriculum for language learning included Pilipino, Spanish, and English and was exceptionally demanding for the youngest students.

One of the highlights of our experience was the wedding of our roommate Mary Baker to another volunteer, Lee Johnson. The anticipation and preparation was happy excitement for us and for our Filipino friends who helped us plan this special day. The guests at the fiesta held at the Sea Breeze Hotel in Bacolod City included volunteers and Filipino teachers as well as many people from our barrio and other cities and towns on Negros.

Such a large group with common goals and hopes creates a lot of fun and good times. It also results in sad times. The volunteers in Negros Occidental especially and all others in our group were devastated by the sudden and untimely death or our friend David Mulholland June 10, 1962. We have lost many since that time including a roommate of mine, Carol Byrnes. Each person we lose reminds us of the camaraderie we enjoyed as members of this very select group.

After Effects

Our Peace Corps service had a great influence on how we perceive the world and our place in it. My own Peace Corps experience changed my career course. Although I continued to use my art in the various employment positions I held, the focus of my employment shifted to social programs. In working here at home and in other countries my Peace Corps experience gave me a new appreciation for my American culture and values. It made me aware of the everyday good that happens in our country and countries around the world. I think Peace Corps Volunteers then and now project an American image reflective of how we wish to be perceived in the international community.

Now I live in Hudson Heights in NYC across from the Cabrini Shrine & Chapel. There is a large Philippine community attending my parish. Several times a year Mass is celebrated in Tagalog. Many of the Philippine people who attend Cabrini are now my friends. It completes the circle of my lifelong connection to the Philippines beginning with my father's experience there.

In the '80s as a staff member at the *Centro del Muchacho Trabajador* (CMT) in Quito, Ecuador, I supervised Peace Corps Volunteers and had a collegial relationship with many other volunteers working in the program. CMT had Peace Corps Volunteers from the 1960s through 2002.

In 1981, while on sabbatical to write a grant for the CMT Women's Program, I also wrote a grant and directed a Peace Corps training program at Howard University in Washington D.C. Volunteers in that program were trained and served in Kenya. One staff member of this training program was a returned Peace Corps volunteer from Uganda.

I have written letters of recommendation for prospective Peace Corps volunteers. I lived with a returned volunteer from Costa Rica. I have many RPCV friends including one who was Deputy Director in the Philippines after her volunteer service in Fiji. Many neighbors are RPCVs. Peace Corps Volunteers will always have a special bond with others who had the experience.

I have great respect for America and The Philippines, my host country. I shared what I had learned about the culture of the Filipino people as a member of the Peace Corps Speakers Bureau in the Wisconsin/Illinois area. The Filipinos welcomed developing new images of their American friends in Peace Corps. Our group definitely left behind favorable impressions of young Americans.

Generally speaking, my parents educated all of their children to believe that we should go out and spread the "Good Word" by reaching out to our fellow human beings whenever and wherever we saw a need. We learned at home that it is in giving that we receive. I have found that to be true.

Upon her return from Peace Corps, Judy Conway was challenged by a Marquette professor "to give as much to the church as you give to your country." His challenge inspired her to teach in Catholic Schools in Milwaukee for several years. Later she taught in Milwaukee Public Schools (MPS), after which, she worked for the Community Relations-Social Development Commission (CR-SDC) as a community organizer and a trainer. During this time, she also co-owned an art business, was the state chair for the Wisconsin Women in The Arts and a board member of the Inner City Arts Council in Milwaukee, Wisconsin. Judy then worked for eight years at Centro Del Muchacho Trabajador (CMT) Quito, Ecuador, in various positions—teacher, human relations skills trainer, director of the women's program, coordinator of the "HOY" newspaper program and director of professional education. After Quito, she was employed as Regional Director of Joint Action In Community Service (JACS) Region II, United States Department of Labor, Job Corps including, New York, New Jersey, Puerto Rico and the Virgin Islands. Presently, she spends a month at Christmastime every year in Quito at the CMT volunteering wherever they need her. At home she assists with grant writing and art designs for the CMT (known in the U.S. as The Working Boys Center.) She has been a catechist and taught in the Hispanic religious education program at St. Elizabeth's Parish for 22 years. She often volunteers for the largest soup kitchen in NYC. She also tutors in Spanish and works consulting on translations.

(The first photo shows Judy doing the Itik-itik folk dance.)

Margo Heineman Daniels and Pera Daniels
Once Upon a Time in a Land So Far Away

A Real "American" Wedding

Undoubtedly the highlight of our Peace Corps experience occurred on April 28, 1962, when we got married at San Juan Baptista Cathedral in Daet, Camarines Norte. Ours was the first marriage among Peace Corps volunteers in the Philippines, but not the last. My mother obtained and kept copies of *The Philippine Herald* and the *The Manila Times*, both of which published many pictures of the event.

Pera and the groomsmen wore white jackets, black slacks and black bow ties that they had to tie themselves. The result: they all looked as though they were helicoptering to the wedding from the other side of the world! Barongs would have made much more sense! My dress was made in Manila by a seamstress cousin of our wedding sponsors, the Calneas. She also sewed the flowered bridesmaids' dresses. On the occasion of our 40th wedding anniversary, I actually managed to get into that dress long enough to have our picture taken.

According to the letters I wrote to my parents, our Filipino friends encouraged us to have a real "American" wedding and we did try our best. We had much help and enthusiastic support from the Camarines Norte community. "The girls" gave us a wonderful shower at Aida Guinto's beautiful house before the wedding that included lunch, gifts, singing and dancing and much heartfelt advice, most of the latter coming from our unmarried friends who had chaperoned us everywhere during our "courtship." We still correspond with many of these friends and were even treated to afternoon tea and ice cream at Aida's home when we returned to visit Daet in 1996. The photographer at our wedding was Igmedio (Iding) Zaldua, whose wife Fay gave birth to a daughter at almost exactly the moment we were saying our vows. Iding was busy snapping pictures when he was given the news and told us proudly the baby was to be called Margo. Margo Zaldua now works as a computer engineer in Quezon City.

We did incorporate at least two Filipino traditions in the wedding plans. Our "sponsors," Mr. and Mrs. Calnea, invited the wedding party and all Peace Corps visitors to a feast the night before the ceremony at their home. They were also very helpful to us when we discovered we had to get permission from the Archbishop in Naga City in order to get married. We met with the Archbishop's assistant, *Father* Jaime Sin, who helped us fill out and sign the necessary documents. Twenty-four years later, *Cardinal* Jaime Sin gave the commencement address at Boston College when Julie, our first born, graduated from there.

We had our wedding reception in the upstairs community room at the Alatco Bus Station. The food was provided by our Filipino friends who made our favorite dishes—*lumpia*, *pansit, flan*, among others. We had a great band that played in a transformed community room full of white bows and ribbons draped from wall to wall.

The second tradition was a beautifully decorated bell-shaped cage housing one male and one female dove that was hanging from the ceiling of the room. As the festivities were winding down, we were asked to stand beneath the cage. Each of us was handed a white satin ribbon to pull. As we did, the doves were freed from the cage and began circling the room. They circled three times and then flew together out the window. We were then told by our friend Yoly the significance of the doves: circling three times meant we would have three children and flying out the window together meant our marriage would last forever.

Having been given the Vice Governor's car and driver for the day, we were whisked off to Daet's airport (the field outside of town) where we boarded a plane for our honeymoon to Manila, Hong Kong, Japan and Taiwan. Many, if not most, of our "out-of-town" wedding guests were on the same plane. It was truly a memorable day and, following those doves, 48 years, 3 children and 6 grandchildren later, it seems Yoly's "reading" of the tradition of the doves was uncannily accurate.

From Whence We Came and Why

Pera came to the Peace Corps from San Francisco after college and employment with Dean Witter and Company. I came from Connersville, Indiana after some graduate studies at Columbia and working in both New York and San Francisco. Incredibly, both of us were born in Indiana (about 40 miles apart) and were regular customers at the Bonanza's "Happy Hour" in San Francisco's financial district in 1960. We were both invited to go to Nigeria with the Peace Corps and both declined for different reasons. We both accepted the invitation to the Philippines and met for the first time playing bridge during our training at Penn State. Serendipity? Fate? Destiny? Who knows? But it was the Peace Corps that brought us together.

In light of the twists and turns in U.S. diplomacy and foreign policy and the vagaries of world events during the past fifty years, it is almost unimaginable to recall the optimism, enthusiasm and excitement in *our* world following the 1960 election. I was energized and excited about JFK's election and was determined to do something to answer the call, "Ask not…." Pera was looking for adventure and travel, having had a taste of being abroad in 1958. Though I had only "traveled abroad" on a one day-visit to Mexico, I had left the Midwest for New York immediately after college and felt that I had learned to adapt to another "culture" already, for "The City" was a far cry from the cornfields of Indiana. The challenge of the Peace Corps—unclear as it may have been in the spring of 1961—was then, in different ways, appealing to both of us. We were both in our early '20s and were confident in our ability to earn a living and cope with being on our own, apart from our families. Rather than fear or apprehension, we both were curious and anxious to discover not only what other types of people would join the Peace Corps but the idiosyncrasies of other cultures and customs as well. We were anxious to participate in a "people-to-people" program that would bring us some education about foreign issues that we sorely needed to understand in the world of 1960-61. It was a heady time—the torch had been passed to a new generation—ours! And we were more than ready to grab it with both hands! Idealism was a motivating factor but it was tempered by wanting to learn from people in another country as much as possible, giving back whatever meager talents we had to share.

Pera was initially dissuaded from joining the Peace Corps because he was being offered a rather substantial raise at Dean Witter. But in talking with his supervisor, he kept having the uncomfortable feeling that he really wanted a new and different adventure—he wasn't ready to settle down to a corporate existence, at least not yet.

I talked about the Peace Corps possibility with a dear friend from college and we both were excited about it. On a weekend trip to Chicago (about the time Sargent Shriver was named Peace Corps director), we met other college friends at a bar and one of the guys had a Peace Corps application form. Unknown to me, he filled it out with my name and address and sent it in. When I got the letter notifying me about where to take the exam, I didn't think twice. I had been waiting for my friend to decide but when the invitation to the Philippines program arrived, I waited no more. Interestingly, my father received a letter from the VFW Post in Connersville when our local newspaper announced I was heading to the Philippines as a Peace Corps volunteer. After soundly criticizing my father for "encouraging" me to join the Peace Corps, the Post Commander claimed that "…only military personnel are trained to withstand the Communist influences abroad." On the other hand, the Connersville Chamber of Commerce sent my parents a letter of congratulations and the Knights of Columbus did too.

Off to the Provinces—I—Camarines Norte

Pera proposed to me with ring in hand on November 28, 1961 at the 1958 Boy Scout Jamboree Camp in Los Baños, Laguna. Stu Taylor trumpeted our grand entrance into the dining hall that night. At this point, I think all the volunteers were ready to get on with the work we came to do and were anxious to leave our classes in Tagalog (which so few of us were ever going to be able to use in our assigned sites) and get down to doing something useful. Little did we know that even though we were leaving Los Baños in three days, it would still be several weeks before we were all "settled" and actually involved in real work. A great test for "rolling with the punches."

When we arrived in Camarines Norte, along with 11 other volunteers who had already become fast friends, we were greeted by Daet's public officials and the school superintendent and head teachers. We were *not* asked to sing the national anthem in Tagalog as we had been when arriving in the country on October 12! We thirteen were housed together initially at the Daet Central Elementary School's Home Economics Building because a typhoon was bearing down on the region and left us stuck at the school for about ten days. We were still there for the feast of the Immaculate Conception when all the teachers in the area put on a magnificent show of Filipino folk dances and songs and we were fed, what I thought at the time, exotic and tasty dishes.

When we were finally allowed to find our "homes" in Mercedes, Basud or Paracale, we discovered we were all housed in nicely built homes and we girls had indoor plumbing! Pera's group had a wonderful house with two floors and a grand staircase. Pera and I spent every moment we could together, riding *calesas* or buses between Mercedes and Basud with dinners with our Filipino friends in Daet at the Sky Garden restaurant in-between. We were chaperoned continually by our young Filipino friends—in the Bicol area unmarried couples were never allowed to be alone together. There were lots of parties and many opportunities for the "Peace Corpses" to respond—how many times did several of us together get through

"Oh, we ain't got a barrel of money; maybe we're ragged and funny, but we're travelin' along, singin' a song; side by side!" Or there was always *Home on the Range*. But we also learned to dance the *tinikling* and the planting rice and rooster dances. When my brother came for the wedding in 1961, he tried to teach the young girls of Basud the twist amid many giggles, for he was 6'4" tall.

Both of us were very fortunate in the schools that we were assigned. In my case, the head teacher, Joe Alejandro, had made up a schedule for me where I was able to make the rounds of all the classes during the week. The training we had received in teaching English as a second language was invaluable to me and I had a great deal of fun in the evenings devising interesting twists to the lesson plans Mr. Alejandro and I wrote. Fortunately, too, one of my housemates, Ethel Gardner, had been teaching elementary school for several years before joining the Peace Corps. She was very helpful to me. Of course, I was given all sorts of roles—that of Commencement speaker/gardener/Spelling Bee Creator and Judge/Assistant Troop Leader for the Boy Scouts and Jamboree Queen!/Kick Ball referee/Tinikling Dancer extraodinaire! The students were so very well behaved and just looking at a roomful of those gorgeous brown eyes made me fall in love with each and every one of "my" boys and girls. The last week of school Pera and I arranged for a "beach day" for the graduating class. We made s'mores with marshmallows, graham crackers and Hershey bars my parents had sent us. It was a wonderful "farewell" party and the children had made beautiful cards wishing us well as we were about to start our married life together.

Plaridel, where Pera taught, was in a very remote area and some of the children walked as many as 10 kilometers to get to school every day. Fortunately, the school district provided lunch for the students there, which was, we think, rather unusual. Pera had a great relationship with his head teacher who often fed him dinner as the bus ride from Plaridel to Basud was a little over an hour and often the bus arrival and departure times were extremely erratic.

In looking through our scrap books and old letters from our first year in the Philippines, I ran across two letters written to my mother from Washington D.C.. Both letters were dated May 1962. One was from Vance Hartke who was a Democrat and a U.S. Senator from Indiana. Senator Hartke was thanking my mother for her letter of support for the Peace Corps and assuring her that he not only wanted to continue to support the Peace Corps but hoped to push for its expansion as well. There was also a letter from Republican Senator John G. Tower of Texas in which he thanked her for expressing her views on the Peace Corps as well as the dismissal of trainee Janie Fletcher. He went on to tell her that he had asked the Senate Committee on Foreign Relations and the Senate Appropriations Committee to examine the concept and administration of the Peace Corps before the 1963 fiscal year funds were appropriated. Interestingly enough, Senator Tower also mentioned to Mother that the preponderance of his mail reflected the negative concerns of his constituents about the entire Peace Corps program. He agreed with their concerns. Years later, Mother laughed about her letter-writing campaign to Congress in those early Peace Corps years. Don't criticize and jeopardize something HER daughter is doing!! But I also found a speech Mother gave to the Business and Professional Women's Club in 1963 in which she praised Congress for their wisdom in continuing to support the Peace Corps Program.

Off to the Provinces—II—Samar

When we decided to marry, the Peace Corps Director asked us if we'd be willing to continue to live with our individual housemates after we were married. Assuring the powers that be that we weren't interested in that arrangement at all, we were finally assigned to the island of Samar where Groups III and IV were soon to arrive. Our friends in Camarines Norte professed great fear that we were going to that "wild place" right in the middle of the "typhoon belt" where there were no paved roads, lots of drinking (*tuba* was a great favorite) and basically rather uncivilized conditions. Nonetheless, off we went!

But what fun we had in Samar. Unlike the strict, almost Victorian mores of the Bicol, the Samareños were open, earthy and clearly *"Bahala na"* fans. We never thought in terms of poverty but one could compare the Bicol to Northern Virginia and Samar to West Virginia coal mining country. We were fortunate in our school situation again and even had the opportunity to teach at the Samar Institute of Technology, which is now the University of the Eastern Philippines. Dr. Asinas, President of SIT, and his wife became fast friends. Pera taught math and I taught English composition at SIT. We taught on Saturday mornings; then we'd drive around with the Asinases visiting small barrios and villages. As a native of Catubig, Dr. Asinas was happy to do repeat visits there plus taking us to the beautiful island village of Laoang—a place somewhat reminiscent of a much smaller San Francisco. The beach was gorgeous and the views fantastic! We joyfully welcomed Dr. Asinas and his wife to the United States in San Francisco when they emigrated in early 1966.

The following is a paragraph from a letter I wrote my mother in 1962: "When we arrived in Samar we found our house was a nipa hut (our own *"bahay kubo"*) consisting of a *sala*, a *kusina* and a bedroom. No indoor plumbing here! Mondragon is a small town with a populace made up of fishermen, farmers, schoolteachers, one doctor, one priest, one judge, and now two *"Americanos."* We live on the bank of the river about a block from the thundering whitecaps of the Pacific. Our house is wooden, with G.I. sheeting for the roof (unlike the typical bamboo woven roofs) and the house beams are gnarled tree trunks." We have in our possession a replica of our *bahay kubo* that was carved by Dr. De Leon's son, Merrill. He used his father's surgical instruments to carve it (glad we never needed surgery there!) and it is something that our children and now our grandchildren have all taken to schools for "show and tell." What a wonderful souvenir!

The bridge over the Mondragon River that flowed to the ocean was the communal commode and the one time we ventured there we attracted so much attention we knew quickly we'd have to make other arrangements. USAID provided us with great plans for a bucket flush contraption so we contracted with Max Atencio, a local carpenter, to help us dig and build a septic tank and then the toilet. He also built a bed for us that took up the entire space allotted for sleeping (he was impressed with our height!).

Pera and our houseboy Pepe (whom we were told we had to hire at $1 a week because we were among the few salaried people in the town of Mondragon) built a chicken house for our egg-laying hens and the three of us planted a fabulous garden that yielded tomatoes, corn and *camotes*. We also dug a well and built a water tower so we could pipe water into the house for showering (after the sun had heated our two 25-gallon drums of water) and washing dishes. I can still see Pepe dashing up that tower and viciously pumping the handle, a broad smile on his face all the time. Dear Pepe, whom we financed through high school and the University of the Eastern Philippines, died in Manila of tuberculosis when he was just 36 years old.

I was often invited to "drinking sprees" with the female teachers and Pera more than once was invited by the male teachers to come "propagate." Since he never accepted his invitations, neither he nor I ever knew just where this "propagation" business took place. But there were several "interesting-looking" houses we passed on the road between Mondragon and Bugko, the small barrio where we taught on Wednesdays. So perhaps…. The Peace Corps provided us with bicycles and we cycled the five kilometers to and from Bugko. Great fun and good exercise to boot. Pepe absolutely adored the bikes and rode them like a fiend doing "errands" for us all around town. When we left, with Peace Corps permission, Pepe inherited one of the bikes. He was thrilled.

We lived on the bank of the Mondragon River that flowed into the Pacific Ocean and not far from shore was a small coral island that surfaced during low tide. We spent many a lovely, warm afternoon rowing to the island in our *banca*. We would picnic there and then jump in without snorkeling equipment to view the beautiful coral. How idyllic it was!

Teaching the children in the Bicol and Samar was a great privilege for both of us. We both came from families that greatly valued books and reading. Pera and I wrote letters to all our relatives—aunts, uncles, cousins, etc.—and asked them to send books for the (at that time) non-existent school library at Mondragon Central School. About fifty boxes and several months later, we were able to set up the first "public lending library" in Mondragon. What fun that was and how rewarding to see how well it was received. Our Philippines Peace Corps Director, Larry Fuchs, even made the trip to Mondragon to be present at the grand ribbon-cutting. How proud we were!

Although we made several trips to various areas of the Visayas and elsewhere, there were just a few people who made the harrowing trip to visit us in Samar: Dr. Fuchs came that once; Lone Castillo came several times from Leyte as Volunteer Leader in those parts; and Maureen Carroll probably made the most unrewarding of all treks as she had exactly 45 minutes to visit before having to make the arduous return trip to Sorsogon during a holiday weekend. Travel to Samar was often downright impossible.

Ang mga kaibigan namin Pilipinas (Our Filipino Friends)

After all the training we received at Penn State and Los Baños, we learned so many more things about our host country and its people living there for two years. One of the amazing "discoveries" about the Filipinos was their uncanny knack of knowing things that we Americans just never got. For example, they knew when the bus might arrive, regardless of what kind of a schedule the Alatco Bus Company might publish. When we did our *Balikbayan* in 1996, we journeyed back to Samar where we were posted after our marriage. We were told that the ferry to Sorsogon would depart Allen at 9:00 am. Naturally, we Americans were all there at 8:45. None of the Filipinos arrived until about 11:15 and the ferry departed shortly before noon. How did they know? During the Cuban Missile crisis, one of our teacher friends at the elementary school in Mondragon, Samar, told us we might be evacuated at any moment. The following day we received a telegram telling us to "be prepared" as the Peace Corps might have to remove us from our assigned sites. During our time in the Philippines, we grew to have deep respect for the sensitive nature of the Filipinos and their ability to cope with so many natural and human disasters, whether typhoons or disease. *"Bahala na"*—never mind—it might happen and it might not but life goes on so stop worrying about it.

We learned that "Filipino time" basically means "whenever." There was one exception at the schools—*merienda* time was always scheduled and only changed in the event of a national disaster. So too were the afternoon downpours when we relocated to the island of Samar. One could almost set a watch to the start of the rains—more or less 3 pm. But the casual nature of coping with typhoons, dysentery and tuberculosis plus the heat, lizards, bugs, rain, humidity and flooded, muddy roads forced us to slow down and look at what was really important in life.

We also learned how much the Filipinos love their fiestas—the Christmas *luminaria* and pageants and town decorations were all things we too loved and we wanted to know all about their traditions. We'll never forget the rubber baby Jesus being whirled from one end of the church into the hands of Mary and Joseph at the altar that first midnight Mass in 1961. There was a tendency at first to think of these things as childlike, or worse, childish. But that wasn't it at all. It is an approach to life that promotes enjoyment in small things and an optimistic view of what might or might not come to be. It is a delight in preserving their customs and traditions as well.

One incident occurred during our time in Samar that still fills us with deep love and respect for the people with whom we lived in the Philippines, and in a sense epitomizes our Philippines experience. We had been to Calbayog in southern Samar and were returning to Mondragon by bus, normally a 3-4 hour, 80 kilometer ride. Unfortunately, it had been raining for days when we boarded the bus along with all the other people who had been waiting for the buses to start running again. No paved roads meant that many of the roads washed out completely during the rainy season. Along with pigs, chickens, luggage and people on the roof and hanging onto the sides of the open, wooden-seated bus we sat with a toilet seat we had found in the market in Calbayog. Everyone on the bus thought that was a very amusing purchase and many jokes were made about it as we started our trip. Very shortly, we realized how very bad the roads really were. We had to stop every few kilometers so that the bus driver, his assistant and some of the young men could push the bus out of the muddy ruts so that we could advance another kilometer or two before we got stuck again. After about five hours, we had only traveled some 10 kilometers. Everyone had been on and off the bus several times and it was raining again. Another five hours passed and we had been on and off the bus another 10 or 15 times.

The next time we had to get off the bus, two of the teachers from the Samar Institute of Technology invited us to go into the home of one of their friends who lived along the highway. We at first demurred (we figured we were only a few kilometers from home by then), but were persuaded by the two women that their friends would be "honored" to supply us with *merienda*. Great activity ensued immediately in the house as they began cooking rice and cutting up mangoes and bananas and setting out a supply of saltines and warm cokes. We had just sat down to eat when the bus careened drunkenly up the road in front of the house. Pera and I immediately but hastily thanked our hostess and apologized for not being able to stay. We began to run through the rain to the bus. Our teacher friends were calling to us to finish eating and the people on the bus were all yelling at us. We thought they were telling us to hurry, but when we reached the bus we realized they were telling us to go back and enjoy our *merienda*. Imagine! We had been traveling, without food or rest stops (although we had stopped often enough to satisfy that need), for almost twenty-four hours and yet there was unanimous agreement among those on the bus that we should eat and enjoy! Many saltines and bamboo gourds of water were passed around the folks on the bus as we lurched on for another two hours and home. What an experience and what a wonderful lesson we learned from these patient, good-hearted, selfless and courageous people.

Epilogue

It is difficult for us (and especially perhaps me) to separate the Peace Corps experience from the personal experience of meeting someone special and falling in love. Add to that the lifelong friendships we have been fortunate to maintain for fifty years, both volunteers and Filipinos, as well as most of the Peace Corps staff that were there 1961-1963, and it is clear why we so cherish the memory of those two years.

We saw quite a bit of the Philippines during our two-year tenure there. In the early months, we were able to enjoy Pagsanjan Falls where our two canoeists were a 63-year-old father and his 39-year-old son. Just thinking about that ride down those rapids still raises goose bumps. We spent Easter weekend 1962 in Baguio and were able to travel through the gorgeous rice terrace country as well. We saw Mount Mayon "the perfect cone" in Albay as well as the beautiful bay city of Legaspi. In 1963 we joined the Bicol hikers who were going south as we traveled north on our "trotte terminale" fitness hike—50 kilometers from Mondragon to Rizal Beach in Gubat, Sorsogon where we all met up. The hike, patterned after the 50 mile hikes that Kennedy Administration folks were taking on the C&O Canal in Washington, was a farewell celebration of our two years in the Philippines. Pera and I stayed on in Manila working in the office until the end of June and then we boarded a boat for a trip down to Mindanao and Jolo, stopping in Cebu as well. Quite a trip with the Philippine Constabulary on the roof of the boat with machine guns at the ready—on the lookout for pirates from Borneo.

When we moved to the Washington D.C. area in 1966, we were able to become involved with many Filipino organizations as well as the PCAFPD—Peace Corps Alumni Foundation for Philippine Development. We were proud to meet our Filipino counterparts when we were in Manila in 1996. We have often attended Filipino festivals and special occasions here in the States. We've marched in Philippine Independence Celebrations in Washington D.C. as well as San Francisco. Through the years Pera and I have made numerous presentations to various groups about our Peace Corps experience and we never fail to point out what a positive and happy one it was.

Did Peace Corps make a difference in our lives? Absolutely! We met and married for one thing and if in no other way, Peace Corps influenced us toward our public service careers and our continuing commitment to volunteering in many organizations. Did we make a difference to those with whom we interacted in the Philippines? We think so. But again, we know that we learned and gained probably much more from the Filipinos than what we had to give them.

To celebrate Iding Zaldua's 80th birthday in October 2009, his children emailed us and asked us to write a memory of our meeting Iding and his wife Fay (who died five years ago). We did and Iding sent us a note shortly thereafter with a picture of him with his daughter Margo and a notation: "I may be 80 but I look pretty good. All the old people in Daet remember you fondly. Won't you come back again?"

Shortly before we left Samar, our landlady and dear friend Epion Echual had her seventh child—a little boy she named Pera. So we could reply to Iding Zaldua that Pera and Margo are indeed alive and well in the Philippines.

In going through other letters that Margo's parents sent us, we found a note describing "great changes" in the states during our absence: it snowed in San Francisco the winter of 1962-3 and Connersville Indiana finally acquired dial telephone service!!!!

Pera and I in Nevada remember our Peace Corps days with gratitude for the opportunity to have served as volunteers and contented feelings that we did the very best job we could.

Margo and Pera Daniels settled in San Francisco when they returned from the Philippines, but moved to Northern Virginia in 1966. Pera worked for the Federal Government, 1964-1994, lastly as a Financial Manager for Health and Human Services. Margo worked for the Fairfax County Public Library System, retiring in 1997. In 1998 they moved to Reno, Nevada, where they instantly became involved in volunteer activities, most especially in the formation of what is now the Osher Lifelong Learning Institute at the University of Nevada, Reno, a learning-in-retirement organization. They both continue to serve on their Board of Directors, Pera as Treasurer and Margo as Scholarship and Curriculum Chair. Pera facilitates a discussion group, Cracker Barrel, addressing (and sometimes solving) all the world's problems and Margo teaches a memoir writing class and facilitates literature discussion groups. Margo also sings with the Reno Philharmonic Chorus (appearing at Carnegie Hall in 2007!), among many other activities. Their oldest child, Julie, and her husband and two daughters live in Roseville, California; their middle child, Christy, and her husband and son and daughter live in Louisville, Colorado; and their son,  *Michael, and his wife and daughter and son live in Ocala, Florida. In addition to driving all over the country visiting their children and grandchildren and many old Peace Corps friends, Margo and Pera have continued to travel the world with great curiosity and enthusiasm. They say Reno is a great town.*

Dolores Ducommun
My One and Only True Home

Making the Grade

Peace Corps was a great opportunity for me. It opened my eyes to the possibilities that the world has to offer. I learned to travel on a shoestring for the rest of my life, alone, and to remote villages or the back alleys of cities, so that I could experience the life of local people. That led to great adventures, as I would attract their curiosity and quickly become included in their daily lives.

I had no idea what the program was when I took the Peace Corps test to qualify. I wanted to go to Africa, and a Nigerian friend of mine told me to take the test and the U.S. government would send me there for free. Great! I took the test at UCLA with about 150 others. The test monitor told us that if we passed, "they" would contact us. I put the test out of my mind and was attending summer school when I got a telegram telling me to be in Pennsylvania in a week. Wow! I was going to Africa. Hurrah! Oops. Wait a minute: I was going to the Philippines?

I called my professors, and they all encouraged me to go to whatever and wherever it was. One of them told me to send him an excellent report on the people, and he would give me the last six units I needed to graduate. My summer school teacher assured me I had an "A" and said, "Go now!" Another paid my fees and filled out the papers required for my degree. They were excited at my good fortune and wished me well. What wonderful people they were. To this day, I love them for their enthusiastic support of an undergraduate student who had no other support system in her life.

I found the training at Penn State to be exciting. I had a great time with a group of people who had been chosen to be America's link to the developing world. They were extremely bright and a wonderful mix in age, professions, and motivations for joining Peace Corps. As someone from an obscure state college with working class parents, a divorcee with no professional work experience, I felt that I would be selected out of this elite group before going overseas. So, I decided to learn everything I could, enjoy the individuals in the group, and be grateful for the experience of the training alone. (Unfortunately, I found what they were offering us was boring and useless for learning about a new culture-—my field was anthropology so I had a good idea about relevance.)

Amazingly, I was accepted. I went home, gave away my car, my Harley, my trailer and everything in it and headed out. There were 128 of us going to the Philippines, wherever that was!

The Arrivals

Filipinos welcomed the first group of volunteers with total enthusiasm. Met at the airport by a group of students from the University of the Philippines, we were given flowers to wear and greeted individually. They seemed genuinely happy to see us. Then we proceeded by bus through the towns of Laguna on our way to our training site in Los Baños, which was a former Japanese concentration camp during World War II and an international Boy Scout jamboree site. In each town we were greeted by school children waving flags, lots of food and much hugging and smiling. By the end of the day, we were totally frazzled. I couldn't wait to find my bunk and crash, exhausted by the 24 hours plane ride and the fabulous welcome.

We were assigned to our communities in groups of four. The Filipinos had a large house in Pili (Camarines Sur, Bicol Region) waiting for us, nicely furnished and including a maid. The whole town came to greet us at the train station. In procession, we went to the large school and were entertained by the children, speeches by all the important people, and a grand feast and dancing. Then we were asked to give a speech as to why we were there. That totally traumatized me at first, but we all did our bit. One of my housemates, Ellen Brindle, was an experienced speaker. She was poised and eloquent. So the rest of us foisted that duty off on her whenever we were in a group. She made us all look good.

Out on My Own

I soon tired of the big house in Pili and moved out to Himao, the village where I worked. Everyone came and went in my house when they wanted; as my door was always open. (To this day, I always have my doors open all day. I live in the desert, so even the animals come in from time to time.) One full moon night, as we all hung out at the *sari-sari* store, an elder asked me very seriously, "Why did Mr. Kennedy send you to our village?" He knew I was not a trained teacher, and the school really had little use for an English speaking person. I just as seriously told him that Mr. Kennedy had asked me to find out about the daily life of Filipinos in the provinces so that he could better understand how he could help them. He told this to the others and they all beamed and clapped and hugged me. They thought that was great!

From that day on, I was taken to every event in the surrounding area. People would come to get me on a school day, and when I told them I had to work, they just laughed. They would send someone to tell my principal where I was going as this was my real job—to find out about the people in the area. So I would go off sometimes for two or three days without a toothbrush, a change of clothes, or anything else. I loved it. I met the farmers in the faraway fields. I met the women who had never been to the village or to Pili. They told me amazing stories about the life they lived. They were so brave and enduring that I was always humbled by comparison to these strong people.

I was only there one school year before I transferred to Sorsogon, still in the Bicol but further south and speaking a different dialect. There I was a formal teacher in a trade school teaching report writing, English and U.S. history. I had brought my maid Asuncion from Himao with me at her request. Because of the language differences, she got homesick for someone to talk to in her own dialect, so with his parents' permission, we took a five-year-old boy, Modesto, from Himao to Sorsogon to live with us. I was boarding with a Filipina, whose 90 year-old mother had been a principal in the American schools and whose husband had been a taxi driver in the United States for thirty years. They all spoke excellent English. They were a great family and were very generous to me, Asuncion, and Modesto. They fell in love with the little scamp and ended up keeping him to go to private school, then to high school and on to college.

(I went back to visit Ayugan/Himao and Sorsogon in 1977. It was touching to see that they had kept some of the things I had given them, and we laughed together at the stories of the capers we had shared.)

The Sulu Period

During the summers we had to have a project when the schools were out. I joined a team of anthropologists form the Ateneo de Manila, a Jesuit university, to do a study of the various people of the Sulu Archipelago in the very southern Philippines. We worked with the Oblate Fathers Mission, which had been in the area for many years. I was assigned to the Samal people in Siasi, Sulu, who lived on reefs adjacent to the islands. One of my associates, Brother Arong, worked with the Bajau, a people who lived their entire lives on boats. The Samal lived in houses on stilts on the reef. At high tide I had to go on a boat from one house to another to interview them. They spoke only Samal so I needed an interpreter. Their life was very simple. They only ate what they could glean from the sea and a bitter root, poisonous to outsiders, which they cultivated in the jungle away from the town and across a tidal stream.

The people initially were aloof and regarded me with curiosity. They had learned to be wary of strangers because they were often harassed when they went to the island to trade fish for other goods. However, when I asked to come into their homes and ask them questions, they were very obliging. They couldn't understand why anyone would want to know their customs. They never asked me about America. I don't think they knew there were other countries in the world that were different from where they lived.

The paper I wrote was published by the Ateneo and is the only one on the Samal, who may have disappeared by now, that researchers have to know they existed.

As a swimmer I loved the Sulu area. It's all islands and I could sometime swim from one to the other—that had its hazards, but was worth it. When my Peace Corps commitment ended, I stayed on in Sulu. I had a job with the Oblate Fathers teaching history and English at their high school. In the summer, when the fathers and the nuns took vacation, I put their entire library on the Dewey Decimal system. People back home had sent them many books, but no one bothered to read them because they were so out of order. Now they would have no excuse not to read! The fathers were great guys—rugged, kind, caring and brave. They were always trying to convince me there is a God. We had many lively discussions on the topic, hooting and hollering, and ending up with them kicking me out if the evening was late.

I also boarded with thee other women related to the Mission. One was a doctor, another, a midwife, and third was the school's bookkeeper, a former Carmelite nun. Each one was interesting in her own right and very dedicated to her profession. They even engaged me in their work on occasion so I learned about the primitive medicine that prevailed in Sulu. People in these cultures were very courageous and they didn't even know it. They taught me what was possible when there are no modern conveniences to do the work. As a result, I am a very resourceful person in my present home of rocks and bottles in the Sonoran desert.

In Search of Another Sulu

In 1981, I again gave away all of my "stuff" for the third time and took off for Asia to live. I travelled to India, Nepal, Thailand, Malaya, Singapore, Bali, Java, Hong Kong and China for a year. Then I headed to Palawan in the Philippines to retire. I lived on an island by myself (plus several animals) near Port Barton. Unfortunately, I had to return to the U.S. because of an IRS problem and have not returned.

In 2001 I checked out the Marshalls, Kosrae, Pohnpei, Yap and Palau, but after three months I was bored with the paucity of these islands. The life was too bland for me, and the beaches could not compare to the beaches in the Philippines, so I returned home to the desert.

The Philippines is a special place for me and no other place overseas will be suitable. As far as my contribution to the Philippines, I don't think I was of much use to the Filipinos. However, they certainly gave me much joy and took good care of me so I thank all of them for being who they are, I also thank all the Peace Corps people I will never meet for having given me this GREAT gift of meeting truly wonderful people at a young age so I could lead my life in a compassionate manner.

Dolores Ducommun lives in the center of five acres in a village-like setting in the Sonoran Desert in Tucson, Arizona, where she says she doesn't have to obey all the rules of society. She owns Anna's Bottle House, which according to one visitor "is the most amazing B&B in existence. The bottles used range from clear Pepsi bottles to amber colored beer bottles to green wine bottles. When the sun strikes them, the effect is quite beautiful. Interspersed with the bottles are smooth rocks completing the very organic cottage." Dolores says the place was built in the '60s by individualists and Mexicans, so it is very eccentric—and therefore she loves it.

Michael Forman
Volunteer and See What Happens

Okay, so here I am almost fifty years later, in our house looking downhill to the back of Diamond Head. I'm writing this at a table that once belonged to Imelda. Yes, her, that Imelda. I know I need to explain, but how?

It all started at another table, a much smaller one, in a dormitory at John Carroll University (JCU), a Jesuit school in a suburb east of Cleveland. I was playing chess and losing badly when friends provided an escape by calling me to watch TV with them. "Hey Forman, come listen to this. It sounds like you." On screen, John F. Kennedy was campaigning from the library steps of the University of Michigan in Ann Arbor. I listened until he wrapped up his speech. I then went straight to my dorm room desk and drafted a letter. "If you do this, remember me. I'm interested." You might think that I would have committed to voting for him too, but I could not. I had a draft card, but I was not old enough yet to vote.

Shortly after Kennedy's inauguration, a telegram came from Washington: "WILL YOU GO TO THE PHILIPPINES? STOP."—or something to that effect. What did I know about the Philippines? Effectively, nothing. I had to go look it up. Did any names come to mind? Yes, Aguinaldo—I have no idea why. I even had no clue as to his first name. No other names came to mind. I was really pretty much a blank slate on the topic. I had to start reading.

Summer came quickly in Ohio and so did the trip to State College, Pennsylvania. The Penn State experience is mostly lost in the fog of the past. Was there a bar on a corner, downhill, maybe one below street level? There was that "survival training" session where we were driven to a spot somewhere in the woods to find our way back alone. I recall being dropped off not far from a paved road, walking back to the pavement, and hitch-hiking back to the campus. There were readings in English as a foreign language. The reading that really stuck with me, however, for its presentation of cultural difference, was Edward T. Hall's *The Silent Language*. I was much too young and naïve either to recognize or to become engaged in several controversies that arose during the training, e.g. potential de-selection of a trainee who had protested against a film about the House Un-American Activities Committee. We had a little schooling in Tagalog, courtesy of several upper class Filipino graduate students from top U.S. universities, who had been recruited as cultural and language informants. Although the "training" was unstructured and informal, I know I was struck by how different Tagalog was from the languages I had studied up to that point—four years of college Latin on top of four years of high school Latin, three years of college French, two years of high school German, and two years of high school Greek. I thought I knew a lot about language, but Tagalog made it clear that I did not. The concept of languages being grouped into families was foreign to me as was the fact that Philippine languages grouped into a very large family that stretched from Hawaiian in the east to languages of Madagascar in the west.

The Long Flight over the Pacific

Following a few days in San Francisco where we were sworn in as volunteers, we took off for the Philippines. A landing at Honolulu International Airport gave us the opportunity to dash in to see Waikiki. I was with a small group who rolled up pants legs and waded at the beach, just to say we'd been there. This was my first glimpse of Diamond Head—from the customary tourist angle rather than the view that I have enjoyed for many years now from my home. Then it was back to the plane, one of those old triple-tail "Constellations." My imagination had made this into a Flying Tiger Express. (Now, having dug up a photo, I see that nothing on the tails supports my guess, and suddenly the name Slick Air pops into mind. (Hmm. Gotta google that.) Anyway, the propellers cranked into action and we were off. I remember the pilot coming on the intercom and chastising us for moving around so much, saying it was hard enough to fly that plane as it was. I skipped out on the card games and settled down for a long nap stretched out on the floor beneath three or four rows of seats.

We landed for a stop on Wake Island "unannounced" and were "honored" with an armed military escort down the runway. Locked up in some sort of cafeteria, I remember being part of a small contingent who cornered the young lieutenant in charge, arguing that he was holding "Kennedy's children" (Well, others had started using that, so why not?). We said that if he did not make whatever calls he needed to make to get us released, we would take advantage of a pay phone hanging on the wall to call the White House. (I don't recall counting up our quarters to see if we could make good on our threat). Not much later, I recall enjoying *kilawen (raw meat or fish dish)* at the beach house of some Filipino laborers from the base.

The Pan Am commercial jet that was carrying about 25 women who could not fit on the "connie" eventually caught up and we all landed at the same time for the welcoming ceremony in Manila on the morning of October 12. I have a photograph of the young me, sleeves rolled up, bounding down the stairway from the plane. A cartoon caption today would read "Bring it on!"

Los Baños

Chartered red LTB (Laguna-Tayabas-Batangas) buses, open-sided, with wooden benches in flat-bed trucks carried us through the countryside. This was my first look at rice paddies, a bit of sugarcane, and the magnificent half-moon mango and acacia trees. Another welcoming ceremony awaited us at our training site, the University of the Philippines agricultural college at Los Baños in Laguna province (UPLB.)

I was standing beside Bureau of Public Schools official Rodolpho Tupas when he was pressed by a skeptical reporter to say what school people thought these PCVs could do that might have any lasting value for Filipinos. Tupas hemmed and hawed; then, glancing at me, a good six to eight inches taller than he, opined that, well, we could hold up maps for the classroom teachers. Some of us thought it was time to go back home right away! We began to realize how hastily this project had been put together.

Later some of us were prodded to evaluate our mission further when we were challenged in a meeting with historian, author, and journalist Nick Joaquin. He was a strong nationalist, anti-colonial in a way I was not yet prepared for. Joaquin's position was forcefully articulated: Philippines for Filipinos! We've already had quite enough of you Americans. Thank you very much, but you can go back home now. It was disturbing, thought-provoking, and stronger than anything I had picked up on during training.

A week or so later, another encounter underscored how unprepared I was for the reality of our adventure. As I was hiking back up Mt. Makiling to the dorm, I was offered a ride in a campus security patrol jeep. We were leaving the area of UPLB buildings, when suddenly the jeep lurched off the pavement and roared across a grassy field. The patrolman in the passenger seat in front of me emptied his pistol at something or someone I never saw. "Robbers—we chased them off," he explained.

An outstanding feature of the training at Los Baños, however, was the outstanding staff from Ateneo de Manila who conducted our training: Jesuits Frank Lynch, John McCarron, and Jaime Bulatao, and others such as Mary Racelis Hollnsteiner and Vicky Bunye. I was deeply impressed by the design of the Tagalog course with its Malinowskian focus on language in context. (Bronislaw Malinowski was a brilliant anthropologist whose ideas about language learning emphasized that meaning is not just in word and sentence structure but is to be found in use in context—an approach I used subsequently throughout my career.) I was to work later with this Ateneo staff both in the Philippines and back in the States. Vicky came to be a colleague in Honolulu. Father Bulatao was my marriage "go-between" and officiated at my wedding (but I'm getting ahead of myself).

Off to the Provinces

At the end of training, we got our assignments. Most of Group 1 was sent to the Bikol region south and east of Manila, but still on Luzon. A much smaller group headed south to the center of the Philippines, to the Visayan (*Bisayan*) island of Negros. On Negros there were at least two different major Philippine languages spoken, one on either side of the island's mountain spine. A Philippine Airlines DC-3 (Flight 816, to be exact—I saved the baggage stub) carried a dozen of us to the coral-rubble landing field of Dumaguete, Negros Oriental. We were met there by Governor Perdices and maybe a dozen officials, including the Governor's sister, who was the supervisor of English instruction in the province's public schools. Her name was Carmen Perdices, but we were told to call her, as did everyone else, "Mameng." Eventually, as I became familiar with language patterns for nicknames, I learned that this was the common nickname for a woman named Carmen, but for the longest time, I mis-heard it as "Mommy." She was indeed a very nurturing supervisor.

I'm not sure why I got included in the Negros group, but it may have been that when asked where I would like to be assigned, I had answered, "the place nearest a Philippine university." Silliman University it was. I was the runt of the litter, the *bunso*, i.e., the youngest PCV in Group I, and I had hopes of continuing to study and of making friends with Filipino peers. Assigned together, the late Len Giesecke, Ralph Thomas (Ralph T), Ralph Cauthen (Ralph C), and I were housed in a newly-built cinder-block house in Maslog, a barrio of the *poblacion* of Sibulan. A couple who were both officials of the Negros Oriental Bureau of Public Schools owned the house. The wife was principal of the *poblacion's* central elementary school, where I was assigned to assist in teaching first and second grade English and sixth-grade science.

Ralph T and Len were both appointed Volunteer Leaders and were often on the road visiting and providing support for other volunteers. Ralph C worked at the Maslog school where we lived and a short walk from our house. My walk to the central school was longer (and hotter).

We all had to adjust to certain quotidian annoyances such as the quasi-greeting from children of, "Chocolates, Joe?" Adults more often called out "Hi, Joe." This could be a bother, as they were holdovers from WWII. It was hard for us to understand that the war was still a part of the lives of many of the adults, although it was close to two decades past. We wanted a military image no more than we wanted to be the "neo-Thomasites." Determined not to be caught up in a stew of pique, I adopted the strategy of a smiling reply: "Hello, Juan," or "Hello, Maria." These generated, "But my name is not Juan/Maria" and so I had the opening to say "Me too—my name is not Joe. I'm Mike." This often led to more personal conversations (as well as invitations to stop for a drink of *tuba*, which I usually could decline with the excuse that I was on my way to teach). Sometimes I even tried this gambit in Cebuano instead of English.

Some of the teachers I worked with, and pretty much all of the children, seemed quite ill at ease with English, beyond the formulaic snippets everyone knew. This had motivated me to plunge into self-study of Cebuano (or *Sinugbuhanon*).

My school principal was proficient in English, but we were not comfortable with one another on different grounds. Often it seemed to me that she was making up any old thing and passing it as fact just to avoid any blemish to her aura of authority. She told me once that she had been observing my methods and had concluded that my goal was "to make the children bold." Certainly it was true that I encouraged the children to go beyond merely answering my questions. I wanted them to become comfortable with asking questions. I wanted them to think about questions, to distinguish questions they knew the answers to from those they did not, and to recognize a question that I knew the answer to as distinct from one I probably did not. It would have pained me deeply to hear the principal's assessment had the contemporary usage of the word *bold* in the Philippines (usually associated with sleazy behavior) been in play at that time. However, I knew that *bold* in my principal's assessment was not a compliment!

After some months in the Maslog house, I moved to a two-story house near my school. I rented the bottom floor and opened a sort of boys-and-girls clubhouse. Books, art materials, puzzles, and a ping-pong table attracted children from the neighborhood. A puzzle map got a lot of play, and I found myself attending to the cognitive moves, or lack thereof, which differentiated each child's encounter with the puzzle. I also started a group project to map our school grounds.

I took my meals on contract with the family next door. I'm sure that family was doing its level best to make me feel at home, but it was quite difficult to persuade them that this young man from Ohio was really not accustomed to a cold fried egg on cold rice with a warm San Miguel for breakfast.

These changes in my living style gave me the opportunity to focus on Cebuano and observe how the language was being used in context. My general impression was that none of the Peace Corps staff was giving much attention to language. It was the Director, Dr. Fuchs, whom I burdened with most of my complaints about the Peace Corps' failure to assist the volunteers in learning the language of their places of assignment (the "dialect"). Eventually, Dr. Fuchs must have grown weary of my nagging. He told me, "Okay, do something about it. You're in charge." Shortly after that, I began to be teased with the sobriquet "the PCV assigned to Philippine Air Lines," for I got to travel all over the country looking for any and all means (language study centers, experts) to assist the PCVs in language learning. I was sorry to leave Sibulan and more or less lived out of a duffel bag from then on. I had been named a Volunteer Leader to accommodate the shift in assignment and got to take on other quasi-staff functions as well as the development of a language program.

Valuable Resources on the Road to a Language Program

I met John Wolff, a Yale graduate student who was working on Cebuano in Cebu City. It was instantly obvious to me that his knowledge of the language was far in advance of mine. We teamed up and offered a summer school in Cebuano for interested volunteers. (Later John was hired by Cornell University and became a member of my doctoral committee.)

I also met Doug Foley (from a later group of volunteers) who was a quick study in Waray, the language in Leyte, where he was assigned. Doug was a top-notch basketball player and used his basketball to work with street kids in Leyte. Doug and I used to compete with one another on learning "green" vocabulary (dirty words). We did so not out of any prurient interest but because we were all too aware of a propensity for Filipinos to have fun at the PCV expense, tricking the volunteer by mis-teaching a "naughty" phrase in place of something innocent that the volunteer had requested. Knowledge seemed the best defense. After Peace Corps, Doug earned a PhD from Stanford in anthropology and education and has had a long and successful career at the University of Texas.

A trip to Nasuli in Bukidnon in Mindanao introduced me to the very large Summer Institute of Linguistics (SIL) and its engagement with Philippine languages. Although Bible translation was the goal for SIL, literacy activities, orthography development, lexicography work, and language analysis all produced information on many Philippine languages that were helpful to me.

The Most Important of My Road Trips

Trips to Quezon City and to Manila made a huge difference in my life. This was especially true of assigned visits to Ateneo de Manila University, whereby I earned another sobriquet, "Peace Corps ambassador to the Jesuits." New Volunteers continued to arrive every several months, and I was responsible for establishing and maintaining liaisons with providers of language and culture instruction. The ties to the Ateneo staff we had met in Los Baños were crucial.

But the really important development was that in Manila/Quezon City I met Sheila. She was a senior at Maryknoll (now Miriam College) and was working as a research assistant for Father Bulatao at Ateneo. We corresponded when I was in Negros or Mindanao—Peace Corps had opened a training center in Zamboanga. And whenever I could arrange it, we met in Manila, sometimes for movies (but usually she'd already seen every film five times, there being a long line of rivals for her attention.) Her coterie of suitors included young men who would pick her up in Mercedes' or Jaguars or Cadillacs. All I had to offer was long walks and cheap stops at the Dairy Queen on Taft Avenue or the Milky Way in Malate with a very occasional dinner at Tasa de Oro if I could manage to save up for it. Near the end of my two-year Peace Corps commitment, when Sheila and I went to discuss marriage and ask her father's approval, he told her that it was "fiscal folly" for her to contemplate this. He was right, of course.

The economic status of volunteers was well known among locals. When Sheila and I went to city hall for a marriage license, we made the mistake of going too close to the noon hour. We encountered a band of "fixers" who presumed that I was from Clark Air Force Base and that we would need to have our business conducted as quickly as possible. They were speaking Tagalog to each other, of course. One of them spoke English to us. When I overheard that fellow saying something about us to others in Tagalog, I spoke up, in Tagalog. I was not military, we were not in such a big hurry. *"Ay, piskorp pala 'to. Wala tayong makukuha sa kanya."* 'Oh, he's Peace Corps. We're not gonna make anything off of him."

Trying to be fiscally responsible, I had backed out of an option to buy a (beautiful) BMW motorcycle from an Irish missionary priest. Also, with help from Mr. Gruy (the security guard at Peace Corps on Herran Street), I was saving money by sleeping on the floor in an office under someone's desk—I think it was Bert Pumento's.

Larry Fuchs asked me to stay on for a third year to continue developing in-country language training. But I was getting married. No problem, said Fuchs. Never mind the Washington policy pronouncements. They could kick up my stipend a bit. More importantly, they would guarantee the same medical coverage for Sheila as I had. So Sheila and I got married in May of 1963. It was a big celebration because it was also my new in-laws' wedding anniversary and my mother-in-law's birthday. If my memory is not too faulty at this distance, it was also the first anniversary of our first date.

The Extension Year

We set up our first household in Pasonanca Park in Zamboanga. Sheila went to work teaching in the Ateneo de Zamboanga elementary school and setting up a pre-school/kindergarten for Father Stan Reynolds, an Episcopal priest who had been very helpful and friendly to many PCVs. As Sheila did that, I continued to work on language materials and in-country training resources.

1963 rushed past. When JFK was assassinated, Sheila and I were back in Quezon City in a little apartment. I remember our late colleague John Bossany running down from Bert Pumento's house to pass on the tragic news. The next time John was to hurry to this apartment, it was to transport us to St. Luke's Hospital for the (premature) birth of Mark, our first child, on January 27, 1964—Peace Corps Dr. Jack Harkness attending.

Before we left that apartment in Quezon City in 1964 there was another adventure. Late one evening, Mark was sound asleep in a drawer which we had made over into a crib. Sheila and I were downstairs packing for the big trip home to the USA. I was using a souvenir *balisong* (*pocket knife*) to cut the Manila hemp with which we were tying up the boxes. We were both tired. All of a sudden, the knife slipped in my hand. I thought for sure that I had cut myself, possibly deeply, in the palm of my left hand. Sheila is very sensitive to the sight of blood. After all, she had lived through the Japanese occupation and MacArthur's battle of south Manila, as a very young child. So I clenched the hand tightly and tried to hide it behind my back. Sheila nonetheless started screaming. The next thing I knew, I heard a measured male voice saying, "Do not worry, Mum. We are protecting you." There I stood with *balisong* in hand, the other hand a fist at my left side. Sheila a few feet away was screaming. At the louvered window at the front of the apartment, maybe ten feet away, there stood two men, one of them pointing a shotgun in my direction. Fortunately Sheila managed to calm down enough to explain to her "protectors" that she was in no real danger.

Getting the Necessary Credentials

Not much later our little family of three was off to Ohio to visit my family and for me to take a summer job in one of Akron's tire factories to save up a little for graduate school. What I had forgotten, or never given much thought to, never really knew about, was that Akron, Ohio had been considerably involved in the northern history of the Ku Klux Klan. We experienced a picket of my parents' house, with marchers carrying signs that read: "Get that nigger out of our neighborhood." Sheila acted quickly, joining the NAACP and boarding a Greyhound bus bound for Ithaca, NY, where I had been accepted into graduate studies at Cornell University in linguistics, anthropology, and Southeast Asian Studies. There, with the assistance of Filipino students in the Cornell-Philippines program, Sheila set up an apartment for us on farmland above Lake Cayuga. I followed as soon as I could.

Cornell was good, very challenging, and a lot of work. With her background in child development study, Sheila became a prototype Head Start teacher for Tompkins County. I had trips to the Philippines and to Hawai'i at Peace Corps-Washington expense to review programs and to conduct language testing. In the summer of 1966, we (now a family of four) went to Cambridge, MA to help with a Peace Corps training and selection program run by volunteers from later groups, Dick Vittitow and Jim Stewart. Most of the money we earned that summer went to good food at Joyce Chen's restaurant.

Toward the end of the 1967-1968 school year, I was working on the proposal for my doctoral dissertation, which was to be a description of Zamboanga Chabakano (Chavacano.) Out of the blue came three offers of employment in academic positions: from Ohio University, from the University of Michigan, and from the University of Hawai'i (UH). I dithered. Ohio had family. I'd been to Michigan and I knew UM had a strong library collection from the American colonial period in the Philippines. Hawai'i? There was a lot unknown except that there were hundreds of thousands of Filipinos residing in the state. I expected that I would be able to continue with Philippine Studies. "Write the letter!" *utos ni missus* (the wife commanded). "What letter?" said I, weakly. "You know," she said. "It snows in Ohio. It snows in Michigan. It doesn't snow in Hawai'i. Write the letter." By then, while living on the farm outside Ithaca the family had grown to five. David had come late (on March 13, 1966), cooperating by waiting until finally a fifteen-foot snowdrift was cleared from the rural route we lived on. Maia (Malaya Paz) had the even better sense to be born on June 20, 1967.

Hawai'i...and Back to the Philippines

The Hawai'i offer was to work as a researcher at the Pacific and Asian Linguistics Institute (PALI). PALI had a Peace Corps contract to produce dictionaries, reference grammars, and language lessons for a set of Philippine languages. One of the languages in the contract was to have been Zamboangueno, and that would have been the ideal assignment for me. Unfortunately, Peace Corps decided that Zamboanga was getting too dangerous for PCVs and cancelled that portion of the contract. What was I to do? Committed to Zamboangueno with my Cornell committee, I had a wife and children counting on my having a job to support them. A colleague suggested that I take another language from the contract set. So it was that our little family (five now) moved to rural Pampanga in 1968. It will come as no surprise, then, when I tell you that more adventure was to follow.

The news magazine *Philippine Graphic* broke the story of the infamous, terrible My Lai massacre in Vietnam. In the same issue, on the page facing the beginning of the My Lai story, appeared a tale (entirely fictitious) of a triple agent based in Pampanga, working for CIA, of course; plus the NPA (The New People's Army, a post Huk Communist Group), replacing Huk education director William Pomeroy; and Malaysia (during the time of *konfrontasi*, when the Philippines and Malaysia were disputing the ownership of Sabah).

Well, guess who was all but named as the triple agent? Space here is much too short to tell the full story of how that came to pass, but my supervisor at the University of Hawai'i decided that I should return there to complete my work. I ended up finishing the two Kapampangan books (1971) and the dissertation back in Honolulu. Being there gave me the opportunity to apply for and win a tenure-track position in instruction (divided three ways: PALI, linguistics, and anthropology). Beyond that, I became involved in many other activities, including establishment of Philippine Studies, first as a "program" and later as a "Center."

Martial Law in the Philippines

At one point we did not consider it safe to return to the Philippines. A friend highly-placed in the Philippine government warned us: "Your accident has already been prepared." It seems the Marcos crowd frowned on some of the things we'd done in Hawaii, such as the time Sheila, as Imelda, paraded in a Pitoy Moreno gown with gold bracelets and watches festooning her arms. The parade went from the Philippine Consulate in Nuuanu to the Philippine Air Lines office in Waikiki. Our boys experienced having the police confiscate their toy rifles. The police department explained that the parade permit did not cover arms. I suppose it's also likely that the Marcos people didn't really appreciate our sheltering Charito Planas shortly after the election in which many say she defeated Imelda for mayor of Manila.

After Ninoy's assassination and the People Power revolution, we were able to return to the Philippines in 1989. We were now a family of six, our youngest, Daniel, having been born on September 15, 1970. He accompanied us and enrolled as an undergraduate student at the Ateneo. Both Lea Salonga and Kris Aquino were in his classes. He used to grumble about forgetting to leave space for the bodyguards. He enjoyed playing shortstop for the Ateneo varsity and was flattered to receive offers to play for other teams. His Ateneo teammates went out of their way to be nice to him. And my Tagalog got a work-out once we realized that most practices and games were conducted not in English but in Tagalog. *Dapa!* (slide!).

During this time, our Group I colleague, the late Tim Peterson, and his wife Tatti Licuanan were a great help to us. Tim was working at the Asian Development Bank. When I found that commercial banks wanted to hold my sabbatical checks for forty-five days before cashing them, Tim cashed checks for me out of his pocket. Tatti as academic VP at Ateneo helped shepherd Daniel through a new system.

During this stay, we lived through the thrills and scares of the *kudeta* which nearly toppled President Cory Aquino. A *kudeta* is the Tagalog version of the French *coup d'etat*. A whole graffiti phrase (seen along EDAS) was *Kudeta Pakana Ng* USA—"coup d'etat, a machination of the United States."

When we returned from this trip, we were met at the Honolulu airport by people who were begging Sheila to accept a job as director of the Catholic Immigration Center (CIC). Here's where the tale of the Marcos table comes in… I haven't forgotten.

Back to the Table

The Marcoses, it was alleged (and I took those allegations to have been made on good authority), were the real owners of two ritzy houses in the hillside residential community in Honolulu called Tantalus. Eventually, after Ferdinand Marcos had died, new officers in the Philippine consulate—as I heard the story—had those houses seized. They were put on the market to try to recoup funds for the Philippines, but prior to any sale, the real estate agent insisted that the houses be emptied of furniture and other contents. Known at the consulate for our efforts during martial law, we were now in their good graces. Their agent asked that Catholic Immigration (Sheila) help dispose of a truckload of books which had been removed from built-in shelves in one of the houses. A big truck came and filled our garage with boxes and boxes of books. Once we found time to examine these boxes, we found scores of royal romances together with scores of books on military history and military strategy. Now I wish we had had the foresight to list them all. But it was a busy time for us and soon enough we realized that very many of these books were borrowed, unreturned property of the State of Hawaii Public Libraries. Sheila, as a member of the Library Board, hastened to put the books back into the libraries. She also was instrumental in having restored the practice of fines for overdue books.

More than books, there was furniture to be removed and disposed. At that time, parishes of the Catholic Church were providing houses as transition assistance to refugees, mostly from Laos and Vietnam, but also from Eastern Europe. The Church accepted a lot of the Tantalus houses' furniture and put them in these houses. But this one table kept going out and coming back. It's made of bamboo and tinted glass. Maybe refugees found it too reminiscent of Asia, of something left behind. I don't know. In any case, each time it came back it took up too much space in the narrow hallway outside the director's office. Ultimately I relieved the pressure on the CIC director's space by making a donation and taking "Imelda's table" home.

These days our kids have no hesitation to join us at this table to feast on *adobo* and *lumpia*. They used to resist dishes with *patis*, but Sheila has developed a salad dressing with (hidden) *patis* that they all love. They won't eat "stink fish" (*bagoong, tuyo, daeng*), but they like some Ilokano dishes they developed a taste for when we lived in the Filipino camp of a pineapple plantation on Moloka'i. They're great kids; we're proud of them all. Sometimes they even bring the San Miguel.

Epilogue

When Mark was born, he weighed only five pounds, but he grew to be strong and healthy. His coach at Pitzer (one of the five colleges in the Claremont schools) said he was pound-for-pound the strongest defensive back the Mudhens had ever had. With an MA from Columbia University's School of International and Public Affairs, Mark went on to serve as aide to Hawaii's Senator Sparky Matsunaga and then for six years as aide to Senator Daniel

K. Inouye. Later a graduate of the UH William S. Richardson School of Law, Mark today runs the Hawaii Medical Services Association Foundation, a job his sister younger sister Maia held before him.

Maia is a strong woman herself. Surviving second and third degree burns as a four-year old, she has shown how strong she is in many ways. From sinking free throws with no time on the clock to lead her high school team to victory, to four years as an All-Ivy volleyball player and three year captain of the Harvard team, to work in graduate classes as an undergraduate there in which she finished a BA thesis on Kalaupapa, on the interface between Hawaiian culture and western medicine, to the skirmish in which she wangled her way into a joint MA in public health and public administration at UC Berkeley, to her current multiple-round battles with cancer while raising two delightful and talented children.

Even though the police had taken away David's toy rifle during martial law, I don't think this had any adverse effect on his life. He serves today as enforcement attorney for the State of Hawai'i Civil Rights Commission. He also serves as co-chair of a Filipino-American lawyers' group.

Our youngest son Daniel later served in the Peace Corps in Madagascar and then taught and coached at a high school on O'ahu's rural Leeward Coast. Today he works in the mountains in O'ahu in resource management and conservation.

Our engagement with the Philippines is obviously life-long. When I retired from the University of Hawai'i, I proudly accepted a plaque from the Center for Philippines Studies that read in part as follows:

> ...in recognition of his significant achievements in and outstanding contribution to Philippine Studies, particularly in the fields of general linguistics, ethnographic linguistics, and Philippine linguistics and languages and in grateful appreciation of his many years of service to the community on human rights, language issues, democratic principles, social justice, cross-cultural learning and Filipino-American issues....The Center also greatly appreciates his outstanding service as acting director of Philippine Studies at various times in the past and his continued commitment of promoting academic studies on the Philippines and the Filipino people.

How could I have ever imagined that such a life would ensue from writing that letter to John F. Kennedy to remember me if he got the Peace Corps underway?

Michael L. Forman was born June 30, 1940 in Kansas City, Missouri, the first son of Lawrence E. Forman and Callista M. Berrigan (both passed on now). He is the eldest of six. He earned a BA from John Carroll University and a PhD from Cornell University. Married to Sheila Maria da Silva, they are the parents of four and the grandparents of four. Forman was on the faculty of the University of Hawai'i at Manoa for forty years (June 1968—June 2008) and is now Professor Emeritus.

(First photo shows Mike and Sheila after their wedding in 1963; the second shows Mike with his grandson.)

Richard Gilbert
The World's Worst Peace Corps Volunteer

Years later, I came back. As was the custom, they roasted a pig in my honor. A banner draped the stage: "Welcome Back, Dick Gilbert." Around the head table were assembled the teachers whom I knew, all now retired, and among whom, for a moment, I had supposedly "worked." Next to me, they placed an aging woman of the town who had once been, reportedly, the pretty, vivacious college student who lived across the street and with whom I had often flirted at various town events. Not lost on me was the sight of her red-faced husband, drinking with the town toughs on the fringes of the event, who glared toward me with increasing antipathy. "Hey buddy," I wanted to say, "loosen up. It wasn't like that then, and it sure ain't now."

Then, the story-telling began. One by one, the teachers took to the microphone on stage and began to recite humorous anecdotes of Dick Gilbert, the town's first Peace Corps volunteer. "Gee," I thought, after the first speaker, "I don't remember that." In fact, hardly anything in the eager testifying rang a bell. Quickly, it dawned on me. These weren't stories about me. These were yarns recalled about all the Peace Corps volunteers who had come to the town in the many years after me, forged by time into one collective memory and ascribed to me because I was the one sitting there. Someone probably even slipped in the tale of a revered Thomasite or two.

Truth be told, hardly anyone remembered a single thing about me. That figures. My good buddy Max and I got the short end of the stick in Los Baños and were assigned to the same town as John and Miriam Kennedy, crazed composters, namesake to the President and the nascent program's showcase "senior" volunteers. In their blazing fame, Max and I disappeared.

The Truth of the Matter

I was surely the world's worst Peace Corps volunteer, at least up to that time. There were three things that interested me in 1961: folk music and left-wing politics and girls, in reverse order. Note that neither saving the world nor teaching English or elementary science in a Philippine barrio school is listed. Still, as I recall, being a debutant PCV was way cool. I mean, I got my picture in *The New York Times* as one of the state's first volunteers, met a lot of swell people (girls mainly) and learned the meaning of *utang na loob*. Now how great is that?

I mean I tried, occasionally at least. Once, finding myself "teaching" the barrio school's sixth grade a unit of science, I asked the class "What shape is the earth?" In a flash came the answer in perfect unison: "The earth is round, sir." Hmmm, I thought, not good. So I invited the class to follow me outside and regard the horizon. "Look around you," I said, "what shape is the earth?" Puzzlement reigned. What does the all-knowing foreigner want from us?

Suddenly, staring into the distance, the smartest kid in the class got it. "Flat, sir. The earth is flat!" "Yes," I shouted triumphantly. "Look around you. Of course, the earth is flat. Our eyes tell us that the earth is flat." Now, having unlearned another piece of spoon-fed "knowledge" for which there was little obvious evidence except faith, we returned to the classroom just as the gong sounded ending the day. Had I returned the next day, my class and I would have proceeded through the endless fascinating series of proofs to discover how ancient peoples, using their eyes, deduced the true shape of the earth. The deeper lesson, I thought then, was about the nature of truth and the danger of blind acceptance. Alas, I probably didn't show up the next day, or for many days thereafter, leaving a classroom full of Filipino children who today, as they approach their dotage, are convinced the earth is flat.

But perhaps I do myself an injustice. I am remembered, in that small town at the tip of Negros, by at least one actual living resident, my namesake, "Jeep" Gilbert Ragay. Here's the story. I had managed to inveigle the Peace Corps jeep from our local rep for a few days' stay in our front yard (jeep, not rep). In the midst of the night, the local midwife appeared to announce rather enigmatically that "Mrs. Ragay is giving birth" and needed to be transported to the hospital in Dumaguete City. The town doctor's jeep was broken and apparently Dick Gilbert possessed the town's only motorized vehicle capable at that moment of movement. Did I jump in the jeep, load Mrs. Ragay and, in the black night, roar off to town, cape flying? No. I just tossed the keys to the doctor who, I figured, was better trained than I (George Guthrie's best efforts notwithstanding) to handle any awkward situation which might develop on the road. Off they went while I dove back under the mosquito net and returned to sleep.

Next morning at first light, like a phantom, there sat the Peace Corps jeep, safely in front of the house. Seems that Mrs. Ragay couldn't wait, or perhaps the bouncing of the unpaved road undid her determination. Somewhere in the night, in the back of the jeep in the back of the beyond, her newest son had arrived. The birth complete, the party just turned 'round and headed back to town. And that's how "Jeep" Gilbert Ragay, as he was subsequently named in my honor, came into the world. Postscript: in a bit of hyperbole of which the Peace Corps was particularly adept in those formative years, the Congress was duly informed in a subsequent annual report about how Dick Gilbert, heroic Philippines Group I volunteer, had himself skillfully delivered the baby on the road.

On the other hand, fortunately for me, my "speech" at the town fiesta in 1962 escaped notice in Manila or in Washington. It was the moment of the Cuban missile crisis and my strong sympathies for the Cuban revolution (undiminished by encountering rural poverty in the Philippines) quite overcame whatever common sense I may have then possessed. So there I stood on the rickety stage, rather superciliously criticizing the Kennedy Administration for its rash bellicosity in bringing all of us, including "innocent Filipino children," to the edge of nuclear cataclysm. As I recall the moment, my words and passion were received with total incomprehension and the town party moved quickly on to a song. Not quite so bewildering was the letter of protest about the Administration's Cuba policy that I dispatched to Manila about the same time. That screed came back to bite me a year or so later when a Peace Corps staffer, called upon to recommend me for an important academic graduate fellowship, suggested to the selection committee that I was a person of immoderate views best avoided. (Who me?)

Truth be told, back at Penn State, I was *doppelgänger* to Charlie Kamen but no one in authority noticed. Charlie, we all remember, claimed the spot-light that summer as the political sore thumb of the Peace Corps' infancy, attacked for his behavior at a Miami showing of the infamous right-wing propaganda film, *Operation Abolition* (go Google it). Heck,

Charlie only laughed in a few places. I led a student "truth squad" in my hometown that attended showing after showing to debate loudly (and immoderately) with sponsors who felt that American youth (like me) were going to hell in a Red hand basket. Only a single journalist for my local paper, reading about Charlie, made the connection to me and he, the reporter, after hearing my protestations of purest patriotism, kindly let the matter drop.

Dr. Doug

The appearance of my new roommate Doug Darling and his guitar in my Negros household was the salvation of my Peace Corps tour. (Tired of my harassment, Max had packed his bags and taken off, along with our cook, to more fertile pastures in Panay.) Together with Don Zelinski, Doug had been blown off the bleak Bicol island of Catanduanes by Typhoon Ellen and had washed up down south with me. Doug was, I believe, the world's second-worst Peace Corps volunteer and, together, we managed to set new standards of service

Our most memorable effort consisted of inventing a weekly 15-minute children's radio program called "The Wonderful World of Science" that we scammed the provincial education authorities into broadcasting during school hours. As script-writer, I had the role of ever-wise Dr. Dick. Doug was the friendly Uncle Doug, sort of a Greek chorus in drawl. We dragooned Arlene Pearson, a vivacious, serious-minded volunteer from a neighboring town, into the madcap enterprise by casting her in the role of "Meling," curious village naïf. Best of all was our theme song, composed over many nights with the help of St. Miguel. The lyrics bear repeating here before these are lost to posterity:

Hello Kids, whaddya' know,
It's time for our old science show.
With Uncle Doug and Dr. Dick,
We'll find out how our world ticks.

Don't forget that I'm here too
Enjoying Science along with you
I'm Meling and I want to know
How to help my country grow.

You ought to know both how and why
What's on the earth and in the sky
So that's why we are here today
Exploring the world in our special way.

So c'mon kids, it's time to go
It's time for our old science shooooow…

So successful was the show that Doug and I wrangled to trip to Manila months later to sell a spin-off ("The Happy Friends of Mr. Health") to the World Health Organization. Thankfully for all involved, this last doubly-dubious venture ran up against the deadline of our impending departure and came to naught, except, of course, for rounding up about twenty eager little kids for a memorable recording session of our inevitable new theme song ("We're the Happy Friends of Mr. Health, clean and neat and strong...").

I must point out, with great haste, lest there be doubt, that goings-on such as are recounted here were not typical of my colleagues in the Peace Corps. Their activities were far more laudable than mine and far closer to the model and idealism that fueled the Peace Corps concept. All around me, other volunteers dutifully went to school every day, worked on worthy barrio projects and unstintingly gave the best of themselves to their assignments. Alas, not me. I found being a living language model of doubtful utility for barrio children, and I never could make a workable piece of science equipment out of sticks and bamboo, no matter how simple the instructions. While more sainted volunteers were spending their precious free summers on storied provincial undertakings like Camp Brotherhood in Negros Occidental, I was off in Manila "working" at the Asian Labor Education Center at the University of the Philippines, bar-hopping in Ermita and pitching radio programs of uncertain efficacy.

Coming Back

Fast forward to the time of the roasted pig. I stood with Mayor Teopisto Yap, the town's activist Mayor, facing distant Mindanao on the beach where I had spent many weekends snorkeling or gathering shells. Proof of the nearly three decades that had passed since my departure from this place were the pens of the Japanese-owned shrimp farm that now jutted above the aqua waters of the lovely inlet where we had swum. There were other proofs, not the least of which was the smooth two-lane paved highway that brought us to the town from Dumaguete City in about thirty minutes. During my first stroll-around, I saw people watching television in their homes and marveled at the small town grocery store with its refrigerated beer and frozen goods. The main streets were now electrified at night and the house where I stayed on my visit boasted a telephone, running water and even a flush toilet. The transformation was remarkable. In time, only a bit more than 25 years had gone by but, in truth, the place had been transported whole from one century to another.

The mayor pointed to the fish farm and asked me what I saw. "Shrimp?" I ventured. "No," he replied like the smart politico that he was, "investment, jobs and progress." Back in town, he proudly showed me other examples of projects underway, new electric lines from the city, an expanded health clinic, a town plaza and a shiny new annex for the central school. I was more than a little impressed.

Meanwhile, at one end of the town, long-since collapsed into disrepair, was the wooden, bamboo and nipa house along the gravely main road that the town had built so many years before to house Max and me, honored first-comers. Standing there regarding the debris (and my past), an air-conditioned bus roared by heading for the city. No more, I noted, the distant rumble on the corduroy strips of the road bed warning of the approaching "truck," no more the huge cloud of dirt and dust traveling in its wake coating homes and humans alike and no more the cries of *"para"* from *macho* conductors climbing on the bus roof or hanging with *bravado* from the sides. I found myself succumbing to an unexpected and quite unwelcome surge of nostalgia.

During my farewell conversation with Mayor Yap, I thanked him for the warmth of my welcome and the hospitality he had engineered for me during the past four or five days. We talked about development and change and the Peace Corps. I no longer recall his exact words or his reflections on such heady topics. I only remember that he said that many other Peace Corps volunteers had come to the town after me, one of whom had been his own teacher, and he was glad that we came. "But did we make a difference?" I asked. He paused and thought. "Who knows," he said, "who knows what makes a difference?"

The Last Word

Not many months after my return trip to the Philippines, newly retired from the Foreign Service, I took a position with Special Olympics International in Washington D.C., the organization famously founded by Eunice Kennedy Shriver and headed at that time by Sargent Shriver himself. Shortly after I arrived, I found myself in conversation with Mr. Shriver and, without thinking, alluded to myself as a former Peace Corps volunteer. "Oh my God," he said with a loud laugh, "not another one."

At that moment, I guess I realized how far from the genuine uniqueness of my early Peace Corps experience (and my own youth) I had traveled. Being just another of many thousands of RPCVs was not nearly the symbol of distinction that came with being among the first chosen, the special, the few.

Unlike many of my colleagues, my "service" in the Peace Corps was neither life-transforming nor did it result in a history of connections to the Republic of the Philippines. Still, like any past honor of great value, the experience is untarnished and persists as an important part of me. Even if I never came close to being, or even aspired to be, the epitome of the perfect volunteer, I am proud to have been selected and to have served. Although my accomplishments were few and my legacy non-existent, my Peace Corps memories are immutable and, when the evenings are cold, dark and lonely, they serve as a welcome source of much happiness and warmth and many, many smiles. A full half century later, that's no small thing.

After his Peace Corps service, Dick Gilbert received an MA degree in Asian History from the University of Hawaii and joined the Foreign Service. He served with the U.S. Information Agency in Thailand, Romania, Finland, Liberia and the Soviet Union in addition to tours in Washington. Since retiring, Dick has continued to write for fun and profit as a free-lance magazine journalist while accompanying his Foreign Service spouse, Carol Urban, on her tours to Germany, Spain (twice), Switzerland and Chile. Dick and Carol live in New York City (where Carol is assigned to the U.S. Mission to the United Nations) and in Rhinebeck, N.Y.

Marianne Gould

Life at the End of the Road...and Beyond

Ay nako! The 50th Peace Corps reunion already! How is that possible? Sometimes I think I'm still there! Just the other day I was winnowing pumpkin seeds and shells, after a breakfast of rice and eggs!

During my teen years I was very active in 4-H Clubs, which is how I first became interested in international exchange programs. When Peace Corps started, I knew I wanted to be part of it and didn't care where I served. I had the good fortune to be selected to go to the Philippines. The hometown library had good information about the country of thousands of islands on the other side of the world! It turned out to be exotic, very friendly and the living was good—a dream come true very early in life.

The welcome we received from the time we landed in Manila until we arrived at our assignments was overwhelming. Filipinos lined the road leaving the airport. The train trip from Manila to Legaspi was the same, Filipinos waving and yelling "Hi Joe" as the train traveled through villages and towns. When the train stopped, people came to the windows and stared. After a minute we would get them to smile and their faces would light up. They were so beautiful!

Anne Hankins and I were assigned to Santa Magdalena, Sorsogon, a small seaside municipality at the end of the road, at the end of Luzon Island, distinguished as the hometown of Provincial Governor Johnny Frivaldo. There were no private vehicles in town or anywhere nearby. An Alatco bus made two or three trips in and out a day, and the last bus stayed overnight so the first trip out could start the next morning about five am. The economy was based on fishing and farming rice, coconuts and abaca. Two or three small *sari sari* stores provided basic supplies of cigarettes, gum, candy, small cans of milk, locally woven hats, plastic sandals, dried fish, bananas, coke, Pepsi, sugar, soap, etc.

A two-story, cement block, tin-roofed municipal building housed the mayor's office, the post and telegraph office, and the constabulary. Other prominent buildings were the Catholic Church, in dire need of repairs, a small clinic, and several two-story homes owned by teachers. Most families lived in small nipa huts with split bamboo floors sitting three or four feet off the ground. Sometimes self-sufficient chickens were penned under the nipa huts

School buildings had wood sides and tin roofs with dirt floors. Grades 1-8 were separated from the high school buildings. In front of the school buildings were large activity grounds where the students played and practiced folk dances for coming events. Folk dances and songs were a very important part of life in the village.

Because of its remoteness, Santa Magdalena didn't have a lot of contact with the outside world. It took a good part of the day just to get to Sorsogon, the provincial capital. The distance wasn't the problem. It was changing buses, making connections, and the number of stops along the way. (Charlotte Hough & Nancy Jeffers lived in Bulusan and were our closest Peace Corps neighbors—five hours by bus or four hours by walking!)

Teaching English seemed to start out well but then became a challenge. The teachers were as curious as the students about the American lady in their school. But some of the teachers were not comfortable with me because their English skills were poor. So I organized an English conversation class for teachers, which lasted a few months.

I spent summer school vacations working with Nick Royal and Dave Christenson (Group II) in Belison, Antique, teaching art at their summer camps. The first summer camp was for elementary age students, who were very creative as we explored and learned ways to use indigenous materials. We had such a good time that I decided to teach art in Santa Magdalena, and that turned out to be more successful than teaching English.

The second summer we had classes for local teachers who were given college credits for their endeavors. Sally Pierce joined us to teach English as a second language. These summer camps were very successful for all parties involved.

Anne Hankins moved to Sorsogon to teach in the high school for the second school year. By that time I had overcome one of the most difficult situations for me, which was always being the center of attention. For the first several months in Santa Magdalena a couple dozen kids lined the fence at the house or followed us wherever we went. When I finally realized we were such tremendous curiosities, my level of tolerance increased. Having to sing at many activities became easier even though carrying a tune didn't improve!

Several teachers became wonderful friends who kept me out of cultural trouble, and there were situations where that was a large undertaking. To this day I shudder at the social blunders I made.

Many of the teachers and I would often go to the church rectory for *merienda*. At 4:50 everyone left to listen to the 5 pm soap opera that started with a woman's voice sobbing dramatically. *"Ang mga Tugan"*—sob—sob. Most of the dialog was lost because of my limited Bicol/Tagalog but the drama was so much fun! The handful of radios in the village were all tuned to the soap opera, which created surround sound.

Before a day of rice planting I put plastic bags on my feet and hid them with socks and shoes to help ward off schistosomiasis!

Visits to the barrio ladies always picked up my spirits where there was much laughter and merry making as we sat on the steps of a nipa hut smoking hand rolled cigars!

At the end of my tour, I had the opportunity to teach art for a semester at the Iloilo Normal School. Lessons were based mainly on the art activities at the summer camps in Belison. To do this I had to ask for an extension to stay after Group I had terminated. Extensions at that time were not being encouraged so it took what seemed forever to get approval. Shortly after this, some volunteers signed on for another two years.

Living in Iloilo City was totally different from Santa Magdalena or Belison. Dottie Dunlap (a PCV from Group V) and five Normal School students and their monkey welcomed me into their city home. Many more activities were available in the city: movie theaters, well-stocked stores, restaurants etc. An ice skating show even came to the city when I was there. The girls at the house attended the show but didn't comprehend gliding across the ice on skates because they had never experienced walking on ice.

My last day in the Peace Corps was the day after President Kennedy was assassinated. That compounded the sadness.

My Peace Corps experience has been one of the greatest influences on my life. It was my gateway to the world. Living in the Philippines sensitized me to respect other cultures and people even if I didn't always understand what was happening. I also learned that patience was an important asset since many things didn't happen quickly or the way they were anticipated. Two phrases from our Penn State Training, "Roll with the punches" and "This too shall pass" served me well then and for the next 50 years! And, most valuably, I carry with me yet today unforgettable sight and sound snapshots of daily life in Santa Magdalena.

- Bougainvillea flowers of many delicate colors everywhere, along with many other flowers whose names are long forgotten.
- Hand-washed, white, starched clothes hanging on fences drying in the sun—the whitest clothes I've ever seen.
- Barefoot boys playing with three horned beetles tied to a string so they couldn't fly away.
- Young girls carrying babies on their hips.
- Men squatting with and stroking their prized fighting roosters.
- Pigs of all sizes wandering around town, squealing when urged with a stick to relocate.
- The rhythmic pounding of rice being hulled with large wooden pestles & mortars.
- Hand woven hats drying on mats.
- Young boys sitting on the backs of their carabaos in the fields.
- People looking out of their nipa hut windows.
- Empty five-gallon kerosene cans being used to make charcoal from coconut shells.
- Women sweeping their yards with coconut leaf rib brooms.
- The mailman ringing the bell on his bike announcing mail.
- The roar of an occasional truck coming into town—usually the Pepsi or Coke man.
- A three or four instrument band playing for funerals and other special occasions.
- Christmas Star decorations made of bamboo stick frames and intricately cut tissue paper glued over the frames.
- Christmas Midnight Mass in Bulusan with the generators laboring & the Christmas star moving from back to front of the church on a wire as the Mass progressed.
- The smell and haze of burning candles during Mass.
- Older ladies wearing black signifying the death of a loved one.
- Men and women coming in from the "forest" carrying bundles of coconut fronds to be made into nipa shingles.
- Ladies who had been sipping tuba & chewing betel nut, merry-making after a day's work in the fields.
- Men carrying long stocks of delicious bananas over their strong shoulders.
- Women in their long colorful wraparound skirts (*patadjong*)
- The high school students going through their ROTC-type drills with handmade wooden rifles.
- Kids playing with ingenious toys made from tin cans.
- Kids playing & laughing in the gentle waves at the swimming beach while staying away from the rocks where the moray eels lurked

- Boys and girls going to the open classroom windows to spit.
- Young girls shooing flies during meals by gently swinging a stick with a small wire hoop at the end and strips of newspaper hanging down from the hoop.
- Fried bananas, *macapuno* (young coconut), ice cream, *bihon* noodles, chicken *adobo* and fresh tuna fish.
- Cold Cafe Pro coffee with canned milk and sugar, fish head soup, chicken soup with head and feet added for flavor, fish cooked in every way possible
- The question repeatedly asked of us, "Do you eat rice?"
- Easter activities: processions, new clothes, bands, a local man portraying Jesus on the cross at Mass.
- A vehicle equipped with huge loudspeakers playing *Ave Maria* in front of the church and for two years the record stuck in the same place.
- Lights flickering in nipa huts at night from little pint size cans of kerosene with cloth wicks.
- Kids listening to their voices that had just been tape recorded—such amazement and disbelief!
- Cigarettes sold one at a time—maybe two.
- Kids scooting around a wood floor, one foot on the top half of a mature coconut husk. The cut side polished the floor that had just had a mixture of wax and kerosene applied.
- CARE packages with dried milk. The kids would eat the dried milk from rolled newspaper cones.
- Tiny first graders sharpening short, stubby pencils with a 12-inch *bolo*.
- Leaving food on the plate to indicate your are full—finished—*tapos na*.
- All the aromas and colors of the delicious mouthwatering fresh fruit.
- The telegrams sent to volunteers during the Cuban Missile Crises to determine how long it took to get communication to different parts of the country should we need to be evacuated.
- A lone fisherman in a small outrigger singing a very haunting song as he paddled on a glassy sea at the break of day.

When Marianne Gould left the Philippines, her grand adventure continued for another year and a half as she traveled overland through Asia when that part of the world was a friendlier place. Upon returning to Massachusetts, she graduated from Clark University, taught for two years and then gave in to the call of the road again, traveling and camping in a van for several years. On January 1, 2010, she retired from the U.S. Forest Service after 35 years as a ranger working with Wildfire Prevention, Smokey Bear programs, and conservation education in the Lincoln National Forest in New Mexico. Since 1974 she has lived in a two room cabin just outside of the small mountain community of Cloudcroft, New Mexico, elevation 9000 feet. The desert is a sixteen mile drive down the mountain where it is 20 degrees warmer—the best of two very different environments, desert and high mountain forest with several life zones in between.

Hans C. Groot
Returning "Home"

When I first arrived in the Philippines, I certainly had no idea that one day I would spend my retirement years here.

When I joined the Peace Corps, I was a young and idealistic newspaper reporter, frustrated because I couldn't get an article published about the plight of migrant workers in California. I was also impressed with John F. Kennedy, having had the opportunity to cover the political convention that brought him the nomination. When his call to service came, I responded, never looked back, and never regretted joining.

Ilog Interlude

My first assignment, upon completion of in-country training, was to an elementary school in Ilog, Negros Occidental, where I lived with John Lagomarsino and David Mulholland.

On our way to Ilog, we first arrived in Bacolod. Some of our co-teachers and the district school superintendent met us and arranged for a taxi to take us the 100 kilometers to Ilog. I soon felt sort of silly. In Los Baños I had acquired a monkey, which I had brought with me. When we got to Ilog, we were met at the town's welcome arch and had to march through the town to our house—with me leading my monkey on a leash, as I could not leave him in the taxi. The house was a two-story nipa hut. We got our water with a bucket from the well in our garden.

We were there as "educational aides"—a somewhat undefined task and one I was not really ready for, never having been in front of an elementary school class, especially one filled with kids who could not comprehend my Ilongo or Tagalog, let alone my English.

We had arrived in Ilog in early December, and some of us were promptly whisked off to provincial and then regional athletic meets and local and regional Boy Scout gatherings. I got invited to these because Jim Turner and I had taken the scoutmaster training course while at the Jamboree site in Los Baños. To be honest, I did not spend much time in the classroom between the time we arrived and the start of summer vacation in March.

Though I was not Catholic, I went along with John and Dave on their regular visits to a local priest, an Irishman of the Dominican order. He had the only refrigerator in town—stocked with cold beer. However, more than the beer must have made a deep impression on "Lago." After his Peace Corps stint, John joined the Dominican order and served back in Negros for a good number of years. When not at our assignments, we occasionally visited Bacolod to enjoy the generous hospitality of Rene and Angie Echaus, owners of the Sea Breeze Hotel. In those days, the hotel was right on the water—now it's sitting 'high and dry' thanks to the local reclamation project. It became a hangout for volunteers from Negros as well as Panay Island.

My roommates and I were not together very long. For the summer vacation, volunteers in Negros Occidental organized Camp Brotherhood for close to 800 children of the migrant sugar plantation workers. I went to the American military bases at Clark and Subic to scrounge supplies for the camp. I made a serendipitous side trip to the campus of the University of the Philippines at Los Baños (UPLB), where I met Dr. Thomas G. Flores, who was in the process of establishing a Department of Agricultural Information and Communication (DAIC). Since that was more in line with my chosen profession, the Peace Corps approved my request for permission to teach summer school at UPLB, rather than to work at the Camp. Tragically, while at the Camp that summer, Dave contracted amoebic dysentery. He mysteriously refused to seek medical attention, got really sick, and had to be medically evacuated to Clark Hospital, where he died a short time later.

Back to Los Baños

Subsequently, the Peace Corps approved my full time transfer to UPLB where I continued to assist with the setup of DAIC and also helped establish the College of Agriculture's agricultural extension information program, working primarily with provincial radio stations and newspapers. It was an ideal assignment and allowed me to travel from Appari in the north to Jolo in the south. (As an aside, the 'baby brother' of Vladimir Velasco, one of our language trainers and honorary Group I member, is now Chancellor of UPLB. The small agricultural college where we had our in-country training is no more—it is now a full-fledged university with some 15,000 students.)

Since I was relatively close to Manila, somebody got the bright idea that I was well qualified to edit the volunteer newsletter *Voluntario*—soon to be renamed *Ang Boluntaryo*. Looking back on that job, I can only dream about what we could have done with that publication had we had computers. We had to make-do with mimeograph machine.

Staying On—Off and On

Upon completion of my extended Peace Corps tour, I joined the U.S. Agency for International Development (USAID) in Manila as rural communications advisor. The timing was great. I became involved in provincial development programs with the late Senator Benigno Aquino. I worked with the International Rice Research Institute in its efforts to help encourage the adoption of the new, high-yielding rice varieties.

I gained valuable experience but soon realized the need for graduate education. My Peace Corps/USAID experience helped me land a scholarship and assistantship at the University of Wisconsin (UW Madison). I was not alone there. The aforementioned Dr. Flores came over for a semester as visiting professor and one of my students and three co-workers from DAIC joined me in grad school.

After two years of course work, I was once again back at UPLB to do field work for my doctoral dissertation. When I got my PhD, I taught at UW for a few years and then joined the fledgling international division of Planned Parenthood Federation of America. That job that had me travel some 60 percent of the time to Asia, Africa and Latin America.

We had a number of family planning projects in the Philippines. I sometimes wonder, though, how successful we were. When I first came to the Philippines, the population was somewhere around 28 million—now it is in the neighborhood of 90 million. I like to tell myself that, without our efforts, it could have been 150 million now. We did some big and successful projects with the Iglesia ni Cristo Church and Protestant hospitals. We even had a project with a Catholic priest, Father Jim Reuter that handed out packages of birth control pills with a picture of the Madonna on the cover. It did not take long for Catholic Church officials to put a stop to that scheme. The then first Lady, Imelda Marcos, was very supportive of these programs, but political conditions changed and the country's leadership was no longer in favor of these efforts.

Then and Now Notes

The Philippines has changed in many other ways since we first came here in 1961. Then, when you'd drive from Los Baños, you'd pass through separate and distinct towns surrounded by rice paddies. The paddies are gone and it's one big megapolis. When you drive around the metropolitan area, the 'trapik' is an experience. No one pays attention to the traffic rules, roads designed for four lanes end up with six cars side by side, buses and jeepneys weave in and out trying to catch passengers, and then motorcycles seem appear out of nowhere. Driver education, driver courtesy and driver patience are unheard of.

When we first came here, the Philippines was one of the more advanced countries in southeast Asia. Sadly speaking, it no longer is. It has a long way to go. I'm still looking for the answer to the question, "What went wrong?" There are no simple answers and many pieces to the puzzle. Political dynasties that make it difficult for new talent to come to power are part of the problem, and so is corruption (the driver who pays the bribe as well as the traffic cop who takes a bribe.) It is also the lack of true entrepreneurship (beyond opening a sari-sari store) among Filipinos—a condition exacerbated by the many overseas workers, who, unsatisfied with opportunities in the Philippines, go to live and work abroad. Their talent, skills and 'drive' are lost to the country.

The Marcos days also contributed to the problem. While a number of positive things were accomplished, Marcos had to keep the generals—who helped put him in power and kept him there—happy and satisfied by appointing them to important government positions and to boards of directors of major companies. The generals, in turn, had to keep others content—the colonels, majors and captains—many of whom also wanted a piece of the pie.

The Peace Corps also has changed, though I have no firsthand experience with the current program except for talking to some of the volunteers during training sessions. In many ways we were very fortunate to be the first group—the rules were minimal and the inevitable government bureaucracy had not yet had a chance to take root in this new organization.

The old office on Herran Street is no more—a high rise condo has gone up in that spot. As a matter of fact, Herran Street is no more—it's now Pedro Gill. A favorite local pastime seems to be changing street names. Dewey Boulevard is now Roxas Boulevard, Buendia is now Gil Puyat, and Harrison Boulevard is now Quirino.

The Peace Corps office is now in the Philippine National Bank complex in an area that used to be Manila Bay before it was reclaimed. The office is considerably larger and fancier. If memory serves me right, the old office had a janitor and a lone night guard. The new office, however, is in a virtual fortress—a sign of the times.

The American compound at Seafront is still there but with a number of new buildings. The American Embassy is still in the same place but the beautiful open lawn on the "Dewey Boulevard" side has given way to more embassy office buildings.

The great jazz bars in Ermita are no more—the area is now kind of sleazy. Most bars now have video karaoke. Jim Turner's *Hobbit House* still features live music, having moved after some 35 years from Malate to Ermita.

Some things don't seem to have changed much. If you look at the 2010 ballot—many of the 'old names' are there. Through a younger generation, it seems some families manage to remain in power *ad infinitum*.

So why did I go back to the Philippines? A good question. Perhaps it was something in the water back in 1961! Here's what I know for sure. The climate is great. I don't have to shovel snow anymore. The food is good. But the main reason is the people. They're tops, always ready with that smile—even in the face of many adversities. Since my Peace Corps/USAID days, I had visited here frequently and developed strong friendships. At one point, I had considered Puerto Vallarta, Mexico, for retirement, but my lack of Spanish skills and lack of local friends, all pointed to the Philippines as a logical choice. The dollar goes a bit further here but is worth less and less each day. While planning retirement, the exchange rate was 56 pesos to one dollar. The current rate is about 44.5 to one. As they say, ouch!

Hans Groot describes himself as someone who started in Holland, moved to California, to the Philippines, to Wisconsin, back to the Philippines, back to Wisconsin, then to New York, around the world a number of times, and now landed safely and happily in Silang, Cavite. Hans serves as a Board Member of the Peace Corps Alumni Foundation for Philippine Development and has played a major role in developing scholarship agreements with universities and in nurturing a fledgling alumni association. Hans is the editor of a coffee-table book about the history of the Peace Corps in the Philippines entitled Huwag Magtanong-Ask Not: 50 Years of Peace Corps Service in the Philippines, *available through www.blurb.com/bookstore.*

Martha Allshouse Hull
Belafonte to the Rescue

Getting In

I got "drafted" into the Peace Corps. In my junior year of college, I had won a Community Ambassador scholarship through the Experiment in International Living (EIL). I had spent a summer in northern Italy under the sponsorship of the World Affairs Council of San Jose and returned home to share my experiences with many community groups. I was also the area representative for EIL. Sargent Shriver had been one of the first Experimenters and was a great enthusiast of the organization. As he worked on turning the concept of the Peace Corps into reality in early 1961, he turned to a number of us from EIL for "input." I answered his questions and completed several follow-up questionnaires. At the end of each he asked, "Would you be interested in joining such an organization?" I always answered yes. I also took the Peace Corps test as part of the "input" process. It didn't dawn on me that I had actually *applied* to the Peace Corps until I received the telegram saying, "Congratulations, you have been selected to be a Peace Corps Volunteer in the Philippines."

When I arrived at Penn State for training, I was scared silly. It didn't help that the airlines had lost my luggage, and my roommate, Mary Baker, was going to be several days late. Who were these people? They all seemed so self-confident, to know so much more than I did. The staff too seemed full of confidence, even though they admitted they had no real idea where we were going or what we were supposed to do. We should just "roll with the punches." My reaction was, "Get me out of here." But then I met Mary and found a lifelong friend. I got to know some of the others and found that they were not much different than me. Except for Wally Allen, it seemed that we were all bluffing a bit. Having last names that began with "A," Wally and I seemed to be always together as we alphabetically went through the training paces. Wally was cheerful, confident, and ready to take whatever came. His friendliness and bravado, whether real or pretend, got me over the rough spots. My luggage finally came, and I began to feel that I was part of the group. I've never regretted my decision to stay.

On the Job(s)

My service was different from the usual two years spent in one community. I lived in three quite different areas: the island of Masbate in the Bicol, a temporary assignment in the Muslim community of Marawi in Lanao del Sur in Mindanao, and Libon in Albay province. I do not feel as attached to my primary locations, Masbate & Libon, as I do to Marawi. It has to do with the nature of the work.

In Masbate, I was never comfortable with the role of teacher's aide, but just as I began to think I knew what I was doing, I was sent down to Marawi in Mindanao for the summer to help establish Mindanao State University. Our group of twelve volunteers had to physically build the university (done by the fellows), teach summer school to the local students, and run a public relations campaign to convince the people of Mindanao that the university would open and that it was safe for students to come to Marawi for school. I loved the work and felt I was doing something of value.

It was a different story in Libon. I lived in the town but took the bus at six each morning to my little barrio school on the top of the hills between Libon and the sea. I took the bus home at about four in the afternoon, arriving home around five pm. The men of the barrio built me a classroom with bamboo walls, mud floor and a grass roof. With the help of some of the students, I made the tables and chairs for the room. I created a library and wrote many of the books we used in our lessons. I had a good relationship with the five other teachers at the school. I did, however, have a problem with the Head Teacher, who taught a combination fifth/sixth grade class. He began to be absent and sent word for me to take his class while he was away. I knew we were *not* supposed to be substitute teachers, but the alternative was to let the students go home. My Peace Corps supervisor told me to do what I thought best.

The Head Teacher's absences began to extend to days and then weeks. I didn't know the curriculum the children were to study. The other teachers said that I should just do whatever I wanted. I looked through the office hoping to find some guidelines, but instead found a lot of playground equipment and supplies that had been given to the school by the USAID program several years before. I gave them out to the teachers and students to be used. I finally went to the district education office and asked for advice. I did not "complain," but asked for a transfer. About a week later, the Head Teacher showed up again—furious. He had been visiting his mistress. He told me that I brought shame on the barrio by telling on him! He was also very angry that I had given out the playground equipment. "The students will lose things, then we can't list them as our equipment on the school evaluations and we'll miss points!" He stopped speaking to me. The other teachers were caught in the middle. They had to work with him after I left. They stopped being as friendly to me. I was very glad that shortly after that I was reassigned to Marawi where I stayed until it was time to come home.

I loved the work in Marawi. It was challenging, exciting, and rewarding. We had actual goals and projects. We really did get the university built and the students came. (Recently, I was delighted when a dance troupe from Mindanao State University entertained us at a Group I reunion in Pasadena.) The university is a real success.

As to Masbate and Libon/San Jose, I doubt if I accomplished anything of value. I know I learned a tremendous amount, not only about the Philippines & Filipinos, but about myself, but I'm not sure I *did* anything of value. I do know I used to hate those Peace Corps evaluations that always asked for what we had accomplished. I didn't have anything to say.

Life Lessons

I had worked hard to put myself through school and to earn the scholarships that helped pay my way. I was involved in many activities and always was first to help and was there to clean up at the end. I was pretty sure of my values and fought for what I thought was right.

However, my time in the Philippines broadened my perspectives and made me realize that my way was not always the only way. I realized that I had been pretty tough on myself and that I could not do everything by myself. I learned to listen before making judgments—and that, horrors, I wasn't always right!

I vividly remember when this self-realization began to sink in. We were on Masbate. I was getting to know many of my Filipino co-workers and was becoming very depressed. I'm sorry, but there were a few people I simply did not like. How could I *not* like a Filipino? Where had I failed? I was sitting by myself thinking about what to do, when I finally realized that I had missed a very important truth. I would carefully explain to Filipinos that we Americans were individuals and we did not do everything alike. There were good Americans and bad Americans. Our government was basically good, but I did not agree with everything it did. I asked the Filipinos to accept me as an individual. But here I was, doing exactly that to the Filipinos! Why didn't I understand that there could be good Filipinos and bad Filipinos? Why couldn't I accept them as individuals and be free to like some and not others? *BINGO!!* Treat people as individuals according to how they act and who they are.

I was a real do-gooder in the beginning. I was going to erase the "ugly American" image all by myself. I resented those volunteers who didn't seem to be quite as serious about it as I was. I was a "follow the rules!" type. The ambiguity of our project drove me crazy. "Tell me what to do and I'll do it!" I found I had to figure out what to do myself, and I had to realize that I didn't always *have to do* anything. It was hard, but I slowly began to bend, to relax. But at one point, I bent a little too far. Thank heaven for Larry Howard—a Peace Corps staff representative.

In Libon, my housemate was spending most of her time working in Legaspi, so I was basically alone. I had those long early morning bus rides up the mountain to my barrio school and the equally long bus ride home each night. I came to *like* the smell of that bus when it rained and they rolled down the oilcloth sides. The smell of the pigs, urine, chickens, spit, and God knows what else that was part of that bus really appealed to me. I also got to thinking that we should not build latrines. People should take care of their bodily functions out in the open so things could oxidize. When I realized I was thinking like this, I decided I had gone over the edge. I gave myself permission (!) to go to Manila. I walked into the Peace Corps headquarters and the first thing I saw was Wally Allen without his shirt on. He was the most awful color!! He looked pink!!! I then realized that I was the same color. I wasn't the lovely brown that the Filipinos were. At that point Larry Howard saw me. I think he realized that I was in culture shock because he started talking to me and invited me out to his house for dinner that evening. Another volunteer, Sue Johnson, came in shortly after I did, and she was also invited for dinner.

Sue and I had both been away from other volunteers and certainly away from city life. We were taken out to the Howard home and made to feel comfortable with Larry, Betty and the children. After a wonderful home-style dinner, Sue and I simply laid down on the floor in the living room and listened to Harry Belafonte records long into the evening. The next morning I went to the Swiss Country Inn for a wonderful American breakfast. I stayed in Manila for a total of three days and went happily back to Libon in a much better frame of mind. Hearing Harry Belafonte perform at the Kennedy Center during the Peace Corps 25th Anniversary in Washington D.C. was an exceptional experience for me!

By the time I left the Philippines, I had a new look on things and I was a bit easier on myself. I knew that rules were important and should be followed, but sometimes they just don't fit. My attitude became: Follow the rules unless there is a really good reason not to. If your brain tells you something is wrong, don't do it. I also realized that I didn't always have to do everything that was on the agenda. I also learned to accept others as they were, not as I wanted them to be.

The Impact

Before I went to Penn State, I had been planning to get a Master's in American Social and Intellectual History and a teaching credential. I had taken one course in Asian Humanities that focused on India, China and Japan. What I knew of the Philippines I had learned from studying the Spanish American War.

Returning home, I started my master's program in U.S. History, but found myself choosing topics such as "Filipino Immigration to the U.S.," "Chinese Exclusion Policy in U.S. History," etc. I decided to get my master's in Asian Studies. I taught Asian Studies in high school for 15 years. My students in World History got a lot more Asian (including Filipino) history than the other classes. My work in Marawi also introduced me to the Moslem culture, and broadened my interest in religious customs and traditions. I traveled home with Frances Boylston who had also been part of the Marawi project. We made a point of looking at Moslem minority groups as we traveled through Southeast Asia and the Middle East. I certainly became better prepared to explain the varieties of Islam (and other religions) in helping my students understand the events our world.

I kept in contact with Miss Serrano, my landlady in Libon. She even visited me in Santa Clara sometime in the 1980s. I also kept in contact with a good friend from Marawi, Mauyag "Tommy" Tamano. Tommy was one of the five Filipino staff members of the university when we arrived in Marawi. After I came home, he kept me apprised of the university's progress. He sent me a book *Muslim-Christian Integration at the Mindanao State University*, written by the first president, Antonio Isidro. Our group is mentioned several places in the book. Tommy visited me here in Santa Clara when he was finishing his doctorate at Stanford. He returned to Marawi, and became the second president of Mindanao State University. He later was appointed Ambassador to Saudi Arabia.

Other than the two Filipinos mentioned above, I had little contact with the Philippines after I left. I did, however, keep in contact with Peace Corps friends. I have attended all reunions except the 35th (a trip back to the Philippines) and correspond regularly with some of them. Mary Baker Johnson and I have remained good friends, visiting each other on several occasions. When our "foster daughter"—a young Chinese student, came to live with us, we took her to visit Bruce Campbell in Oregon and to Washington D.C., where we met Maureen Carroll and others. I cherish the friends I have who were part of Group I.

All in all, the Peace Corps was a fantastic experience for me. Not only was I proud to be part of Kennedy's call to service, but my high school students later benefited from the spirit and excitement of that time. Several of them joined the Peace Corps themselves. The Corps broadened my horizons and taught me about the world. It also taught me about myself. I shall ever be grateful for the opportunity to be one of the first volunteers. I may not have been successful as a teacher's aide, but I do believe I met the other two goals of the Peace

Corps: Helping promote a better understanding of Americans and helping promote a better understanding of other peoples on the part of Americans.

Following her service, Martha Allshouse Hull returned home to Santa Clara Valley, also now called Silicon Valley. After several years at San Jose State University working with foreign students, she left to teach at Los Gatos High School where she was Department Chair for Social Studies for 15 years. She took advanced work at the East West Center in Hawaii, Sophia University in Tokyo, and Poona, India and earned a Masters in Asian Studies from San Jose University. She was named the district's Outstanding Teacher in 1991 and retired from full-time teaching in 1999. From 2000-2003 she taught/supervised student teachers at Stanford University and now spends time volunteering at the local library, reading, gardening, and enjoying life.

In 1975 Martha married Keith Hull, an engineer at Lockheed. In 1989 they sponsored a high school student from China who became their "foster daughter." Hui (now Julie) finished high school and went on to get her master's in Computer Engineering at San Jose State. She now works for Microsoft in Seattle. She has become a U.S. citizen, married and has two children who consider Martha and Keith their grandparents.

(The first photo shows Marty with Tommy Tamano, a Filipino staff member at Marawi State University who has remained a longtime friend; the second photo shows her with her husband, Keith.)

Martin Hurwitz
Undeterred

> *"You can't make much of a dent, but it will be good for you."*
> —GEORGE GUTHRIE, Peace Corps training staff at Penn State
>
> Quoted from *Voluntario*, the magazine of the
> Philippine Peace Corps Project, December 1961

What! Was that all we could expect from two years in the Philippines? What did George Guthrie mean? We would have virtually no impact but it would be "good" for us? Volunteers would be successful, he added, if we left the Philippines speaking a few words of the dialect, and looking back on some nice days in the barrios.

None of us joined the Peace Corps expecting a pleasant, extended stay among friendly people on a tropical island, at government expense. Many had quit jobs, interrupted or postponed careers. We left friends and family and were prepared to make sacrifices. We took seriously the notion of service to our country so Guthrie's words were unsettling, even demeaning. Moreover, his notion of success—speak a few words of the dialect and remember nice days in the barrios—seemed, at the time, deeply unsatisfying and cynical.

With the benefit of hindsight we all know now that the odds against us making a dent on Philippine society or the schools or the economy or anything else were very high. There were no precedents. We were relatively unskilled. Nothing was known about how Americans might fare living long term in small provincial towns. We were the first group in Asia in the first year of the Peace Corps. Despite all of that uncertainty, as I remember, none of us was deterred, which is just as it should have been.

We needed a positive attitude because, although we didn't know it then, there were going to be bumps in the road. The first bump was the so-called training period at Penn State.

Training

Our time at Penn State was certainly not a training course. It was, in fact, a selection process. I don't recall learning anything of value but was acutely aware of being observed, scrutinized and evaluated constantly. It was very stressful indeed, especially for those of us who had quit jobs and were draft-eligible. Vietnam hadn't yet heated up but the Soviets had just begun building the Berlin Wall.

The interlude at Los Baños wasn't particularly useful either but it was more agreeable. At last we met and interacted with Filipinos. We learned a few words of Tagalog (Pilipino).

However, since I was assigned to the Bicol region, that too, was of little value. I certainly got no training for our jobs as a "models of spoken English" in the elementary grades—a role which was ill-defined, nebulous and, in retrospect, trivial. I think we all looked forward to being on the job in the provinces.

On the Job

Not so fast. Before the classrooms came a dizzying array of welcome ceremonies and introductions followed by receptions, then dinners and parties followed by dances, speeches, festivals and more speeches. Finally, finally into classrooms which were filled with curious, eager, friendly and smiling but, I soon discovered, uncomprehending faces.

What to do next? I don't actually remember, especially after nearly 50 years, but somehow I managed, somehow, with help from teachers, I muddled through, day after day. It sounds awkward but actually it was not unpleasant. The kids were delightful, everyone was friendly. However, the job as model of spoken English had to be embellished so I added a little geography (the oceans, continents, mountain ranges) a bit of biology (the human body, health, sanitation), a dash of astronomy (the solar system, day/night, eclipses) and anything else I could think of. It became obvious that without a syllabus and curriculum and, at least, rudimentary teaching materials this, by-the-seat-of-the-pants approach was unsustainable (at least by me alone).

Remaking the Job

I could not conceive of doing only that job for the balance of my stay in the Philippines so I had to make changes.

Prior to the Peace Corps I had worked as a reporter on a Connecticut daily newspaper and when I learned that the Legaspi City High School senior English class published a monthly school paper, I asked the instructor to allow me to teach news writing to her class one day a week. Done.

Next, I got permission from a Tabaco High School history teacher to teach a current events unit once a week to her senior class. I gathered my material from the *NY Times News of the Week in Review*, *The New Republic*, *Time* and *Newsweek* thanks to subscriptions provided either by those publications or by the Peace Corps. I prepared a one-page summary of a recent major news event which the school staff typed, mimeographed and distributed and I was in business.

In both the above situations I worked with high school seniors whose English was good. It was a far more appropriate job than talking at third, fourth and fifth graders.

I also organized an adult evening class in Barrio San Jose, where I lived, and taught English and elementary science by kerosene lanterns once or twice a week. It was fun, and I was pleased with my situation.

During summer vacation I was a photographer in Mindanao for the College of Forestry supporting its program to halt deforestation caused by mountain-dwelling farmers who cut trees and clear land for crops. The cut and burn practice, especially on sloping land, causes the rich topsoil to be washed away in rainy seasons and accelerates deforestation. The farmer then moves on to clear again.

A Low Point

In August 1962 after about five months' experience in the elementary grades (I do not include my "extracurricular" teaching jobs here) volunteers in the Bikol region gathered in Legaspi City to meet Sargent Shriver and some Washington staff who flew in for a whirlwind visit. Shriver must have been surprised and displeased when he heard several of us speak of problems with our designated assignment as models of spoken English, of how the job was ill-defined and we were not trained adequately and that the local teachers *were as puzzled as we* and did not know how to use us.

Clearly we wanted to be effective and were genuinely committed and passionate about the Peace Corps. But Shriver did not hear that. After a pause he sternly told us if we were not happy with our assignments, we should go home.

That was stunning in its blunt delivery, shocking in its insensitivity and inappropriate for volunteers who were so eager to be effective. From Shriver's statement and demeanor it was obvious that the Peace Corps was not going to change our mission or retrain us.

His dismissal of our concerns cast a pall over many of us, but for me it was turning point. I resolved that I would work at only those activities that I believed in wholeheartedly, that I would not go through the motions to fulfill a faulty mission. It was liberating.

Yes, George Guthrie

Creating those embellishments and "extracurricular" jobs was a source of personal satisfaction. I had confronted problems in an unfamiliar place and found or fashioned a set of solutions. In so doing I tapped resources I didn't know I had, I stretched and grew under circumstances I could not have imagined or would ever have experienced had I stayed safely at home. That experience stands me in good stead to this day.

Yes, George Guthrie, the experience was "good" for me. But that's not all.

Friends

I was fortunate to have made a few Filipino friends to whom I grew close and could share confidences. In the latter part of our stay I moved in with an extended family (husband, wife, four kids, a grandmother plus various relatives numbering 10 and more during fiesta time). Together we relaxed, celebrated holidays, marriages, fiestas, christenings, new babies. We shared disappointments and sorrows, even death. We danced, we sang, we ate and ate and ate, and we held hands (sometimes). We laughed and smiled a lot.

Throughout my stay in the Philippines I took chances, made mistakes, was embarrassed, then recovered. I misunderstood, I *was* misunderstood, I explained, they explained. I learned to deal with the unfamiliar. This all took place largely in full view of lots of curious eyes, virtually no privacy.

Filipinos are warm, open, generous people and we were readily welcomed. I was fortunate to have made friends with the Bien family which became very important to me. And, as I learned only recently, I must have been important to them.

Unexpected Reunion

In early June 2010 my wife and I had an unexpected reunion with members of the Bien family. The occasion was the ordination, as a Catholic priest, of the last of *seven* Bien children. Ysrael, born in 1980—long after I left—had trained at an abbey near Portland, Oregon. His mother, Amparo, (I called her "Par-ING," her nickname) and several siblings traveled from Malilipot. Another, the only girl among six boys, came from Saudi Arabia, and the fourth son, Daniel, whom I knew as a four-year-old and is also a Catholic priest, traveled from Guam for the event.

Beforehand, Ysrael and I exchanged e-mails to which he attached scans of old photographs of family groupings, including several of me from 1963! I told him I was deeply touched that he had brought with him to America photographs of his mother, father, four siblings and of me as if I myself were a member of the family. He wrote back immediately: "Indeed, my parents spoke of you as truly part of the family."

That's not all. I learned in Portland that the fifth son, Jose Martin, (nicknamed Jomar), born after I left, is named, in part, after me, and Martin Hurwitz is declared his godfather on the baptismal certificate. I was stunned, I was moved.

Yes, relationships matter.

Questions

Did I make much of a dent or any dent at all? As a personal friend, I seem to have made a modest, long-term impression. As a teacher, none. But, then again, can any teacher be certain of his effect?

Was I "successful"? By George Guthrie's slim definition, yes, moderately. After all, I did learn a few words of Bicol, which I used shamelessly whenever I could, and I have many pleasant memories of days in the barrios. As a group the volunteers were certainly successful. I believe we were well regarded by our hosts, left behind positive impressions and paved the way for successive volunteers, all of which I assume was helpful.

Was the experience good for me? Decidedly, yes. I grew, stretched and met personal challenges. More importantly, I brought home a vivid picture and sympathetic understanding of life in an underdeveloped land, of people who have fewer possessions and comforts and may struggle more than we but who, nevertheless, live rich, full lives. America might not have stumbled as it did in Vietnam and Iraq if more of us knew, understood, and appreciated other people.

Would I do it again? Absolutely!

After Peace Corps, Martin Hurwitz resumed his journalism career, first at United Press International in Columbus, Ohio, then with the esteemed public broadcasting station WGHB-TV in Boston. He switched to government work as an information officer for the New York City Model Cities program. He partnered for a while with an industrial designer of exhibits and graphics, and after a brief stint in the printing business he made his final career move to the exhibit business (trade shows, museum installations).

Now retired, Martin is currently a volunteer at the Brooklyn Navy Yard, helping to outfit a new exhibition space and visitors' center. Thanks to a willingness to "pioneer" 40 years ago in a marginal neighborhood, he lives in an 1850s' brownstone in the now "hot" neighborhood of Ft. Greene in Brooklyn. He also spends time in a second home in Shelter Island on Long Island—where he's reminded of the Philippines as he manicures nearly a half acre of bamboo which thrives through snowy winters. He keeps it under control with an old friend, his "bolo" (machete) brought home from Malilipot. Martin's wife, Natalie, is a commercial real estate broker, and he has two grown sons, one who is married and one who caught the volunteer bug and spent a year with Americorps in Vermont where he met his wife to be. Only a "grand-dog" so far.

Ellen Brindle Jeronimo
Fifty Years—Are You Kidding?

My entry in a remembrance booklet prepared for the 25th Anniversary of our Peace Corps service noted: At 22, I was not over-concerned with others' opinions of the Peace Corps. With the confidence of youth and the vague sense that something important was happening, I joined….To JFK, we were "The New Frontier" and to Barry Goldwater we were the "Kiddie Corps." We were both. If pessimists got that way by funding optimists, both fulfilled their destinies in 1961.

In the years since this was written, my view of our great adventure has not changed, despite profound changes in my life.

When I came across a photo published in *Life Magazine* in September of 1961, showing five female trainees relaxing at a dam during our Penn State training and another of Gerry Thomas and me at Camp Brotherhood one year later in the *Manila Bulletin*, I remembered that these had prompted a friend to write: "When are they going to pry you out of that bathing suit and put you to work?"

There are so many memories. Some are incredibly sad, like the loss of Dave Mulholland. Some are hilarious, like a photo in the Penn State bulletin captioned "Susan M. Johnson, Steubenville, Ohio locates the Philippines on a globe for other volunteers." Presumably the rest of us had no idea where we were going.

From my totally disorganized memorabilia, odd information emerges:

• We each had five inoculations—smallpox, typhoid, tetanus, influenza and tuberculosis—and additional shots for cholera, typhus and yellow fever. (A Penn State bulletin).

• A songbook from the Bureau of Public Schools in Manila that includes *"Ili-Ili."* I must have sung this lullaby about a thousand times—and will never do it again.

• A ribbon that proves that at least on March 28, 1963 I was indeed a member of the faculty of Camarines Sur High School.

• Photos showing Pili's Municipal Elementary School teachers, including fellow volunteers Jan Wright, Mary Teasler and me.

Having started with a quote from our 25th reunion, I'll end with thoughts from that same time, when my I went to Washington D.C. for the anniversary celebration. I recently came across a card from a florist that accompanied a beautiful bouquet sent to the Marriott Hotel from eight good friends in New York. It was addressed to "Mr. and Mrs. Robert Jeronimo." Bob was indeed at the reunion but spent a great deal of time at the Folger Library, doing research for his project involving the heraldry mentioned in Shakespeare's works. Bob will not be with us this time; he died unexpectedly almost two years ago. We had 40 wonderful years together, 38 of them legal!

The card that came with the flowers read: "Have a nice weekend, but try not to upset the delicate balance of world power." Sage advice for all of us as we plan for the 50th reunion.

Ellen Brindle Jeronimo is living in New York City, where she settled in 1963, right after returning from the Peace Corps. There, she received her Master's degree, settled into a long career in the management of nonprofits, and met and married her late, wonderful husband, Bob. As she puts it, "I'm lonely, but a ton of friends and family keep me from becoming downright maudlin.

(The second photo shows Ellen with her brother and his children.)

Mary Baker Johnson
A Life-Changing Experience

On the day that President Kennedy was elected, I was in Rome at the American Embassy. Everyone there was elated, and indeed, as I traveled throughout Europe, the enthusiasm for our new President was palpable. I arrived home in time for the inaugural address, and like many of my fellow Peace Corps Volunteers, I wanted to answer his call, "Ask not what your country can do for you; ask what you can do for your country." I had taught high school for four years before taking a six-month odyssey in Europe. While waiting to hear more about the President's new plan, I was substitute teaching and acting in local theatre. As soon as I heard about the national tests to be given in Cleveland, Ohio, I immediately signed up.

My "fifteen minutes of fame" occurred when I discovered I was the first woman from Cleveland to go into the Peace Corps and wound up appearing on television and in the Cleveland newspapers. I was first selected for Ghana, but when I heard about the program in the Philippines, I asked to be sent there instead. I knew about the strong ties between the Philippines and the United States, and teaching English as a second language there appealed to me. Peace Corps granted my request, and I set off in the summer of 1961 for the training program at Penn State.

The First Few Months

The extensive training we received in the U.S. and the Philippines was so helpful that I felt adequately prepared for our new adventure. One thing I was not prepared for on our arrival, however, was the overwhelming reception given us as President Kennedy's Peace Corps. As we rode to our training site, Los Baños, on Luzon, children lined the streets waving flags and shouting "*Mabuhay!*" (Welcome!), and we were given receptions at many schools on the way.

Our Assignments

There were 128 of us in Group I. Most were assigned to various locales in the Bicol region on the main island of Luzon, but some of us went to the Visayan island of Negros. Twenty-five of us were assigned on the western side of the island, Negros Occidental, scattered in households of two, three, or four. Judy Conway, Carol Byrnes, Edmee Hawkes, and I lived together in Hinigaran, a fishing village on the Sulu Sea. An elderly couple owned and occupied the house. They gave us two small bedrooms and a sitting room upstairs, and use of the kitchen, dining room and living room downstairs. We had a flush toilet, shower, and electricity for about four hours a day. Carol was assigned to the central school in the town; Judy, Edmee, and I took jeepney rides every day to our different barrio schools a few kilometers away.

School Experiences

Although our official assignments were as aides to the teachers in the elementary schools, the teachers were very happy to have us take over in the classroom teaching of English. I felt very comfortable in this role, as I had had several years of teaching experience behind me. The school day began about eight in the morning. After a two-hour break for lunch and siesta, classes began again about 2 and went until about 5 pm. The times were always approximate.

After observing the way lessons were taught, we soon learned that the children absorbed everything by rote, memorized from the blackboard. There were two or three children crammed into one desk, often sharing one pencil and one sheet of notebook paper divided into eight pieces. (The children learned to write in very small script.) The few books they had (discarded American textbooks) were also shared. I showed how one book could be read by the whole class with each child reading one page at a time. I had the children learn English dialogues, which they picked up very quickly; comprehension took a little longer!

The social life of the school was just as important as the academic life. There were *merienda* breaks every morning where coconut milk, rice cakes, and fruit were offered. Many days were "program days" when all classes were suspended, usually in honor of a visiting dignitary, and the children performed by singing, dancing, and reciting. During "Community Days" we were also expected to give speeches and sometimes perform in native dress. On one occasion I donned *patadjong* and kimono and, much to the delight of the spectators, attempted the *tinikling* (two long bamboo poles clicking together as the dancers step between them).

One year I was put in charge of the Christmas pageant. I wrote a short play based on the story, *The Littlest Angel*. I expected rudimentary scenery and costumes, but on the day of the performance I found the steps to the school decorated with banana stalk pillars, stage scenery of palm trees and stars, and a decorated white sheet on a throne. Jesus was in a pink dress with a gold crown borrowed from a church, and the angels had blue dresses with gold paper halos and wings made from cardboard and cotton. The play was a great success!

During summer vacations (in March) one group from our island started Camp Brotherhood, which gave children their first camping experience. The rest of us taught language arts and science at a Christian Brothers college (La Salle) in Bacolod, the capital city of the province.

Home Life and Social Life

The Peace Corps staff in Manila often sent American visitors to our house and schools. Among them were notables like Sargent Shriver, Bill Haddad (chief assistant to Shriver), Lawrence Fuchs (director of Peace Corps in the Philippines), Jay Rockefeller (desk officer in Washington for the Philippines), and Eugene Burdick and William Lederer (authors of *The Ugly American*, the book that was partly the inspiration for the founding of the Peace Corps).

We had a cook and *lavendera*, so we didn't have many housekeeping tasks. Our cook went to the market everyday, so we had wonderful fresh fish, prawns, and fruits like bananas and mangoes. We didn't even miss the scarcity of beef; we had chicken and on special occasions, *lechon* (roast pig). Our drinks consisted of coffee, cokes, and water we ourselves had boiled. Once every few weeks we made a trip to the city to buy canned goods.

Our evenings at home were spent mostly by reading, writing letters, talking, and playing cards. Sometimes we visited other Peace Corps households where we ate American food and played games like charades or Pick-up-Sticks. For outside entertainment we went to the local cinema where we saw first-run American movies. Sometimes the reels were mixed up so we saw the ending of the movie before the beginning.

We went to more barrio fiestas and parties than I can remember. We were invited to every social event (a baby's baptism, neighborhood party, and even the mayor's birthday). Since Negros was the chief sugar-cane producing island, we were also invited to tour and be feted at the sugar-cane plantations. We learned to say "yes" to every invitation even when we knew we would be unable to go because it was not polite to refuse. All Filipinos (rich and poor alike) held Americans in high esteem, and socially reaching out to us may have been their way of thanking America for its aid in World War II. They still talked about General MacArthur as their hero.

Most Memorable Event

The most memorable event for me, of course, was my wedding to Lee Johnson, a fellow Peace Corps volunteer from Long Beach, California. Lee lived in Pontevedra, a town about 30 kilometers away. The wedding combined both Philippine and American customs and took place in Bacolod, attended by all the teachers from both our schools and the PCVs from our island. After the wedding we moved into a brand new nipa house that Lee had built with the help of Filipino friends and neighbors.

Life in a Nipa Hut

Our house consisted of one room, on bamboo stilts, with nipa palm leaves lashed together for the walls and roof. The floor was made of split bamboo. Walking on it (only barefoot) was very comfortable. Lee had made a rattan bed; the only other furniture was a table with two chairs and a bookcase. The bookcase served to separate the "kitchen," which housed our Coleman stove, ice chest, and a metal pan as a sink to let water run down to the ground. He also built a sliding door inside in one corner to close off our "shower," an oil drum filled with water from a well and a tin can for rinsing.

Our cook prepared the food on a wood fire outside and we often had guests who would sit on the bed or floor. After serving American food (hot dogs and spaghetti), we discovered they didn't like it very much, so we had the traditional Filipino dishes thereafter.

When we propped the two windows open or opened the front door, it was an invitation for anyone to come visit us. The neighborhood children, especially, liked to come and sit on our porch reading the comic books sent to us by our parents and friends. When the door and windows were closed, everyone respected our privacy. We also felt very safe there; "Neighborhood Watch" was in full force. The house was in the middle of a coconut grove and the mosquitoes were rampant. Of course we slept under a mosquito net and practically bathed in insect repellent.

One innovation was the water-seal toilet Lee had built in the back yard of the house. In the "outhouse," a pit was dug, with a gas drum and a metal funnel inserted into it. Over the hole was a seat made from a fruit crate with water for flushing in a container. It was very sanitary and the only one in the neighborhood. (We hoped it would be a model for others to build.)

Notable Moments

- Lee had bought a bird to enter in the local cockfight. Women were not allowed to watch cockfights (thank goodness). One day he came home announcing the bird was a champion. It died a few minutes after the fight, and was later cooked. (I didn't eat.)
- Because our house was so new, it was stronger than many others, so some of the neighbors came to our house to wait out the typhoons in case their houses blew over.
- The Peace Corps furnished an open-air jeep to the volunteer leader, which was used for necessary trips, such as to the doctor. One time twelve of us piled in the jeep to go to the city hospital for enemas. (The Peace Corps staff was very solicitous about our health.)
- We got news of the outside world by transistor radio or weekly news magazines. Since there were only a few telephones in the village, we all had to go to a house with a phone during the Cuban Missile Crisis to get instructions on what to do in case of an evacuation.
- We attended many fiestas and although the invitation was for 8 pm, we were always the first ones to arrive at 10 pm. There was a sign outside the entrance that said, "Please leave deadly weapons outside" and specially marked places for honored guests: Governor's Box, Sugar Planter's Box, Peace Corps Members' Box. All the popular music of the '60s was played. To prevent creating a bad impression, our Volunteer leader instructed us not to do the "Twist," until it was evident that the Filipinos were already doing it.
- The most unusual hair salon experience I ever had was my visit to the barrio beauty parlor. I sat with my head out the window for the shampoo; the hair was set with rolled-up papers, and dried by two girls waving palm fronds. I later had my parents send some beauty supplies for the establishment.
- At our farewell dinner with the teachers we knew we had finally "arrived" when we were served fish and rice on banana leaves—with no eating utensils.

A Sad Memory

Dave Mulholland was one of the first deaths in the Peace Corps. He had lived in a town on our island, and had been taken ill and sent to Manila. Since we all considered ourselves as family, we were very saddened when he died.

Impressions

- The buses were converted Army trucks or jeepneys, which could be stopped anywhere on the main road by waving your hand downward. There was always room for one more so we were often crammed in with the nursing mothers, chickens, fish, and fruit baskets. One time I had to sit next to the bus driver, and while looking in his rear view mirror, I saw everyone staring at me and suddenly realized why the children called me "Round Eyes." My eyes looked like saucers!
- I learned how to say "Slow down!" in the local dialect and used it for a driver of the Good Luck Bus Company, well-named because many times the drivers tried to race each other.
- I was impressed with the ingenuity of the children. They were able to make sandals out of old rubber tires and rope. There were multiple uses for tin cans; bottle caps were used as

wheels for toy cars or checkers played in the dirt. The children performed all the custodial tasks at the schools, from polishing the floors with coconut shells to cutting the grass.

Quotable Quotes

"Are you related to Marilyn Monroe?" (a Filipino knowing my last name was Baker)

"I know someone from Ohio."
"Really? What city?" I asked.
"Illinois."

"It's bad to be black" (a child putting her arm against mine).

"Na, Na" (short for "Ari Americana—here comes the American"—toddlers calling out as I walked down the road).

"How are you this morning?" (English lesson response to question, "How are you this morning?").

Return Visit (35 Years Later)

On a short visit back to Negros, I noticed many changes! When I asked to go back to the barrio school where I had taught, it didn't look familiar. I was told that it had been moved to another location. All the beautiful coconut palms also had been cut down to make room for growing more rice. Our nipa house had been moved long ago to a school to be used as a home economics building. Where many nipa houses had been, there were now cement block houses. Many houses had more hours of electricity, televisions, and indoor bathrooms. There were new methods of transport—three-wheeled motorized vehicles, air-conditioned buses, …and pollution.

I went back to my *barrio* without telling anyone I was coming, but somehow the word got around quickly and I was greeted very warmly, almost as if I had just left a short time ago. Upon very short notice, the last school where I had taught had a huge reception for me with welcoming banners and an elaborate program in my honor.

Did we make a difference? I believe we did. In the two short years we were there, I think the Filipinos we encountered got to know Americans as we really were, not as Americans portrayed in the movies. Perhaps the impact on us was greater; we were able to understand another culture because we had lived in it. The friendships we have made with Filipinos and PCVs have lasted for fifty years. Peace Corps in the Philippines was indeed a life-changing experience!

Upon their return from the Philippines, Lee Johnson became the principal-superintendent of a small school district in California, and Mary went back to teaching high school. They raised three children, who all followed in the footsteps of their parents and now have careers in education. Lee died in 1992, and Mary retired in 1994. She has six grandchildren and now lives in San Diego, California.

(The first photo shows Mary with the bridesmaids at her wedding; from left to right Judy Conway, Mary Baker, Edmeé Hawkes, and Carol Byrnes.)

Pat Joslyn Johnson
Scholarships, Seminars, and Salingogon

A Special Memory
We were quite a sight on the train from Naga City to Manila—twelve excited, first-year high school students and four Peace Corps Volunteers (Barb Mitchell, Sondy Williams, Evie Mittman, and I). It was the first visit to Manila for all of these students, and for most of them, the first trip outside their province.

These students were receiving scholarships from the Cooperative Education Fund (CEF), which we set up to help young people continue their studies. They were selected near the end of our first year in the Philippines, and began attending high school during our second year. This "field trip" to Manila near the end of our two years in the Philippines was a chance for us all to have an enjoyable—and educational—time together before we PCVs returned to the U.S.

It was a great visit to Manila, and though the logistics were a bit daunting, everything worked out fairly well. We travelled around the city by jeepney, bus, and foot, exploring the main sights and trying not to get lost or separated. Each evening we returned exhausted to the home of a Peace Corps staff family who generously let us sleep on the floor of their big porch. It was quite an experience to see the capital city with such an eager, enthusiastic group of young people, and it was also a wonderful capstone to our experience as Peace Corps Volunteers in the Philippines.

Motivation
I was in college (Oberlin, Ohio) when John F. Kennedy was elected President, and was intrigued by his announcement of a new international service program called the Peace Corps. With graduation approaching in the spring of 1961, I was undecided about the next step. When the Peace Corps actually took shape and started seeking volunteers, I knew that's what I wanted to do if possible. It seemed much more interesting than trying for graduate school or seeking a job!

The Philippines
I admit to knowing very little about the Philippines before I received the invitation to become a volunteer there—mainly that it was a country made up of islands, and that it had been involved in WWII. Also it turned out that no one I knew had much knowledge about it, and therefore several people suggested I should request a place better known (and perhaps closer to home)!

After six weeks of training in the U.S., it was thrilling actually to arrive in the Philippines. I remember being amazed by the welcoming people, lush vegetation, warmth & humidity, colorful jeepneys and markets, strange but tasty foods, beautiful children, rough roads & wild driving, new languages yet a surprising amount of English spoken, and wonderful music. These initial impressions turned out to be fairly accurate, but as time passed we found the country and the people to be even more interesting and complex. Of course, by the end of our stay we had become aware of some negative aspects, but I continued to feel very positive about the country in general and especially the many wonderful people I'd come to know.

My three PCV housemates and I have had continuing connections with the Philippines especially through the family in whose home we lived and the dozen students whom we helped continue their studies through college/university. Although communications have been intermittent, two of us were able to reconnect with many of the people we knew and have some wonderful reunions during our return visit in 1996, the Peace Corps' 35th Anniversary.

Four of us lived together in one community and then travelled to serve several different schools in the area. Milaor was a small village about 10 kilometers from Naga City, the provincial capital of Camarines Sur. Near the village center was a small plaza, with the city hall along one side and the large Catholic Church and rectory nearby. Across the road was the trim, spacious elementary school. There were no large stores or businesses, just a few very small shops located at the homes of enterprising local residents. The village did not have a public clothes washing area or bathrooms—most people just headed for the river along the edge of our village.

Because of that river and its frequent flooding, the "ground floor" of the houses was typically 5 to 7 feet above the street level. Some houses had wood floors—polished by "skating" with a coconut half—but many had bamboo floors, and almost all had nipa roofs. The "streets" were hard packed dirt (except when they were waterways!) and of course there were no street lights or signs.

Small farm agriculture—mostly rice—was a primary occupation of Milaor residents, but a number of people had jobs in Naga City, while most of the local teachers and community officials lived in the village. The Catholic Church was a major center of community life, with daily Mass and holy day celebrations that included parades, music, and bountiful meals.

A wonderful family—the Claros—allowed us to use their house, and then they took very good care of us by cooking Filipino meals, cleaning the place, taking care of the pig living below, and helping us learn the local customs and language (Bicol). They lived just across a dirt yard—squeezing into an older family home—and we all became very close. Since four of us volunteers were living together, we had the challenge of getting along in close quarters but the benefit of support in dealing with some of the challenges we faced.

The volunteer assignments helped us go well beyond our foursome since we each served separate elementary schools. Three of us travelled by bus daily to reach the rural elementary schools where we worked with teachers on improving the teaching of English and Science. Yet we also worked together effectively in providing seminars for teachers in these subjects.

Effects of the Peace Corps Experience
...on the Philippines

What was the impact of our presence on our community, on the teachers and students with whom we worked and interacted? A natural question but it's hard to answer. Fortunately, most people seemed to appreciate our presence and our volunteer efforts. At my two schools, most of the teachers were very friendly and interested in interacting with me, but at each school there were three to five teachers who really wanted to learn new ideas and to work on changing some of their teaching techniques. The children were always eager to interact with me, to practice their English, and to have me teach a class or assist their teacher. Those teachers who made the extra effort to learn about more effective ways of teaching science and English, improved their instruction methods. Thus, their students benefitted from our presence, and hopefully that benefit continued for many additional children taught by those teachers over the years.

A significant impact as far as our core assignment—to help improve the teaching of these two subjects in the Philippines—occurred as a result of the seminars we designed, arranged for teachers from our seven schools to attend, and taught during our second year there. The four of us developed "methods and materials" seminars for the teachers of each grade level and held them at our home. We prepared sample lesson plans, a set of simple science experiments, tools for teaching English using an active verbal approach, and a set of materials for them to take back to their schools. This approach seemed to give the teachers a significant boost toward improving their teaching of these two subjects.

A different way in which we had an impact was through the CEF scholarship program we set up during our first year. We learned that many students from our rural schools were unable to continue beyond sixth grade since the only high school in our province was in Naga City and there were significant costs involved—for uniforms, books, tuition, and living expenses. We wrote home to family and friends and talked with people we'd come to know in the Philippines, explaining the scholarship idea and requesting contributions. We identified a dozen students who were at the top of their class in sixth grade but who were unable to continue their education because of these costs. During our second year, they all began high school in Naga City and three of them lived with us. Later on, all 12 of these students graduated from high school, and most of them were able to also graduate from university with the continued scholarship program assistance. Certainly their lives were changed through this opportunity with ripple effects on their families and communities.

Milaor did not have a library so we helped to get one started for the village. We began by lending the books given to us in a locker by the Peace Corps. We set them up on shelves in our house and developed a card system to keep track of the borrowing. Also, we wrote home to request more books, especially for the eager children who came every day after school to our makeshift library. Toward the end of our stay we arranged for the books to be transferred to a central space in the village so that people would have their own library in the future.

When school was not in session, we had to find different volunteer work to do, and one summer we arranged with a coastal community (Salingogon) to teach an informal "summer school" consisting of such courses as swimming, health & wellness, music, art, etc. (We had learned that many of the people along the coast did not know how to swim despite the fact that they needed to travel by boat frequently—to fish and to reach the nearest road.) We spent the summer there and had a pleasant time in this lovely village teaching the children—and some adults, too—the basics of swimming plus other extra-curricular subjects.

...on me

After serving with the Peace Corps in the Philippines, I felt more focused on a career path. I attended graduate school in social work at the University of Michigan with a primary focus on community development. While there, I met and married another PCV, Paul Johnson, who had served with the second group to Ghana, West Africa. As former volunteers, we were drawn together by our experiences and our concerns about international issues. So my life partner and subsequent family are a very direct result of my Peace Corps service!

Since then we have lived abroad three different times and places for extended periods of time—another likely effect of the PC experience. Also, all three of our children have lived and worked abroad for many years, and one served as a PCV in Guatemala during the 1990s. Even now, two of our children live in other countries with their families—in Sweden and China. It seems that the Peace Corps experience started an international streak in our family!

I've tried to incorporate an international perspective into my work in a variety of ways. As a professor of social work at Luther College, I urged the expansion of study-abroad opportunities, and advised students on international experiences. Also, I developed a short course in comparative family studies and took students abroad to Scandinavia for a month-long learning experience for several years.

The Peace Corps experience certainly helped increase my understanding of cultural, social, and religious differences among people and countries. It has led me to follow international news more closely and to be more open to various perspectives. Unfortunately, it has also led to a certain amount of discomfort and even sometimes anger about the way our nation views and treats other countries. And my husband and I often lament the fact that most Americans have such a high-consumption lifestyle, oblivious to the struggles and suffering of millions around the world.

But overall, the opportunity to serve as a Peace Corps Volunteer was truly the experience of a lifetime, and it has greatly enriched my life. It helped me find a wonderful partner, developed an international outlook in our children, and expanded my contributions to college students. Only rarely now do people ask me about my PC experience but when it happens, they get an earful of positive comments!

Pat Johnson lives on the Iowa farm she and her husband bought 35 years ago, soon after finishing graduate school at the University of Michigan—an MSW for Pat and an MS in forestry for her husband, Paul (Ghana II). Initial jobs included school social work, medical social work, and foster care & adoption services. Later she shifted into education and taught social work for 25 years at Luther College in Decorah, Iowa. On the farm Pat helped milk cows, take care of the sheep, run their Christmas tree operation, and raise a big garden/orchard to provide most of the family's vegetables, fruits and jams (frozen, canned & preserved for winter use). She and Paul raised three children who are now raising six wonderful grandchildren (no bias of course!). One son lives in Shanghai, a daughter lives in Sweden, and their second son is now taking over the farm—allowing Paul and her to retire gradually.

David King
Adjusting to the Peace Corps Life:

**Letters Received and Assembled by
Nancy Jeffers Schmidt and Charlotte Hough Stocek**

Dave King was not only a colleague of ours, but also a dear and close friend. Dave was charming, bright and talented. He played the piano and loved to sing. He had a touch of irreverence about him that endeared him all the more to us. We three established a bond early on during the initial training at Penn State. That friendship flourished and lasted well beyond our Peace Corps days.

Dave was born in Waterloo, Indiana and grew up on a farm there. He went to Ball State University to prepare to be a teacher. Dave always wanted to travel and after teaching a few years in Indiana, he became a teacher with the Department of Defense schools in Germany. He was in Germany when he learned about the Peace Corps after having heard President John F. Kennedy's inaugural speech that included the words, "Ask not what your country can do for you—ask what you can do for your country." The words resonated with Dave and he was inspired to apply to be a Peace Corps Volunteer. He had no hesitation about leaving his DOD teaching position and accepting his assignment to be a teacher's aide in the schools of the Philippines.

Dave's first assignment was to schools in the Municipality of Bato, Camarines Sur. As did others of us, he found his first few months fitting into another culture uncomfortable and trying at times in spite of being warmly welcomed by the locals. Excerpts from two of his letters reflect this.

Bato, Camarines Sur, December 9, 1961

Dear Nancy and Group,
   We're sitting here waiting out a typhoon or rather the outskirts of one.
   It's not so bad as the one in Los Banos—only bad enough to make a rainy, miserable, gloomy day. (That's why I'm writing letters.)
   They're building a brand spankin new nipa hut for us to live in. It's more than half done in just a week's work. Meanwhile we're living with Wally's principal and family. I think there are twelve of us (it keeps changing) in this smallish type nipa. We're getting a lot of insights into Philippine family life, which is good, but I can hardly wait until we move into our own little hut
   Stay sober,
   Dave

Bato, Camarines Sur, December 10, 1961

Hi Sweetie—
   We got the news today that the two flowers of Sorsogon had been transplanted to Bulusan. From Char's letter, it sounds as if you're in much the same situation that

we're struggling with. Life in the aquarium is just a bit too public to suit my taste. People even know when we bathe! But, at least we do! We're living with Wally's principal—a really great guy—and his family. There are approximately twelve people living in his smallish nipa—about eight too many for comfort.

I'm toiling away here in the kitchen by the light of the old oil lamp. If Abe Lincoln could do it, so can I! That damned typhoon knocked down the light wire.

Hey, let's play nostalgia. How's this—toilet seats that lift up—or toothbrush holders—or another pitcher of beer—or cement sidewalks—or Gig and Rene—or "No Exit." Enough? These kinds of things I miss, but I can get along without them. I see so clearly now, that the thing that will get me is the human element—all the "aye—sayers," the complete lack of privacy, and the constant stares. I certainly hope that we will come to the point where we can be our normal, uninteresting selves. Maybe as we find our places as "teacher's aides" things will level off.

Any big plans for the holidays? We'll have to get together and swing a little. Legaspi isn't too bad—a few night clubs and a nice hotel. We'll have to check them out.

Well, it's 8 pm. Time for bed. There's a big fiesta for me tomorrow at La Opinion. Must be at my charming best.

Stay sober!

Love from Dave

Dave experienced some of the same frustrations others of us did searching for that "right fit." He finally found his niche in Nabua teaching at the high school and was really happy. He describes his work there below:

Nabua, Camarines Sur, January 29th, 1962

Dear Char and Nance,

High school is heaven, or as near as we'll ever get to it in the Philippines. My principal is a good man with ambition and drive. I've really enjoyed charming my way into their good graces, and I'm not selling myself short this time. They expect me to be expert in many fields, and I find that I can be just that. In one and a half weeks' time the activities have been staggering. I've made so any speeches in almost all the classes on everything from American birds to how to make good instant coffee, to why American Indians aren't white. I've discussed Communism, compared the industrialization of the U.S to that of the USSR, showed how to write a good news story (glad you didn't hear that one, Char), talked Peace Corps til I'm blue in the face, done the dating bit, showed them some real slang, gave a talk on segregation—and on and on.

The physical ed classes had me teach square dancing. I taught the three I know—The Bunny Hop and the Hokey Pokey. I'm going to organize a club of student librarians to open the barricaded library. The municipal council asked me to help develop a program to combat juvenile delinquency. Now my big project is High School Day. The committee asked me to write up a pageant to present the queens for the coronation ceremony, so I came home and whipped up a sort of Moro fairy tale, working in songs and folk dances with Moro décor—the gimmick is five grand processions—up the center isle with queens carried on chairs with many attendants fanning, etc. I'm eager to see how it turns out. The teachers really like the idea. Some are talking about a Nabua Playhouse. Wish you were here Nancy; I'm on shaky grounds there. So, my enthusiasm has been reawakened. It's so much better than my elementary school was. I can't believe it. The four of us are going to have a "Saturday Seminar"—lectures and discussions for any interested students or teachers in the area—that's still in the talking stage.

P.S. My yaws are really bad—could mean a trip to Manila, I hope, I hope. Barb Bassett went for that. Oh yes, Wally is really a ball of fire at his school—he's fitting my idea of a real Peace Corpsman. Guess he's feeling better.

Loves,
Dave

Quite often some of us wrote to one another sharing our more personal thoughts and philosophical musings. Dave did just that in this letter.

Nabua, Camarines Sur, July 19, 1962

Hi Ducky—

Sorry you missed the conference in Legaspi. It was so-so. The best part was afterward and the hour I spent in the hot pool with Char and the Far East representative of PC. That picked me up and flung me back into the spirit of things with new wisdom. He was so fine—ask Char what he said—especially the Oriental attitude toward time. Up to the talk in the pool, I think I had been judging Filipinos by western standards, but making plenty of allowances because they are foreigners. I tolerated and went along (with) their quaint customs, thinking these were the differences I had to understand and adjust to. But that's not true. The customs and tradition of the land are influenced by the climate, the long years of colonial reign and other outside factors; but more important, they're a reflection of the philosophy upon which they base their adjustment to those situations. For instance, bahala na is not the result of frequent typhoons or an inherent tendency to indolence; it's an expression of the deeper attitude which says. "Don't sweat it!"—"Relax!

So, instead of peeking unhappily out of my rut, I've leaped out, looking boldly around me, and found my place. I teach three classes every day now and do extra—curricular stuff. More significantly, perhaps, I see Filipinos around me just as right as anyone in the way they live. I'm the foreigner here and according to their code, I'm the one with quaint customs—one of which is impatience.

I'm over it, Nanc, and mighty glad for this new outlook. I'm happy again—no more bitching from Nabua!

They're twisting at the H.S. tonight. Wish you were here.

Love to the whole household, Dave

This last letter, short and succinct, indicates that Dave was keeping very busy and was quite content in his role as a teacher.

Nabua, Camarines Sur, September 18, 1962

Hi Chick—

I don't write because I'm busy teaching six classes a day, and more important, I'm happy doing it. You're involved in the same thing, aren't you? Still doing the 7th grade bit?

I like teaching, too. I've discovered that my former dislike of teaching was not because of the job, but because of my attitude.

I'm lonely to see you. Care to come to Legaspi some weekend? I've met some fantastic people and we're welcome anytime. Maybe Char told you about them. Are you going to Manila for physical exam? If so, when? Let's coordinate.

Gotta grade 53 themes tonight—grades are due tomorrow.

Stay happy—Love, Dave

Dave became a field representative with the American Book Company after he returned from the Philippines. He served an area of colleges in the Midwest. He later earned his Masters of Library Science and became a writer and librarian for the Encyclopedia Britannica in Chicago where he and his partner made their home. He loved to travel and often visited southern France.

Dave stayed in touch over the years with his Peace Corps friends, traveling to visit them from time to time and attending the 25th Peace Corps Reunion in Washington D.C. in 1986. He also remained close to his family in Waterloo, Indiana.

Dave died August 26, 1998 in Chicago.

Biographic information on Nancy Jeffers Schmidt and Charlotte Hough Stocek can be found elsewhere in this volume. In addition to calling her "Nance," Dave used the terms "Sweetie," Ducky," and "Chick" when addressing Nancy Jeffers.

(The photo shows Dave with Group I friends Nancy Jeffers Schmidt and Charlotte Hough Stocek.)

Rayna Larson
Life of a Wife—Volunteer Style

Why I Joined the Peace Corps

In the orientation at Penn State, I remember being told that people never do anything for just one reason. We all have multiple reasons for doing everything we do, including joining the Peace Corps. Today we might call these "talking points."

To See the World: Just before our final departure my husband Blaine and I were asked "Why we joined the Peace Corps?" by a reporter from *The Arizona Republic*, who came to take our photo and interview us. We dutifully gave the reporter multiple reasons for joining, but the only one printed in the story was that we wanted, "to see the world." This resulted in a nasty letter from a reader who was angry that his tax money was going to be spent for us to take a two year vacation to "see the world." And to think that all along, we thought we were "doing something for our country!"

A Family Tradition: Some of those multiple reasons included my Mormon heritage. I had read my great, great grandfather's journal written in the mid 1800s. He was called to go on a mission to Burma but ended up teaching English in India and couldn't get home to America for several years. In the late 1800s my grandfather saved his money as a teacher and went to Samoa on a mission. I probably would have gone on a mission, too, but in those years, a young woman had to be 23 years old before she could go and I was married by then. When the Peace Corps was announced, it seemed like a second chance for me to "do something good for the world."

Presidential Junkie: Another reason was that I was a political junkie—really a presidential junkie. I even wrote a letter to President Truman when I was in elementary school. On one summer vacation, our family ended up in the same city as a national convention of governors and I saw Thomas Dewey in the parade. When he ran against Truman, I wanted him to win just so I could say I had seen a president of the United States.

In February of 1959, a banquet celebrating the Sesquicentennial of Lincoln's birth was held in Washington, D.C. It was announced that all three living U.S. presidents were going to be in attendance. Two students from every state would be invited as guests to represent their home state. Through a nomination from my school, American University, I became one of the two students representing Arizona. Herbert Hoover wasn't at the banquet, but Truman was there and Eisenhower gave the major speech. I not only got to see a U.S. president but I sat down to dinner with two presidents, albeit at a distant table.

When Kennedy was elected, I was living in the Washington suburbs. The night before his inauguration, a huge snow storm hit the area. Newscasts were filled with stories of people who where snowed in. I was determined to attend the inauguration, but no one wanted to go. I finally convinced my sister, who was an English major, with the promise of seeing Robert Frost in person. So very early that morning, we left her one-year-old baby with our husbands, dressed in our warmest clothes and snow boots and drove through the snow bound streets. It was a great day. My sister got to see Robert Frost and I got to attend a U.S. Presidential inauguration in person. "Ask not what your country can do for you, but what you can do for your country," became another reason why I joined the Peace Corps.

A Married Couple Joins the Peace Corps

I have often been asked what it was like being in the Peace Corps as a couple. Some assume it was a romantic adventure; others think it might have proven difficult because of too much togetherness. Let me relate some experiences that illustrate our life as a Peace Corps couple.

Penn State Memories: At Penn State, where our training began, we were housed in the girls dorm with bunk beds—enough said! Someone even thought we were brother and sister since we had the same unique last name, Larson-Crowther, which was a combination of Blaine's father's and stepfather's names. When everyone went camping, Blaine went with the men and I went with the women, which worked out fine.

Then, when it came time for the flight over the Pacific, our group was divided into males and females, and this time, Blaine and I were put in the male group. We flew in a prop jet which was very slow and had to stop for refueling at places made famous by World War II—Midway, Guam, Wake, and Pearl Harbor. My memory is that it took two nights and a day or maybe more to get to the Philippines. After we arrived, we were not allowed to deplane, but had to sit in the hot plane on the tarmac in Manila waiting for the female volunteers to arrive by jet from Hawaii. Although the females left at the same time, they were in a faster plane, which gave them a layover in Hawaii for a day at the beach so that our two planes would arrive in Manila at the same time. All this was carefully planned so that rather than getting photos of tired, grumpy guys with two-day-old stinky, sweaty clothes, the news photographers could get pictures of pretty girls, newly suntanned and wearing fresh clothes, coming gracefully down the steps of their more modern jet airplane. Eventually we were allowed to deplane and join in the ceremonies planned for us at the airport. We were welcomed as the second wave of "Thomasites," a group of 500 American teachers who had come to teach in the Philippines in the early 1900s.

Los Baños Memories: During our in-country training at Los Baños, we didn't live with the other volunteers, but were assigned to live in the International House for foreign students at the college. This meant that we were somewhat isolated from the other members of our group, especially during the evenings; however, we met and became friends with some of the foreign students living there. We never saw a menu, but every night, when we went to the dining hall, a plate of food was placed in front of us. We noticed that friends sitting next to us were served entirely different plates of food. One night when we arrived at the table we pointed to their plates and asked if we could have the same thing. We were told that Pakistanis eat Pakistani food and that Americans eat American food. We laughed inwardly because nothing we had eaten had a familiar taste to it.

Wives Are Supposed to Know Everything: After Blaine was chosen to be one of the volunteer leaders, he went to our assigned province, Sorsogon, ahead of the main group of volunteers, which meant I was left alone at the International House for a period of time—long enough for Blaine to write me letters. One evening a knock on the door brought a Peace Corps staff member holding one of Blaine's letters clearly addressed to me. On the back was written something like, "Tell so-and-so that I am working on it." To my surprise he demanded that I open the letter and let him read it. When the letter didn't reveal whatever information he was seeking, he demanded to know what Blaine had told me about this situation. Apparently, one volunteer had previously asked Blaine to arrange a transfer from her assignment to one in Sorsogon. I didn't know anything about it. The leader insisted that I wasn't telling the truth and that Blaine would certainly have discussed this with me. I really had never heard a single word about it. After my visitor left, I started crying—maybe from loneliness or maybe because I had been treated so rudely or maybe because Blaine hadn't told me anything about it. In a few seconds, there was a soft knock on my door. Two Filipino members of the International House staff had come to comfort me, having heard this entire conversation through the wall. Then, I began to wonder what else they had heard through the wall in the previous weeks.

"Get Me to the Train on Time": After the Filipino elections the day finally arrived when all the volunteers were to leave Los Baños for their assignments. Our group was to take the train to Legaspi and then travel on to Sorsogon by bus. As directed, I packed my suitcase and sat on the steps of the International House. I waited and waited, but no one came. Finally I went inside and called the Peace Corps office. They had completely forgotten about me. Shortly thereafter a driver arrived in a jeep to pick me up. Off we went flying through the jungle trying to beat the train to the next station. A bumpy zigzagging road and no seat belts meant that I had to hang on for dear life. Of course, there was no way that a jeep going on a rough road through the jungle could beat a train. Someone had phoned the train to wait for us, but the train had a schedule to keep. I was just happy to have arrived in one piece and that my suitcase hadn't fallen out.

Whoever was in charge, decided against taking me back to Los Baños and the International House. Instead, I was taken to a very lush private home with marble floors. I don't know how this house was chosen. Maybe it was the local mayor's house, or perhaps, a wealthy relative of the jeep driver. No matter, they graciously took me in, gave me food and a bed. They accomplished their assignment of getting me to the train on time with no mishaps, but the trip was not pleasant. It was the overnight train, which might explain why I was the only female in the dining car full of beer-drinking men. I stayed awake the entire night answering questions from strangers.

As the train reached Legaspi, I saw two memorable sights. The first was a beautiful pink and yellow sunrise behind Mayon volcano framed with tall coconut palm trees. The second was Blaine waiting at the station to take me to Sorsogon in his jeep.

Sorsogon Stories

A Home of Our Own: Although Blaine had arranged housing for all the other volunteers in our district, there seemed to be no affordable housing in the provincial capital, Sorsogon City, where we were assigned. At first there was talk about the Peace Corps building us a small house. In the meantime, we were to live temporarily with Dr. Leocadio, the Superintendent of Education. I remember that we had a breezy second floor bedroom that looked out onto the convent across the street. Every morning we awakened to the chanting of prayers and the singing of the nuns. We were soon embarrassed to discover that a young relative of the family, who was acting as their maid had given up her room for us and was sleeping in a closet on the floor. This information spurred us to work harder to find our own quarters.

Because of flooding, Filipinos usually lived on the second floor of their homes leaving the first floor basically empty, unfinished, or sometimes as a shelter for farm animals. We ended up renting the lower half of such a place, but it needed a lot of work. Neighbors, other volunteers, and curious Filipinos who were passing by stopped to help. We had to remove junk, scrape layers of dirt and finally paint all the walls and unfinished surfaces. I remember that the paint was blue. Although some homes had flattened sea shells set in wooden frames for windows, our windows were just open to the outside. There was a basic toilet and a cement shower that drained directly into the side yard. This allowed snails and other small organisms to enter our shower from the yard.

The kitchen was in the back yard separate from the house. We learned that this was the custom because fires often started in the kitchen and when such a tragedy happened, this would prevent the whole house from burning down. After we moved in, we discovered one minor flaw—our home had no ceiling. When the family swept the floor above us, the dust would float down between their floor boards onto our heads. I never remember any water coming down. Maybe they never mopped their floor. It mattered little, however, because rain, wind, and numerous living things came in through the windows.

We had several lizards that moved in permanently and ran unimpeded across our blue walls. We were told that they kept the insects under control. Eventually their little clicking noises became comforting rather than frightening. However, spiders were not comforting. One day a huge five inch spider came walking across the floor. I smashed it with our broom and suddenly—what seemed like hundreds of little spiders, were running in every direction. It turned out that this was a mother spider carrying a sac of baby spiders on her back.

We bought a bamboo couch, but could not find a table. We went to a "furniture store," where we were taken immediately to the back yard and shown huge hardwood logs, four feet in diameter. We were asked to select the log we wanted them to use for our table and chairs. We also ordered a double bed, but when it came it was the size of an American twin bed. At first I thought this was a translation problem. Double and twin could have been misunderstood. It turned out that a local single bed was a very narrow cot size. We had to order a second "double" bed. Our home was complete when Blaine painted a picture to hang in our beautiful blue living room.

Glimpses of Romance: In spite of the critic who thought that the government had sent us on an extended honeymoon, we rarely experienced anything that came close to a romantic vacation, but in fairness I will mention a few instances.

In the first few days after arriving in Sorsogon, Blaine invited me for a jeep ride during a typhoon. It seemed dangerous, but I joined him anyway. Everything was unique and beautiful. There was no one at all on the road—no cars, no people, just palm trees and jungle vegetation. Everywhere coconuts had been blown down by the strong winds. As the storm began to abate, a little boy came walking down the side of the road holding a gigantic leaf over his head as an umbrella. It was a magical moment. My immediate thought was, "Mad dogs and Englishmen go out in the noonday sun," only, in this case, it was, "Mad Americans and little boys go out in a typhoon."

Although Blaine was often away on Peace Corps business, visiting other volunteers, going to the regional office in Legaspi, or even attending meetings in Manila, I do remember one weekend we had to ourselves. We found an isolated beach—no huts, no boats, just a beautiful beach not too far from the main highway. We had worn our swim suits under our clothes, but ended up swimming in the nude. Almost immediately, we heard the squeal of brakes. Peering into the distance we saw a public bus unloading a group that we recognized as Peace Corps volunteers. We barely had time to retrieve our swim suits, swim into deep water, and pull them on before our friends arrived. We had a good time that day, but it wasn't the romantic get-away we had planned.

Although we lived in a city that had recreational possibilities I never remember having time to go to dinner or the movies with Blaine. We did go to midnight mass on Christmas Eve at the local Catholic Church and once were invited for dinner by a group of volunteers who lived not too far from Sorsogon City.

Writing My Own Job Description: I never learned how it came to be that I didn't get assigned to a specific school—as had all the other volunteers. Maybe it was assumed that I was to be the supporting wife of a volunteer leader. Or maybe I was supposed to be assigned to the local school. It was the "model" school for the entire province and the teachers there regarded themselves as "model" teachers and perhaps didn't really want a Peace Corps Volunteer assigned to their school. The school superintendent told me that I was to work in his office. My first duties were to write letters to Manila to try to get money for some teachers who hadn't been paid. The thought of working for two years as an office assistant was too dismal to contemplate.

Somehow, I arranged to present a few science workshops for groups of teachers from outlying villages. I saw the need for some handouts, which inspired the idea of printing inexpensive pamphlets for teachers. I gathered up some science books and began to write, *For Teachers Who Are Attracted to Magnets*. They could be produced for less than three cents each. The Peace Corps reproduced a large quantity and offered them to other volunteers and local schools. A Jesuit Priest came across one and wrote me a very complimentary letter encouraging me to write more of these. I began working on, *For Teachers Who Are Sparked by Electricity*. A publisher in Manila also came across the pamphlet and asked me to help edit some high school science textbooks written by Filipino science teachers. The Peace Corps office in Washington even wrote me a letter asking my opinion on what to provide new volunteer teachers. These affirmations helped make up for a lack of a "real" assignment.

The Toaster: When I was in elementary school, one of my favorite magazines in the library was *Popular Mechanics*. It told how to make marvelous toys and useful household items. The Peace Corps had given all of us a UNESCO book that detailed all sorts of wonderful things to make when living in primitive conditions. I remember it told how to make a slide projector for a school with no electricity, using multiple mirrors to reflect the sun. It also had directions for making a toaster which did not use electricity. I decided to make one. I found some resistance wire at a local radio repair shop and the other supplies at a hardware store. Of course, the bread didn't pop up. You had to turn it over to toast the other side. You can't imagine how good the familiar taste of toast was after a few months of Filipino food. About this time someone gave us a can of butter from Denmark. Afterward we kept a store of guava jelly on hand at all times. Our weekend guests all loved making toast at our house.

Day to Day Problems: Lack of money was a problem for us. Most of the volunteers lived in smaller towns in groups of four and pooled their allowances to cover the cost of a cook and other household help. Although Blaine got extra money to cover the cost of gas and the upkeep of the jeep, we didn't have money for a cook and had to get by with Manny, the 19-year-old son of the landlady as a house boy. He cleaned, washed dishes, and boiled our drinking water, but he didn't really know how to cook. I usually had to do all the cooking as well as the shopping. I never remember getting to drive the jeep, even once, but I was thrilled when I got a bicycle. Now, I could ride to the market for food or to the pier for fish and clams. I remember that beef was available only on Saturdays. The entire carcass hung in the market and you pointed to the part you wanted. There was a set price per pound whether you got the choice cuts or the soup bones. After I learned this, I got up early on Saturdays and pedaled to the market so I could buy a tender cut.

Running a Bed and Breakfast: Because Blaine was the volunteer leader for the surrounding area, our home became a kind of bed and breakfast with visitors almost every weekend, some staying overnight. One volunteer became very ill and moved into our extra bedroom. Manny became his practical nurse, until he had recovered sufficiently to return to his assignment. Volunteers stopped by our house whenever they were in Sorsogon City, mainly to see each other, eat together, and exchange stories about their assignments.

Besides the volunteers, we often had visitors from Manila, sometimes social and sometimes official. Blaine's parents had apparently complained to a senator that they hadn't heard from their son who was far away in the Peace Corps. Diplomatic wires buzzed and a young man was sent all the way from Manila to Sorsogon to check on Blaine, in person, and to tell him to write a letter to his mother.

A Not So Happy Jeep Story: A short time after we came to Sorsogon, Blaine had a not-so-pleasant experience with a jeep. At a meeting of volunteer leaders, he was riding in the back seat of a jeep driven by another volunteer. The jeep hit and killed an elderly man. The collateral damage consisted of the side view mirror coming off and flying into Blaine's face. He came home with stitches and a bandage. The headline in the local paper read, "Peace Corps Volunteer Injured in Accident." instead of "Peace Corps Jeep Kills Local Man." The rumor was that the man's family had been paid a good deal of money. From that time on, young men would pretend to push their friends in front of our jeep, saying something like, "His family needs the money." Even though they were joking, Blaine had to be a careful driver because, in their horsing around, the boys sometimes actually stumbled into the road.

They Came Bearing Gifts—Turkeys! Cheese! A Baby?

It Took a Whole Village: During a visit to Legaspi, an American Mormon family who lived nearby heard about us and showed up one day bringing a huge turkey from their farm as a gift. We thanked them profusely, but were extremely happy they had already butchered it because I was still learning how to kill, pluck, and dress the much smaller chickens from our market in Sorsogon. After taking the turkey back home, the real problem began. What could we do with this huge bird?

Luckily for us Philippine culture is full of FOAF (Friend of a Friend). Someone in our neighborhood knew someone who knew someone who was in the business of renting out freezer space. So off went our turkey to the freezer. In the hassle of trying to get a place to live, we forgot about the turkey until one day word came that we should come and get our turkey. Now the same old problem returned, except it was "What to do with this huge frozen bird?" We did not have a stove big enough to cook it. Peace Corps volunteers either cooked with charcoal or used the little camp stoves given to us as part of our gear, even though the required fuel was not available in the country. FOAF to the rescue! Someone knew someone who knew the owner of the local bakery—one of those huge wood-fired brick ovens with long wooden spatulas. Off went our turkey for the second time.

Now everyone, including our house boy and his mother, began to prepare the other fixings. I don't remember the menu, but I am pretty certain that we did not have cranberry sauce. The turkey came back, beautifully roasted and delicious. Volunteers, our land lady's family, neighbors, and some of the FOAFs were there.

It had taken an entire village to prepare this Thanksgiving feast, but the funny part was that it didn't take place on Thanksgiving Day. It might have been Christmas, but I think it was just a random day dictated by when the freezer man needed more space.

The Great Cheese Chase: On another occasion we received a large rounded waxed cheese from the Netherlands, a gift from a Professor of Linguistics who had befriended us at Los Baños and had decided to visit us in Sorsogon with his family. It was a welcome gift—even fancier than the canned butter from Denmark that someone else had given us. Although we didn't have a refrigerator, we put the cheese with our other food supplies in the cupboard of our backyard kitchen.

The next day after our guests had left for Manila, I looked up and saw a big stray dog running past our open door with the cheese in its mouth. Right behind him went Manny, chasing him with a machete. They were halfway down the block when he threw the machete with surprising accuracy and the wounded dog dropped the cheese. Manny came back, triumphantly holding up the cheese. The wounded dog was howling so pitifully that I began to cry. Off Manny went to find his uncle who was watching a movie at the local theater. They came back almost immediately and put the dog out of his misery with the gun that his uncle always carried. To end the story: in spite of all that happened, we actually ate the cheese.

Could This Be True? Since it was obvious that the Peace Corps wasn't really prepared for couples, I felt certain that they weren't prepared for pregnant volunteers. Blaine and I had decided that the Peace Corps was to be our big adventure before starting a family. Nothing specific was said to us about official policy, but I do remember getting birth control pills in Manila.

After we settled in at Sorsogon, we were constantly asked by Filipinos, why we didn't have children. They began sending us cards with pictures of babies on them and cards with prayers that God would send us a baby. Somewhere along the way, we were told about another childless American couple, who came home, one day, to find that someone had left them an anonymous gift—a Filipino baby. I always suspected that this was an urban legend, but the possibility that it might be true was unsettling.

Our Summer Proposal and University Teaching

The Peace Corps office asked all the volunteers to submit a proposal for spending the summer break in a productive way. Blaine and I proposed to produce television programs focused on English as a Second Language. I planned to produce and write a puppet show for children and enlisted a beautiful volunteer who agreed to be the star. The Peace Corps approved our proposal, but at the last minute, the beautiful star of the show went off to Zamboanga for the summer and I ended up as "Miss Rayna" on a weekly show called, *For Children Only* with Blaine working the two puppets, Toto the sassy dog, and Fred the slow talking horse. I made the puppets and Blaine painted the sets. Blaine also had his own show, *English as a Key* for high school students in which he co-starred with Rosie, a staff member from the Bureau of Education. We learned about story boards, script writing, set making, and about the hard work that goes into producing television programs.

The project required that we relocate to Manila for the summer. We found a small apartment over a beauty shop which was convenient since I had to get my hair done just before our show was taped at the PBS studios in downtown Manila. Every night nearby hawkers called out, "Baloooooot, Balooot" as they peddled this Filipino specialty, a fertilized duck egg, almost ready to hatch, complete with feathers, beaks, and legs. This is one thing you need to try only once in a lifetime, if ever.

Our programs on the PBS (Philippine Broadcasting System) were so successful that the Bureau of Education requested that we stay and continue them during the next school year. The Peace Corps thought that doing television programs was too glamorous, but agreed if we also taught college classes at the University of the Philippines (UP) in Quezon City.

Living on the UP Campus: The University, which was building small two-bedroom houses on campus for faculty members, provided us the first completed one as our quarters. We were both assigned to teach English classes to incoming freshmen. Second semester I was assigned to the graduate college and, as a presidential junkie, valued the hand signed transfer letter from the new UP President, Carlos P. Romulo, who had previously been the President of the United Nations General Assembly.

Although we were busy writing scripts, rehearsing, preparing lessons and grading papers we had more time for normal living. We sometimes went to movies or ate Filipino fast food on the way home from the television station. We met a young Filipino poet and his wife, who sometimes double dated with us. We became friends with Leno Brocka, a Filipino student who spent a lot of time at our house, sometimes staying overnight. He later became a very famous movie director. We also met several American families who reached out to us socially, as a way of thanking us for our service as volunteers.

Beware of Empty Bedrooms: After we had been teaching at UP for a while, a group of female volunteers from a later Peace Corps group moved into the new house next to ours. One was a grandmother who was having difficulties with the younger volunteers. Someone's idea of the solution was to give the older woman her own bedroom. Since we had an empty second bedroom, it was decided that she would move in with us. I know that I did not volunteer or agree to this arrangement. We were told that this was to be a temporary arrangement—just until a new house was built for her.

So now, we had a "mother-in-law" living with us who wasn't related to either of us. She complained about my cooking, gave advice to us on personal matters, and to my recollection never helped with any of the housework, which fell on me since we had, long ago, given up on the maid who put leftovers under the sink instead of in the refrigerator.

I began to long for the lonely, but quiet, times in Sorsogon. I was especially homesick for our Sorsogon family of volunteers with their humor and funny stories.

Day after day, I watched as our "mother-in-law's" intended house was being built. When it was finished, she still didn't move out, claiming it had no electricity. More time went by. Finally, I was so exasperated that I went over to the house and turned the lights on. She moved out in a few days.

Tales from Clark Air Force Base

My Introduction to Vietnam: During the second semester at UP, Blaine began losing weight and came down with an unidentified ailment that allowed large amounts of blood to seep into his urine. Since his father had died of kidney failure at a fairly young age, we of course, quickly sought medical help. At first he was hospitalized in Manila where they checked out his kidneys. Later he was moved to Clark Air Base hospital where they began looking for symptoms of various tropical diseases.

This was a difficult time because I had to continue teaching my classes plus some of Blaine's. Several days a week I would catch a bus for the two hour ride to Angeles, the nearest town to Clark Air Base, and then take a jeepney to the airbase gate. After the doctors did a biopsy on Blaine's calf muscle to look for parasites, he was temporarily in a wheel chair. As I pushed him around the grounds of the hospital, I had one of those literary romantic moments. I felt like I was a nurse in some World War II movie caring for a wounded soldier.

In the hospital Blaine was sharing a two-person room with a real American soldier who had been wounded in Vietnam. At that time I knew nothing about Vietnam or for that matter that American soldiers were fighting anywhere. Meeting this soldier was my introduction to a whole era of American history that was just beginning to unfold. The next time I came back to the hospital, the soldier's bed was empty and Blaine told me that he had died during the night.

The Ugly American Jeepney Ride: One evening when I was leaving Clark Air Base, I got on a crowded jeepney that would take me into town where I could catch the bus to Manila. An American serviceman walked up and shocked everyone, including me, by telling the Filipino passengers to get out of the jeepney. I protested, but he waved me off and hired the jeepney privately for me alone. I know he thought he was being kind, but it was a typical "ugly-American" thing to do. Such events wipe out much of the goodwill that the Peace Corps was trying to establish. At the time I couldn't think fast enough, but in retrospect, I wish I had asked the driver to go around the block and come back to pick up those abandoned passengers.

A Smoking Hot Bus Ride: Another time when leaving the Air Base, there was no jeepney waiting. In hope of getting to Manila before dark, I walked out to the main highway and flagged down a bus. It stopped and I climbed on. It was coming from a northern village heading to Manila. I am sure the passengers thought it was strange that an American woman was on the highway flagging down buses, but I also thought it was strange that nearly everyone on the bus was smoking cigarettes with the lit end inside their mouths. During our orientation sessions at Penn State, we had been told about certain groups who smoked this way, but this was the only time that I ever saw this phenomenon.

Going Home: When the doctors at Clark Air Base Hospital couldn't diagnose Blaine's problem, it was decided that going back to the U.S. was the best choice. The Peace Corps staff was probably influenced by the fact that one volunteer from our group had already died and the organization didn't need any more scary publicity.

I remember being called to the Peace Corps office and given the choice of staying in the Philippines or going home to the U.S. with Blaine. Of course, I chose to go home with my husband.

Some of the new volunteers at UP took over our college classes. Blaine's co-star got another co-star and went on with their TV program. My TV show, *For Children Only* ended. I packed Toto, the sassy brown dog, Fred, the sock puppet horse; and the TV guide with a picture of "Miss Rayna" in my suitcase as souvenirs.

And so our "honeymoon" in the Peace Corps ended with Blaine in a Public Health Hospital in Baltimore, Maryland surrounded by sick Coast Guard retirees. His final diagnosis was "idiopathic bleeding" which I was told by the doctor translates to "nobody knows." Blaine did, however, recover fully.

Useful Things I Learned in the Peace Corps

I learned how to cut a mango and how to skin a pineapple with no waste, but these skills were not as impressive as opening a coconut with one blow of a hammer. Someone taught me to turn a coconut so that you can see the "face" and then hit one hard blow to the left eyebrow. Sure enough the coconut pops wide open. This was always an impressive trick that I enjoyed performing for my children and their friends.

One night after my shower I discovered that my hairdryer wouldn't work anymore. The thought of sleeping with wet hair and the "bad hair day" that would follow, motivated me to use the skills I had gained making the Sorsogon toaster. Sure enough, I was able to repair it. That is why a broken toaster sits on my kitchen counter, right now, waiting for the same skills to be applied.

I have not, yet, had an occasion to cut down a jungle vine and get the water to drain out in just the right way, but I still remember how to do it. I've told my friends that if they ever get lost in a jungle and are thirsty, they can call me on their cell phone and I'll tell them exactly how to do it.

When I confessed to having no talent at speaking Tagalog, a linguistics professor taught me three rote sentences in Tagalog that were useful on a daily basis in Manila. "What is your name?" "My name is Rayna," and "I don't smoke cigarettes." This last one was used to fend off the many street venders. I still know all three sentences. I have used the first two to open conversations with Filipino Americans I meet, only to disappoint them when I can't remember any more Tagalog. Little kids just go on talking to me, thinking that I can understand their Tagalog.

Although I never became one of the noted Peace Corps volunteers in Peace Corps publications, what I learned has had a lasting effect on what has taken place in my life. I now have a great-grandchild and with luck, will pass on to him some of the things I learned in the Peace Corps. His mother, however, will get the lovely embroidered tablecloth.

After leaving the Philippines Rayna Larson taught school in Fairfax County, Virginia during the county's first efforts at racial integration. She and Blaine separated in 1965. Having written science pamphlets in the Philippines, she was inspired to return to college for pre-med courses and entered the Medical College of Pennsylvania, but quickly found that raising two children as a single mother, attending school eight hours a day, and studying in the evenings was too much. After two years, she returned to Fairfax County and worked as a school psychologist until she retired in 1991. After her retirement from Fairfax County, she continued working off and on as a psychologist and college instructor in Arizona and California.

Having joined the Peace Corps as one-half of a couple, when most everyone else was single, Rayna spent two years in China as a single woman with a group of mostly retired couples. She taught English in 2002, at XISU in Xian, and in 2004 at CFAU in Beijing, as part of a service project sponsored by Brigham Young University.

In addition to her two children, eight grandchildren, and one great grandchild, she stays in touch with many of her former Chinese students on the internet and through Face book.

(The first photo shows Rayna with her then husband Blaine being interviewed by a local radio station in the Philippines; the second shows her with her great grandson Charlie.)

Stanley Mazaroff
Risks Worth Taking, Rewards Worth Remembering

A New Breed of Pioneer

Although fifty years have elapsed since I volunteered to serve in the Peace Corps, the confluence of events that influenced that decision happily remain as fresh in my mind as a dip in a cool stream on a summer day. In the early summer of 1960, following my graduation from college and before starting law school, I embarked on cross-country trip in the style of Jack Kerouac living existentially day to day by digging ditches, chopping wood, bailing hay and working at any odd job that would provide me with enough loose change to reach my next destination. Aware that the Democratic convention was in Los Angeles, I headed there hoping to befriend a delegate who might permit me to carry his or her bags or provide some other service that might help to pay my way but more importantly to catch a glimpse of Adlai Stevenson, whom I then viewed as a paragon of political virtue. I met a woman who offered me neither money nor work but something, as it turned-out, far more valuable—a ticket to the convention.

The Los Angeles Memorial Stadium was packed with over 100,000 people on that memorable day on July 15, 1960, when John Kennedy delivered his acceptance speech. My seat magically was so close to the podium that I could see his youthful face, hear the lilt of his voice and feel viscerally the impact of the words he expressed. Even today, those words, phase by phrase, remain carved in my memory. "We are not here to curse the darkness but to light a candle," he said. We were at a "turning point of history," he proclaimed. And he called upon a "new generation of leadership" to serve as "pioneers" to America's "new frontier." The speech not only set the elevated tone of his campaign, but also served as the precursor to his more famous, "Ask not" speech that he delivered upon taking the oath of office on January 20, 1961, some six months later. It was, of course, President Kennedy who inspired me, like thousands of other idealistic young people, to join the Peace Corps.

Following the establishment of the Peace Corps by President Kennedy on March 1, 1961, I believe that I was among the earliest to volunteer. My parents did not share my enthusiasm. I had finished first in my law school class, and my father, distraught over my decision to temporarily leave law behind in favor of an adventurous life in a third world country, questioned my sanity. I remember him asking me point blank why I had chosen, in his words, "to commit suicide." My mother, on the other hand, asked for only one favor. Write to her as often as I could, she implored. It was a promise I kept, and it is the one hundred and fifty letters that she saved in three ring binders that allow me to now turn back the clock and re-examine my experience.

The Peace Corps as a Coat of Arms

After leafing through these letters, I am reminded that the Peace Corps, in essence, was not a job, but a transformative, once-in-a-lifetime experience. Our job was to serve as a "teacher's aide," which entailed teaching English as a second language to elementary school children in remote barrios in the Philippine countryside. The mission had a ring of idealism, but in reality, it was an innocuous, feel-good project that did no harm and accomplished very little except for satisfying the platitudinous goal of "winning friends for America." As my letters confirm, the volunteers in my group as well as some of the staff became increasingly skeptical about the merits of this program. I wish otherwise, but I cannot state with any conviction that I made any concrete contribution to permanently improve the lives (except for the one I tried to save) of any of the Filipinos who were my friends, neighbors and students.

Yet I cherished my tour in the Peace Corps and life in the Philippines—and still do. When asked what I have done in my life, I usually bypass my work as a legislative assistant on Capitol Hill, my tour of duty as an Army JAG in the Pentagon during the Vietnam era, my 30 years of law firm practice, the awards I won, the courses I taught, the books and articles I have written and the service I have provided on non-profit boards. Instead, I raise the banner of the Peace Corps, as if it were my personal coat of arms. My tour of duty as a Peace Corps Volunteer in a very real sense helped to define me; it shaped my values and became an inseparable part of my persona. Here's why.

A Village Called Telegrafo

The small barrio of Telegrafo, as I remember it, rested imperceptibly among a grove of palm trees that were a stone's throw from a white sandy beach that ran along a crescent shaped lagoon under the watchful eye of a massive, perfectly coned volcano of breathtaking beauty known as Mayon. Having traveled to the four corners of the globe, I still remember Telegrafo as an unspoiled paradise rarely visited, but, for the fortunate few who saw it, never forgotten. I discovered this barrio while travelling in my old WW II-vintage jeep though the province of Camarines Sur in southern Luzon where I served for the initial six months of my tour as a Volunteer Leader. Upon the completion of this work, I requested permission to teach and reside in Telegrafo, and my request was granted. There was no place in the Philippines that I'd rather live.

There were about 100 families who resided in Telegrafo in a cluster of small houses, constructed of bamboo and the large leathery leaves of local nipa and elevated above the ground on the trunks of coconut trees, which enabled those inside to catch the sweet breeze of the sea and avoid the menagerie of goats, pigs and other animals that were penned thereunder. The families were headed by fisherman and tenant farmers who, like generations before them, subsisted on the fruits of the ocean and land. It was, of course, an insular, some might say primitive world unconnected to the conveniences of the twentieth-century. There was no electricity, no running water, no clocks, no telephones, no newspapers, no televisions, and no sanitation system. But what I found there was something far less tangible but significantly more valuable. It was that a peaceful yet simple life among loving friends and family was its own reward.

I designed, and with the help of neighbors, built a small split-level, three room house on the edge of the beach about seventy-five yards from the sea. I drilled an artesian well that generated water for drinking and cooking and that was connected by a large bamboo shaft to my nearby out-house (the first and only one in my barrio).

I acquired a Coleman stove for cooking and Coleman lanterns for night time reading, writing and, perhaps most importantly, casting light on my chess board, which, together with rum and coke, became a regular source of evening entertainment among the many young men in Telegrafo who loved the game and who loved even more to sit and share remarkable stories, some truthful but mostly fanciful, late into the night. I also had a short wave radio that enabled me to listen from afar to the conflicting views of world affairs expressed on Radio Russia, Radio China and the Voice of America. I remember how my ear was virtually glued to this radio during the Cuban Missile Crisis.

I became acclimated to my hard bamboo and rattan bed on which I slept without a mattress and a steady diet of fish and rice. I shared my house and my food with my dog Chico, my cat Midas and a baby goat whom I adored but can't remember his name.

I swam and jogged on the beach early each morning and usually played pick-up basketball (a popular sport in the Philippines) late in the day on a court that I constructed for the community. Except for a brief period of time when my ankles were horribly swollen due a systemic infection, I was in good shape.

The most important part of my day was spent with a small group of perhaps 10 to 15 children between the ages of five and ten teaching—or more realistically trying to teach English as a second language. Because the small one room school in the village had a mud floor and a leaking roof, I used my house as my classroom. Of course I loved the kids, and I think they liked me. I will never forget the note that one child left behind on her last day of class. Before she departed, she wrote on my blackboard: "Stanley is the very good American." It was and remains the most gratifying compliment that I have ever received.

But it was not what I did, but the cultural environment in which I lived that generated my most lasting memory. It was a way of life that was starkly different than mine. It is fair to say that for most of my life, I have been driven by goals, one after the other, the product of what some disparagingly call a "Type A" personality. I sadly admit that at the age of 71, I still am awakened at night by nightmares of being unprepared to take an exam, to teach a class or to try a case. My life as a Peace Corps Volunteer in the Philippines not only was an idyllic interlude of the Robinson Crusoe variety, but more importantly, a healthful counterweight to my incessant drive to achieve.

Life in my small village was not driven by lists or timed by clocks or subject to deadlines or judged by superiors. It was an existential life that used the rhythms of nature as its guide. With no clocks or numbers on buildings, meetings were not arranged at a particular place or a particular time but in the vicinity of some familiar location and at some indefinite time in the morning, afternoon or evening. With this in mind, I rarely would go anywhere without a book to read while reclining comfortably on the ground with my back against a tree. And the authors I loved, such as Somerset Maugham, Lawrence Durrell, Graham Greene, Jean Paul Sartre and Dostoyevsky, became not only my regular companions but, in my mind, best friends as well.

There was in this environment one rule that was most important of all. In the western world where quarrels and arguments and the stress and strain of confrontation were part of daily life, none of this was permitted in Telegrafo or in most other rural villages in the Philippines. The maintenance of smooth interpersonal relationships and the avoidance of conflict was an overarching societal goal. This might have slowed progress in a conventional sense, but it increased the pleasure of living, and strangely it made my small village both backward and highly civilized at the same time. It was this unwritten code of human relations that made people so friendly, life so pleasurable, and a small place on the globe so peaceful. It was a way of life that I wish more people would share.

Twists of Fate

The picture I have drawn from memory so far leaves much outside its frame. It needs to be broadened to also reveal some of the hazards as well as the occasional fear, pain and sadness that punctuated my two years of service. There were three incidents that are worth mentioning. I remember them well because each traversed the thin line between life and death. These were incidents that I did not write home about because to have done so would only have added to my parents' anxiety.

The first incident involved my responsibilities as a Volunteer Leader in the province of Camarines Sur. There were, I believe, five households of volunteers in my province, and I was obligated to visit each at least weekly to check on the health and safety of the volunteers and to offer my advice and assistance in resolving any issues pertaining to their duties as teachers. To reach one of the households, I had to drive my jeep through a small stream which usually was no more than six inches deep and easy to navigate. A strong typhoon accompanied by torrential rains struck my area, and when I reached the stream that I needed to cross, I badly miscalculated how deep and treacherous it had become. Recklessly, I attempted to drive my jeep through it. Almost immediately, I was submerged in a torrent of water up to my chest, my jeep stalled and I could do nothing but hold on to the steering wheel for dear life. It was not just my pounding heart that told me that my life was in jeopardy, but the stark realization that my jeep was on the verge of being swept off the road into the swirling river with me in it. Seemingly from out of nowhere, a group of strangers, like guardian angels, plunged into the water, surrounded my jeep and pushed it to higher ground. They saved my life. I thanked them all, but they quickly departed before I could get their names.

At end of February, 1963, I spent two days at the Peace Corps rest and recreation center located on a lovely beach outside of town of Zamboanga on the island of Mindanao. My primary goal was to learn more about the Muslim culture that dominated that large island. I met a fun loving and interesting new volunteer whose name was Phillip Maggard, and we quickly became friends. He invited me to catch a flight with him to another part of the island where he lived, and I accepted. The landing field near Zamboanga had none of the characteristics of a modern airport. It had no lights, lines on the ground or control tower. It was simply a flat field where water buffaloes ordinarily grazed and were chased away when an airplane was approaching. I recall standing on that field with Phil and twenty-six other passengers (including another volunteer whose name was Nancy Boyd) on the morning of March 2 as the plane approached. I am not sure why, but at the last moment I changed my mind about spending any more time in Mindanao. I apologized to Phil and told him that I hoped to see him again on another occasion. I waved goodbye and watched the plane depart. I did not see it go down. But I learned about one-half hour later that it crashed and all were lost. I mourned for Phil and railed against whatever fate or force so suddenly and arbitrarily took his good life but spared mine.

The last incident that deserves remembrance involves the heroism of another volunteer and friend, Bruce Campbell. In April 1963, I, along with five other volunteers, established an overnight camp for 50 boys between the ages of 11 and 14 in the hills overlooking the town of San Jose. Running through the campgrounds was a river around 30 to 40 yards wide. We roped-off the shallow side of the river for the campers, whom we attentively safeguarded from cobras and other hazards. One day while standing on a boulder on the edge of the river and serving as the guard, I saw a hand—only a hand—of a person in the deep part of the river who was desperately reaching skyward for something to grasp in order to save himself from drowning. Although not a strong swimmer, I instinctively dove into the water and swam toward the victim hoping to save his life. Bruce also dove in, and we reached the person around the same time. What ensued for the next minute or more was an exhausting, nightmarish, underwater struggle with a drowning man. I will never forget it. I doubt that I would have survived this struggle but for Bruce's intervention. I remember coming up for air at least twice, hoping by this time to save at least myself. Bruce was also gasping for air but somehow managed to wrap a rope around the drowning person enabling someone on shore to pull him to safety. We both were shaken to tears by the experience. And I continue to wonder whether Bruce ever realized that he saved not one but two lives that day.

The Unforgettable

My last day in Telegrafo was May 22, 1963. I finalized the sale of my house (contributing the small proceeds to the barrio), found a home for my dog and sadly said good-bye to my friends. One week later, I boarded a plane and headed for Vietnam, Cambodia and elsewhere in Southeast and Southern Asia before heading home. Although my Peace Corps tour was over, the way of life I experienced, like the invisible inner-clock that determines when we sleep and eat, remained inside me.

I recall extending an offer to a hotel porter in Agra, India, to allow me to sleep on his mat under the stars in return for my hotel room, an offer that he quickly accepted. When I returned home to the States, I had more trouble psychologically adjusting to daily life than I did upon arriving two years earlier in the Philippines. Although my life seemed to be returning to normal (I re-entered law school, earned good grades and became Editor-in-Chief of the Maryland Law Review), late at night the tremors that kept me awake told me all too clearly that I was going through withdrawal from an extraordinary experience that was in my veins and that I could not and did not want to forget.

Looking backward, I have no illusion about what, if anything, I accomplished as a Peace Corps Volunteer. To the people in my village, I was, I suspect, little more than a passing curiosity—an American who for a brief period of time provided some pleasure and added a very small element of knowledge into the fabric of their lives. But this experience has meant much more to me. That's how I remember it, and I cannot imagine it otherwise.

In 1965, Stan graduated from The University of Maryland Law School, where he served as Editor-in-Chief of the Maryland Law Review. In 1966, shortly after Lyndon Johnson escalated the U.S. commitment in Vietnam, Stan entered the U.S. Army as a tank commander and JAG lawyer. For three years he served as a legal advisor in the Pentagon. During these years he obtained a master of law degree from George Washington University.

In 1969, Stan was requested by U.S. Senator Joseph Tydings to join his Capitol Hill staff and assigned to provide advice to the Senate Judiciary Committee. In this capacity he was involved in defeating two of President Nixon's nominees to the Supreme Court. Most importantly, he met his wife, Nancy Dorman, who has had a distinguished career in government, business and public service.

In 1971, Stan joined the law firm of Venable Baetjer and Howard, where he remained for 31 years. He also taught equal employment law at Maryland Law School, wrote a treatise on employment law (that is now in its second edition), was annually recognized in Best Lawyers in America and chaired two civil rights organizations. In 2002, he retired early from his law firm to pursue graduate studies in art history at Johns Hopkins University. He subsequently wrote a book entitled Henry Walters and Bernard Berenson: Collector and Connoisseur, which was published in 2010 by The Johns Hopkins University Press. Stan presently serves as a Trustee of The Walters Art Museum.

(The first photo shows Stan providing nutrition to his pet monkey in Camarines Sur.)

Sally Pierce McCandless
Letters Home

When I was a freshman in high school, my mother took me out of school for an extended trip to Europe and the Middle East. I remember being so embarrassed about leaving my school because growing up in Vermont, none of my friends had ever done any traveling outside of the U.S. As a result of the trip, I was fascinated with the Middle East and that experience formed my desire to go back to a developing country.

I had planned to join a work camp sponsored by the United Nations after I graduated from college, but I was so fortunate to be a senior in college when President Kennedy was elected and the Peace Corps was formed. Again, I remember my mother sent me the application and it was perfect timing for me to join the PC.

In preparing to write this, I read many of the letters that I sent to my family during the two years. My mother would type up my letters and send them off to my five siblings. I'm fortunate to have them all to reread fifty years later. This has been an unusual experience for me because I have forgotten so many of the details. It is as though this was another person, not me. The experiences that I had could never have happened if I had stayed in the States and just followed a conventional career and marriage.

I am reminded in reading my letters about the time that I was the queen of the Philippine-American Fiesta that we had in our town. There was also the Filipina queen who was far prettier than I, but I was the token American. What an excruciating experience, but one that I had to do. (Making speeches was nothing compared to that!) This is what I wrote to my family on February 12, 1962:

> Good God, I've never spent so much time, effort and MONEY trying to look pretty and to no avail. Saturday afternoon, Mrs. Ledesma assigned her car and driver to take me from the hairdresser's to the make-up man, etc., and then she drove with me from Bacolod to San Enrique that night to help me dress for the coronation. The ceremony was around 12:30 AM and I was scared stiff that I wouldn't be able to sit down in my dress but I managed, and the only accident was that I tripped on it once while going up the stairs. My proclamation address was nice and short since I had

pleaded with the mayor to tell my proclaimer my wishes concerning this. But then, two congressmen bigwigs got hold of the mike and decided to turn the affair into a political rally. The speeches went on for one and a half hours, and my smile became dimmer and grimmer but I did manage to maintain my sense of humor. After the royal dance (my escort was very nice to me, poor fellow), I then had to dance with the politicians whom I definitely disagreed with their political positions.

Being at my barrio school didn't necessarily mean that all that time was spent in the classroom. I wrote my family:

> I've had a very busy time at school. I spent five nights from dusk to dawn Christmas caroling with my teachers. Here people carol to earn money and so we covered four different towns and raised about 700 pesos. I was an important part of the act. I sang "White Christmas" and joined my teachers in a couple of native dances.

What I didn't write because I was too embarrassed to relate a conversation that I had with one of my teachers and that was that she and others (probably everybody) thought that I enjoyed singing White Christmas because I missed all of my white friends and family!

I will always look at my country in a different way from most Americans that I know and read about. Having the opportunity to live among another people in another country for two years has been invaluable. I would like to think that I am more tolerant and understanding of others who have different backgrounds than I. My interest in politics and international relations developed during these two years.

I always said, even in my dark moments, that those two years would be the most eventful and memorable years of my life. And that is still true. I wrote my mother and siblings on April 24, 1963, near the end of stay, to ask their opinion about my extending my tour because I had been offered an interesting position and I said, "At the rate I am adjusting here, a year more could develop into a lifetime." I really needed sound advice. My mother wrote back, "You have had a priceless experience these past two years, but the final decision is yours. Of course we want to see you and it would be a much more comfortable feeling for all of us to have you within easy reach, but this is purely a selfish point of view and certainly not a typically Pierce one."

Needless to say, I returned home and after a year of a rather difficult adjustment, I have had a wonderful life. I continued in education, teaching at the United Nations International School, and then here in Houston being involved in both international education and public school education. I also married a loving, supportive man, and we have three daughters that are native Texans, a far cry from our New England upbringing.

Stan and Sally McCandless have lived in Houston for the last 40 years. They moved there from NYC when Shell Oil moved its headquarters to Houston. They have three daughters and four grandchildren. Their oldest daughter lives next door with their two grandsons. Two other daughters live in San Francisco and Los Angeles.

After the Peace Corps, Sally went to graduate school at Columbia University Teachers College to get an MA in Teaching English as a Foreign Language. She taught at the United Nations Inter-

national School during the '60s. Then in Houston, she taught at an international school for 17 years, coordinating the International Baccalaureate Program. Since 2000, she has been on the teaching staff of a non-profit educational foundation. She has coordinated various grants to set up family literacy programs, follow up our teacher training classes which support inner city schools, and participate in research projects for the efficacy of reading programs. She hopes to stay in the field of education…as long as she can be of service.

Stan and Sally love to travel and Sally loves to walk, read, and eat! Both are politically active and also enjoy being with our family and friends. Both look forward to the 50th anniversary reunion!!

(The first photo shows Sally dancing as the queen at the Philippine-American fiesta in San Enrique, Negros Occidental in 1962.)

Ray McEachern
The Time of My Life

Talk about a life changing experience: The Peace Corps was a Godsend, stuck, as I was, in what seemed like a dead end job as a first year English teacher at St. Petersburg High.

Oh, I was an okay teacher. I still have mementos from some of my students who were shocked that I was leaving to join the Peace Corps. But I was only there because of the trauma that ended my lifelong dream of becoming a professional pilot. I already considered myself a hotshot pilot in a Piper J-3 high wing airplane, having gotten a private pilot's license at the age of 16. My only interest in English then was the cute English teacher. As a college sophomore the dream crashed like the plane I had once flown as part owner in a flying club. The results of an eye exam for Naval Air Cadet training determined that I was color blind. Needing money to finish college, a teaching scholarship had been the only way forward.

The announcement of the Peace Corps was like a siren call! I couldn't wait to sign on the dotted line. It didn't matter where they sent me. The thought that I would now have a chance to work for world peace, instead of waiting for my draft number to come up at the local draft board, seemed to be God's way of paying me back for the lost dream of flying.

My only knowledge of the Philippines was that it was half way around the world.

Arriving on Philippine soil and being confined to Los Baños for training gave me my first glimpse of what lay ahead.

Abruptly, I became aware that our mission was not to teach English, but to serve as a model for how English should be spoken. The Filipinos knew English. It was spoken throughout the land, and my first thought was, "Hey, just get me out of this irrelevant training and let me go to my village and start living like a native." The fear that many of us would start "living like a native" was apparently why Peace Corps Headquarters assigned us to central towns in groups of four.

The Household in San Jose

My assignment was to San Jose, the *poblacion* for a group of barrios in the central Luzon province of Camarines Sur. My three roommates and I got a very sturdy two story house (with an outhouse) near the *parada* (the town square) and also near the homes of several of the wealthy land owners. We became instant celebrities, being wined and dined by the local power brokers. While we felt the allure of being friends with the upper class, who were generally well educated and fun to be around—plenty of Johnny Walker Black Label and American cigarettes—we soon came to feel that we weren't fulfilling our true Peace Corps role to live and mix with everyday Filipinos.

After a few months, the group split up; we each moved to separate barrios several kilometers from our previous location. One of the volunteers continued to live in what came to be called the "Town House," while another moved to a nipa hut on the beach at Sabang, which became our "Beach House." A third PCV took a house between the Town House and the Beach House which, of course, we referred to as the "Halfway House," and I moved to a nipa thatched three-room house in San Ramon, a barrio of the *poblacion* of Lagonoy.

As this house was the most distant, it inevitably was dubbed the "Out House." Ironically, it had no outhouse at all. My first project—after being embarrassed when I mistakenly found my visiting landlady relieving herself on what I thought was a back porch—was to build a bathroom with a water-sealed toilet. The landlady had once lived in the house, and the back platform, that I called a porch, had in fact been used as she was using it. This was my first observation of the much talked about "pig toilets," which I choose not to describe further.

Snapshots

- The memories of the two years I spent as a Peace Corps Volunteer are by far the most vivid and varied of any period of my life before or since. There are so many that I can only briefly summarize some of them here:
- The way my pet monkey, Okay, would turn his back and sulk if I passed him by on the way to the outhouse without stopping to allow him to groom me.
- The sounds of the hawkers at each train stop on the ride to Manila as they walked the isles shouting *"Tinacpay, Mainit Pa"* (Fresh Bread, still hot).
- The teacher who commented to me as we walked together down a street that women would stare at me from their windows in hopes that they would conceive a light-skinned child.
- The time I stood before a classroom of fifth grade students and was told to look out for the cobra that was crawling up the wall behind me. (If I had been in a U.S. school, I would have thought it was a joke—It wasn't.)
- My first trip back to Manila from Camarines Sur to stay for a few days with an American family in the upscale community of Forbes Park. This was a Peace Corps ordered therapy session for volunteers who might be going into "culture shock." How horrified the American family was when I brought along some *balut* and offered them one before eating one of the partially incubated duck eggs that are considered a delicacy.
- A trip through the islands on an inter island steamer where I met some wealthy young men in Dumaguete on a round-the-world adventure on their schooner, the *M/V Collegiate Rebel*. They had just come from Borneo and told me the story of the death of Michael Rockefeller at the hands of cannibals after, according to what they claimed, he had paid to instigate tribal warfare for his anthropological studies.
- Being robbed as I slept with dozens of other people on the deck of a crowded steamer on the way to Jolo. There, my complaint to the mayor got no results, but he told me about his two fast power boats named the Kennedy and the Nixon which he used to smuggle blue seal cigarettes from Borneo. (American made cigarettes, called "Blue Seal," were highly taxed and were very superior to the local brands.)
- While staying in Jolo and waiting for funds to be wired to pay for a return trip to my village, I visited one of the most beautiful white sand beaches I had ever seen. On the way back from the beach we came upon a road block of several fallen coconut trees. A local who loaned us bolos to clear the debris advised us that the road block was put in place by bandits to rob a bus. When we happened along before the bus came, the bandits chose not to rob

us because we were Americans. (They loved Americans, and may have known that we were broke Peace Corps Volunteers.)

• The night it got too dark for me to continue a trip in my small sailing *banca* (an outrigger canoe with a sail.) Belying the name I had given it (the *Bahala Na*, meaning "What Me Worry?"), I pulled it up on the beach where I saw the light of a fisherman about to go out for his nightly fishing trip. Struggling to use the Bicol dialect to tell him that I wanted to leave my boat at his house for the night, I learned that he spoke better English than I spoke Bicolano when he replied. No doubt he realized he couldn't possibly mess up English any worse than I had messed up Bicol.

• The month I spent in the hospital at Clark Air Force Base in a hepatitis ward filled with young American pilots from the nascent war in Viet Nam, and being asked to hold down the feet of a dying young man as a technician attempted to insert a catheter. The hospital and all of Clark AFB were later covered by volcanic ash from the 1980s eruption of Mount Pinatubo.

• The commotion at a bus stop one day as I was passing by which turned out to be a crowd consoling a woman with an infant who had a seriously bleeding open wound. The mother seemed resigned that the baby would soon die as there were no doctors nearby and she had no money to go to one. How rarely does one have the opportunity to help another human being—especially with so little effort on my part. Convincing her to let me help, we boarded the bus and went to a doctor's office in Goa where the baby's life was saved.

• The difficulty the San Jose volunteers faced in trying to secure funding for our summer boys' camp designed to encourage worthy teenagers to learn more about the world outside the Philippines. During sessions lasting into the wee hours we brain-stormed until we had the name we wanted—ORIOX that combined the orient with the occident—and the funding scheme that gave the landowners the opportunity to pick one camper for every three campers we picked—and the money flowed like the water over the Cagaycay dam at our campsite.

All these memories and more come to mind from a period in my life lasting not much longer than the combined gestation periods of my two sons, a period during which I can now recall not one thing other than their births.

A Child's Funeral in Lagonoy

Yet there is one more memory that stands above all others as summing up a period when the Peace Corps and I were both young and the unlimited promise of youth was yet to be tempered by the reality of life. It was the funeral of my Godchild. I wrote about it a few days later in a diary from which I now quote liberally. The story was written in the style of a stream of consciousness. I wrote:

> I'm not Catholic, so why am I standing here. I'm not even very religious, so why am I standing here in the burning sun in front of a wall of burial vaults watching the *portero* (a laborer who carries things) use a claw hammer to break open a vault. After a half dozen-or-so swings the cement breaks away and I am overwhelmed by the foul smell.
>
> "It has been five years since that vault was last used. Three years is long enough for a child," says the priest. He is standing on one side of me. I can't remember his name.

"I think your godchild died because you had a beard when he was baptized," the priest continues laughing. My godchild's father, my *padi* (the local word for a compadre), is standing next to me. He is barefoot and beardless as are most Filipinos, and I, too, have shaved the beard I wore for awhile before I decided the beard was more trouble than shaving in cold water.

The *portero* pulls out the rotting coffin and tosses it, piece by piece, over the wall. We watch as he pushes the brown, disintegrating, tiny skull of the previous occupant toward the back of the crypt, and slides the coffin of little Fredericko inside.

It was just seven month ago that I stood in the shed that had been built inside the walls of the old, roofless church in Lagonoy holding little Fredericko Panuncio in my arms as the nameless priest touched his forehead with holy water.

I had moved to barrio San Ramon to escape the landowners in San Jose who had filled most of my nights with parties and outings with exotic foods like the *kanding* (a goat stew) that I disliked but ate as long as there was plenty of Tanduay Rum or San Miguel Beer to wash it down. They had record albums of the latest hits from back home, and generators to provide electricity so they didn't have to rely on the city electric company that provided electricity for only three hours a night.

The parties didn't stop when I moved to my little nipa hut across the street from the school house where I taught, but instead of Tanduay Rum, now it was tuba, the homemade brew that everyone drank from a common cup. Instead of modern hits from home, there were native songs and stories of leprechaun-like creatures who watched from the fields as we made our way along darkened roads. There were many men who called me their '*padi*,' but only one who got the courage to ask me to actually be his compadre—to be the godfather of his first-born who was due very soon.

He wasn't concerned about my religion. He may not have even realized that there was any other religion but Catholicism. Eager to fit in, I had accepted without knowing much about the tradition behind it. Then, yesterday, Fredericko's mother had stopped at my house on her way home from Goa where she had taken the baby to the health clinic. He died there of bronchitis. He was with her, stiff in the arms of a friend, eyes open, not seeing. I went with them to their house and stood mute as her husband, my *padi*, learned that Fredericko had died.

He ran his hand over the little lifeless head and then squatted beside the body in the Filipino tradition without speaking.

"*Diang Suerte*," (no luck) I had said. "*Sayang*" (such a waste). I, too, squatted beside him for awhile and then left as people gathered and a carpenter arrived to craft the tiny coffin.

The next day I returned to the house of my *padi* to find a festive atmosphere. There was roast pork and someone suggested it might be my pig that had been stolen several months before.

A drunken member of the Philippine Constabulary who had come to enjoy the food claimed that I must be a spy sent by the USA instead of just a simple teacher. Why was I there, he asked, pretending to be like the poor farmers when everyone knew I could leave whenever I wanted to but they could not. I realized he had a point but I just laughingly replied that I hadn't learned any secrets and that I didn't think the CIA needed to know how to plow with a carabao. An old lady folded some *buyo* (betel) leaves around a piece of a lime and gave it to me to chew. I hadn't tried it before, and the sweet taste of the mild narcotic gave me a slight rush which I quickly spit out to the delight of those who chewed it often.

Soon a bus arrived to take everyone to the church. The father explained to me that he felt he had to hire the bus despite the expense because the day was hot and the distance to the church far. I gave him a few pesos, and felt guilty that I could not afford more.

The requiem mass began with the clanging of bells, shaking of water, and waving of incense. I thought to myself that with a priest and five assistants this must be a 10-peso funeral service. I tried to put such thoughts out of my head, knowing that ritual should inspire spiritual.

Afterward, as we walked to the cemetery, my *padi* explained that he could not afford the usual band of musicians to play the upbeat music that would normally be played at the funeral of a child. He said when a child dies, people play happy music because the child is surely going straight to heaven. I resolved to give him a few more pesos as soon as possible.

The *portero* covers the opening of the burial vault with new cement and the service is over.

Ray McEachern is from Plant City, Florida, a town which bills itself as the "Winter Strawberry Capital of the World." Retired from the ownership of several small businesses, he lives with his wife, Pat, and two dogs, Blossom and Febe, not far from his hometown. He still attends his high school class reunions annually, dotes on his grandchildren all under the age of four, and spends much of his time advocating for the release of a wrongfully convicted man on Florida's death row for 34 years for whom he maintains a website, www.freetommyz.com.

After his service as a Peace Corps Volunteer in the Philippines in 1963, Ray spent 5 years on the staff of Peace Corps/Washington and several more years with other federal agencies before returning home to raise his family.

(The first photo shows Ray standing with fellow PCVs Tim Peterson, Bernice Koffler, and Barbara Gladysiewicz at Camp Orlox, where they were serving as counselors in the summer of 1962.)

Barbara Bassett McIver
Some Old, Old Memories

I find it very difficult to write of my experience as a Peace Corps volunteer in the Philippines Group I contingent from 1961 to 1963 because that experience seems but a stitch in the fabric of my 75-year life. After training at Pennsylvania State University and then Los Baños in the Philippines, four of us were dispatched to our assignment in the small town of Magarao, Camarines Sur at the southern end of the island of Luzon.

Once we had arrived, we began getting acquainted with our hosts who seemed intent on displaying us at endless rounds of parties and fiestas. These social events intensified during the 1961 Christmas holiday season, leaving us mentally and physically exhausted. One excursion in January 1962 took us on a one-day visit to 21 barrio schools over rough roads with the District Superintendent, several school principals, and teachers. We were all bright eyed and bushy tailed before we left. After the trek, which included a *merienda* snack at each school, I think we lost some of that enthusiasm. At the time though, we were young, thoughtful and trying to please our hosts, who were also doing everything they could to please us. Adding these social activities to six  months of training, the long journey across the Pacific and down the Luzon Peninsula to our communities, the unfamiliar countryside and people, and the minor discomforts along the way created a strain, which made some of us wonder just what the hell we were doing!

As I look over my old Peace Corps papers, letters, photos, and memorabilia from that time, I have the distinct recollection that much of the Peace Corps program in the Philippines was not planned, but grew out of a general outline scribbled in place in Washington D.C.. After all, we were the first of the volunteers. As is Washington's wont, when they have a plan, the protocol is to make the plan operation ASAP while the general enthusiasm is on the uptick.

Meanwhile our kind and hospitable hosts tried to figure out what they would do with this influx of willing and enthusiastic volunteers of various skills (which did not necessarily include teaching English as a second language) in order to satisfy Washington and make the program work. As usual "the devil was in the details' and this became more apparent to our hosts and the volunteers within our first six months of on-site living.

I often thought that our Filipino hosts, who had little pre-knowledge, little pre-planning, and little certainty of the skills the volunteers would bring to their assignments were extremely kind and generous to us with our frequently grandiose schemes which often didn't meet the Filipinos' real needs. They always tried to make us feel welcome and comfortable and were willing to adapt their homes and communities to our invasion. I'm not sure I would have been so generous.

I cannot say, even today, that the Peace Corps was, or is, a great program. It certainly captured the imagination of the United States and other countries around the world. While in the Philippines I received a letter of inquiry from a group in Germany. However, as in all firsts (i.e. tests, experiences, trials, and new programs,) there must be a first endeavor. Nothing ventured, nothing gained. We were the venturers.

As we four volunteers struggled with our assignments after the first of the year, it became quickly apparent that Pat Nash (who was a medical professional) and Karen Cole (who had expertise other than teaching) wanted to find work in their respective fields of expertise. Brenda Brown and I both had some teaching experience prior to coming to the Philippines and were prepared to work in the original education program. Before everything was settled, we received word that we were being evicted from our house in Magarao. Although I was not yet attuned to the subtleties of Filipino cultural interactions at the time, I think the landlord wanted more rent! As a consequence of the eviction and the desire of Karen Cole and Pat Nash to find work in the fields elsewhere, Brenda and I heard of a rental opportunity "down the road" in the teeming metropolis of Naga City.

Naga City wasn't a barrio. It was the provincial capital of Camarines Sur, a real urban community with a population of about 55,000 people. It had a movie house, jeepneys (the multiple fare jeep taxi cabs gloriously decorated in the driver/owner's own inimitable art work), a soda stand that sold San Miguel beer and ice cream (both delicious), a public high school, a girls' private high school, and a boys' private high school, the Jesuit run Ateneo de Naga. I guess I'm a big city girl because I loved Naga and obtained a teaching job at Naga High School. It was a little harder on Brenda because she continued to work at Magarao elementary and intermediate school, requiring her to use the jeepney back and forth between Naga and Magarao every day.

In spite of our eviction we put some programs in place in Magarao during that first summer. Brenda and I started a free community library and a free summer day-camp. Two of our fellow volunteers, Mary Teasler and Janet Wright came to Magarao to help us get our programs under way. Brenda's mother and mine separately went out into their respective communities and beat the bushes (and other people) until we had many books coming to our library and sports equipment coming to our summer camp. We also obtained the support of some fine young men and women from the private high schools in Naga City who gave freely of their time to supervise the young campers.

I am able to recall many memories as I go through memorabilia of these grand, but sometimes sad times. I especially miss my dear friends Tom Carlton and Carol Byrnes, who each passed away well before their times. Many times during those two years they made my heart sing with laughter: Tom insisting that we go to the Naga movie house because they had a film with a "cast of thousands" and Carol's frequent and raucous greetings to me in her inter-island letters: Dear Gunga Din!" (I was affected with a mysterious, creepy, crawly skin ailment at the time).

We had some great times: the spas at Los Baños, the white water ride at Pagsanjan Falls, and our inter-island cruise to Mindanao where we slept on the boat's deck and found it terribly relaxing. I also fondly recall a Mrs. Smith who had lived in the Philippines for forty years with her engineer husband who was then working at the iron mines in Larap, Camarines Norte. They had both spent World War II in the Ateneo de Manila as prisoners of the Japanese. Despite this cruelty, the Smiths assured us their home would always be in the Philippines.

On that last Memorial Day in 1963, Tom Carlton and I (along with some others) went to the island of Corregidor off the Bataan Peninsula. On this desolate island we saw the terrible, corrugated steel tunnel where General Wainwright and the Filipino and American soldiers were trapped for so long before they began their horrible death march into Manila. One could imagine the horror of the noise from the constant bombardment. After 20 years the trees that then grew on the peninsula were small saplings. We heard no birds sing.

Later in Manila, we went out to the American Cemetery, which was glorious. We saw thousands of white crosses set in rows and surrounded by magnificent red flame trees. We took pictures which I sent to my mother to share with her contemporaries, many who had lost their sons in the Asian Theatre. My mother told me it was comforting for them to see that magnificent cemetery where some of their sons had been buried.

Finally, I still believe in the vision of a better world as I did in 1960 when President John Kennedy issued his call. In the message put so succinctly by Reverend William Hollister and quoted in our 25th Anniversary bulletin:

> Go into the world in peace and of good cheer.
> Do not give back evil for evil.
> Strengthen the faint hearted and support the weak.
> Fight injustice wherever you find it.
> Do not stifle inspiration in yourself or anybody else
> And be very tender to yourself and everyone else.

Upon returning from the Peace Corps, Barbara decided not to go back into teaching. At the suggestion of her father, she signed up for what she considered the quirky idea of becoming a policewoman in Detroit. After her acceptance she attended the Police Academy for training and simultaneously returned to Law School at night. Although she hated shooting guns and lost her police badge during the training program, she became a police officer. During the Detroit riots of 1967, she was shot wearing plain clothes while entering the 14th precinct station. Following the riots, Barbara was elected to the Policeman's Union, where she quickly started an unfair labor suit against the Department, which the union won, but made life less enjoyable in the Department.

Having finished law school and passed the Bar Examination, Barbara left police work in Detroit and became an Assistant Prosecutor in Jackson County, Michigan. She ran for Probate Judge three months after arriving, but lost the election. The local Circuit Court judges, however, liked her work and asked her to become a "Friend of the Court," where she worked on the support provisions of broken marriages. While living in Jackson County she got married. She returned with her husband to the Detroit area where Barbara was hired by the Michigan Attorney General to become an Assistant Attorney General, working on Treasury, Labor and Liquor Commission issues.

Barbara gave birth to a son Matthew in 1970 and because her husband thought it would be a great idea, moved with the family to a northern rural part of Michigan. She found work 50 miles away, but he could not find anything. Working at Legal Aid, she was supervisor to the civil division. While she enjoyed the job supervising the junior attorneys, the commute became too much to bear. She returned to Detroit where she became the Chief Deputy Judicial Assistant for the 36th District Court.

Separated from her husband, Barbara and her son survived his obnoxious teen age years. He subsequently married a woman who keeps him on the straight and narrow. There are no grandchildren, but Barbara has said that at this stage of the game, she would probably drop them. Barbara has travelled extensively in Europe, Turkey, Egypt, Africa and Russia. She still golfs "in her own fashion" and works at the local food pantry.

(The first photo shows Barbara to the right of fellow volunteer Pat Nash and surrounded by other teachers on a visit to Calabanga, Camarines Sur in December 1961; the second photos shows Barbara at her 75th birthday in 2010.)

Warren McNeely
What I Took Away From San Jose

We were a very loose household of four young men in San Jose Partido, Camarines Sur. Or was it only two? Or three? Nope, in the end just one, me and Jose, the house boy. I don't really remember how many of us started out in the San Jose house, I kept no diary or journal, but it must have been four. Soon, however, Ray McEachern was off to Lagonoy and Tim Peterson to Sabang. That left Bruce Campbell and me until Bruce was romanced into a nipa hut in Kinalansan. We all saw each other occasionally, or that's how I remember it. They had moved off to the barrios and I maintained the group house with the help of Jose. San Jose was a town of about 2000 people in a rice growing section of Camarines Sur, just inland from the Lagonoy Gulf and about two hours by road from Naga City, the Provincial Capital.

We had gotten a number of recently published books via the Peace Corps and started a lending library out of the house. That brought in adults and kids to keep Bruce, Jose and myself entertained. In fact, we always had a contingent of kids hanging around, just outside our front door. We did our daily school routines, which consisted of helping students and teachers with their English, math or science. We also attended all the social events we were invited to—which were inordinately many by our thinking, but great fun, unless we had the trots. There were a lot of interesting things that happened and since I did not keep a journal, I have forgotten so many of them. There is the one really big thing that happened; it came the last week I was there, but more on that later.

My most memorable trip in Camarines Sur took several of us to the municipality of Caramoan, located on the peninsula almost due east of San Jose, but only reachable by a 2-3 hour boat ride across the bay. We stayed there with Dr. Nilo Roa and his family. From there we took a short, less than one hour, ride in a dugout to Haponan a small island with a large population of fruit bats. Upon arriving we had lunch of fish and rice in the small nipa hut of the local headman. Afterward we went hunting and came back to Dr. Roa's with several fruit bats which were fixed adobo style. Eat your heart out Andrew Zimmern (Zimmern is the host of the Travel Channel's TV show Bizarre Foods)!!

I spent one school vacation in Davao City at the Ateneo de Davao assisting in the training of science teachers. The field trips there, which took us to study tidal pools were great fun. While in Davao I occasionally enjoyed the notorious durian fruit. Beat you again, Andrew. I spent my second school vacation period at the International Rice Research Institute in Los Baños doing a statistics project. I enjoyed that very much because it was located very near our training site on the slope of Mt. Makiling. This project permitted me to visit Mrs. Bautista, our old friend from town during training days, who had enjoyed cooking hamburgers for us in her little café.

The last week of my stay in San Jose, a railroad car arrived in Naga City filled with books from the U.S. My friends David and Carol Smith from the Seattle area had set about collecting books from all around the Pacific Northwest and induced the Navy to carry them, I think via aircraft carrier, to the Philippines. The Navy presumably loaded them into a boxcar; when they arrived in Naga, the Philippine Constabulary loaded them onto a truck and brought them out to San Jose. After they were dumped in the bodega of our good friend Miguel Obias, I spent what little time I had left sorting them out for delivery to the different schools where we had worked. The principal of San Jose School had organized the construction of a library because we had told him that the books were coming but not when. I remembered many of the books I was sorting from my days in elementary school. Yep, they were old! The schools were really quite happy to get them, however.

In 1969 my wife at that time and I visited old friends in Camarines Sur. We spent six weeks in the province, going again to Caramoan by boat and being hosted in San Jose by Tomas Obias, who also took us around Mt Mayon. We had travelled south from Manila by train, spending half a day sitting at the nowhere town of Candalaria due to problems on the track. I remember the joy of boiled peanuts, maize, sweet rice and fried bananas as we sat there waiting for the train to move. In fact some of my best memories from the Philippines come from bus or train rides and all the people, animals and food along the way

I learned a bit about myself and about helping others complete community projects while in the Philippines. I had thought about becoming a missionary, but my PC experience convinced me otherwise. I did become a teacher and taught high school math and science until 1978. The most enduring lesson I have taken from the experience is that host country projects started by host country citizens are usually more enduring than projects started by outsiders. There are exceptions to that, but not many. The library at the San Jose elementary school, for instance, was a project which was built by the locals. Well, I guess when you know a boxcar full of books is coming your way, you do what needs to be done to make use of it.

After the Peace Corps Warren returned to the University of Puget Sound, obtained a teaching certificate, and started working toward a Masters Degree in Science which he acquired in 1969. He taught high school science and math from 1965 until 1978. In the fall of 1978 he spent three months hitchhiking in England and Scotland. In the early 1980s, he began a second career in sports photography specializing in photos of runners in 10K races and Marathons, which he pursued until 1998. Since 2002, he has been retired and living off social security.

Warren married in 1964 and got divorced in 1977. The marriage produced a son in 1970 and a daughter in 1972. Since 1984, he has been living and playing tennis with, but not married to, his business partner.

Ray Meyer
On Becoming a Peace Corpz

A half century ago? It's a little hard to imagine, let alone remember. But we were there in 1961. I remember that I wasn't shaving yet, the Cold War was raging, and, if somebody had given me a map and asked me to find the Philippines because that's where I would soon be spending the next 10 years of my life, I might have said, "Yeah, and typewriters will soon become obsolete."

I also remember quite clearly one evening in early March of '61. I was getting ready for my classes the next day. Someone at school had mentioned that Mr. Kennedy was speaking, either live or at a press conference recorded earlier—I didn't know, but it would be on the radio. I had listened to his Inaugural Address a couple of months before and felt I "knew" this man. My idealism was running unchecked at the time. He had spoken directly to me. So put aside the stack of papers, the textbook, and books from the library scattered around my chair. This was President Kennedy visiting my little Hollywood apartment.

The Peace Corps? That's what he said: I think he invited me to join it. So before I did another thing, I found a blank piece of paper, probably mimeograph paper, and wrote: "Dear Sir (yes, I'm sure it was just 'Sir'), please send me information about how to apply for the Peace Corps." I've wondered many times since what the volume of mail was at "Peace Corps, Washington, D.C." (That's how I addressed my inquiry.) after President Kennedy's announcement.

And then I waited. I told Wilma Schneidermeyer, another English teacher at school, what I had done. It felt almost conspiratorial; it would, after all, involve "serving in a foreign country." I was only vaguely aware of what espionage entailed. The big envelope arrived before the summer recess; I filled out the papers and agreed that the FBI could check my "references" and background. Would they find out about what I did in high school?

Then I enrolled in two literature classes at Sacred Heart College: Medieval and Romantic. I would have to take 'Incomplete' in both, because sometime in July the "You have been selected" telegram arrived. Wilma S. and her husband took over the payments on my 1960 Vauxhall, I let my family in St. Louis know, called Sacred Heart College to see if I could come back in a couple years and finish those two courses, and asked a school counselor if I could store a few things with him until I got back.

I can't remember exactly when we "reported to'" Penn State for training. But I do recall my first ride in an airplane. My ears hurt. And I never knew before that I was afraid of heights. Dave King and I were roommates. The term anthropology was used a lot in classes. And I 'discovered linguistics, the concept of culture (I hoped nobody would find out that my liberal arts background omitted these things completely.) and names like Margaret Mead and Ruth Benedict. I'm sure that I fell asleep in class, but that training opened many doors for me. I became much more certain of why I had 'joined the Peace Corps'. Quite simply, it was to change the world! That's what we were all there for.

After the experience in Bato, the fishing village known for the tiny tilapia that grew in the lake, and where I learned from an old woman with a radio that Mr. Kennedy had been shot, and where Wally Allen, Doug Schmidt, Dave King and I had gotten off a Beltranco bus not many months before and walked with our umbrellas in hand down the street to the nipa house that Mr. Pili had built as a rental to the new Peace Corps volunteers, only after that did I realize our true purpose: We were there in the Philippines to learn, not only about reciprocity and shame and Aguinaldo, but about ourselves. We all did that, didn't we!

It's 50 years later, of course. And there's the possibility that we might celebrate our golden anniversary together next year. I regret that I will come, knowing that I haven't done a thing in all this time to contact anybody. I still don't know why that is. Because of all the people I've known in my life since the Peace Corps, only a dozen or so would measure up to the dozens of people I came to know in those two short years.

After leaving the Peace Corps, Ray Meyer remained in the Philippines till the end of the 1960s. He married a Filipina, attended a grad program at the Ateneo de Manila and became an English teacher at several universities in the Manila area. Three of his four children were born during these years.

Ray spent the years from 1969-1979 as an English and Social Studies teacher for the Department of Defense Dependent Schools, starting off at Clark Air Base in Pampanga. He also taught in Okinawa where a fourth child was born and then headed to Mannheim, Germany for five years. Before going to Germany, the University of Maryland granted him an MA in Counseling.

In 1979, Ray returned home: the '60s and the '70s had come and gone! He woke up as a broker for insurance and financial services, living in Duluth, Minnesota, his marriage finished, and his kids heading for high school. He began buying running shoes and eventually started running ultra/50 mile races. He met Cathy Montgomery, a school psychologist, in Minneapolis. They commuted the 160 miles for 11 years until he moved to Minneapolis in 1995.

In Minneapolis, Ray returned to the field of education, first as a substitute teacher and ESL teacher for adults. He spent three years as an English/Language Arts teacher at the Hennepin County Juvenile Detention Center, an activity that rivaled the Peace Corps as a personal challenge. In 2008, he retired from teaching and married Cathy.

The four children survived the hectic years. The oldest, Stuart, is a stay-at-home dad now after working as an engineer for seven years. Ray's second son, Vince, graduated with a degree in fine arts and chose to work in sales. He went back to the Philippines five years ago and married a girl he met in grade school in Legaspi, Albay. Ray's daughter Cheryl spent a year in high school in Germany and later a year in France, graduating with a degree in modern languages. Cheryl earned another undergrad degree in photojournalism and is now also the recipient of two Pulitzers. The youngest son, Terry, has a PhD in engineering and teaches at Iowa State. All four speak Bicol.

Gerald W. Mullins

A Grand Adventure: A Peace Corps Memoir

How It All Began

You might say it all began aboard that propeller driven Slick Airlines plane from San Francisco to Manila. As I recall, we were in the air some twenty-eight hours, with stops in Hawaii, Wake Island and Guam. The year was 1961. Our Peace Corps group, 128 in number, had just completed eight weeks of training at Penn State University. Being together that length of time, we were a tight-knit group. Bonds were formed that in some cases led to marriage, in many others to life-long friendship. That long flight—though exhausting—was fun-filled and the mood was light-hearted. A number of people had stashed refreshments in their belongings. I remember a quart-sized bottle of Southern Comfort being passed around in my section. (To some degree that Peace Corps movie with John Candy that came out a few years later was not too far off base.) The stop-over on Wake Island was particularly memorable. Several of the macho-type guys (yes, I considered myself one) decided to take a quick underwear dip in the ocean near the runway… until a Navy guy came running toward us yelling "Sharks!" I still have this vivid picture of my friend Frank Krajewski bolting from the water so fast he nearly lost his Jockey shorts.

Then again, you might say it all began as we headed out to our barrios (villages) following another session of training at the University of the Philippines College of Agriculture. For the group of us heading to the Bicol region, this involved another long trip… this time by open air (therefore dusty) rail travel from Manila to Legaspi. Again, a very tedious journey, but "oh so interesting." It was a great way to get a feel for the rural Philippines. Upon arriving in Legaspi, we were greeted by host families for the night, prior to heading out to our assignments the next day. Ted Kelly and I spent the evening with the Dr. Javier family and joked privately that this would be our last taste of civilization for awhile… a warm shower, White Horse scotch before dinner and a marvelous feast of Filipino delicacies in a living room with a "to die for" view of majestic Mayon Volcano.

Actually…I'm getting way ahead of myself. The real beginning of my Peace Corps experience was perhaps rooted in the visit by then presidential hopeful, John F. Kennedy to the Marquette University campus in March of 1960. It was during the important primary election campaign in Wisconsin. I was part of the huge crowd when Kennedy spoke in the old Clybourn Street gym on the campus. Yes, I found him charismatic and "likeable." I joined the Kennedy bandwagon and, in the months that followed, worked on the Kennedy campaign as a member of the campus Young Democrats. When the Peace Corps idea was aired some months later, it was not surprising I got caught up in it immediately. I graduated from Marquette in June of 1961 and entered the Peace Corps training program for the Philippines project the following August.

On Assignment in the Bicol

The time I spent in the Philippines as a volunteer was divided between two assignments. Together with Stu Taylor, Jim Sousane and Duncan Yaggy, I was assigned to Santo Domingo, Albay in southern Luzon, in the region known as the Bicol. Santo Domingo is a beautiful seaside village at the base of Mayon Volcano and along the Albay Gulf. During the second part of my Philippines assignment, I teamed with John Bossany and worked with staff member Bill Warren as a Volunteer Leader (PCVL) in Mindanao and Sulu. Our job there was to lay the groundwork for volunteers who were to follow some months later.

Each of these assignments was special in its own way. In Albay, the four of us volunteers were housed with the Balin family in what was to become known as the "Shriver House." Director Shriver and a small advance group had visited our site several months earlier and personally selected the location as a spot for the assignment of some of the first volunteers in the Philippines. We were the fortunate ones to land where we did and to become adopted sons of the marvelous Balins, led by family patriarch, retired teacher and principal in Santo Domingo, Diego Balin.

Each of us was assigned to a separate school. Mine was in barrio San Fernando, some four kilometers from Santo Domingo. What a warm reception I received as I became a member of the small school staff (six teachers), and part of the barrio community.

On the whole, the four of us in the household got along fine. Though it was challenging at times to find "independent space," somehow we managed. It helped that we were able to pursue our individual interests in addition to the work we did in the schools. Among my favorite pastimes was walking the quarter mile or so from our house to Kalayukai Beach, a beautiful palm-fringed black sand beach in Santo Domingo. Before too long, I was greeted by dozens of children who wished to communicate with me as I walked along. *"Jed dy, Ma sa In Ka?"* (Where are you going?) With my few words of the Bicol language, I would respond, *"Sa dagat"* (the beach). This got to be quite a ritual, repeated dozens of times on each trip to "the *dagat.*"

Among other highlights of my stay in Santo Domingo was a summer scout camp (held at Kalayukai Beach) and a three-day trek to the summit (yes, the actual tip) of Mayon Volcano.

As an Eagle Scout back home in Wisconsin, the camp idea was one I took to with much enthusiasm. While scouting was big in the Philippines I found that opportunities for actual "camping" were somewhat limited. Together with a number of Filipino scout leaders from Legaspi, we put together quite a good program (ocean swimming, trekking, nature study, survival skills, etc.). Overall, it was quite a success—and a lot of fun.

Climbing Mount Mayon—from sea level to the southeast, not from the rest house to the northwest—was quite an adventure. Together with a friend from the scout camp program, Ramon Balquin, we set off on what would be an arduous but exhilarating three-day trek. We set up a base camp at the mid-way point up the volcano and spent the first night there, with plans to ascend to the summit and back to the base camp on day two. As sometimes happens, day two required far more time than we anticipated. Yes, we made it to the top—a somewhat scary experience due to the uneasy footing near the crater and the strong smell of sulfur. Getting there, however, proved to be only half the battle. The real challenge was getting back to base camp before nightfall. We were unsuccessful in doing so and ended up working our way back to our tent and camp in darkness. Fortunately, we had a fair amount of moonlight on this particular evening and made it without incident—totally exhausted but without major injury or harm.

Years later, a principal friend posed the question to me, "What was the most challenging outdoor experience you've ever had?" Immediately—without hesitation—I cited the Mayon Volcano experience.

Mindanao, Oh Mindanao

The second phase of my Philippines Peace Corps experience was as a Volunteer Leader for Mindanao and the Sulu Islands. While I was very much enjoying my time in Albay in the Bicol region, I nevertheless accepted an invitation from staff member Bill Warren to work with him as a PCVL. Perhaps that continuing "spirit of adventure" prompted me to do so. I was also influenced by the respect—and friendship—I had developed for Bill and Jay Warren from our working together in the Bicol. What great people they are! Then when I learned I would be teamed with John Bossany in this new assignment, I knew it was the right decision. John and I eventually became "like brothers" and though we worked hard we also had lots of good times together. The job we had was huge—laying the groundwork for a large contingent of volunteers (Group VII) scheduled to arrive in September of 1962. Our travels entailed airplane, inter-island ferry and ground transportation (jeep). We were stationed in Zamboanga; however our territory encompassed all of Mindanao and Sulu. It was indeed adventurous. I personally covered most of Mindanao by jeep with the exception of the far northeast part of the island. Some time later, Ralph Thomas was recruited to cover this northeast area around Surigao.

With a schedule of constant travel and a return to Zamboanga to "recharge," John and I decided we needed to put down some roots in the Zamboanga area. (We had been living in the Normal College dormitory.) From a few beach trips around Zamboanga, we discovered a place called Caragasan Beach. Voila! We decided to put up a small, humble beach house there to have a place to call home. It was a great decision. We again became part of a barrio community and enjoyed the most idyllic beach house imaginable. It was a house on stilts, literally on the water during times of high tide. We had a great lanai overlooking the Sulu Sea with a million dollar view of the sunsets and our own coral reef for snorkeling. Outside, in a seaside coconut grove, we strung a hammock. As I later joked with people about this paradise setting, "I peaked too early." At twenty-three years of age, what in my future life could possibly top this?

The Caragasan Beach house later became somewhat famous as assorted photographers captured it for "cover photo" opportunities. (Friends sent me copies after my departure). Among the photos is a large cover picture from a Caltex calendar, a cover photo on a copy of the *Philippine Journal of Education*, and the cover picture of the *Stars and Stripes* newspaper (September 6, 1964). The description of the house on stilts usually mentioned it being a "typical Filipino nipa hut." They were unaware that it was the creation of these two *Americanos*, John and Jerry from the U.S. Midwest. I might add that John met his wife-to-be, Cely, at about this time. Since he was frequently away spending time with her and her family, I ended up having the beach house much to myself.

In hindsight, being assigned to these two distinct locations, Albay in the Bicol and Zamboanga at the southern tip of Mindanao, was a unique experience. In many ways, it "doubled the fun" for me. I put down roots and became part of each of the two communities, establishing friendships in both places that have lasted to today.

Looking Back...and Ahead

A question frequently asked of returned volunteers is, "What do you see as some of the benefits of the Peace Corps?" What effect our Peace Corps project had in the Philippines is difficult to assess. As an education project, measurement of "results" is not easy. One hopes, however, that our presence there did make a difference—particularly in the lives of the children.

For me personally, in addition to leading me toward a career in education, in a very real sense the experience contributed to my being a global citizen, a credential I have maintained throughout my adult life. I also maintain that an often-overlooked benefit to our larger society as a result of service in the Peace Corps is that we are developing a huge contingent of "area specialists" among our citizens. One cannot help but have an endearing attachment to the people and places where one has lived, worked, celebrated—and commiserated—over a two-year period. As a Peace Corps volunteer, I personally have come to love the Philippines and the Filipino people. I feel fortunate the Peace Corps provided me with the opportunity for such a grand adventure, and to get to know the Philippines so well.

In closing, while I may not necessarily have "peaked too early" in my career as a result of the Peace Corps, it was, nevertheless, an experience of a lifetime and one that was formative in terms of my future. I have genuinely enjoyed working with children and young adults throughout these many years, much as I did in those early days with the Peace Corps. I stayed in the education field far longer than most of my colleagues, recently retiring in 2008.

The sense of adventure and wanderlust developed during those Peace Corps years hasn't totally left me. At the time of this writing, I am preparing for a trip to Hawaii for the 50th Anniversary of the East-West Center and an International Conference in Honolulu. A side trip I am planning while there is a visit to Kauai and a hike along the Kalalau Trail on the Na Pali Coast. The spirit of adventure continues....

After leaving the Philippines in June of 1963—following some travel in Asia and some free time at home in Wisconsin—Jerry accepted a position with the Peace Corps Training Staff in Puerto Rico. He was an instructor in the Outward Bound program there for trainees prior to assignments in Latin America. Following a year in Puerto Rico, his island hopping continued into the fall of 1964 when he headed off to Hawaii for a two-year grant at the East-West Center. He received a master's degree in Asian Studies from the University of Hawaii in 1966. Eventually, his travels led him back to Wisconsin where he embarked on a long career in education. With a PhD in Education from the University of Wisconsin, his career included positions from principal at various levels to Superintendent.

Throughout his career, Jerry continued his interest in Asia—Philippines, Japan and Korea in particular. He currently is serving on the Board of Directors of Wisconsin—Chiba, Inc., a sister-state program between Wisconsin and Japan's Chiba prefecture.

In retirement, Jerry lives with his wife Gail in a suburb of Milwaukee. Their son Brian is an attorney with the Federal government who lives nearby on Milwaukee's east side.

Patricia Nash

Mission Sunday

It was Sunday, October 20, 2002, and as I was watching CNN, various, sometimes bothersome, intrusive, distracting news and information strips progressed across the bottom of my television screen. Suddenly, one caught my attention and provoked a vivid memory of an October Sunday exactly 40 years ago. The item was a news release from the Roman Catholic Papacy that it was Mission Sunday—a day the church set aside to promote evangelism—mission efforts—in various parts of the world.

The words on the screen quite literally grabbed me—whisked me away—transported me immediately back to that late October Sunday in 1962, when I was a Peace Corps volunteer stationed high in the northern mountains of the Philippines. I instantly turned the TV off, seated myself in front of my word processer and began to write, starting, if you will, by setting the scene.

Yes, I was back in the northern part of the Philippine main Island of Luzon in the tiny settlement of Mayoyao in the Ifugao sub-province of the large Mountain Province. It was a place quite isolated from the outside world—a three day bus trip from Manila and, most of the time, the nearest other Peace Corps volunteer.

Mayoyao was in an area that was fascinating to me for many reasons—but primarily because it was situated in rice terrace country, an area of extensive terracing of the mountain sides. The Ifugao people were historically responsible for construction of these wonders and worked and maintained them to that day.

These terraces were indeed something else—considered by some on a par with the Seven Wonders of the World. They were incredibly amazing structures—kilometer after kilometer—thousands of kilometers of them. Rice terracing hand built over a period of some 1500 years by native peoples—truly magnificent engineering feats.

They could be described as very small fields dug out of the sides of mountains—some buttressed with stone walls—walls 20, 40, even reputed to be as high as 80 feet. In the immediate area where I was located, the terracing was accomplished for the most part by using sod in the absence of plentiful large stones. As time passed, however, the carefully positioned sod blocks became strong enough to essentially act as stonework.

And even more awe-inspiring were the Ifugao people—the twentieth century descendants of the original builders, still living in very much the same way as their ancestors.

Life truly had changed little for these mountain dwellers over the centuries. Most lived on small family patches of land handed down for generations in the larger terraced scene. A family's property would consist mainly of a portion of irrigated rice terrace land and a small hut. Much of the irrigation water was captured high in the mountains in the form of rain, moved downward in streams and extensive irrigation ditches and channels.

Living on their small properties, the Ifugao effectively utilized every square foot of land and space available. Their pyramidal huts were elevated on strong posts some four to eight feet above the ground—interior living space dimensions about ten by ten with high roofs. The posts, walls, roof frames and floors were made from first class hard wood brought in from stands of trees often some distance away. Roofs were woven from a native grass-like plant called cogon, while the ground under them and the immediate surrounding area were often covered with closely placed flattish stones.

Beneath each hut would be a large, hand chiseled, stone mortar and pestle for grinding the rice grown in the surrounding terraces—the main staple, of course, of their diets. Also, more than likely, some chickens, a few pigs, perhaps a mongrel dog, would be in residence. Affixed below the elevated hut were various sized hand woven baskets used for storage or to transport goods. There was also often a frame in place for the weaving of brightly colored cloth for clothing unique to their tribe.

Clay fire areas were located inside—smoke passing on up and out through a roof opening—fire wood obtained from treed lands remaining higher in the mountains. Ladders would be put in place for entering and exiting the huts.

Interior furnishings were generally scant; three or four six-inch high wooden blocks provided seating. There would be a few handmade wooden utensils and bowls, woven mats, and handmade pottery pots and vessels. Iron and metal pots and porcelain plates and wares were more recent acquisitions. In the peaked roofs rice was stored.

Banana trees produced fruit on their plots—betel nut trees as well were also highly desirable. Onions, beans, and *camotes* (sweet potatoes) were raised on nearby plots for personal consumption. A fresh water fish pond would at times have been dug and kept stocked.

The men wore hand-woven G-strings, and when out and about, would have a bolo knife at the waist and carry a five to six foot long spear. The women wore brightly colored hand woven wrap-around skirts and belt affairs—in warmer weather, tops were optional. I perceived these Ifugao people to be pretty self-sufficient. Some had converted to Christianity, but most still practiced their pagan rituals. The taking of heads in serious disputes or warfare had only recently been abandoned.

The only other Caucasian within a day's journey was a Belgian priest singly in residence at a small mission not far away. Every Sunday I'd make the trek down from the ten bed Jaycee-Care hospital and residence where I lived to his small hand crafted chapel for Mass, about a half hour walk.

Father Louis Mellebeek was the priest's name, and we had become good friends—treasuring our after Mass chats, exchanging magazines, books and news from the outside world. He often generously shared cheeses and Belgian goodies he'd received from family and friends back home.

I knew Father Louie hiked to small settlements some distance away for his mission work. So I recall asking—pestering—to accompany him. He finally relented, and just once I was able to join him. Over the course of several days we were to trek some 40 kilometers—an arduous and grueling hike to a mission he'd established—up and down mountains, crossing streams, carefully making our way atop narrow terrace dikes. Well, he had warned me it would be extremely difficult, and sure enough, I was barely able to walk by the time we reached our destination, and then there would be the equally arduous return trip.

Fr. Louie was well over six feet tall, with long legs, and he routinely traversed like a fast moving nimble mountain goat. But there was no whimper from me. As the tag-along on this journey, I couldn't impede his travel. My eyes rarely left his booted feet moving forward in front of me. Scenic? No doubt it was, but I had little chance to gaze around as I desperately struggled to keep pace. Perhaps I need not add, I never asked to trek to an outlying mission with Father Louie again!

At any rate, Father Louie was a preeminent soul—a one in thousands—a truly energetic and remarkably able, albeit humble person—a fine, fine man. To his converts he offered medicines and health care, education, and spiritual guidance. I've met no one in my lifetime I've held in higher esteem.

So much for some scene setting and on to events more closely related to Mission Sunday.

So it was on a Sunday in October of 1962. I was in his small chapel in Mayoyao along with his congregation. And at one point among his announcements he stated: "Next Sunday is Mission Sunday. I'm passing out envelopes for your offerings. Please donate what you can to help with the church's mission work worldwide."

The following Sunday, October 28th, Mission Sunday dawned, and I hiked down the mountain—was once again on a hand hewn bench in his most modest church. When the collection basket came around for mission offerings, I did notice the woman beside me had placed a rather bulgy envelope as her offering, but I did not think too much of it. After Mass Fr. Louie showed me the bulgy envelope and its contents: a single tan colored egg!

Yes, right there—smack dab in country that couldn't be more mission like—these beautiful people had stepped up to the plate and generously donated to others in need. The woman next to me had wanted to contribute something. Later when I glanced her way I noticed that she was not a young person—shoeless, long hair wrapped around her crown as was their custom, lips and remaining teeth stained rust red from betel nut chewing, hand woven skirt, a faded old long sleeve flannel top, a few strands of the small red and white beads they treasured. But it was important to this woman and others there that day that they help a mission elsewhere. I was deeply touched. It's still a scene I vividly remember although it took place decades ago.

How I Ended Up in Mayoyao

I had originally been assigned as a teacher's aide, like all my Group I colleagues, to Camarines Sur Province, but because of the vagueness of the education project and my desire to provide service in my field of training as a health professional, I began looking for alternative projects. At the end of the first school year four of us from Groups I and II chose to volunteer for the summer vacation at the Jaycee Care Hospital in Mayoyao. We painted the structures, completed a thorough inventory of equipment and supplies, and with the help of the other three, I set up a small laboratory and wrote a lab manual for some basic procedures that could be performed there. A small hand operated centrifuge and an old single ocular microscope utilizing day light and flashlight luminescence kept things very basic!

At the end of summer, I wanted to stay on as I felt unfulfilled as a teachers' aide. And, I wanted to do more in my area of education, training and work experience. The Peace Corps reluctantly allowed the transfer.

Upon returning from the Peace Corps, Pat worked as a microbiologist primarily in Spokane, Washington. She retired from laboratory work in 1992 after some 34 years in the field and moved across Washington State to Camano Island in the Puget Sound. There she began a second career of nearly full-time volunteerism, first as an AIDS' helper and peer counselor, but found herself gravitating toward work in the natural world. She started taking classes, attending lectures, going on numerous field trips, and buying a small library of natural world books (native plants, marine life, birds etc); before long she was referred to as a "naturalist" by local groups. She became active in the Native Plant Society and on the boards of the local Audubon Society, Island County Beachwatchers, and Friends of Camano Island Parks. She has led interpretive beach and trail walks, mostly for elementary students and picked up vast quantities of litter along miles of beaches. She has written natural world articles for the local newspaper, for four newsletters and the internet (www.beachwatchers.wsu.edu). She has also written, illustrated, and distributed several informational and interpretive brochures for Washington State parks. Pat has volunteered at the local senior center and swimming pool, earning awards for some 5,000 documented hours during the 17 years she lived on Camano Island. She now makes her home in Wenatchee, Washington, near the home of her daughter, son-in-law and two teenage grandchildren.

(The first photo shows Pat leaving the Philippines in 1963; the second shows her with her two grandchildren at the river cottage in 2007.)

Philip Nicholas

Language and Love: My Peace Corps Experience

It always feels great to put "Philippines I" after my name. Being in Group I gave us certain bragging rights. I'm sure subsequent groups accomplished great things, but we told ourselves that we were the first, the pioneers.

And that may be why our group had such cohesion, such a great spirit. Until today, we hold reunions every couple or years. And when we meet, our conversations continue as if we saw each other just yesterday.

Looking back, our selection process, training and, on the whole, our outstanding staff were pretty good. Because when we got to our in-country we were able to hit the ground running. Sort of.

There were minor glitches as both staff and volunteers improvised as we went along. But most were flexible and able to make adjustments. A big reason for this was the support of our teachers and principals.

One of the most important things I learned was the importance of language and the importance of being seen to try to speak it. That was certainly stressed in our training, along with respect for the Philippine culture.

While we learned some of the national language, Tagalog, most of us were sent to non-Tagalog speaking provinces. Still, it gave us a foundation on which to build other languages.

Catanduanes

I was first assigned to the province of Catanduanes in the Bicol region, with my roommate Frank Krajewski from Rhode Island.

We had gotten along in training and the assignment in Catanduanes had to be voluntary.

Being a New Yorker, I found Catanduanes quite an exotic place. It also appealed to Frank and me that we would be quite far from any staff.

Catanduanes was known as "typhoon island" because it got a lot of typhoons on the Pacific side. In fact, on the second day in our barrio, Calolbon, we had a big typhoon (about 220 kms/hour). We awoke to find an entire family sleeping in our small living room.

In Calolbon, I learned to speak the Bicol language by talking with the little kids who used to follow me when I was running or walking along the beach with the German shepherd I had bought in Manila.

After about a year, I was asked, pressured, strong-armed into giving a speech at our barrio fiesta. Afterward, when I asked my principal how I did, he said: "everyone was impressed but they all mentioned that you spoke like a little kid."

Mindanao and Afterward

After about 20 months, I became a Volunteer Leader in Mindanao. I learned a few phrases of the language of one of the Muslim provinces, which helped when my Jeep broke down and a truckload of armed men came along. (Jeep? Did I say Jeep? That was one of the perks of being a Volunteer Leader, because I had to visit around 30 Volunteers in seven provinces on a regular basis.)

My base in Mindanao was a hotel in Iligan, run by a couple who later became my aunt and uncle. When a new group of volunteers arrived, I joined them for language training in Cebu. My future aunt suggested I stay with her sister. And that's how I met my future wife, Donette.

While a few objected to her marrying a foreigner, most supported me because they knew me first-hand.

Three of my four children were born in Manila, and one in Montreal, where I worked after the Peace Corps.

How to sum up my Peace Corps experience? What were my memories? When I was taking a French language course in Montreal, we had an assignment to do a slide show for the class, in French of course.

I chose to use my slides from the Philippines. After the show, I noticed a girl in the front row sobbing. I jokingly asked her if my French was that bad. She said no, but how could you leave such a place? She explained that in spite of the poverty, everyone was smiling—especially the kids walking barefoot to school.

I checked the slides later on and she was absolutely right. Most were poor and barefoot but everyone has broad smiles on their faces.

I truly loved every minute I spent in the Philippines and serving alongside such a great group of people. And I often ask myself the same question: why would you leave all that behind?

After his Peace Corps service, Phil remained In Manila for five years working at J. Walter Thompson (JWT) Advertising and studying nights at the Ateneo de Manila University toward a master's degree in Communications. He transferred to JWT in New York where he also worked on the successful reelection of New York Congressman John Dow.

Phil helped found the League for Economic Assistance and Development, which initiated several self-sustaining projects in Guatemala. He transferred to the JWT Montreal Office in 1972 and later to BBDO in Toronto before starting his own agency, Royal Piranha Jockey Advertising in 2005. He retired in 2010 and has been currently writing a children's book for his eight grandchildren. He is also enrolled in Spanish classes in the Spanish Centre in Toronto.

(The first photo shows Phil enjoying himself with Filipino friends; the second shows him with the wife, Donnette.)

Lee Ann Justice Pelea

An American Life in the Albay Town of Tiwi: With the Peace Corps and Afterward

Introductions

Shortly after my high school graduation, my career Air Force father was assigned to Japan and later to Hickam Air Force Base in Hawaii. This was fortunate for me because it gave me the opportunity to attend Sophia University in Tokyo, Japan as a freshman and finish the next three years of my college career at the University of Hawaii in Honolulu. These exposures to Asian cultures increased my interest in that part of the world and led to my choice of International Relations as a major. After graduation in 1960, I returned home to Dayton, Ohio with the intention of pursuing post-graduate work. After the election of John F. Kennedy, however, my attention became focused on the Peace Corps. The prospect of traveling to far-off countries, living with local populations, and, hopefully, providing help for them, was very appealing. Having met Filipinos in Japan and Hawaii, I felt particularly fortunate to be assigned to the Philippines.

Penn State provided our introduction to the Peace Corps. The training was excellent, but I was extremely concerned I'd fail the psychological segment, which evaluated our ability to assimilate into an unfamiliar culture to the level where we would be effective at our assigned jobs. I can't recall a single class we took, but remember Peace Corps leaders from Washington D.C. checking in once in a while. Also, I can't recall any building/classroom/dormitory we used even though I've been on the Penn State campus several times in the past 15 years.

We all met in San Francisco for the flight to the Philippines. While most of the women flew on a jet, I travelled on the prop plane with the men, an unforgettable ride in bucket seats, with box lunch meals and stopovers at Wake and Guam.

I remember well Los Baños Agricultural College in Laguna where we continued our training, particularly the dormitory style lodging and the call of resident lizards in the night. The most stressful memory of Los Baños involved where we would be assigned in the Philippines for the next two years and with whom. I was hoping for the Visayas (sounded exotic) but ended up in the Bicol Region in the town of Tiwi, Albay with Patricia Lutz, Elaine Gilvear and Melinda Meyer as my housemates. The latter sang and played the guitar and, thus, was the most popular simply because of her ability to entertain without an introduction.

Life in Tiwi as a Volunteer

The four of us initially rented a large two-story house on a corner lot near the center of town. The owner was Peña Villanueva, who owned the largest grocery store in town. The house had windows facing the intersecting roads and we often were serenaded by local young men, particularly Orping Competente, whose father became my first Head Teacher.

In a couple of months, we decided to build our own house using local materials and partly financed by our families back home. We enlisted the help of the family of the Industrial Arts teacher at Tiwi Central Elementary School, Ramon Pelea, whose father and two brothers were carpenters by trade. Within a short time we had our own "Bamboo House," called that because the walls were made of large, thick bamboo trunks split in half, each half nailed to a wood framework, the only house of such design in Tiwi. The roof was nipa and we had a 'dirty' outside cooking section where rice was cooked over a wood fire.

The outside bathroom consisted of two separate stalls, one containing a toilet & the other a shower, with an open outside basin for washing, all also made of bamboo. Huge spiders with equally huge attached egg sacks frequented the lavatory ceiling. When the sacks would break, hundred of tiny spiders would scurry into dark, wet hiding places.

The main floor of our new house was the traditional red cement with wood floors for the two bedrooms and loft. Since Tiwi had no electricity, we depended on Coleman lamps for light.

We had a maid, Remy, who shopped at the market each day for our meals and washed and bleached our clothes by hand on a vacant lot across the road. We ate fish for lunch and dinner, but our breakfast consisted of locally made bread, called pandesal, which was delicious. We also had our furniture made of bamboo and wood (it lasted for decades).

The town of Tiwi, organized in 1776, had not one, but two Patron Saints, St Lawrence and Our Lady of Salvation which meant both August 9 and 10 were yearly feast days. Tiwi's most prominent family was the Pacis Family, which produced a bishop (Bishop Teotimo Pacis), a parish priest, and a couple of sisters—all siblings—and all well known throughout the Bicol Region. The family home was located in the barrio of Libtong and we were often invited there to meet the priests and sisters, as well as other family members. In 1961 the Mayor of Tiwi was Mariano Cirujales, a rather heavy man who loved to dance—and CLOSE at that.

There was one car in Tiwi when we arrived, owned by Dr Ciocson, the brother of a fellow teacher, Amparo Ciocson. The main source of transportation was the open, wooden-sided buses, with bench seating. Families used the bus to get to Tabaco, about six miles down the coast and the closest big town, for marketing and general shopping. Riders continually got on and off the bus (no such thing as bus stops) with young men clinging to the sides. Tabaco was also the site of the closest public high school, Tabaco High School. Though "public," all post elementary schooling in Albay cost money which meant most students stopped their schooling at the sixth grade. Tiwi's only high school was private, the Virgin of Carmel High School, located next to the old church.

The tricycle, a bicycle (sometimes motorized) with a side seat attached, was also used for transportation. It was commonly used for in-town transportation, particularly by teachers. Since school hours stretched from 7 am to 5 pm with a two hour lunch period, students and teachers alike went home for lunch and a siesta before resuming afternoon classes. Due to the extreme heat, no woman left home without an umbrella to provide protection against the heat/sun and rain alike. No matter how heavy the rain, men, however, never used an umbrella—it was considered too effeminate. Unlike other areas of the Philippines, the Bicol enjoyed year round rain which meant two crops per year were possible.

Teaching and Pursuing Community Projects

I went to Tiwi as a teacher like everyone else but never felt confident in my ability to teach. I envied those PCV's who were trained teachers, Eleanor Whitlatch in Catanduanes being one. Nevertheless, if I wasn't particularly good, no one seemed to notice or care—all were happy I was there to help.

We all were assigned to different schools, with Pat traveling each day by bus to the neighboring town of Malinao. I can't recall where Elaine & Melinda were assigned but within a year the two left the Philippines and Pat was re-assigned to Peace Corps headquarters in Manila, leaving me and our maid Remy alone in the large Bamboo House.

Tiwi was famous for its hot springs, widely respected in the region for their medicinal attributes. The hot springs were located near Naga, one of Tiwi's 24 barrios. This was important because Naga Elementary School was the location of my first teaching assignment. Near the school was the "Boiling Lake" where locals often boiled eggs and chickens, and where carabaos would occasionally wander, likewise to be boiled alive (so I was told).

My co-teacher was Carmen (Maling) Olarte, daughter of the town treasurer, who, within a year married her longtime boyfriend, Jose (Ping) Villanueva, a relative of our first landlady.

We quickly learned the importance of school events such as graduation and other special days in the school year. Being polite and punctual, we'd arrive for such events at the scheduled start time, usually 6 pm; only to wait for an hour before others started trickling in for what would turn out to be an 8 pm program. Eventually, I skipped the punctual part and like my fellow friends/teachers, arrived sensibly at least an hour late (popularly known as "Philippine Time").

I quickly found out that nearly all my students had last names beginning with the letter 'C' (dating supposedly from Spanish times), which made making up student lists somewhat complicated. Eventually, I learned to recognize which students with identical family names were siblings (same middle name) and which were cousins (different middle name) as the middle name of offspring was the maiden name of their mothers. I later learned that most Tabaco family names began with the letter 'B' and Legaspi City family names often began with letter 'A'. Thus, I had a reasonably good idea where someone lived by the last name since families tended to stay close to their hometown.

It wasn't all work—we had fun also. I've ridden a carabao, walked the rice paddies in our town, and also camped overnight in a mountain ravine with several local young people. The latter was particularly memorable because a cloudburst quickly flooded the ravine where we camped, forcing us to run for our lives.

On vacation trips, I have traveled to the Visayas, Baguio, the Banaue Rice Terraces and to Mindanao (Cotabato and Zamboanga). Loving musical theater, I took the train one time to Manila for the sole purpose of watching *West Side Story*, immediately returning home following the movie. My favorite trips were to nearby Catanduanes, reached by boat out of Tabaco, to visit Eleanor Whitlatch. Typhoons often passed through Albay but Catanduanes seemed to be the preferred target. Each trip there brought different scenes because of the damage typhoons inflicted, regularly altering vistas and changing landmarks.

After a year, I began teaching in the barrio of Joroan, a mountain seaside village about ten miles from the *poblacion* of Tiwi. I took lodging at a teacher's house during the school week, my room being about as big as a closet—just long enough for a wood bed and small dresser. Joroan was also the location of the only other church in Tiwi, a beautiful one overlooking the coast, whose priest, Father Rafer, watched over me during my tenure there.

Joroan was one of several seaside barrios in Tiwi, all reached by a pock-marked winding road. I loved to bicycle (I had my own bike shipped to Tiwi from the U.S.) and in the company of the local Philippine community development officer, Oriel Clutario, would bike up and down this road to reach these barrios.

Oriel Clutario (who later became Mayor, like his father decades earlier) was unusual in that he was very energetic and smart, with the ability to get something from nothing, attributes which would easily qualify him to work in any U.S. community. With his help, I began a project to introduce a library into the community, called, fittingly, the Tiwi PHIL-US Library. The library was housed in a large one-story concrete structure next to the Municipal Building that at one time was the "PuriCultural Center," used to provide pre-natal care for mothers. By removing the "Puri" from its name, the building became the "Cultural Center" and the home of the new successful library, filled with books sent from my hometown in Ohio.

I worked to establish Youth Clubs in each barrio (thus the reason for the aforementioned bike rides to outlaying seaside barrios). I also helped the Youth Groups create revolving libraries with books being rotated among the different barrios. It was fun and well appreciated while it lasted. Finally, I felt confident I was making a real contribution to the town of Tiwi.

Remaining in Tiwi after the Peace Corps: 1963-1977

We all arrived in the Philippines in October of 1961 and the memories of those Group I PCV's who left 2 years later are limited to that period. For most of the volunteers there was a definite beginning and a definite ending.

In my case, I married a local Filipino teacher and remained in Tiwi for an additional 14 years; thus, my Peace Corps and subsequent experiences as a private Tiwi citizen (albeit foreign) tend to merge together and, in fact, the latter dominates my memory at the expense of the former. Generally speaking, the experiences and friendships that evolved at the beginning continued to impact the later years.

I married Ramon Pelea, whose family had built our Bamboo House. Our Peace Corps house became the Pelea family home. Like my fellow teachers, we had three generations living under one roof. Ramon and I had four children, all with the middle name of "Justice," my maiden name.

A few years later the seemingly indestructible Bamboo House became infested with termites, discovered in the middle of a birthday party for my oldest daughter, when a swarm of flying termites forced the party outside. After years of experiencing destroyed class lesson plans/research papers/etc., I learned to soak the back of wood cabinets/shelves with kerosene on a yearly basis to keep termites under control.

The split bamboo walls harbored native animals including at one time a huge poisonous rice snake (the Bamboo House was next to a rice field). Our elderly neighbor grabbed its tail, snapped it out, and killed it.

New Projects and Old Friendships in the post-Peace Corps Years

I established a Kindergarten in 1968, using the Cultural Center (still used as library) as my classroom. My students were the children of my fellow teachers and friends from my Peace Corps years, including the sons of Mayor Oriel Clutario (Totoy) and Peña Villanueva (Jaime), our Peace Corps era landlady. As was the custom, first and second honors were given out at the end of school; Jaime was 1st Honors the first year. He is now the very popular and progressive Mayor of Tiwi.

The Kindergarten ended on the 13th of October 1970 when one of the most powerful typhoons of the century, Typhoon Sening, made a direct hit on Tiwi, destroying schools and many structures throughout the town, including the Cultural Center. Only a few books could be salvaged from the library. For two years, classes in Tiwi were conducted in the few surviving private homes.

Friendships developed through the Peace Corps continued on through my married life.

• Along with other teachers, I became close to Lorenzo Competente, my first Head Teacher at Naga Community School. He confided to me that he was retiring early to enjoy a long retirement but in fact died less than a year later while playing cards at the corner *halo-halo* store.

• As a PCV, I became close to two young women, our lives often crossing as we each married, had children, and went about our daily lives. I thought I knew them very well. Years after my return to Ohio, both women became public figures, each eventually running and winning election as Mayor of Tiwi. Regrettably for Tiwi, both ran corrupt and graft ridden administrations, including the personal use of city funds, exposing character flaws that shocked me.

• Central School teacher, Dehlia Mercader, co-teacher of Elaine, married Felix Pacis, nephew of the bishop, and their children were playmates of mine. The year I taught the eldest child in kindergarten, Dehlia miscarried and died, leaving four children, the youngest a two-year-old named Minerva (Minnie), who some 25 years later, became my daughter-in-law.

• Later Felix Pacis married a niece of Peña Villanueva, and their six offspring, half-siblings of Minnie, mean that I am now related (by marriage) to the often-mentioned Peña Villanueva.

• Lilia Pacis, wife of Felix's brother, Canuto, who sold us volunteers a wonderful assortment of baked goods from her bakery, now lives 40 miles away in Fort Myers, Florida with her daughter, Tipin, also a pupil of mine, and Minnie's cousin.

I became completely assimilated into the Philippine culture/life. By the time I left, I could ride public buses free of stares. My only American contact was with the occasional PCV that stopped in to check out this "oddity" living in the Bamboo House in Tiwi.

In l969 Tiwi got a new PCV, Allen Schorff, an agriculturalist who accomplished a lot in that field. Allen also stretched out his tenure and married a young woman from Tabaco, who happened to be a distant relative of the Pelea family.

Other American contacts occurred following Typhoon Sening in 1970 when American servicemen came from Clark Air Force Base, I think, to rebuild the water system destroyed by Sening. One of the members of the group was black—Tiwi's first exposure to an African American.

As with everyone else, the Marcos Era of Martial Law required life adjustments. I delivered my first child during that time. Because of curfew restrictions, my brother-in-law, Senio, a Tiwi motorcycle policeman, escorted us to Legaspi. The oldest child was born in Legaspi City at the hospital that was the official designated Peace Corps medical facility selected to treat Peace Corps Volunteers.

The second and fourth children were born at the Senir Clinic in Tabaco owned by a Spanish doctor who served wonderful Spanish soups. The third child was born at home, with the aid of the local midwife and under the light of a lantern—the way most Tiwi teachers had their babies delivered.

Our family was exposed to the same diseases and hardships as the rest. Two of Ramon's young cousins, who lived next door to the Bamboo House, died of TB. Ginger (the third child) took TB drugs for a couple of years to prevent the disease from erupting.

And Life Goes On

I can only speculate that the new English my old pupils learned from me did them well. My three oldest children (ages 9-13 at the time I departed) attended Tiwi Central Elementary School and later on were able to adjust to Ohio public schools. They all went to college, the youngest joining the Peace Corps and serving in Honduras. Upon my return to Ohio, unbeknown to me, I had developed an accent from 16 years exposure and use of the Bicol language. For the first 4-5 years, acquaintances and strangers would ask me "what country do you come from?" Regrettably, the accent eventually disappeared.

The year before I left, Tiwi finally got electricity, but it was haphazard at best with two hours daily of electrical usage available if we were lucky. Several professionals from Tiwi have moved to the U.S. including our family doctor, Dr Tomas Madrilejos. Many of these professionals are the children of teachers I worked with.

Every two years a "Tiwinion" Reunion is planned in different areas of the country, each one hosted by a resident of the host city. 2009 was the last reunion and took place in Anchorage, Alaska. The next one will be in Tiwi itself in 2011. My family has attended several reunions, giving me the opportunity to renew old friendships. Each time someone approaches me and asks, "Do you remember me?" They remind me that I had taught them as grade school pupils, but I, of course, don't usually recognize them. But it always brings back pleasant memories as we briefly relive the past.

Every few years I visit with the Templado family, who were our closest neighbors in Tiwi. They live with their daughter May in Houston. I taught the older Templado children and the younger ones were playmates of my children.

Life continues as if I'm still sitting outside the Tiwi Bamboo House on the roadside bench, greeting passersby....

After sixteen years in the Philippines, Lee Ann returned to the U.S. in 1977 with her four children. She settled in her old hometown, Dayton, Ohio, where her parents still lived. Her husband, Ramon Pelea, remained in the Philippines. They divorced 15 years later, but he has visited the U.S. several times for family weddings and other special occasions.

Lee Ann worked as a Civil Service employee at Dayton's Wright-Patterson Air Force Base. She was a computer programmer/analyst. Before retiring in 1999, she had spent the previous 13 years assigned to AFSAC (Air Force Security Assistance Center), which provided assistance in the management of requisitions procured by U.S. allies around the world.

In 2001, she escaped the bitter Ohio winters and moved to Bradenton, Florida where her son, Mark, lived with his wife, Minnie Pacis, and their son, Alleque, now 14. Both worked in nearby Sarasota: Mark as a computer manager for a medical facility and Minnie as a nurse at a re-hab center. The family returns to Tiwi, Albay every 3-4 years for a month's visit—the next one planned for August 2011, the time of the Tiwi Town Fiesta.

Lee Ann's eldest daughter, Jeanette, returned to Tiwi for her first two years of college. She is now the only one living in the Dayton area with her family, including her daughter, Alexianna, now 13.

The middle daughter, Ginger, is living with her family, including eight-year old son, Tyler, in Hardin, Montana. Her husband, Brian, is manager of the local Pamida store. Ginger returned to Tiwi about 20 years ago for a two-week visit to meet her many cousins.

The youngest daughter, Bernice, who was four when the family left Tiwi, is the only child who's never returned to the Philippines. She was a Peace Corps Volunteer/Leader in Honduras for three years, beginning in 1997, specializing in Public Health. She later worked at PC Headquarters in Washington for a year. Bernice earned a Master's Degree in Public Health from John Hopkins University in Baltimore, where she currently resides with her musician husband, Kevin Gift.

(The first photo shows Lee Ann with housemates Elaine Gilvear and Pat Lutz at "the Nipa House" in Tiwi; the second photo show Lee Ann flanked on the left by grandson Alleque and daughter-in-law Minnie and on the right by granddaughter Alexianna and daughter Jeanette.)

Ronald J. Peters
Taking My Uncle's Advice:
My Lifelong Adventure with the Philippines

Motivating Factors

My motivation for joining the Peace Corps was both personal and ideological. I was a commuter student from the western New York industrial suburb of North Tonawanda while attending Buffalo State College. After graduating in 1959, I taught junior high social studies in a nearby school district. Being single and 22 made me quite eligible for the military draft—which would have meant two years of army service plus an additional four years of active reserve. I volunteered instead for the U.S. Army Reserve, which required six months of active duty training plus five and half years of reserve duty. My six months started in July 1960, and finished the next January, just days after the inauguration of President John F. Kennedy. Inspired by Kennedy's speeches and events taking place around the world, I wanted to ply my teaching trade in a developing country.

The other motivator was that I had hardly travelled outside my hometown. My army training at Ft. Dix, New Jersey was the farthest I had ever been from home. My uncles had been in World War II, as had been many of my professors at Buffalo State. My older brother and his cohorts had been in the Korean War. All these guys had stories of "far away places, with strange sounding names" (as the song lyrics went). And here I was at age 23, having hardly been any farther from Buffalo than New Jersey.

In the spring of 1961 I applied for about every overseas teaching opportunity I'd heard about including this new government program called the Peace Corps. Sub-Sahara Africa captured my imagination. I really wanted to go there. In mid July when I received a telegram from a guy named R. Sargent Shriver (at 9 pm on a Saturday evening), saying I had been selected for Peace Corps training to go to the Philippines, I was disappointed. It wasn't Africa. I was in the middle of my summer school courses, and slated to teach that fall. I had strong doubts about going.

The next day I discussed this with my uncle (one of those WWII guys), and told him I wasn't sure about going. He bellowed at me, "This is the chance of a life time, man. What do you mean you're thinking about not going? Give me that damn telegram; I'll go in your place." I thought it would be difficult getting released from my Army Reserve commitment. To my amazement on the basis of the Shriver's telegram plus a phone call to some unknown command center, I was transferred to a "Control Group," a paper unit consisting of a list of names and ranks of servicemen who could be activated in a national emergency. The time I would spend in the Peace Corps would count toward my six-year obligation to the Army. So with my uncle's advice and my reserve obligation in place I was ready for Penn State and Peace Corps training.

The director of graduate study at Buffalo State where I was taking courses was so enthused about my going that he arranged for a tuition refund when I withdrew. Barbara Swanekamp and I became the first Peace Corps volunteers from the Buffalo area. We were on the local TV news, and we were written up in both Buffalo daily papers. This was the end of July 1961.

Two weeks after I arrived at Penn State, the Soviets built the Berlin Wall causing the first major international crisis for President Kennedy. In a show of strength Kennedy placed the armed forces on full alert, and put over 100 reserve units on active duty. I bought a *New York Times* the next day. The inner pages contained a list of reserve units being activated. Jumping off the page was "432nd Ordinance Company, Kenmore NY," the unit I had been released from just 21 days earlier. I later learned those poor guys sat for the next year and a half at Ft. Jackson, South Carolina before being sent home. They never even got overseas. Had it not been for the Peace Corps that's where I would have been.

Training at Penn State and Los Baños

What I knew about the Philippines at the time was quite minimal. The only Filipino I had known was my First Sergeant at Ft. Dix, Raphael Holaso. My father's brother, Charles Peters, was in a National Guard unit that had been activated in the summer of 1940. He was sent to the Philippines later that fall. Unfortunately, he was there when the Japanese invaded, was subsequently captured, and died in a Japanese POW camp. He was buried in the American Cemetery at Makati, near Manila. Shortly after arriving at Los Baños, I commandeered a Peace Corps jeep and drove to that cemetery. I found his grave, took several photos, and sent them to my grandmother. It turned out I was the only one among her eleven children and 30 grandchildren who ever visited Charlie's grave. When I left for the Philippines in October 1961, it was slightly over 20 years after my Uncle Charlie had left for the same place. I didn't realize it at the time, but my departure must have weighed on my mother and father as they saw me off.

On balance I found our instructors at Penn State to be knowledgeable and effective teachers. I paid pretty close attention and took extensive notes, thinking that this information was going to be useful in the very near future. Another thing happened to me at Penn State. This was the first large university campus where I'd ever spent much time. I felt the campus and State College as a community were nice places. The positive Penn State experience helped attract me to similar places. As my life evolved, I spent the next fifty years working for universities and living in places like State College, Pennsylvania.

I found most of my fellow volunteer trainees quite congenial and easy to get along with. Most were like me, college graduates within the last three years and eager for some kind of dramatic change in their lives. I had never been around so many people from such a wide range of places. They all seemed quite excited at the prospect of going overseas. Only a few had previously travelled outside the U.S. Most of us were getting our very first passports.

I found our training program at Los Baños (the Agriculture College of the University of the Philippines) to be of a much lower quality, but at least we were in the Philippines. For the most part, academics from prestigious Philippine universities presented lectures on various aspects of Philippine life and culture. The faculty members from the Ateneo de Manila were probably the best of this lot. The three hours of Tagalog language training each morning turned out to be not particularly useful; as almost all of us were sent to non-Tagalog speaking areas. In retrospect my guess is that the Filipino speakers from various government agencies including the Bureau of Public Schools (BPS) must have been terrified having to appear for an hour or more before 126 Americans. We spent seven weeks at Los Baños. We later learned that the principal reason for keeping us there so long was due to the Philippine Presidential campaign going on at the time. Filipinos take their politics very seriously and campaigns can get deadly violent. I realize in retrospect that Embassy officials were wise in not to allow us out into the provinces during such a time. Nonetheless, we were eager to get to our assignments "in the field" and away from the confines of a college campus.

Living and Working in Casiguran, Sorsogon

I was assigned to Casiguran, Sorsogon, on Sorsogon Bay with three other volunteers. Our household consisted of David Jett from Richmond, Kentucky, Foster Wiggins from North Providence, Rhode Island, Doug Watts from Laconia, New Hampshire and me. We were among the 16 volunteers in the Sorsogon province of the Bicol Region at the extreme southern tip of the main island of Luzon. Casiguran was mainly a fishing community where large fish were caught, iced, and shipped to Manila. The principal cash crop was abaca fiber, known also as Manila hemp. The hemp produced in Sorsogon was considered the strongest. For years it had been prized for making the best ropes for ships. When powerful navies were considered the vital component of defense, hemp from Sorsogon was considered a strategic commodity. That era had passed by the time we arrived, but a number of large houses in the town in varying states of disrepair, were indicators of this bygone wealth.

The town got its name from when the first Spanish sailors arrived. When the sailors asked the name of the place, the locals didn't understand the question. Thinking they were asking the whereabouts of young women, the town elders deflected their inquiry and replied *"casi guran"* meaning "mostly old." The Spaniards recorded the elders' response on their map and the name endured.

We soon learned that our purpose for being sent to Casiguran was that the BPS Division superintendent's brother was the town's high school principal. They needed a physics teacher at the high school. Since Foster had been trained as an electrical engineer, he could presumably teach physics. So we were all assigned to Casiguran. Foster taught one class a day of physics to third and fourth year students in the mid morning. That became his assignment. Dave, Doug and I were assigned to work with elementary teachers. I was to go to the central school in the center of town. Dave and Doug were assigned to large barrio schools. Doug eventually built a small house in his barrio and moved there for the second year of our tour.

We lived in a modest two bedroom apartment in a frame house above the owners, the Marteriez family, the wife being the sister of the BPS superintendent. Our clumsy feet must have sounded like a thunder storm when we walked around at night. The Peace Corps sent us a crate of household goods, which included a Coleman gasoline camp stove that worked off a hand pump pressure tank. Mrs. Marteriez was convinced the thing was going to explode and burn down the house. Fortunately, for everyone, the stove required white (non-leaded) gasoline. The leaded gasoline available locally soon clogged the burner jets. This forced us to buy a conventional kerosene wick stove used by the locals. The Marterez family was all quite relieved when we decommissioned the Coleman.

We had electricity. It came on at 6 pm and then dimmed at 10 pm. That was when the old Ford truck engine powering the World War II surplus generator was set to half throttle. There were frequent power failures, either caused by high wind storms or for unknown reasons. We kept a kerosene fired lantern (called a Petromax) for our power failure times. The town's mayor owned the power company. Customers were charged a flat monthly rate (in advance) by the number of light fixtures and plug outlets. The mayor was always investigating whether people had more than maximum allowable 60 watt bulbs. Someone in town, he was convinced, was using an electric iron during full power times. Search as he might, he never caught the culprit.

We were supposed to introduce a new curriculum to elementary school teachers that included English as a second language and science. The general outlines of these curricula were discussed by representative of the BPS who lectured at us at Los Baños. But when we arrived there were no materials, course outlines, or any printed materials. All we had were some sketchy handouts and the notes we had taken at Los Baños. The four of us were warmly received by the teachers and the town officialdom. They had no idea (except for Foster's physics course) why we were there, only that we had been sent by President Kennedy. The latter was all these folks needed to immediately befriend us.

I put together some simple exercises on spoken English for the teachers, which I tried out in an informal workshop following a faculty meeting. The teachers seemed to be interested at first, but soon were talking among themselves. I didn't realize until years later that I probably talked too rapidly and with my American accent they had a hard time deciphering my words. Eventually materials arrived and I was able to assemble systematic presentations on how to teach English as a second language.

Teaching science was a little easier. We had materials with which we could perform basic experiments and demonstrations. The kids seem to respond quite well to the little demonstrations we set up. I consulted with teachers on their lesson plans but I had no real way of knowing just how much got through to them. I think they perceived us as personable oddities. We were asked to speak at graduations, award ceremonies, and other public events. We were on committees and served as judges at various athletic events during the town fiesta.

One of my more interesting experiences was when we did a series on a commercial radio station in the provincial capital, Sorsogon City. The station's owner thought it novel if we could do a few shows. As part of an expanded definition of English as a second language, Nancy Jeffers and I scripted fairy tales for broadcasting. We didn't have much for sound effects. I recall that when we did *Rapunzel*, I played the prince. When I said "Rapunzel, Rapunzel, let down your hair" I ran a ruler down the broadcast booth's venetian blind, and it went "bloop, bloop, bloop." When Nancy picked up the Rapunzel line, listeners must have visualized Rapunzel's hair unfolding in sections from the tower's turret. I never ran into any one who ever heard the broadcast. All I could conclude was that the station owner was hungry for local programming.

Continuing the Sorsogon Connection After 1963

It is hard to assess if I had any lasting impact in Casiguran. After leaving in 1963, my first time back there was in 1978. The town had noticeably improved in the intervening 15 years. Electrical power was available 24 hours a day off a national grid. The jerry-rigged Ford truck engine was long gone. Concrete roads had been built making auto travel faster and safer. Television antennas stood above the nipa (thatched) shingled and galvanized iron roofed houses. A TV station had been established in Legaspi that transmitted programs from Manila. Life had definitely improved there, if one used housing and amenities as the measure. I was remembered, and the teachers especially were glad to see me. We took pictures and shared stories about the "goings on" in our lives since we were last together.

Since 1984, I have visited Casiguran every three years or so. Many of my teacher friends have died, but I visit one or two to catch up on the latest news. Life has definitely improved. Most recently a new market place has been built, somewhat akin to an urban renewal project in the United States. The housing stock has definitely upgraded, hardly any of the dwellings now have nipa roofs. Cable television service is available throughout the town, and a cell phone tower permits easier communications with family and friends. When one inquires further, however, it is quickly apparent that in just about every one of the neat little houses (and true throughout the country), there is a family member working overseas. The work destinations include the Gulf States, the U.S., Europe, Australia and Japan. The remittances these folks send home help generate a relatively decent standard of living for many folks in places like Casiguran. But one worries if this way of life can be sustained given the uncertainty of the global economy.

One significant take-away from my Peace Corps experience involved finding my wife and life partner. I met Lilia briefly while she was working as a nurse at Sorsogon Provincial Hospital. In one conversation she indicated that she had applied for several nursing opportunities in the U.S. After I completed my master's program at Syracuse in 1965, I took a job at Roosevelt University in Chicago. Through happenstance I ran into another Filipina nurse from Sorsogon who ran down the number of Sorsoganias working in Chicago. She mentioned that Lilia Estipona had already completed her second year at Cook County Hospital, but was still in the Chicago area. She gave me Lilia's forwarding address, an apartment on Chicago's West Side. Since my job required visiting union offices in the area, on one of my rounds I stopped off at the address. I rang the bell. A Filipina answered. She was very hesitant when I asked for Lilia. Since they all were overstaying their working visas, she thought I was an immigration officer. Lilia had just come home after working a night shift at a hospital that was not very particular about their nurses' immigration status. The roommate woke up Lilia saying, "There's some big white guy with a necktie asking for you." Lilia got up, put on a robe and greeted me. At first, she didn't remember me, but soon made the connection. She asked if I had a car. It seemed there was a party that Saturday night and she asked if I would I be willing to drive her and a couple of the other nurses there. I agreed—and that was how things started between us.

At the time we re-met in Chicago she and two other nurses had Canadian papers to work in a town about 200 miles north of Toronto. The following month I took them to Windsor, Ontario. One of the nurses had a cousin working there. As jobs for nurses were plentiful in Windsor, they all decided to take jobs there rather than in rural Ontario. This was October 1965. I spent nearly every other weekend the next year travelling to Windsor. We were married in September 1966. That was 44 years ago. And here we are now—two grown children and three grandchildren later. Harking back to our re-meeting in 1965, Lilia has had her own car now for some years, yet she still likes me to drive her places.

Lilia over the years has straightened out the perceptions about the Philippines and Filipinos that I had wrong. The amount I have learned from her and other stateside Filipinos dwarfs any knowledge I had gathered during my time at Penn State, Los Baños, or Casiguran.

Ripples of the Peace Corps Connection in Recent Years

With visits to Lilia's family in Gubat, Sorsogon over the years, I've been able to keep in much closer touch with the Philippines than most other former volunteers. It turns out my First Sergeant at Fort Dix, Raphael Holaso, was also from Gubat, and was a friend of Lilia's father.

During my visits I established contact with the School of Labor and Industrial Relations (SOLAIR) at the University of the Philippines Diliman. In the mid 1980s I helped arrange for two of their younger faculty members to do graduate work at the University of Illinois. Each of them did a term as dean of their school in subsequent years. I try to visit SOLAIR about every time we are in the Philippines. They generally ask me to do a seminar for the students and faculty on the latest developments in collective bargaining in the U.S. or some such topic. I really value this connection and have made some lasting friends there.

Throughout the years Lilia and I gotten to know some very fine Filipino graduate students from Michigan State and Illinois. Lilia became an honorary big sister for many of the young women, offering them advice on their problems of the moment. I have helped many students find jobs or assisted their navigation through the university bureaucracy. Lilia has gone out of her way to entertain Philippine visitors. Over the years she has cooked tons of *pancit (a noodle dish)*, barrels of *sinigang (tamarind based soup)*, and countless other dishes that Filipinos miss when away from home. Our house has served as a gathering center for scores of graduate students and nurses over the years. Our back yard was the venue for one wedding and at least four wedding receptions. Young people have met at our house, fallen in love, married and had children. Our refrigerator door has photos of many of their kids. Folks send us Christmas cards with the latest photos; and we stick them there for the next 11 months. On about the first of December all the photos come down and the most recent ones get stuck up for the next year. Some of the kids are now in college, so we might very well soon be putting up the second generation's photos on our refrigerator.

We've had the privilege of befriending numerous bright and promising graduate students. Many have returned to the Philippines and have gone on to prominent positions in business, government and universities. It is very satisfying to know that we may have helped many of them in some small way.

Another very satisfying activity has been serving on the board the Peace Corps Alumni Foundation for Philippine Development, a foundation that grants college scholarships to low income but qualified Filipino kids to study in the Philippines. On our trips to the Philippines we've met with some of the scholarship recipients. The optimism and cheerfulness they express is heart warming. Maureen Carroll and other Washington D.C.–area former Peace Corps volunteers have worked hard to keep this program going. Our man in Manila, Roland De Jesus, is an unusual individual who dedicates a considerable amount of his life's energy to the Foundation. At any one time there might be 45 scholars at some stage of their studies. It turns out Roland's wife, Ning, has a cousin who is married to one of Lilia's cousins.

Dave Jett, Doug Watts and I remained close friends over the years since the Peace Corps. Our kids were about the same age and our spouses got along well when we got together.

Unfortunately Dave lost his wife Genie to cancer after about 20 years of marriage. Doug Watts died from a massive heart attack in September 2002. We still keep in touch with his widow, Liz. Our fourth housemate, Foster Wiggins died of a stroke in 2008. Dave and I have joked that we should have formed a last man's club.

It is hard to contemplate what I would have done had it not been for the Peace Corps. I am certain my life would not have been nearly so interesting. I'm very glad I took my uncle's advice and answered Shriver's telegram in the affirmative.

Ron Peters retired in 2002 as Head of the Labor Education Program at the Institute of Labor and Industrial Relations at the University of Illinois at Urbana Champaign, a position he held since 1976. His main focus over the years was conducting off-campus leadership training and continuing education for union leaders.

Ron was previously at Michigan State University where he obtained his doctorate and briefly taught. Upon returning from the Peace Corps he completed a Masters degree at Syracuse University, and from 1965-69 worked at the Labor Education Division of Roosevelt University in Chicago. He married Lilia Estipona, a registered nurse in 1966. They have two children, Emily and Franklin, and three grandchildren.

In recent years Ron has been active in local Democratic politics. He also serves as a board member for the local mass transit district. He and Lilia visit their grandchildren in Glen Ridge, New Jersey often. They take about one international trip a year.

Dave Pierson
Delayed Contribution

I was the only person in our group who had just completed active military service when I joined the Peace Corps. I had joined the Massachusetts National Guard, expecting to teach and coach in Greenfield, Massachusetts after my active duty service. I was at Fort Dix when I read about the start of the Corps, and felt that maybe I could make a contribution.

When we were at Penn State in training, I was very impressed by our whole group, but disappointed with the training, especially with the lack of language immersion. When the final selection was made, and we met in San Francisco, and we found that some of our best people were cut, I felt like just walking out. I remember a few outstanding people who  none of us could believe were left out of the program. My many experiences with government programs and politics over the years have cemented into my mind how many idiots have been allowed to make personnel decisions regarding government programs, Democrats and Republicans alike.

I recall that we were strictly instructed to stay out of politics in the Philippines, but several of our group openly supported Macapagal and Pelaez over President Carlos Garcia in the election that occurred shortly after our arrival. Some thought Macapagal to be "Kennedyesque."

I know I was one of the biggest hell-raisers of the group and enjoyed sitting and drinking San Miguel with the people in Los Baños, where I picked-up some Tagalog before being sent to a Visayan area. I was fortunate to be stationed with three great guys: Leo Pastore, Jim Turner and Pat Rowe. The teacher's aide job was little more than being a walking-talking audio-visual aid, but most volunteers expanded their roles in their communities by using whatever skills they had.

I was once asked to be a basketball official at the Visayan Games in Iloilo and received a fine ovation when I stepped on the court. I had a license in Massachusetts and Ohio and was pretty confident of my ability. Well, after a few calls, the cheers turned to boos and I couldn't figure it out. Then, at the half, it was explained to me the international rules were different. I had to adjust quickly!

Shortly before the end of my tour, I was quite sick with something, but no one would tell me what! At the hospital in Manila, I caught the mumps and Dr. Fuchs advised me to return to the States. I did not return to Negros after my hospital visit. Back in the States, I hoped to work with the Peace Corps on recruiting. I went to Washington D.C. and met with a Peace Corps official, but he had no job for me. I was bitterly disappointed. It took me many years to get over it, but I have never stopped supporting the Peace Corps.

The only real contributions that I made while in the Philippines as a volunteer were organizing our basketball team at Los Baños and writing a pamphlet on Filipino games. Years later, I discovered that the pamphlet was still being used by PCVs. We had one great basketball game at Los Baños between our PCV team starring Lee Johnson and Jerry Mullins against the Los Baños Team starring Vladimir Velasco. Vlad was great. The Filipino team beat us by a few points.

My real contribution to Filipinos came 20 years later when I was an administrator for the F-5 Fighter Support System in Khamis Mushayt, Saudi Arabia. My entire staff, except for a translator, was made up of Filipinos. They were great friends, terrific workers and helped me translate a Christmas speech into Tagalog, which I delivered to a standing ovation. I also campaigned to get better housing for our Filipino firemen on the airbase and after many teas and tennis matches with Saudi officers, I was successful. The only negative was that my boss (who was married to a Filipina) was very jealous that my Christmas speech was so applauded.

The Philippines has not changed too much over the years. I visited in 1990 and saw as much or more poverty as in the 60s, but the kindness, spirit and friendliness were there in abundance, and everyone who had come in contact with PCVs, regardless of their skills, had a high regard for them. The Peace Corps was more for us to learn than for us to facilitate change. We came in total innocence and left with a variety of feelings and experiences. I wish I could have been more of a contributor and less of a critic, but I did learn a lot, which helped me work and lead in Iran and Saudi Arabia in the years that followed.

Dave Pierson lives in Ajijic, Mexico, about an hour from Guadalajara. His Peace Corps service was cut short by illness, and he then continued his six year military obligation with the Army Reserve in Hawaii. He's had an eclectic work life including about 16 years of teaching, managing the Hawaii islanders- a San Diego Padres AAA team, the Maui Tropical Plantation, and the Kona Reef Hotel. He served a year as State Finance Director for the Hawaii GOP and ran for Mayor of Mesquite, Nevada, in a non-partisan election. He founded the Mesquite Madness Auction in 1999 to raise funds for the prevention of child abuse and serves yet as its auctioneer each year. He was also one of the founders of the Mesquite Senior Games, which now has over 800 participants. He is divorced (a long time ago) after 23 years of marriage. He has one son, who has recently returned from Afghanistan where he won a Bronze Star. He describes living in Ajijic as slow and relaxed, a great, SAFE place to retire. He reports that he has stopped diving off buildings into shallow water as he once did at the Boy Scout camp in Los Baños.

(The first picture shows Dave standing behind fellow Group I volunteers John Siedensticker and Tim Peterson as part of a group picture taken upon arrival at Penn State in 1961.)

Beth Sorenson Plummer
Sketches from the Philippines

Rather than writing an essay about my life as a Peace Corps volunteer in Philippines Group I from 1961 to 1963, I feel that a series of short sketches taken from my letters to my parents about some of my experiences will provide a more interesting understanding of the times and my observations. I have taken these sketches from pieces I wrote as a volunteer and left them in the present tense so readers might sense the original flavor of my words.

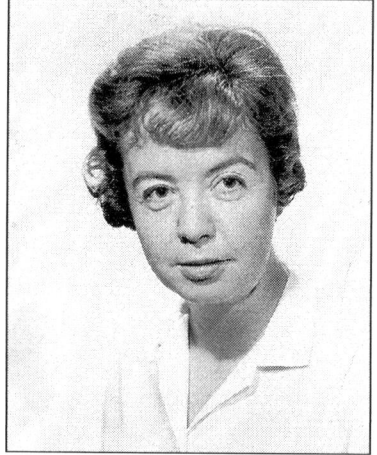

I had grown up in Methuen, Massachusetts and taught reading for one year in Burlington, Massachusetts before joining the Peace Corps. I lived with two other volunteers in the town of San Enrique in Negros Occidental Province of the Visayan region. I worked at a school in the town of San Enrique. The other volunteers in my household were Ann Snuggs from Alabama and Sally Pierce from Vermont. Marge Pfankuch also lived with us for a very short time, but she left to become a Volunteer Leader. San Enrique was 37 kilometers from Bacolod City, which was in turn an hour and a half from Manila by air.

Folk Dancing (February 1962)

We're busy getting ready for San Enrique's fiesta. Miss Velmonte, one of the teachers in charge of the entertainment, asked us if we'd try to learn a folk dance to perform on the final evening. So we are learning the *itik-itik*, which is supposed to resemble a duck's walk. We are having costumes made for our grand performance. Miss Velmonte was over Saturday morning to teach us the steps. Now she is going to work for the next 12 days until the fiesta to teach us "grace."

A few days later I wrote:

We're still busy practicing our dance for the fiesta next Friday. It's supposed to be a big surprise number, but everyone has found out, and the whole town has been going around singing the music. We're also teaching a group of children the Virginia reel. Everyone we've met has promised to come, so we hope to have a good time at the dance.

And on the day after the fiesta:

The day of the fiesta, it rained all day, but by 10 pm it was only drizzling. The cement floor was wet, however, and a little slippery. Miss Velmonte hustled us home to change into our costumes. They are really attractive—yellow and brown checked dresses with big sleeves. We were a little worried about dancing on the slippery floor, since some of the steps are fast. But the band played real slowly—too slow actually. We got a little mixed up, especially at first, but we didn't think we were too bad. One man later asked me how long we practiced and when I said two weeks, he responded, "Oh, not bad for two weeks." Another told me that it was very good, except I was always one step behind. I only goofed on the first set, though. (Sally went off in the wrong direction once.) (No, no, I can't be comparing myself to SALLY. What, do you think, I'm CRAZY? My point is that I was drifting one way and Sally was drifting another. Maybe it would be best to just delete the whole sentence.)

We learned another new folk dance to perform with the schoolteachers. Mr. Rivera, my school principal, was my partner. He's a short plump little man and had some trouble kicking his leg and looking graceful at the same time. Half the dancers and their partners were in a line on one side and half on the other. We had one figure where we're supposed to come together and meet side by side in the center. But we were too close and it looked like we were all going to charge into one another for a minute there. But somehow we all survived and I think the audience enjoyed it more because they had a chance to laugh.

Sally's Birthday Party (August 1962)

Yesterday was Sally Pierce's birthday. This was the social event of the century in San Enrique. What a hectic time it was! Things started happening in the middle of the night. We were all peacefully sleeping and then our slumbers were abruptly terminated by the sound of hammering and the voices of Santa (our maid) and Boy (our landlady's son). I don't know whatever possessed them to start hanging curtains in the dead of night. Sally thought maybe it was some kind of birthday surprise, but was let down when she discovered in the morning it was only a doorway curtain. Someone loaned us her bright orange curtains. I guess she thought our green ones were too drab.

The next thing I knew it was the crack of dawn and naturally was Sally's cue to rise and shine. She just barely bounced out of bed in time this morning, though. She almost didn't beat Mrs. Bedayo our landlady and Boy to our living room. Boy was impatient to sit down and start playing his ukulele. Fortunately, he decided not to favor us with a vocal solo. He was saving his voice for the evening performance.

People started arriving in the early morning hours with the dishes which we had to borrow in order to have enough to go around. At one point, we were expecting about 100 guests. I decided I'd better get out of bed while the house was still relatively un-invaded. It was getting pretty late, anyhow. It was at least 6 am already. As it was, I didn't have enough time to get dressed before the coconut husk floor polishers swept in. This crew consisted of about a dozen young boys. They were ready and eager to begin work, but we had to restrain them temporarily while we moved some of the furniture. Our main problem was the beds. Since we planned to use the bedroom as a dining area, it was necessary to dispense with the beds. We intended to put them in our dressing room, but this proved to be too small. Thanks to Filipino ingenuity, though, our problems were neatly solved. Giovanni (Mrs. Bedayo's son) and Henry (the young man who lit our propane lanterns, or more succinctly our maid's cousin) climbed up on the rafters and secured the beds with a few strips of rattan. So our beds dangled overhead while the birthday festivities went on below. Not too many people seemed to pay much attention to them, although a few guests slyly commented that we might encounter a few difficulties when it was time to "climb" into bed.

After the floor polishers settled down to work, little girls started arriving with flowers. Sally had broadcast an appeal for flowers, and the children rallied to the demand. From the first brief flurries to the final avalanche, we scurried around locating all available containers and shoved the bouquets inside with the only the merest semblance of arrangement.

The essentials of our menu consisted of two local specialties: chicken adobo, and lechon, a pig slow roasted over an open fire on a spit. We were eating breakfast when the pig arrived—led on the end of a rope. I didn't look at him. I didn't want to have any prior acquaintance with him until I met him on the table. Nevertheless, the pig strove to make himself known, chiefly through his loud cries of protest. It seems he objected to joining the party as part of the menu. When I went downstairs for a minute, the chickens were in the midst of getting their necks cut. Like the pig, they also weren't too happy about the situation. One flew madly across my path, in a last ditch escape attempt. But he was quickly retrieved by one of the capable little girls who helped us all day to get ready for the party. (And who helped us all the next day to clean up after the event).

My companions and I have agreed that it's really no problem at all to give a party. As usual, everyone else took charge and we were left standing around helplessly. One woman volunteered to make the salad, another made a chocolate cake, one made a pink and white birthday cake and yet another made *leche flan*. Giovanni took charge of roasting the pig, which took all day. The Mayor sent a man over in the morning to put in electricity for the party. He hooked it up to the private generator in the municipal building. The Mayor was one of the first to arrive at the party. He kept saying, "We'll never eat all this food." As it was, we had just about enough. We had to send out for extra coke, and we'd ordered four cases. People kept coming and coming. We could barely move around in our humble little abode. I think the party was a success, though. One of the teachers remarked, "This is better than a fiesta."

Camp Brotherhood—the Beginning (Three letters from April and May 1962)

First letter: A group of Peace Corps volunteers from Negros and other provinces are going to have a summer camp for boys at Mambucal, which is a popular hillside resort where people escape the hottest months of the year. When I try to explain the camp at Mambucal, all my teachers say, "Oh, you're going to spend your vacation at Mambucal." They can't shake the image of Mambucal as a holiday resort. I've made arrangements to go around with the social worker to some of the barrios recruiting the neediest boys for the camp. They'll be between the ages of 10 and 16.

Mambucal is a really wonderful site. It's in a natural setting with lots of trees, even pine trees, which are unusual in Negros. Everyone is always telling us how cool Mambucal is, but it gets hot enough during the day. The nights get really cold, though, and you can use two blankets. They have two swimming pools which blend into the natural setting. They are made of stone and oval shaped. There are about 15 young Filipino college students working as counselors. I know I'm going to have a wonderful summer even though all the Peace Corps volunteers are such independent characters that there won't be any Indians; they'll all want to be Chiefs. (They won't necessarily be Chiefs, but they'll want to be.) They're usually scrapping about something.

There are many different guest cottages around the camp. Until we get settled, the women are sleeping on the floor of the Governor's cottage. The Governor had sent up some extra mats the night before Ann Snuggs and I arrived. It's so pleasant to be falling asleep while outside hearing the sound of voices serenading to the soft strum of guitars.

The boys who will be our campers haven't arrived yet. They come next Sunday. We've got all our tents pitched and now everyone's busy lashing bamboo benches and fences. They keep sending us out to straighten up our campsites. I'm sure there's a lot to be done, but it looks complete to me. I helped Ann yesterday. After she requested me to make a bench, I asked our friend Sammy for his saw. He ended up by making the whole thing. I tried to help another friend Francis lash together a fence, but I guess I got in his way and he did it all. Sometimes it's nice to have the boys do all the work we think up, but sometimes we'd like to do a little ourselves.

Second letter: We went to "fetch" a group of prospective campers on Sunday morning. We were divided up into pairs—a Filipino and an American. I was assigned to the farthest outpost—Sagay, which is about 134 kilometers away. Eight of us went in a jeep and got dropped off along the way in different towns. The trucks for the boys were supposed to be waiting in the towns already. We waited for about two hours and when the trucks didn't show up I had to get a bus to take 29 boys to camp. I didn't have too much trouble since the scoutmaster went out and rounded one (a bus, not necessarily the last bus) up in a jiffy. All along the way, I watched to see if any of my "companions" were left in a similar situation, but I didn't see anyone nor did I see any trucks.

The bus that I hired only went as far as Bacolod, which is about 40 kilometers from Mambucal. I had to do something with them from there. I took them to our old standby, the Sea Breeze Hotel. I thought the owner could help me out, but he was at Mambucal. When I mentioned the name of Mr. Miranda who had supplied some of the trucks, the man at the desk just happened to have him on the line. When two more groups arrived outside, Mr. Miranda promised to come over and straighten things out with a truck.

We now had about 60 boys on our hands. It was about noon and they were hungry. John Lagomarsino took charge. He got them all lined up and we marched them two by two along the streets of Bacolod to a Chinese restaurant. The proprietors were a little taken aback by the mass invasion, but we herded everyone upstairs where every four boys shared a big dish of *pansit*.

After lunch we returned to the Sea Breeze and crammed the boys on a truck. There wasn't enough room left for us, so one of the men rode in the back of the truck with the campers and we followed later in the jeep. Those boys from Sagay were bigger than the Filipino counselors. I think some of them lied when they said they were only 16 years old. Anyhow, they got to camp okay, although they were a little crowded on the truck. And I think a little rain was an added bonus for their trip.

Third letter: Now that the boys are here we've met a few problems. Some of them are homesick, but they don't just talk about being homesick. Since they are very self-sufficient, they do something about it. We've grabbed several of them just in the nick of time, heading for home. We had quite a time getting them here in the first place—we hate to see them leave without giving the camp a try.

We're struggling, trying to raise money for the camp. We have a very nice group of about 45 boys from Bacolod in my campsite. Some of the other groups have had trouble with fights, but my group is wonderful. They're winning all the prizes at camp—the neatest campsite, the best skit and so on. They think it's a lot of fun when they try to teach me words in their dialect and hear the funny ways I pronounce them. But they're very patient. It's a nice feeling when one of them will come up and grasp your hand and look up at you and smile.

Dave Mulholland's Death (June 1962)

We were in bed Sunday night when Leo Pastore, our volunteer leader, drove by in the jeep and called up to us. He said, "I have some bad news. Dave died this afternoon." Of course, we were very upset. It was worse when I went to send a telegram to Marge Pfankuch telling her about it. Monday afternoon, Dr. Howard and many others descended on San Enrique, telling us that we could go to Manila for the Memorial Service. We got travel vouchers for our tickets and flew to Manila Tuesday afternoon.

Wednesday morning we went to the service. Dave's parents had been with him a week before he died, but they decided not to stay for the service. His mother was pretty overwrought. It's just as well she didn't stay, because even though the service was very touching, it was an extremely emotional occasion. Ambassador Stevenson gave a eulogy and so did Vice President Pelaez. The church wasn't dark and dingy at all. It was comforting to be in such a bright place, rather than a gloomy dark church. The sunlight was streaming in on the white casket and flowers and the birds were flying around overhead. It made you think about God. Just the same, it was very sad. Going to that funeral was the hardest thing I've had to do here. I keep thinking of his parents when they saw him off at the airport in Boston and how proud they were of him. Now they were on their way home from the Philippines without their son.

When Dave first felt sick, he didn't do anything about it; then he didn't take his medicines. Eventually when he started to feel pain he didn't tell anyone and by the time he got to the hospital it was too late. He had amoebic dysentery and it infected his liver, eventually bursting it. Doctors had done an exploratory operation, but afterward he got pneumonia. Nonetheless, we heard one report that he was getting better. The day before he died, his best friend, John Lagomarsino, had returned to Negros, thinking Dave was going to get better. They were very close. John had "mothered" Dave. We got to know them very well this past summer at Camp Brotherhood. Dave was in my campsite group and John was in Ann's. Poor John took it very hard.

Typhoon Lucy (November 1962)

We had our first typhoon in Negros on November 26, 1962. San Enrique got just about the worst of it. They don't report storms well here. Before the storm came, we didn't know what time it was expected and afterward, we didn't hear any complete reports on the extent of damages. I think the newspaper said there were three dead, but Father O'Connell said that in Isabella, 15 were killed in a flash flood.

A lot of nipa houses were destroyed in San Enrique. Our two-story wooden house has a nipa roof. Nipa is a palm which local people use to thatch the walls and roof of buildings. Nipa buildings are cool and airy but flimsy in strong winds. We were very excited at first, but it was really worse than any storm I've ever been in, and we were a little afraid. Bits of the nipa roof kept falling down around our ears. We were a little concerned that one of the coconut trees swaying beside the house might fall on the house. But they all stood firm. The mango tree in the backyard was uprooted, though. Typhoon Lucy had winds reported at 75 mph, but there were pretty strong gusts. The galvanized iron roof blew off Ann's school.

In Bacolod, there were hardly any signs of the storm. People riding south from Bacolod were surprised to see the damage. A lot of banana trees fell down, since they have weak fibers. The people near the sea took shelter in a safer place, since they were afraid of the coconut trees. No one was killed here. It was certainly enough excitement to last awhile.

Upon returning from the Peace Corps, Beth worked at the Medford, Massachusetts Public Library and began taking graduate classes in Library Science. Before finishing her degree she was bitten again by the travel bug and soon left to spend a year in Korea with U.S. Army Special Services as a recreation director at a missile base about an hour's drive from Seoul.

When she returned stateside in 1967, she continued working with Special Services at Fort Belvoir, just outside of Washington D.C., where she met and married her husband Paul. They moved to Washington State where they lived for 17 years and Beth worked for the state Utilities and Transportation Commission. Paul and Beth were divorced in 1981.

In 1989 Beth returned to the DC area and worked as an executive secretary for a manufacturer of small airplanes. Because her parents were in ill health, she returned to Massachusetts in 1996. Finally having enough of ice and snow, she retired to Pensacola, Florida in 2005 where she has been happily pursuing "senior" activities such as bowling and line dancing.

Karen Long Santos
A Lifelong Adventure Launched by the Peace Corps

When I filled out the Peace Corps application and took the required test, I never dreamed that my life was about to begin a multi-cultural adventure that would lead to marriage in the Philippines and continue for a lifetime down an unpredictable path which still amazes this Nebraska small-town girl. For all of these experiences and memories, I am grateful.

A Young Republican Joins the Peace Corps

The telegram from Peace Corps Washington arrived as I was walking out the door of my parents' house in Diller, Nebraska to go to Rock Creek Station to watch the reenactment of the "Pony Express Riders and Life on the Prairie." It was July 1961. The telegram was an invitation to train for Group I Philippines.

Although an officer in the Young Republicans Club at the University of Nebraska, as news editor of the *Daily Nebraskan*, I had to cover Democrat John F. Kennedy's campaign in Lincoln. I was both impressed and inspired. When I heard his inaugural address that included "Ask not what your country can do for you but what you can do for your country," I was ready to join his program. Idealistic and adventuresome, I had done summer volunteer work in church camps, and youth and educational programs in the U.S. and Canada. As a child, the first book I ever checked out of a library was about children in Uruguay; I decided right then that I wanted to meet children all over the world.

The decision to accept or not had to be made quickly. My parents were silent—two years away and half way around the world must have seemed like an eternity. I had just started a job with the Nebraska Education Association and was doing part time work for the State 4-H office. A sorority sister and I had set up an apartment together and were planning her wedding. I was studying for finals and preparing for summer graduation. I was looking forward to the social life after college and waiting to see if things would work out with the guy I most admired. These were all factors. But my friends, who would never have gone on such an adventure themselves and who were with me at the Pony Express station that day said "go for it," and I did.

The morning after graduation a series of several connecting planes flights took me to Penn State in State College, Pennsylvania. My suitcase didn't make it. Another plane would not arrive for three days. But no worry, some of the friendliest people I had ever met were there with clothes and necessities to help me out. It gave me a very warm feeling to know we were all in this together to help one another and "roll with the punches," which became an often used slogan for all of us. When training began for this Peace Corps program, it was apparent that no one knew exactly what to do or how to do it. Each day brought expectations and new plans, which all seemed to change the next day.

Many of us knew little about the Philippines but after a few weeks we thought we understood the culture quite well. Ironically, Rolando Santos, a Filipino graduate student, who later became my husband, had been asked to train our group, but he declined and instead led a group to Europe with the Experiment in International Living.

Gathering at the Fairmont Hotel in San Francisco in mid September, we were given a grand send off the last night when we left for Manila, some on a Flying Tiger Cargo prop plane and others on a commercial jet. Dr. Larry Fuchs, Country Director, welcomed us at a ceremony outside Manila International Airport. We then got on busses that took us to Los Baños and nearby Mt. Makiling, the site of a former Boy Scout Camp, where we spent the next few weeks listening to experts on education and Filipino culture, studying Tagalog with native speakers, and going on field trips.

Fortunately I had the opportunity to serve in four very different assignments during the next two years. They were in Libon, Albay Central School; at Welfareville Children's Village, Mandaluyong, in Metro Manila; at Bicol Teacher's College Elementary Lab School and at the University of the Philippines Quezon City Elementary Lab School. During the second summer I enrolled in classes at Baguio Teachers Camp.

The Original Assignment: Libon, Albay

Libon was a small inland town, hot and dusty, where Mount Mayon volcano, with its perfect cone, was far enough away that we were protected from danger but close enough for a spectacular view. The Peace Corps assigned us to a house that was owned by a teacher, Andrea Serrano, a first grade teacher. She was a devout Catholic, a Girl Scout leader, and a very respected member of the community. She was embarrassed, however, to hold conversations and so she giggled as she gave commands. She and many of her relatives lived in a room adjacent to our five-room two-story house.

We were the town curiosity. The first night armed guards stood in front of our house and crowds filled the road out front, watching our every move. The next day we dismissed the guards.

Life was not easy in Libon. Little food was available locally. There was a bakery and a few small *sari-sari* (convenience) stores, but the nearest open market was a bus ride away. We travelled on open third-class buses, which accommodated people, animals, and anything else that needed to be moved. The schedule was unreliable. Sometimes I waited at the dusty stop all day, dressed professionally in nice clothes and heels, only to have to return the next day hoping that a bus might pass. Supposedly there was one car in town that belonged to the priest, but it never seemed to be working. Just like the unused refrigerators that stood in living rooms, the car was a prestige symbol.

The church was in ruins, only a shell of it being used for worship. Carabaos and workers passed our house on the way to the nearby rice fields. Some nights we had electricity for a few hours, but these nights were the exception. Beautiful orchid plants lined our outside stairway. There was always lots of gossip. The biggest news when we arrived was that the former governor, who was from Libon, had died suddenly and his ghost lived in the Seva family house down the street from us and kept doing strange things.

Mail from the U.S. took months. To help us get settled the Peace Corps sent trunks of supplies and books for use in the house and classrooms. We received complete sets of china and glassware, which looked like luxury items, but were really government surplus. Some of the volunteers just closed up the trunks and left them in corners. On Christmas Day, the first year, the Libon Postman brought me a stack of Christmas cards from the States. He said he had gone down to sort the mail that morning. This was a very nice gesture, but people soon learned we did not give the expected tips or other things away for favors.

The school was not far from our house, but when it rained we waded in water up to our knees to get there. The streets were often muddy. The shoes we'd brought with us quickly got moldy and ruined. Most village children were so poor that they could not afford pencils or pads of paper. They sat quietly and listened. I saved every scrap of paper, even gum wrappers, for them to do math and practice writing. Most girls wore the same pink dresses each day as once a year they were required to have new dresses (all alike) for the Mass Demonstration and Athletic Competition for District Officials to judge.

Our work, as I understood it, was to be teachers' aide's in the schools and do community development in our villages. That was broad enough for interpretation and imagination. One day I got a note during a meeting that said "Miss Long, You are the second American to sit in this building. The other came fifty years ago."

Though teachers said they liked our frankness, it was hard to get to know them and learn what they really felt. They wanted to please, and though poor, they showed their love and respect. They did not shower us with gifts as we made it clear that was against Peace Corps policy. The children loved to be around us and touch us, but were usually too shy to carry on conversations. In the classrooms they did answer questions and often recited the lessons in unison.

Years later we heard again from Miss Serrano, our landlord/teacher friend. She had invested her money in sending a niece to school. When the niece later became an overseas worker and paid her back, the niece advised her to invest the money in land in Alabang, a growing metro area, just south of Manila. Out of the blue Miss Serrano wrote a letter to me from a niece's house in New Jersey about 25 years after I had worked with her. When I called her back almost immediately, she was walking out the door to catch a plane to visit me in San Marino. There had been no news for years. After retirement, she had sold that land and used all the money to take a religious pilgrimage to Europe and then set out to find her Peace Corps friends and relatives in the U.S. For almost the first time she spoke openly. She also was out of money, having sent Holy Water and small items back to all her friends in Libon from everywhere she had travelled. When I asked her why she spent all her money, she said, "I have my house and a small rice field and some papaya trees. My pension pays for my Parkinson's medications and I own a burial plot. The only other thing I needed was to see you and the Holy places. Those were my dreams and they came true."

In 2005 my husband Rollie and I went back to Libon for our first visit since we'd left in 1963 after our marriage. We were surprised by the progress. The streets were cement, and the church was beautiful. The town was full of new homes, which had been built because of the remittances from the many young people who had become overseas workers. We went to the Mayor's Office and met the secretary, who had been my first grade student. She made a call and up the stairs bounded the Town Policeman, who had pumped my water as a seven-year old boy. An assistant took us to all the former teachers' homes. Tears, laughter, hugs, and picture taking filled what was one of the most memorable days of my life. The policeman's house was the last to be visited. It was Miss Serrano's Peace Corps House. Even though Miss Serrano had died, every piece of our old furniture was still there, but there was also a computer and television set. On the sala table were photo albums. Yes, they were filled with pictures of the Peace Corps volunteers and pictures sent after we'd left Libon.

I would like to think that the examples we set, the stories we told, and the hope we gave led some of our students in the '60s to go out and realize their potential and fulfill not only their dreams but the needs of their relatives.

A Second Job: Working with Filipino Youth on a Social Welfare Project

The Peace Corps/Philippines staff encouraged us to do special projects away from our assigned provincial schools during summer break. During our training in Los Baños the previous year, a newly formed group, Philippine Youth for UNICEF, came to see what Peace Corps was all about. A few of us did a day project with them. During our first few months in the provinces, some of the more curious members of this group came to visit us in our villages and wrote news articles which sometimes circulated internationally about our living and working with the Filipino people. The group included recent college graduates, who were potential future leaders, sons and daughters of prominent families, and young journalists. That group was doing a summer project at the government social service institution, "Welfareville for Children" in Mandaluyong, a suburb of Manila. Peace Corps volunteers were invited to join them. I joined the group as did some members of other newly-arrived groups.

During the first two weeks we were invited to stay in homes of the Filipino group members while special Peace Corps housing was being arranged. Another volunteer and I were asked to stay at the home of the late President Magsaysay with his widow, Luz, their son Jun (a member of the young volunteer group) and her two married daughters, Teresita and Mila, their husbands and children. I will never forget how Jun picked us up at Peace Corps Headquarters, treated us to halo-halo (the Filipino shaved ice dessert for which I have never acquired a taste) and then took us to their home. There Mrs. Magsaysay opened the door, held out her arms and said, "Welcome home." She also took us with her and the family to Baguio for Easter week where we visited as many churches as possible on Good Friday and observed traditional Lenten customs. On Sunday we attended the opening of the latest movie. Jun would talk for hours about how he wanted to help the poor by changing customs and the Filipino mind set.

Later, after moving with other volunteers to housing at the University of the Philippines campus, a fire destroyed all our belongings and the house where Peace Corps volunteers were housed. Mrs. Magsaysay again welcomed us back to stay in her home. Since clothes and shoes in our big sizes were not easily available, Filipino friends gave us a few necessities, but we also successfully appealed for help to the American Ambassador's wife. She got money for us and arranged a trip to Clark Air Base PX to get supplies.

That summer was a learning experience of how things get done Filipino-style for an organization like Welfareville. This run-down, overcrowded government institution housed juvenile delinquents, the offspring of lepers, orphans, and handicapped children. We spent time knocking on doors of influential individuals and organizations, appealing to the people who seemed to be in positions to help. We succeeded in getting the swimming pool reopened, reading and sports programs set up, crafts taught, and programs planned. Those kids had a good summer.

Some of the Peace Corps and Filipino youth volunteers formed close friendships. In fact, the Magsaysays still greet me with "Welcome Home" when I visit. During this past year they again took us to Baguio. Another member of that group, Jorge Ledesma, has become the godfather of our first child. One of our sons and his family who live in the Philippines coincidently have become friends with many of the children and grandchildren of my friends from that project.

One of the great things to come from projects like this is the commitment of many of these Filipino young people to stay in the Philippines. They have worked hard for 50 years to support and start charity programs and businesses which support nutrition projects, health clinics, education, housing, and sports competitions for less fortunate children and adults.

The Third Assignment: Working at Bicol Teacher's College Brings Romance

Going back to Libon after the summer program in 1962 was both a letdown and frustrating. The teachers and administrators, having become adjusted to us living and working among them, had gone back to their old habits, such as keeping books locked up so they wouldn't be charged for damages. They answered our suggestions by saying "yes," which really meant "no" or "maybe." Our helper in the house, who had cooked for us, disappeared presumably because she had been given such a hard time by relatives for working for the Americans. We began taking our meals with various families and paying them for food.

One day a telegram arrived saying, "Come to Legaspi to Bicol Teachers College tomorrow." It was addressed to my housemate Marty Allshouse. I said it must be just for her, but she convinced me to go along with her. On arrival we learned U.S. Peace Corps Director Sargent Shriver and a delegation from Washington were coming for a visit. We had been invited as part of the welcoming program. The problem was that the Peace Corps Director seemed to be having such a good time in the beautiful city of Zamboanga that he didn't want to leave. The plane did not arrive for 6 hours. The only thing to do was to sit and talk in the cafeteria while we waited. A newly arrived Professor, Dr. Rolando Santos, who loved to talk and tell stories, entertained us. He was in charge of the program for this welcome event. The next day back in Libon, I told Marty I would like a date with this professor; Marty said she'd like to debate him.

A few days later we were invited along with other Peace Corps volunteers to a party at the lovely home of a prominent landowner and businessman, Alfonso Carbo, and his wife Sophie. The Carbos were hungry for intellectual stimulation and found Peace Corps volunteers, out of town visitors, and again Rolando Santos great company. Bicol PC Director Bill Warren, his wife Jay, and their family had previously been our refuge and strength during the first year, but he was off to a new assignment in another part of the country. A new regional representative, Charley Dey and his wife Phoebe and family had replaced them.

Ray Meyer, the volunteer leader for Albay, and Charley decided that I needed to have more challenging and satisfying work. They arranged for me to teach at the Elementary Lab School at Bicol Teachers College two days a week. That third assignment would bring new cultural experiences because the teachers and students in this school were much more anxious to learn and talk. There were also many field trips and special ceremonies.

Other changes were taking place among the volunteers. Households were changing. Volunteers were getting sick and picking up diseases. One member of our group died. Several others quit or got sick and had to return to the U.S. I ended up in the hospital in Manila. Some volunteers got married. Even though we'd been in the Philippines for a year, we still had many questions and problems. Fortunately staff members were there to help us through them.

Rollie and I had a brief courtship during this period which is still the subject of local conversation. All the cultural barriers that we had studied were overshadowed by two people who wanted to be together. We married in April of 1963 in Legaspi at the home of Alfonso and Sophie Carbo with Mount Mayon in the background. Reverend David Schneider from the Lutheran church in Manila who happened to be in Legaspi at the time performed the ceremony. We went separately to the Archbishop's office for a parallel Catholic ceremony. Charley Dey stood in for my father, walking me down the aisle. The Peace Corps staff doctor, Dr. John Harkness and wife, who had become friends and advisors, came from Manila as did Jay Warren. The Filipino Dr. Baylon (married to an American) furnished the beautiful car for transportation. The reception was at the Albay Governor's Mansion. The cake was flown in from Zamboanga, courtesy of a favorite relative on Rollie's side. The ceremony/event was put together by Peace Corps friends, local teachers, local and international friends living in Legaspi. Mrs. Magsaysay had her dressmaker design and make my dress. The only family member present was Rollie's father who was afraid he might go to hell for attending his son's Lutheran wedding. Students and children too shy to come to the ceremony watched from the roadside and from behind bushes. No one thought our marriage would last.

This memoir seems a good opportunity to express thanks to everyone who stood by us all these years and contributed to that meaningful day—whether you picked the flowers for my bouquet, took photographs, stretched the shoes, gave advice, served the cake, played and sang love songs, or just showed up to be with us.

The Fourth Assignment: Working at UP and Establishing Lifelong Ties

We had no idea what we would do after Rollie taught summer school and I attended classes for the summer at Baguio Vacation Normal School Teachers Camp in 1963. Most of my group members would be going back to the U.S., traveling through various countries. A few extended, as I did. I knew that Annie Gison, the Filipino Peace Corps Secretary, who had gone out of her way to make some of us feel so welcome and close to her by taking us to her home, to social occasions, All Saints Day Celebrations and teaching us what to do and not do, would be there for me. She later became the godmother of our daughter when she married a Group I volunteer, Emery Bontrager, and moved to Los Angeles. Other meaningful supporters at the Peace Corps office in Manila were Dr. Larry Howard and his wife Betty, Mrs. Borneo and Dahlia. Dr. Manny Escudero, the Peace Corps psychologist advised us against the marriage, but later became the godfather of our second baby. He surprised us after the baby's birth when his good friend, my obstetrics doctor declined accepting any charges for the delivery. Bert Pumento and wife were very special and we visited together often after they moved to Hawaii.

The fourth assignment fell into place at the end of the Baguio summer session when Rollie was approached by the University of the Philippines (UP) President, Carlos Romulo, and the Dean of the University of the Philippines College of Education, Alfredo Morales, to teach at the University of the Philippines and be Dean of Men and Foreign Student Advisor. I learned I could co-teach fifth grade at the UP Elementary School. That would be a lot of work, but very low pay. For a while, Rollie and I shared a bedroom in a Peace Corps house with three volunteer leaders on the UP campus. When a separate house became available Rollie and I moved. This house became a center for some of the Peace Corps volunteers, Rotary scholars, Rollie's students, and my fifth grade students who often came over to sit on our patio and talk. I later would see one of those students in Los Angeles as a news photographer.

John Cort was a new Peace Corps staff member who arrived in 1962 with nine children and another born in Manila. Helen Cort would come over in her van, pick us up and take us to their house for dinner, or to educational lectures and art programs. She also became a godmother of one of our children. John's daughter Barbara who had attended Peace Corps camp in Negros as a child helped us organize a Philippines Group I reunion in Pasadena in 2009, where she made a presentation about recent development among the Muslim community of the Philippines.

Continuing Family Connections with the Philippines

In September 1965, Rollie and I along with our first two children and our Philippine helper, Virginia Afable, boarded the American President Lines ship, the President Wilson, to go to Los Angeles for a year and to visit my parents in Nebraska who had not seen me for four years or met my husband and children. Rollie would teach at Cal State University, Los Angeles and I would get a Masters of Education. We brought only five cardboard boxes of our things as we couldn't afford suitcases. We left most of our belongings in the Philippines since we thought we would return. While we've returned to the Philippines many times over the years, California has been our permanent address since 1965.

I look at our children and grandchildren and know how they have been impacted by our Peace Corps experiences. First and foremost, they all love Filipino food and the Philippines.

Our oldest son, Rolsky, who went to San Diego State University, has much contact with Filipino employees in the Navy Exchanges throughout the country as a civilian District Manager for the Department of Defense. He recently asked his Dad to give a cross cultural workshop and has requested follow-up sessions. His office wall is filled with pictures and medals for his rescue work during Florida hurricanes.

Our second son, Rick, who studied at the UC/Berkeley, London School of Economics, and Oxford, has taken Philippine citizenship and now lives there, but thanks to instant communication, often calls us as a sounding board on his business and charitable causes. He started and built up a large company with over 500 employees, which directly supports their families and indirectly many more. He has been President of the American Chamber of Commerce four times and is often looked to for property investment, interviews for TV and the media. He supports many charities and youth programs. One of his sons plays on a Rugby team with orphans. I can go to the Polo Club now on his membership and watch my three grandsons compete in many sports, but I was in big trouble for appearing there in the summer of 1962. Dr. Fuchs happened to be there and saw two of us as guests. We were called into his office the next day as he feared our presence might cause an international incident like the Ghana postcard saga shortly before.

Our daughter, Lei Lani, who obtained her Bachelor's and Master's degrees from UCLA, worked with the American Field Service, the international exchange program. She has also done multicultural programs for several companies and many volunteer community programs in Hawaii and California.

Our son Rob, who studied at Harvard, where he played football, works in international finance with Asia and Southeast Asia as his territory. He and his wife sponsor Inner-City (Los Angeles) Scholar/Rugby teams. They encourage and finance sending these teams to international competitions in Hong Kong and Europe. He says they've seen remarkable changes and results in academics and admittance to colleges—even Ivy League schools.

In the 1990s when we spent each fall, following Rob's football career at Harvard, we stayed in the apartment of one of John Cort's children. John was absolutely thrilled that he could be there to celebrate Rob's heroic play that won the Harvard-Yale game his senior year. It was during one of the Harvard games that I had the chance to sit near Ted Kennedy and his wife. We talked about the Peace Corps and how our son on the field would not have been there if his brother John F. Kennedy had not had the vision of bringing people together through Peace Corps.

Making a Difference

It is impossible to measure how successful we were or what differences we made. Some doubted the value of our service. From 50 years of speaking with people from various parts of the Philippines, I know each individual that served made some definite impact. I hear remarks like, "My English is good because a PCV taught me," "I would like to find Jane because she lived with a relative and we loved her so much," or "John gave me an incentive to do my best." We were not the ugly Americans. We were the genuine Americans that could cross cultural boundaries and cross economic divides. We did not have to wear designer clothes and our makeup did not have to be perfect. We were not the images they'd seen in the movies. For many of us, and Filipinos too, we learned and experienced that skin colors did not matter at a time when in many places it still did. Language barriers could be bridged. Politics and government did not have to divide us. We helped our students and co-workers feel the world was accessible. The remark that "he is not from this place" was not as significant as it use to be.

It is a big thrill for me now to see that beautiful books and stories for and about Filipino children in Pilipino and the regional dialects, as well as in English, are now available in bookstores in the Philippines. A National Peace Corps workshop with Filipino teachers in Ayala in 1963 tried to do just that. Another of my projects the year after Peace Corps, PAMANA, an organization that promoted Philippine heritage awards in the Philippines, also attempted to publish and promote children's books. Sometimes ideas planted or examples given, take a long time to get good results.

Lasting impressions came from smiles that were given, words that were spoken, opinions that were voiced, games that were played, foods that were shared, projects that were undertaken and completed, pictures that were taken, words from a dialect that were learned, a kilometer that was walked, songs that were sung, pats of approval that were given, and silence that was understood…

Karen Long Santos grew up in Diller, Nebraska. She married Dr. Rolando A. Santos in Legaspi in 1963. Since 1965 they have been in the Los Angeles area. They now divide time between homes in San Marino, California, and Pacific Beach (San Diego), and the family farm in Nebraska. Rolando is a Professor Emeritus at Cal State University in Los Angeles. He is a consultant for various educational and governmental projects and has just completed writing a dictionary and compendium of Chavacano, the principal dialect of his native city of Zamboanga. It will be published by the Ateneo Zamboanga Press.

Karen has been a San Marino volunteer and board head for many community organizations. Rollie and she run a small antique business in Ocean Beach, California. For twenty-two years she worked in wholesale trade, promoting mostly Philippine products. She is currently involved in CARES at County–USC Medical Center, where she was named the 2010 Volunteer of the Year. She is assisting in the 90th Anniversary Year for Pasadena College Women's Club, Membership Chair of San Marino City Club, Board Member of Zamboanga Hermosa Club and assisting the Historical Society of Diller, Nebraska and the Diller Community Foundation. They have 4 children, who are all working in international business and volunteer services. All have Filipino employees or co-workers. They have eight grandsons and two granddaughters.

(Both photos show Karen with her husband Rollie Santos; the first at the time of their wedding in 1963 and the second in 2010.)

Nancy Jeffers Schmidt
An Unforgettable Journey

The Journey Begins

What triggered my decision to join the Peace Corps? I graduated from high school in 1956. I had been accepted to Pasadena Playhouse so I could pursue my dream of being in the theatre. At the last moment, I changed my mind and accompanied my best friend to Texas Christian University. This didn't pan out for either of us, and I returned to Las Vegas and began taking classes at Nevada Southern University. By the time I'd heard about the Peace Corps I had attended three different universities with no degree to show for it. My big dream of becoming a highly successful character actress wasn't going anywhere. I was certainly at sixes and sevens. Perhaps that was it, or perhaps it was the idealist in me—maybe it was JFK's charisma—a combination of all three, I suspect.

Accepted for the initial training at Penn State University, I returned home, waiting for the fateful telegram. When it came, and I had been accepted into the Peace Corps, feelings of elation, trepidation and downright fear engulfed me. Clouds of doubt began to form. I was ready to change my mind. Soul searching conversations with my mother finally convinced me to gamble on the unknown and just do it. I did it, and so began an unforgettable journey.

How vividly I recall the day we landed in Manila. I remember lines of smiling, hand shaking people who greeted us. After several speeches we were herded onto buses, headed for final training at Los Baños. In spite of the pouring rain people stood along the road cheering and welcoming us. Upon arrival we immersed ourselves in classes and intensive language training. Several of us teamed up with the local theatre folks and staged the play *No Exit* by Jean Paul Sartre. I was cast as Inez, the lesbian. That had to enhance my reputation with the locals.

The Los Baños experience seemed like a "Never Never Land" between what we left behind and what was to come. We were all eager and anxious to get to our assignments. In a letter home to my mother I wrote: "We still have lots of questions about our assignments, what we'll be doing—our specific duties. I don't think that has been made very clear to us. " As a number of us would soon discover, it wasn't all that clear to the Filipinos either.

Training completed, all of us going to Southern Luzon boarded the Bicol express train. There were two classes, first and ordinary, the difference being that first class seats were softer and reclined. Other than that, the odors, the insects, the clutter were the same. There were many friendly Filipinos on the train who were naturally curious about us. I met a Filipino dentist whose goal was to marry an American. I was literally proposed to halfway through the trip. One of the railroad policemen took an interest in me. I was tired. He found me an empty seat where I could stretch out. He sat opposite me, running people off so I could sleep. Well, the darned seat collapsed and I rolled off, landing on my behind. Needless to say, I brought some comic relief to those around me. Everyone had a good laugh.

Volunteers got off the train along the way. The last of us proceeded to Legaspi City, the end of the line. That night, staying with a Filipino family, I was unable to sleep. I felt pangs of excitement and anxiety. Did I know enough about the culture? Was I a strong enough individual to take it? Time would determine.

Settling Down in Bulusan

My housemate Charlotte Hough and I arrived in Bulusan and waited several days before our house was ready. The house, constructed of nipa and wood, was on stilts. Moving day was a spectacle. Hordes of curious people watched us unpack our U.S. government household supply box. One item that caused amazed glances was a spray can of bug killer. People were also very curious about our toilet, considered a luxury. After you used it, you filled a bucket with water, poured it down the toilet, and the contents flowed into the river and out to sea.

As it grew darker, I hauled out the Coleman lantern. However, there was no white gas in town. So we used regular gas. After almost losing half a finger and breaking a few fingernails, I finally got the lantern assembled. Then I lit a match. Ssst-Blam. Lighting that match and turning the jet on too early resulted in singed eyebrows and burned fingers. We soon discovered that the lamp and the Coleman stove were bad news because we couldn't get the right fuel for them. The Coleman lamp was replaced by a kerosene lamp and the stove by four huge stones and coconut husk fuel that became the source for all of our cooking.

Other times we would discover that stuff the U.S. government thought we should have just didn't work in the barrios. On the other hand things that we really could use were not available because someone at the Embassy in Manila made the decision that they couldn't be used in the barrios. I remember the time we went to the Embassy in Manila to get kerosene lamps for some of the indigent families in our village. We were told kerosene lamps were considered passé and had been relegated to storage. Fortunately, we were able to find a "friend" in the Embassy who managed to acquire lamps for us to take back to our families.

Getting settled in our house was a milestone. Now, we were ready to get to work. After numerous delays, the principal of the central school finally worked out a schedule for us. I set out that first day, my spirits high, full of good intentions, looking forward to working with everyone. When I arrived, the principal was not there. No one seemed to know what I was to do. I warmed a seat for a while and finally went home. The next day I went back and was assigned teaching English to fifth and sixth graders. One of the teachers in particular seemed to resent me—one who had influence over the others. He tried to embarrass me several times. This lasted about two weeks. I decided to pull up stakes and began making the rounds of the barrios, looking for a place where I would be welcome.

To complicate things with the central school, there was an issue with the distribution of CARE milk. Children were paying three centavos a glass for it when it was available. Much of it was stored and rotting away. Charlotte and I began mixing the milk ourselves and giving it to all the children in the community. We expressed our concerns to CARE staff. Basically we were told that they couldn't do anything about it since the milk was distributed through the Philippine Bureau of Public Schools.

Another issue with CARE related to our community garden project. During training, CARE officials elaborated upon resources they had available to us, including garden kits. Our plan was to get the community involved in establishing and maintaining a garden. The food we grew would be distributed to local indigent families. We requested the kit, and received the following reply from CARE's Assistant Chief of Missions:

Regarding your letter requesting garden tools, we offer the following: We interpret your request as a personal one. I am sure you understand that a person in the United States who donates money does not expect that the money will be used for equipment for the personal needs of Americans abroad. I am afraid we cannot be of assistance to you.

We did not take kindly to this curt reply, and wrote a response that did not mince words. It worked. We received a kit, and had our garden.

In the meantime, we established a nursery school. It started with 10 children and grew to 40. We established a relationship with the wealthy family that had a private high school and I began teaching English classes for them.

It didn't take me long to find what became the "perfect fit" for me. It was the Barrio San Roque at the foot of the Bulusan volcano. My first day was unforgettable. At 6 am, I boarded the rickety bus along with other teachers commuting from Bulusan every day. It was full of people chickens, coconuts, and reeking with the smell of fish and petroleum. One of the teachers told me the bus comes through anywhere from 6:45 am to 8:15 am depending upon the engine, the tires or the number of glasses of tuba (the local palm wine) the bus driver had consumed the night before.

The bus rattled and creaked up around the coastline providing breathtaking views of the beaches and the ocean. Soon after, the ocean was hidden from view and a lush, mountainous area overgrown with tropical plants, flowers and palm trees took its place. The main part of the school was an old wooden structure. To one side of it were some prefabricated buildings and out in the back was a nipa hut, which served as my first classroom.

In a letter home, I described my first impression of the children:

> They are really something—naïve and innocent, their faces the faces of the poor and underprivileged, but also the faces of the gentle and the humble, most of all they are the faces of the eager, the willing. They swarmed about me, many not having seen an American before. They are simply dressed, most are barefoot. I noticed swollen bellies and open sores on some of them. And the teachers—eight of them—dedicating their lives to these children. One is a product of the Thomasite missionaries. One of the teachers told me how grateful they were because I had come to work with them. At the end of the day I thought to myself how grateful I was to these people for having accepted me with such open arms.

I had found my school in the school at San Roque, and our daily life in Bulusan continued. Some of my most vivid memories include:

- The wonderful relationship Charlotte and I had with our neighbors, Inoysidro and Oyaloly, and their nine children.
- Lubing, our 16-year-old hired helper who transformed during our time there from a cowering, shy, fearful soul into to an assertive, confident young woman.

- The night I woke up to get a cup of water in the kitchen and reached for the clay pot. Something wriggled through my hand, something alive. I screamed and Inoysidro came racing over. There, writhing though the slats was a huge python. Inoysidro felled it with several strikes of his bolo.

- The night thousands of ants invaded and completely covered our house. With the assistance of many neighbors, we burned them off with kerosene—a miracle the house didn't catch fire and burn.

- The infection in my foot. It produced gooey pus-filled cankerous sores that soon spread to my legs and face. I went to a doctor in Legaspi City. He told me I had yaws and put me on sulfa drugs and penicillin.

- The cholera epidemic that hit the area causing the death of many children.

- The day Ari came to live with us. Ari lived in a nipa hut with his parents and 12 siblings. His father died and his mother went to Manila leaving the children to live with relatives. One day he appeared at the kitchen door with his few belongings and literally moved in with us. Ari was kind and generous, but fierce as well. He had a beautiful smile, a voice like raw silk, and very bad breath, which improved when I took him to a dentist for the first time in his life. When I asked him how old he was, he said he thought he'd had six or seven summers. One regret—I tried to adopt Ari, but at the time, it was an almost impossible undertaking for a single woman. I should have persevered.

- The story of Juan. Juan was the village waif. He'd fallen from the roof of the municipal building when he was very young. People said this was why he "couldn't talk right." Neglected by his family, he wandered around begging and stealing. Ari began bringing Juan to the house. He responded immediately to being fed and getting some attention. I did have to teach him that stealing from me was not a wise thing. One afternoon I heard a great commotion. Ari came running in the house yelling that Juan was in trouble. We went down the street where a crowd of people was gathered laughing, shouting and throwing stones at something. The something was Juan. He was huddled in a ball holding his head in his hands, sobbing plaintively. I was furious. I screamed at everyone to stop. I raced over to Juan and picked him up. He was as limp as a rag doll. I carried him to the house, Ari following behind, shouting at the crowd. Ari shut the door, went over to Juan and said, "Don't cry, we are your *kaibigans* (your friends). No one will hurt you here."

- The time I went through a period of despair and depression. I was feeling lonely and isolated and sensed that the world was passing me by. Things were not going well with my students. My best friend was getting married back in the States and my two young nephews were growing up without their Auntie Nan. I wanted to go home, to be back with my friends and family and back in school. I spent several days in Manila where I received support from Peace Corps staff and was finally able to pull myself together. As I got off the bus back in Bulusan I was surrounded by a swarm of children greeting me with "tita Nancy, tita Nancy." Several of them had bouquets of flowers for me. They acted as if I'd been gone for months, not just a few days. I felt that I was home once again, and there was no question that I would be staying.

- The realization that prejudice is universal. Once I told my neighbor how beautiful her daughter Nina was. Her reply was "Oh, that can't be, she is my darkest child." I spent a month in Manila teaching at the National School for the Deaf and the Blind. My students were all deaf and/or blind. They were so excited when I arranged to take them to the American Embassy pool for swimming lessons. We had two certified swimming instructors, and the kids were extremely grateful and so well behaved. After our second visit, the head of the school informed me that we could no longer use the Embassy pool. There had been complaints about all those Filipino kids using "their pool." My first reaction was a feeling of indignation. Then a sense of sadness overtook me as I tried to figure out how I was going to explain this to my kids.

A Summer in the Muslim Heartland

My summer project took me to the Sulu Sea and the island of Jolo, a predominantly Muslim area. I lived with the Valbuena family and taught speech and drama at Notre Dame de Jolo College run by American Oblate Catholic Fathers. My Filipino friends up north were shocked to hear where I was going. They were convinced I would be harmed.

Getting there took us to Mindanao where we changed planes, and got on a rickety old thing that was bound for Jolo, but couldn't land because it was raining so hard. I was really scared. We finally landed in a rice field and one of the priests, Father Billman met us. The first question he asked was "Do you bowl?"

Jolo was hardly what I had expected after all I'd heard from people up North. It was a busy, bustling city full of industrious and progressive people. The beaches were the most pristine, spectacular ones I'd ever seen. You could wade several feet, look down and see incredible fish and vibrant colors. Getting to the beach was interesting. We experienced an ambush one time. Fortunately, we were in the priest's jeep, and we were allowed to pass. Another time, an armed guard accompanied me when I went down to the beach. I asked why, and was told it was just a temporary precaution. I befriended a number of Moslem families, and was fortunate to become the godmother to a Moslem child. I directed my drama students in Thornton Wilder's *Our Town*. It was a fascinating experience working with these young college students in this extraordinary part of the world.

Saying Farewell in Bulusan

I returned to Bulusan after the summer in Jolo and picked up where I had left off. Time flew by. The end of the second school year was almost over. My last few days in Bulusan were unforgettable. The realization of the inevitable, my leave taking began to envelop us all. We'd all been through so much together, especially Ari, Lubing and I.

San Roque graduation day finally arrived. The ceremony began late in the afternoon, and was very long. Afterward dinner was served. Then my seventh graders performed my play, *The Golden Goose*. The kids were great. By this time it was getting dark. The crowd moved out into the field behind the school and formed a huge circle. A table and chair were set up in the middle of the circle. I was asked to sit at the table. Then, my wonderful barrio families began paying tribute to me—songs were sung, dances were danced, poems were read. A hand written proclamation was read, making me an adopted daughter of San Roque. Every family had signed it. Then people came forward laden with handmade gifts, eggs and chickens—all gifts from the heart. Then the circle of people joined hands and began singing "Auld Lang Syne." I rose from my chair and walked toward my seventh graders—I broke into the circle and grasped the hands of two of my students. I needed to be part of the circle, not separate from it.

By the time it was over and I was on my way back to Bulusan, it was after 2 am. Ari and Lubing were there waiting for me. Ari took me by the hand and led me to his little room where he slept. He pointed to his woven mat and said, "No more here." I replied, "No more after tonight." He quietly stooped over, grasped the corner of his mat and pulled it into the room where Lubing and I slept. He said, "In here with you and Lubing. It's the last time." He lay himself down on the mat, said the little prayer I had taught him, and cried himself to sleep.

I was up at 6:30 the next morning. Soon after, my house was full of people. My students from San Roque had taken the first bus down the mountain to be with me that morning. It was good that they were there. I needed them to cook the 70 eggs I had acquired the night before. My students cooked a huge batch of scrambled eggs—fixed lots of coffee and toast and fed those who came to say goodbye. I scurried around the house to see if I had left anything. Finally the bus arrived. The house emptied as everyone rushed to the bus to wave me off. Suddenly I was left all alone. I looked around and for a precious second I reflected upon all that had happened here. Tears came to my eyes. Then the voices of Lubing, Ari and some of my students broke the spell and I hurried out to catch the bus.

Afterword

When I began working on my essay, I pulled out all my old letters and my diary. While reading the diary, I kept anticipating descriptions of deep, profound statements and philosophical thoughts that defined my experience. Well, that didn't happen. My diary was pretty mundane. It was an account of daily life, repetitive, and frankly, a bit tedious at times. I realized the deep reflective and the philosophical aspects of my experiences were not necessarily written down in my diary. Those occurred in all-night intense discussions and debates with my Peace Corps colleagues. They occurred the many times Charlotte and I sat up late at night pondering and sharing some of our deepest fears, doubts and frustrations as well as our successes and accomplishments. They occurred in personal and confidential letters we sent to one another, and in the letters I sent home to my mother.

What the diary does reflect, however, is the revelation that the human condition, the life we live in our own environments has its parallels in every culture. No matter where one is, despite the living conditions—there are commonalities. We must eat and drink. We experience the same range of human emotions whether we live in a nipa hut or a two story brick home. We laugh, we love, we cry, we have our ups, we have our downs. That's what happened to me in the Philippines living in the barrio, and it was the case when I returned home to the United States. As a matter of fact, often times when I returned home and someone asked me about my experience, I would reply that I had some of my highest highs and lowest lows as a Peace Corps Volunteer.

Shortly after returning to the States, I became a new bride married to a Navy pilot. We moved to Hanford, California in the middle of the San Joaquin Valley. I found a position working for the Armona Union Elementary School District as the Director of their new Language Enrichment Program. The classroom space was a converted WWII barracks. My students were children of migratory farm workers, low-income children and those with physical and/or emotional disabilities. I recall that first day. I gathered the children together and what did I see? I saw a rag tag group of kids, some in clean, but threadbare clothing, some paying more attention to the smell of freshly baked bread coming from the cafeteria than they were to me. I was to find out later that many came to school without having had any breakfast. A remark made by my principal came to mind. It seems that none of the teachers wanted to be relegated to the converted barracks. They were also not interested in this new position that would have to deal with such a hodgepodge of challenging children. When the principal introduced me to the teachers, he said, "I have every confidence in Nancy and her taking on this new position. She can do it; she has served in the Peace Corps." I was to discover in the next two years that the Peace Corps had prepared me well for my challenging new position at Armona. From that point on, my ensuing career became an extension of my Peace Corps experience.

A fourth-generation Nevadan, Nancy was born in Reno, and grew up in Las Vegas. She graduated from Las Vegas High School and attended Nevada Southern University (now UNLV). She met her first husband, a Navy pilot, in Manila before returning home from the Peace Corps. Her first post Peace Corps job was as a teacher in Armona, California. When her husband returned to civilian life in the 1970s, they moved back to Las Vegas, where she went to work for the Clark County Library District. After attending 11 schools in many places, she got her degree from UNLV in 1973. She obtained a Masters in Library Science from San Jose State University.

After a divorce from her first husband, she moved to Yuma, Arizona to take the position of Library Director for the city. In Yuma she met her current husband, Dr. Elwood Schmidt, a family physician. They were married in 1994. With this marriage, she inherited three fine sons and four grandchildren. They moved to Reno, Nevada in December 1994, where she became the Director of Washoe County Libraries the following month. While Director, she had the opportunity to build five new libraries as well as remodeling others. Three of the libraries received regional and national design awards.

After both retired, Nancy began blissfully re-engineering her life. She serves on the Nevada Humanities Board of Directors, the Nevada Council on Libraries and Literacy, and is the Chairperson for Northern Nevada Reads, a one book, one community project. She enjoys gourmet cooking, planting flowers in her garden and traveling the back roads of the West with Elwood.

(The first photo shows Nancy flanked by two Philippine school officials in Sorsogon; the second shows her in her library office in Reno, Nevada.)

Brenda Brown Schoonover

On Being an American

Changing Worlds

I had grown up in Halethorpe in Baltimore County, Maryland, in a predominately African-American neighborhood. It was a small community where everyone knew their neighbors, many who were family and where a number of the homes had been built by my great grandfather and his business partners. That part of Maryland was not as racially-divided as the Deep South, but it was definitely a segregated environment. Eating facilities were separate and department stores in nearby Baltimore would let Blacks purchase clothes, but we were not allowed to try on garments nor return them.

Until 1955, area public schools were segregated. My first ten years of schooling was in a school designated for Negroes (as we were called then). Kids in my neighborhood were bused from Halethorpe to the Benjamin Banneker Elementary, Junior and Senior High School in the "Colored" section of Catonsville. En route, we passed the Catonsville High School campus, a sprawling, state-of-the-art facility for white students. When Baltimore County enacted its school desegregation law in 1955, students at Banneker had the choice of remaining there or transferring to Catonsville. I was one of the nine students who decided to integrate Catonsville High, population 1500 as I recall. The situation was not as difficult or tense as in some parts of the country. Yet, it was not easy. For the most part, the nine of us were not met with open hostility, but there were few open arms. Over time, things did improve somewhat and by my senior year I was even selected to narrate the commencement pageant at graduation. I had also done well enough to secure a senatorial scholarship to any college under the umbrella of Maryland's state university system. I seriously considered the University of Maryland at College Park. However, because Catonsville High had been so socially isolating for me, I decided to go to the historically black college, Morgan State in Baltimore. So to speak, I came back to the fold, where I could feel welcomed.

But once I joined the Peace Corps, I felt part of a team whose players had a shared purpose and like values. We became a very special family as illustrated by the fact that many of us are dear friends who still keep in touch. I learned something I could not have learned at home during that period in our history. I learned to be an American as opposed to being a "Negro in America" negotiating the restrictions imposed by racism. I began to perceive my identity from a wider context than the nurturing community and school where I had lived and studied during my formative years.

The Peace Corps offered me a freedom denied to me in my own country at least in my part of the country during that era. I am under no illusion that people ever forgot my color; nor would I want them to; nor did I. The point is that I was less and less defined by my race. There were fewer assumptions based on how I would react as a Negro—more about how I would relate as an American.

In adjusting to the Philippines, unlike most fellow volunteers, I was accustomed to being in the minority. I now see that my response to being one of a handful of African Americans among an overwhelming majority of white students in Catonsville High turned out to be excellent training for living abroad. Instead of being intimidated because I was different, I chose to hold my head high and to wear my uniqueness with pride and as a badge of honor.

Daring to Take the Plunge

In hindsight, I realize that I really did not know what I was getting into when I joined the Peace Corps. How could any of us have known? It was all so new then. Yet today it is hard to imagine how my life would have been without that initial voyage into living and working outside of the United States.

So much has happened since that muggy, rainy day in October 1961 when we landed in Manila and took the long bus ride to the Los Baños training site with multiple stops in small towns, each treating us to a *merienda* (a small meal). I have had a rich and fulfilling career, much of which I can attribute to that life-changing start as Peace Corps Volunteer.

During our Peace Corps training, we had been steeped in cultural awareness by Professor George Guthrie. Once on the ground, it was time to apply that training. Nevertheless, there were at least two occasions that come to mind in which I flunked "Cultural Sensitivity 101."

Clueless One:

In our assigned town, Magarao, Camarines Sur, one Peace Corps Volunteer housemate and I brainstormed the idea of establishing a community library. Thanks to the cooperation of my mother and other family and friends in the U.S., the Baltimore Enoch Pratt Library, the Asia Foundation and the United States Information Service, we amassed a large number of book donations for the project. We set up a community library taskforce, held numerous planning sessions and assumed our Filipino colleagues were equally keen. Things seemed to be progressing well—or so we thought until we discovered that some of Filipino members had reneged on their commitments. In fact, in earlier meetings, a number of the town leaders and teachers had only been polite—telling us what they thought we wanted to hear. Pleasing us for the moment in order to avoid possible unpleasant disagreements was their gentle way of going along with the program but not owning it—perhaps hoping the issue would resolve itself or go away. It had not occurred to the Filipinos that we would see their actions as deceitful or dishonest. Unfortunately, when we learned that not everyone was on the same wave length, we volunteers became outraged and let it all out. One Filipino male teacher responded in kind, resentful of young American women telling him what to do. Ultimately, through the graciousness of most committee members, we managed to save the day.

From that experience, I learned to probe more gently, but more deeply to get forthcoming answers when soliciting cooperation from others. Had I not been so taken with the project, so full of my own "bright ideas," I might have picked up on the cultural cues, subtle signs of reluctance, faint unenthusiastic polite compliances. It was never easy, but I became more sensitive, more adept at communicating with my hosts. In the end the library was a success. Not only did the town provide space and shelving for the books, but also assigned the over-qualified town hall janitor as library attendant. The library remained intact for several years until it was hit by a typhoon, which I learned 15 years later when as a Foreign Service Officer, I had the chance to visit Magarao.

Clueless Two

Another example of miscommunications occurred in our own Peace Corps household only a month or so after my three housemates and I arrived in Magarao. It was early January 1962, by which time we were barely settled into our new house, a simple sturdily-constructed dwelling with a nipa (thatched) roof and the luxury of electricity, in-door plumbing and one small screened-in room. As with most volunteers and as was expected of us, we had a maid/cook. Rita Brabante was hired in advance of our December 1961 arrival by fellow Magarao teacher, Mrs. Barameda. Rita was quiet, pleasant and very helpful as we tried to adjust to our new surroundings. She made a great effort to please us, unaccustomed as we were to managing household help. Unfortunately, in just a little more than a month, Rita decided to quit because, "Her mother needed her at home." In an effort to get to the real reason for Rita's departure, we sought the advice of a "go-between," Mrs. Barameda. To our surprise, Rita had several complaints. For starters, we had left her for the weekend with no food. (She did not usually stay overnight; so, we had assumed she would eat at home with her family). Second, we had failed to provide expected bonuses for the movies or recreation. Third, the four of us constituted too many uncoordinated bosses giving confusing and conflicting directions. And last, but not least, we talked too fast!

Looking back, I believe we were so focused on establishing relations with our fellow teachers and community leaders that we had neglected to concentrate on basic communications with a person supporting us in our own home. Unwittingly, we had reserved cultural awareness for a certain segment of the population. We were able to resolve our differences with Rita thanks to the invaluable skills of Mrs. Barameda, who helped us maneuver through that situation as well as a few other scrapes. Rita turned out to be a good sport, tolerant of our "peculiar" ways. For me, Rita became such a confidant and part of our household that she was one of the people I sought out when I returned to the Philippines in the mid-1970s.

Re-Entry

Back home, not too long after my return from my volunteer assignment, there would be one last comeuppance on the racial front. Another African-American returned volunteer and I went to our alma mater, Morgan State College, on a Peace Corps recruiting trip. Afterward, he and I stopped at a very casual restaurant for a meal and we were refused service. Bluntly reminded that segregation in my country was alive and flourishing, I was hurt, disgusted. I had left our country to represent our great democracy. Yet, less than 35 miles from our nation's capital and only one mile away from my old campus, I could still be refused service because of the color of my skin. Fortunately for me that was the last such unpleasant encounter of its kind.

At the end of my volunteer stint in the fall 1963, I joined The Cardozo Project in Urban Teaching, a year-long pilot program in curriculum development utilizing returned Peace

Corps Volunteers in an urban setting, Cardozo High School in Washington D.C.. I had grown up in a small town. So, while the project was an invaluable experience, I must admit to a degree of culture shock. For me, working in the rough and tumble of an inner city American high school was quite an adjustment. I found the students a stark contrast to the well-behaved youngsters I had taught in the Philippine classroom.

However, nothing was more devastating that year than the senseless death of President John Fitzgerald Kennedy on November 22, 1963, a tragic day stamped in the memories of so many. For me it was made even more poignant because I had the honor to be one of the two returned Peace Corps Volunteers selected to represent the Peace Corps at the President's funeral three days later. The other returned volunteer was Thomas Scanlon who had served in the first group in Chile.

My recollections of my emotions are more vivid than of the proceedings of that sad occasion handled with the utmost elegance and dignity. The funeral was held in Washington D.C. at St. Mathews Cathedral and the burial at the Arlington National Cemetery. Cardinal Richard J. Cushing conducted the requiem mass. The cathedral was packed with dignitaries and distinguished guests, family and friends. I could not help but be in awe of the array of American leaders as well as foreign luminaries such as Emperor Haile Selassie, the Duke of Edinburgh, and King Baudouin of Belgium, all who had gathered to pay tribute to our President.

The assembled group left St. Mathews and was led to the motorcade that took us to the Arlington National Cemetery. Tom and I were honored to be assigned to the same car as Astronaut John Glenn and his lovely wife, Annie. As the solemn procession of more than 100 vehicles moved slowly along the route, I was profoundly touched by the throngs of bystanders, mourners, lined along the passages to pay their respects to our fallen leader. Despite the crowds, the city was eerily hushed on that cold winter afternoon as we passed through its elegant spacious boulevards, by its monuments and across the Potomac to the final tribute to John Fitzgerald Kennedy, who had been a beacon of hope for so many around the world.

The Kennedy Inspiration and the Peace Corps

One event that brought home to me the full significance of the impact the Kennedy era and the Peace Corps experience had on my life occurred thirty years later when I had the occasion to tour the Texas School Book Depository in Dallas and view the exhibit of events related to President Kennedy's assassination.

The longer I stayed on the sixth floor of the Texas School Book Depository, the more it struck me how much President Kennedy had influenced my life. Eventually, I stopped viewing the exhibit and sat on a side bench. I thought of how Kennedy's call to service in his inaugural address had heightened my interest in volunteering. Even earlier in my junior year in college I had seen two moving television documentaries on volunteering: one about *Crossroads Africa* and the other about *Teachers for East Africa*. Plus, I had gotten to know a number of African students on Morgan's campus. Those I met were incredibly dedicated and mature compared to American students. These encounters enhanced my interest in working abroad, preferably in Africa. And then as I was about to graduate from college, the Peace Corps was being formed—just what I had been looking for. I took the Peace Corps examination at the earliest possible opportunity. Twelve hours later, I had a telegram offering me an assignment in the Philippines! So, I located the Philippines on the map and responded in the affirmative. It was not Africa, but it was the answer to my wanderlust to serve abroad.

The Peace Corps had set me on a path that otherwise I would most likely never have dared to embark upon. As a liberal arts graduate with a minor in education, I was destined to teach in the public school system—a respectable, secure profession, which I accepted as the natural career path for many women college grads at the time.

Sitting there in the book depository, as all those memories surfaced, I found myself weeping, not caring who noticed me or what they thought. That day in Dallas seemed to solidify my realization of the dramatic effect the Peace Corps had on me. I thought of all of the wonderful people, fellow volunteers, other Americans and countless foreign nationals who have been a part of my life during my volunteer years and subsequent overseas experiences; of how the Peace Corps was the foundation for other major decisions such as my joining the Foreign Service. Even more importantly, it was while I was on the Peace Corps staff in Tanzania in the mid-1960s that I met my fantastic husband, Dick Schoonover, who was serving in our Embassy as Cultural Affairs Officer.

And, I also reflected on how much I had learned from my gentle and gracious Filipino hosts who had helped me develop an understanding of the importance of cultural sensitivity—knowledge that has served me well, especially as a diplomat, in the many countries I have lived and worked.

Yes, I thought of the moving funeral ceremonies of November 25, 1963. Yes, I was crying for our country's incredible loss of our vibrant President. But, I was also overcome with gratitude, a profound appreciation of my good fortune to have had the unique opportunity to be a pioneer, a part of Kennedy's brilliant creation of the Peace Corps at its inception. It was my gateway to many other far-flung places and encounters with so many fascinating people. It allowed me to be a citizen of the world- and a very lucky one at that.

Brenda Brown Schoonover, a native of Maryland, retired from the U.S. State Department Foreign Service in 2004 after more than 30 years of U.S. Government service. In addition to her volunteer assignment, she was also on the Peace Corps Staff in Washington and in Tanzania. There, she met her late husband of forty years, Foreign Service Officer Richard (Dick) Schoonover. She accompanied Dick on his tours with the United States Information Agency in Nigeria and Tunisia. After

Brenda joined the State Department, the couple had tandem assignments in the Philippines, Sri Lanka, Tunisia, and Belgium. Brenda was also U.S. Ambassador to Togo in West Africa. She currently lives in Chapel Hill, North Carolina and is on the advisory boards of the University of North Carolina's Global Education, the International Affairs Council in the Research Triangle, IntraHealth International and Carolina Friends of the Foreign Service. She is President of American Diplomacy Publishers, an on-line journal created more than a dozen years ago in Chapel Hill by a group of retired Foreign Service Officers.

(The first photo was taken in 1964 when Brenda was working on the Peace Corps staff in Tanzania in the mid-1960s; the second is her official photo as a U.S. Ambassador.)

Clair Whiting Sharpless
On Being a Teacher's Aide in a Rural Barrio

A New Volunteer (PCV# 04747) Settles In

I applied to the Peace Corps after reading an article in a Sunday Parade-type magazine on President Kennedy's concept of the Peace Corps. I was a recent college graduate, idealistic and full of energy. The idea of going to a foreign country, living with the people and working with them toward a worthy goal was just what I thought the youth of America needed to channel its energy and contribute to a better image of what Americans were really like. For me it didn't matter where in the world that might be. I had traveled quite a bit, thought I was rather flexible and didn't mind bugs.

On December 1, l961, in the town of Saravia, Negros Occidental, four rather tall, good-looking young women moved into a small second floor apartment above a family. We hired a housekeeper who shopped, cooked the evening meal for us, and washed our clothes. We had a toilet, a cold water shower, screens on the windows and electricity from 5:30 pm to 5:30 am. Saravia was about 24 kilometers north of Bacolod, the provincial capital. Negros Occidental was known for its large sugar cane haciendas owned by wealthy Filipinos. The sugar was sold to the United States at an inflated price (because of special diplomatic arrangements), making the rich richer while the cane workers earned a minimum of 2.50 pesos per day (about $0.85) during the harvesting season. Saravia was located between two large sugar mills, Victorias Milling to the north and the Hawaiian-Philippine Sugar Central, just south of us in Silay. Raising fish in ponds was also a means of livelihood for some of the townspeople. Elected officials traveled with body guards carrying automatic weapons, giving a frontier flavor to the town. We quickly learned that it was wise to stay indoors during election time.

The town of Saravia had 16 barrios, probably each with an elementary school, making each barrio a potential candidate for our assignments as educational aides. One day after our arrival a teacher took Patricia Horne, one of my roommates, to Barrio Nunca. They first rode a bus, then a jeepney, next a flat car pulled by a donkey and then walked a quarter of a mile to the barrio. That barrio was not chosen as one of our sites. Our house was directly across from the Central Elementary School where Patricia was eventually assigned. Jackie Melvin, another roommate, preferred the high school and eventually transferred to Bacolod to teach and produce plays at Bacolod High School. Betty Sherriffs was assigned to a barrio school, Tanza, a longer bus commute from our house and I was assigned to Alicante, with a small barrio school about ten minutes away by jeepney and a short walk.

At Alicante three classes were held in a large nipa building with a leaky roof, but the other buildings were cement structures. The sixth grade teacher and some of the boys were building a shop building which was soon completed after I arrived. The teaching staff of ten was supervised by a head teacher. There were two teachers for Grade 1, two for Grade 2, one for Grade 3, one for Grade 4, two for Grade 5 and one for Grade 6. Classes were large, with about 50-60 children in each. Children in Alicante seldom went beyond the fourth grade and rarely went to high school which in 1961 cost some 85 pesos per year. I found the teachers to be dedicated, energetic and generally good sports, eventually accepting me and my personality. I did speak English and could help them there, but I had never taught kids in school a day in my life! Peace Corps training included barely an introduction to learning the dialect spoken in our province. Could I implement what the Bureau of Public Schools defined as our job description as educational aides? Where to begin?

Teaching English as a Second Language

For a week or two I observed the methods of teaching in classes in the Central School and in Alicante. The rote method of learning was routine: recitation, simple questions and answers followed by a test ("Pencils up! Begin!"), exchanging of papers to be graded by their fellow classmates, and then the teacher exhorting the students to study the answers because the test would be given again the next day. The teachers said "If the children do not learn, what can we do? It's not our fault! Look at the odds. No equipment. No textbooks." The children seemed bright and eager to learn, but by Grade 3 when the medium of instruction changed to English, the children were unable to express themselves in anything other than their vernacular, Hiligaynon. The teachers were hardly good role models because they did not speak English with each other.

Before the Christmas vacation the teachers and I met to discuss where I could help them the most. In biweekly seminars at the end of the school day I implemented a program to practice English pronunciation and intonation, eventually graduating to a simple course in phonemics and structural analysis of English using Donald Lloyd's method learned in training. My first lecture was on the aural-oral approach to teaching English as a second language. We practiced patterns to improve their English and to demonstrate the application of the approach. Eventually each teacher took over the seminar and demonstrated a language lesson using the other teachers or using students from his or her class. We evaluated the demonstration using the outline of a language lesson that I had received from the English superintendent of the province who came to the barrio to help me and also help the teachers.

I had the extreme good fortune to have had teachers who were flexible enough to try new methods in their classes and who could tolerate suggestions from me. I had one Grade 1 Guide from the Bureau of Public Schools given to each of us in training which I passed on to the teachers. The Grade 2 Guide and material for Grades 3 and 4 came later. I emphasized planning units of lessons that followed a logical sequence. By February the two Grade 1 teachers planned all their English lessons through the end of the school year. As I remember, I was extremely pleased with the teachers' progress in implementing the new method of teaching English and much more confident of my own ability to teach and work with the teachers in a meaningful way. I often took over the English class for a teacher to demonstrate a concept. In fact, when a teacher was absent for some reason, instead of dismissing the class the head teacher did not mind if I took over the class all day and taught all the subjects. There were no substitute teachers in the barrio!

The next school year some of the teaching faculty changed and I started over with the new teachers. We were at ease with each other and the demonstrations and lessons generally went well. But my diary shows I was often frustrated and impatient because the new teachers were not catching on to the new methods as fast as I would have liked and occasionally were teaching a class without being prepared. For a while I considered asking for a change in assignment, but instead asked the district supervisor for an additional school not too far away.

One week I walked several kilometers alongside fishponds to a small elementary school in Barrio Tuburan to observe the English lessons and then help plan some lessons using the aural-oral approach. The Grade 1 and 2 teacher who brought her own two little well-behaved children to class everyday, seemed to catch on to the new method. I later visited the school to demonstrate some lessons. The second year I also participated in training sessions for Peace Corps volunteers in Zamboanga on the island of Mindanao, Dumaguete across the island in Negros Oriental and in Manila. It was a busy year.

Teaching Elementary School Science

I introduced new methods for teaching elementary school science in Alicante by working individually with teachers on their units. First, the Grade 5 teacher had a unit on magnetism and electricity. Producing static electricity in the classroom was a challenge because of the humidity. The kids loved constructing a circuit with a borrowed dry cell, a bell, and a switch made by a local machinist. As part of the unit the teacher, the kids and I went on a field trip to Saravia to see how the electric generator lit up a light bulb (of course, there was no electricity in Alicante that they could go to see). The kids also got to speak to the telephone operator, and check out the telegraph, a lawn mower, the town water tower, and the electric refrigerator in the Mayor's house! The kids eyes really lit up. Teachers wondered what the fun was about and came to me to work hands-on experimentation into their units.

Another unit on space and the constellations with a Grade 6 teacher generated a discussion with the kids that I will never forget. A youngster from the back of the room asked the teacher "Why do the planets stay in their orbits around the sun?" This was impressive because the student had processed the facts learned in the lesson and was able to formulate this question in English! The teacher and I had a small celebration. The hands-on experimentation encouraged the kids to raise questions and seek other possible explanations for the results they were observing. These new methods were catching on, especially since the classes were fun for everyone. One day I watched a demonstration of the "what-to-wear-on-a-rainy day" lesson when the Grade 1 teacher dumped some water on a properly dressed child to the hilarity of the other kids.

During my year and a half at Alicante I was witness to some changes in teaching methods, but also to the delivery of 250 text books from California. Each child now had a reader! Teaching English Guides for Grade 2 and 3 were provided later by the Bureau of Public Schools. We even had a small library in the curriculum office where I had my table-desk. My best friend and teacher, with whom I boarded for the last six months of my stay, wrote me a letter at the start of the next school year. She had attended the beginning of the year teacher seminars and wrote that "we are so proud enough that we can do better job than any of the demonstrators…due to the chances we had acquired from the Peace Corps. We can challenge any of them….Is there any objection Miss Clair Whiting?" Well, I don't know. I was conscientious, probably to a fault. If I helped her and others, it was my pleasure and that was my job. The teachers taught me also, how to slow down, how to ask questions and provide choices and how to be patient. They taught me what good friends are and the meaning of hospitality and generosity.

One of my major accomplishments at the school was to promote the construction of boys' and girls' toilets. When I arrived the "pits" were closed. The kids peed anywhere in the schoolyard and, since all were barefoot, they probably walked in it. All children had intestinal parasites as confirmed by a CARE doctor and pathologists who visited the school. The preferred method of the teachers was to encourage the children to urinate in a pot, add water and heave the contents out the window. I noted that kids stood outside and peeked in that very window to watch what we were doing at lunchtime. I told the school nurse who visited monthly, there had to be some sanitary changes and she agreed. Finally, by the end of my assignment one of the hacienderos (an owner of a sugar plantation) agreed to build some concrete toilets for the school. While these toilets were finished after my departure, I hope their construction made sanitation more a part of everyone's daily life.

Smooth Interpersonal Relationships (SIR)

Reading back over my diary and my letters home, I am amazed at how many people my roommates and I met, how many visitors we had at our house everyday, how many fiestas, dances and dinners we went to (how many times I came home exhausted from doing the twist) and how the people of Saravia accepted us and protected us. On our arrival the town council passed a resolution declaring us "adopted daughters." Our two best friend teachers often visited to tell us what the townspeople were saying about us, who had an active case of TB, who was a womanizer, etc., all things to make our relationships easier. When Betty developed a 104 degree temperature and we requested a doctor, the surgeon at the Hawaiian-Philippine Sugar Central hospital immediately drove out to pick her up (she had the measles!) and oversaw her excellent care. We were young women who liked to dance and sing; and we liked to listen and talk. We were interested in the politics of the country, the town, the elections of barrio councils and the discussions of President Kennedy's lowering the price of sugar (an all-consuming topic among the hacienderos and sugar mill executives). We could discuss religion in the schools, racial discrimination in America and the Vietnam War. There wasn't a topic that wasn't discussed including World War II which so many Filipinos had had a part in. In fact, it seemed that the war had ended only a short time before.

In my barrio I formed a group of teenagers who enjoyed speaking English. We met twice a week to discuss a topic of their choosing. My notes show we covered communism, America, and evolution among other topics. We also planned an excursion to the beach and had a marvelous time. I heard about their troubles finding employment and about their disputes which unfortunately sometimes ended in violent solutions. Gradually the school children began to feel comfortable coming to visit me in my curriculum lab. Even a few of their parents showed up. I felt like the Peace Corps was a people-to-people project and on that score was certainly successful. No one was "ashamed" or shy to approach us at home or at school.

Part of forming friendships and good personal relations had to do with learning the language, Hiligaynon. Early on our two best friend teachers and later the parish priest gave us language lessons each week. I also spent several weeks at a language institute at Central Philippines University in Iloilo City, Panay, which really helped me with vocabulary and grammar. Talking with townspeople and conversing in the jeepneys helped to integrate us into the life of the town and barrio.

Looking Back

To this day if I happen to mention to friends or acquaintances that I was in the Peace Corps, I elicit responses of awe and wonderment and, of course, many questions about where and when I served. The Peace Corps experience is an important part of me. My two years in the Philippines as an educational aide in a barrio school are still the most concentrated, adventurous and exciting times of my life. I met my life-mate and best friend, Tom Sharpless, in training and we have never in forty-six years of marriage ceased to talk (and laugh) about our shared experiences and to remember our Filipino friends and the volunteers in our group.

On returning to the States, Clair spent some time looking for a job teaching English as a second language in Chicago where she had many friends from her college days at Northwestern University,

but the Chicago public schools had a full roster of tenured teachers in the field. After being advised to pursue a graduate degree, she entered a master's program in Speech and Language Pathology at Northwestern. After her marriage to Tom Sharpless, she transferred to the University of Florida Department of Speech. Upon graduation she became the speech therapist in the Starke County Public Schools, and eventually supervised student therapists in the schools at the University of Florida.

Clair and Tom moved to Connecticut in 1968. While their two daughters were in school, she was a leader for their Girl Scout troops. She also was a charter member and later program manager of her Connecticut town's cable access TV station. Gardening is her current hobby and her three grandchildren the delight of their retirement years.

(The first photo shows Clair on the far right with her housemates in Victorias, Negros Occidental. From the left are Jackie Melvin, Pat Horne, Betty Sherriffs, and Clair; the second photos shows Clair with her husband Tom.)

Tom Sharpless
Teaching Science in the Philippines

Joining Up

Having just graduated from the University of Miami with a BS in Chemistry, I was interviewing for various positions in the summer of 1961 when the Peace Corps programs were seeking volunteers. The one job I turned down upon acceptance into the Peace Corps was as a quality control tester in a Coca Cola bottling plant in Bermuda. My plan was to work a few years and then pursue a Masters degree in chemistry. I would decide later whether to become a research scientist (not fully realizing then that I would need a PhD to do that) or teach chemistry in a high school.

The Peace Corps offered the chance to experience teaching and to delay making this decision. The factors that predisposed me toward becoming a volunteer were an eagerness to see the world, experience a foreign culture, participate in my country's seemingly more enlightened foreign policies, and no felt need to make money.

Encountering the Philippines and the Island of Masbate

I certainly knew a lot more about the Philippines after reading Little Brown Brother at Penn State, than I did before. Previously, I knew its location and I had heard of the Bataan "Death March" and the landing at Leyte, but I did not personally know anyone who had been to the Philippines. I probably thought their language was Spanish. I recall going to a lounge in Miami featuring a Filipino band just to see what Filipinos looked like. My first impressions of Filipinos came at Penn State where several Filipino students introduced themselves and attended some of our classes. I recall how a few of their feathers were ruffled when our social psychology professor described some of the lengths to which Filipinos may go to preserve smooth interpersonal relationships (SIR). I began to realize that one could not analyze SIR without violating SIR.

The Filipinos treated us like celebrities when we reached Manila. We quickly gained a sense of the importance in Philippine culture of music, oration, and feasting. From their point of view, we arrived at a most opportune time because we could participate in a province-wide event called the All-Bicol games by performing traditional dances with scores of other teachers. This was our first big act in Masbate where we were initially assigned. Masbate, an island slightly larger than the State of Rhode Island, is located south of the Bicol Peninsula in the Sibuyan Sea, the site of a famous air battle against the Imperial Japanese Central fleet during the landing of American forces at Leyte and Samar.

I was assigned to the central elementary school in Milagros, Masbate, a coastal fishing town. The principal there was also the principal of all the schools of the outlying barrios, including several that could be reached only by sea. He was very pleased to see me and tried to make me comfortable by providing me a desk near his office. Whenever he was called to visit other schools for various assemblies, he took me along. One of these visits entailed an hour's ride in a banca, a canoe-like boat with an outrigger. Among the songs we sang along the way was You Are My Sunshine.

We were in Milagros when the Cuban missile crisis took place. A Filipino family, who learned of the situation before we did, came to our house and asked if we had news as they were worried about their son in the U.S. Navy. Perhaps they took our ignorance as a sign that the crisis couldn't be that bad.

Masbate is known for cattle ranching and fishing. Mike Rosenthal, one of my roommates, made the discovery of how fish were caught in this part of the Philippines. Our neighbor, who was the captain of a fleet of fishing boats, invited Mike to go out with the fleet one night. Mike had even brought his fishing rod. The next morning an ashen Mike told us they use dynamite in coke bottles. "The shorter the fuse, the bigger the fish." It was only then we realized why we encountered so many men without hands. The other major economic activity in our town was smuggling "blue seal" cigarettes from offshore freighters.

We learned about guerilla activity on the island during the Japanese occupation. My principal, Mr. Froilan, and the social studies teacher, were both officers in one of the guerilla bands. They described how during a battle with another guerilla band they were surprised by the Japanese and nearly captured. My principal also spoke of his participating in the trial and execution of an important political figure who had been accused of collaborating with the Japanese. Anyone of means at the time found it much easier to live in Manila than on Masbate where food was in short supply and the local Japanese commanders were cruel. We were all impressed with how the Masbateños spoke of the war as though it had just ended.

Our group of four was in Milagros for nearly eight months when we were ordered out because of a local breakout of cholera. I doubt we were in any real danger as the disease seemed to discriminate against the poor. The teachers gave us a send-off party and seemed genuinely sorry to see us leave. I hoped that the science teachers would continue the hands-on science teaching projects we had started and that the tools I got from AID would be used to set up a woodworking shop.

Teaching Science in Albay

Mr. Garcia, the principal of Albay High School in Guinobatan happened to be at the provincial supervisor's office in Legazpi, Albay, when I was interviewing for a science teacher's aide position. He was delighted that I had decided to look into his school. Thus began phase two of my Philippines experiences.

Being in the first group of volunteers had definite advantages from my point of view. I liked the freedom to mold my own mission. I recall Dr. Fuchs, the project director, calling a meeting of volunteers who happened to be in Manila at one point. He wanted to discuss the need felt by some volunteers for more direction and support. I never considered myself to have those needs.

My roommate, Brian Johnston, and I selected quarters on a small farm near the high school. Copra and pigs were the main products. The Reantazo family, who ran the farm, became good friends. Brian elected to work at the provincial hospital in Legazpi, a harrowing thirty-minute bus ride away. We were soon joined by two additional volunteers from Group V, John Laing and Henry McFadden, who had been trained to work at the high school level in science and math and were assigned to Albay High School. Years later, the school was renamed the Marcial O. Ranola Memorial High School. Mr. Garcia introduced me to Mr. Nelson Yap, the teacher of Industrial Arts.

Nelson and I quickly became friends and undertook several projects together, one of which was to construct a six-inch reflecting telescope. Again I emphasized laboratories with hands-on experimentation. I was surprised to find a storage room filled with expensive science teaching equipment such as a Hooke's Law apparatus that could give you the change in spring length to the tenth of a millimeter and used very accurate, chrome-plated weights. The physics teacher had never used any of it because the equipment required careful handling and would soon be damaged. The apparati did serve, however, as trophies and a reminder of the generosity of USAID. With Nelson's help, I had the students construct the instructional equipment they needed using materials at hand.

In my quest to find simple equipment for the teaching of science, I learned about a Silesian brother at the Don Bosco School in Tarlac City in Luzon who had developed an impressive array of science instructional materials using everyday items. I traveled to meet him with Jennifer Grant, a volunteer from our group who had become a group leader. There, among other things, we learned that the suitability of a plastic coaster as an insulator for an electroscope depended on its color. Apparently some dyes enhance the conductivity and allow the charge to leak away. From this visit I got the idea that it would be useful to provide volunteers with kits consisting of simple materials and instructions for building various simple pieces of equipment for science experiments. That project faltered essentially because the $65 price tag per kit was considered too high by Dr. Harville, a science teaching consultant hired by the Peace Corps. I suspect Harville's lack of enthusiasm was due to the fact that the kit was oriented toward the physical sciences whereas Harville was a biologist.

As had been apparent from the beginning of our training at Penn State, even though English and science shared equal billing as objectives for our program in the Philippines, there were only a few of us with science backgrounds who were teaching or assisting in science education on a full time basis, particularly at the secondary school level. That was about to change with the arrival of the Group V volunteers who were specifically trained to teach secondary school science and mathematics. Warren McNealy, Ann Hankins, Foster Wiggins and I participated in the in-country training of these volunteers and also in an abortive "National Science Development Board Summer Institute," which was supposed to recommend changes to the Bureau of Public Schools' Science curricula. The Institute turned into a political scramble to decide which schools would get the resources provided by the U.S. Agency for International Development. Curriculum reform seemed to be of minimal concern to many of the participants.

During the summer break of 1962 I took part in a teacher training institute that Sally Pierce, another volunteer leader, had set up at the La Salle school in Bacolod, Negros Occidental. I conducted workshops in which science teachers from all parts of the province of Negros Occidental came to study and learn, among other things, how to construct science teaching equipment. Teaching in Bacolod had the added benefit of the opportunity to court Clair Whiting, a volunteer teaching in Negros, who would become my wife.

The Effect of the PC Experience

I'm sure the Peace Corps has had a positive effect both on the volunteers and the people served. I suspect the main effect is that it put faces on people that you might otherwise pay little attention to. The Filipinos who met us were able—perhaps—to see us as persons who may not have fit their preconceptions. When I returned to the Philippines in 1980, I was mightily impressed with the durability of the friendships I had among the teachers at the high school in Guinobatan. The comradery took up so much time that I was not able to see whether there was any evidence that hands-on experience in the science labs had displaced rote learning to any degree. I did note that the high school was much more crowded. There were unmistakable signs of progress in the town, such as the concrete highway and 24-hour electricity. It was apparent, however, that many of the current problems were connected to the country's rapid population growth because of a high fertility rate. It is encouraging to note that the fertility rate was down 25% in 1980 from its level in 1962. (It has approximately halved between 1962 [6.8 children per woman] and the present [3.3 children per woman]). Fertility levels were (and still are) well above replacement level and less progress in controlling fertility was made in the Philippines than in neighboring countries. I suspected that future economic progress would be constrained by both population growth and regular natural disasters.

I have remained in contact with the families of several Filipino friends from Albay in recent years. Two of the children of the Reantazo family who were our landlords in Guinobatan remain Facebook contacts. One of the children and one grandchild of Nelson Yap, the industrial arts teacher in the high school are also friends on Facebook. I have on one occasion "chatted" with Nelson on the computer when he visited one of his daughters in Manila. We also correspond by regular mail, especially after Mt. Mayon erupts or a typhoon goes through.

Guinobatan was covered with ash from an eruption of Mt. Mayon in 1968, and again in 2000. Typhoon Durian brought ash and water down on the town in 2006. Each time I read of these catastrophes my mind flooded with the memories of those places and I have felt great sympathy for the people who have to struggle against these adversities.

Tom Sharpless married Clair Whiting, a volunteer stationed on Negros Occidental, in 1964. They currently divide their time between Simsbury, Connecticut and Miami, Florida. Tom received his PhD from the University of Florida in 1968, the year their first daughter was born. Their second daughter was born in 1969 in Hartford, CT where Tom taught in the Chemistry Department at the University of Hartford. He retired in 1998 to pursue other interests including helping to raise his grandchildren.

(The first photo shows Tom demonstrating the use of a telescope to students at Albay High School in Guinobatan, Albay; the second shows him with his wife Clair.)

Claire Horan Smith

(In collaboration with Jo McMakin Brooks)

Remembering Gini

In the small, unassuming barrio of Nato, Camarines Sur, Philippines, there is a legacy of love. Among the beaches, waving coconut palms and outrigger fishing boats, school children enjoy a full functioning library and seniors share memories of a great lady. The library project was begun and sustained by the love and deep bond that bloomed between Miss Virginia Lee Hopkins and the people of this small fishing village. The memories are of an educator and a role model who gave three years to the children of Nato and who by her very presence and encouraging words inspired children and adults to see themselves as beautiful and accomplished human beings.

Virginia Lee Hopkins (1940–1999) grew up in Portland, Oregon. The somewhat rarified air in Portland in terms of race relations in the late fifties and early sixties allowed Gini to escape some of the racist realities experienced by other African Americans throughout the United States. However, even in Portland, to achieve as an African American you had to reach higher, be smarter and work harder while always being extremely proper, and respectful to those with whom you interacted. Gini graduated with honors from a predominately white high school serving as class historian. She received her BA from Oregon College of Education and then brought that discipline and strength with her to the Peace Corps.

We were four in our household, three songbirds and a mother hen. Gini, Jo McMakin (Brooks), Sue Johnson (Johnson), the three songbirds, bonded at Penn State and quickly became the musical voice of Philippines Peace Corps 1. With their quick mastery of Filipino folksongs, they were sought after for every welcoming ceremony. Their sound was delightful. Gini's voice especially was rich and resonant. I was added to the threesome and quickly became the designated speaker for the group since the others were the performers. I can't say I was thrilled with my role but then I couldn't sing. We were a close group, bonding in a way that a significant shared experience will create. There were long nights of rehashing the day's events, analyzing each and every comment, figuring out our latest faux pas. There were conversations about things that were awkward such as being 5'9" in a country full of exquisitely delicate 5-foot 4-inch females and conversations about how the humidity caused

Jo's hair to curl in clumps. Gini's response was that we had no clue as to what constituted a bad hair day.

All points of the U.S. map were represented in our house from Portland, Oregon, to Providence, Rhode Island (me), from Spartanburg, South Carolina (Jo), to Steubenville, Ohio (Sue). Catholic, Protestant, public school, private school, racially aware, mostly clueless, we brought it all to those evenings in Tigaon, Camarines Sur. We frequently discussed the level of self-consciousness about skin color so prevalent in the Philippines. The conversations, however, were on an intellectual level not a personal one. Gini's natural reserve held her back from sharing incidents and feelings, especially ones that were painful. It took several months into our assignment before we realized that our "tower of strength" was feeling under siege. Sue and Gini are gone now. Both Sue's infectious laughter and Gini's "regal" self are very much missed. It is, however, Gini's experiences that Jo and I feel are important to share. It is a story with some difficult moments, determined coping, understanding and love.

Our household was not unique to Peace Corps, but it certainly did not represent the reality of race relations in the U.S. We, in a way, were the future but there was to be a long road between then and now. *Life* magazine, which was found in many Filipino households, told a different story. African Americans when pictured in *Life* in 1961 would probably have been shown in subservient roles, or an occasional vocalist or musician. As the Civil Rights movement heated up, the face of violence against African Americans would be shown in *Life* as well. The disconnect between *Life* and the picture we were presenting made for some funny moments as well as for some difficult conversations. The third or fourth day after we arrived in our assigned community, a small delegation of folks from a nearby barrio came to visit. Gini was outside attempting to do something with our small patch of garden. Most politely, one member of the group ask Gini if she would "Inform her mistresses that some neighbors had stopped by." I remember Gini, ramrod straight, indignation oozing from every pore coming into the house, asking, " Please, someone inform these nice folks that I am not your maid!" Of course, clarification was quickly made all around. Gini was absolutely charming, laughing with our visitors reassuring them that no offense was taken. Afterward, you can be sure, there was much joking and teasing about avoiding the appearance of servitude by not weeding the garden, which was a hopeless case anyway. A confusing moment eased by openness, clarification and laughter.

In the early weeks we did most things as a group, then as time passed we moved out into our individual school assignments. Hopping the Alatco bus to get to school, running to the market, church on Sundays, day trips to Mt. Mayon with Filipino friends became more frequent. This is when Jo began to notice the change in Gini. She was closing down, avoiding crowds, trips, and invitations especially if she had to go alone. We knew she loved her school and yet more and more frequently failed to catch the bus in order to get there. This went on for quite a while. Unfortunately, that reserve of Gini's forestalled discussion. She didn't share and we didn't push. Jo talked her into taking a field trip with Jo's school. The trip was an eye-opener. While stopped at a roadside stand, Jo heard the Bicol dialect equivalent of "super dark" being called out several times with accompanying laughter. Then she noticed Gini hunched over on the bus "tying" her shoes. The same thing happened on the return trip. With gentle encouragement from Jo, she admitted that this type of thing had been going on from the beginning. Crowds, buses, public places, especially if she were alone, had become occasions of possible ridicule. Places of comfort were our friends and neighbors, our home and her school, but getting to school had become almost paralyzing. The open-air bus offered no protection from curious eyes.

Gini regrouped, drawing on some deep inner strength uniquely hers. There was a small Evangelical Church in our very Catholic town. Gini joined, sharing that magnificent voice. She was quickly loved and treasured by a group of young women from the church. During a visit to our home, one young woman, obviously enchanted by and adoring of Gini, was holding her arm, rubbing it. I remember the woman saying, "So dark, what a pity for you." Gini covered her hand and gave her a hug perhaps recognizing that it wasn't about Gini's darker pigmentation but about the young woman's insecurity with her own brown skin. Although "Black is Beautiful" did not arrive as a movement until much later in the United States, it quietly bloomed in the Philippines under the auspices of Miss Virginia Lee Hopkins in 1961.

Toward the end of the first year, some of us moved out into our assigned barrio communities. Gini built an adorable nipa hut in her fishing village of Nato, Camarines Sur and began immersing herself in the life of the community. The problem of the bus ride was solved. I suspect that the fact that the folks in this fishing community were of a darker skin tone gave Gini a sense of mission as well. Jo recalls sitting on the beach one evening with Gini while a group of children were putting flowers in their hair. Giggling, a shy little girl told Gini how pretty she was. Gini replied, "Just like you, do you have any idea just how beautiful you are?"

By the end of the second year when most of us were heading home Gini was in full swing. She had signed up for a third year in Nato. The library project, which she was committed to for the rest of her life, was underway. She had a couple of students on scholarships at the local high school. She was even appearing on Philippine Television. All concerns as to "comfort zones" seemed to have vanished. Gini was not an activist; she was a presence. Jo would call her "Duskily Regal." She was dark skinned and she was beautiful. We were her housemates proud to have shared those special years beside her.

All four of us went on to careers in public service. Sue became a social worker; I returned to teaching; Jo became involved with environmental quality issues; Gini found her niche in higher education. Winning a Study Fellowship in International Development from the Ford Foundation, she earned her Masters in Education from Columbia University. Gini fell in love with New York and with George Roland Hayes, a young actor. George passed away early in their marriage leaving Gini two beautiful gifts, Amanda Rose and Gregory Austin, the greatest joys of her life.

Gini spent twenty years working for the State University of New York Educational Opportunity Center in Brooklyn as a teacher, counselor and mentor. While coping with an increasingly debilitating disease, Gini served at the Center as Assistant Director for the Office of Student Affairs. Her fellow teachers and counselors felt that the Center allowed Gini to indulge the primary passion of her life, supporting, nudging, pushing, young people to believe in themselves and their future.

Church was always very important to Gini. Calvary Baptist Church played a central role in her life until her death in 1999. There she served in a variety of capacities, Head Teacher, Youth Coordinator, Bible School Director. She was much loved and according to church members, touched the lives of hundreds of children in a significant and personal way.

Sue passed away in the late eighties. Jo and I are retired, enjoying friends, family and grandchildren. We appreciate this opportunity to salute an incredibly caring and giving human being: Virginia Hopkins Hayes.

(The first photo shows the four volunteers assigned to Tigaon, Camarines Sur. From left are Sue Johnson, Virginia, Hopkins, Claire Horan, and Betty Jo McMakin; the second photo shows Gini flanked by her two children Amanda Rose Hayes and Gregory Austin Hayes.)

Ann Snuggs
Joining the Peace Corps Twice

Life before the Peace Corps

My first job after graduating from Auburn University in June of 1960 was with the Social Security Administration. It was a good job with the chance for regular promotions—and at the conclusion of a career, an excellent pension would be forthcoming My training took place in Atlanta. Before this training program, except for a few short vacations at Panama City Beach in Northwest Florida, I had spent all of my life in South Alabama. For someone who had spent four years in college, I was about as ignorant of the world as Gomer Pyle on the Andy Griffith show. Most of my information about the lives of people who populated other parts of the world came from books, especially mystery novels. To transfer from South Alabama to the big, I mean really big to me, city of Atlanta was in, retrospect, a more reckless step than actually joining the Peace Corps. Which brings me to this question—why did I join the Peace Corps?

After three months of training in Atlanta where, in theory, we learned what we needed to know to help untangle the laws by which the government gives money to retirees, disabled persons and spouses and children deprived of their livelihood by the death of the person who was supporting them, we received our assignments. I was assigned as a Social Security case officer in West Palm Beach, Florida. I found this part of Florida lovely in the 1960s; life there moved at a much slower pace than in places like Miami and other more industrialized areas in the state. It did not take me long to learn that the really rich lived in Palm Beach and we servant types were located in West Palm. I would take walks on Worth Avenue in Palm Beach and marvel at the wonderful stores which offered nothing at all that I could afford.

I was not unhappy in West Palm Beach. My coworkers were all extremely kind and welcoming. The interviews with clients were often interesting and allowed me to meet people from a variety of ethnic groups who had never come my way before. For some reason, South Alabama did not have many residents of Italian or Middle European descent—people who had arrived in America much more recently than my family and our neighbors in my hometown.

After several months of living and working in West Palm Beach, I found myself restless. I had a desire to move to a place with more young people than I was likely to meet in South

Florida with its large proportion of retirees. Remember, I was young then. Today I might find West Palm Beach a more satisfying place to live. In addition to a dearth of young people who might have become friends, I spent my working hours interviewing retirees, people who were injured or ill and bereaved relatives of deceased insured workers. This could, at times, be a sad and depressing experience. I was ready for some sort of challenge that would include adventure and travel. One day I spotted an article in the newspaper about the Peace Corps. The description of the type of jobs that Volunteers would be doing, the chance to travel to foreign countries and the opportunity to help people made me want to become part of this experience. After obtaining an application, I completed it and sent if off. In a fairly short time, I was invited to join the Peace Corps although I had not taken the requisite "qualifying" exam. In fact, I took the exam some months later at Penn State when I was already in the training program.

It might have been my family situation that kept me from having many qualms about my decision to join the Peace Corps and go about as far away as possible from everything and everyone I knew. My parents were both dead—my mother died in 1955, my father shortly after I graduated from college. My older brother was in the Air Force, my younger brother in college and living with my aunt. Since nobody depended on me or my income, I quit my good government job (to the chagrin of my relatives) and flew to Penn State to start a new chapter in my life.

Training, Penn State and the Philippines

I enjoyed both training programs very much despite some difficulty in understanding what portions were relevant and what were thrown in to fill up some space in the day. It was sometimes a little hard to "go with the flow" without feeling that I could cope very well if I could find out what the "flow" happened to be. I relaxed about the ambiguous directions we received when I realized that almost all of the other Volunteers felt as I did. The training did allow us to become confident that we would be able to live and work in this different culture once we had settled in at our sites and become familiar with the people who would become our neighbors and coworkers.

Negros Occidental

Four of us from the group were assigned to San Enrique, Negros Occidental. Marge Pfankuch, now Bakken) was one of the four, but since she had already been selected to be a Volunteer Leader, she stayed only a few weeks before she went away to assume the duties of her new position. She visited San Enrique several times during our first year in Negros, but after that she was put in charge of training for new Volunteers and did not have much free time. The other three assigned to San Enrique were Sally Pierce (now McCandless), from Vermont, Beth Sorenson (now Plummer), from Massachusetts and me. Sally was a worthy daughter of a state known for its self-reliant citizens. Sally never met anything or any situation that caused her fear and probably to this day still has not. Beth Sorenson was a soft-spoken teacher, and she quickly became a favorite of our Filipino hosts because she reminded them that some Americans were "normal" in size and not the usual giants seen so often when a group of Volunteers was in the area. I was the third member of this trio—a southern girl—though never a belle—from Alabama, tall and lanky with red hair. If Central Casting had ordered someone with a peculiar appearance who would stand out in a land with a dark-haired, brown-eyed populace, I would probably have gotten a call-back

We had to fly from Manila to Bacolod, the capital of Negros Occidental. To go to Negros by boat would have taken a long time. We spent the first few days in Bacolod at the Sea Breeze hotel which later became a favorite gathering place for the Negros Volunteers.

Sugar cane was one of the principal crops of Negros Occidental. There were a number of very wealthy owners and managers of the facilities where the raw cane was processed into gleaming white sugar. The grand haciendas and sugar centrals to be seen in the countryside were responsible for the opinion that Negros was a more prosperous place than the other provinces. However, many of the men and women who worked in the cane fields had little to live on and no job security. Sugar cane is a cruel crop to cultivate, harvest and make into sugar. It is a crop subject to the political climates in the countries that import sugar and to the supply and demand cycles which can make for a prosperous year followed by a lean one. A popular new sugar substitute can influence the fate of all of those who work with the processing of the cane crop.

San Enrique was 37 miles from Bacolod and was one of the poorest towns in Negros. Growing rice, fishing and making tuba were some of the ways people living in San Enrique made a living. Our original housing in San Enrique was a converted garage beside the home of a well-off family. Mr. And Mrs. Silos were wonderful people and were good friends during our entire stay in Negros, but we were behind a fence in a house that had been made very comfortable for us with running water, electricity and a flush toilet. We wanted a more traditional Philippine house.

After living in the Silos property for several months, we rented the second floor of a house owned by Mrs. Virginia Bedayo, a teacher at the Central School. The house was wooden with a nipa roof. We had more space than in the first house, and we had bookcases and even curtains, so we made it a comfortable home. The "running water" in this house was available when Henry, our boy of all work, pumped the water up into a tank. When the tank was full, we could turn on a faucet, take a shower and flush the toilet. The three of us slept in one room—a large one to be sure. Beth and I were at one end of the room and Sally was at the other end. A friend of ours came in one day, looked at the bedroom and said to Sally, "Miss Sally, you have no companion."

Santa, a young girl who lived with us did the laundry and some cooking. She also bought a few supplies for us at the *sari-sari* store, the only market available in the town. A few vendors would grill chicken in the afternoon, and we often had that for supper (with rice of course). We bought many of our groceries in Bacolod including these canned goods—cheese and corned beef. I might still be able to eat canned cheese, but corned beef is off my menu forever.

The new house was right on the main road from Bacolod to the southern part of the province. That location allowed us to be a "friend to man" and anyone else who wanted to have a look at the crazy American girls. Early in our stay in San Enrique, two young men knocked on the door and announced that they (along with their mother as chaperone) would take us on a trip to Iloilo on the following Saturday. OK, we said, and it turned out to be a very nice excursion. We never saw those people again, which was actually unusual. Negros was like a small town in many ways, and we were constantly running into acquaintances wherever we went.

Beth was assigned to the Central School, Sally was at Tabao, a barrio of Vallodolid, and I was at Sibucao, a San Enrique barrio. I took the bus to Sibucao, Sally rode a bicycle to Tabao, and Beth walked the short distance to her site. Beth was a great help to me in making lesson plans because she had worked as a teacher. She had a number of teaching aids that she had brought with her and some that her family sent her, which she shared with Sally and me. At Sibucao I concentrated mostly on the second language drills that were in the very useful book given to us. I also did some remedial reading exercises for small groups. Although I find it hard to believe now, I taught some American songs and dances to the older children. Beth concentrated on teaching reading. In addition to the second language assistance, Sally did a lot of science projects. She took to heart the "science is fun" motto from our training at Penn State. Sally was the only one of us who conquered and used the Cuisenaire rods to help teach math. I can only plead "math fear" from my early schooling for my failure to understand how to work with the rods.

During the school vacation, Beth and I worked at a camp for boys in Mambucal, a mountain village not far from Bacolod. Mambucal was a good place to spend time not only because the climate was cooler, but there were wonderful hot spring pools where we could relax after helping to entertain and teach young boys all day. Sally worked at La Salle College in Bacolod managing enrichment seminars for teachers.

Sally, Beth and I were able to provide entertainment at several fiestas and other events by learning some Filipino dances and performing them in public. We also had two numbers that we would sing—"I Don't Know Why I Love You like I Do" and "Moon River." It was certainly very brave of us to do this among people who had danced and sung practically from birth. Our dancing was actually better than our singing, and both appeared to entertain our audiences since there was always a lot of merriment when we were performing.

I'm not sure if we made any significant changes in the Philippine education system. However, I do think that our living in much the same way as rural Filipinos lived showed that some Americans would put time and effort in understanding and respecting other cultures of the world. We learned that all ethnic groups and religions deserve to be treated with respect. Also, we were made aware daily that people in many countries around the world can live happy and decent lives without many of the consumer goods considered necessary in the United States.

Trying the Peace Corps a Second Time

After coming back to the states from the Philippines, I moved to Washington and worked for a short time at Peace Corps Headquarters. I had always been interested in working in a library, so I got a job with the District of Columbia school system. While I was working as a school librarian, I went to Catholic University as a part-time student and received my Master's Degree in Library Science in 1968.

In 1972 my desire to work overseas again prompted me to join the Peace Corps for a second tour. I went to Malaysia where I taught Library Science at Mara Institute of Technology (MIT), located in Shah Alam, a suburb of Kuala Lumpur in the state of Selangor. MIT was a new school established to provide higher education at minimal cost for students who might otherwise have been denied a chance to go to college because of their family's poverty. The mission of Mara was not only to provide a college education to Bumiputras (defined as Malays and the tribal peoples of Sabah and Sarawak) but to send its graduates out with degrees that would make them more competitive for jobs in local businesses and industries. Besides Library Science, Volunteers from my group taught English, Architectural Drawing and Computer Skills.

At the time I was in Malaysia, the education system for college curriculums was still based on the British model. We gave lectures and had tutorials for students in our chosen fields. After the lecturer marked the examinations, they were sent to an outside examiner, in the case of Library Science, usually an expert from an English or Australian university

My Peace Corps experience in Malaysia was quite different from the way we lived and worked in the Philippines. In Malaysia we were treated as employees of the government. We had hardly any interaction with Peace Corps staff unless we needed approval for some unusual expenses (treatment for my broken tooth for example) or there was some personal emergency in a Volunteer's life. We had housing and transportation allowances from Mara. My friends and I lived in a four-bedroom house, and all of us had cars or motorcycles. I'm sure we often terrified local drivers as we maneuvered around on the "wrong" side of the road.

I am glad to have had both of my Volunteer experiences. I was exposed to two quite different cultures in Asia. The major religion in the Philippines was Catholicism derived from almost four hundred years of Spanish rule, and a majority of the population was of Malay origin. In Malaysia, there were many different ethnic groups and religions, but most of the highest governing positions were held by Muslims. After a devastating riot in 1969, the government took action to try to bring all groups into a better understanding of religions and cultures so that the citizens of the country could live together with tolerance and peace. Courses in multi-ethnic studies were taught in universities and schools all over the country. The Prime Minister wrote a play demonstrating how respect for all made for a more peaceful and prosperous place to live. Differences in religions and cultures may still cause problems, but the Malaysian government has taken steps to try to reduce strife among its multiethnic population.

After returning from Malaysia, Ann worked for the Agency for International Development (AID) in Washington D.C. as a librarian in the training division. She studied law at Catholic University

at night and after graduation passed the DC bar. Although she never practiced as a lawyer, she believes that her degree helped her get a job with the Freedom of Information Office (FOIA) at the State Department. She notes that while she enjoyed the work there and found it very interesting, the FOIA office was often a stressful place because so many people—State Department employees, Congressional offices, the press, and the public often disagreed about the declassification of foreign policy documents. Ann retired in 1996 and since then has been doing volunteer work at the Smithsonian Institution and the National Gallery of Art.

(The first photo shows Ann with fellow teacher Evangeline Jucal on graduation day in March 1963.)

John Stickler
The PCV Who Wasn't There

My parents were both physicians who dedicated their lives to caring for others. So I was raised in a household where serving one's fellow man was a given; it was never preached, only taught by example. My latent pacifist, do-good tendencies had been brought to the fore by Yale's chaplain, the Rev. William Sloane Coffin, Jr. who urged all Yalies to work overseas in the developing world for a year or two after graduation, preferably for a non-profit organization. I determined to do just that.

Returning to Tucson, Arizona, after graduating from Yale in 1959, the Selective Service System loomed over my consciousness. Registering as a conscientious objector (CO) was a major step, even in peacetime. I was still undecided. The law in those days was very narrow: a draftee could be offered two years of civilian alternative service if a background investigation confirmed that he was sincere in his objection to military service. That sincerity had to be based on a record of church attendance and a belief in God. My résumé in those categories was sorely deficient. I'd never attended any church. I called myself a Humanist.

One morning I dropped in on my local Draft Board to inquire about the CO application form. (You couldn't just print it out off the Internet.) The woman behind the desk was "Nurse Ratched."

"I can give you one," she said coldly, "but I'll have to record in your file that you took one."

Unh. Backpedal. "Maybe you could just show it to me," I suggested hopefully. "I don't have to take it."

"I can do that," she replied, studying me carefully, "but I'll still have to make a note in your file."

"Never mind," I said hastily, making a bee-line for the door.

Wham. Nailed by the Thought Police.

"Ask Not What Your Country Can Do for You…"

Sometime before his inauguration President-elect Kennedy announced the formation of the Peace Corps and called on young Americans to serve their country. He was talking to me.

My plan took shape: I would register as a CO, join the Peace Corps, and request that my two years in the PC qualify as Alternative Service. I'd be establishing a legal precedent for generations of peacenik do-gooders following in my footsteps. Maybe even give the Peace Corps a boost in the process. I applied and sat for the federal examination. On July 14, 1961, I became the first Arizonan to be selected.

It seemed like a good idea at the time.

The Peace Corps may have saved some money on my background check; the FBI was well along on its investigation of my sincerity as an objector. The only part of the investigation involving me was the FBI interview, held at the Federal Building in Tucson in the same room where I'd taken the Peace Corps entrance exam. I remember feeling a little sorry for the interrogator (not an apt term for him, he was trying to be kind) because of the questions he was required to ask:

"Do you believe in God?"

"How would you describe God?"

"How many angels can dance on the head of a pin?"

These are not easy questions under any circumstance. They are even tougher when your answers determine whether you go into A) the Peace Corps, B) the Army, or C) prison. I could commiserate with Joan of Arc: D) Burn at the stake.

If my folks had taken me to church, or even if I'd attended Reverend Coffin's Sunday services in Battell Chapel (now I regret not), I might have been better prepared for this. I told him I was quite sure there was no God looking down on me, monitoring my ethical humanist behavior. I was on my own.

Penn State

The seven weeks at Penn State were exhilarating for me. It seemed we were all brothers and sisters with the same cause, like Moonies, except we were devotees of JFK setting out to save the world for him.

Aside from those nasty inoculations every Friday, there were two obstacles I had to face during our training. The first was the psychiatrist, remember Dr. Gordon? "Flash" Gordon? We sat on the grass under a tree (first put the subject at ease) and chatted about my goals and feelings. I told her I had registered as a conscientious objector and that I hoped my two years in the Philippines would be accepted by the Selective Service as Alternative Service.

Psychiatry is an inexact science at best and anyone's words can be taken in many ways. I knew that Dr. Gordon held all our futures in her hands, especially mine. Yes, the Peace Corps wanted idealists to volunteer, but how far along that I'm-a-do-gooder spectrum could one stand before being classified as *too* idealistic (i.e., weird)? Would my CO application, now in the hands of the FBI, push me over that psychiatric boundary?

I thought my interview with Dr. Gordon went well. I was open and sincere—always risky.

My other obstacle, quite unexpected, was a steadily increasing itchiness in my groinal area, as Woody Allen might say. It got to the embarrassing point where I could not stop scratching, so I went to the university medical center to have it checked out. The doctor quickly diagnosed the problem: pubic lice.

Just fine. I imagined the final admissions panel back in Washington reviewing my record: "Not only is he *way* too idealistic, he's got crabs! Do we really need this guy?"

Graduation

Our graduation was a downer. First, we did not receive our diplomas in the Rose Garden from President Kennedy as advertised, something I've lamented all my life. (Seeing that old film of 4H Club member Bill Clinton shaking hands with JFK in the Rose Garden made it even worse.) Then Sargent Shriver cancelled his trip to Penn State to do the honors because he had to stay in DC and lobby for the initial PC budget bill when it came up in congress.

So we ended up with Ambassador Carlos P. Romulo who railed at us because the Filipino soldiers who had fought alongside U.S. forces in WWII had not been paid yet. (What would he have said if he'd known that in 2010 they'd still be waiting for their checks?)Second, was the word that some of our fellow volunteers were being washed out even as graduation day approached. It was a gloomy ceremony.But I had made it through! Crabs and Dr. Gordon notwithstanding. I treasured that diploma and headed back to Arizona with it and my ticket to San Francisco. The lull before the storm.

Enroute, I stopped in New Haven to see Reverend Coffin. The door of his office was ajar and I peeked in. He was sitting with three young men who appeared to be Jewish grad students and they were arguing that Christianity was a failure. "That's because no one's tried it yet!" he countered. I didn't interrupt.

The Peace Corps had suggested that before assignment to some remote jungle island I should have all four wisdom teeth removed. Back in Tucson, after coming out of the general anesthetic, I was given some pain pills and my mother drove me home. Groggy and weak, I lay on the couch. The phone rang. It was a telegram from Washington. The operator read it to me. I had been deselected.

It wasn't enough to have my dreams shattered, the arc of my entire life derailed, but insults had to follow the injury. I didn't make *Time* magazine, as Charlie Kamen did, but the local media was all over me. I was page-one news for several days. My poor parents were mortified.

Eternal Arizona Senator Carl Hayden called a press conference in Washington to announce my deselection and I've often wondered if my dismissal was traded for Carl's vote for PC funding. I hadn't planned to serve my country that way, but it may have been the case. I can't blame the Peace Corps; they were under pressure from Arizona's Goldwaterites. They had not voted for JFK, they were dismissive of his ideas, and particularly did not like me

My draft board was ecstatic and called the newspapers to let them know how delighted they were that I had been rejected by the Peace Corps. They boasted that they had assisted by refusing to allow my overseas travel and I was now 1-A, eligible for the draft. Heh, heh. (Sound of hands rubbing together.) The vice chairman of the board told *The Arizona Daily Star*, "I couldn't name a human being in the world who is more unfit for the Peace Corps."

Letters to the editor split down the middle. Some said, "We don't want draft dodgers representing our country overseas!" Others said that it seemed I was just the sort of volunteer who belonged in the Peace Corps. The local chapter of the American Humanist Association wrote a nice letter in my support. The American Legion Hall was horrified that I had suggested letting PC service substitute for military duty, thus dishonoring all the blood spilled to date by our patriotic servicemen and women.

The local chapter of the ACLU broke up because half of the attorneys wrote to General Hershey accusing the head of the draft board (a very prominent state senator) of breeching his oath of office. He was quoted in the press as saying that he did not recognize conscientious objection, an accepted draft classification, and they demanded his firing or at least a reprimand. The other half didn't agree.

So the Peace Corps would not be my Alternative Service, nor anyone else's. No precedent would be set. I now had three options: lie on the tracks until the Army enlistment train arrived; take a moral stand and go to jail for two years; or enroll in graduate school. I seriously considered incarceration, but received an invitation from my father's cardiologist. "Your father has had two heart attacks already," he told me. "Would you want to be the cause of his third, his final one?"

That left grad school. My hard-nosed draft board had never granted me a student deferment during four years of college because I wasn't in the top half of my class.

"But I'm at Yale."

"Doesn't matter."

The rules then were that if you reached your 26th birthday you were no longer draft eligible. Further, if you'd never received a student deferment they were obligated to give you one for graduate school. I was pleased to learn that the University of Arizona planned to introduce a new master's program in Community Development in January of 1962. I applied and was accepted. I was 25.

Classes began and I had not heard from my draft board. I was home free.

"Greetings"

The induction notice was postmarked the day before classes began and thus trumped my new student status. My last refuge. The Army enlistment train was coming down the tracks.

U.S. Army Personnel File, 1962

"Private Stickler does not project proper military bearing."

John Stickler served the second year of his two-year Army obligation with the Korea Military Advisory Group in Seoul. In the evenings he spent his time working off his pent-up PC energy, teaching English and advising Korean college students at the USIS office. He took his separation in Seoul early in 1964 and ended up helping launch Korea's first advertising agency. In 1966 he opened his own agency, primarily helping Korean companies promote tourism and export products overseas. In

1967 he was hired by CBS News to file radio reports for the network, which he did in his spare time for the next nine years.

After his favorite English student, Miss Han, became his bride, he found he'd married into one of Korea's aristocratic families. During the Yi Dynasty, 1392-1910, there had been six queens from the Han family. They were known for their beauty, their intelligence and their decisiveness.

John and his wife moved back to the United States in 1976 with their two sons and he began a writing based career: publishing, journalism, editing, advertising and public relations. In the 1990s he worked on travel books for Fodor's and Berlitz, international trade books for Global Sources in Hong Kong, and in 2003 wrote a picture book on Korea illustrated by his wife, who had become a talented fine artist. Land of Morning Calm: Korean Culture Then and Now *is published by Shen's Books, www.shens.com.*

(The first photo shows John after he'd been inducted into the army; the second shows him with his wife on a book tour where they were autographing copies of their book.)

Charlotte Hough Stocek
Remembering Life in a Small Filipino Village

Sick, but Not Alone

My most profound memory from my Peace Corps experience occurred when I was sick because of food poisoning. I had eaten crab *relleno* that was made from crabs sold by a man walking on the beach in front of my little house in Tagdon. Soon my palms started to itch and then I had stomach cramps, vomiting, and diarrhea. I weakened as the fluids drained from my body to the point that by nightfall I could not walk. I asked Segundina, my housegirl, to go to Mamay or Cabeza for help. They owned the only store in Tagdon and were like family to me. Segundina told my neighbors about my illness on her way to the store.

The neighbors came quietly into my house and squatted in a circle around the bamboo cot where I was resting. "Charlo, Charlo" (with Char as in charcoal) they chanted over and over as they swayed back and forth. I looked into the flickering flame of the little jar lamp Segundina put beside me and thought, "I am going to die right here on this faraway island, in this grass hut with these people squatting around my bed chanting my name." Cabeza and Mamay returned with Segundina and I was carried to their house. A neighbor, Domingo, ran to the wealthy man's house and borrowed his jeep, the only vehicle in Tagdon, and drove to Gubat. I wondered how he learned to drive. Domingo returned with the doctora. "Don't drink milk," the doctora said as soon as she entered. We had no milk in Tagdon. They thought I had El Tor or cholera, the killer. I had food poisoning and began to feel better when the poison left my body. I wanted to go back to my house. As I neared my little house, neighbors came to me from their sleep and kissed my hands and hugged me. I had returned from the almost dead.

It is now nearly five decades since I lived in Tagdon; yet I remember with vivid detail the people and my life there and especially when I look up at a full bright moon here. Sleep came early in Tagdon because there was no electricity. The little glass lamps were snuffed out when all light left the sky. Tagdon was covered in darkness and quiet except for the ever rolling soothing sounds of the ocean breaking the night silence.

Nights of a full moon were a different story. The light of the moon called us out of our little houses and we celebrated the light and life by the sea. It seemed that everyone in the tiny village gathered by the ocean on such evenings. The adults drank tuba, the homemade coconut wine, sang the haunting *kundimans*, danced, told stories, and laughed together under the moonlight. The children raced down the bank into the surf over and over again, laughing all the while. People then returned to their little houses to sleep as the moon moved higher and covered Tagdon in light.

I thought of my family in Vermont and missed them when I gazed up at the full moon while in Tagdon just as I think about Tagdon and miss it now. The people of Tagdon and other places in the Philippines became my family while there and touched my life forever. This connection with another culture shown so deeply to me when I was very ill illustrates the bond of caring and concern the people of Tagdon and I shared during my stay there. It lingers and remains with me to this day.

My Motivation

I graduated from Texas Woman's University in August 1960 with a degree in English and started a job as a newspaper reporter in September in St. Johnsbury, Vermont. I did not have a teaching credential because I did not want to be a teacher, but there were few options for a liberal arts graduate. Having decided newspaper work was not a career path for me, I applied for a high school English teaching position in Ludlow, Vermont. I went for the interview at the same time I received the invitation for Peace Corps training. I decided to take the unknown path and join the Peace Corps.

I had first learned of the Peace Corps from my mother. She drew my attention to a column in the *Boston Globe* after President-Elect Kennedy spoke at the University of Michigan in October 1960. "This sounds like you, Charlotte," she said as she handed me the article. "How would you like to trample in the jungles of Africa," the column began and went on to describe Kennedy's proposal of the Peace Corps. I was immediately interested and wrote for information. After completing the application, I had an all day testing session at the Montpelier post office.

I waited for news, then received a letter about a project in Ghana and thought it would be my assignment. I wanted to go anywhere in the world. Ghana was fine. Soon a telegram came with the news that I was selected for training for an education project in the Philippines. I was to wire my acceptance if I wanted to do it. I did although I knew little about the Philippines. There were few books about the country in the local library. The next telegram invited me for training at Penn State.

There were 156 in our Philippines education project. We had classes in history and culture, American politics, health and safety. Each weekend a group of us was taken into the Allegheny Mountains to test our survival skills. A survival expert from the Navy went with us and supervised our stay. We were taught how to get water out of vines, make a shelter in the woods, and find our way out of the woods with a map and compass. There were psychological tests and rounds of shots to protect us from tropical diseases.

We left for home in early September not knowing if we had been accepted by the Peace Corps to serve in the Philippines. After calling each other around the country to discuss our fates, I finally got word that I had been accepted. Upon meeting up in San Francisco in October, I learned that 128 of us had been accepted and 28 of those who trained with us did not meet the requirements for reasons unknown to us.

The Philippines

We left for the Philippines October 12 and were taken by buses to the University of the Philippines at Los Baños in the province of Laguna. I remember that it was very green everywhere, like a jungle with blue-blue sky and cookie-cutter shaped intense white clouds. The natural world surrounded us; it was vivid and beautiful. The training site had been the place where the World Boy Scout Jamboree had been held two years earlier. There were still large dormitories to house us and separate buildings for classes and a language laboratory. Geckos ran across the rafters at night and I feared one would fall on me. I was in an upper bunk and hoped the mosquito net would protect me. We ate Filipino food, listened to Filipino music, and studied Tagalog during the day along with other classes about the Philippines. It all fascinated me. We remained in Los Baños until we left for our assignments in the field on December 1, 1961.

I was assigned to Bulusan poblacion (a municipality) in the province of Sorsogon in a household with Nancy Jeffers. Our closest Peace Corps neighbors were Marianne Gould and Anne Hankins who lived in Santa Magdalena, which was about twenty miles down the coast at the tip of the province and the end of the road. It could only be reached by bus, which was true of Bulusan and in fact all of towns in Sorsogon. Located on the Pacific coast, Bulusan had an open market, a Catholic church, a post office, a few stores, a bakery with fresh bread daily, a public elementary school, and a private high school. I worked in the elementary school there and Nancy worked in a school in a nearby barrio.

Jaime Borja and his family, who owned a store in Bulusan, were very good to us. He was a head teacher in a barrio, Tagdon, which was a 45 minute bus ride, traveling west from Bulusan. He invited me to work in his school the second year of my Peace Corps stay. I liked the idea, but it was a long bus ride, a beautiful one with an ocean view all the way. I began helping in his school and decided I wanted to live in Tagdon. I was ready to live there alone and Nancy agreed. She would stay in Bulusan with Lubing, our housegirl. I asked Jaime if there would be a place I could live in Tagdon rather than make the daily commute from Bulusan. I had a vision of living by the ocean in a little nipa grass house, a bahay kubo. At first I was told that there were no places for me to rent in Tagdon by the ocean, but then a family decided to rent their house to me (for $20 a month) and their daughter, Segundina, would help me for another $20 a month. Segundina's father, Papay, and neighbors put new thatch on the house, built an addition with a toilet, and added a porch. There was a little kitchen with a tabletop of cement where we could build a wood fire between three stones to cradle a cooking pot. At the well we lowered a bucket on a rope to gather water. Segundina did all the cooking and household chores, washed my clothes in the river, and ironed them with a charcoal iron.

The school was nearby. My neighbors were helpful and kind. The children followed me everywhere and visited me at home. We took great delight in each other. (The bond with these children influenced my decision to become a teacher of young children.) All of the houses in my neighborhood were small and built also of nipa and bamboo. There were dirt paths through our neighborhood with pigs wandering everywhere. Papay built a bamboo fence around my yard that kept the animals out. I made a little garden. The school had a bigger garden that the children tended and harvested.

The one store in town was owned by Mamay and Cabeza and they sold everything needed by the people in Tagdon. Their home was above the store, a building made of concrete blocks with a tin roof. Mamay and Cabeza were like family to me. If Cabeza went to Legazpi City, he would bring me an apple or something he knew I missed from home. Most of my neighbors were fishermen who took their handmade boats out at night with lanterns to attract the fish. They often brought me pieces of coral and special shells from the ocean. There were rice fields around Tagdon that were tended by my neighbors in exchange for rice for their families. People brought me orchids in coconut shells that they found in the mountains and I hung them on the porch. I loved the little house I lived in and named it *"Kaibigan Dalam Pasigan"*—"friend by the sea." When I think of my stay in the Philippines, I think of the little house in Tagdon by the sea and my neighbors there.

Reflections on the Peace Corps Experience

I would like to know the impact or effect of my presence in Bulusan or Tagdon and how the people there perceived the Peace Corps. I know there was genuine respect and affection between us. It pleased me greatly that Jaime Borja, the Tagdon head teacher, visited my young family in Vermont in 1969. Mamay and I have exchanged letters and photos through the years.

I learned a great deal about living simply from my experience in the Philippines. I liked how the people there used resources and did not waste materials. They could live joyfully in the midst of difficulties, disappointments, and lurking death from diseases and disasters.

My Peace Corps service has influenced my life in important ways. I wanted to enlarge my interest in world cultures and share it with others after I returned. I have invited foreign students and visitors to our home and helped my children develop a respect for others. My son, while in college, invited a fellow student from Pakistan to spend the summer with us. We also had a Japanese student spend a year with us and attend high school in Montpelier. I have made a great effort over the years to open the world to young people at my home and in my classrooms.

While teaching at the elementary school in Montpelier, Vermont and serving as social studies coordinator for three years, I initiated and directed (with the help of other teachers and all the children) three Peace Corps Partnerships with Peace Corps Volunteers serving in Liberia, Nepal, and Ecuador. Each year a primary school was built in one of the countries and the school children in Montpelier collected pennies to raise over $1000 each year to build a school. Throughout the school year, letters and packages were exchanged and shared with all school classes. Each project culminated with a festival for the school and Montpelier community. The African Festival included exhibits and talks by many area Returned Peace Corps Volunteers (RPCVs) who had served in Africa.

I believe I have gained the ability to view my country through the eyes of others. I strive to bring critical thinking and reasonableness to political and international issues. My Peace Corps experience moved me toward Simone Weil's inquiry of others, "What are you going through?"

My hometown of Danville, Vermont and nearby St. Johnsbury, Vermont took a great interest in my Peace Corps work and sent packages for the children at my schools. My parents even thought of joining the Peace Corps while I was in the Philippines. My experience in the Philippines engendered an affectionate and positive feeling about the Filipino people in all my family and friends. They all are supporters of the Peace Corps.

I have recruited a number of volunteers for the Peace Corps and been part of RPCV groups in Vermont, Arizona, and now New Mexico. I was the RPCV newsletter editor in Vermont and Arizona for several years. I have advocated for additional Peace Corps funding, spoken in schools and to groups about my Peace Corps experiences, whenever possible, and worked "to bring the world back home."

I think the value of the Peace Corps to the Philippines and the U.S. is the value of love and friendship in the lives of human beings. Peace Corps Volunteers may have completed helpful projects and modeled certain practices, but the greatest value is that of forging bonds of caring friendship that sustain and endure.

Since Peace Corps days, Charlotte worked in the field of education. She studied the Montessori Method in 1965 and has used this method to teach children in Connecticut, New York State, Vermont and Arizona. She left the classroom in 1993 to study Teaching and Teacher Education at the University of Arizona, obtaining a Master's in teaching ESL and a PhD in 1997. She worked for the next decade in teacher preparation at the Community College of Vermont, Vermont College in Montpelier, and the University of Arizona (UA) South in Sierra Vista.

Through the years, while teaching and raising four children, Charlotte wanted to live in another culture again and to improve her Spanish. After retirement from UA South in 2006, she taught a semester at the Universidad de Sonora in Hermosillo, Mexico, where she developed an appreciation for the strong connection between Mexico and the Philippines. She found it satisfying to end her teaching career in Mexico after beginning it the rural schools of the Philippines.

Charlotte is now living in Albuquerque, New Mexico where her second daughter, Natasha, and her family live. She claims the births and lives of her four children as the greatest gifts of her life. Her oldest daughter, Damariscotta, lives in Vermont with her family and is 42; Natasha is 40; Gideon lives in Los Angeles and is 37; and Aaron is 35 and lives in Portland, Oregon with his wife and two daughters. Her daughters are teachers and her sons are engineers. Charlotte now has ten grandchildren—the youngest, Noemi Charlotte, having been born the 26th of April, 2010 in Portland, Oregon. She continues to do occasional teaching on topics related to children and facilitated, for example, a seminar, Doing Philosophy with Children *with Vermont College of Union Institute & University students in the summer of 2010.*

(The first photo shows Charlotte with a Filipina friend in Tagdon, Sorsogon; the second show her in Arizona visiting with fellow Group I volunteer Wally Allen.)

Stu Taylor
Finding a Role in Rural Albay

In the Beginning (Slick Airways)

The beginning, 1961, was an exciting time as the Kennedy administration was novel, especially for young Americans. I had filled out my Peace Corps application and taken the Peace Corps test the first time it was offered in downtown Spokane, Washington. I took it on a lark on the first day after my college graduation. I was not ready for graduate school and didn't want to teach. My majors (political science & education) along with my strong interest in international relations and a deep seated wish to go around the world made me, at least in my mind, a prime candidate for the Peace Corps.

Imagine my surprise when a telegram arrived one Friday evening later in June, saying that I had been selected for training at Penn State University for elementary education work in the Philippines. My initial reaction was shock at being selected and disappointment that it was for Asia and not Africa. A great uncle criticized my decision to join the Peace Corps, calling it a "Kidde Corps" and warned me that by associating with this "political boondoggle," my career in any worthwhile endeavor would be forever tainted!

Training at Penn State took place from the end of July until mid-September. I had a few weeks at home and on October 10th at midnight we (128 in "Group I") boarded two airliners for the flight to Manila. (Ironically, we landed in Manila on October 12th—Columbus Day.) We had worked to be ready for a job that we really didn't understand. Our project description was: Teaching English & Science to grades 3-6. Why this? The Philippines with its myriad of dialects taught grades 1 and 2 in the local dialect and then switched to English as the language of instruction in the third grade. When asked by a Peace Corps advance official what Peace Corps volunteers could do, the Philippine Superintendent of Education reportedly answered (or so I was told), "I don't know—pull maps down, wash the blackboards, etc." Since we, at this late date (mid-October), did not know where in the Philippines we were going, there had been no language instruction.  When we arrived at the University of the Philippines (Los Baños) we began Tagalog language training, although almost none of us would live in a Tagalog (Pilipino) speaking area. Needless to say, to be flexible was a prerequisite!

This midnight flight conjured up a scene from the movie *Casablanca*. San Francisco fog swirled around the airport, planes, and passengers. I was one of the few volunteers that had family to see them off on this unknown and unsure two year adventure. I remember well as I boarded the plane and sat in my seat looking out at the fog shrouded runway the one thought that pounded my psyche,: "you are embarking on this mission/endeavor/adventure…your family is here and you can exit this plane…but understand that if you don't exit the plane, you are going for the full two years. You are not a quitter and you will do your best as a "Kennedy Kid" to represent your country and to make your family proud of your time spent in the Philippines."

Middle: Mid-term Self Evaluation

As I reflect back on my Peace Corps training I knew at the time I would learn a great deal about a different culture, but I'm not sure I thought about how it would help me gain an insight into my own culture or myself. The midpoint of my tour of duty coincided with the end of the school year. Being in education, I wondered what I had imparted to the teachers and the students in my school. I was conscious that the teachers wanted to emulate my "blue seal" accent. ("Blue seal" comes from the seal on a pack of American cigarettes—and just as American cigarettes were considered the best, anything of top quality was often called "blue seal"). But what had I accomplished?

I remember vividly reading Peace Corps literature highlighting what other volunteers around the world had done and were accomplishing. Two stories I remember were about a road building in Africa, where so many kilometers had been built, and a poultry project in South America, where chicken production had increased by X%. I did not have a benchmark to compare results. No one went into the Peace Corps without the strong purpose of serving and helping the host country. I only had one school year left to make my mark: that is when the realization set in that my culture is "results driven." Unless we can *quantify* whatever we do, we are frustrated. I was surprised at this answer for it was like a window that had suddenly opened and I could understand more of what made me who I was.

What then did I do in the second year? I would continue with the normal school days and the classroom work. In addition, after seeking out the Agricultural Extension Agent, we designed a project for the sixth grade boys at my school to work on an agricultural experiment relating to rice cultivation. Rural Filipinos in Albay Province were and are subsistence farmers for the most part, and there was little room for experimentation in daily life on the farm. This experiment was to test four rice plots on the school field. On the first plot the students planted the normal rice seedlings. On the second plot they planted certified seeds from the International Rice Research Institute, an institute dedicated to increase rice yields throughout Asia. On the third plot the students used fertilizer with the normal rice seedlings and on the fourth plot they used the certified seeds and fertilizer. I was excited to see what this experiment would yield. The boys were charged with planting the seedlings in the four plots as well as seeing that they received enough water. Imagine my dismay when one of the boys came to me one evening about halfway through the experiment to say that a local farmer had opened the gate to the field and allowed his water buffalo to graze on our "experiment." There is a Tagalog phrase *"Bahala Na"* which means "that's life"! In addition to this agricultural experiment I spent some of my spare time, accompanying the same Agricultural Agent as he tried to convince farmers to use the certified seeds and to use fertilizer in their rice patties.

I also worked with the local Community Development worker as he attempted to convince the townspeople to buy water seal toilets (very inexpensive ones) which would help the sanitation situation in the town. Being an American my presence alone would help him draw a crowd.

Lastly, I had made a close friend in the nearby provincial capital, an American missionary priest who had built a boy's high school. He asked me to coach his school's basketball team.

How ironic it is to look at my after school endeavors and see that they all fit within my American cultural mores: that of being able to *quantify* the work!

End: Reflection on My Two Years

I arrived at the provincial capital airport of Legaspi. Goodbyes had been said. The parish priest in our town of Santo Domingo had celebrated a *Te Deum* Mass for me. The mayor and the council had made me an honorary son of Santo Domingo. The school principal and a few of the teachers had wished me God speed. Most of all, I spent some time with the Balin family, the family with whom I had lived for almost two years. Behind me was Mt. Mayon, the most symmetrical volcano in the world, with its ever present smoke billowing across the blue sky. Evening was approaching with its yellows and pinks and reds of the sunset becoming visible. I looked east to Legaspi Bay and the myriad of rice fields with the occasional water buffalo dotted by the many growths of coconut trees. Past the fields in the Bay I saw the *bankas* (canoes with outriggers on one side), which meant the fishermen were still hoping to add to their catch for the day. I thought then that there had not been a prettier day.

I was excited to be going because in a few short days I would be leaving the Philippines to embark upon a boyhood dream of going around the world. I had planned this trip for a long time. I would be travelling alone as I didn't want to compromise my one chance to see everything I could. I was planning on travelling up to a full year. (I had a ticket from Manila going west ultimately landing in New York and on to my home in Berkeley. I would live on $200 a month debited from an American Express card that an American copra industrialist had loaned me).

Apart from the excitement of the upcoming trip I was confronted by thoughts about what I had and what I had not accomplished. I had worked hard at being a solid Peace Corps Volunteer. I had worked hard at building a concrete {"typhoon proof") basketball and volleyball court near the market in my town. I had built a library at the school. Through my American family a California school district had donated hundreds of learn-to-read textbooks, the U.S. Navy had transported them to the Philippines, and the Philippine Air Force had flown them to Legaspi. I had coached a Peace Corps basketball team assembled in Manila that played (and beat) two of the finest local university teams and the Philippine Air Force team. (This brought widespread fame for my town). I had worked with Filipinos in Health & Sanitation and in Agriculture.

There were disappointments too. I had not learned to speak the dialect (Bicol) as well as I should have. I also knew that I could have been a better science teacher to the faculty and students at my school.

The Philippine Airlines DC-3 started its engines and abruptly interrupted my reflections. The time had come to say the final goodbyes bringing an end to this Peace Corps Volunteer's tour of duty.

Stu Taylor graduated in 1961 with a bachelor's degree from Whitworth College in Spokane, Washington, having majored in political science and secondary education. Following his service in the Peace Corps he traveled around the world from June to December 1963 and then enlisted in California National Guard April 1964 as an alterative to the draft. After his six months of active duty training, he enrolled in American University to study international relations, earning an MA and by 1968 completing his course work for a PhD.

Between 1968 and 2001, Stu worked for Procter & Gamble in the Food and Beverages division and Pharmaceuticals Division. Following his retirement in 2001, he worked as a substitute teacher in local high schools, served for many years on the Board of the Peace Corps Alumni Foundation for Philippine Development, plays golf, and takes care of his garden.

(The first photo shows Stu in a fragment of his group picture at Penn State, flanked front to back by Doug Watts, Sondra Williams, and Clair Whiting Sharpless.)

Ralph Thomas

Reflection on a Peace Corps Life in the Visayas and Mindanao

Two Learning Experiences

I was invited by a school principal in Siaton, Negros Oriental, to see the installation of a fish corral that was about 1000 feet offshore. We went out in a local banca, a six-person outrigger canoe, to where the men were attaching the woven thatch netting to the bamboo posts that had already been driven into the sea floor. I was impressed that these Filipinos could stay underwater for 90-120 seconds while tying the netting to the posts.

After watching for two hours, I said that I wanted to swim to shore—a bit of recreation for me. The school principal and the fishermen didn't want me to do it, saying they would take me ashore in the banca. Neither felt comfortable telling me *not* to do it. The principal didn't want to offend me, his guest. There were no dangerous sharks or swift currents, but the fishermen couldn't imagine anyone swimming a distance for fun. Interrupting their work, one banca with a seasoned fisherman and the principal followed me all the way to shore. The principal kept yelling to ask me if I was all right.

When we all got ashore, I realized how truly worried they had been and how I had disrupted their work. As an American guest, they had no choice but to try to protect me in the midst of my irresponsible action, if not craziness. I had ignored the clues in their initial expressions of concern. As a "special" person, I should not always indulge my ways of doing things. In hindsight, I am struck by the sense of responsibility of these poorly educated, rural Filipinos and how much they would have benefited from a better road and transportation to get their fish to market in Dumaguete City.

During my second year when I was living on Mindanao Island in the southern part of the country, I rented a jeepney with a Christian Filipino driver in Cotabato City in order to visit some PCVs in the interior of the province. Coming back late in the afternoon, we lost a wheel and were laid up about two kilometers outside the small town of Pikit and 60 kilometers from our destination, Cotabato City. The driver was convinced that he had probably lost the jeep forever. While some Christian Filipinos lived in Pikit, the surrounding area was dominantly Muslim. We stayed overnight in the equivalent of a rooming house. The next day the driver left at dawn to see whether his jeep had been stolen or vandalized. I caught a bus to the capital city and only learned on my next trip that the driver's worst fears hadn't materialized. The jeep was safe, his cousin having come to tow him back to Cotabato City.

That fear and enmity between Christian and Muslim Filipinos in Mindanao was also represented to me in a neat row of bullet holes in the trunk lid of a Philippine Constabulary

Chief's car. I was intrigued with these Christian-Muslim relations because of my experiences in Mindanao and later studied them in greater depth when I did research for my dissertation.

Joining the Peace Corps

When I applied for the Peace Corps in March 1961, I was in my first year of graduate school at the University of Pennsylvania studying European history. I had previously considered teaching English in a Protestant mission school in Sierra Leone. I also knew about Senator Hubert Humphrey's proposed legislation to add another category of young Americans to the U.S. Point Four foreign aid program. After five years of college-university education, I was ready for a study break. When President Kennedy announced the Peace Corps, I was primed.

What I knew about the Philippines beforehand could be reduced to: 1) the most significant result of the American grab for colonial empire and 2) General MacArthur's return during World War II. Since the Peace Corps also contacted me about the initial programs in Nigeria and Malaysia, I didn't bother to study the Philippines before the final notification for training.

Impressions from Work and Life in the Philippines

My first impressions of the Philippines were the enthusiastic welcome and Filipinos' desire to make us happy—especially since we were so far away from family and the luxuries to which they assumed we were accustomed. Many Filipinos told me of their appreciation of American teachers or their connection to GIs at the end of the war. They were always positive and laudatory. I saw Filipinos as very family and tradition-bound, deferring to authority in a manner that I rejected, even though I had been told in training about *utang na loob* [sense of obligation or indebtedness from past assistance].

By the time I left, I understood Filipino relationships a little better, especially how persons found security in family and place, to a degree that I did not share. I still disliked the corruption and political control based on family and status relationships. However, my idealistic view of American politics and culture needed some realism. During my first summer I met with the editor of my hometown newspaper, then in Manila on an agricultural tour. He told me how a township trustee had secured a change of venue for a court case to an adjoining county, where the judge was his cousin. The result was another year of court-ordered delay preventing the state-mandated consolidation of the township high school of less than 100 students. I told that story to many new PCVs to illustrate that we had our problems with special interests and influence in American politics.

I was originally assigned along with two other PCVs to assist Filipino teachers in a large elementary school not far from the capital city of the province of Negros Oriental. With no shortage of Filipino teachers, our job was to assist them in teaching English—the language of all texts and classes after the first grade—and health & science. I was also a so-called, Volunteer Leader with the added responsibility to keep in touch with other PCVs in my province and to deal with the provincial school authorities when necessary. After only two months in Negros, I was reassigned to participate in the in-country training of the second group of PCVs, who were to teach in schools on the island of Panay.

I never got to the point of joint lesson-planning with Filipino teachers. Even though they would correct my mispronunciation of Cebuano *when I asked*, they did not want to co-teach with me. Probably they were afraid of my correcting their English in front of students. In health and science we left our fellow teachers with some additional ideas and group activities to illustrate "the facts" that the children were to "learn/memorize."

I have no doubt that we helped many children to stay interested in school and be prepared for secondary school, which most could not afford. Like many other PCVs, my housemates and I paid the tuition for our "houseboy," whose father had chosen to kill a pig (his son's trade school tuition) to prepare a big dinner for his friends as part of a successful campaign to be elected barrio lieutenant.

The sanitary toilets that we had installed at schools were a definite improvement over the pits without proper drainage. Hopefully our activities suggested that life could change for the better rather than the resignation—known in the Philippines by the expression *bahala na*—and negativism that characterized many of our poor neighbors. In observing other Volunteers, I was convinced that the projects we did *with* Filipinos would be far more lasting than those we did *for* them.

As a Volunteer Leader, I lost out on the depth of cultural experience—e.g., I never became even a beginning Cebuano speaker—that I would have gained, had I remained in one community. On the plus side, however, I had a different perspective on the overall PCV experience and the difficulties and constraints of the original "teacher's aide" position. Working with the incoming Philippines Group II, and later with Groups III, IV, and VII assigned to the central Visayan Islands and Mindanao and Sulu in the south, I had opportunities to translate my experience and that of other Group I and II volunteers to others to ease their adjustment.

One of my Volunteer Leader assignments was surveying locations for new PCVs on Panay and in northern Luzon that had been pre-selected by Philippine school officials. In rejecting any selections, I had to deal with the traditional hierarchy of provincial politics and family networks. In general, I would say that I failed. However, I remember once using my "authority" to threaten a provincial school superintendent/supervisor. Three Peace Corps women were assigned in the hometown of the Speaker of the Philippine National Assembly. They told me that they had been unsuccessful in stopping the supervisor from taking small liberties with them—such as putting his hand on their knees while riding in a vehicle with them. The supervisor never acknowledged my direct approach—I stated that I would move the women from the town if he didn't stop, but his behavior changed.

After months of dreamy praise from Filipinos of all things "American," I found true Philippine nationalism at a Rotary Club in Cotabato City. The club president introduced me *after* citing American prevention and postponement of Philippine independence and calling for the removal of American military bases in Luzon. I acknowledged the colonial past and stated my hope that the Peace Corps was showing a different face. Of course, afterward, the club president apologized for embarrassing me with his introduction and praised his Thomasite teachers in his hometown region of Ilocos in northern Luzon.

My parents shared some of my letters with the local newspaper in Decatur, Indiana. The headline of one article—"Decatur Boy in Earthquake"—exemplifies the lack of impact I had on my hometown. Friends and relatives, however, didn't seem to pick up on any of the cross-cultural observations made in my letters or comments. On my return, my relatives were amazed that I had survived and, indeed, had enjoyed the two years. One repeat question that bothered me was: "Did you have to eat rice all the time?" Nevertheless, I would like to believe that commenting on our experiences added a little leavening to the otherwise "white-bread" cultural experience of many Americans. Later, as a teacher of Asian history in a small college, one of my goals was to get students to discover more about themselves as they studied a different culture.

Reflections

In the Philippines I learned patience—waiting for buses, enduring long speeches, and sitting through accolades for undeserving individuals. The two years definitely slowed my "Type A" personality. I came to recognize that democracy will be shaped by the cultural setting. It definitely enhanced my understanding of the limits of American economic, political and cultural influence in both the Cold War and post-Cold War worlds.

I believe that the early Peace Corps/Philippines experience was one of the best "first jobs" that we could have had. We found our weaknesses as well as our strengths and had to confront them on our own. We were stretching ourselves as we dealt with the bad planning of others. We would have experienced much less self-learning and cultural awareness, if we had taken that other job in the U.S.

I know we offered a positive offset to both American movies and the prevailing image of the American military among Filipinos. This came home to me in Cagayan de Oro, where a small U.S. military weather station was located adjacent to a Dole pineapple plantation. Here, in relative isolation, the Air Force personnel had to mix with the local population, and they did. There were no bars and brothels set up for them. From my limited perception, the result was beneficial.

I certainly had arrived with an exaggerated idea of what I and the Peace Corps could do to *help* the Philippines. I left with greater self-awareness, an enhanced understanding of the commonalities of different cultures and the distinctiveness of my own, and an enduring appreciation for many things Filipino.

I still track the news from the Philippines. My only return trip was in 1988, when I was visiting a Vietnamese refugee camp in Palawan. This was post-Marcos, when there was great hope for political change. The refugee camp was an economic boon to the local economy, but otherwise I could see no economic progress anywhere that I visited. Motorized bikes had replaced pedicabs and horse-drawn *calesas*, but poverty was even more visible in Manila and the provinces.

My greatest sorrow is the ongoing conflict between Christians and Muslims in Mindanao and Sulu. It is only superficially based on religion; the real issue is political control over the division of the economic pie, which has not been growing as it could and should. After each election report, I am disappointed by the continuing dominance of family, provincial/language group, crony favoritism. When I meet Filipino nurses and doctors in the U.S., I only regret that they could not/did not find their future in the Philippines.

After leaving the Philippines in 1963, Ralph returned to work for Peace Corps/Washington for 14 months, recruiting new volunteers and handling various tasks in the Volunteer Support division. He returned to graduate school at the University of Pennsylvania and received his PhD in Asian history, having written a dissertation on the integration of Muslim Filipinos into the Philippine body politic prior to World War II.

He spent the next seven years in education—college teaching, social studies curriculum development, and working with a citizens group helping the Detroit Public Schools.

When his fellow Philippines Group I volunteer, Leonel Castillo, was named Commissioner of the Immigration & Naturalization Service (INS) in 1977, Ralph joined INS and spent 25 years involved with immigration policy.

Now retired, Ralph lives with his wife, Janet, in Chula Vista, California. His main contact with Peace Corps is limited to letters to Congress regarding funding.

(The first photo is Ralph's college graduation picture; the second shows him with his wife Janet.)

Anne Wilson
Fifty Years of Hindsight

Ever see a banana leaf running down the road? A banana leaf with two tiny bare bottoms and four sturdy legs on little feet scampering as fast as they could go? Fifty years ago, I glimpsed just such a sight from a rural bus in the Philippines—two small playmates caught in a rainy season downpour were high-tailing it for home beneath a broad green leaf they'd grabbed to stay dry. They paused just long enough to peek out from under their makeshift umbrella, grin and wave as the bus went past. That delightful cameo makes me smile every time I think of it, even these many years later.

How did I happen to see it at all?

The Kennedy Inspiration

Following the dull stodgy Eisenhower years, John F. Kennedy catapulted us into an era of promise, vibrant with fresh ideas. His concept of a "new frontier" resonated with me and everyone else in my circle of acquaintances. A junior high English teacher in northern Vermont, I had enthused about JFK to my students during his campaign. I even pasted a "Kennedy for President" bumper sticker on the front of my desk! When Senator Kennedy flew into Burlington, Vermont in the "Caroline" for a hasty late-October campaign stop, some of my eighth grade students begged me to take them to see him at the airport forty miles away. Once there, I pushed them through the crowd to the chain link fence so they could shake his hand. How they bragged the next day to their schoolmates! Their pride almost equaled mine when a week later he was elected President.

In January 1961, right after that memorable inauguration of snow and Frost, I was home for a weekend on the family farm. My parents and I were closet Democrats in the rock-ribbed GOP Vermont of those days, and my dad mentioned that he thought our new president had a great idea with this "peace corps thing." Why didn't I look into it? He suggested that I write to Vermont's Senator George Aiken to ask his help. Following my dad's inspired advice I wrote to ask the senator to forward my name to the Peace Corps, so new it didn't even have an office. Senator Aiken promptly responded that he would do what he could, although he believed that interest was high, competition would be fierce, and I shouldn't be too optimistic. But the senator, true to his word, followed through, and on March 1, the day the Peace Corps "began," I found an application in the mail, daunting in its length! The cover letter noted that I had been assigned identification number 00073.

In late June, having taken both batteries of entrance exams (one general, one specific for potential English teachers), I received another letter from Peace Corps. I was being considered for training and possible assignment to an African nation; was I interested? As it happened, just days before I had read in "Newsweek" that the first program in the Far East was being organized for volunteers to teach English in the Philippines. I immediately wrote back to say that while certainly I would accept service wherever it was deemed appropriate, with several years of experience as an English teacher and having grown up in a rural environment, I felt better suited for and was more interested in the new Philippines program.

My knowledge of those far-away islands was sparse: Vermonter Admiral Dewey was a hero of Manila Bay in the Spanish-American War. Corregidor and Bataan were by-words for heroics in the terrible atrocities of armed conflict. General MacArthur had promised, "I will return." Carlos Romulo was the Ambassador to the UN. Imagine making a major life decision founded in such naïveté! However, soon after came the telegram that I had been accepted for the Philippines Group I training program at Penn State, so off I went in eager anticipation, along with three other women from Vermont. We were Vermont's first-ever Peace Corps Volunteers.

The media gushed about the flocks of altruistic youngsters (I didn't consider myself that young; I was twenty-five) who responded to JFK's exhortation to "ask not" what their country could do for them but rather what they could do for their country. Although I would like to claim otherwise, the honest truth is that if altruism did enter my head, it was only a fleeting thought. I'd always had life goals. One was to teach English at the post-secondary level. Another was to circumnavigate the globe and to see as much of the world as I possibly could in my lifetime. Perhaps this offered a chance to make strides toward both. I could learn and get paid as well. What a deal! I went for it, most assuredly out of pure self-interest. While the prospect of a far-off adventure was infectious, I caught only a touch of the idealism virus, a very mild case with few symptoms and virtually no residual effects for the duration of my Peace Corps service.

Trying to be a Teacher's Aide

Perhaps, then, if my motives had been more high-minded, my frustrations would have been proportionately less. Transitioning from the role of experienced and successful classroom teacher to the ill-defined assignment of "educational aide" was such a reversal of my career path that it tainted nearly every aspect of my outlook as a Peace Corps Volunteer during the first year. I liked my three housemates (two from Jersey City, one from Chicago), and the people of Castilla, Sorsogon, in the Bikol region of southern Luzon. Our village was several kilometers off the national road; we lived with few amenities. Having grown up on a farm in rural Vermont, getting along without electricity, running water, flush toilets and other such "civilized" niceties was no big deal. That rudimentary life had not been my own experience, but I had acquaintances who lived just so on hill farms.

The real problem for me was the educational aide non-job. Rising to catch the pre-dawn bus to get to my schools was a necessity. But to arrive before daylight, wait for a couple of hours for the teacher to arrive and the school to open—or not, a more routine occurrence—knowing that all I would be allowed to do would be to observe, listen and occasionally correct a child's pronunciation was more than I was prepared or willing to accept. At one of my schools, the one and only teacher was an avid fan of cock-fighting; he raised prize roosters. For him this meant late nights, hard drinking and heavy betting. For me, it meant taking over all his classes when he didn't show, with no warning or lesson plans. If he did appear (never before noon), he would almost certainly open with a plea for *pesos* to cover his losses. As if I had *pesos* to loan on a Peace Corps living!

These frustrations were compounded by what seemed to me to be serious inconsistencies in Peace Corps policies and management: for example, how logistics such as getting paid or dealing with unforeseen expenses were handled, how personal concerns or problems of Volunteers were resolved, how some Volunteers were allowed certain latitudes and others in like circumstances were not, to name only a few.

Other aggravations came from the occasional communications emanating out of Manila from junior staff with no volunteer experience—or any other relevant life experience for that matter. One particularly irksome memo dated March 16, 1962, notified us of an upcoming four-day "Reorientation Conference." It read, in part, "… Every Volunteer will be responsible for attending every session. The staff has decided that attendance will be taken and that unauthorized absences will be rewarded with deprivation of vacation time and the entrance of a record of irresponsibility in the Volunteer's personnel file." This threat rallied a good many of us to arrive in Manila for the conference indignant and loaded for bear. One creative household brought very clever lyrics they had written to "Hey, Look [Us] Over!" In part the ditty went "…We've all been called to your conference/ Threats you have tried/ We're all here to bitch now/ We're after someone's hide…" We sang with gusto. Perhaps the message got across. Not long after, the staff signatory on the letter was on his way home for good. (The memo and the lyrics are in my Peace Corps scrapbook on facing pages.)

True, the organization was so new that most issues were handled pretty much on an *ad hoc* basis. It's also true that, at the time, whether my personal perceptions were accurate or not had no significance in the larger picture. Except to me.

As a result, at the end of my first year of service early termination loomed large. The idea of being a quitter was distasteful, but the thought of another year of an unproductive, unsatisfying assignment rankled. I met with a staff member for direction. The discussion was cordial; I was assured that of course early termination was a choice. I needed to understand, however, that Peace Corps would not subsidize my return home—I'd have to make the arrangements and underwrite all costs myself. That fried any notion of early termination.

Finding a Better Role

If, however, I could arrange an alternative assignment that conformed to Peace Corps guidelines, a transfer might be approved. Some fast letter-writing, and shortly after, I relocated to Manila to work at the Bureau of Public Schools Educational Radio/TV unit as my primary assignment. Another PCV and I prepared, recorded and filmed ESL scripts coordinated with the English lessons being taught in the public schools. This proved a far more rewarding placement. The work was interesting. It required some creativity. I learned much. My Filipino co-workers were energetic, ambitious, professional, compatible and fun.

For both summer vacations I worked at the Ateneo de Manila Graduate School in its English Language Institute program in ESL attended by teachers, legal, medical and business professionals, and other graduate students. Three other Volunteers and I had responsibility for developing the curriculum, and for preparing and editing all print and audio-visual materials. We modeled spoken English for the students and led small group seminars to explain the cultural contexts and nuances that distinguish American English from Filipino English. I welcomed the professional challenges and stimulating environment. The BPS and Ateneo assignments allowed me to feel more positive as a Volunteer while expanding my own horizons. Best of all, they rehabilitated my outlook about whether joining the Peace Corps had been the right decision.

Would I do it again? When he retired, my husband and I applied for Peace Corps when the programs in Eastern Europe opened. He has an MA in Business; mine is in TESL. Both of us have lived abroad, had careers in education as teachers and administrators, and speak other languages. In a startling twist, we were told that we were "too over-qualified." I found that curious, if not bizarre, and I've wondered how "over-qualified" translates in some arcane internal Peace Corps code. So the answer is that I tried but probably won't do it again. Opportunities for short term, task-specific assignments with Peace Corps intrigue me, though. I do keep that option open. Am I glad I did it the first time around? Oh, yes. I'm also grateful, although I certainly wasn't at the time that circumstances prohibited my giving up early.

I doubt I made any difference at all as a result of my Peace Corps service. I enjoyed and took pride in our work at the Ateneo and at the BPS Radio/TV Unit. I learned a great deal in both assignments. It would be nice to think I made a small contribution somewhere, but I have no hard evidence to support that notion. I do believe that Peace Corps around the world has made and continues to make differences, one volunteer at a time, as a global presence and with better-informed, more culturally aware Americans as world citizens. Whoever actually came up with the concept of the Peace Corps should have received a special medal for sheer brilliance disguised in simplicity. It continues to inspire Americans into service beyond themselves. If ID numbers were still in use, they'd be a whole lot higher than 00073.

Having been a Peace Corps Volunteer in those earliest years made a significant difference in my own life. While I had traveled around the U.S. for six weeks the summer before I joined Peace Corps, my world view was limited. My values reflected the rural New England, small college, female of the 50s, WASP perspectives of my upbringing and environment. Exposure to the broader social, cultural, intellectual and philosophical spectrums of other Volunteers and the very special, beloved people of the Philippines expanded my horizons enormously.

And certainly if I hadn't been in Peace Corps, I never would have had three of the most unique experiences of my life, before or since: 1) a trip to the island of Corregidor, 2) an unexpected visit to our village by the American ambassador and his wife, and 3) a week in Mt. Province as part of a medical mission team. Highlights of each follow.

Seeing Corregidor

Over Easter Week in 1962 four of us used the break to visit locations we'd not seen. We took the pre-dawn train from mobbed Tutuban Station in Manila and spent a day and night at Hundred Islands on the South China Sea. After being stranded for twelve hours in Santa Cruz, Zambales, (no buses from noon till midnight in observance of Good Friday), our route proceeded south, with a stop at Olongapo. At two in the morning its bus station teemed with travelers; vendors hawking fruit, food and flesh—and American sailors from the U.S naval base at nearby Subic Bay.

Sunrise found us in Cabcaban at the southern tip of the Bataan peninsula. Corregidor loomed across the water. For a few pesos, we arranged with a local fisherman to land us on "The Rock" and return at noon to pick us up. A squad of Filipino marines stationed there agreed to take us around the island in their open truck in exchange for our pooled packs of Lucky Strikes and Camels.

In 1942 General MacArthur had left Corregidor under cover of night for his own safe haven in Australia, sacrificing Jonathan Wainwright, American and Filipino troops to an impossible defense and the infamous Bataan Death March. Now, twenty years later almost exactly to the day, time had taken its toll. Derelict barracks and an overgrown parade ground marked the Topside compound. Inside massive Malinta Tunnel, original signs with faded paint indicated doors leading to "General Headquarters, U.S. Army/Pacific Theater," "Hospital" and "Nurses' Quarters" located in corridors radiating off the main tunnel. In the jungle undergrowth, dismantled gun barrels eroding in rusty flakes lay on the broken concrete floors of anti-aircraft batteries. We stood in these ravaged surroundings trying to conjure up the noise, smoke and fury of defensive battle. Our attempt was futile. The sky above was clear. All was quiet. We heard only the trill of tropical birds in young trees just beginning to hide the devastation of twenty years before. Our return to Manila by bus along the Death March Highway passed through the town where a notorious prison camp had held the hundreds of emaciated, sick, exhausted GIs who managed to survive. Their American and Filipino comrades who had fallen by the roadside were shot, beaten and left to die. That day and its sights shook this exceedingly naïve young woman. Those images are as sharp in my mind today as they were then. I will never forget.

Receiving the American Ambassador

In August 1962 Ambassador William Stevenson visited Sorsogon province for a USAID something-or-other (I have no clue what!). Two of us decided to attend the event in the provincial capital, half an hour by bus from our village. Maybe we'd get to mingle with the big-wigs! When we arrived, the Filipino hosts of the event greeted us warmly, assuming that, as Americans, we belonged with the ambassador's entourage. Already gate crashers, we did nothing to disabuse them of that idea and found ourselves in the front row with the real dignitaries, just a few seats from the ambassador. When the program ended, on a whim we extended an invitation to the ambassador and his wife to stop on their way back to Legaspi, meet our other two housemates and "see how the Peace Corps lives." To our huge surprise, they accepted and asked us to ride with them in their large and comfortable vehicle. (Fortuitously, I might add, since the last bus to Castilla had left hours before.) We regaled them with tales of barrio adventures during the ride and found them gracious and down-to-earth. Mrs. Stevenson gave us to understand that they called each other "Billy" and "Bumpy" and that she expected us to address them thus. We did draw the line at calling the ambassador "Billy" and continued to address him as "Mr. Ambassador." I don't remember that we called her "Bumpy," either.

Our arrival after dark in Castilla was a spectacle. A forward escort of police motorcycles, all lights flashing, was followed by jeeps filled with armed soldiers. Then the official car, U.S. flag conspicuous on the front fender. More lights, security, soldiers brought up the rear. Every barking mongrel in town contributed to the ruckus. Within minutes the entire population had gathered outside our house to observe, chatter away, and get a glimpse of our distinguished unexpected visitors.

After showing off our quarters—deemed "charming" by Mrs. S. and considered a marvel by both (no surprise there!), we sat our guests down for a "natural cold," i.e., room temperature, San Miguel. Our irrepressible *lavendera* Jacinta kept peeping around the kitchen door, curiosity barely in check. I stepped to the doorway and asked her if she would like to meet our visitors. Well! Jacinta smoothed down her faded dress, swanked into the *sala* as though she owned the world and everything in it, bowed, opened her arms wide and piped, "Good EVE-ning to all!" She shook hands all around, bowed again and vanished back into the kitchen where she dissolved in giggles. By the time the last flashing lights disappeared down the road later that night, Jacinta's social status in Castilla had peaked! And four Volunteers stared at each other in disbelief that in a tiny house in a tiny remote fishing village 13,000 miles from home they had entertained the Ambassador of the United States of America!

Joining a Medical Mission

The lengthiest entry (twelve pages) in my casually-kept journal of those Peace Corps years records an experience which had nothing at all to do with Peace Corps. In April 1963 good fortune just happened to put me in the right place at the right time with the right connection. I had met an American medical student in the College of Medicine, University of Santo Thomas (UST). He was one of the founders of "Medical Missions, Inc.," an organization whereby medical professionals from UST volunteered their vacations to travel to remote regions of the Philippines providing free medical services and supplies not otherwise available. He suggested that I sign up with a team going to Lubuagan in far north-central Luzon for the week preceding Easter. I had no medical background at all, but I could serve as a "pharmacist's mate," counting and dispensing pills, dosing children with de-worming potions, checking patients in and out, and doing whatever non-skilled tasks needed doing to spare the true professionals. Since I'd never seen northern Luzon beyond one quick trip to Baguio, and the mission coincided with vacation time from my usual assignment, I jumped at this chance. The group numbered twenty-two in all. It included doctors with a variety of specialties (orthopedics, anesthesiology, surgery, pediatrics, internal medicine, dermatology, etc), several equally well-qualified nurses and a couple of motivated med students. And me.

We left Manila by bus at 7:15 pm and travelled north all night, stopping once in Nueva Vizcaya to join a convoy for security against robbers. Just before dawn someone called out, "*Is bu, is bu!* Men on the left; women on the right!" (Let your imagination translate.) The bus pulled to a stop. We all piled out, separating as directed. We took an extra few minutes to stretch our cramped limbs, watch the new day break over desolate Isabela province, and then continued on to the mountain town of Bontoc where we stopped for fuel. Distant rice terraces sparkled in the sun. We arrived in Lubuagan in late afternoon, just in time for *merienda cena*—rice, something unknown (dog was a local specialty; I didn't ask), fried *camotes*, bananas and coffee—sustenance we welcomed after the arduous trip. Work started early the next morning. Scores of patients appeared outside the provincial hospital. Their afflictions ran the medical gamut. Days were long and busy with short breaks only for meals. No siestas! Nights were cold, but I slept well in the nurses' residence under heavy covers, walked to breakfast in dense fog, and dispensed meds and de-wormed little children all day.

One patient in particular intrigued us all: a lovely young Kalingan woman whose otherwise perfect features were marred by an ugly growth the size of a grapefruit on her neck beneath her right ear. She had walked a long distance out of the mountains to this special clinic at Lubuagan. For several days, without one word of complaint, she appeared for treatment, and each day I asked the chief surgeon when she would receive care. On the last afternoon, as I was counting out pills, a messenger handed me a note telling me to come immediately to the operating room. I ran across the hospital grounds; the receptionist pointed to a door and told me the surgeon had said that I should go right in. Protesting her mistake—the sign on the door said "Operating Room—No Admittance!"—I gestured: no scrubs, no mask, no gloves. Just then the doctor stepped out, crooked his finger and said, "Get in here! That young woman you've been asking about is on the table." I started to object about steri—but he cut me off, "Come on! You're as clean as anybody else here! We're ready to go!" He placed me at the head of the table right between the anesthesiologist and himself, glanced around to see that everyone was in place, reached for a scalpel, and bingo—the operation was off and running. "Surgical precision" suddenly became very real. The OR team functioned with nary a hitch. The surgeon removed the huge tumor and sent it for biopsy. Fingers flying, he nimbly knotted the stitches with one hand, right and left equally skilled. I was mesmerized, completely enthralled. I never felt a queasy moment nor gave a thought to the vocal, coughing and spitting audience watching through the outside (but thankfully screened) open windows on two sides of the operating theater. When he finished that procedure, the surgeon motioned me over to the second table, and I watched again as he performed the last surgery of the mission, a thyroidectomy. I left the hospital in a trance, walking back to my pills and worm cathartics, astonished at what I had just witnessed. As a grace note, the tumor proved benign. On quite another note, I came back with amoebic dysentery.

Concluding Reflections

And my original purposes for joining Peace Corps? Yes, I circled the globe and saw parts of the world I would not have seen otherwise. Yes, I taught English at the post-secondary level as a PCV, albeit not in the traditional sense. Because of the Peace Corps experience and the two summer sessions at the Ateneo, when I came home a Catholic men's college in Vermont offered me a full graduate fellowship. I served as international student adviser to the several hundred men and women from all over the world who came there annually to learn English.

That Peace Corps ethic of trial and error, risk-taking, and learning to "roll with the punches" gave me confidence to take on brand new ventures, to seek start-up jobs in which I could, in a sense, draw the maps and write the how-to manuals. My career took me to educational program planning, development and evaluation, an expanding field in the late '60s. Again, there was a lot of on-the-job learning. For the next two and a half decades of my professional life, I worked as an independent contractor in educational program planning and evaluation.

Given the luxury of fifty years of hindsight, I treasure the memories associated with having been part of that very first Peace Corps effort in the Philippines. Unpleasantries have faded with passing time; the many good times remain lively in my mind. Most precious to me are the people I met, the friends I made. For that privilege alone I gained far better than I gave as a Peace Corps Volunteer. I am grateful to have had such a singular opportunity.

Those two rainy day playmates may have silver hair and arthritic joints these days, just as I do. But in my memory they stay forever young under their banana leaf umbrella, a delightful reminder of that time long ago when I was a Peace Corps Volunteer.

Anne Wilson grew up in rural northern Vermont; there were six boys and five girls in her 1953 graduating class at Craftsbury Academy. She attended the University of Vermont, Lyndon State College and received a Master's degree from St. Michael's College in Winooski, Vermont, and followed a career in education.

She returned to her hometown in 1977 after designing and helping to build her home on hill-top land that was part of the family farm. Anne married Warren Williams in 1981; they have three sons and three grandchildren. She and Warren enjoy summers at their lake property in West Barnet, Vermont. They travel a bit here and abroad when the mood strikes.

Anne serves as the Church Clerk for the United Church of Craftsbury and is active in the Craftsbury Historical Society. She has been elected to a variety of town offices. She chaired of the Board of Civil Authority, was a Justice of the Peace, a Select Board member for nine years, and has been Moderator of the annual Town Meeting since 1994.

Anne suggests going to www.townofcraftsbury.com for a virtual visit to her hometown. A personal visit would be even better!

(The first photo shows Anne sitting at the dinner table with fellow volunteer Hope Gould with Filipino friends in the background.)

Evelyn Mittman Wrin
Milaor Memories

This past August, I received a surprise telephone call from Gloria Rada, an old friend from the Philippines, who is now living in New Jersey. Her family owned the Moderna Bakery in Naga City, which her sister still runs (now known as Casa Moderna). Naga City is about two miles from Milaor, my Peace Corps home for two years beginning in 1961. Gloria and her husband, Dr. Wing Chu had seen the notice in the *Filipino Reporter* (New York City) about the 50th Anniversary of the Peace Corps and the request that Filipinos who had stories and memories about Peace Corps volunteers in their areas submit them for publication. This prompted Gloria and her husband to "google" the names of the Milaor volunteers, which led to their telephone call to me.

When we were originally asked to send in recollections about our Peace Corps service in the Philippines, I had decided that I would enjoy reading what others wrote but couldn't imagine finding the time to prepare my own essay. Gloria's phone call changed my mind. Since she and her sisters were about the same age as my fellow Milaor volunteers and me, we had become good friends during my Philippine years. Not only was I taken by surprise by Gloria's initiative in contacting me after so many years, but also by the extent of her memory about what we did together at her home in Naga City, the visits she and her sisters had made to Milaor, and the time we'd met after she moved to the States in 1964.

Gloria's call led me back to read the diary I'd kept as a volunteer, which I thought would be a good first step to putting together some thoughts. Lots of memories, which had become vague over the intervening years, came clearly back to life.

First, there were, of course, the school-related memories:

• My assigned elementary school of San Fernando was a relatively short bus ride away, depending on "if" and "when" the bus came and how well it could hold up on the bumpy roads.

• School staffing was a mix of talented, interested teachers and some less so; establishing a role for myself as a teacher's aide was therefore a challenge.

• Overall, I felt the frustration that came with seeing needs among the students—and their families—that went far beyond learning English.

• The children were great; I enjoyed the opportunity to be with them and share what I could.

• One of my small but fond memories was the gift of a bunch of bananas from a young student who was physically handicapped and at quite a disadvantage in the school, but he and I worked well together and I admired his strength and efforts.

• A joint activity among the four Milaor volunteers was the Cooperative Education Fund (CEF) that we set up to assist 14 sixth grade students from our elementary schools with the costs of attending high school the next year. We raised funds from friends, families and organizations in the States and from local families and businesses.

• Another activity that went beyond being a "teacher's aide" in our elementary schools was participation in teacher-training programs in English and science at the University of Nueva Caceres in Naga City.

• And then there were the many boxes of books, including a series in elementary science that were sent by friends, families and organizations in the States for use in libraries that we worked to establish in Milaor town, our elementary schools and other nearby schools.

Second, there were the reminders of many friendships in Milaor and Naga City:

• I enjoyed the occasional *merienda* with Gloria, Erlinda and Teresita Rada at their home; visiting with Loli and Nenita Fabregas—and borrowing a dress from one of them for a dance; other meriendas with Mrs. Bichara and Emily; and dinner with Jaime Sarthou, head of the Coca Cola operations in Naga, and his wife.

• I found great pleasure using real ovens at the homes of friends in Naga City to prepare baked goods.

• We also enjoyed hosting friends at our house in Milaor—as long as it was not the flood season when we needed to use a *banca* to get around.

• Gloria Rada and I concluded in our recent communication that the Rotary Club may have been the common connection with many of the families we came to know in Naga City. I see in my diary that we were invited by Jaime Sarthou early on to a Rotary Club meeting in Naga City. So, Rotary was a connection, and my diary reminded me that some invitations also came from the Kiwanis and Lions Clubs.

Third, there were, of course, the friendships made during Peace Corps days with many Volunteers:

• It was a special joy to be a bridesmaid at the wedding of Margo Heineman and Pera Daniels in 1962 in Camarines Norte;

• And on November 11 to celebrate a joint birthday among Sondra Williams, Wally Allen and me along with Santiago Patasin, one of our CEF students.

• It was fun to travel to the Banaue rice terraces; to take a boat with Sondra Williams to the Visayas where we met up with Ann Snuggs; to go on to Zamboanga where we visited Dirk and Lila Ballendorf; and to visit or be visited by other volunteers in the Bicol area.

Fourth, there were lots of memories of events:

• The typhoon in a remote part of Camarines Sur that could only be reached by boat (Since the house where we were staying still had part of its roof in place, many people were gathering there. But without much else to do, we had breakfast about 6:30 am, *merienda* about 8 am, and dinner about 10 am.);

• The time we received a pig as a gift (We kept it in a pen attached to our house and next to our "shower," which was little more than a bucket of cold water with a cord attached to turn it upside down over us.);

• The stir created by the "peeping tom" article in *Time* magazine in December 1961 (This story told about the Peace Corps girls in Milaor and the alleged restrictions imposed on Filipinos walking near our house.);

• The opportunity to have my first-ever piano lessons, thanks to a local piano teacher and the piano at the home of Attorney Tena in Milaor;

- The trip to Manila where we went to watch jai alai with Bobby Tañada, who had been one of our Filipino cultural informants at Penn State;
- While in Manila, also going to see the newly released film, *West Side Story* with Sondra—and then seeing it again for a second time in Naga City. (As I recall, however, Sondra may have set a record for the number of times she saw the film.);
- And the serenades outside our living room window, the dances in the local municipal square, and all the singing performances by volunteers.

And finally, there were many memories that involved food:

- At the barrio fiestas and the *meriendas,* I remember the bananas fried on a stick that were so good (but what were they called?), the wonderful green leafy vegetables, and the festive *polvoron* (a shortbread made with powdered milk and other ingredients, shaped in a mold, and wrapped in colorful tissue paper).
- At the *Noche Buena* celebration I recall the great beef tongue prepared by Father Ramin, the Milaor's parish priest.
- When bats were living in our attic (one disadvantage of having a ceiling) and flying around our house, Santiago (one of the CEF students), caught some and served us fried bats that tasted quite okay.
- And then there were the "splurge" items. The one I remember best is Magnolia ice cream, but my diary reminded me of the number of times I splurged on hamburgers and chocolates as well.
- When I heard myself referred to, however, as *"mataba"* (fat, although I understand it was used as a positive reference), I decided it was time to do some serious weight control. As a result Sondra (although she was *"maniwang"* or thin) and I started a diet and exercise program. This brought me down more than 20 pounds, but I was probably never referred to as *"maniwang."*

Looking back, I enjoyed the many opportunities offered as part of my Peace Corps experience. Although I regret that Spanish was not really useful (beyond giving me a "head start" in the Bicol language), the geographic location of the Philippines gave me the chance to travel home through many countries that I would not have visited had I been assigned to Central or South America. Most importantly, perhaps, is that on my way home I connected with relatives in France, where my mother was born, and in Germany, ancestral home of my father's family. The French re-connection continues to this day.

Following her return from the Peace Corps, Evelyn worked as an assistant buyer for Marshall Field Company in Chicago, preferring that to a 9-5 office job so soon after the Peace Corps. She attended the 1964 Democratic Convention in Atlantic City as a "Johnson Girl" and subsequently worked at the Office of Economic Opportunity (OEO), then headed by Sargent Shriver, in an office that served as liaison with the Vice President's office and private organizations.

In 1966, Evelyn married Robert Wrin, a former volunteer from Nigeria (1962-4) and joined him for six months in Malawi where he was serving as Associate Peace Corps Director. After returning the U.S., she went back to OEO where she worked with the Job Corps, Head Start, and Community Action Programs. When their first child was born in 1969, she became a temporary stay-at-home mom, but did substitute teaching and voluntary work in the Washington D.C. area. She returned to school in the 1970s, earning a Master's Degree in American Government in 1975 from University of Maryland and a JD from George Washington University in 1975. As an attorney, her practice focused on real estate, housing, land use and economic development. She did work with the National Trust for Historic Preservation and Potomac Electric Power Company. Since 1988 Evelyn has worked for the Department of Housing and Urban Development.

Evelyn and Bob have two children: Martin (who lives in the Boston area) and Anna Marie (who is married to Ernest Yombo and living in the DC area). They have two grandchildren, Rachelle and Leo Yombo.

Evelyn's other activities include the Committee of 100 on the Federal City, the Historic Preservation Subcommittee and the DC Preservation League. She is a past president of Chevy Chase Citizens Association and the Woodrow Wilson High School PTA.

(The first photo shows Evelyn with fellow volunteer Sondra William and Mr. Soler outside a Filipino school; the second photo shows her with her husband Bob Wrin.)

Deane Wylie
Life Beyond California

Answering the Call

In 1961 I was looking for a way out of California, a way to escape the humdrum, predictable years of the 1950s. At 26 I'd barely left the state—a couple of trips to Oregon and Nevada. In 1956 I thought the Army might do it; a friend drafted before me went to Germany, another to Italy. My unit was sent to Oakland, California, where I typed discharges for the balance of two years while living at home since the base was crowded.

With John Kennedy's call for the Peace Corps, I saw a different future. As I graduated from UC Berkeley, I dispatched an application and waited with high hopes. When word came that I could join a project for the Philippines I was ready to leave the next day.

But first came phonemes at Penn State, and all the other topics that were held necessary for Volunteers going off to work in Philippine public schools. State College, Pennsylvania was a good training site because July and August there compared in heat and humidity with our eventual worksites abroad.

It was also a good site for me, since I met Carolyn Ekdahl, a Volunteer from Moline, Illinois, who a year later became my wife. After we got to the Philippines and had more training at Los Baños, eight of our group of 128 were dispatched to the island of Masbate, off the southern tip of Luzon—luckily Carolyn and I were in this group of four men and four women. She accused me of rigging the assignment, but it was the luck of the draw (and I'm forever grateful to those who stacked the deck).

Finding a Turkey

Masbate, as it turned out, was not then a great match for Volunteers. Assignments were tenuous and an outbreak of cholera on the island concerned Peace Corps officials; eventually all of us were dispatched to new posts in Albay, Sorsogon and elsewhere (in later years, however, Volunteers served again in Masbate).

After our marriage in July 1962, Carolyn and I stayed for a time in the provincial capital, Masbate City. I worked with English teachers at the high school, just a few yards from our second-floor apartment, and Carolyn commuted to a primary school in Mobo, about 10 kilometers north of the capital.

In November of that year, we decided to have a traditional American Thanksgiving dinner, turkey and all. This promised to be a novelty, since turkeys are not a common item on the bill of fare in the Philippines. They were known, however, but usually regarded as exotic pets.

We asked local friends where we could buy a turkey, and finally someone told us to try "the priest's wife" at a *sitio* about eight kilometers over a cross-island road. We had a World

War II-era jeep at our disposal, so one Saturday about two weeks before Thanksgiving Carolyn, I and Patria Perez, who cooked for us, set off in search of a turkey.

Sure enough, the woman who answered the door at the parish house did indeed have a turkey she could part with—I can't recall now what the cost was, but it was nominal.

We got the bird into the jeep, despite its objections, with Patria holding it on her lap. This was a messy journey, since the bird was justifiably nervous.

We kept it in an improvised enclosure till the big day came. Then there was a problem—since we all had become better acquainted with this turkey, no one wanted to be the executioner. Finally a neighborhood youth who occasionally did chores for us was persuaded to do the job. We gave him encouragement from a distance.

The next problem was how to cook it—our little Primus oven wouldn't have held a wing. We asked the local baker (and supplier of our morning *pan de sal*), George Ng, if he could help us out. He'd never roasted a turkey, let alone any other kind of bird, but compliantly agreed.

Masbate at about that time was getting telephones for the first time. We had one installed although there were few places you could call—maybe a dozen connections in town at that point. One of them was George Ng's bakery. As the time for the holiday dinner approached, I remember calling George several times to check on the turkey's progress. Finally he pronounced it done and we brought it home to great acclaim.

And we had most of the trimmings—my mother had mailed us a can of cranberry sauce that actually made it through the postal system intact. Our Filipino friends declared it all very good, kindly folks that they were, for it was strange fare for them.

Mindanao and After

The highlight of our time in the Philippines was a vacation assignment in Mindanao, at the Mt. Apo Science Foundation School near Davao. In contrast to Masbate, our jobs there were well-defined and we had real classroom responsibilities. We also found the students far more responsive—it was a boarding school where all of the students lived on campus. Delighting in children who would ask questions and take part enthusiastically in exercises, we made a pitch to the Peace Corps for a permanent change of assignment.

That wasn't possible, as it turned out, so after that assignment we went back to Masbate, packed our things and made a storm-tossed voyage to Legazpi City in Albay, catching the tail end of a typhoon as we passed through the San Bernardino Strait. That was probably the low point of our experience, since we were certain the little inter-island ship would soon capsize—a feeling heightened when the radio operator came out and lashed himself to the deck. Never have I given thanks as I did when we rounded the tip of Luzon and the sea was calm again.

We spent the remainder of our time in Legazpi, living in a little house in the shadow of Mt. Mayon's then-perfect cone. We found a small radio station in town that agreed to give us some weekly time for a program on English that we aimed at school teachers. We called it *The Active Voice*, and I'm rather glad I don't have any recordings or transcripts, because I'm sure it was pretty clumsy. We got no feedback, so have no idea if anyone ever heard it.

It all seems very distant now, as we come up on the 50-year mark. The pictures are fading, the memories too. Did we help anyone? A few, I'd guess. Certainly we corrected some impressions of life in the U.S., and on return were able to give a more accurate picture of how people live in a Third World country. Perhaps most of all it gave me a much different perspective of the privileged lives we lead in this country and how we relate to the world at large.

For my wife, working at the little primary school on Masbate led to a career in education, first in an innovative program in Washington D.C., where former volunteers both taught and studied for master's degrees, and later in California where she was involved in early childhood education for nearly 30 years, right up to the time of her death in 2004.

I'm still keenly attuned to any news about the Philippines and was able during my working years as a journalist to bring some Philippine topics to the fore, especially during the Marcos years when I kept in touch with writers in the Philippines. In recent years I've been privileged to be involved with the Peace Corps Alumni Foundation for Philippine Development, which funds scholarships for students in the Philippines who would not otherwise be able to afford a college education.

Deane Wylie is from Berkeley, California. Upon returning from the Peace Corps he served as editor of the Peace Corps Newsletter, The Volunteer, *in 1963-64, the first former Volunteer to hold the position. He next worked for the UN Food and Agriculture Organization in Rome and then returned to California to report and edit for a number of newspapers, including twenty years at the* Los Angeles Times *as assistant opinion and Op-Ed editor. He lives in Riverside, Calif.*

Carolyn Ekdahl Wylie from Moline, Illinois became the director of the Children's Center at University of California, Riverside in 1973. She spent 20 years with the Riverside County Office of Education, becoming assistant superintendent for children's services. In 2000 she was named executive director of the Riverside County Commission for Children, Youth and Families (First Five), a post she held until her death in 2004.

(The two photos show Dean and his wife Carolyn Ekdahl Wylie in 1962 and in 2004.)

Duncan Yaggy
Innocents Abroad

Beginnings

I signed up for the Peace Corps because John Kennedy held out the opportunity to make the kind of difference that we wanted to make—and because I did not want to continue in the credit and collection business. I had no idea what project I might be chosen for or where I might end up or what I might be asked to do, and I didn't care. In fact, that mystery was part of the appeal because I was sure we could learn to do anything. Like others in our group, I would have signed up for any project, whether building roads in Africa or teaching teachers in the Philippines.

And that was despite the fact that we all knew that the Peace Corps might die aborning. When we began training, the bill creating the Peace Corps was being debated in the Congress, and we all knew that, if the bill failed, we would be sent home instead of abroad. The uncertainty continued right to the end. I remember the night we graduated from training at Penn State. Harris Wofford, who helped Sargent Shriver set up the Peace Corps, came from Washington to speak at our graduation, and he began with a long face and a solemn statement that the Senate had earlier that day voted 47 to 46 NOT to fund the Peace Corps. The room fell absolutely silent. Harris quickly realized his "joke" had fallen flat and told us the truth, and the celebration then began.

Even before Group I completed training, the Peace Corps realized that a staff of five would be unable to support 128 volunteers in households of two, three and four scattered across eight provinces. Several of us were appointed Volunteer Leaders and deployed as field staff, to support Group I volunteers where they were assigned and to find schools and homes for volunteers in groups that quickly followed ours. I lived near Legaspi and visited volunteers in Albay, Sorsogon, and Catanduanes for several months, then moved to Tacloban on Leyte to provide support for volunteers coming to the Eastern Visayas, and then moved again six months later to Laoag in Ilocos Norte to open Northern Luzon. These transfers may explain why the memories that come first to mind involve:

Travel

The flight over: Twenty-nine of the women volunteers went by jet, and the rest of us filled every seat, nook and cranny on a 99-passenger Constellation that took us from San Francisco to Manila. Our route involved refueling stops in Alaska, Guam, and Wake, and the trip took 38 hours. The ventilation system was not really geared to support 99 passengers, and by the time we got to Manila the inside of the plane smelled like a moist, recently used sweat sock. But we were all so excited that it could not have mattered less.

Trips to see Don Zelinski and Doug Darling at the north tip of Catanduanes: The road from the capital Virac, which was about a lane and a half wide, wound through the mountains in the middle of the island. There were three buses that left the north early each morning. The first to fill, with people on the seats and pigs, chickens and goats underneath, would take off, driving 20 miles an hour faster than possible. The others would follow immediately, and passed the first as soon as its driver stopped to pick up someone by the side of the road. When the second stopped, the third would overtake it and race ahead, hoping to get far enough in front of the other two that he could stop to pick up a passenger and still stay in the lead. As we neared Virac, the buses were so full that the last passengers literally hung on the side, swaying with the bus.

Our jeeps: Volunteer leaders were provided jeeps that had been discarded by the Air Force at Clark Air Base after being dropped from planes in training exercises; their steering and suspension reflected their experience. They were loose. That turned out to be important because a lot of the one-lane bridges we crossed consisted of two boards, one for the tires on the left and the other for the tires on the right, laid over planks spaced a bit wider than railroad ties. When the boards were wet, they were slippery, so you didn't want to brake or accelerate. We learned to line up the tires with the boards and hit the bridges going fast enough that we could coast over. But that didn't work going from Albay to Sorsogon because we had to cross a long one-lane bridge arched over an ocean inlet and thus drive a bit more cautiously. Rain made this road especially exciting because the windshield wipers couldn't keep up with the rain, and the jeeps were completely open on the sides.

The road from Tacloban to Calbayog: Finding houses and schools for the Group III volunteers coming to Samar and Leyte was especially challenging. The road that ran from Tacloban south to Dulag, where MacArthur waded ashore, was two lanes and well paved, but more typical was the road from Tacloban on Leyte across the San Juanico Strait and then 62 miles north to Calbayog, the capital of Samar (known as the West Virginia of the Philippines). Not believing the stories I was told, I took the bus with all manner of people and livestock. The trip took nearly six hours, over roads that pitched and rolled like a small boat in an ocean storm and rope-tow ferries that once were landing craft. After that I flew to Calbayog.

The plane out of Calbayog: Flying in and out of Calbayog was easy enough, but there were only three planes each week—on Monday, Wednesday and Friday. If you missed the Friday plane out, you were stuck until Monday unless you took the bus. As that was not an experience I wanted to repeat, I made sure to arrange for a jeepney that would get me to the airport in plenty of time. But one Friday the jeepney was late, and as we approached the airport I could see the DC-3 that Philippines Air flew to Calbayog pulling away from the gate and taxiing to the end of the runway to take off. The road we were on actually crossed the other end of the runway, and a policemen stood there three times a week to make sure that no vehicles crossed as the plane was coming or going. He waved to my driver to stop, but I persuaded him to turn on to the runway and drive straight toward the plane, to prevent its taking off. That worked like a charm. The stewardess who lowered the steps to let me on was a bit put out with me, but the jeepney driver loved his tip!

The ferries between Tacloban and Bohol and Cebu: For Group IV Volunteers, three of us from Group I—Len Giesecke, Lone Castillo and I—had to find houses and schools on Bohol and Cebu. Len did most of the work there, but Lone and I would go over to help now and then. Ferries were the way to go. Leaving toward midnight and arriving about 7 in the morning, the ferries had broad decks, which were filled with folding cots that were put up beginning around 9 pm. You needed to arrive early to be sure of getting a well-positioned cot. I went myself at 9 until our Tacloban chief of staff (and later Lone's wife), Evelyn, told me to "send a boy," which she did for us. The boy (a teen-aged connection of Evelyn's family) would go over at 8, get a good cot, and sit on it until one of us arrived at 11 or 11:30.

The small planes: Philippine Airlines used small planes seating 8 or 12 to serve some of the smaller communities where we placed volunteers, like Catarman on the north coast of Samar. These planes were flown by young, hot-shot pilots who loved to explore. Whenever I could, I would buy the copilot's seat and try to talk the pilot into detours that would take us down lush valleys, past gorgeous waterfalls, and over the coast. I never had to do much persuading.

The Rabbit: Those of us who opened northern Luzon were based in Laoag, Baguio, and Tuguegàrao. Those travelling between Laoag and Manila learned to treasure the Rabbit, a Greyhound-like bus that made the trip overnight. I think it even had a bathroom. After weeks on open-sided buses with hard wooden benches, a night on the Rabbit seemed like pure heaven.

The Fokker flight from Manila to Zamboanga: After the Peace Corps developed its center in Zamboanga and began holding meetings there, we'd fly from Manila on a plane that left after dark. Most of the flights were completely uneventful, but I remember one flight through a thunderstorm that was especially violent. In the middle of it, I was looking out the window down the wing and saw lightning strike the wingtip. The engines stopped, the lights went out, the air turned off, and the plane was completely silent for a moment—and falling. As panic set in and screams and prayers began, everything came back on, and the flight continued.

The water buffalo cart in Laoag: The cart rolled past our house in a barrio of Laoag about four in the morning on market day every week. It moved very slowly, creaked and bounced, so I got to listen a long time. But the sound I remember most was that of the nose flute played by the old man who drove the cart. As he surely knew, his music was the perfect counterpoint, played by starlight.

Sights

The place I first lived: In a barrio of Legaspi City three other volunteers and I were quartered in an old two-story house with views of the ocean to the south, a 1560s Spanish church to the west, and the perfect cone of Mt. Mayon to the northwest. It was spectacular. I've often wondered whether the barrio survived the eruptions since we left.

A snake: One day I encountered a group of four men standing behind an official jeep parked by the side of the road to Legaspi. Thinking that their jeep might have broken down, I stopped and walked back, to find them standing in a circle and taking turns throwing a large stone at the head of a "three-step snake" (the popular name for a snake thought to be so deadly that its bite would kill somebody before three steps could be taken) trapped in the middle of the circle. As the asphalt was hot and soft, the rock stuck where it landed, and that made it more challenging to pick it up. The trick was to snap your fingers on the opposite side of the snake's head and then grab the rock when he turned to strike. I watched!

A million stars: I'll never forget the darkness that settled over our house in Ilocos Norte when the lanterns were extinguished at 9 or 9:30. Or the extraordinary light that followed, from stars that I had never seen before, and have never seen since. In the foreground, rice paddies; in the distance, hills that defined the landscape.

A boy of 12 or 13 who danced in a barrio festival: He flew over the ground, lifted our spirits and showed us why he would soon be a Bayanihan dancer.

A tree full of mangoes behind our house in Laoag: Using a bamboo 15 or 20 feet long and split at the end to form a basket, a neighborhood boy brought us a ripe one every morning for a month or more, and those mangoes tasted better than any I've eaten since.

Tiny children guiding enormous water buffaloes

Typhoon winds: I recall looking out the window of a boarding house in Virac (the capital of Catanduanes) over 24 hours and watching typhoon winds raise the nipa roofs of hundreds of houses straight up, which meant that the rain went straight through. We were later told that the winds reached 170 mph at the U.S. Coast Guard base off the island's north coast.

Moments

The *merienda*: The first step in opening a new territory for Volunteers was to find and negotiate the selection of the schools in which they would work. That meant going with the superintendent, the district supervisor, or both on a round of schools in the area, chatting with principals and teachers to see who was interested and why, and taking merienda. In the library the tables would be pushed together and covered with the favorite dishes of the teachers, who would stand around the perimeter of the room watching as the visitors filled their plates. And the visitors had no choice but to take a little of everything, lest by skipping a dish we shamed the teacher who made it. The day we visited nine schools was the high point. Fortunately most of the schools were small, so we were sampling 8 or 10 dishes rather than 20 or 25. And washing them down with warm Cokes or San Miguels. (I remember a book of short stories that included one called "The Visitation of the Gods" that perfectly captured a superintendent's visit to a rural school.)

The discovery of the Chapman house: When I first went to Tacloban, I needed to find a boarding house that we could make the base of PC development for Groups III and IV in the Eastern Visayas. Some kind soul directed me to the Chapman house in downtown Tacloban. It was a large and rambling establishment, with the family and boarders upstairs and country kin and connections staying downstairs when they needed to come to town. Come to find out, the Chapmans we came to know were the children, grandchildren and other kin of an American serviceman who stayed on and his Filipina wife. They thought that the Peace Corps was terrific. Lone and I were immediately taken in and became star boarders. And Evelyn Chapman soon became our staff assistant (read manager)—and a few months later (without any prior notice to me!)—Lone's wife. The short version is that the Chapmans took care of us and became the base on which we built the Peace Corps in the Eastern Visayas!

The triumph at Dulag: Not the triumph pictured on the 1962 calendars, which showed General MacArthur wading ashore in 1944, but the triumph of the three volunteers we assigned there. They moved into their house six weeks before school began, hired a house boy, and agreed among themselves not to speak English in the house until school began. That meant that they had to get their house boy to teach them Waray-Waray, then an unwritten language, and he did. But the first any of us knew about it was just before school started, when the three PCVs took a jeepney from Dulag to Tacloban. Confident that they knew no Waray-Waray, the other passengers made jokes about the PCVs, many involving their sexual appetites and capabilities. Not until they reached Tacloban did the volunteers let on that they understood perfectly what had been said about them. Needless to say, that disclosure and their command of the language changed their entire experience in the Philippines.

A conversation about birth control: During a discussion in Ilocos Sur with a Filipino husband and wife, both schoolteachers, awaiting the birth of their first baby, they said they wanted to limit the size of their family, to give their kids the best education and a chance for a good career, but that their Catholic faith would not allow them to do that. They were despairing because they saw no way to prevent the birth of six or eight children.

A chance encounter with a group of priests: When I first went to Calbayog, I arrived in the late afternoon, found no room in the boarding houses and hotels, and was directed to a mission. The priests gave me shelter for a couple of days in a nice accommodation. They had a generator, refrigeration, and food shipped in from Europe (including individually wrapped pats of Danish butter). They were responsible for the local mission church and school. Most of the priests were German, devoted to a strict interpretation of their mission, and frustrated. Their frustration seemed to come from trying to teach their brand of Catholicism to the Filipinos in their congregation, who believed in a different version of Catholicism, animism, and other things as well. It was like trying to persuade people who knew how to swim that they did not know how to swim and to start over. But for their duties in their church and school, they stayed in their residence. The exception among them was an American priest who wore the same habit (white with a knotted rope around the middle and sandals) and was as happy as they were depressed. He attended every barrio celebration in reach, drank enormous quantities of *tuba* (the local palm wine), and was welcome everywhere. He was barely on speaking terms with his German colleagues, who regarded him as an embarrassment, but unlike them he spoke Waray-Waray. During our time in Tacloban he compiled and published the first Waray-Waray/English dictionary.

A card from PC headquarters in Manila: Volunteer leaders visiting women Volunteers in rural areas delivered sanitary supplies because there were none available locally. One month we ran short, and I sent a telegram asking that two cartons of sanitary napkins be shipped on the next plane. Sure enough they came, right on schedule, addressed to me, and covered by a tasteful get-well card.

A visit from our landlord and his wife soon after we arrived in Laoag: They were much older than we were then, and a bit younger than we are now, and as sweet as you can imagine. That morning they brought shot glasses of a sugar extract made in a building behind our house. True to our mission, we drank it, and then were told that it was a rum liqueur—150 proof. The rest of the morning passed smoothly.

A visit in Catarman on the north coast of Samar: As it was the only way to get a house for the Volunteers to be stationed there, I commissioned the construction of a traditional bamboo and nipa house, despite advice that cutting bamboo at that time of year was to invite the destruction of the bamboo and house by the *buk-buk* (termites on steroids). Sure enough, when I visited later, I got to hear the *buk-buk* eating the house. I can't remember if I commissioned the construction of another house, with bamboo cut at the right time of year or why the Volunteers didn't shoot me. I could not have lived or slept with the sound and dust of the *buk-buk*.

Reflections

Living in three places and travelling much of the time fragmented my experience. I got to see much more of the country, and to know many more volunteers and Filipinos than I would have otherwise, but I never learned more than a few words of any of the languages and never dealt with the constraints or enjoyed the benefits of living 18 or 20 months in a single small town with the same neighbors and working with the same teachers.

It's been a wonderful life: Thanks in great measure to the Peace Corps.

After leaving the Philippines, Duncan worked first as a teacher in a special project at Cardozo High School in Washington D.C. along with Brenda Brown, Judy Cridler, and Carolyn Ekdahl Wylie from Philippines Group I and a number of former volunteers from other groups. Duncan later joined former Peace Corps/Philippines staff member, Harvey Pressman, working on the first Upward Bound program. Although he obtained a PhD in American history, he decided to forego a career in education and instead joined up again with Harvey Pressman on the Model Cities Project because working again with Harvey would be more fun than working in education.

Duncan later went to work for the Commonwealth of Massachusetts where he got to try to make the difference he had always wanted to make, primarily for the developmentally disabled. Transferring to the Duke University Medical Center in Durham, North Carolina, Duncan has for many years been the organization's Chief Planning Officer and has also been teaching as an adjunct professor of Public Management at the Terry Sanford Institute of Public Policy.

He says he has gradually realized that he has come full circle. He came from a family about half devoted to business and half devoted to the law, rejected all that for the Peace Corps and a career in education, and now finds that without any graduate training in anything except American history, he's gainfully and happily employed in jobs that are about half law and half business. This has allowed him also to teach and mentor graduate students.

Clockwise from top center: 1. Larry Fuchs greets Group II volunteers at Manila Airport. 2. Mary and Lee Johnson moved to this nipa house in Negros Occidental shortly after their marriage. Many volunteers lived in similar houses. 3. This rural school in San Joaquin, Iloilo Province was newer than most buildings where volunteers worked. 4. Rural buses like this one, which plied the road between Daet and Mambulao in Camarines Norte, were typical throughout the country. 5. The Peace Corps Headquarters at 728 Herran Street in Manila.

Philippines II

July 1961—Arrival of male volunteers in Puerto Rico for training

September 1961—Arrival of all volunteers at Penn State for training

January 3, 1962—Arrival in the Philippines for training at Los Baños

February 1962—Arrival in Panay

June 1963—Completion of Peace Corps service

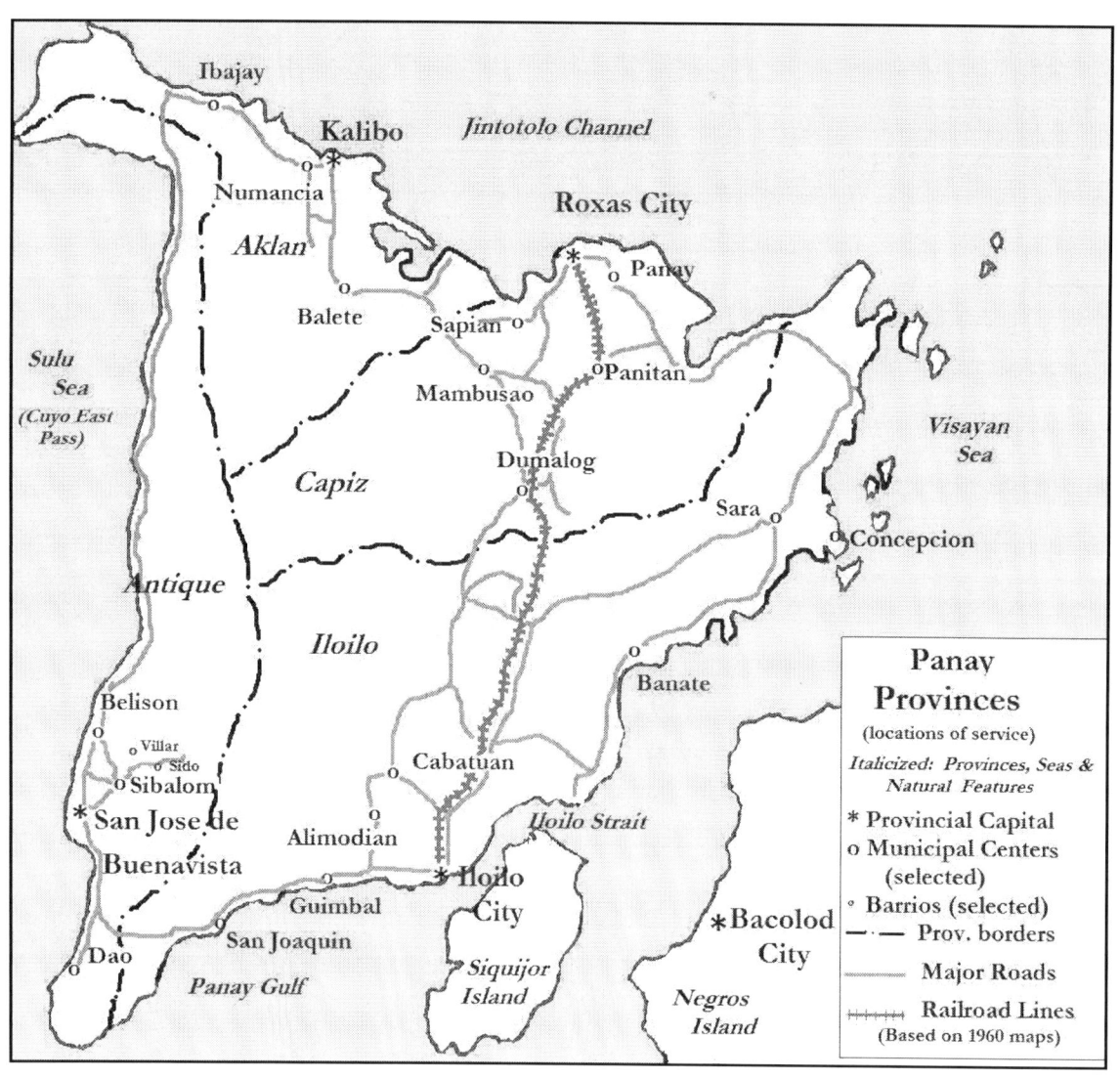

Joan Aragone
Thank you, President Kennedy

Joining the Peace Corps in 1961 was the most important decision I have ever made. To use the term "life-changing" is to understate the case. The idea of the Peace Corps came at a perfect time for me—a very young (age 20 in 1960), female, sheltered, college senior at a small women's Catholic college in California. My protective, i.e., smothering, hyper-religious, Italian-Catholic, San Francisco family had one dream for me: teach school and remain close to home.

I yearned only to leave. I wanted to travel and have adventures. I wanted to save the world.

So when soon to be elected President John F. Kennedy told an audience at the Cow Palace in San Francisco in November 1960 of his plan to establish a corps of young Americans who would go abroad to undeveloped countries and teach and serve, I was electrified. I was in the audience, and I felt he was speaking directly to me. President Kennedy himself was giving me permission to leave home.

Accepted to a graduate program in history at UC Berkeley, I saw ahead of me only additional years of schooling to be followed by a career in—yes, school. I admitted my plans to nobody, taking the Peace Corps exam in secret and going through the motions of planning for Berkeley. When Sargent Shriver's telegram arrived, inviting me to serve in the Philippines and to report in a few weeks to training at Penn State, chaos ensued. My mother took to her bed in wailing despair. Everybody else in my family was furious.

I recall when Group II left from San Francisco Airport for the Philippines how surprised I was at the other volunteers' families' apparent joy and pride at their offspring's decision to join. Only my father and sister came to the airport, sad and exhausted from the constant emotional turmoil our family had undergone in the previous weeks.

Of the Philippines I knew nothing. I had requested an assignment in Asia, based on a fascination with China. So when the invitation arrived, I searched my map in the vicinity of Hawaii and continued uncertainly across the Pacific until I found myself in the South China Sea. At that point, the implication of my decision began to dawn.

To pacify my parents, I told them (and myself) that I would probably not go beyond Penn State in this process. But once there, my perspective changed.

The culture shock I experienced at Penn State was as great as any I encountered in the Philippines. Away from California and my family, meeting a previously unimaginable assortment of other trainees, attending coed classes, I found almost every encounter a surprise. The smiling, polite and docile Filipinos who participated in the program as models of that culture seemed more familiar to me than the Americans in my group. But by training's end, I was determined to go.

After the long plane ride from San Francisco, my first impressions of the Philippines: oppressive heat, a dank smell, and poverty.

Gripping the seat on that initial open-air bus ride along the rutted National Highway toward Los Baños, I stared at flimsy wooden huts, barefoot children and pregnant women in plastic sandals stepping from canvas-curtained doors. I was shocked at what I saw as the entrapment of poverty. For the first time I realized my good luck at being born American.

Los Baños was difficult. I hated the food; I missed my physical comforts; I wanted my daily dose of fog.

The low point occurred one sultry evening as I was ironing in a dorm common room lit by a dim overhead light bulb when something moving and alive fell on my head. I reached up to find a gecko, the small lizards that scurried along the walls 24/7, writhing in my hair. I screamed and ran from the room.

A PCV came to my aid. "You need a drink," she said, and offered to pour me a glass from the bottle of Scotch whiskey her mother had sent. She hadn't yet opened it. "I need one myself." She had received a letter from the boyfriend she had left to come to the Philippines.

We commiserated, and, by the end of the conversation, I knew that I was going to stay.

My original assignment was in Ibajay, Aklan, in a remote northwest province, separated from adjacent provinces by a string of mountains. More than 30 miles from the provincial capital, Ibajay was a prosperous community with a large plaza in the center of town, the focus, I would learn, of countless gatherings and celebrations that would feature the Peace Corps volunteers. At one end stood the municipal stage, and in the center a tall statue of Ramon Magsaysay, the "Kennedy of the Philippines." Little did we know as we got off the bus that we would become the equivalent of rock stars.

We were three recent college grads plus another who had worked in Manhattan, sharing a two-story wood frame house with a cement floor, windows with wood panels that rolled back to let in the light and a windowless kitchen where food was cooked on a fire. We read by Petromax lantern or flashlight and washed our hair amid the banana and mango trees at the backyard water pump.

In two rooms upstairs, two each slept on narrow wooden bed frames topped with mosquito nets and nipa mats. The third room, which faced a canopy of trees, was our place to talk, read aloud or play music into the night.

Behind the house a path wound through a thick grove of bamboo trees and opened onto a long stretch of pristine white beach lined as far as the eye could see with coco palms. The water was high and clear. From my bedroom window, I looked onto a nipa hut nestled in that grove, almost hidden by lush foliage. At night, I heard the bamboo trees rustling in the breeze and the waves washing the shore. The moon was so bright it often woke me. I felt I had landed in paradise.

Like all the volunteers, we experienced an absolute loss of privacy. Neighborhood children sat on the windowsills and watched our daily lives. Hordes followed us everywhere. "You cannot be alone, mum," somebody inevitably said the moment we stepped outside. "I will be your companion."

How was life? We danced the twist with the mayor, we gave parties so huge that neighbors were climbing in the windows and spilling into the yard. We were wined. We dined non-stop. In between, we taught in the schools.

In the first weeks packs of wild dogs prowled the streets and howled into the night, we discovered a bat colony in the attic, a disturbed local man tried to break into our house "to find the love" of one of the volunteers. Two and three-hour bus trips were often extended by many hours when buses broke down. Invited constantly to sing/appear/speak/smile at public events, we arrived on time only to find the audience and officials arrived two or three hours later. We got sunburned, we got sick, we ate too much; we were in constant confusion. It was horrible. It was wonderful. It was the Peace Corps.

The head teacher in my barrio had been a translator for the Americans during World War II, and when he met me, the first American he had seen since 1945, he grabbed my hands and burst into tears. He told me stories of the Japanese occupation. Throughout the time I remained in Ibajay, he educated me about the Philippines. He was a kind friend who died several years ago.

After six months in Ibajay and a summer in Manila working on a UNICEF summer project as a counselor for delinquent teenagers in Welfareville, the state orphanage, I was transferred to a small village in Iloilo Province on the other side of the island. It was a completely different setting.

A volunteer in a two-person household there had left her post to get married, and the Peace Corps sought somebody to take her place. Months before, uncertain about my recently announced assignment to the remote Ibajay, I had submitted my name as interested in moving if the Peace Corps should ever "need" me. So when such a situation arose, I felt obligated to follow my word.

The new assignment was a poor, small fishing village bifurcated by the National Highway, its tiny plaza overgrown and tired. There was a *sari sari* store, a small market and a flat, dirty beach. Again I shared a wood frame house, but with one other volunteer, also a recent graduate of a Catholic women's college, who had been there since the beginning. With her former housemate, she had undergone the welcoming frenzy we all had known.

I moved into the house and the barrio school with little fuss, and life continued. I walked to my school along the beach. My housemate Pat rode a *banca*. At night frogs croaked in our swampy yard. By day a carabao flopped in the mud.

Despite differences in the pace of life, Peace Corps basics remained: a simple house without electricity or running water in a community removed from the "outside world." As in Ibajay, we were energetic, sincere and well-intentioned. Children visited our library and stared in our windows. We opened the house to the community, and we were warmly welcomed.

I recall conversations about "free time." While some believed we really didn't have any—we represented the Peace Corps 24/7—not everybody agreed.

We learned lessons in unexpected places, including the circa World War II reconverted, open-sided buses that somehow, always managed to break down. In those rattletraps, I was forcibly introduced to patience and the art of "letting go."

After sitting cheek by jowl with other passengers, our feet nestling on sacks of live chickens, we were often forced to wait, sometimes for hours, in sugar cane fields, on stark mountain roads, by the side of the National Highway, while a ragtag crew of passengers hammered rusty bus parts back to life. There, despite my American need to "get on with it," I learned to appreciate the incandescent blues of the skies and the greens of the rice paddies.

Once, while on a shopping trip with my housemate, a precious gallon of Magnolia Super Mocha ice cream melted and dripped over our dresses and down our legs as a two-hour bus ride turned into four or five. When we finally got home, we ate the dregs with a spoon, laughed, and had a party—typical Peace Corps reaction, I learned, when things went wrong. Like other volunteers, I incorporated into my vocabulary the term Filipinos used when plans collapsed: *"bahala na,"* which I took to mean *"C'est la vie,"* "It doesn't matter," "Never mind." I use it still.

A highpoint in Aklan Province each January was *Ati Atihan*—a pre-Christian ritual to honor an ancient warrior who had defended Ibajay against invasion centuries before, but adapted by the Spanish colonial church into a Catholic festival to honor *Santo Niño*, the Christ Child, in the form of the Infant of Prague, a Catholic icon of no known connection to Southeast Asia.

It was Aklan's *Mardi Gras*, and the town rocked. For three days of non-stop celebration, townspeople blackened their bodies with ash from smoked coconut husks as a symbol of anonymity, dressed in fantastic costumes and, fueled with alcohol and drum beats, danced and chanted in a kind of conga line through the streets. They carried a huge picture of the Infant of Prague.

In January 1963, when I had come to visit, the revelers stopped in front of the Peace Corps house. "Join us," they called. Our faces and arms rubbed with ash, the volunteers stepped outside, hooked arms, joined the line and moved through the town to the hypnotic rhythms of chants and drums. In the distance, guns went off.

Celebrations culminated with Mass in the Cathedral. There I stood next to a man in blackface with a bandana on his head, dressed as a pregnant woman. On my other side stood a sweaty man, naked except for skimpy shorts. He held a chicken crucified on a bamboo cross. All around me townspeople wearing feathers or holding spears stood praying. At the consecration, the most solemn part of the Mass, where the wine is turned into the blood of Christ, a trumpet played a soulful "taps." At Mass's end, when the priest said in Latin, "The Mass is over," a boom rocked the church. It was the cannon in the plaza.

Whatever my assignment during those years, when I crawled under my mosquito net at night armed with insect repellent, a shortwave radio (to listen to jazz on the Voice of America), ear plugs (for the frogs and/or the mosquitoes) and a flashlight to check for holes in the net lest an errant mosquito invade, I knew I was where I wanted to be.

The volunteers taught in the schools, ran home libraries, counseled teenagers who confided their dreams, organized field trips with children who hadn't been five miles from their villages, tried, not always successfully, to explain water seal toilets to the town elders, helped in medical projects and mental hospitals and orphanages. We served as role models. We worked hard.

In return we were feted, awash and sometimes amazed at Philippine hospitality, befriended by colleagues, townspeople and students, exposed to experiences few of us would otherwise encounter. In a benign environment we were free to explore and learn, about the Philippines and ourselves.

The Peace Corps experience changed me profoundly and permanently, but to my family and friends it was something to get out of my system, like the flu.

I went to the Philippines believing that the USA was "superior" to other countries and that it could/would save the world. I arrived home after travel through the Middle East and Europe to view the USA as one in a complex tapestry of countries and cultures. I saw Americans as lucky, not superior, because of opportunities available. I recognized that place of birth and native intelligence are accidents of fate. And my perceptions of the Catholic Church were permanently changed.

In Group II, I had entered into a world of peers where, for the first time, I felt comfortable. This "botch" of strong-minded individuals became, in a real sense, a family, and I made lifelong friends whom I treasure to this day.

Forbidden as a teenager to apply to colleges that weren't Catholic or close to home, eventually I did graduate work at schools that had been beyond my ken. I became a journalist and teacher.

Yes, the Peace Corps in the Philippines has enriched the lives of many Filipinos, teachers and friends, but in my view those most enriched have been the volunteers themselves.

Joan Aragone was born in San Francisco, attended Catholic schools until she was 21 and graduated as valedictorian from a women's college 25 miles from home. Then she joined the Peace Corps. After returning to the States, she attended Columbia University and earned a master's degree from Stanford University. She has taught at the high school and university levels in the U.S. and at a university in Beijing, worked as a staff writer and editor on magazines and newspapers in the San Francisco Bay Area and in Hong Kong, and freelanced articles for various publications. She currently writes a column for a Bay Area newspaper and teaches adult school. She hopes she will always be a traveler, not a tourist, a distinction she learned from her Peace Corps experience.

William Austin
Carabao Bill

I took the Peace Corps exam at the post office in the spring of 1961. It was long and hard. By mid-afternoon the math section was in front of me. Giving up, I turned in the unfinished exam, went away discouraged and returned to teaching high school world history in Western Kansas.

I had a summer job hauling wheat. The depot agent hand delivered a telegram to the house. From Peace Corps, Washington, it said, "Report to Berkeley, California for training in 'Chana' project." The depot agent had made an error and it was Ghana, not Chana. I told the farmer to find another truck driver. He said they would get the Kansas wheat crop in without me.

A Peace Corps Official called me in on the last day of training and told me the Africans didn't want me. They considered me a threat to overthrow the government of Kwame Nkrumah because I had taken courses in political science. I didn't care that President Nkrumah had the opposition locked up and that his motto was, "Seek ye first the political kingdom and all things else shall be added unto you."

Then I got the chance to risk life and limb in the rain forest of Puerto Rico, and if I survived the "outward bound" experience, to go to Penn State for Group II Philippines training. I survived jumping off a cliff backwards and was "drown-proofed." I was excellent on the rope obstacle course and ran two miles before breakfast.

At the beginning of Penn State training, I was almost sent home because I refused to take the shots. I had recently taken the shots at Berkeley and had my shot record to prove it. The Peace Corps wasn't happy but let me go to the Philippines with Group II.

Basketball is the national sport of the Philippines. A game was scheduled between Group II and the Los Baños varsity. It was like the Olympics. The teams marched in amid great fanfare and pageantry. I felt like I was 6' tall but I was only 5'6". All of their players were my size. I lost the game in the final seconds by dribbling out-of-bounds. They won 65-63. It was a great victory for the boys of the agricultural college. They beat us at our game. Filipinos had an inferiority complex when they compared themselves to *"Amerikanos."* My poor play helped them overcome this complex. Perhaps it was my greatest accomplishment, but I was devastated at the time. After a month at Los Baños, I had more training than any other PCV. I failed to pass the language exam, but PC/Manila felt sorry for me and let me go to permanent assignment: Mambusao, Capiz on the island of Panay, Western Visayas.

In our nipa/bamboo hut on 4' pilings, we had a four-man household. We were the only four-man household in Group II. Richard was a gregarious, ambitious, mover type, while

Tom, "Bolivar" and "Carabao Bill" were more patient with smaller plans. It was a beautiful balance. Our steadying influence was a check on Richard's driving ambition, and at the same time, he demonstrated how positive, concrete changes are effected. Richard encouraged our house boy to go to high school. O'Ning later became Mambusao police chief.

Josie Lapidez, our cook, was afraid of me at first. I was too serious, unsmiling and depressed. Finally, I cheered up and she didn't hide her face when I looked at her. Josie was an enjoyable girl and great cook. One of the things I miss most is Filipino food. We learned much about the culture from Josie. She gained much confidence associating with us. Unknowingly, she was the adhesive that held us together. Often we were broke at the end of the month and Josie lent us *pesos* out of her meager salary.

When it didn't rain enough to fill our 55 gallon barrel, we went to the city well. I tried carrying two five-gallon buckets of water at the ends of a bamboo pole slung across my shoulders, but failed. Demonstrating the dignity of labor and a little ingenuity, I placed a bucket of water on the handlebars of my bike and pedaled home. It required eleven trips. Perhaps the meager efforts of this *"Kano"* inspired a Filipino student to make a magnificent effort and become another Jose Rizal or a President Ramon Magsaysay!

Bill Austin dated his wife briefly before leaving Kansas for Peace Corps training. They corresponded while he was in the Philippines, and their relationship blossomed to the extent that Bill proposed by mail and was accepted by mail. They were married a month after he returned. Bill taught junior high and high school in Kansas for ten years after Peace Corps service then earned a master's in education at Kansas State University. He later worked for Union Pacific Railroad and in his spare time volunteered to entertain nursing-home residents by playing his trumpet. He retired in 1997 and volunteers to teach math and social studies in GED programs. He also volunteers at the Philippine Cultural Center of Greater Kansas City, where he is the flagman who pulls up the American flag on one pole and the Philippine flag on the other pole. He once played the Philippine national anthem on his trumpet at a gala banquet in the Hyatt Regency ballroom downtown; wearing his Barong Tagalog, *he stood proudly beside the Philippine flag—"It was grandioso!" he reports. He can still sing half of* Lupang Hinirang, *the Philippine national anthem, in Tagalog, but says no one wants to hear it.*

(The second photo shows Bill with his granddaughter.)

Phyllis Smith Baer
Precious Time Warp

April 13, 1962

Sometimes, one just stops, confronts the moment and says, "Hey, how did all this happen?" A few months ago, I was swinging in The Peppermint Lounge in my native New York City doing the Twist, mesmerized by the cacophonous beat of Chubby Checker and now here I am, light years away in a place populated by a primitive people who have never left the land, whose identity is the land and who feel they belong to the land. All this would be incomprehensible to me, were I not here, living and slowly identifying with them. Sanity necessitates we backtrack a bit.

My boyfriend at that time was very much of an idealist with a passionate pursuit of whatever it took for him to be able to contribute and make a difference in the short period we all are given. Hence, he was one of the first in line to take the Peace Corps exam in the early '60s. Without his idealism, drive and dedication, I went along with the plan. I saw it as an adventure; he saw it as a fantastic opportunity to begin his journey. However, being the youngest son of a very strong Italian family, his brothers let him know in no uncertain terms that his primary responsibility was to the family entity and lofty goals were wonderful but family came first. Hence, he declined his acceptance, and I, with great trepidation, went off to the Philippines with his encouragement and blessings and with great plans for "when I come home."

February 1, 1962

This marked the beginning of my first few months in the field, spent in Guimbal, Iloilo, in the school system, where I was wined, dined, fed, clothed and made happy and paraded about as the American Peace Corps volunteer. The school system was very intact and functional and my contribution was actually minimal other than a pleasant exchange of language, culture, clothing and "gifts from home" with the locals. My house-mate and I lived in a nipa hut on the beach *sans* electricity, running water, etc., and we enjoyed the local food, rice, fish, chicken, *calamanci*, mango, *pancit*, *adobo*, and whatever was offered, especially at fiestas. In short, we were very well cared for and "prized" by our hosts.

April 6, 1962

This was the end of the school year, when we were encouraged to find a 'project' to work on for summer vacation. We were the first groups in the Philippines, and not much was actually formalized about projects—so we all branched out to various areas of interest. I learned that two volunteers from Group I were planning on helping to set up a makeshift lab/clinic in Mayoyao, Northern Luzon, an area populated by native Ifugao Tribes. I was interested in health care (I have since become an MD) and tagged along. One of my companions had been a lab tech in the states and the other was, as was I, without much knowledge, but dedicated to providing "something" in the way of basic health needs. So, we set out for Mayoyao.

Mayoyao is situated in the rice terraces of northern Luzon, in the Mountain province. From Manila it is an all day trip to Banaue and from there, 44 km to Mayoyao—but that journey can take anywhere from three to eight or ten hours depending on the road conditions and the weather, and sometimes the "Dangway" doesn't run at all. The "Dangway" was a large red, yellow and black bus which was our means of transport from Mayoyao. It was mostly populated by pigs, chickens and other similar transport items, along with humans sitting on wooden seats or hanging off the side. The upper part of the vehicle carried large burlap sacks of rice, tuba, rice wine, camotes and whatever one chose to haul. It was a very sturdy vehicle which travelled very slowly and made a great deal of noise, mainly by shifting gears to prevent accidents such as going over a cliff.

The drive can be quite harrowing as we noted a few World War II U.S. Army jeeps rusted and overturned at the bases of the terraces. We came face to face with the enormity and beauty of the stunningly spectacular rice terraces and the magnificent power of the land as slowly we made our way, with some apprehension to the people who were the caretakers of this wonder. Our "place" in Mayoyao was to be on the very top of one of the rice terraces, high above the clouds. On arrival in Mayoyao, the "Dangway" having let us off at the base, we hiked up a winding path through the terraces for the next hour or so. The path was populated by many large green iguanas (some of them easily two feet long), with piercing red eyes. There were moments of mild terror probably for both us and the Iguanas who stopped, looked at us squarely and fortunately ran off the path.

A guide met us on our arrival at the top and presented us to locals, who were barefoot and dressed in tribal finery—G-strings, copper wrist, neck and ankle bracelets, beads, earrings—both male and female, and all chewing betel nut. Most of the men were heavily tattooed, and wore bolos and carried spears as the tribes until recently had been head-hunters. Some of the men wore old World War II Army jackets, likely taken from abandoned jeeps or given to them by U.S. soldiers many years ago.

After the initial curiosity on both parts, we were ushered into a small wooden structure with one room packed with cartons (which we later learned were donated by Dr. Tom Dooley's clinic in Laos—Dooley having recently died at the age of 34 after dedicating his life to health care in Southeast Asia); this was to be the lab and small clinic. Our job was to unpack all the supplies and organize them into some sort of dispensary and to set up a make-shift lab, using the donated materials. The "hospital" room was very small with a few beds and a small enclosed side area for "operations." There was another room for the doctor and we had an adjacent room.

The doctor was a resident from the University of Santo Thomas in Manila who was assigned on a "hardship rotation" for a two-week tour. He gave us instructions about our room; we had three beds and were told to place them in the middle of the room and at night always to cover ourselves with whatever papers we could find as the rat population was very curious (and hungry), came out at night and ran along the shelves lining the walls. This was all precautionary—just in case one of the rats made an error—the sounds of the paper would frighten them and us and we would all be safe. He said someone had brought cats up there at one time but the cats had all disappeared. We found that the big drawing factor for the animals was the large boxes of powdered milk from CARE which had been brought up many months ago and left there (obviously only partaken of by the animal population).

We were told that our main staples would be *camotes*, bananas, oatmeal, rice, and CARE powdered milk. We were given a Petromax lantern and flashlights. We were able to boil water and had a makeshift shower. Our place was a good distance from the base of the terrace where there was a post office and with luck, mail came once a week. There was a small *bodega*, a *sari-sari* store where we were able to purchase tea, coffee and other simple supplies.

As we settled in to our home—we no longer were regarded as curiosity factors and went about our business unpacking and doing the best we could under the circumstances. It was very impressive to see the stamina and tolerance for adversity of the Ifugao people which would be incomprehensible in our culture. To get to the clinic, they had to be carried up the terraces by family or friends in makeshift litters—some journeying for hours with broken bones, shotgun or knife wounds, animal bites. They were then treated with no anesthesia and most survived. If one did not survive, he was carried on litter back to his home on another terrace which we could easily see but which may actually have been a day's journey down one terrace and up the other. We could see and hear the ritualistic ceremonies—fires, wailing, clanging of metal drums and general universal grief.

At one time, our nurse, Josie invited us to attend a memorial service for an elder who had donated significant land to the tribe. We were honored and dressed as we thought was appropriate for the occasion only to be greeted by our nurse who usually came to the clinic in a white dress and a hair net, arriving in full Tribal regalia—multi-painted in native skirt, wearing ankle, neck, and wrist brass bracelets and bare-breasted. The ritual consisted of exhumation of the remains of the lady who had died many years ago, on this particular date, placing her body on a chair where all could view her, and surrounding her with flowers. Dancing ensued around the remains to music made by clanging metal pans and the sounds of a nose flute. A wild boar was slain and all imbibed local rice wine. We were very tempted to take pictures of this event but felt it would be disrespectful to our hosts as we were very closely watched by the guests. We wondered if other outsiders had ever been invited to such a ritual. We definitely felt a strong sense of acceptance at this point.

We learned many of the traditions of the people—a people who had become highly sought after by the "bible translators" who sought to "cure them of their paganism." One evening, returning from a visit to Banaue, we found we were too late for the bus back to Mayoyao and became unwittingly privy to the intensity and pervasiveness of the bible translators when we were guided by a kindly elderly Ifugao woman to one of their places. We arrived at the home of two women who immediately relieved our guide of the cigarettes we had given her in gratitude and warned her with strong condemnation about "tools of the devil." That evening we were both captivated and terrorized as we sat in the middle of a small room illuminated by a flickering candle and listened to many tales of the devil's prowling about looking for souls in the areas where Christianity had not yet had a stronghold. Perhaps the greatest impact on the ladies had occurred one night when a group of Ifugao were apparently participating in a ritual around a fire and likely had a bit too much to drink. One of them became "possessed" and our host, noting the battle between good and evil, ran into their midst holding up a crucifix. She re-enacted her action with crucifix in hand, eyes blazing in the waning candle-light—the whole scene seemed more like a scene from *The Exorcist* than the hallowed duty of a missionary. The possessed man fell to the ground writhing, then was still and lay there until the morning when he awoke and was "himself" again. None of us was able to sleep that evening without waking up every few minutes to make sure God, or someone, was on "our side."

Many attempts at Christianizing the tribal people were not really successful. We heard from the Ifugao that one member of their tribe who had become a Christian had gone to Manila to work. He came down with a severe illness and saw a doctor in Manila; he was told he was dying of advanced metastatic cancer and should settle his affairs. The man came back to Mayoyao, went to see his local tribal elder who told him what to do, and he was alive and well ten years later, or so the story goes. The tribal way of life was very strong.

Sometime in Mid 1962

We left Mayoyao, not really knowing if we would ever be back, and wondering if we really had contributed anything. At that time, we became part of something else—our frames of reference no longer were our support systems. We felt for a time we had "crossed over" and become "one" with the tribal people, and ironically, could continue to do so, at the same time questioning our own sanity. One of my companions wrote a diary while there which she perused many months later and decided she better burn it as she felt she had definitely gone "off the beaten path of sanity." It was good to hear that and to know that neither of us was alone in our feelings. We were caught in a place between two worlds and could not stay in both.

It has been a long time. The person who went to the Philippines in no way resembles the person who came home. I never saw my boyfriend again when I came back. Again, the person who left was not the person who came home. In a very short period of time a lifetime of probing, questioning, floundering, soul-searching, gains, losses, joys, miseries all have been realized with no real answers. But, did we ever seek answers or were we just on a road and somehow found direction through mutual closeness and caring and unwittingly building bonds which in no way was our aim in joining in the first place? We seem to have built a structure among ourselves which pervades any obstacle and holds us together—we are conditioned by each other and that alone could be the best part of the whole experience.

I did go back. In Mayoyao the terraces were no longer kept up as the young people all had gone to Manila and given up on their tribal ways according to the elders. The iguanas had all been eaten and were no more. The women pose for pictures for the tourists and the men wear ties now under their Army jackets. In Iloilo there are no more *calesas* and very few horses are to be found. Motor bikes are everywhere. Shopping malls with escalators and elevators stand where the trees once stood. Most of what we knew has changed and some gone forever. So where does that leave us? Again, we have a great treasure—we have each other.

Phyllis Smith Baer was born in New York City. She attended St. John's Elementary School and Bronx High School of Science. She graduated from Pace College with a degree in Business Administration and worked in the field of advertising for two years, simultaneously taking premed courses  *in the evenings and on weekends. She joined the Peace Corps, was part of Group II (her house-mate was from Group I). Upon her return to the U.S. she had a fellowship to Columbia University and graduated with an MA in Biology. Phyllis met her husband at Columbia and together they embarked on Medical School at Hahnemann in Philadelphia. She did a residency in internal medicine, had a fellowship in hematology and managed to have three children during that time—Jeniffer, Heidi and Jesse. Phyllis and family went from Philadelphia to Boston, where she earned a master's in public health from Harvard University. She has been working for more than 25 years in a neighborhood health clinic in Boston. She helped to start the Program of All-inclusive Care for the Elderly (PACE) at that health center and is currently the executive medical director. Her three children are all doctors. She has received numerous awards in the field of medicine from her various affiliated hospitals and clinics. She likes to travel and spend time with her children and two grandchildren.*

(The first photo shows Phyllis blowing out the candles at her birthday party in Guimbal, Iloilo in 1962 with Patricia MacDermot behind her and Geri Thomas at her side; the second photo shows her in New York with Joan Aragone.)

The Adventure Continues
Linda Cover Bigelow

Clinging to the side of the rock face, I contemplated my possible end on the rocks in the ravine far below or springing to a tiny tuft of grass that might hold my weight for the few instants needed to scramble to safety. How did I ever allow myself to get into this predicament? Whatever was I doing on this rock face at age 68? My whole life flashed through my mind as I took a deep breath, counted to three, leaped to the tuft, and pulled myself up and over the top. This adventure was a supreme act of imprudence and poor judgment. I had not applied the most basic of rules for hiking in the mountains. But let's go back to my life flashing through my mind.

A girl of six sits in front of a slide projector watching pictures of Alaska, from where her aunt had just returned. I was that little girl. Enthralled by these pictures, I determined to see the world. A U.S. Steelworker's daughter decides to go to university, the premier criterion being that this university should be located as far as possible from her home town of Gary, Indiana. I was that daughter, and I made what could be viewed as a bad choice. Southern Methodist University was rich and expensive. The emphasis was on the Greeks, and I could not, and did not want to, participate.

Working part time during my junior year in the Presbyterian office, I learned of a summer work camp experience called Operation Crossroads Africa. Offered a subsidy of half the cost of the trip, I canvassed all the church groups and moneyed establishments in Dallas and pulled together the other half. Six weeks of digging street-drains and making mud bricks in cooperation with a Ghanaian group of youths further enhanced my childhood desire to see the world.

After graduation in 1961, and with an Elementary School Teaching Certificate in hand, I prepared to teach Grade Four in the Denver Public School system. I spent that summer nearby, in Rocky Mountain National Park, working in a lodge. President John F. Kennedy had recently announced the creation of the Peace Corps. My acceptance telegram arrived two weeks before the start of school. I blithely called the Denver Public School system and announced that I had joined the Peace Corps and would not be teaching. They were not upset!

And that brings us to our Philippines, to our roommates, to our Filipino friends, to our colleagues, to our struggles to overcome the ambiguities of the appellation "teacher's aide". In my *poblacion*, that meant dance partner, speaker, place-holder on stage for all VIP visits. Although my original assignment was as a "teacher's aide" in the Central Elementary School, I spent my time sitting in the back of classrooms, "observing" and occasionally offering a correct pronunciation for an English word. To vary this routine, my roommate and I offered initially well-received science teaching workshops at home, using UNESCO materials. After about a month, one of the teachers told us that the principal would no longer allow them to attend. Why? The teacher was very uncomfortable, but he gave us to understand that the principal felt threatened by our presence and by the independence of spirit which we represented. For their part, the teachers at the central school, nearing retirement, did not wish to jeopardize their future. They obeyed the principal's orders. Deeply discouraged, my roommate and I decided to seek new teaching situations where the younger, newer teachers were, at the far-flung edges of the school district. I moved to the farthest barrio of Santa Ana, in the hills, nine kilometers away on foot, with no road, no water, and no electricity—total calm. There I found bright, inquisitive minds, a big welcome, and lots of work. My fondest memories are from here, of meals with Nanay, Tatay, and Manang, bathing in a nearby spring, living in the home economics bamboo house, and having sweet children repeating everything I said.

For a summer project, Bob Miller and I accompanied our Filipina friend Cora and a young Filipino to the small island of Taloto-an where we were to initiate a community program of building outdoor toilets. No sooner had we arrived than we found ourselves administering first aid. The island had no health care at all. Any cases of illness or injury had to be cared for on the main island of Panay. Most of the men on the island were fishermen who used explosives to stun and/or kill the fish, which was the origin of many injuries. On one occasion we saw a burning boat arrive in front of our house, and a badly-burned and frightened man was brought to us. Clearly this was beyond our expertise, but I accompanied him by boat to the nearest clinic on Panay where he could get good care. All I could do was to offer soothing, reassuring words. He survived. Overwhelmed by first aid requests, we never dug a single toilet.

Near the end of the Philippines stay, I met Lee Bigelow who was doing dissertation research on Manila city politics. We quickly discovered we shared the same curiosity about the world and its people. With the U.S. Foreign Service we were posted in Rangoon, Burma (now Yangon, Myanmar); Bangkok and Udorn Thani, Thailand; Ouagadougou, Upper Volta (now Burkina Faso); Paris, France; and, of course, Washington D.C. Later, with the private sector, we lived in Vientiane, Laos and Hanoi, Vietnam.

To comprehend the people of these countries and their customs over the years, we learned Thai, Lao (closely related to Thai), and French. We traveled to as many nearby countries as our budget would allow and we raised three children. My Peace Corps experience interfered at first in adapting to the Foreign Service lifestyle. Our Rangoon house was entirely too grand. Did we really need engraved calling cards? Do I have to attend all these chatty coffee parties? Do I have to be pleasant and speak meaningless nothings at all these receptions? (Trying hard to do my best, I had a delightful discussion at a Paris reception with a handsome Asian male with a beautiful head of white hair. When I later told Lee of him, he remarked that this handsome Asian was the head of the Khmer Rouge delegation, and that we were never supposed to engage any of them in conversation. Oh well…)

Our life was not always merry. We were threatened, robbed, and briefly held hostage. Our adolescent children enjoyed the worst that Bangkok had to offer. But these adult children are now strong, responsible citizens, and we are proud of them.

Drawing on that Peace Corps experience of making unintelligible speeches in front of an adoring audience, I was persuaded to make intelligible speeches in front of critical audiences on the subject of Thai traditional art in Bangkok. The necessity of visual aids sent me prowling all over the countryside with a camera looking for obscure, overgrown, Buddhist temples. This evolved into a passion for photography; I eventually exhibited, published, and printed photos. Totally portable, photography has been an excellent hobby, a real joy.

Suddenly it was time to retire—but where? Did this mean the adventure was over? We were hooked on the daily language challenge; on the math acrobatics of a different currency; on understanding what that little nod of the head meant; of eating chicken soup for breakfast or of eating dinner at 21:00 (that's nine p.m.). We eliminated countries with harsh climates, unstable governments, or unreliable access to things such as banks, hospitals, international transportation, and cultural activities. We had once been smitten by the Cote d'Ázur, but never ever for a moment thought we could possibly live here. It was for the jet setters, the suntan fans. On the other hand, by living in a village; by renovating an old, village house; and by living modestly (no restaurant flings); we could have the charm of a small village, the amenities of a large city, a wonderful climate, and the sea and the mountains.

Now, let's return to that rock face in the south of France, not far from where we live and hike regularly. All these things flashed through my mind. If that little tuft of grass did not hold up, the adventure was all over. But, the little tuft did hold, and the adventure continues.

Linda and Lee met in a Manila bookstore and married after she saw how well Lee engaged with the inhabitants of her barrio. Lee joined the U.S. Foreign Service, which sent them to Burma, Thailand, Burkina Faso, France, and the United States. Later, with the private sector, they lived in Laos and Vietnam. All three of their children were born in Thailand. As the spouse of a U.S. diplomat, Linda was not permitted to work by the local national governments, but could have a hobby; she chose photography. While in Bangkok she was a National Museum volunteer, guiding, helping to start a slide library, and giving lectures. In Udorn, Thailand, she participated in the organization and assistance of hundreds of refugees who flowed over the border from Laos. While in Paris, Linda and Lee traveled throughout France, and when the time came to retire, chose the village of Saint Jeannet, near Nice, to settle down and finally plant roots.

Marthlu Bledsoe

Lessons

It was all new and no one, not staff and certainly not the volunteers, had a handle on what to do. Lots of memories, one in particular still grates—those psychologists! Not a whole lot older than the volunteers. I was terrified. Mine, a guy, had on the topic list: "How are you going to survive with all these older people?" I was 20 at the time as was one other trainee. All I could do was to stare at him—heart sank. Next question: "How are you going to handle young kids running around with no pants on?" Answer: "I grew up in the country: one room school—12 grades, electricity, but water was at a pump outside and 50 yards away out-houses." Didn't register, he was a city kid. Asked again—and this time I was into his program. Answer: "Just spent the summer in Europe and most of that in the south of France on the beaches. Most of the beach people didn't have any clothes on—no problem." His language, so it worked. First Peace Corps lesson: important to use the hearer's frame of reference.

Expect all groups feel this way, but we had a spectacular group of volunteers: city and country, private and public schools, talented musicians, hockey players, genuine, and some very, very smart folks.

Three housemates and I were posted in Panitan, Capiz. Two important lessons here:

First, you're twenty years old, but you don't know everything, such as how to wring a live chicken's neck. Fortunately, one of the house mates did and we had dinner for several visiting volunteers; and second, sometimes you do what you have to do. While in Panitan we had local guys under the floor—bamboo—at bath time. We poured boiling water on them. Unfortunately, one of the guys was the sheriff's son. The sheriff said, "Boys will be boys." We were moved in short order to a different town, Dumalog.

Dumalog was about half way down the island and maybe a mile walk from the rail line. Lots of visitors showed up. The house had cement floors and the town had a serious sheriff.

Nice town, good place to be with some bad memories for residents since just a short way to the south had been a Japanese concentration camp for locals. The Sugar Central folks (Basques) had been interned in Santo Tomas, Manila. As "teachers aides", my house mates and I each had a school. Mine was close to the rail line. The Principal was Chinese and well thought of by teachers and students, but not really a part of the social fabric. The school closed twice for earthquake warnings, but only small tremors of 3.2 or so.

The teachers and I, after awhile, had discussions at lunch or after school about the difficultly of pronouncing English. They concluded that their tongues were too long. So I asked the English teacher to measure my tongue. She thought it was fun. Then we measured volunteered teachers' tongues; slightly over half volunteered, if I remember correctly. No particular difference in length. It did generate almost daily discussion on language and some cultural differences—useful.

Because Dumalog was close to the rail line, within commuting distance to Capiz City and every other town in easy travel distance, teachers were ordered to give up their houses to participants and visitors for the country-wide school Olympics. Teachers were unhappy at being summarily displaced. So, I organized my teachers to strike; they talked most other teachers in three nearby schools into joining, a new idea for all of them. It worked, but all of us got into considerable trouble. I suggested they blame me, especially my principal who was about to be fired. After some lobbying, we semi-apologized, and I think some of the teachers were fined—for the cost of housing elsewhere for the game participants. The teachers, including my principal, thought it worked out pretty well.

One fun thing happened. The central school administrators in Manila were going to "visit" for an inspection of all four schools. Talk about hustle: in town and in the schools, to replace all signs including city signs that were in *Visayan* and NOT *Tagalog*. They removed all *Visayan* designations and put the signs back as soon as the administrators departed. Way to go!

During the summer school break, folks could opt for various assignments. I served in a home/school (large) for non-leprous children of leprous parents. The children had a limited understanding of the reason they were there. "Daddy, or Mother, is sick." One tyke wanted to know why I had corn silk for hair. I let her pull and pat, just to prove it was really hair. The school had limited resources and several other volunteers and I were able to "liberate" from USAID some nonperishable food. How does lots and lots of chocolate Ovaltine sound? We also liberated Lifesavers and such.

We were staying in University graduate housing when the small house caught fire, fortunately while we were out. We lost our clothing and whatever else each of had brought. Dresses were easy—all we had to do was find a *modista;* other items such as underwear and shoes, impossible—we were too large. We ended up going to the military commissary in Subic Bay for those necessities. We stayed in a variety of places, mostly with nearby families, until permanent housing could be located. Several of us ended up in a boarding house where a number of the *Jai Alai* players stayed. Interesting! Manila was a busy time. I ran around with new friends, one a lovely gal engaged to President Magsaysay's son, and his school chums from the Ateneo de Manila. Jesuits at the Ateneo were a new breed of cat for me. I took a class that summer and was the only non-religious-order student. Even the baby Jesuits in training were highly educated and verbal. They had attitude!

After that summer all of us returned to our towns. Going home was good—for awhile. Then Dumalog began losing volunteers. The first housemate got married and moved to another island. The second volunteer left to marry a Filipino. The third housemate resigned—totally disappointed by PC staff and its mismanagement. Town folks wanted to know, reasonably so, where their friends and teachers had gone and why. I talked a lot about one who had gotten married, but there just wasn't any real way to tell the truth, have it make sense, and not offend the townspeople.

During the in-between, there were several visits by volunteers and staff—helpful. Eventually, Dumalog got two new volunteers from a later group—great gals, but only two not three. Life settled down, the schools, the town and the volunteers got back to business. We did adopt a pregnant cat. And while in Manila getting ready for departure, I received a telegram saying "Mother and four kittens doing fine."

I flew back the long way: Viet Nam, Thailand, India, Lebanon, etc.—a great trip, great fun to circumnavigate the globe. Ended up at home in Missouri for about five months and ran the family bookstore so my parents could take a vacation. Then I took off for D.C. to see what those "damn" jerks at the Peace Corps thought they were doing. There were not yet many volunteers returning and I was more or less hired on the spot for recruiting. I stayed at the Peace Corps for five years. After doing on-the-road recruiting, I became head of small college recruiting, and then program officer in for East Asia and Pacific Region.

Since five years was the limit staff could remain at that time, a former PC boss asked me to join the McCarthy Campaign for President. I did, as the head of Advance, where I met some really great people and some who were not so great. I stayed with politics for two more unsuccessful campaigns: Muskie and Sanford. If you can't win, fold. I then spent several years with the National Committee for Support of Public Schools in a successful effort to obtain federal funds, not just local money for public schools. Agnes Meyer, of the *Washington Post* Meyers (very much the *grande dame*) deserves great admiration for having the idea and getting it passed by Congress.

About that time, I got married to a returned volunteer who served in Guinea and we moved to an historic house in the slums built in 1870. We survived transvestite prostitutes, dead bodies fore and aft and lots of K-Y jelly, assorted left-behind food and clothing especially wigs and always a shoe. Go figure. Out of this my husband and I, along with a few others, created a now-great community. We all like each other and get along 99.9% of the time. We are proud of the Blagden Alley and Naylor Court Association. We worked hard to get where we are today.

Somewhere in there, I served on the staffs of various local candidates, successfully this time. Eventually had different positions in the District of Columbia government including on Mayor Marion Barry's staff. Retired from the D.C. government and joined a think tank working on the city's assorted problems. There were other jobs in there but not all that interesting. Before retiring for the final time, or so I think, I served as the Director of a foundation supporting job readiness and job training. Second best job, I ever had.

As for now, I am trying to be a good enough Texas hold 'em player to win a seat in the World Series of Poker. Filipinos seem to like poker, and I have played with several. One of our directors is from Iloilo City.

Wish me luck!

After Peace Corps service, Marthlu Bledsoe spent five years on Peace Corps staff in Washington D.C., recruiting, as head of Small College Recruiting and as Program Officer for East Asia and the Pacific. She then headed the advance team for Eugene McCarthy's Presidential campaign and later worked on Senator Muskie's Presidential campaign. She spent several years with the National Committee for Support of Public Schools in a successful effort to obtain federal funds for public schools. She also served on the staffs of several successful Washington D.C. candidates. She held several positions with the government of the District of Columbia, including on Mayor Marion Barry's staff, and worked for a think tank focused on the District's problems. She then was Director of a foundation contributing to job readiness and job training. She is married to a returned volunteer who served in Guinea. They live in the Shaw neighborhood of Washington, where they have been very active in forming and maintaining the Blagden Alley and Naylor Court Association. In retirement Marthlu is a dedicated Texas hold 'em poker player.

(The photo shows Marthlu sitting astride on a carabao.)

Philip Bloom

As I Remember—Days in the Peace Corps

Key experiences

Living and working with the community of Dao. Learning many life experiences, especially "self reliance." One of the key moments occurred when I visited outlying communities by foot to teach and learn. Coming from one of the largest cities in the world, New York City, this was an eye opener for me. Everything I learned I kept with me the rest of my life.

Motivation

JFK and his speech, "Ask not what your country can do for you, ask what you can do for your country" was a profound influence at a time when my college friends and I were choosing careers. I was in New York when I applied and never will forget the "telegram" I received indicating I was chosen to serve. I was heading to grad school and then wasn't sure—I was and still remain a liberal democrat, so my focus was on doing something creative and productive. Peace Corps helped change everything.

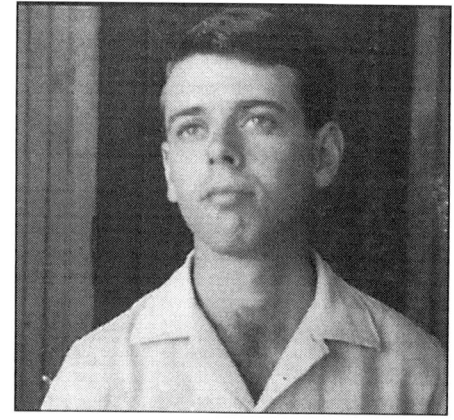

Philippines

I knew very little about the Philippines until I went to a library. I knew about MacArthur and the war, Bataan, The Death March and what I'd seen in movie houses. I knew Filipinos were allies and friends. I arrived on a Pan Am flight and was met at the airport by the Minister of Education. We were whisked away to Los Baños. What a first night—very exciting. I can't comment on the Philippines today since I have never been back and have no personal reference other than the media.

I lived and worked in Dao in Antique Province. I enjoyed the entire experience. I lived with Harvey November who now resides in Israel. We became friends and remain in contact. Dao was a small town with a central square and a Dutch priest. I remember playing basketball with the current senator from West Virginia, Jay Rockefeller. He was the Philippine desk officer for Peace Corps and he visited us and stayed for several days. We had a lot of good times together. He certainly towered over the local population. The town was located at the tail end of Antique province; its main occupation was fishing. We introduced mushroom farming as part of a project I started. We successfully grew mushrooms for the Chinese markets in large cities.

Effects of the Experience

I believe strongly we had an impact although it was hard to calculate in terms of points. Everyone learned from each other, one culture from another. The teachers and politicians were divided on how they perceived us. The former welcomed us; the latter were leery, although at the end of my tour everyone understood our purpose for being there. The real shame is we left and no one took our place. There was no continuity.

I learned self reliance, independence and, most importantly, the ability to understand others. This was and remains a valuable asset.

Peace Corps experiences remain with me today, stronger than ever. I certainly believe it has stayed with me because it was a true example of cross cultural adaptation.

My experience had very little impact on my parents or brother or New York City.

I remain in contact with the local Peace Corps contingents in Romania. I have attended their graduations and invited them to my home for dinner from time to time.

Lasting Memories

I enjoyed being with Harvey in Dao. When he got sick, we rushed him to Manila where he was put in a Catholic hospital. Harvey, however, was an orthodox Jew and his presence at the hospital was quite interesting. He would take the cross down from the head of the bed and when the nuns came to visit, they would return it to its original position. This went on till he was finally released. Actually, I think he let himself out of the hospital.

I also remember writing for *Ang Boluntaryo*. The first edition had reported openly on controversial issues. After that, publication was taken over by staff and ended "investigative reporting." (The first issues were called *The Voluntario*). The first edition that I worked on covered David Mulholland's death and its causes.

I am lucky that I am alive and here to enjoy the 50th. We shall all remember those who won't be with us: John F. Kennedy, Buckminster Fuller, Bill Coffin, and the wonderful team that taught me so much in the mountains of Puerto Rico.

Philip H. Bloom is living in Romania with his wife, Anda, and his two daughters—Susan, age five, and Stephanie, who is eight months old. He is currently retired and enjoying the beautiful city of Bucharest.

Sylvia Boecker
Peace Corps is Powerful

In Naperville, Illinois at thirteen years of age I decided I wanted to learn French and eventually join the Foreign Service. When I was fourteen my parents asked me, "When are you going to start traveling?" That summer I went to Canada for three weeks on a canoe trip. The following year I was chosen to represent my area of Illinois at the 100th anniversary of the YMCA in Paris. I spent two weeks in Paris with two thousand young people from fifteen to eighteen years of age from all over the world. I then traveled within Europe for an additional two weeks. Paris at fifteen certainly made an impression on me. I was determined to return to France. When I was eighteen I applied to the Experiment in International Living to live with a French family for the summer. The France program was full. I was invited to go to Chile instead. I eagerly went and was quiet for three months because I did not know Spanish. At nineteen I decided to do my junior year of college at the University of Mexico. I studied and spoke Spanish day and night. I was determined to learn that language. And in 1961, just as I was graduating from college, the Peace Corps accepted me to go to the Philippines—perfect timing.

I knew that the Philippines had been part of the Spanish Empire. I think that was all I knew when I was accepted into Peace Corps. We trained at Penn State University and then flew off to Manila from San Francisco via Hawaii, Wake and Guam. It was always dawn each time we landed and then in Manila it was 7:30 am, still dawn, as we stood on the tarmac and were welcomed to the Philippines. The sun was intense. The green of the countryside was also intense. The sun and the green burned into my brain and fifty years later those memories are as intense as they were at the beginning.

The tremendous freedom I experienced was the key event during those two years. Peace Corps literally told us, "You have two years. Go out and fill them." That was the greatest gift I could have received. I taught English, Spanish, science, swimming and helped the rural health doctor. I went to market day each Tuesday, reviewed ROTC troops, opened fiestas and dances, spoke at a high school graduation, hiked to far barrios (villages), attended every fiesta that I could and even welcomed Filipinos who had emigrated to the U.S. and were back to visit. There was no end of the activities in which I was involved. I was the guest singer for two years with the Ibajay Academy Rockers. During free time I traveled from Zamboanga to Batanes and also visited other volunteers. I even had a family planning clinic that fortunately was not successful and procreation was not impeded in any way. Today Filipinos work all over the world as a result of excess population.

For the first year I lived with three other volunteers in Ibajay, a rice growing area about 22 miles from the provincial capital of Aklan on the Island of Panay in the central Philippines. After my housemates, Joan Aragone, Barbara Litrop and Jan Everett transferred to other towns and for the second year, I lived in San Isidro, a barrio of Ibajay. A teacher's husband built a nipa house in a coconut grove for me. It faced the sea, not the road, so I would not think of leaving. I had a bicycle and rode each afternoon into town to teach Spanish at the high school. The path to town started through the coconut grove, crossed the Ibajay River that flowed from the mountains into the sea and passed some barrios before reaching the town. I passed the market, the bakery and various stores. Along I pedaled greeting people and stopping to chat along the way. Those two years were filled with intense freedom, intense responsibility, emotions that tore my heart out and attention that spoiled me for the rest of my life.

On market day people would approach me, tug on my skirt and simply say, "Thank you." Then they went on their way. This happened time and again. I finally asked someone, "Why are the people thanking me?" I was told they were thanking me for "Liberation." I was the first American they had seen since World War II ended and they were extremely grateful for the Americans who helped liberate them from the Japanese. The war had ended in 1945, but was still very much a topic of daily conversation in 1962 and 1963.

The Filipino people are the reason I return often to the Philippines and the reason I keep in contact with Filipino friends in the U.S. and the Philippines. I am a member of the Aklan Society of Chicago and also of the *Ibajaynons* of North America and meet with them regularly. Weddings, funerals, reunions and birthday parties bring invitations to join friends from all those years ago. Lenny Villanueva grew up in Ibajay and immigrated to Hawaii after he received his engineering degree. I see him often and he has always told me, "The Peace Corps was the best thing that happened in Ibajay."

Across the street from the Peace Corps house in Ibajay lived the family of Nestorio Tirol. They had a large family and the children seemed always to be at the Peace Corps house. We four volunteers loved them as they loved us. Maybe it was partially a result of all the English spoken and all the books read that resulted in their migration to the U.S. Eventually, they all settled in New Jersey and Illinois. All these years later, when we get together, we talk of those days in Ibajay when the Peace Corps lived across the street from their family. The youngest was a precious little girl named Dinah Bonita. She was about four years old and just came to our house and looked at us. Today she lives in New Jersey, is fifty-four, has her own family and has survived breast cancer. We still phone each other to chat and I always remind her of fifty years ago.

One day a high school student invited me to go home with him to meet his parents. Johnny and Elmina Tirol and their seven children became my very close friends. They lived in San Isidro and I eventually taught with Mrs. Tirol in the San Isidro Primary School. Mr. Tirol built my bamboo/nipa house in a coconut grove near their home and insisted, when the winds blew hard during the rainy season, that I sleep at their house to avoid injury from a coconut falling through the roof of my little house. Their son, who was almost always at my side, was Elmer, a third grader. His nickname was Pic-Pong, the sound the Japanese guns made during the war. When I rode my bike to town, Pic-Pong was on the back. If I went for a swim, Pic-Pong also went for a swim. If I sang with the guitar, he also sang. If I read or wrote, Pic-Pong drew pictures. People referred to him as my shadow. His older brother Billy was in the fourth grade. He had a bike and would ride around and around my house but would never come up into the house. I always encouraged him to come up, but he never would do so. I finally asked his mother why Billy would not come into the house. She explained that he knew I would leave some day and he did not want to be too close to me and then see me leave. Peace Corps is powerful.

When I return to the Philippines for visits, I always visit the Johnny Tirol family. I mourned when Pic-Pong died at age seventeen from hepatitis. I mourned when Billy was stabbed to death in a case of mistaken identity. I have watched the other children marry and have children of their own. In 1967 I returned to the Philippines and stayed with the Tirol family for several months. When I said that I really should leave and they said no. I asked how long they wanted me to stay. They said, "Forever." We played many Scrabble games. If I won, Mrs. Tirol would say, "Of course you win, you are a native speaker of English." If she won, I would say, "Of course you win, you are a teacher of English." Mrs. Elmina Tirol was forty when I met her, now she is ninety. We are still in contact after all these years. I still refer to her as my co-teacher. We email and write and speak of fifty years ago as if it were yesterday.

Filipinos whom I met thought that President Kennedy had sent me as his personal representative to Ibajay. If I was typing and people would pass they would tell me to say good things about them to President Kennedy. I left the Philippines in September 1963 and President Kennedy was killed that November. The outpouring of grief from the people of Ibajay was huge. He had sent a personal representative to them. Nothing could have been more powerful.

In January 1964 I began recruiting for Peace Corps and traveled all over the USA to tell people about Peace Corps and encourage folks to apply—at the University of Vermont, the University of Utah, one city after another, back and forth across the country. It was great. In Cleveland I was on a talk radio program and afterwards, Oberlin College phoned the studio and invited me to apply for graduate school. They wanted a returned Peace Corps volunteer on campus. I received their Master of Arts in Teaching in 1965.

Teaching high school Spanish in the Virgin Islands was my next adventure. Then for eight years I worked for the Experiment in International Living. I took high school and college students on study abroad programs to Mexico, Argentina, Ceylon, Greece, Italy and England. I must have quietly recruited for Peace Corps because a number of those students eventually joined the Peace Corps.

In my own family, two of my nieces joined the Peace Corps. Michelle was in Sierra Leone for three years. One of her projects was to build a market place. I went to visit for the opening because it was the first time in our family that anyone had built a market. Rebecca was in Yap for three years. She wrote a history book as one of her projects.

My older brother, Donald, Michelle's father, was a U.S. Navy pilot in Southeast Asia during the Vietnam War in the 1960s. He asked me the exact location of Ibajay and he flew over the town, the shoreline and the surrounding mountains and took photos from the air.

I married in 1989 and thought it best that my husband visit Ibajay so he would know what I was talking about almost every day. We visited the Philippines twice and you can imagine the excitement when my husband, named Michael Jackson, visited Ibajay. All the attention turned from me to him! He had studied in high school in Illinois with Vicente Araneta. Meeting the Araneta family in Manila was a pleasure and yet another connection to the Philippines. When Michael told me about Vicente I explained that the Araneta name in the Philippines was similar to the Kennedy name in the USA

In the Philippines I met many women professionals who left a real impression on me. Attorneys, physicians, deans of colleges, high school principals, mayors, governors and businesswomen were some who inspired me. In 1977 I graduated from DePaul University College of Law in Chicago. After graduation I wanted to visit the Philippines to attend an International Law Conference in Manila. I contacted a group of Silliman University graduates in the Chicago area who had a special fare to return for their reunion in the Philippines. (Before the conference I visited Ibajay and the good news spread quickly: "Miss Boecker has changed her title!" "Oh, did she marry?" "Better, she is now Attorney Boecker!" There was much joy and celebration).

Freddie Aquino organized the Silliman University reunion flight to Manila. He was an insurance salesman in Chicago, who was interested that I was an attorney and had lived in the Philippines. He started referring Filipinos to me who wanted help with immigration matters. Singlehandedly Freddie Aquino started my law practice which has spanned thirty-three years of specialization in Filipino immigration to the USA, and all by word of mouth. So every day I have the pleasure of meeting with, speaking with and emailing Filipinos all over the world; they are either already here or waiting to immigrate. Today most of my clients are nurses from the Philippines. Some are even from Ibajay.

Peace Corps truly is Powerful!

Sylvia Boecker was born and raised in Naperville, Illinois. A graduate of Naperville High School, she proceeded to finish college in four years, transferring each year. She received a B.A. in Latin American Studies from the University of Denver in 1961. Sylvia immediately joined the Peace Corps and was assigned to the Philippines which she enjoyed immensely. Sylvia received her law degree from DePaul University in 1977 and since then has had her own law practice with emphasis on immigration law. She has written and spoken widely about immigration of foreign nurses, especially nurses from the Philippines. In 1989 Sylvia married Michael Jackson and they have lived in St. Louis, Chicago, Virginia Beach and, since 2001, in Williamsburg, Virginia. When Sylvia is not working she spends her time staying healthy and pushing her nieces and nephews and great nieces and nephews to travel, learn languages, study abroad, work abroad and save money. She has had limited success. Of her three major travel goals, she has crossed Russia on the Trans-Siberian railroad and traveled up the Amazon River. She has yet to cross the Sahara Desert. Her most recent dream is to take a full World Cruise on the QM2. Sylvia thinks that the great thing about travel is that it is endless.

Al Bradford
Peace Corps Stories

Why I Joined the Peace Corps

I joined the Peace Corps for two reasons: to postpone being drafted and to see whether I could learn to communicate with and be useful to persons from backgrounds different from mine. The second reason was important because I was involved in civil rights work and thought that I might continue such work after the Peace Corps. As for the first reason, if General Hershey, the head of Selective Service, had not personally intervened for me, I would have been drafted, since my draft board had never heard of the Peace Corps or read the memo about Peace Corps deferments. (I had *two* Army physicals before matters were settled.)

Something I Learned

My time in the Philippines taught me several profound lessons. One is that there is more than one way to be a human being. That revelation hit me after around three months in Numancia the small municipality where I was assigned in the province of Aklan, less than ten miles from the capital city of Kalibo on the north coast of Panay Island, where, in legend, the first settlers from Borneo settled the Philippines. During those initial months, I had viewed my students and neighbors as wannabe Americans and felt that my job was to help them climb out of their ignorance to be more like Americans—like me. I would never, never have admitted that, at the time, even to myself—I thought of myself as open-minded, respectful of other cultures, and humble, and even trained in anthropology. But underneath all that, and diametrically opposed to it, I was a missionary for Western values and behaviors. This stance had developed for one simple reason: I could not imagine doing things *any other way* but my way, the South Carolina, United States, Western way.

The big change finally came when, after a few months of feeling more and more frustrated, disoriented, and "at sea," I realized that it was I, not the Filipinos, who was ignorant; it was I who had a huge amount of learning to do; and that my neighbors—despite a surface colonial mentality—did not want to be Americans. They were doing just fine as Filipinos and as Asians. This realization completely changed my behavior. I began a life of sharing and being shared with, sending and receiving signals and learning across the cultural chasm. My neighbors and I grew to care about one another and trust one another and enjoy one another, even though we often did not truly understand one another. It was like holding hands in the dark.

I am a different person because I learned the lesson that just because someone doesn't think like me or look like me, it doesn't necessarily mean that he or she is inferior, bad, or scary; and that perhaps I can learn from that person and he or she can learn from me, to our mutual benefit. (But sometimes not: I lived in the Philippines long enough to see that the percentage of jerks there is the same as here.) And my four years of immersion in Philippine culture still mean that part of me sees things somewhat as a Filipino sees them. I feel fortunate to have this alternative to my fundamentally Western view, even though it can be confusing sometimes or cause me to behave inappropriately if I forget where I am (e.g., to settle a dispute via an intermediary rather than directly). I am still a Westerner, but not *just* a Westerner.

Was the Peace Corps's Investment in Me Worth It?

Has the transformation in my thinking described above been worth the Peace Corps's investment in me? Has my life since the Peace Corps made a good difference to others? I think it has, but in countless small, un-dramatic ways, stemming from my ability to understand people and situations—and myself—better than my non-Peace Corps self might have. Perhaps, without this ability, I might not have sought, much less succeeded at, the jobs that I pursued after returning home. And some of those jobs have given me the chance to make a good difference to others in my own country.

And what of my time in the Philippines? Did I make a difference there? In my formal job as a science resource person in elementary schools, I saw three teachers bloom and outpace me in creative science teaching, and I helped several more learn to cope with the new science curriculum. But my main contribution, especially during my first year, was to provide comic relief in the lives of my town-mates. My groping to understand and be understood, and my being so *different*, was a frequent source of entertainment and novelty.

That court-jester-like role lessened over time as my neighbors—some of them now friends—began regarding me less and less as a white American, a Peace Corps volunteer, and an honored guest and more and more as a real *person* with strengths and flaws. I became a strange sort of citizen of the town. Becoming an adopted *Numanciahanon* brought many joys but also the kinds of complexities and problems that everyone else faced. For example, I became aligned with certain groups and distant from others, and was subject to Filipino-style interpersonal difficulties that my earlier guest status had shielded me from.

This journey from outsider to insider was summed up well by a good friend in Numancia, who confided, "Al, when you came here, you were like an infant—you knew nothing. But we were patient with you because we could tell that you liked us and were trying so hard to learn. Now you are 'Al' to us, no longer the important but sometimes ridiculous '*Cano*'."

None of us who served in the Peace Corps will ever know many of the good (or not so good) effects of our time as volunteers. But sometimes we do find out. One of my *Aklanon* godchildren, now a married woman living in California, wrote me the following message a few years ago. Needless to say, I treasure it.

> I am sure that you have touched people's lives in Aklan as much as they have touched yours. I am a living example of that. You infected me with your sense of adventure, empathy for others, and a childlike wonder for things. You were enjoying

your life in a place different from your own, with people who were different from you. I think that gave me the idea that I might do the same some day. I wish the younger generation had "experienced" you as I have. As I have told you before, I am what I am in part because of you and the idea of you.

Good Stories.

First Story: It's the school vacation after my third year in Numancia. I have been spending some of my free days with fishermen—the fathers and brothers of some of my students—as they build large bamboo fish corrals a half mile out in the ocean. I swim back and forth from boat to boat and to and from the beach, delivering water and tools and food—despite all their diving and fishing skills, these men cannot swim, and they marvel that I can.

All this time in the sun gave me a deep, bronze tan. As I was returning home one day, I stopped to chat with a friend, who looked me over and said, "Well, Al, when you first arrived here, you were much too pale. But now you are just about the right color." We laughed and I walked on, amazed that I had been given an insight into a deeper level of my neighbor's values, a level untouched by the surface colonial mentality where white skin was best.

Second Story: It is a moonlit evening, and I am sitting on the balcony of a nipa hut with one of my high-school students, her brother, and her parents. The only artificial light is from a couple of kerosene lanterns; all around us, coconut palms glint in the moonlight. I have my flute and my voice, they have their guitars and other stringed instruments and voices, and we spend the evening singing and playing, with a snack now and then. They teach me beautiful songs about lost love, which are hard to sing because they are so sad. Forty-five years later, my student and her siblings, now all grown with families, invite me to come back to Numancia to sing and play in a concert honoring their parents. I did not go, but the invitation meant so much.

Third Story (excerpted and adapted from my article in the October 1963 *Ang Boluntaryo* about participating in Aklan's *Ati-Atihan* celebration):

> "How do you do that limping dance step?" I asked, since I kept tripping over my feet trying to keep up with the bodies bobbing up and down in unison all around me. "Just keep dancing and you will feel it," a red-white-and-blue Cherokee Chief answered. I watched them, persons of all classes wearing all sorts of costumes, mingling and dancing together without shyness or distinction, and I tried to get the shuffling step but just couldn't. My legs started getting tired and the whole affair was beginning to seem foolish, my soot-blackened arms were getting too hot in the sun, and my head hurt—when suddenly the group shouted in unison, *"Viva, viva Santo Niño!"* What a shout! The thrill of being in a happy mob shouting a happy shout bolted through me and suddenly I had the dance step. It was effortless; I was flying. Our smiles and eyes fused us; instantly we were all brothers and sisters, these carabao herders, politicians, children, teachers, street-boys, bus drivers, and me, the American. We swung out from our side street into the plaza, dancing and singing and beating our drums, joining so many other groups that were already there, heads moving in waves to the same beat.

Before I knew it, we were dancing toward a group coming from the opposite way. It was obvious we would soon meet, and I wondered what would happen. *"Viva!"* everyone in both groups shouted, and then we just plowed right through each other, waving to friends, smiling in that way of greeting which flashed out to all and made us one. Suddenly a chum tugged me and yelled, "Come with us, Al," so I waved to my old group and reversed direction, not missing a beat. Ah, what a change! My new group was dressed like pirates and bandits and called themselves "The Terrors." The leader quickly yelled "Charge!" and we broke the dance step and ran screaming across the plaza, brandishing knives and sticks and veering to the right and left as we dodged other groups. Everyone stopped short at a signal I could not see, and we began laughing, then danced once again—the drumbeats of the different groups were blending into something loud and insistent beyond sound, and then the shout again, *"Viva!,"* laughter, and smiles. I just began laughing, and then sang and danced more furiously, for I felt I would burst with spirit. We locked hands and arms, dancing through the market, jostling each other, and singing "Happy Days are Here Again." Our group was overflowing with strong feeling. Indeed, in my ecstasy, I was finding truth in an old saying about the *Ati-Atihan*: that if the celebrant, in blank nakedness or rich costume, abandons himself to sincere and fervent participation, he will be blessed in the moment of wildness.

Al Bradford was one of the first Peace Corps volunteers from South Carolina. After returning from four years in Numancia, Aklan (three as a volunteer, the fourth on his own as an English teacher), he held a wide variety of jobs, from waiter and receptionist to science writer for an environmental group and director of an artists' retreat. He now works as one of the editors of a scholarly journal of medical education and health policy, Academic Medicine. *He sings with professional and amateur choruses in Washington D.C.*

(The first photo shows Al playing his flute while Filipino musicians play their guitars.)

Nancy S. Dunetz
Colossal Chutzpah

Being treated like royalty can be quite dangerous for the ego. It makes you feel more important than you are. It makes you feel like you can do more than you are capable of. It helps you understand (many years later) the story of *The Emperor's New Clothes*. That's what happened to me in the Philippines. Never in my 21-year-old life had I received so much attention and affirmation. Never had I experienced such self-confidence (call me naive). Never had I felt such a sense of community. Never had I felt such peace.

We were very young. Here we were, "educational consultants" (We were called educational *aides*, but that came to have a different meaning a few years later in the States.) with no experience, with the mission of counseling people twice our age, who had 25 years of teaching experience, on how to teach. Colossal chutzpah!!!

Other volunteers were not as gullible as I. I believed our professors in PC training who told us that we could teach English because we spoke English. Now, 50 years later, I have a doctorate in teaching English as a second language. I have written a textbook. I have 43 years of experience teaching English as a second language from kindergarten through college; 35 years of experience in teacher education; as many years in curriculum development, professional development, and developing new schools devoted to the needs of English language learners.

This, all to create some perspective—back in the Philippines 50 years ago, I had the privilege of experiencing opportunities that would not have happened at home. Now, at the age of 70, I am considered an expert in many of these areas.

As a violinist, I was invited to give a concert at Central Philippines University in Iloilo City. I remember I played the Mozart Violin Concerto #3 in G, and I played to a full house, but I don't remember much else, except that I was a pretty mediocre violinist. Colossal chutzpah!! It wasn't until 30 years later that I felt I could perform credibly in public. By then I had transitioned to viola, and am now secretary of the NY Viola Society. In Concepcion, the town where I eventually made my home, I had many godchildren. One of my *compadres* had a dance band. I could only play by reading music, whereas the band could only play by ear. I would perform with them at *fiestas* and my *compadre* would stand behind me and call out the notes.

During my summer project in Malaybalay, Bukidnon, Mindanao, I taught a course in art education at the normal college (Mind you, I had never studied art.) and performed a solo dance at their fiesta, never having performed a dance before. Colossal chutzpah!! The highlight of that experience was living with a family, which contributed a lot to my worldview. I remember one time I was so amazed at how beautiful were the children of one of the people I met, but was tactfully scolded for making the compliment in the presence of other people who had children that I wasn't complimenting.

When I first arrived in Iloilo, I was assigned to a household with 3 lovely volunteers. Linda was about 5 feet; I was 5'7"; Joyce was about 2 inches taller than I, and Susan was about 5'5". Two of us were blonde, and two brunettes. Three had light eyes, and one, dark eyes. We also differed in body types. Yet, the Filipinos couldn't tell us apart, because we all looked alike!!!!! Likewise, we were treated as if we were one person.

Feeling a wedge between myself and the culture, I opted to move out and live with a family in a town that had no other Americans. I was referred to a family in what was then a remote town. I visited with them and declared I wanted to live there. They made it clear that they didn't want a boarder, but I insisted, so what could they do? Having forced myself upon them, I succeeded in breaking the glass top on the dining table by sitting on it, keeping the family awake drinking and telling jokes all night with my Peace Corps friend Chuck Gostlin, and generally disrupting the family routines—colossal chutzpah.

Then there was the *fiesta* queen fiasco. I had no idea that it was "rigged". But there I was, riding around town on a *fiesta* float, sporting my *patadyong* and kimono, and depriving an innocent young beauty of her rightful honor. My title was Miss Concepcion (no laughing, please), as the name of the town was Concepcion—sad and colossal chutzpah.

I spent 10 days in Iloilo Mission Hospital with amebic dysentery, sharing a room with my buddy Susan Thompson. Hospital employees—nurses' aides, etc.—would find many an excuse to come to our room, because we were the *"canás."* We were invited to give an "inspirational talk" at the nurses' Sunday morning service. What did I know about Sunday morning services? What did I know about inspirational talks? Again, colossal chutzpah, but I loved the attention. At some point we became stir-crazy, and snuck out of the hospital to go downtown to a movie, and eat chocolate bars. It wasn't as easy to sneak back in, but we managed it. We never did find out if anyone knew we had gone.

Once a month we received a check from the Peace Corps. We had to go to Iloilo City to cash our checks, as there were no local banks. Transportation was erratic, and very often depended on economics. When there was a good catch of fish, the bus (called "truck") raced to the city in the middle of the night, getting there in 5 hours as opposed to the usual 7 hours. One weekend Chuck and I took the fish bus, and arrived in Iloilo City at 5:30 AM. We often visited the Gonzaga family, who hosted us our very first night in Iloilo. We went directly to their house on the campus of Central Philippines University and, without their knowledge fell asleep on their living room couches—more chutzpah. When Mrs. Gonzaga woke up at a reasonable hour and discovered us in her living room, she said we smelled of fish and ordered us to shower.

So what came of all this? I returned to the Philippines 35 years later, in 1996, to find a completely different country. At this point Concepcion was only 1 hour from Iloilo City due to improved roads and transportation services. There were flowers all along the road thanks to running water. The streets were paved and there was electricity; there was an elementary school, a high school, and a community college; a gas station and a bank. And a clay tennis court smack in the middle of the town plaza. The teachers now lived in concrete buildings rather than the nipa huts in which I visited them in the '60s and in which I had my first cooking lessons and my first (and last) sampling of betel nut. It was as if I had been there before and after the Industrial Revolution.

Two teachers from the college greeted me and informed me that because of me, they had become science teachers. I was greeted by a former elementary school student who had become an accountant/auditor for Coca Cola. She took 2 days off from work to hang out with the returnees, and when she said goodbye to me at the airport, she took off her Coca Cola jacket and put it around my shoulders.

You can't have everything in life, but I think I have what's most important to me—I have fond memories of the Philippines and Filipinos. The experience launched my career as an ESL (English as a Second Language) specialist. I discovered a part of the world that filled in some gaps in my Eurocentric education. I am constantly learning. I have my career, I have myself, I have a Gagliano viola, I have freedom, and I have some wonderful friends—many of whom are from my Peace Corps cohort. All this because of the experiences in my younger life and what I learned from them. There's no telling where chutzpah might take you.

Nancy S. Dunetz holds a BA in music from Syracuse University, an MA in TEFL (Teaching English as a Foreign Language) from Teachers College, Columbia University, and an EdD in Language Education from New York University. After serving as a Peace Corps volunteer in the Philippines 1961-63, she spent her basic career in the New York City public school system teaching English as a second language, and training teachers at various universities throughout the city. An active violist, she serves as secretary of both the New York Viola society and the Broadway Bach Ensemble.

Lila Dulaney Gardner

The Onwacan ("The Awakening," Middle English)

Now Let's Begin

Did the Peace Corps experience shape my life? You bet it did! Getting that call, summer of l961, to come to Penn State University to train for the Peace Corps/Philippines dramatically changed and charged up my life (but where did you say the Philippines is?). I had no idea!

I had just graduated college, had voted for John F. Kennedy, and listened to his speech about giving back to your country. I was deeply moved by him and his words. While I had some options awaiting me in Boston involving both love and work, I was not as excited about these as the chance to travel, learn about other cultures, and to use a cliché, "see the world"—so I said yes and off I went in a bumpy small plane to State College, Pennsylvania.

I guess that bumpy small plane trip was just warming me up for what lay ahead! My father was supportive of me but didn't want me to go so far away. Others, friends and neighbors, thought I was crazy to do this—the great unknown—just too much—and think of all the awful things that could happen to you out there! I was the first girl from Arkansas to go into the Peace Corps. Anyway, when I arrived at Penn State, there was Bob Tyler helping us off the plane, grabbing our suitcases and telling us what a great group of people had already gathered there; I was excited and reassured. It was in getting off the plane there that Tyler mentioned this great banjo picker/guitar player—Dirk somebody—and what great songfests we'd be having along with our studies. Penn State was a remarkable experience—the training, new language, people from all over the US, and it was there I fell in love with that banjo picker Dirk Ballendorf.

This was an exciting time, for us and for the country. Penn State had the familiar and the strange. I thought it really odd that we were being trained for the tropics and our survival training was on a mountain in Pennsylvania in snow, putting up pup tents and eating steaks. And there were always the looming questions: would we be up to the tasks ahead and would we be selected? Several were not selected, as it turned out, people who I thought would have made great Peace Corps volunteers, as good as any of us who did go. I have always wondered about them and what this de-selection did to their lives—especially the Greens, Wally and John.

Then it was on to San Francisco and staying with Joyce Edwards' family, exploring the Bay Area, as it was my first trip there; and off on that long flight in a propeller plane, a wonderful respite and banquet in Honolulu, refueling in Guam, and touchdown amidst coconut trees, safely in Manila. I can still see in my mind's eye us coming down at Manila airport and feel the moist tropic air on my face as the door opened and we were greeted. Then it was on to Los Baños, where we were over-trained and acculturated very fast. I was stunned at our meals at Los Baños—such big plates of rice and tiny pieces of fish, but banana bread at the local store and garlic peanuts from a street vender made up for the food deficit.

Part of our training included going out to the field to visit Group I volunteers. For some of us this involved a long train journey to Camarines Sur and on by *banca* to Calabusao. The *banca* trip scared the daylights out of me. I was terrified of getting "schisto," and that tiny *banca* ride across a schistosomiasis-laden (I imagined) lake had me really paying attention to every little splash and spray that came my way. The household there was scary too, but local people and the volunteers were kind and wonderful; they eased my fears.

Panay Days

Out in the field, in Panitan, Capiz, walking to my school was a wonderful sensation. A sense of vastness stretched before me—the road was dirt, empty, narrow, ahead of me were maybe thousands of acres of rice paddies, water in between rows. There didn't really seem to be any people to speak of, but I was going to the school where I'll be helping out. Recently in 2009, a TV program that stated the Philippines in the future would probably not be growing rice shocked me! Arkansas is a rice-growing state and that day walking on that road, no doubt I was reminded of home—my father would always drive around outside our town pointing out various large rice growers he knew and did business with.

As it turned out we had problems in Panitan with men going under our house at night (the house was raised up off the ground), peeping toms, watching us which was very upsetting. Larry Howard and Bob Tyler came down from Manila to check on us and our situation.

They decided to move us to Dumalog, Capiz. The Fords, a mestizo family, owned a big plantation and were very solicitous of us. Trying to get food, we'd go with the Fords on back roads into Iloilo in a beat-up vehicle with guards in front with carbines on their laps, watching for bandits. One of Mrs. Ford's plantation managers, Ramos, came to the house one day and brought a huge basket of local mangoes and we sat outside gorging ourselves—my first and the best I've ever had! Otherwise, food was definitely an issue there! We'd go very early, 4 or 5 am, to the local market and find a tiny strip of very tough carabao meat left for sale. My roommate Frances McDonald was very creative in making interesting dishes for our household out of all kinds of canned goods.

The Peace Corps had some very curious ideas about how to deal with volunteers. Everything was all so new that I don't blame them. With regard to Dirk and me, they seemed to think they should break us up and put us in households very far apart. This did not work because our love and hormones had already kicked in; their efforts made us work even harder to get to see each other. These visits were amazing; they only sealed our love for each other and our determination to marry. After we were married in Manila in August 1962, the Peace Corps moved us to Pasonanca Park, outside of Zamboanga on the island of Mindanao.

Life in Mindanao

There is one very scaring story I'd like to share (having just read *An Unfinished Life: John F. Kennedy* by Robert Dallek)—the Cuban Missile crisis. In October 1962, we got a telegram from Dean Rusk asking us to determine the quickest way out of the Philippines and wire that to the State Department. This was particularly scary—I was pregnant and not eager to take a *banca* to Malaysia or Sulu, so we waited for further instructions until we got something that said the situation was OK.

Being pregnant, I became more aware of everything around me. I knew I wanted to have a completely natural childbirth, so on a daily basis I worked out using Grantley Reed's textbook, which was very helpful with exercises. As the time got closer, Jerry Poznak, our "group leader," loaned us the Peace Corps truck to keep nearby. That fateful early morning when the pains started coming closer and closer and closer, Dirk and I got ready, but first Dirk decided we needed to start out our journey on a full stomach, so he calmly cooked us scrambled eggs and toast with *calamansi* juice, good, rich in vitamin C. We got to the Brent Hospital in Zamboanga and urged the nurse to get Dr. Henerosa. He came in very slowly and casually in his pajamas. I heard him and Dirk talking, whispering. Since I was in increasing agony, they put me in the room and prepped me and somehow, half an hour later, Heidi was in my arms. I found myself in a private room recovering after no anesthetic. We were all happy and amazed at such a short delivery. (Later Dr. Henerosa came to stay with us in D.C. while getting further training at Johns Hopkins.)

As a couple living in Pasonanca Park, we had our most rewarding Peace Corps experiences. The community took us in much more as a family, protected us, watched over our child and loved her as dearly as we did. Our school work helping others greatly improved. One of my jobs was to instruct children how to use the newly installed water seal toilets from USAID. (I imagine that even now, as we know how our mothers instructed us to use toilets as children, those adults still remember Mrs. Ballendorf showing how not to stand on the seat but how to squat!)

It was always a thrill when Bob Tyler, Al Bradford, Nancy Dunetz, Carl Rogers (an eminent psychologist and Director Larry Fuchs's father-in-law) or Natalie and Larry Fuchs came to visit our little nipa hut, and inspect our outdoor water seal toilet (with the distinction of Carl Rogers having used it!). The striking poverty of people and their deep, soulful kindness to us can never be erased. My next door neighbor, Mrs. Lacastesantos, made a hammock for Heidi out of silk parachutes she had saved from WWII. She would sit on the porch, while Heidi slept in her mosquito-wire covered crib, and watch over her so we could go nearby to a school function.

Rogelia and Bert took care of our household—Bert would find us fresh-caught fish from the markets; Rogelia kept the house spotless and Heidi happy while we ate lots of *meriendas* and were treated like royalty at our various schools. Pasonanca Park is where we hung out and introduced Heidi to her first experience swimming. She screamed her head off while Dirk just laughed. She saw Indonesian bears at the zoo and our parrot Grumper and lots of other birds, a fantastic experience for us.

Yet by the end of our tour of duty, we were eager to get back to the States. We departed remembering what wonderful, kind, caring, loving and giving people the Filipinos were and no doubt still are. JFK said somewhere that the Peace Corps would bring home to America a new understanding of the world when these volunteers came home. This was true in my life and for others; and it continues to be true today. While no doubt we left our mark on the barrios where we lived and worked and in the schools where we taught, yet when we returned home, we were not the same—we had been transformed. We saw our own culture differently; we began to understand the lure of materialism and reject it in many cases; we also remembered people in the barrios who had so little of life's luxuries, yet had such joyous spirits, laughter and genuine happiness in going about their daily lives. It was quite something to ponder and to have been a part of and to share in our communities as we came back home. It still is, after all these years, quite marvelous to ponder!

Lila Dulaney Gardner was born and grew up in Paragould, Arkansas; graduated from high school at the Lausanne School for Girls in Memphis, Tennessee; went on to earn a BA from Northwestern University with a major in American History/English; much later in life a Master's Degree from the University of Hawaii/Manoa in Pacific and Asian Art History. She was married to Dirk Ballendorf; they had three children—Heidi, Anton (deceased) and Hans. She is divorced, has lived in Micronesia and currently resides in Honolulu, Hawaii. In l997 she took a break from Honolulu and moved to Mt. Shasta, California where with others she helped establish the Siskiyou Arts Council which continues to support and encourage artists and the arts in Northern California. On returning to Honolulu in 2000, Lila became a supervisor for the Moiliili Community Center where she sported a number of hats—director of Informal Education, Manager of the Thrift Shop, editor of the quarterly newsletter and co-coordinator for the Moiliili History Project which culminated in a book, Moiliili—The Life of a Community. *In 2008, Lila retired from the community center, and currently volunteers at the Lyon Arboretum, maintains a garden with the Makiki Community Gardens, and enjoys photography, ceramics, and various writing projects.*

(The second photo shows Lila with her daughter Heidi Ballendorf in 2005.)

Phyllis Clemensen Halton
Engaging the World

Motivation

When I was in third grade, some manufacturer stamped out two-inch plastic figures of women in red and blue national dress. I fell in love with their 'exotic' attire. Each time I entered Woolworth's I begged my mother to buy one. On my father's meager factory worker's wage, I now realize that 25 cents was a big investment, but with these "dolls" I embarked on my first tangible fascination with the rest of the world. By the time I was a college senior, I had failed to convince my parents to let me participate in Operation Crossroads Africa, had learned to make *dolma* (stuffed grape leaves) and had friends from Africa, the Middle East, Europe, Asia and Latin America. I participated in MUN (Model United Nations) and was secretary of the International Club, all of which fed my dream of working abroad.

One day, John F. Kennedy spoke on the steps of the Michigan Union, and, although I studied at the arch rival, his words about the Peace Corps electrified me. The Peace Corps was what I wanted. I lived in the richest country in the world and wanted to be sure all the poor had a roof over their heads, food on their tables and access to "good" schools. I had these benefits through American democracy and now I could right some of these wrongs. We were going to make the world a better place—that is what drove me, that and a curiosity about what else was out there. At some point I filled out a form and mailed it. Weeks later I was invited to sit for a Peace Corps entrance exam in the Lansing Civic Center. It was a cold April morning (it was Michigan so of course it was cold). My boyfriend offered to drive me for the 8 am reporting time—his departing words, "I know I must wish you good luck, but I wish you would not go," have echoed in my memory for fifty years. He went on to become prime minister of his country, fulfilling the dreams we all had for him.

Meanwhile, I prepared to graduate and half-heartedly searched for a job; refusing a teaching position for fear I would have to honor a contract. I was bound and determined to have no ties so that I would be available for the Peace Corps. My mother was openly hostile to the fact that her college graduate daughter had no work. As Peace Corps legislation crawled through Congress, each word in the newspaper gave me hope. My *alma mater*, Michigan State University, had been selected to serve as a Peace Corps training site for the Nigeria program. I dialed the head of the project only to be told that my name had not appeared on the list of candidates for Nigeria. But I grasped the straws of hope with his words, "Perhaps you are eligible for another country."

As July dragged into August the tension at home grew until the evening we returned home to find a telegram stuck in the door. Unfathomable joy erupted on my part. As always, my father remained quiet. My mother became a fountain of tears. When I left the room, she stopped, but each time I entered, Niagara Falls poured from her eyes. I tried to reason, to be altruistic, but nothing changed her hysterical state. When I emerged the next morning, the deluge returned; so I rushed back into my room and sought refuge under my covers. No matter how strongly I felt about joining the PC, guilt entered my consciousness whenever I considered my younger sister and father dealing with a hysterical woman for two years. Later, when my father knocked on my bedroom door to say it was time for Sunday lunch, I started to talk with him about my desire to join the Peace Corps. He shocked me when he said that if that was what I wanted, I should do it. Stunned by his encouragement, I asked about how he would handle his wife's hysteria. To which he responded, "We can deal with it." Six months later he was interviewed for an internal company newspaper in which he said we would like to have her closer to home but can appreciate the necessity of the type of work being done by the Peace Corps.

If the Peace Corps had not existed, I would have accepted a friend's offer of an English teaching position in Baghdad. I cannot even begin to speculate on what might have been. I was determined to learn about the world first hand. My international circle of friends had ignited my curiosity. As a teenager I had dreamed of living in Europe, but by the time I had graduated from college, I was more interested in Asia.

The Effect of the Peace Corps Experience

For 25 years, the Peace Corps was foremost in my mind; those two years nuanced all I did, all I thought. At times I wondered if this was strange or abnormal. At least once a month I wondered if I was emotionally balanced because it was a constant presence (Ruth Useem, where were you when I needed your TCK [Third Culture Kid] theory?). It was not until I attended the Peace Corps' 25th anniversary in Washington D.C. that I discovered others in our group had the same feelings. Overnight my Peace Corps experience was finally incorporated into my being rather than haunting my life. The PC experience has colored my view of the world for almost a half century; it has reminded me of how I should or could view other countries, people or cultures. At times, it has made me feel guilty about my work of the last 25 years in Brazil where much of my contact is with the elite. The Philippines is never far; my ears pick up when I hear the country mentioned on the news; I have an immediate bond with the few Filipinos I encounter in this part of the world. One of my best friends is a Filipina who worked with the Peace Corps in Cebu. She and her husband live in the interior of the state of São Paulo so our visits are infrequent but the Philippines is the strong tie that binds our friendship.

My Peace Corps experience directly impacted one of my college friends (she was a frosh when I was a senior; a senior when I returned for grad school). She asked me every possible question about my Peace Corps experience and, when she graduated, trained and served in the Peace Corps in Brazil. And although she returned to the U.S. after her Peace Corps experience, today she lives in Rio with her Brazilian husband, whom she met when they were both working in the U.S. for the Peace Corps.

Some Important Memories and Incidents

As I write this I am bombarded with memories, flashes of events and people, but what always stood out was the warmth the Filipinos felt for Americans. No matter where we wandered, where we lived, there was always a bed, a meal and a warm welcome for us.

In 1962, my school in the barrio of Villar had a huge influx of students so a second section was created for first year students. At the end of the school year, I was stunned when I heard one girl, Natalie, speaking in unaccented English, she sounded like an American. When I pointed this out to her regular teacher, her bemused face made me laugh at myself because the child had learned her English from me. If a teacher can do that, what else can we do?

During those first weeks in Sibalom, (a rice growing area in Antique Province on the west coast of Panay), many local residents came to introduce themselves; some became mentors, some became friends, and others, keepers of history.

It was our elderly, end-of-the-street neighbor, Dr. Jorge Massa, however, who stunned me with the information that he had completed his PhD at Yale. A grandfather, he lived in a two-story wooden house that featured a shortwave radio. He listened to Voice of America on a regular basis, but it was our mutual love of jazz that drew me to his home. He taught me the value of that "cold war weapon." However the biggest draw was my curiosity. I wondered how someone with such educational credentials could have returned to this town without electricity or running water, a town with no apparent future or even a past. Our Peace Corps group had visited IRRI (the International Rice Research Institute at Los Baños) and learned about "miracle rice," as had Dr. Massa. He had planted miracle rice and it did provide two plantings. However, the local farmers were suspicious of such a plant. What kind of bad spirits inhabited the seedlings? How could earth support two plantings? Questions I had not imagined as an urban 22-year-old, but he had. Dr. Massa understood the value and implications of miracle rice; he wanted to better his fellow citizens' lives. Through his example, he hoped to implement change. My first lesson: Change was not brought about by two years in the Peace Corps. It could take a lifetime, and Dr. Massa would be sure his lifetime brought positive change. He taught me to carry the richness of my culture with me, no matter where I lived; to listen to others; to respect others' ideas.

The Peace Corps had taught us to ask why something is done a certain way, not crash in and make changes because we think "our" way is better. Today, I teach those lessons to others. Sadly, today I laugh at an America that thinks it can show the rest of the world (Where did that arrogance come from?), when we should be looking at others respectfully to see if they can offer us advice. And I suppose that is the greatest lesson of the Peace Corps, that each one of us, no matter how humble, should be respected. What a different world we would live in today if that lesson had been learned by all of us not just by the handful who served in the Peace Corps.

When the monsoon rains came, the province of Antique was no longer accessible as all the major rivers flooded their banks. We crossed a roaring river on rickety bamboo "pathways" which were washed away at least once a week. I learned that life for most of the world meant struggling to survive and fighting for the opportunity to practice a profession. Although I always had new shoes to begin the school year, many of the children in my school did not even have a pair of flip-flops. So strong was their desire to learn, they came to school barefoot. Perhaps their clothes were threadbare and they had not eaten for days, but they came to school.

When the annual floods did not close the roads, Millie, the home economics teacher, and I, shared the morning *jeepney* ride to Villar. At the beginning of each school year, she received the annual supply of CARE powdered milk that the people of America had contributed to better the lives of Filipino children who did not have access to milk on a daily basis. I soon learned that each year the students suffered from diarrhea for a few days after they drank the milk—still it was something unusual so they all wanted a sip and besides it was supposed to be good for you. Sadly, the American people, the Filipino villagers and CARE apparently knew nothing about lactose intolerance, which caused the annual diarrhea. What would have been better?

Months later, Millie asked me why Americans are all tall and healthy. My ready response was that we drink milk everyday. Seven years later, when I returned to Sibalom, her two tall children surprised me (stretching, Millie might be five feet tall). Her response, "I did what you told me," left me confused. When I asked for clarification, she explained that her children had one glass of milk everyday—that was the difference. So apparently CARE was right, but did not have sufficient milk to grow all Filipinos tall!

In Sibalom, four of us resided in a two-story wooden house, huge by local standards. A pump and well next to the house was our water supply, and Estelita boiled water to pour into our "water cooler." Almost fifty years later, that ubiquitous ceramic cooler is a constant in all Brazilian homes, reminding me that I have not travelled far—life in the 'developing' world is no different from life in the "underdeveloped" world fifty years ago, except that we have become aware of the need to be politically correct. Will the poor always be poor? If you answer "yes," does that mean there is no hope for the future? Many of my students dream our dreams, of righting the world's wrongs, of bringing food, water, homes to those in need. I tell them to continue to dream those dreams because even though I, through the Peace Corps, was more than one, we were not enough to make all the changes we thought we could make. I see hope in them and want to share the lessons I have learned and to encourage them to continue the path we created fifty years ago.

Those who served in the Peace Corps with me were idealists; we were going to make the world a better place. Together we could do it. In Sibalom there had been a relatively new trade school, where one of the men who worked there had been employed in Laos and Cambodia. As one of my heroes was Tom Dooley, I was anxious to learn about this fabled doctor. Since this man had been working with Americans in Southeast Asia, he was anxious to talk with us. One evening he started talking about something I did not understand: Air America, the war in Vietnam, the American war in Southeast Asia, the CIA. He soon understood we knew nothing of this, but my curiosity was piqued. I asked him to explain everything, which he did, under the condition that I never repeat any of this. From the Philippines, I returned to a university deeply involved in training the Vietnamese police and befriended some of the Vietnamese students. Remembering my promise, I never spoke, as the U.S. spiraled into the quagmire of Viet Nam. I lived in Thailand at the height of the war all the time trying to understand the duplicity of the country I had proudly served in the Peace Corps. My belief in what the U.S. stood for was corroding, but no one could understand. I kept silent, until forty years later in São Paulo, when three of us were invited to share our Vietnam stories (protests, conscientious objectors) with our school's advanced history students. It was not planned; I just started talking about my first knowledge of the U.S. involvement in Southeast Asia back in 1961 and went from there. So while the Peace Corps taught me hope, in the back of my mind was the knowledge about the war that would eventually divide America a few years later.

After Peace Corps service, Phyllis Clemensen returned to Michigan State University for a master's degree with the idea of becoming a university foreign student advisor. With degree in hand she spent the next five years changing jobs or cities every six months, trying to find a career and a place to live. Working as a high school counselor resolved her first dilemma but it took her longer to realize she wanted someplace warm. In 1970 she became a counselor at the International School Bangkok, where she remained for four years. It was during her travels to and from Bangkok that she met the Englishman who would become her husband and ask her to move to London, then Portugal and eventually Brazil. As "accompanying spouse" she worked in local American schools or language centers. For the last twenty-five years she has served as the college counselor at the Escola Graduada *(Graded School) in São Paulo.*

(The second photo shows Phyllis with fellow group II volunteer Janet Karon standing on her left.)

Richard Holzman
My Peace Corps Journey

My Peace Corps Journey began in August 1961, shortly after service as an Army lieutenant. After induction in Washington D.C., a small pilot group of PCVs was sent to Arecibo, Puerto Rico, where we received one month of Outward Bound experiential education to prepare us for the work we were to do in the Philippines after further training at Pennsylvania State University.

In Puerto Rico, we were inspired by the Rev. William Sloane Coffin, and Captain Freddy Fuller, one of the founders of Outward Bound. The exemplary lives and work of both men were committed to the ideals of President John Kennedy, Bobby Kennedy, Martin Luther King, Jr., and Sargent Shriver. It was in these rain forests that I, from New York, connected with three other PCVs—Bill Austin from Kansas, Bill Melhoff from Oregon and Tom Kincaid from West Virginia.

We were different people from different places but with the shared goal of doing work that would hopefully contribute to healing the world. Yes, we were caught up in the spirit of the times inspired by JFK, RFK, and MLK. We would soon be challenged to see if we could promote freedom from want through service to others. We soon found out that the people we came to help were also our teachers as we learned about ourselves and made new friends.

There was yet another training session at Los Baños, then to the town of Mambusao, about 36 kilometers from Roxas City, the capital of Capiz Province on Panay where my three fellow PCVs and I would be "models" of English language in local classrooms and work with our new friends in joint educational efforts that would often turn out to be mutually beneficial. We found out that we would get at least as much as we gave in ways we never anticipated. We would learn about others and in doing so learned about ourselves. So it went during our tour. We learned to live with ourselves and others in meaningful ways that would help us follow the compass as we charted a course for our personal and professional lives. For that reason, with deepest gratitude I say that the Peace Corps transformed my life as it did for many other PCVs.

There are three memories that stand out in my mind beyond the day-to-day quest to enhance learning and make a difference in the lives of students in the small barrio school where I was assigned which was six kilometers from where we lived.

The first was working with the families of Barrio Caidquid to construct a new two-classroom school building using the Cinva-Ram Machine developed at the Rockefeller Institute that would compress one part of cement to seven parts of soil creating the equivalent of adobe bricks. After much bartering, volunteering, and donations the building was successfully completed with great pride and fanfare and a keynote address by the Minister of Education. Little did I know at the time that this gave me the experience and confidence to successfully tackle numerous multi-million dollar school construction projects as a school superintendent in the United States and in Venezuela.

The next memory is of starting a chicken project—raising week-old chicks (Rhode Island Reds) transported from a Manila hatchery, which became a successful pilot poultry project demonstrating efficient, effective and economical poultry production that had not been attempted in Mambusao previously.

The third is the memory that has perhaps had for me the most powerful impact. It was the friendship that I developed with the late Dr. Ravelo Argamaso, who became a renowned plastic and reconstructive surgeon. We first got to know each other at the Central Philippines University Baptist Mission Hospital in Iloilo where I approached him to help needy children in Mambusao who had cleft palates and other deformities to see if he could transform their lives through corrective surgery. Of course I told him we had little money to pay. He said he understood since he had little money as well. So we went ahead with the project. In particular, he transformed the life of one girl named Candelaria, the daughter of an impoverished water carrier. I believe that his work with me was the precursor of other worldwide initiatives of doctors in service to humanity which started through my friendship with this extraordinary man. Dr. Argamaso went on to do groundbreaking work in transforming the lives of countless numbers through plastic and reconstructive surgery, including prisoners at Sing-Sing prison in New York through a grant from the National Institutes of Health. Acting on the belief that eliminating disfiguring scars and deformities would change self image and thereby reduce the rate of recidivism, Dr. Argamaso's theory was proved accurate. Until his retirement, Ravelo continued to return home on his "vacation" to do multiple surgeries daily for one month every year to continue the work we started decades earlier in Iloilo. Ravelo Argamaso, graduate of Central Philippine University, University of Santo Tómas Medical School, International Diplomate in Plastic and Reconstructive Surgery, had a distinguished career as a surgeon and educator and Chief of Plastic Surgery at Montefiore Hospital in New York City.

Now as we enter the fourth quarter of our lives and reflect with pride on what we have tried to do, we should continue to envision and inspire a world where new generations focus on the major issues of war, overpopulation, depletion of natural resources, and pollution, which then as now, are central to universal well being and survival.

Richard B. Holzman worked in the field of education for 50 years serving as a teacher and administrator, then as a superintendent of schools for 32 years in Schenectady, NY; Teaneck, NJ; and the American International School of Caracas, Venezuela. In 1986 he was named one of the Top Executive Educators in the U.S. He was a Fulbright Scholar in China in 1981. Dr. Holzman earned an International Diplomate in Education. Currently he is Dean of Special Academic Projects at

American International College, Springfield, Massachusetts. He and his wife, Shelley, have three children, Jason Moss, a singer/songwriter in Los Angeles, California; Erica Eckman, a psychotherapist in Belmont, Massachusetts; and Jessica Holzman, an ELL (English Language Learner) teacher in Holyoke, Massachusetts. They have two grandchildren and live in Chester, Massachusetts, on a dirt road in the foothills of the Berkshires, where he welcomes RPCVs, remembering the hospitality extended to him as he connected with people around the world.

(The first photo shows Richard with Dr. Rafelo Armagaso.)

Patricia MacDermot Kasdan
Tasting Rice

Hail and Farewell

The first memory that comes to mind is of my farewell party in the small barrio where I worked as a Teacher's Aide. The principal and teachers proudly announced that, to hold the party, they had defied the District Supervisor who had planned another of his innumerable meetings that required cancelling school to attend. I had often encouraged the teachers to skip these obligatory meetings in the interest of keeping school open. They had always patiently explained that they needed to keep their jobs to survive and did not have my freedom to choose what they wanted to do. This time they had done exactly what I usually urged, more to please me I suspected than to keep school open, yet a touching way of thanking me for living and working among them.

It was a wonderful party, enlivened by a ferocious dog fight under the picnic table which required that we all stand on the table or benches to avoid being bitten. From that vantage, the barrio seemed unchanged since the first day I had seen it, so poor it had shocked the Peace Corps Director who thought the children's orange-tipped hair indicated malnutrition. The view across the water to the island of Negros was as stunning as ever. Although I felt profoundly changed by having lived and worked there, I doubted I had had any real impact.

When, Where and Why

The Peace Corps was announced at an opportune time for me. In my final semester at a Catholic women's college, I discovered that all my classmates had plans after graduation, some to marry, others to attend graduate school or take a job they had lined up. I, however, had neglected to consider life after graduation. My panic was eased by President Kennedy's announcement of the Peace Corps, which not only could bail me out of my predicament, but also promised travel and adventure while doing good (my high school's motto had been *noblesse oblige!).* Dr. Thomas Dooley had visited my high school, talked about his work among Vietnamese refugees, and inspired me to share my considerable advantages with those who had few. Joining the Peace Corps would also provide a good excuse to leave home. My mother was delighted with our first Catholic president, so could not object to my responding to his proposal. I also found John F. Kennedy irresistibly attractive.

The Reality of the Philippines

When I received an invitation to go to the Philippines, of all places, I was disappointed because it had been an American colony. I assumed it would be similar to the States and not at all exotic. Yet I dared not ask for another assignment lest I be rejected.

My first glimpse of the Philippines was through the window of the old bus that took us from the airport to our training site at Los Baños. I was shocked by the ragged crowds, dirty children and ramshackle huts that lined the dusty road. I remember wondering why human beings would consent to live in such an ugly place. I marveled, (irrationally) that the people, jeepneys, trucks and landscape looked exactly as they had in the pictures we had been shown during training.

The best part of training was the week we spent in the field with members of the first group of volunteers. The long voyage to the Bikol region in third class carriages on the "Bikol Express" was a sudden immersion in heat, poverty and discomfort. The train was packed, babies cried, children ran about, smells abounded, food-sellers shouted, toilets overflowed, and I wondered what on earth I was doing there. The four-woman household where I stayed was reassuring—the comfortable wood house was well organized, each volunteer went to a different school and seemed to work well with their teachers, and the young Filipina helping the volunteers keep house was charming and sweet. However, they reported that the town seemed aloof compared to other places and wondered why. During my visit they learned that some townspeople who had collaborated with Japanese occupiers during World War II had been executed by American liberators, accounting for the atypical anti-American mood in that town.

In the Field at Last

I was assigned to a small fishing village in Iloilo Province on the Central Philippine island of Panay. Fifty-two kilometers and four-and-a-half hours by bus from the provincial capital of Iloilo City, it had a market, central and barrio elementary schools, a municipal building, and a typical "earthquake baroque" Roman Catholic church. Most other structures were nipa huts. There was no electricity or running water, but views of the island of Negros across the strait were spectacular. The house I and Sandy Phillips were assigned was wood with cement floors, sturdier than most in town, but with a leaky nipa roof. Our water collected in a rain barrel or was brought from a well. There was no water-seal toilet which volunteer houses were supposed to have, so we had to use bed pans until a toilet was eventually installed. This was so mortifying that we dared not ask where they were emptied; however, a morning stroll on the beach at low tide revealed how most of the village dealt with this issue.

At first I was desperately unhappy in this little town where no one spoke English except the teachers. Even the elderly mayor knew no English, nor did his niece, who was assigned to be our housekeeper, a job she clearly did not relish. We could barely communicate, but we gave her money and she purchased fish and rice to cook for us three times a day. We went to school to observe classes and try to figure out how to work with the teachers. They were happy to turn over their classes to us, but we were not supposed to take over, only to assist them. We were taken to interminable meetings at distant barrio schools where we were told we were the first Westerners to visit. We were escorted to numerous parties and dances at which we towered over our dance partners.

After the first week of bickering over minutia such as the last scrap of peanut butter, we admitted to each other that we hated our assignment, the country, and especially ourselves for feeling this way. I had expected to love being a Peace Corps volunteer and was shocked at my unhappy reaction. I found everything ugly, uncomfortable, and uninteresting. I longed to go home but could not face the censure I felt sure would await me. Admitting my misery helped, as did growing familiarity with the teachers and the town, in spite of a drought during which the women teachers lent us tube skirts to bathe with them in the sea for lack of well or rain water. Then our monthly checks were lost (filed under "peach crop" at the Embassy, I heard) and we had nothing to eat for 10 days but bananas. Coping with these once unimaginable challenges actually improved my mood. Mail from the Peace Corps included a thoughtful article by author Norman Cousins about Peace Corps volunteers facing unsolvable problems in developing countries. This provoked a flood of soul searching and the realization that I was far more provincial than I thought when removed from my urban comfort zone, and that my values were utterly superficial and the root of my distress. I felt humbled and grateful to the villagers who were not so much intruding as trying to help us.

After six weeks in the field, the school year ended and we had to find summer assignments. Two male volunteers in a nearby town invited me to work with them in a summer Folk School that their Principal was starting. This was based on a European model of continuing education in life skills and culture for young people who had finished elementary school but could not afford high school. We had great fun teaching the kids American songs and learning Filipino tunes, directing plays, organizing games, and helping with sports. At first I lived with the boys in their large ramshackle house that was so open the townsfolk could, and did, observe our every move. Eventually, I lived with a lovely young widow and her eight sons, which, to my great surprise, I enjoyed immensely.

After summer break, I returned to my little fishing village to discover that Sandy, who had spent the summer working in Manila, planned to marry another volunteer and had moved out. The Peace Corps doctor had visited the village and declared the water unfit for volunteer consumption (even though we boiled it for 20 minutes). The Peace Corps Director suggested I join several women volunteers in a distant town. I longed for an easier assignment, but feared villagers would feel shamed if both their Peace Corps volunteers quit. The Peace Corps Director visited to convince me to move—he was shocked by poverty he had not seen elsewhere, but agreed that I could stay if another female volunteer would join me.

Soon another volunteer, Joan Aragone, arrived and we settled into a daily round of school, meriendas, fish, rice, fiestas, serenades, barrio dances, and being followed everywhere by hordes of giggling children. She worked in the central school and I went to a distant barrio, hiking two kilometers along the beach then riding a small dugout across a river and climbing a hill to the school. I showed the teachers what I could contribute and asked them to decide if they wanted me to help with pronunciation in English and practical experiments in science. The third, fifth and sixth grade teachers asked me to work with them, but the fourth grade teacher remained aloof. She was a recent Normal School graduate so may not have wanted anything I could provide.

When our monthly checks arrived from the Peace Corps, we had to travel four-and-a-half hours by overloaded bus into Iloilo City to cash them. The insides of the open buses contained church pew-style benches packed with people; produce, fish and livestock were tied on the back and loaded onto the roof. Chickens often ran around the floor and pecked our toes. On one memorable trip, I was wedged firmly into the middle of a pew when I felt a sudden shower, but noticed it was not raining. People began giggling and I realized that the pig oinking above me on the slatted roof was urinating on my head. The bus was so packed that I could not move, just endure, so I sat back and thought about the Filipino attitude of *bahala na* (never mind) for situations one cannot control.

My Impact in the Philippines

It is impossible to gauge whether or not I had any impact on the village where I lived, as almost no one spoke English but the teachers. They taught me Hiligaynon (the local language) during lunch breaks, and I figured that I learned enough to converse at about second grade level. I think the villagers I lived among were impressed that a couple of American young women could live and eat as Filipinos did. Nonetheless, we were dumbfounded by the recurring question, "Have you tasted rice?" Of course we had, as there was hardly anything else to eat; it was the basis of every meal, yet had such symbolic significance that we had to repeatedly assure folks that, yes, we had not only tasted but actually lived on rice!

It is also hard to tell how much, if any, impact I had on individuals. If my reception 33 years later is any measure, I may have had some success. I was greeted at the Iloilo airport by a delegation of eight (including the aforementioned District Supervisor) waving a sign welcoming me by name. The Mayor of Manila was on the same flight and reportedly assumed this welcoming committee was for him! My historic return to the village was likened by the Mayor to that of General MacArthur returning to the Philippines during World War II. It included a feast of quail eggs and delicacies unheard of when I had lived there, followed by a program of 1500 dancing, singing children, and, most touchingly, a number by the retired teachers who sang "my song" (which I had completely forgotten), *Moon River*. Then the former District Supervisor mentioned that we PCVs had been supposed to go to a larger town, but that he had "stolen" us for this village in his district!

Upon graduation from sixth grade, I had awarded the top six pupils piglets to raise and sell for the approximately $25 needed to attend the nearest high school in a larger town. A couple of these children wrote to me for a year afterward to report how they were doing in high school. I often wondered if there had been a great *lechon* feast after I left. When I returned thirty-three years later, I showed photos of the piglet awardees to teachers at my barrio school. They recognized several children and reported that one had become a customs official, another worked in a different town, and a third was a Navy Frogman who had drowned in service. One teacher recognized her mother, the only girl in the group, who had spent one year in high school and currently had a stall in the market. Children were sent to fetch the mother and we had a touching reunion of returned PCV and former pupil.

Recently, I heard from a PCV currently serving in the village and teaching English in a high school that did not exist when I lived there; she wrote:

> I heard about you within the first 2 days… :)… I do wish I was in an elementary school like you were, but right now PC Philippines doesn't have an elementary program, but I think that will change again in the next 2 years. I guess that now the main medium of instruction in the elementary schools is Hiligaynon until 4th or 5th grade so they stopped putting volunteers in the elementary schools. Hopefully they can put volunteers in 4th-6th grade in classes within the next couple years. I figure the sooner we can help the students with their English the better.

The Philippines Impact on Me

Luckily, I was changed profoundly by my experience in the Philippines from a naïve and superficial New Yorker, who fancied herself a cosmopolitan citizen of the world, to a humbler, more realistic person who could appreciate the Philippines for its beauty and Filipinos for their strong, brave and caring traits. As I experienced more of life, I began to appreciate aspects of Filipino culture that I had questioned while there. I had encouraged a young teacher to leave home for the Mindanao frontier that she dreamed of, and was baffled by the loyalty to her family that stood in the way of her dreams. Years later, when I had a baby, I thought enviously of the extended obligations and support that ruled Filipino families and that I could have used at that time.

I have kept in touch, on and off, with a couple of the teachers I knew. Returning to the Philippines on the 35th anniversary of the Peace Corps, I was stunned at the changes—Manila had evolved from the fun, bustling city I remembered to a smoggy, filthy scene out of the apocalyptic film "Blade Runner." On the other hand, Iloilo City had become an attractive, busy place with malls, theaters and many good restaurants. My former small fishing village of nipa huts, bare-bottomed children, and adults whose few teeth were plated with gold, had grown into a large town of cement houses with running water and electricity whose population all wore shoes and pants and revealed beautiful white teeth when they smiled.

My experience in the Philippines taught me humility, wonder, and admiration for the Filipinos whose lives seemed so much more difficult than mine, yet they accepted their situations with grace and good humor, saying *bahala na* to most adversity. My Peace Corps service undoubtedly shaped my choice of social science as my field of study and work. It also introduced me to the man I married—while working for the Peace Corps in Washington after completing service, I was asked to represent the volunteer experience for an Asia Society program; there I met a former Fullbright scholar who had studied in India; we married eight months later.

Initially, my experience in the Philippines made me extremely grateful to have been born and raised in the United States, for our freedom, democracy, personal independence and general affluence. However, on returning to the US, I was horrified by the gross excess in drug stores, supermarkets, and department stores overflowing with "stuff." My country's hypocritical military involvement in the Dominican Republic and Vietnam appalled me and led to involvement in various anti-war activities.

On returning from service, I worked for the Peace Corps in volunteer support, recruiting, and evaluation. At home in Washington D.C., I have Filipino friends and neighbors with whom I feel a special bond which seems to be shared. Thirty years later I again worked for the Peace Corps, this time designing and conducting surveys of returned volunteers and volunteers in the field. Visiting volunteers in Uzbekistan, I realized how easy we had it in the Philippines, given the balmy climate and welcoming culture. Despite many changes over the years, I was pleased to find that the volunteer experience remained one of tremendous learning and appreciation.

In retrospect, I think the value of the Peace Corps to the Philippines is to show that Americans are not rich and disinterested like the movie stars they associate with the US, but rather ordinary folk who appreciate Filipinos and want to share their lives, food, culture, and future. I think the value of the Peace Corps to the U.S. is the extraordinary learning experience that immersion in another culture can bring. I count myself extremely fortunate to have served at a time when Filipino culture was still undiluted by improved communication, and to have circumnavigated the globe before many cultures became homogenized through access to such modern developments as the Internet.

Patricia MacDermot Kasdan was born and brought up in New York City. After Peace Corps service, she worked for Peace Corps Washington, married, and moved to the Dominican Republic where her husband worked for USAID. Returning to New York, they had a son, then lived in Mexico and eventually moved to Washington D.C., where they have lived ever since. After obtaining a graduate degree in psychology, she worked in medical and social science research at George Washington University Hospital, the National Institutes of Health, and the Peace Corps. On retiring she helped found a senior "village" in her neighborhood modeled on Beacon Hill Village in Boston, providing members with the services they need to age-in-place in their own homes. Otherwise, she dotes on her two adorable grandchildren aged one and four.

(The first photo shows Pat with Peace Corps Director Sargent Shriver in her Peace Corps house in 1962; the second shows her with granddaughter Olivia in 2010.)

Thomas Kincaid

A Philippine Journey Renewed

Most Important Memories and Critical Incidents

One of the most important memories of my Peace Corps service was formed at the very moment I first touched Philippine soil. We disembarked from our plane and were immediately greeted by dozens of cheering Filipino school children and school officials waving American and Philippine flags, a gesture repeated in virtually every town along the route to our training location at the University of the Philippines College of Agriculture at Los Baños. This warm outpouring of welcome, friendship and goodwill was almost tangible. It was encouraging and created in me a feeling of confidence that our mission truly held promise of success. It was obvious they wanted us to be there!

I cannot recall a specific incident that captures the totality of my Peace Corps experience. However, there were a number of instances that still linger in my memory for various reasons. On one of my first bus rides, an ancient looking Filipina lady saw me and immediately jumped up and offered me her seat; this was embarrassing to me but I realized her actions reflected the high esteem and respect with which Filipinos regarded all Americans. It was only with some patient effort that I convinced her to keep her seat. Although this was a minor event, it was an early indication of the difficulty I would face in encouraging my Filipino friends and colleagues to accept me on my own merits, rather than embrace me just because I was an American. Another memorable experience was the two months I spent at Los Baños during summer school break. I worked with the Agricultural Extension Service, learning how to help farmers get better yields from their crops and livestock and also how to build water-seal toilets, projects I implemented upon returning to my assigned location (my mentor was a German national who had been a tank commander with the German army during World War II).

I did have one critical health-related episode that will remain in my memory. During an International Scholastic Sports Event in a nearby city, I helped to coach a regional baseball team and spent many hours with the young players, including sharing meals with them. This was unwise as I contracted amoebic dysentery and became quite seriously ill after returning to my hometown. Luckily, a missionary doctor about 20 miles away diagnosed my illness and I eventually recovered—one of the medications used was arsenic!

I believe it is problematic to look back on an experience so profound, multi-faceted and unprecedented and try to identify specific events and incidents that stand out above all others. Each day brought different challenges and satisfactions, as well as frustrations. One of my favorite memories is of a day during the dry season when my PCV colleagues and I carried water to our house using poles across our shoulders with water cans balanced on each end—the local people were astonished that Americans would soil their hands in this way. Although this was not a "critical incident", I'm sure it lives in the memories of our neighbors as it does in ours, just one episode, but an instructive one, in the cultural laboratory that was our home for 18 months.

Motivation

When I applied for the Peace Corps in the spring of 1961, I was a senior at Bridgewater College in Virginia, but had no clear career path in mind. Although I majored in history and had a strong concentration in the Spanish language, I really had no idea what I'd be doing after graduation. I still lived with my parents but looked forward to independence and being on my own. At that time, I had also considered the possibility of a career in professional baseball. In terms of personal growth, it was a time when international affairs came into focus for me—the Cuban Revolution was in progress, the space race with the Soviet Union was in full swing and the wars in Southeast Asia loomed more menacingly. This was the first time I had contemplated how my life and career might intersect with what was going on outside my "comfort zone" of family and friends.

If I hadn't served in the Peace Corps, I'm sure I would have made a career in teaching or some type of social service work since I've always been "people oriented". Although I had no international experience, my career would have involved work that impacted the worldwide community in some respect.

Prior to submitting my Peace Corps application, I already felt strongly motivated to serve my country in some international capacity. I had read *The Ugly American*, a novel critical of many aspects of American foreign policy and culture, especially as reflected by government officials and businessmen whose international activities often featured an offensive arrogance and insensitivity to foreign cultures. I was impressed by the fact that the "good" American in the story was a man who worked very effectively, and in relative obscurity, with Asian farmers at the "grassroots" level. Having already given some thought to an international career, I was inspired by John F. Kennedy's "Ask not what your country can do for you" speech and felt Peace Corps service offered a perfect vehicle for my desire to help change the negative international perception of Americans. That speech encouraged me to submit an application for Peace Corps service. Another factor in my decision was the challenge the Peace Corps offered in the face of all the "naysayers" who doubted Americans could endure the emotional and physical hardships attendant to living at a "grassroots" level—I wanted to help prove them wrong!

To be sure, the opportunity for adventure played a role and I was eager to test my own limits and capabilities. Being part of the Peace Corps vanguard certainly lent a sense of excitement since there were no guarantees the concept would work.

The Philippines

My pre-PC knowledge of the Philippines was quite limited. I knew it was a former U.S. colony, a Southeast Asian country whose culture had also been heavily influenced by centuries of Spanish colonization. Like most Americans, I realized the country was a World War II battleground that forged a strong US-Philippines bond as the two nations fought jointly against Japanese invasion and occupation.

Probably my first impression of the Philippines was the unbounded generosity and friendliness of the Filipino people. This impression grew stronger as my experience in the country unfolded and remains so today. I will never forget the many kindnesses shown to my colleagues and me by our good neighbors and friends.

Without question, the most profound initial impression was the immense socioeconomic gap between the rich and poor segments of the population; it permeated every facet of everyday life. This impression remained with me throughout my Peace Corps experience and bothers me still.

I was and am impressed by the struggle of Filipinos to find their own identity after absorbing so much American and Spanish influence over centuries of occupation.

Since leaving the Peace Corps, I have had business contacts with the Philippines, traveled there often, and maintain an abiding affection for the country and its people. I wish I could be more optimistic about the future. However, the political system continues to ill-serve the majority of the people, the abysmal gap between rich and poor persists and most of the "best and brightest" citizens leave for better opportunities abroad.

I continue to maintain very close personal relationships with many Filipinos, especially my in-laws. I seek out Filipinos at every opportunity and try to reciprocate the kindness and hospitality shown me during my time in "The Pearl of the Orient".

My community was a municipality that housed the District Government and was the focal point for a number of smaller nearby communities (barrios). Even though the population included an unusually large number of college graduates and professionals, the economy was agricultural, based on rice and sugar cane. I lived with three other PCVs in a large house built of bamboo and nipa (the living quarters were raised a few feet from the ground to keep animals and flood waters out!). The town had no electricity or running water. We supported the local economy by paying rent and hiring a cook, house-boy and laundress. The town was not far from the ocean and we were able to purchase fresh fish most of the time—our cook was also able to visit the local marketplace daily and buy fresh vegetables and meats. Medical needs were attended to by an excellent government doctor. It was a very friendly community—we were warmly welcomed and everyone, especially the teachers, was very attendant to our needs. My favorite pastimes were playing basketball and conversations with local people and colleagues. The beauty of the surrounding countryside was spectacular, offering many opportunities for hiking and photography.

The Effect of the Peace Corps Experience on Me and Others

From the outset, I received the unstinting cooperation and friendship of teachers and school administrators. Although difficult to quantify, I did have a positive influence on the teachers, as well as some of the students, particularly those in advanced and gifted classes. My positive impact in other aspects of community life was more evident, especially in terms of personal relationships. Initial curiosity turned to full acceptance as we got into the routines of everyday life. I made many lifelong friends with whom I continue to be in touch and am especially pleased that many of them were students who felt comfortable in talking about their personal lives and ambitions. Many Filipino friends have told me about the profound effect I had in presenting a more favorable view of Americans.

The most important thing I learned from my Philippines experience was that all people, regardless of race, nationality, religion, etc., have the same fundamental goals and aspirations. I also found that all peoples have something to learn from each other. Personally, I learned I am adaptable to changing circumstances and can persevere in the face of hardship and self-doubt. I was fortunate to have good PCV "housemates".

My Peace Corps service had a profound and lasting impact on my life. Most importantly, six years after completion of my service, I married my Filipina wife, a daughter of the government doctor in my town! Professionally, my experience created a lifelong interest in Asia which led to a Master's Degree in Southeast Asian studies and years of living and working in the region. In a broader sense, my life since the Peace Corps has been internationally oriented and continues to be so.

Completion of Peace Corps service made me more confident that Americans, with a proper dose of humility and dedication, can be more empathic and effective in our interactions with foreigners and project a more positive image.

My parents and siblings shared my Peace Corps experience via a weekly exchange of letters. They also became ongoing direct correspondents with my Filipino friends. I was pleased that many school children from my hometown became "pen pals" with my students.

Since completion of service, I've had no formal or informal connections with the Peace Corps but have made a number of presentations, sharing my experiences with various groups.

In retrospect, I believe the Peace Corps has made, and continues to make, valuable contributions to the Philippines, especially in projects that have an immediate impact on the daily lives of Filipinos (irrigation, forestry, etc.). I am certain that the cumulative effect of having volunteers "in country" for so many years cannot fail to enhance Philippine-American relations. In my opinion, benefits to the U.S. have far exceeded those to the Philippines. Each one of us has come home with greater appreciation of our own country and a better understanding and appreciation of the Philippines. This makes for a better American society all around. I feel very proud and privileged to have been part of the vanguard!

The Effect of the U.S.-Philippines Relationship on My Experience

The historic U.S.-Philippines relationship impacted my Peace Corps experience in both positive and negative ways. On the positive side, the genuine fondness felt by Filipinos for Americans, based on a relatively benign colonial experience and familiarity with our culture, led to a ready acceptance of, and cooperation with, our mission. However, the unquestioning esteem for all things American, and the attendant perception of infallibility, made my job more challenging in some respects. I sometimes felt my hosts expected perfection from me and were disappointed when things didn't always go as planned. Furthermore, there were unrealistic expectations of me simply because I was an American. At one of my very first meetings with local officials, someone asked "Where are the tractors"? I still recall the disappointment when I had to explain that no tractors would be coming.

A teacher asked me if the Peace Corps was a rebirth of the Thomasites (a benevolent group of American teachers whom the U.S. government had sent to the Philippines in 1901). She had misunderstood their role in the Philippine school system, believing they had replaced Filipino teachers, and was fearful of losing her own job. I was able to correct her misperception of the Thomasites and convince her that the Peace Corps mission was to assist Filipino teachers, not replace them.

Although both of these incidents, and others, were indicative of the "growing pains" of early Peace Corps communications, there was always an underlying tendency of Filipinos to unfavorably compare themselves with Americans. This was an ongoing source of frustration in efforts to have Filipinos take pride in their own heritage.

I believe the historic US–Philippines relationship made the Peace Corps effort there uniquely challenging.

Midlothian, Virginia, has been Tom Kincaid's home for 25 years. He retired in 2006 but remains active with volunteer work through his church, assisting with refugee families; he also does some advisory work for small companies engaged in world trade. His post–Peace Corps career involved 20 years in international banking and 12 years in international economic development. He reports he is blessed with a wonderful Filipina wife, two children and three grandchildren.

(The first photo shows Tom with teachers at a barrio school in 1962-63; the second shows him at the McKinley Cemetery in Manila in 2009.)

Hazel Mae Land

Immersion

One Sunday morning in the spring of 1961 as I was preparing to attend worship services, I received a telegram inviting me to participate in training for a Peace Corps project in the Philippines. Training would begin in the fall. Although I had applied for participation and had taken a test, I could not believe the offer—I wanted to help, I wanted to travel, I wanted to visit Africa! I just did not internalize such an offer. I told my sister with whom I was living in Trenton, New Jersey, and she was excited about the possibility. The telegram asked for an immediate response. I did attend worship services that morning.

At the time, I was teaching at a training school in Bordentown, New Jersey. I had planned to attend summer school at Springfield College, Massachusetts, to pursue a Master's Degree in Physical Education. I completed the summer school. Additionally, the Civil Rights Movement was picking up some speed in 1961, and I definitely planned to become actively involved in the struggle. It took only a little time for me to realize that the struggle would be alive and well years and years longer than a few years spent with the Peace Corps.

Prior to my leaving for Peace Corps training, the local newspaper, *The Trentonian*, having interviewed me, published a short article about my participation in the new Peace Corps project in the Philippines. The newspaper listed one other person from New Jersey who had been invited to participate. I shared the newspaper article with Phyllis Clemensen when we met. We both were later assigned to the same town in the Philippines.

I traveled by train to the training site at Penn State located in State College, Pennsylvania. Another Peace Corps trainee was on that train, Lennie from New York. Upon arrival, Lennie and I shared a taxi to Graduate Circle Apartments on campus, where we received our room assignments. One of my roommates, Sylvia, was already there and taking a nap when I arrived. Becky was the last of the three of us to check in. Our apartment seemed miles away from the main campus; there also seemed to be miles between the women's cafeteria where we ate and the classrooms. I and several other trainees rented bicycles for ten dollars a week; at the time the bike saved me! I was 27 years old and I had finished college six years earlier—I was not in shape to pull those hills.

Peace Corps training was hectic, to put it mildly. As I recall, we had courses in English with emphasis on phonemes (taught by a professor with a false British accent), science,

Philippine Studies, American Studies, and physical education. Additionally, much reading was required; nearly all our time was planned! One Saturday afternoon we had a "break" (unscheduled time). Mike Menster led us on a climb of Mount Nittany—my first experience with mountain climbing, as I was born and raised in Florida. Along with a few others, I finally made it to the mountain top with lots of pushing, shoving and pulling from Mike and others.

Nearly every week we were given inoculations, sometimes as many as four in one day. We also had various checkups such as dental and hearing in preparation for our stay abroad, including encounters with psychiatrists! The weekend we spent outdoors camping (survival training) was a trying experience as we tried to sleep under tents we had pitched which kept falling while it rained nearly the whole miserable night!

Our training group consisted of about 60 men and women. Two of us were African American, Richard and me. Having been born and raised in the Deep South, where schools, colleges and universities were racially segregated, being part of this training group was my first experience in being a racial minority. I experienced no recognizable slights in this setting, however; I felt at ease and comfortable. The trainees were as friendly as I was.

After training, my flight from Trenton to Philadelphia was on a small plane for the short trip. This was my first plane ride. In Philadelphia, I boarded a jet to San Francisco. There several of us spent the night at Becky's parents' home in Palo Alto. After departing the shores of the USA, our next stop was Honolulu where we spent the night. Following a *luau*, the stopover was uneventful. After a rest stop on Guam, we arrived at Manila airport on January 3, 1962, having skipped a day. Being a Floridian, the climate in Manila was no real adjustment for me. After less than 24 hours in Manila, we ate hamburgers in a club, prepared just like home. After eating the hamburger, I thought I may make it in the Philippines after all.

We traveled to the University of the Philippines in Los Baños for another few weeks of training. The people in Manila and at the University seemed cosmopolitan in that they seemed to be going their way about their business, not likely to stop and stare endlessly. There seemed to be a variety of edible foods such as fish, meat, vegetables, fruit, rice, basic foods nearly always available for all meals of the day. *Meriendas* (snacks between meals) and *siestas* required some getting used to.

Eventually we were assigned to our towns; eight Peace Corps volunteers were assigned to the Island of Panay and province of Antique. I was among four women who were sent to Sibalom. Nick and Chris, our nearest neighbors, were assigned to Belisan and Phil and Harvey were further away from us. We four women resided in a two-story wooden house which was spacious and met our needs. We had a maid and cook, Estelita, along with her minor son, Francis, who lived in the house with us. Ann was assigned to Sibalom Central School. The other three of us worked at barrio schools. I worked at the school in Sido-San Juan barrio. I taught English as a Second Language in all grades, assisted in experiments in science classes and instructed in games and exercises. I organized a class called "Out of School Youth." The class was comprised of young men and women who had completed elementary school but no longer attended any school. From my savings I provided two promising students a scholarship of 200 pesos each to begin further study: Filipina, a current graduate from our school, and Lucy, an out-of-school youth. The funds came from my living allowance savings.

The Philippines is predominantly Catholic, but I was assigned to a town which was predominantly Protestant—Anglican. There was one Baptist church a block from where I resided. I am a Baptist and I attended this church. I sang in the choir. We met American missionaries in the Philippines; they welcomed the Peace Corps.

Recreational activities were about the same as found in most other cultures: parties, weddings, dances, school activities, harvest festivals, religious celebrations, and folk dancing (for which the Filipinos were well known). One unique activity that we volunteers enjoyed was serenades by young men at night outside our windows. Our favorite song was *Dahil Sa Iyo* accompanied by guitar. We volunteers enjoyed singing, too—after dinner we would remain at the table and sing song after song; our neighbors, men, women, children and babies, would gather outside watching and listening.

The Peace Corps provided bicycles for us; public transportation consisted of buses and jeepneys. Many times I walked to my barrio which was three kilometers each way.

The beaches were beautiful: white sand, black sand, gray sand, blue water, green water— take your pick. Our town had major market day on Mondays. People from villages far and near would come to shop and spend the day enjoying themselves. Food, furniture (usually made from bamboo), clothing, and many other items were sold on market day.

In closing, I will say the experience of Peace Corps was fulfilled in ways anticipated by the original goals: to grasp the opportunity to know people of other cultures in ways learned only by such an experience as afforded by Peace Corps; secondly and conversely, to become known by others in ways best afforded by the Peace Corps; and thirdly, possibly impart in some way a bit of truth which may be of significance to the hosts.

Hazel Mae Land lives in Brooksville, Florida. After serving in the Peace Corps in the Philippines as a Teacher's Aide in English as a Second Language and in science, she applied for a second tour in West Africa. She was accepted for the Nigeria Peace Corps program, for which she trained at UCLA. She served from 1963 through 1966 as a teacher at Bishop Tugwell Teacher Training College, Igbudu, Warri, in the Mid-West region of Nigeria. Upon returning to the US, she became a full-time civil rights employee with the NAACP National Office as Field Director for the state of Tennessee. She was working with the movement in Memphis, Tennessee when Martin Luther King was assassinated; she was caught in the halted traffic minutes after Dr. King was shot. Hazel left active work with the NAACP to study law at the University of Florida College of Law from 1970 to 1973. She then practiced law in her home state of Florida through June of 2002. Currently she participates in church-related activities, the NAACP, and volunteers with the Retired Senior Volunteer Program (RSVP) where she works with the Hernando Museum Association, Inc., researching local black history.

(The first photo shows Hazel speaking at the Commencement of the Sido-San Juan Elementary School in 1963; the second shows her speaking at an NAACP Conference.)

Owen Maher
Reaching Out

In 1961 I had become disillusioned with our society. I was disappointed in adults and frustrated that things couldn't be done better both in the school where I worked and in the community. I had lost faith in people.

When President Kennedy announced the establishment of the Peace Corps I was skeptical. I told my family to expect me back in three days, but I went to Washington to see if this would be another disappointment. Fortunately for me I was very impressed and stayed.

I soon met fifty of the nicest people imaginable. There are good people in the world and I had just met a bunch of them. Together we embarked on an amazing journey.

A few of our group leaned toward the missionary attitude, but I was anxious to see how Filipinos organized themselves to foster individual, family and community development. I was in an agricultural village, primarily sugar cane, in the central islands. There were few middle class people in our area. The plantation owner made decisions for everybody, although that included inviting me to work at the school. The sexes were separated after elementary school. None of the local children had gone to high school before I arrived.

I was pleased to discover that the language had a strong Spanish influence so I quickly developed some basic communication and could work with students. Eventually I became fairly fluent. I had the opportunity to teach a college class and was incredulous that the students didn't dare ask questions no matter how hard I tried. Being from New York City and comfortable with criticism, I was slow to learn that the answer to "How do you like …?" was a positive adjective. Whether it was their English, an object or an activity, I was never expected to express a real opinion. It disgraced them if I responded negatively.

The incredible journey home included visits to Hong Kong, Bangkok, Athens and Nuremberg as well as three weeks in India and one in Egypt. After I arrived, my Peace Corps service was everywhere regarded highly.

After a five-week journey home from the Philippines, Owen Maher received a fellowship from Columbia University. He then taught students who had not previously been successful in school. He married Juanita from Puerto Rico; they have seven children. Their oldest son, Owen Jr., is a graphic artist and video game designer living in Guadalajara, Mexico. Their youngest daughter earned a BS in herbal medicine, is a performing classical Indian dancer and is married to a young man from India. She has a three-year-old child and lives in Berkeley, California. Since retirement Owen has worked as a Spanish-English translator and more recently as a tutor of English to Asian graduate students at the University of Virginia. His avocation is language study. He is currently studying Italian. Owen enjoys playing tennis doubles and swimming competitively. Owen and Juanita's nest is empty but there are lots of visitors.

(The first photo shows Owen with his wife Juanita in the 1960s.)

Leonard Mirin
Notes on a Few Days in Sara, Iloilo, and Washington D.C.

The slightly dissonant sounds of a small brass ensemble were among the saddest moments of sultry afternoons in Sara. Like a slow motion Doppler-effect they originated in the distant reaches of the barrio and grew louder and more plaintive as they neared our windowless house and slowly passed on. Cholera—*El Tor*—was the terrible catalyst of these melancholy moments. Leading a small line of clean clothed farmers and their families, the two or three musicians set a slow dirge-paced walk on the uneven stony dirt road. Two or three of the men toward the middle of the group carried a wooden box, the size of a violin case.

Seeing this for the first time after my arrival in Sara, I connected the aural and visual clues to be an informal, quiet, rural funeral cortege. The death of this infant or a small child was an early moment of sadness. An unusual event, I thought. It hardly was. During that year and more that the cholera pandemic ravaged the Philippines, these depressing scenes occurred with near clockwork at least once or twice a week. Among the infinite reminders of Philippine poverty, ignorance and indifference, these evanescent melodies and marches still linger decades later as among the most poignant.

In the barrios where infant mortality was highest during these deadly months, the government, such as it was, set up a makeshift network of health clinics. A rural nurse whom I had befriended, asked if I would like to accompany her on some of her weekly visits into these far flung mountain communities. The news that a *"Cano,"* white skin, big nose and all, visiting their village would be the chance of a lifetime for residents (and their babies) to experience this neo-World War II soldier. Like bees to honey, the clinic days had large turnouts when I came along. And the infants were inoculated with professional, medical skill.

Back in Sara, an older gentleman and neighbor of ours had gotten word of my occasional excursions and asked if I would like to accompany him as well. A request in pursuit of health education was hard to turn down, especially in the face of the pandemic. Besides the gentleman had a calm, confident demeanor as well as an authentic doctor's black bag. I became a bit curious when, rather than at one of the "health stations" I had visited with the nurse on earlier outings, we met with patients at a relative's nipa house. Reaching into his black bag, the kindly gentleman produced a syringe, a small bottle and a candle. After a short conversation in Hiligaynon he casually injected each of those waiting in line—mothers, infants, and children for the most part. To my horror, the needle was neither changed nor sterilized from patient to patient. My protests were laughed off and I was shown the candle that, after 10 or more injections, would be used to eventually attempt some sterilization. One visit with this gentleman was too many, and I never went out on these medical excursions again. Though cholera is generally transmitted through infected wastewater, I can't help but feel I was being used for private profit (he charged for injections) and forgive myself for being, through my presence in this situation, perhaps a causative factor in the spread of some disease.

Having been involved in sports in high school and college, I thought I could assist the Sara High School girls' softball team in their quest for the provincial tournament championship. Playfield facilities were rough. Games were played on a relatively flat field near the elementary school. Old pieces of clothing were used as bases and foul lines were marked with dried milk sprinkled from the cut corners of a USAID plastic surplus food supplement. The girls would take turns dusting a baseline on the grass with the white powder and then holding some up above their mouths to dribble a bit of nutrition in. I coached well enough, or more likely they were quite talented, and we earned a chance to play for the championship in Iloilo City, four hours away. The bus ride from Sara was akin to a live movable feast. As with many Philippine buses, livestock was everywhere. For the extended stay in Iloilo, a supermarket of edible delights was travelling along with us on the team bus. Bunches of chickens, strung together under the seats, lay side by side with fish frolicking in cut out kerosene cans. Pigs crowned the rooftop much to their displeasure. Rice and all manner of vegetables competed for space with players, teachers and coaches. Along the road, as we passed any church, the group in unison would cross themselves and recite several times "Hail Mary, full of grace." Living and sleeping in local schools, the girls and chaperones turned the classrooms into two star motels, complete with all of the transported food supplies. Breakfast, lunch and dinner were cooked and served on the lawns.

The actual game ambience was a bit more disorganized. Rules, it seemed, were *ad hoc* from minute to minute. Sara's team was behind in the early innings and then it was discovered that distances to the bases were substantially shorter than regulations called for. The pitcher's mound was likewise too close to the plate. Despite our protests, bases and mound were moved to their required distance. While the outcome remained close, Sara eventually lost the championship game by one run.

Though the Japanese presence in the Philippines still evoked bitter memories and almost mythically horrible stories, there were two pieces of that country's memorabilia, locked behind glass classroom cabinets that provided me with real world educational opportunities. As part of war reparation payments, Sara Elementary School had come into possession of a reasonably good microscope and telescope. Fearful they might break one, or not familiar with their uses, these items seemed like real, but untouchable, trophies of war. At least my college education had introduced me to the practical manipulation of these mechanisms, and I was otherwise still somewhat fearless regarding their safekeeping.

In a class of fifth grade science, I took the microscope out of its cabinet and asked one of my students to search his friend's hair for what I knew resided there. He scraped a small, black wiggling object from a strand of his neighbor's hair and we placed it between two glass plates. One by one the students looked through the eyepiece and observed sinister outlines of a louse, with blood still pulsating through its body. The impact was clear on each of the student's faces. Not only did we make practical use of the *objet d'art*, but introduced a hidden world associated with biology and health. I believe that after we left Sara, the microscope was much more in demand.

The political standoff with the Soviet Union was at a peak during our years in the Philippines. With the crisis over missile bases in Cuba and the continuing competition in space occupying daily headlines (a week after the fact) I was in all likelihood frequently looking at the night sky. I remembered the telescope behind glass at the elementary school and asked to borrow it for an evening. After dark, I set it up in front of my house and invited the neighborhood kids to look through it at the moon. "*ABOW!*" was the universal reaction upon seeing with such clarity the moon's distant craters. Extended lines of children and adults waited long minutes for just the chance to peer into what was ultimately to become the symbolic base of triumphant American space technology. In a convoluted sense, for the Filipinos, World War II had brought them closer to the moon.

External events, four years after the creation of the Peace Corps, still strongly color my experiences in Asia and my judgments of the officials associated with its founding and goals. In March 1965, a conference was held at the State Department in celebration of this anniversary and to explore the role of the returned volunteer in American life. Dean Rusk, Bill Moyers and other Johnson administration officials were invited to speak. A savage war was raging and escalating in Vietnam. Many of the speakers were directly responsible for this Kennedy/Johnson policy. How hypocritical! Using young Americans in the developing world as feel good propaganda, while at the same time bombing and burning the youth of Vietnam, Laos and Cambodia, poisoning their water and food and bodies, while Peace Corps volunteers introduced clean wells, advanced agriculture and progressive health standards.

How shameful! How we had been used!

A small group, no more than a dozen of us, around noon during a break in the conference, gathered and marched in protest to the war with signs in front of the White House on Pennsylvania Avenue. It was a brief event, but nevertheless attracted the District's police force. With red lights flashing several policemen confronted us. We were told to leave, mostly for our own safety. The anniversary events drew the attention of the media, but only a brief paragraph buried inside the following day's *New York Times* noted that "…Around noon, a small group of returned volunteers protested United States involvement in Vietnam by picketing the White House."

What is the role of returned volunteers in American life? Here we are. Fifty years after the Peace Corps. Still at war in Asia!

Leonard Mirin grew up in Brooklyn, New York and attended Abraham Lincoln High School and Columbia University. While serving in Sara, Iloilo, with the Peace Corps, he taught English as a second language at Sara Elementary School and science at the high school. During the summers, he ran a swimming program at the University of the Philippines and assisted in a television series, Salmagundi, *which explored conditions at a Manila correctional facility called Welfareville. After serving in the Peace Corps, Leonard worked for UNICEF and* Scientific American *magazine, among* others. In 1969, he returned to school, earning a master's degree in landscape architecture from the University of Michigan. For about three years, he practiced landscape architecture in Michigan and New York City. In 1974, he joined the faculty of Cornell University and helped to establish the Graduate Program in Landscape Architecture there. He is still teaching a variety of courses in this field including the History Sequence, Design Studios, Modern Landscape Architecture and Japanese Architecture and Garden Design. For many years, as co-director of Cornell's Summer Program in Japan, he led eight-week intensive design courses in Japanese architecture and garden design. Leonard is married, living in Ithaca, NY, and learning about BUZZ and texting from his 12 year-old daughter, as well as new techniques of emergency medicine from his son in Philadelphia. Lauren, his wife, is currently chair of the Department of Art History at Ithaca College.

(The first photo is Lenny in Masbate in 1962; the second is with his daughter Alley in 2006.)

Zvi November
Abing November Remembers

My wonderful *nanay*, a spinster teacher, gave me the Filipino name "Abing." I liked it because it made me feel that I belonged.

A few months after Phil Bloom and I landed in Dao, Antique in 1962, just before the start of the rainy season, a poor neighbor who lived directly across from our nipa hut explained that the small parcel of rice paddy he owned could barely provide enough grain for his wife and five children. He went on to tell us idealistic New York City slickers how important it is to prepare the paddies before the first rains come pouring down. He said that tomorrow he and his two teen-age sons were going out to the paddies at dawn to move sod from one spot to another because it is important to level out the fields before sowing the seeds. Bloom and I jumped at the opportunity to help our friend and neighbor. We instantly volunteered to join him to relocate lumps of soil. At daybreak the next day all five of us were out in the fields working hard. But after only two hours, when the tropical sun began to make its presence felt, our neighbor (who was definitely not a lazy *Juan Tamad*) called a halt to our endeavors. He said it was too hot to work and that we should return to the *poblacion*.

I was greatly surprised, to say the least. I thought that we should have put in a full day's work because there was plenty to do. This was my very first lesson in Third World poverty dynamics and it still provides me with food for thought.

Interestingly, at the same time we were in the Philippines, China was struggling through Mao Tse Tung's "Great Leap Forward." Peasants were ordered to melt their metal possessions (even pots and pans). Millions of Chinese died of starvation in that period. Not long after, Pakistan expelled its Peace Corps contingent lest the feudal system that prevailed in the rural Punjab and elsewhere be disturbed by young American agitators. The primary reason for creating the Peace Corps (if I remember correctly) was to fight poverty and help raise socio-economic standards in the "developing world." It was understood axiomatically that the USA could, should and would serve as a model worthy of emulation. However, it was just about this time (the 1960s) that America began losing its steel shipbuilding, automotive and electronics industries to competitors in the Far East and Europe. But Filipino doctors and nurses were imported to staff U.S. hospitals because American doctors make more money in their own clinics.

When it comes to good-heartedness, human warmth and joviality the Filipinos take the cake. (The pineapple upside down cake made by the always cooperative home economics teacher was my favorite).

There are presently tens of thousands of *pinoys* and *pinays* (these terms seem to have lost their negative connotation) here in Israel taking care of our old people (including my father-in-law before he passed away). These care-givers send money back to the Philippines to help support their families. Indeed, remittances are now vital to the Philippine economy.

Now approaching old age, I know that stimulating economic development is an awfully complicated matter. Neither the World Bank nor the IMF has made much progress in figuring it out and they're supposed to be experts. Be that as it may, whatever cross-cultural insights I have gained over these many years have their beginnings near the rice paddies of Dao where the carabaos graze.

For Harvey (Zvi) November the Philippines Peace Corps experience transformed a straight Brooklyn boy with limited horizons into a young optimist hungry for more intercultural encounters. Indeed, while teaching English at the Hong Kong International School in 1969 Harvey made many Chinese friends and acquired the name: LUNG WEN BAW (The Dragon that Studies Culture).

From 1970 onward, Zvi (Harvey) returned to his Jewish roots by moving to Israel where he has worked as a teacher, counselor, probation officer and employment advisor. Upon retirement (2004), Zvi presented his lecture series, "Cultures around the World," in old-age homes in Jerusalem.

Now seventy years young, Zvi rides an electric bike, is a highly competent, dedicated baby-sitter for his two brilliant grandchildren, and volunteers with Israel's Media Watch and Professors for a Strong Israel, two poverty-stricken organizations dedicated to Israel's survival in a world divided by those who would shrink the country so it is no longer a viable, defensible entity and others who want to destroy it completely in one massive missile barrage. Expanding on this topic, Zvi self-published Israel in Reality *in 2008.*

(The first photo shows Zvi with Richard Lewis on his right en route to Dumaguete in 1962. The second photo shows him with his two grandchildren.)

Anne La Barre O'Connor
A Charmed Life

The Philippines—of course the most critical incident of my stint in the Peace Corps was meeting my husband, Rod O'Connor, a young executive with Caltex Oil Company. As far as joining the Peace Corps is concerned, I signed up the minute I graduated from college. I wanted to travel, have some adventures and excitement. The Peace Corps seemed like a good idea and at the time I was a bit fired up by John Kennedy's administration. If I had not joined the Peace Corps, I don't know what I would have done. Joining was the right decision because of all that ensued.

When the Pan Am plane carrying "Batch II" landed in the Philippines in January of 1962, I was shocked. I had never seen such poverty or experienced tropical heat. It was definitely a major culture shock even though we had been briefed as to what to expect at Penn State.

On the positive side, my roommates and I had some fun and experienced lots of amusing incidences. Living in the province, I learned a lot about World War II, Philippine history and culture plus my viewpoints on life and people in general were broadened. Nevertheless, I did not like living in Sibalom, Antique. I missed my former way of life, friends, family and culture. In addition, I did not like being stared at and being called *"Cana"* all the time. I never really got used to it. It was when I was assigned to work in Welfareville outside of Manila that a lucky set of circumstances occurred wherein I met my future husband.

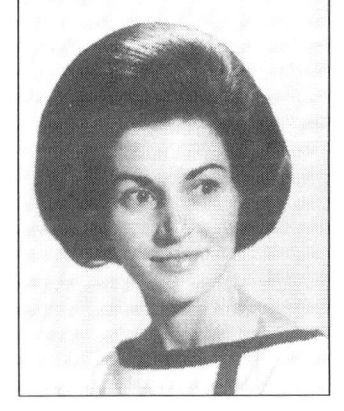

Although I don't think I was really cut out to be a Peace Corps volunteer, I'm basically glad to have had the experience. I personally don't think I had much impact as a Peace Corps member in the community of Sibalom, Antique. I was teaching English where they already knew the language and had excellent English teachers. I felt what I was doing was not something that the people there needed and wanted. Their needs were more in the economic arena, and that was not my area of expertise. I think the Philippine people were glad to have us there as they are just nice people; the hospitality is there and, for the most part, they like Americans. They recognized that we meant well. As far as actual "help" is concerned, I believe it was negligible overall.

I actually fulfilled my original reason for joining the Peace Corps which was to have excitement, travel and adventure albeit this came about more due to my marriage. I consider myself very fortunate to have achieved this goal. Along the way, I met some incredibly fascinating, professional, competent, fun, talented, intelligent, unusual and eccentric people. I was lucky enough to have traveled the world with my husband and indeed, consider that I have lived a charmed life.

Anne O'Connor lives in a suburb of Dallas, Texas. She met and married Rod O'Connor in the Philippines; originally from New York City, he was a young executive with Caltex Oil Company. They married in the Malate Cathedral on December 21, 1962. Anne was then hired as a substitute teacher at the American School. Later she worked for JUSMAG (Joint United States Military Advisory Group), which was under the auspices of the American Embassy in Manila, until 1970, when they were transferred to New York.

After one year, they were transferred back to the Philippines, where her husband became Vice President of Caltex, Manila. They lived in Dasmarinas Village in Makati, where they made lots of friends, both Filipino and foreign, some of whom they have retained. Anne recalls that they absolutely loved the life they led in Manila. In 1975 they were transferred to Wellington, New Zealand. In the two years they were posted there, they traveled the whole country and made many lasting friends. In 1977, they were once again transferred to Manila, where Rod was promoted to President of Caltex, Manila. Anne found it great to be back in Manila as they already had many friends and associates there. They lived in North Forbes Park in Makati. All together, they lived in the Philippines for 18 years.

In 1983, Rod's company transferred them from Manila to Dallas, where she became a paralegal and worked at that profession until 2007. Anne and Rod had been happily married for 39 years when he died in 2002. They had one son, Rod O'Connor Jr., born in Manila in 1964, now married and living in Sydney, Australia, with his wife and two children. Now retired, Anne is involved with her church, family, friends, travel, golf, tennis, and several other hobbies and interests.

Linda Henry Perron
What the Peace Corps Meant To Me

Motivation

As a kid who grew up in the countryside with only 19 in my high school graduating class, I felt a strong need to find out about the rest of the world before I contributed to it. Also, stories my grandfather told about China, having landed there during the Boxer Rebellion, whetted my appetite for travel, as did thorough perusal of every *National Geographic Magazine* I could get my hands on. I applied to study abroad during college, but couldn't find a sponsor.

I had always been told I would be a good teacher, but I did not really know what career I wanted. I really wanted to be a performing pianist, but I knew I probably couldn't support myself on that. I took a liberal arts degree majoring in English, because it seemed like something I needed in order to support myself.

After my graduation, I took a summer internship with an international newspaper, partly to experience living in a big city. It was here that I got the Peace Corps call.

To me, the Peace Corps filled my need to find out about the rest of the world. In addition, on the way home after service, I traveled by myself on five dollars a day for four months, visiting 16 countries throughout Asia, the Middle East, Africa, and Europe. I came home with exactly ten cents left to my Peace Corps readjustment allowance.

My Town

I was assigned to a small, tropical village on the sea coast. Having never been in the tropics, I was most impressed by the flora and fauna. The people did not impress me, because my aunt and uncle from New York City had made sure since I was very young that I encountered people from all over the world on the city streets. I believe that it was easier for me to adjust to village life than for city folk, since I grew up in the country. At first we were a novelty and people came into our house day and night to see what we were doing. Did we eat the fish eyes in the soup? (Yes) Did we manage to sleep on string beds? (Yes) One fun thing was figuring out how to keep the ants out of our food. Finally, after the ants built a bridge across a basin of water, we set the table legs in kerosene. However, that did not keep the gecko from falling into the batter. We also had a friendly, furry tarantula resident in the toilet area.

At first we were herded here and there by the important people in the barrio and province. Later we took our stand to do what we were sent to do, and we were no longer novelties, but viable members of the community. My Filipino best friend and I kept in touch for years until the Philippine government began to censor our mail. Then one day, years later, I was walking on a small street in Manhattan when I heard a voice calling my Filipino name "Lin." There she was! She was here as a nurse in a hospital!

The Effect of the Peace Corps Experience on Me

I am sure that what I was able to give in the Peace Corps at least adequately fulfilled the mission. But what the Peace Corps gave me was worth every last penny the government spent on me those two years. I gained confidence, savvy, knowledge, management skills, and more, beyond anything I could have gained elsewhere.

Otherwise I would not have been able to contribute 23 years as manager in a large corporation, raise a family, serve as church organist, teach piano, and many other activities. If I had not had the PC experience, I may have ended up as a teacher in an isolated little country school, with unfulfilled dreams and unrealized capabilities.

After Peace Corps service, Linda Perron taught school in Scarsdale, New York; Greenwich, Connecticut; and Florida. Later she married and raised a family while working as a project manager for AT&T, analyzing cell phone and calling card systems in Central New Jersey. She served as organist in her church, restored old Victorian houses, earned an MBA, and then moved to the marketing department at AT&T. She is now retired and lives in Emmaus, Pennsylvania, where she teaches piano, conducts church services, and is president-elect for the Lehigh Valley Music Teachers Association and manages their annual music festivals. She and her husband are designing and planting a shade garden in the back yard. They hike locally, in Europe, and in Central America. Linda visited almost every country in Asia and the Middle East on her way home from The Philippines, but couldn't enter mainland China. Last year Linda made that trip, hiking over 70 miles in various parts of the country.

Eric Peterson
Diin ka makadto?

"Where are you going?" Everywhere we went the question was thrown at us to the point that it became comical. We were a bit sensitive those early days but soon realized it was meant as a friendly greeting.

Now, in the larger sense of our lives at that time, I see that it was a good question. We were liberal arts graduates with few boundaries. Our assignments to barrio schools in the Philippines were not directly "career-building." Although many of us went on to contribute in education, I think most of us, like me, were not yet sure what we might do with our lives, other than wanting to be of service in some way. Maybe my housemates and I did in fact look a bit lost as we wandered the dusty roads around Sara, Iloilo, where we were assigned.

But by the time I left, I knew where I was going, thanks to an unpressured environment and wise words from Lenny Mirin, my housemate, who must have been getting tired of my musings about architecture as a possible path: "Eric, why not just decide to do it, and see how it feels? You can't act on it for two years, anyway." The Peace Corps enabled me to do that—enabled me to read more seriously, but most of all to think: to think on my own and shape my own views. We could absorb the environment and the way people thrived in it—I have the Filipinos and the Peace Corps to thank for getting me on a satisfying path.

It soon became clear that our personal experiences were likely to outweigh any impact we might have. Fifty years later, vivid memories remain to confirm this—how easily we were drawn to everyday events unrelated to our work. In retrospect these events did more to shape my life than I could have imagined at the time.

Lenny and I had received a gift of two doves and had shackled them to a crude roost on our open bamboo porch. It was time to make them a suitable cage of split bamboo shaped and tied with rattan. We envisioned it as a huge teardrop, light and spacious, hanging under the eave by our table.

It was the beginning of the wet season and the morning was a slow and ominous prelude to the rains. Across the rice paddies at the edge of the town was a grove of large bamboo where our neighbors said we could find the material we wanted, and after a roundabout hike through the undergrowth we came upon a nipa hut in a clearing, surrounded by stacks of the trimmed poles. A young woman sat at the window nursing her child, the only sounds a clucking hen and the rising wind high in the bamboo. We found a good 30-foot pole, paid the graceful woman, and decided that to beat the rain we would have to cut across the rice fields.

With the long pole on our shoulders we started off single file along the dikes, frogs plopping into the shallow water around us at each step. We pictured ourselves from a distance, marching along reflected in the water, the springy pole bouncing between us, the dark sky behind us cut now by sharp bolts of lightning, and we kept a wary eye on a grey curtain of rain moving in our direction. As we crossed the last dike it was upon us. Ahead stood a small two-room schoolhouse, very white against the black sky, its grounds meticulously groomed by the hands of many children.

The rain came quickly and heavily as we hurried up a mossy bank and took refuge on the school's covered porch. We stood looking out into the steady rain falling hard on the huge wet leaves. One tiny barefoot girl holding a long banana leaf over her head ran lightly along the grass.

A patient calm pervaded the air, and we became aware of a boy behind us with an invitation to come into the classroom. We were greeted by excited shy smiles, accommodated quickly in homemade bamboo chairs, and, like guests of the highest honor, were served delicious bananas fried in sugar. I wished the rain to last forever, falling inexorably but so gently on the roof and over the eaves, and out across the open fields and shimmering paddies. It seemed that nothing could be as gentle and perfect as these quiet moments, these soft children and the rich earth under their small feet.

When I returned home from the Philippines, and was asked what I might have accomplished there, I had to suppress an impulse to say that the question was irrelevant. The vivid memories are of the ways of the people, of the beautiful land and a depth of hospitality that I had never before experienced. Maybe we learned to receive these moments with a whole heart and to recognize our dependence on our environment and the communities that are found around us. This, and the strong friendships we started 50 years ago have shaped my choice of work and the way I have pursued it. They continue to sustain me. In the Philippines, I decided that architects have a unique contribution to make in the resource allocation process, particularly where resources are scarce. After nearly 50 years, I still believe this.

After Peace Corps service, Eric Peterson earned a Master of Architecture at Columbia University. He married while in graduate school and worked as a licensed architect in New York City. In 1976, the UN year of Human Settlements (Habitat), he got involved in architecture in economic and community development, leading to assignments under USAID contracts for housing and urban development. Accompanied by his wife, Jane, and two young sons, he accepted an assignment as advisor for housing reconstruction in Beirut, Lebanon for two years. They stayed on for two more years, Eric working for a private architecture firm and his wife as an editor for the UN. Returning to the U.S. in late 1981, Eric combined working as a consultant for the World Bank and USAID with self-employment as an architect in Washington D.C. World Bank assignments took more of his time as Eastern Europe opened to the West and needed assistance in the transition from central planning to more market-based systems, particularly in housing and municipal services. By 1985, he was consulting nearly fulltime for the World Bank, in small Pacific Island nations, Eastern Europe and Turkey. The continuing World Bank work led eventually to a staff position, focusing on housing, cultural heritage, earthquake mitigation and reconstruction, and the physical planning/architectural aspects of judicial reform. Now retired from the Bank, Eric still consults part time, mostly in Russia, Romania, Armenia, and Croatia. He and Jane have three grandchildren and their parents to keep up with and enjoy.

(The first photo shows Eric, on the right, in 1961 during Peace Corps training at Penn State; fellow volunteer Bob Tyler is on the left.)

Jerry Poznak
Three Filipinos and Me

I was born and raised in a large extended family of five uncles and one aunt on my father's side, four aunts and three uncles on my mother's side, and twenty-two cousins—all within walking distance from my home on Lyons Avenue in the Weequahic section of Newark, New Jersey.

From the age of twelve or so, I knew well the streets of Newark, both tough and tame, as I ranged the city from one end to the other wherever baseball and basketball were played. Until I joined the army at nineteen, I had never been more than one hundred and fifty miles in any direction from my home nor, with the exception of sports, had I any experience with a culture other than my own.

In the ensuing years between the army, college graduation and one year of teaching seventh and eighth grades in rural New Hampshire, I had spent time in half a dozen states and several foreign countries. Furthermore, I had experienced many different cultures with people from all over the world, but none of this prepared me for what I would experience in the fantastic two year period with the Peace Corps in the Philippine Islands.

After eight weeks of largely irrelevant training at Penn State and six more at Los Baños, Eliot Putnam and I were sent to the barrio of Balete on the island of Panay. About a month later, at the end of the Filipino school year, Harvey Pressman asked me to assist in the preparations for the arrival of Group III later that spring.

My first responsibility was to arrange for a Peace Corps office, classroom space, and some additional housing at the Diliman campus of the University of the Philippines in Quezon City. After meeting with the head of buildings and grounds and two other administrators, I was getting nowhere. Everyone was sympathetic, but no one was willing to make a decision so I decided to go right to the top to speak with Carlos Romulo, the president of the university.

I entered the office of the president and told the secretary that I wanted to speak with President Romulo. I told her I didn't have an appointment, and that I was a Peace Corps volunteer (the magic words) and it was important that I speak to him.

"Just one moment," she said as she picked up the inter-office phone and began speaking to Romulo, telling him there was a Peace Corps volunteer in the office who was eager to speak with him. She hung up the phone and directed me to go right in.

I entered a large office and across the room sitting, dwarfed behind a desk the size of an aircraft carrier, was President Carlos Romulo. I told him what I needed and the difficulty I was having getting a commitment from the university officials I had spoken with. Then, in an effort to ingratiate myself, I told him I was from New Jersey and I had heard him speak at the United Nations and was very impressed.

President Romulo replied: "I know New Jersey very well. I have traveled on the New Jersey Turnpike many times. The whole state stinks!" With that he picked up the phone and spoke briefly to an underling and arranged for me to get everything I requested.

The whole thing was marvelous.

I never did go back to Balete. I spent the next two months living on the Diliman campus and doing all manner of Peace Corps work that included a trip to Hong Kong with Bert Pumento to purchase assorted items needed for the program, including a high quality microscope for the Peace Corps doctor.

Shortly thereafter, with the coming arrival of Group VII, Bill Warren relocated to Zamboanga to set up a Peace Corps office and begin scouting Mindanao for further volunteer placements. At the same time, Larry Fuchs decided to establish an in-service training center for volunteers and their Filipino co-teachers and the decision was made to secure a location and construct a suitable building close to the Peace Corps office in Zamboanga. The responsibility for getting this done fell to me.

I moved to Zamboanga in May of '62 and having no accommodations, I went to the Mayor's office and speaking to him directly I once more repeated the magic words telling him I was a Peace Corps volunteer assigned to Zamboanga to establish an in-service training center and, until we constructed a building, I needed a place to live.

I asked him if it would be permissible for me to sleep in the tree house in Pasonanca Park until more appropriate housing was available. The Mayor explained that the tree house was a tourist attraction, but he would happily make an exception for the "US Peace Corpse." The tree house had all the amenities of a small motel room and it became my unofficial residence for the next several weeks.

The next order of business was to engage an architect to design the Center and a residence for Larry Fuchs and his family. Luckily that turned out to be a cinch because in 1962 there was only one architect in all of "metropolitan" Zamboanga.

The architect was quite an amenable gentleman who quickly managed to do two things at once. He had a good sense of what we required and he happily realized he was about to contract himself out to the Peace Corps and the very wealthy United States government. Clearly, here was a man who would have no trouble chewing gum and walking to the bank at the same time.

The site selected for the Center and the Fuchs residence was a working coconut grove of approximately five hectares on a lovely beachfront property in the barrio of Ayala some twenty minutes from the Peace Corps office in downtown Zamboanga.

The architect informed me that there were more than forty people who had an economic interest in that coconut grove and some monetary arrangement would have to be made with all of them. Given the constraints of time, the necessity to get the Center and the Fuchs residence quickly built and the considerable language barrier, there was no way I could handle that problem so I simply suggested to the architect that he handle the negotiations.

So here was the deal: The architect was going to design two buildings, negotiate the use of some prime beachfront property with a large group of Filipinos and handle the construction project all in the space of five weeks. It took less than fifteen minutes to come to an agreement for the cost of the entire project.

At his office several days later he showed me the plans for the Center and the Fuchs residence. It was remarkable. His design for the Center was near perfect needing only the most minor changes. He had designed a nipa roofed building of perhaps four thousand square feet with sleeping accommodations for about twenty-five people, set back on a small rise fifty meters from the shoreline. The whole project from start to finish took less than five weeks. Upon seeing the place several months later, Sylvia Boecker dubbed it "the largest nipa construction in the whole world."

When the architect sat down with me to settle up, he handed me a bill for quadruple the agreed upon costs. I smiled, realizing this was just his way of taking a shot at the mother lode. I knew and he knew that the costs were outrageous and we quickly came to a reasonable settlement.

There had been no lawyers, no written agreement, no signing of papers, no accounting of the monetary arrangements with the many owners of the coconut grove, no building permits, and no electrical inspections. We had simply come to an agreement and shook hands on the deal.

Amazing—and only in the Philippines!

As with most volunteers in the Philippines, I met more than my fair share of interesting, even remarkable Filipinos, but in the nineteen months I spent there the most remarkable person I came to know was an illiterate Filipino Muslim man of indeterminate age named Ricardo Cruz.

I first came upon Ricardo when I was visiting the building site where he was a laborer working as part of the construction crew. He was an arresting character, a few inches shy of six feet, lean and hard with a body taut as a suspension cable. He moved with an easy grace and wore a perpetual smile. I knew that once the Center was up and running we would need to hire someone to handle the many chores that would arise out of such a large and busy place so I offered Ricardo a full-time job and we entered into a yearlong relationship that was, to say the least, fascinating.

Ricardo became friendly with me and Jenifer Grant and soon it became clear that whenever we roamed any distance from Ayala more often than not he would come along. In his own quiet way there was no doubt he was being protective and looking out for us. He never voiced any concerns, and personally I never gave it much thought until one day when Jenifer, Becky Johnston, Ricardo and I were eating lunch in a small cafe near the docks of Zamboanga.

While we were eating, three young men in their early twenties came in, nodded a greeting to Ricardo and took a table not far from where we were seated. Although Jenifer and Becky were oblivious, it soon became clear that these guys were leering at them and making whispered comments among themselves.

In a few moments, Ricardo got out of his chair and walked over to their table. As far as I could tell, he evidenced no anger nor any emotion at all as one of the men got up and, in a gesture of respect, reached out to shake hands. Ricardo took the man's hand and with a look meaner than cat shit on a doorknob, he began speaking softly while gripping the hand with increasing force until the man's face was contorted in pain. I have no idea what he said, but by the time Ricardo sat down the three men were already out the door. It happened so smoothly that Jenifer and Becky never noticed it at all. It was immediately clear to me that Ricardo was not a man to be fooled with.

Some months later a group of volunteers were sitting around drinking iced tea and conversing and the subject turned to the kind of food we missed in the Philippines. One person opted for a New York kosher pastrami sandwich, another for some sweet Kansas corn and so it went until I turned to Ricardo who was quietly sitting by and asked him what was his favorite meal. Ricardo paused for a moment and said, "Ah—a sixteen-year-old Japanese boy."

For a moment it felt like all the air had been sucked out of the room. There we were, a half dozen Peace Corps volunteers absolutely gob-smacked while Ricardo, in a state of complete equipoise and cooler than James Dean, sat unaffected by the enormity of what he had just said.

He put his right hand on his upper left arm and said, "Here, Jerry, is very good." And then pointing to his thigh he said, "and here, too, but we can not do that any more."

And then, Ricardo explained how it came to pass that he and several of his teen-age friends had come to kill and cannibalize a young Japanese soldier.

During the war, just a few miles from Ayala, the Japanese had a small airbase that was patrolled day and night by the soldiers. One night a good friend of Ricardo's was in the wrong place at the wrong time and was shot dead by a Japanese sentry.

The death of the boy by a Japanese soldier saddened and enraged the boy's friends and one night they met to discuss a proper means of retribution. After some discussion, it was decided that the most degrading thing they could do was to kill and cannibalize a Japanese soldier. And so they did.

Thus ends the legend of Ricardo Cruz.

The day before I left Ayala I went for a run along the shoreline about three quarters of a mile north and then back to the Center. I paused for a moment and looking both ways, all I could see was pristine beach and coconut groves. The only sound was the water gently creaming up the shoreline and the natural sounds of birds in the trees, and I thought this was the closest I would ever come to heaven.

The Ayala I left in 1963 was a sleepy little tropical barrio set amongst coconut groves with no schools, no paved roads, and no electricity. It was a place completely unrecognizable today.

"If visited today, Ayala is a thriving community of seventeen thousand people with a police station, fire department, Zamboanga City Hall extension, four canning factories, the Ayala National High School, a grade school with an enrollment of twenty-five hundred students, well lit roads, and a supermarket named Dreamville." Zamboanga City website

I love the Philippines, and I loved the Filipinos, and I feel blessed to have been in the Peace Corps—in the Philippines—in the beginning.

Jerry Poznak was born and raised in Newark, New Jersey. After an extended stay, he graduated from Weequahic High School in 1951. He joined the army in 1952 and following airborne training at Fort Campbell, Kentucky, he spent five months in Korea and a year in Japan with an armored field artillery battalion. He graduated from Fairleigh Dickinson University in 1958, spent two years working in construction and skiing in Stowe, Vermont and Kitzbuhel, Austria. He taught seventh and eighth grades in Tamworth, New Hampshire and joined the Peace Corps in October, 1961. Following the Peace Corps, he received a Master of Arts degree from Harvard's Graduate School of Education in 1965. He spent several years teaching senior high school English in Sudbury, Massachusetts and Northbridge, California. He directed the Northeastern University Upward Bound Program from 1970 to 1975, followed by four years as the Assistant Director of the Roxbury-Harvard School Program at Harvard University. He is retired and living in Watertown, Massachusetts.

Eliot Putnam
A Guest in Another Culture

Important Memories and Critical Experiences

My most lasting personal memory has nothing to do with Peace Corps service, except of course that it made it all possible. It is of standing under a hot sun in a dusty market place in Ibajay in Aklan Province, asking fellow volunteer Jan Everett not to wait until we got back to the U.S. to get married, as we had been planning in an unorganized sort of way, but to do it there and then. The idea of starting life together as PCVs (and of cutting out the hours-long, muddy, bone-jarring weekend bus rides from my town of Balete to Ibajay) was too enticing.

Happily, she said yes. Not long after, we presented ourselves to the town clerk of Kalibo, the capital of Aklan, to get legal certification to wed. I remember he was wearing a dirty t-shirt and was so nervous his hand shook as he signed our authorization, but not before consulting a letter from my father approving the union and attesting to the fact that, baby face notwithstanding, I was indeed over 21. We were married in Manila on a sweltering December day in 1962, and moved into my little house in the Balete town square together, immediately becoming part of the local community in a way that PCV single sex households never could.

I have always said that one of the most important lessons Peace Corps taught me was the meaning of culture and cultural sensitivity. My most painful memory is of a time that I let my western impatience get in the way of that learning process. Late one Saturday evening, shortly after we moved into our house as a married couple, we were trying to go to sleep when a party in the town hall across the square got out of hand. There was loud music and lots of carousing, clearly fuelled by large quantities of *tuba*, the potent local palm wine, which led to noisy bickering among a group of young studs. Determined to have our peace and, I suspect, show off a bit to my new wife, I marched across the square and asked, nay demanded, that the locals tone it down.

Needless to say, my intercession was out of line and entirely unappreciated, subsequent explanations and apologies notwithstanding. I got yelled at by the partygoers as an arrogant, insensitive gringo, and on several occasions in the ensuing days stones were lobbed at our house. Soon enough the furor passed, but the event was a sobering reminder to me that there are lines that must not be crossed and sensitivities that must be respected when a guest in another culture, even one as cloyingly pro-American as was the Philippines in those days.

Motivation

When I learned of the Peace Corps in the spring of 1961 I was a naive college student nearing the end of senior year, largely clueless about the future, except that I knew I had no stomach for graduate school. I'd like to say I was full of altruistic yearnings to do "good things", but basically I was looking for adventure. To this end I had applied and been accepted for naval flight training in Pensacola, Florida when the chance to apply for this other unexpected, untried, but undeniably exciting opportunity came along.

In the end, the choice between two such different types of adventure was not hard. If there was a tipping point it came when my father, a great admirer of the military although (and perhaps because) he had never been able to serve, nonetheless allowed as how he thought the Peace Corps made a lot more sense for me than the Navy. When I think that, had I made another decision, I might have ended up dropping bombs on Viet Nam, I thank God for his wisdom and this opportunity.

But first I wanted the summer in which to hang out, earn a little money, and revel in the prospect of no school in the fall for the first time in my life. When a Peace Corps telegram arrived in June of 1961, inviting me to training for Philippines Group I that would start almost immediately, I asked if they could call me later. Thinking back on the possibility that they could have thrown my name in a dead file at that point, I wonder that I could have been so cavalier. As I said, I was naïve. Probably still am. But as luck would have it, they did send another cable later that summer inviting me to Penn State University to train for Philippines II. I had wanted adventure, and I got it. I was to be sent about as far away from hearth and home as was possible, and asked to make a job there out of whole cloth. And in the process I was to meet and marry my life partner, who had similarly turned down Group I and been accepted for Group II. As the old saying goes, it is far better to be lucky than good!

The Philippines

When invited to be a PCV in the Philippines I knew the country consisted of a lot of islands a long way off, and had read about Bataan and the role (often wildly mythologized) of General MacArthur in liberating the country in World War II. That was about it. Training at Penn State gave us grounding in the country's history and culture, an introduction to our intended role as "teachers' aides" in primary school English and science instruction, and a primer in the importance of S.I.R., or "smooth interpersonal relationships", to successful entry into a new culture. But I was quite unprepared for the all-embracing warmth of our welcome when our Pan Am 707 landed in Manila a couple of days after New Year's Day 1962, after a two-day trip across the Pacific via Honolulu and Guam.

Emerging from the plane into the thick, moist tropical air, our band of Group II PCVs was greeted by a long receiving line of Filipinos (presumably politicians and other dignitaries) who gave us sweaty handshakes while earnestly saying "welcome home." I remember thinking that seemed a bit much from people I had never met in a place I had never been. But subsequent experience showed that it was very much in keeping with Filipinos' adoration at the time of all things American, in a country only 15 years removed from the war, where a portrait of General MacArthur (and sometimes John F. Kennedy) hung beside those of Jesus and national hero Jose Rizal in many a Filipino household. Most volunteers would say that adoration was both our blessing and our curse. It meant we could basically do no wrong, at least in our work, but also that we could expect little objective analysis by our hosts of our performance, except when we made egregious cultural missteps (see above).

After further training in Los Baños, Group II was sent to the island of Panay, in the Central Visayan Islands. With fellow volunteer Jerry Poznak I was assigned to the village of Balete in the Province of Aklan. I remember all too well our flight down from Manila to Kalibo, the capital of Aklan, on an aging Philippine Airlines DC-3, because the zipper on my pants broke, with no opportunity to make repairs. It made me feel and look at far less than my best at this most pivotal life moment, as we faced another effusive airport welcome.

Balete was, and probably still is, a quiet village in a rice-growing community on the rutted "national road" between Kalibo and Panay City to the south. The town had constructed a little house for us on the site of a former building in the central square, with a bamboo frame, plywood walls, and a thick nipa roof, and assigned us a houseboy—Sam Bantigue, whom we quickly named "Sam the man"—to cook for us. From the beginning, the house became a magnet for kids, drawn by our novelty, our open door, and by the various "things" with which Peace Corps had wisely equipped us—games, a radio, a trunk full of books. Our Peace Corps medical kit was also a magnet, and many was the cut, scrape and worse that we tended over time, since such supplies were hard to come by locally.

It quickly became apparent that Mr. Cortes, the Superintendent of Schools, and the principals and teachers of the rural schools in and around Balete to which we were assigned, were not fully clear as to our roles. "Teachers' aides" was a foreign concept to them, and very much a work in progress for us as well. They tended to try to get us to take over their classes, while we tried equally hard to explain that we were there to supplement, rather than replace, what they were doing in the teaching of English and Science. Each volunteer, in his or her own way, eventually worked out an accommodation, by helping with lesson plans, doing special projects, etc. I taught a little, helped a lot, but all in all don't think I made much of an impression on the educational process in the Balete schools. But I made wonderful friends among both teachers and students, and I think we all enjoyed the ongoing process of trying to figure out what the other was all about, personally, culturally and professionally.

As with many volunteers, we also looked around for other projects with which we could contribute to the community. Early on, contemplating the scrawny native chickens that made their living in the streets, we decided to show the community how to raise fat, good eating birds. We had a coop constructed from bamboo next to the house, bought a bunch of pedigreed, newly hatched chicks, and nursed them along with store-bought grain. They got fat and tasty, all right. They also developed rashes and warts and other afflictions such that people didn't want anything to do with them! We soon went back to eating the hardy, ubiquitous local fowl, and actually learned to appreciate their sinewy taste.

I have so many memories of the time in Balete: the lush, comforting sound of rain on a nipa roof; the timeless rituals of planting, tending and harvesting rice going on beside the road as I walked to school; the sight of school children running through the rain holding huge banana leaves over their heads as umbrellas; the lumbering grace of carabao, their haunches crusted with mud as they worked the fields (and the toughness of carabao meat when passed off as beef); San Miguel beer, cooled, if we were lucky, by some ice cubes from the *sari sari* store across the square; Pilipino English; bathing with a jerry-can of sulfurous water from the well behind our house; bus rides sharing a wooden bench seat with chickens or a goat, or being sprayed with betel juice when someone spit out the window; stories of the war, still so vivid and painful, from our neighbors; the hypnotic emerald green of new rice plants.

Above all I remember and will always be grateful for the warmth and hospitality of the townsfolk of Balete. They didn't always know what to make of us, but they seemed to genuinely enjoy our presence. And, as I said, when Jan and I lived there as a couple, our acceptance as normal members of a community was palpable. People were always dropping by to chat, and to drop off gifts of mangoes or star apples or those delicious, fat little local bananas, with paper thin skins, that would melt in your mouth. And they would inquire on an almost daily basis if we were yet "in the pamily way" (Filipino English makes an "f" sound like a "p"), expressing incredulity when we said not yet. Indeed, one neighbor took me aside and suggested, in a fatherly way, that "perhaps we did not know how!"

A couple of those visits were especially memorable. On one occasion the local priest came to call, and we were sitting with him having refreshment when our mongrel dogs, a male and a female, became stuck together *in flagrante* under the table. The other was from a family from a distant village whom we had helped with a medical emergency, bringing us a thank you gift of a tiny palm civet cat. "Sherwood" became our delightful companion, mashing bananas with his little paws, hanging over our heads on our mosquito net at night, sipping San Miguel and retiring to the rafters to sleep off his hangover. We loved him so much we couldn't imagine leaving him behind when we started home. We were going to travel the other way around the world, and so sent him to my mother in Boston via Pan Am Clipper Cargo. Not the most thoughtful thing we've ever done, but she was a good sport about it until he got a bit too "jungley" and started biting ankles, when she gave him to the zoo.

The Effect of the Peace Corps Experience

I will always believe that Peace Corps service in the Philippines had a far more demonstrable impact on me and my life than did any of my efforts on Philippine society. That this could be true is, to me, part of the beauty of the whole Peace Corps idea. The experience introduced me to the concept and reality of "culture," how one invariably differs from another, and the respect one must give to those differences if one has any hope of acceptance. Whereas one could not have chosen a more welcoming culture in which to spend two years, I proved that it was possible to make missteps. I think the lessons learned from them made me a more considerate person and have served me well since.

Another thing that immersion in another society for an extended period of time made possible was the chance to take an objective look at my own country and culture. It's no secret that we Americans can be awfully insular and self-satisfied, and I found it valuable to be able to recognize and contemplate our strengths and our imperfections from afar, through the eyes of others. One particularly searing realization was of the obscene amounts of everything we consume in this country, and of the obscene amounts of what we consume we waste. For a long time after coming home—maybe even to this day—when I saw something as prosaic as a cardboard box being thrown away or burned I would think of all of the uses to which people in Balete would have put that box, over and over.

Finally, the Peace Corps experience set me on a career course in international development that I almost certainly would never have otherwise contemplated. When we returned to the States in 1963 we found ourselves still smitten by the international bug, and lived abroad again for most of the '60s, first in Haiti and then Tunisia, where I worked for CARE. My work since has been in international public health, for the last 15 years as a consultant, traveling widely, using and building on those lessons I learned so long ago.

While I feel that I was by far the greatest beneficiary of this experience, I don't mean to suggest that I think I left no impression. We made many good friends in the Philippines, friends with whom we worked and played and talked and laughed. To them, I hope and think I gave an impression of openness and interest in their lives and country. Many were, I think, sad when we departed, and made an effort to keep in touch and let us know what was going on in Balete. Filipinos wear their hearts on their sleeves, which leads them to be open about anything and everything. In this vein, one of our friends took it on herself to write us some months after we had left to tell us that one of our dogs, whom we had left with another family, had been pickled and eaten with beer by local *borrachos*!

Personally I kept in touch for many years with Mr. Cortes, the School Superintendent and my best Balete friend. We would exchange long, soulful letters every Christmas (Filipinos do soulful very well), reliving those days and pretending that we might renew them at some point. Eventually his letters stopped, which I assume meant that he had died, leaving me with the memory of a wonderfully and typically kind man with whom I shared two memorable years.

Other Reflections

The Peace Corps and the PCV experience changed my life. They opened my eyes to the world, set me on a career path, and, by far best of all, brought me to my life partner. I have been back to the Philippines a few times since on consulting jobs, but never to Balete. It remains in my mind somewhere between dream and reality, quiet and hot under the tropical sun. I can see rice drying on woven mats by the side of the road. I can hear the click of tiles as our neighbors engage in spirited midday games of *MahJongg*. I can taste the fried rice and Rocky Road ice cream at our favorite hangouts in Kalibo. And I can recall with great clarity the uniquely Philippine warmth of the hospitality that was extended to me throughout my time as a volunteer.

Since 1971, after several post-Peace Corps years spent living and working abroad, Eliot and his wife Jan have lived in a comfortable brown shingle house in Wellesley, Massachusetts. In it they raised four children, two who themselves became PCVs (as did Eliot's brother), and to it they now welcome, whenever possible, seven grandchildren. For the past thirty years Eliot has pursued a career in international public health, first working for health-related NGOs, notably Pathfinder International, more recently as a consultant specializing in assessing, evaluating or writing about primary health care programs, primarily in Africa. Eliot's local involvements have included many years as a Little League coach and administrator, current service as board member of a local hospice and of an agency specializing in foster care, and active volunteer involvement with the Wellesley Food Pantry. Thanks to Jan's previous employment at Wellesley College they make almost daily pilgrimages to work out in the college gym, when they are not spending time in Maine or escaping to wild places such as northern Alaska.

(The first photo shows Eliot with a Filipino child; the second shows him with his wife Jan Everett Putnam hiking in Yellowstone Park.)

Janet Everett Putman
Just What the Doctor Ordered

I was working in New York for CBS Television when the idea of the Peace Corps was proposed. Just what the doctor ordered, I thought. I'd taken the Foreign Service exam, but it was very clear in those days that women were not strong candidates for placement overseas. The assumption was that we would last only a few years, then drop out to become wives and mothers. And of course wives and mothers couldn't be uprooted every two years and sent to new assignments. So the Peace Corps sounded just right. I applied immediately, took the test with a vicious hangover on a Saturday morning in downtown Manhattan, and was amazed when I got the telegram offering me service in the Philippines Group I. Philippines? I didn't ask for the Philippines. I wanted Africa! So I took a chance and responded that I wasn't available at the moment—I was, I said, involved in a television show I couldn't abandon—but that I'd welcome another opportunity. A few weeks later I got the second telegram: "Congratulations you've been chosen for Peace Corps service in the Philippines." Okay, I thought. I guess that's it. Philippines it is.

I went looking for adventure, really honestly wanting to be of service in the world and eager to combat the disastrous image of *The Ugly American*. Imagine the hubris! What I found was that there was an abundance of caring, dedicated people already working in the Philippines—teachers and artists and musicians and USAID workers, politicians and town officials and school principals and shopkeepers and priests and parents—a whole, rich community that graciously, unselfishly welcomed us as neighbors, overlooking or excusing our cultural blunders and genuinely liking us for ourselves as well as for the fact that we came from that grand, exalted land called "States."

I learned humility in the Philippines—not a trait I'd particularly treasured before then. "Teaching" alongside Mrs. Salador, I got, right away, how much she knew and how little my U.S. education and Peace Corps training had to offer the students in her class. The only thing I offered was the nerve to break open the glass case that contained a microscope she had received from central headquarters some years before and put it to use in the classroom. We giggled as we loaded the slides and peered through the eyepiece.

In the village, we learned to make use of everything. When we got letters from Peace Corps headquarters, we turned the pages over and wrote lesson plans or made maps or wrote poetry. The biggest culture shock I had, on returning to the US, was to walk down the aisle of any store, viewing what felt to me to be an obscene overabundance. It was way too much. Just as we returned to the US, my sister got married and my Dad went out behind the garage every night to burn the beautiful white boxes all the gifts came in each day. I'll never forget how that made me feel.

Funny little vignettes still make me laugh out loud remembering how Lourdes saved Sylvia, Joan, Barbara and me from boiling water in a chamber pot; how we ordered a Thanksgiving turkey from a local farmer to feed twenty visiting PCVs, only to receive a tiny, eight-pound bird stuffed with cocktail hotdogs; and how our dear dogs "stuck" together under the dining room table when the priest came to visit.

Gosh it was fun.

As PCVs, we did not teach as much as we learned. And the lesson I hold dearest is that simplicity rules. I learned how to discriminate between wants and needs—a lesson so well learned that our children grew quite tired while they were growing up of being asked to consider how each new purchase, trip or acquisition fit into that scale. I came back to the U.S. from the Philippines with a patience and contentedness I never had before. That hasn't stopped me, in my life, from railing against wrong and injustice, but it has given me a sense of balance and understanding I don't think I would have had otherwise. I can actually see another point of view and honor (if not agree with) it.

Peace Corps service started my husband Eliot and me on a life-long commitment to not-for-profit adventure. Our first jobs on returning to the U.S. were with the James Weldon Johnson Community Center in East Harlem. It was there that we heard, in a room full of African American colleagues, that John F. Kennedy had been shot in Dallas. The first, doubly-horrifying rumors suggested that he was shot by a black man. If anything could have made that day worse, that was it. Our friends were devastated. We all were. Eliot and I, like so many other idealistic young people, felt intimately connected to Kennedy. He was our personal President. We had responded to his call to "Ask not." He'd given us the opportunity of a lifetime—one that had changed us forever. And we were deeply grateful.

After New York, we went to Haiti where Eliot worked for CARE and I taught at the American School, then Tunisia for another CARE assignment. In 1968 we were a happy family of five with two sons and a daughter and lots of good, international friends. Then Martin Luther King Jr. and Bobby Kennedy were shot and we thought, "What are we doing here outside the US, we need to go home and work there," once again believing that we had an obligation to try and change things for the better.

We have been blessed, throughout our life, with the opportunity to do work we believe in. We know it, we celebrate it and we never take it for granted. Eliot has been involved in family planning and international health for more than 40 years and I've worked on increasing opportunities for women at the Wellesley College Centers for Research on Women and the National Museum of Women in the Arts. In the 70s we co-chaired the Hunger Action Team of the Episcopal Diocese of Massachusetts and have served on a number of national and local non-profit boards. A rite of passage for all four of our children as they grew up was trekking the 20-mile Boston Walk for Hunger.

Finally, and most importantly, it was in the Peace Corps that I met Eliot, the person I still, after all these years, admire more than anyone I've ever met. We came from different backgrounds and parts of the U.S. to train and travel and teach together. Our shared commitment and sense of mission has made our life rich and meaningful. I wouldn't trade a minute of it.

Jan Putnam lives with her husband Eliot (also Peace Corps Philippines Group II) in Wellesley, Massachusetts. After Peace Corps service, she worked at a community center in New York City, taught at the American School in Haiti, lived in Tunisia, co-chaired the Hunger Action Team of the Episcopal Diocese of Massachusetts, and directed development efforts at the Wellesley College Centers for Research on Women and the National Museum of Women in the Arts in Washington D.C. She has served on a number of boards including Leadership Greater Washington, National Campfire Boys and Girls, Women's Review of Books, Ford Hall Forum, National Women's History Project, Open Door Housing, and Project Bread/The Walk for Hunger . Jan and Eliot spend their summers in Maine and travel as often as possible to the Brooks Range in Alaska. They have four children (two of whom have also served in the Peace Corps) and seven grandchildren.

(The first photo shows Jan to the left of fellow volunteer Barbara Litrop in Ibajay, Aklan in 1962; the second shows Jan recently with husband Eliot.)

Nick Royal
The Peace Corps & Me

Motivation

I can remember very clearly my motivation for applying to the Peace Corps, and how I followed through with it. I had been in Venezuela from 1959 to 1960 as a YMCA staff member, and when I came home, I wanted to spend more time abroad for both the cross-cultural learning experience, and to continue to improve my Spanish speaking ability. After the YMCA work, I did not want to get drafted, and so joined a six-month Medics Training program in the Army. I was at Fort Sam Houston in San Antonio, almost done with my active duty, when the formation of the Peace Corps was announced.

I took the test in San Antonio, and was offered a post in the Philippines—had to look that country up on the map! I asked Peace Corps Washington about going to Latin America, and was told that a post there would open up in maybe eight or nine months. I didn't want to wait around, and thought, "Well, the Spanish were in the Philippines for 400 years, so Spanish must be spoken there." False assumption, but off I went to the Philippines, hoping I could use my Spanish.

What might I have done if I had not joined the Peace Corps? I am not sure, but the Peace Corps at that time seemed exactly like the right thing for me.

Our Community and the Impact We Had on It and It Had on Us

My housemate, David Christenson (Chris), and I were assigned to the small town of Belison, on the island of Panay in the central part of the Philippines. In the early 1960s, Belison was quite rural with no electricity and only one phone located in the town hall that worked from time to time. (When I went back to Belison in 1993 with my family, there was electricity and some TV and videos were available.)

I think the impact that Chris and I had on the town was to add some excitement to a fairly quiet community as Americans with different ways. We carried out two summer projects which I thought were useful for the community. The first summer we worked with some local teachers and ran a summer prep program for students going on to high school the coming fall, in San Jose, the larger town near us. The second summer, with staff from a teachers' college not close to Belison, we ran a summer school offering courses to local teachers.

I look back with very good feelings about being able to spend close to two years in Belison. It was such a different world for me, and I learned a lot from being there. I was sorry though, that I never was very good at the local dialect, Kiniraya, nor did I follow through with a research project collecting songs from the region. It wasn't until I was working at Merrill College assisting students to design projects related to their international studies that I really had a sense of what I might have done with that music interest of mine. I did come away with a few small reels of tape—songs I had recorded.

Some Final Thoughts

One memory I have had is how young we were when we went to the Philippines to be teachers' aides. We were also somewhat judgmental about what we were seeing. We noticed quite quickly the corruption we saw, or at least it was corruption to us. It wasn't until we got back home and started thinking about things in our country related to our Peace Corps experiences, that we could see corruption and problems here.

When I asked a fellow Peace Corps friend of mine if he was going to write something, he said he hoped to get around to it, and he would focus on the personal side of the experience. In many ways most of what we were experiencing was largely personal. For example, getting to know and learn from my housemate, David Christenson, was very important to me. He and I would spend hours talking about what we were trying to do and what we were learning; and I profited from his love of art and poetry.

As with many other Peace Corps volunteers who were in the Philippines, I have a fondness for Filipinos when Ruth and I meet them. I also have a small collection of friends from Groups II and III who are my close friends. That closeness comes from having shared special experiences with them in the Philippines.

Although Ruth and I didn't meet in the Philippines, we were there at the same time, and over the years we have shared many stories and conversations related to our Peace Corps experiences and our time with Filipinos and fellow volunteers. This has been important to me.

Nick Royal has been married to Ruth Kesselring Royal since 1965. Ruth was in Peace Corps Philippines Group III, though they never met in the Philippines. They have two adult children, Suzy, living in Berlin, Germany and married to Guenther Primig, and David in Seaside, California, nearby, married to Aparna Sreenivasan. David and Aparna's four-year-old son, Ravi, takes up some of their time, and lots of their thoughts. After Peace Corps service, Ruth and Nick both entered the University of Chicago's MAT in education program. In 1966, they helped to start a Project Upward Bound program in Milwaukee for low income high school students who demonstrated college potential. They were invited to join the staff by Professor Larry Howard, who had been Nick's Peace Corps staff leader in the Philippines. Upward Bound was not only a learning experience for the students in the program, but also for the staff. In the summer of 1969, Nick and Ruth moved to Santa Cruz, California. Nick directed the Merrill College Field Program for

Experiential Learning, at the University of California, Santa Cruz, which was then in its second year. This was an internship program placing students in local non profit agencies and public schools, assisting some students to go abroad for their field work. Nick ran the Merrill Field Program until budget cuts at the University ended the program in 1993. Since retiring from UC-Santa Cruz, Nick has devoted his time to choral singing, learned to read music for mandolin; and along with a friend, played music for seniors and children.

(The first photo shows Nick with school principal, Mrs. Rosario Pacete in 1963; the second shows Nick with his grandson Ravi in 2009.)

Frances McDonald Santos de Dios
Memories of Rural Life on Panay

My first eighteen years were spent growing up a mile outside a small town of 1500 near Yosemite. In January 1961 I graduated from the University of California–Berkeley and went to work for University Extension. In early summer that year, I applied and was accepted to the Peace Corps.

When I left for Penn State to train it was my second trip out of California. I flew from San Francisco to Chicago and then to Pennsylvania. I remember a very rough flight to Black Moshannon Airport near Penn State.

During-training memories—orienteering in the Nittany Mountains (it was so beautiful in the fall); walking across campus to the dining hall with new fallen snow on the ground; at least twenty vaccination shots and playing volleyball after! Before Thanksgiving I wrote my Mom for her bread dressing recipe. I have no recollection of how I got the groceries to make this dressing. I put the stopper in the kitchen sink in the Graduate Student apartment and mixed up the dressing hoping the stopper would not come out. I roasted a turkey to take to our Thanksgiving dinner. It was in a stone building in the woods as I recall. The faculty brought food and we had a lovely dinner. Some of the kids were homesick as it was their first Thanksgiving away.

We split up after training and reassembled in San Francisco on January 1, 1962. There had been 65 of us in training but now there were 55 going overseas. We crossed the dateline and missed January 2, 1962 arriving on January 3, 1962. I remember seeing a very green patchwork below the Pan Am jet before we landed in Manila.

The next few days were a blur—swimming at the Balara Filters where one of our group lost a contact lens. We had orientation and then went to the University of the Philippines at Los Baños. We were hot and the local girls were wearing sweaters! I remember poinsettias as high as the houses, very friendly people and wonderful food. We were sent to Masbate to visit the Peace Corps Philippines I group before we were sent to our assigned area.

The 55 in our group were sent to the island of Panay in the Visayas. Our household of four had a minor misfortune. The Peace Corps rented the house we used from the ex-mayor—a definite mistake! We were moved from Panitan to Dumalog.

Memories of rural life on Panay—no electricity, no running water, a rice *bodega* in the house, a *sari-sari* store with Vienna sausage, Spam and little else. There was a market early on Sunday morning. One of my roommates grew up on a farm in Virginia—thank heavens! Once in a while we would buy live chickens and stake them until we needed them. Once they got loose and the "*Canas*" (us) chased them down. After all, it was dinner. I rode a carabao and carried water in a five-gallon gasoline container.

I remember riding a bike to school and the faces of the kids—forever I will remember the faces. Philippine schools seemed to take every Philippine, American and Catholic holiday. There was a wide age range in each class as kids stayed out of school to help plant or whatever else was needed. Rain came down in sheets. I also remember the postman coming to our house reading our mail as he came down the street.

One time we invited the whole group on Panay to come to our place in the province of Capiz. About 15 came and it must have been scandalous to the locals—boys and girls sleeping all over the place in one house! I have no idea how we fed them. One day we spent the entire day making *lumpia* wrappers and their filling. We had about a dozen *lumpias* to show for our work!

In April, three of us were sent to the Philippine Normal School in Zamboanga to work for the summer. We flew from Iloilo to Bacolod and on to Cebu. There we stayed overnight and left early the next morning for Zamboanga. Quite by accident in Bacolod on that Good Friday, April 13, 1962, I met Captain Nicanor Cano Santos de Dios, a Philippine Airlines pilot. He became my friend, companion and husband of 42 years.

American cigarettes on which taxes had not been paid had a blue seal, a term often used to refer to Americans. When Susan Thompson, Joyce Edwards (who is about 6 feet tall) and I were walking down the street in Zamboanga we passed three boys. One of them said, referring to Joyce, "blue seal, king-size!" We had a good laugh.

We rubbed elbows with everyone from wonderful local people to Ambassador Stevenson to Eugenio Lopez, Jr. Mr. Lopez was the nephew of Fernando Lopez who served as Vice President of the country under both President Quirino and President Marcos for a time. The Lopez family owned TV and radio stations. They also owned land and the *Manila Chronicle*. It was all confiscated under Marcos. Eugenio Lopez, Jr. was thrown in jail primarily because he was on the wrong side of the political fence. He eventually escaped from jail and went to Hong Kong and the United States. He was away from his family for approximately 17 years. I visited his wife in Manila while he was jailed. One night I caught a piece on the news regarding his return to Manila. I wrote him to tell him how glad I was he was home. Despite all he had to do he wrote a very nice letter back to this PCV who stayed in his home while in Manila. He said he was busy (an understatement) but do stop by next time I was in the country!

My memories include wonderful food and an endless variety of fruit. I remember warm Cokes and pineapple juice. After flying on Philippine Airlines quite a bit I learned not to like pineapple juice!

I have been asked many times if I would join the Peace Corps again. My answer has always been, "In a minute."

Mostly, I remember the people and their kindness, both in the provinces and later in my very large in-law family in and around Marikina, Quezon City and Manila. I have been back to the Philippines many times and enjoyed sharing it with our two daughters. I have always said that we as Peace Corps volunteers probably gained more from the experience than the students we taught!

Frances has lived at one time or another in Hawaii, the Philippines, Japan, California, Florida, Pennsylvania, New Hampshire, back to California and finally Houston, Texas where she lives today. She has two daughters—Anna Lisa Santos de Dios, age 41, who lives in Arlington, Virginia and Amy Santos de Dios Goldstein, age 37, who lives in Houston with her husband and family. Frances has two grandchildren—Ethan, age 4, and Zoe, age 4 months at this writing (July 2010). She participates in water aerobics at the "Y", travels to see friends and family and happily does a lot of babysitting. She works on the family tree when time permits and has 2,200 names on the branches so far.

(The second photo shows Frances with daughter Amy and grandson Ethan.)

John Schweitzer
Did My Peace Corps Experience Make a Difference?

In volunteering for the Peace Corps I had several motives. First of all, I was responding to President Kennedy's challenge to "Ask not…" I wanted to serve my country and my fellow citizens of the world, and additionally I thought that it would be the adventure of a lifetime for me. Flying across the Pacific Ocean in early January, 1962 with my fellow volunteers of Philippines II, I pondered these motives and wondered what would be the impact of my service on me, on my country, and on the Philippines. Could a co-teacher of English and science in an elementary school in the Philippines really make a difference?

After completing our in-country training at the College of Agriculture in Los Baños, the members of Philippines II were anxious to learn where we would be assigned and who we would be living with. I was delighted to learn that I was assigned to the little town of Sapian, Capiz on Panay Island, and my housemate was to be Richard Lewis, an African American from Birmingham, Alabama. Although we came from very different backgrounds, we had become close friends during our training in the camp in Arecibo in Puerto Rico, at Penn State, and at Los Baños.

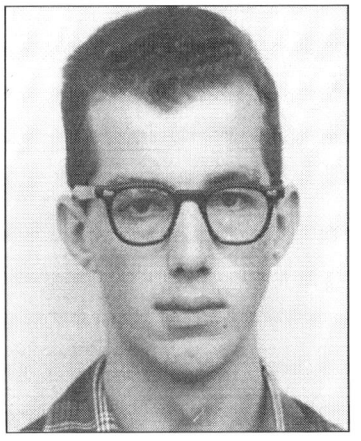

When we arrived in Sapian, we instantly attracted lots of attention from the townspeople who were not used to seeing outsiders. They were especially intrigued with Richard's dark skin (they affectionately called him "the burnt American"). Many Filipinos were amazed that a dark skinned black from Alabama and a white northerner from New York could be such good friends, considering the civil rights unrest and racial violence in the United States in the early sixties. I realized that in our little way we were improving the image of race relations in the U.S. As one of the few two volunteer households, Richard and I had to rely a great deal on each other. During many evenings of conversation as the kerosene lamp faded from brightness, Richard and I learned a great deal about each other and our very different backgrounds, and our friendship grew even closer. I realized that growing up in a white suburb had limited my understanding of the pervasiveness and harmful impact of racial discrimination. I began to realize that much work was needed to help heal the wounds that racism had inflicted on our society. As we were leaving the Philippines, Richard and I had a conversation about the things we had missed about life in the US, and the things we were *not* looking forward to. Richard said that he dreaded being addressed by the n-word epithet.

After traveling through Asia, the Soviet Union, and Europe, I arrived home in August, 1963, just in time to attend the March on Washington. Two weeks later I called Richard in Birmingham, Alabama to discuss the bombing of a church that had just killed four young black girls. In that conversation I asked Richard if he had been referred to by the n-word, and he said it had happened when he first landed back in the U.S. at Los Angeles airport. These events demonstrated to me how much work needed to be done in the area of race relations.

Twenty years later as a Fulbright grantee to Singapore, I was able to travel to Asia, and of course I took the opportunity to return to my little town of Sapian, Capiz in the Philippines. Flying into Roxas City, I again pondered whether my service had made a difference. I had written to the mayor and the school principal telling them that I was planning to visit. When my plane landed, to my surprise there was a car full of people waiting to welcome me and take me back to Sapian.

Arriving in Sapian, I was struck by how the town had changed. It retained its beauty and cleanliness, but there were signs of economic progress. Streets were paved, houses had electricity, there was a high school which the town hadn't had before, and the plaza had new statues and buildings, including a clinic and a day care center. I soon found out that some of this economic progress stemmed from the impact of Bruce French, a Peace Corps volunteer who came to Sapian some ten years after we were there. As an ocean biologist, he developed a new way of growing green mussels (*tahong*) in Sapian Bay, and now the town was exporting them to Manila. Bruce clearly had left an economic impact, but what was my legacy on the Filipinos of Sapian?

As a Catholic in the Philippines, I was asked to be godfather to many of the babies born while I was volunteering in Sapian. Twenty years later I would occasionally meet a young man or woman in the town who told me that I was their godparent. They knew who I was, but had I really made a difference in their lives? Still pondering my legacy one afternoon, I climbed the hill behind the town to visit the new high school. There I began to speak with a young teacher. As we were talking, I said, "Your English is so good. Your pronunciation and grammar are perfect." She replied, "Well, sir, you were my teacher." That was the point when I realized that, indeed, I had made a difference.

Looking back on the last fifty years of my life, I realize that my Peace Corps service has had direct and indirect effects on me, both personally and professionally. I began a life-long interest in addressing the evils of racism, and I was exposed to the use of social science research methods to answer important questions and to address critical issues. In addition to exposing me to racism, my Peace Corps experience introduced me to social science research methodology. During our service in the Philippines, Max Klass (a volunteer from Group I) and I became interested in the impact we were having on the Filipinos and were encouraged by the Peace Corps staff to conduct a study to try to document any impact that volunteers were having. Thinking that our greatest effect might be on the workers who lived with each Peace Corps household, we designed a study to measure various attitudes and expectations of workers in Peace Corps households compared to similar workers in non-Peace Corps households. The results of the study were unremarkable, but carrying out the research engendered in me a life-long interest in measurement and research design as part of the social science research process.

In my work, I have combined my concerns about racism and my interests in social science research by studying the impacts of racial segregation and using research to promote effective schools in low income and minority neighborhoods. I have been privileged to serve as a mentor or adviser to dozens of students of color. I am thankful that I have been able to play a small part in the progress we as a nation have made in addressing the race issue. I continue to work because I still enjoy using my knowledge of social science research methodology to effect change by studying critical societal issues of equity and justice. A particular area of concern is promoting a sense of community and pro-social behaviors in urban neighborhoods. My life has been full and rewarding. I have truly been blessed.

Following Peace Corps service, John earned an MA in psychology from Fordham University and a PhD in educational psychology from Michigan State University, where he has been a social science research professor for over 40 years. He has been married for 43 years to Liz, who was a city council member and mayor of East Lansing and served 30 years in Catholic campus ministry. Susan, their eldest, is conducting linguistics research and completing her doctorate at the Sorbonne in Paris. Daughter Ellen teaches high school in New York, is finishing her doctorate in economics, and is the mother of Louis, their six-month-old grandson. Their son, John, is a basketball coach in the Lansing area. John and Liz live in East Lansing, Michigan.

Martha Spencer
Double the Challenge

Many people wonder what the Peace Corps did for other countries when, more importantly, it is a matter of what it did for an immense number of young Americans who had experiences that would serve them for a lifetime. Being thrust into a diverse group of people with different backgrounds, though from one's own culture, can be enlightening. To then deal with the differences of one's own culture with fellow Peace Corps members, while living in the midst of a foreign culture can double the challenge.

One is caught up short when finding that the American way isn't always the best way. Other cultures established far longer than ours are not so easily adjusted to the rapid, results-oriented tendency of Americans. To observe a people accepting of circumstances readily intolerable to us was not easy to face. The diligent planning, so much a part of getting somewhere in the United States when you are a college graduate, does not dovetail well into the Eastern way of the 1960s which showed little sense of long term planning.

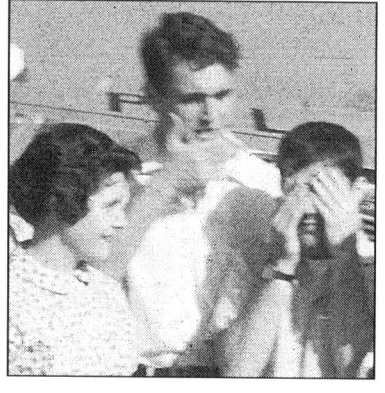

Having gone to the Philippines to be an educational aide, it was difficult to accept the fact that Filipinos only wanted to entertain us with *meriendas*, not have us do a lick of work. The training we were given to teach Filipino children how a doorbell worked seemed ludicrous in a barrio of nipa huts. There was always the lurking suspicion by teachers that we were going to replace them when teaching jobs were very "dear" in the Philippines in the 1960s.

I recently overheard a woman saying she was going to Manila on a vacation. I didn't dare say a word since I am sure the Manila I experienced will not be the one she will. I might have told her of the delicacies of *calamansi* juice, papayas and mangoes which are among the pleasant memories I hold of the Philippines along with the beautiful sunsets on the beach outside Rojas City in Capiz, Panay. But she will surely not go there.

Among the many humorous moments which were a part of this life-long learning experience were:

• Life in a nipa hut, definitely not substantial enough for the average American, where you could throw the dirty wash water through the floor
• No running water and paying five *centavos* for every Caltex can filled with water
• Being the only person in Group II who knew how to kill and dress a chicken
• Leaving town because the mayor and his henchmen had you on their blacklist
• Watching the perfect papaya ripening on the tree in your yard, only to find that it was considered community property and fair game for anyone who picked it
• The ubiquitous gecko that would land on your head, down your back or in your dinner, and he wasn't selling GEICO, nor was he as cute as the GEICO gecko

- Constantly being told the bus would be there in a few minutes when in fact it had already left
- The chorus of "'Cana, Cana" and "Ma-pa-oli" when you boarded the bus
- Trying to step across baskets of rice, chickens, vegetables as you found your place on the church pew style seat of a public bus
- The poor goat tied to the top of the bus tossed to and fro at the mercy of the bus driver
- The wild jeepney rides around Manila
- The war reparation train that chugged from Rojas City to Iloilo and poured sand on the tracks to brake
- Walking a muddy path across rice paddies to get to a barrio school and walking out of your shoes
- Teaching children how a door bell worked when they didn't even have doors on their nipa huts and by no means a door bell
- Eating off (Peace Corps supplied) Noritake china in the barrio and using knives (also Peace Corps supplied) that could only be sharpened at the factory
- The dinner table delicacy of canned margarine while dreaming of chocolate cake

After leaving the Peace Corps in 1962, Martha returned to her previous teaching position in Santa Clara, California. From 1964 to 1998, she was a teacher in Lafayette, California, where she taught fourth grade for ten years and junior high school English and history for twenty-four years. Her winters were spent skiing whenever possible, enjoying the wonderful Sierra snow as well as other beautiful parts of northern California such as Yosemite, Lake Tahoe and the Napa Valley. Her travels included Europe, the Soviet Union and Finland. She now lives back in Virginia, her native state, where she still has many family members. Martha has immersed herself in the history of Rockbridge County and spends much time doing research in the archives of Washington and Lee University and Virginia Military Institute. Lexington, her hometown, is the location of much historical material since both Robert E. Lee and Stonewall Jackson lived and are buried there.

(The 1962 photo shows Martha en route to Dumaguete in 1962 looking toward Bob Tyler and Nick Royal.)

Susan Thompson
Ah, Memories...

As with many of us, the Peace Corps was not my first overseas experience. In 1955-56, my father held a short-term United Nations job, and we lived in Manila. In 1959-60, I spent my junior year of college at the American University of Beirut, Lebanon. So Peace Corps life wasn't the total eye-opener to the world it might have been had I never before strayed from home. Nor was life in the Philippines totally new, although I learned more about traditional Philippine culture living in the barrio (as we said then) than from living in Manila. Certain facets of small town rural life weren't a total surprise either, since I had grown up in a town about the size of Alimodian, my Peace Corps assignment. Some experiences and attitudes weren't a total surprise to this native of Wadena, Minnesota.

That being said, this experience was different. I was older. I was not under my parents' wings or that of an *in loco parentis* college. I was living and working within a different culture, and attempting to navigate all that with housemates whom I didn't at first know well and who themselves were dealing with the same newness and adjustments.

I had been interested in the Peace Corps from the time it was announced. It had originally been the idea of one of my Minnesota heroes, Hubert H. Humphrey. Also, I had enjoyed the overseas experiences I'd already had. And finally, the Peace Corps was an attractive option since I had not passed the foreign-service exam!

One stumbling block was my father who, despite the strong attraction more overseas service held for him, at that point was much more committed to my getting a "real job" and earning money. So he said "one thing you're not going to do after graduation is join the Peace Corps." I don't know if he was surprised or not when a friend came up to him after church one Sunday and said, "I saw the picture of your daughter in the paper taken after the Peace Corps exam in Minneapolis yesterday." For that act of independence (disobedience?), I am forever grateful to my college friend and our Botch Two companion Bob Hoyle. A few days before the exam, Bob said something like "I know what your father said, but this is a natural for you. Come with me to the exam." Thanks again, Bob.

Initially we were four and later three volunteers assigned to the inland Panay town of Alimodian, Iloilo—Linda, Joyce, me, and Nancy, who left a few months later to live with a family in another community. The base of Alimodian's economy was small farms, local commerce and education, with a large central school in town and barrio schools in the outlying areas. Whatever the community may have thought about these strangers moving into their town and schools, they welcomed us graciously and were patient as we learned.

An initial embarrassment for us was the fact that the town had built a new two-story wooden home for us in the center of town and surrounded it with a fence. The condition and newness of the house and the existence of the fence troubled us because of the wrong message it could easily convey. It surely did that to Robert Shaplan, a *New Yorker* writer who came to Panay to write about the fledgling Peace Corps. His article praised most Philippine volunteers and panned us. As I recall, I wrote a three page single spaced letter to Larry Fuchs in our defense! Included in the letter was the fact that we had felt we could not refuse that house, since the town leaders' intentions had been to make us comfortable. If I were to name a "critical moment," it could be that experience of feeling misunderstood and unjustly maligned, not by Alimodianites, but by our own countryman. We were on the receiving end of the outsider who comes to a new place and after a few days decides he knows all about it. Just what the Peace Corps taught us NOT to do.

A few months after we arrived in Alimodian, our volunteer leader, David, asked another volunteer, Eric Peterson, and me to work with him. Our main task was to visit volunteers, finding out if there were things our colleagues needed that the Peace Corps could help provide (this was pre-internet and cell phones), and hearing how things were going. We were given jeeps for our travels and since mine was baby blue I called it, in true Philippine style, Baby Susan.

I was no longer assigned to the Bancal Barrio School, but did return to Alimodian every couple of weeks to visit, do laundry and sleep under my own mosquito net! People have asked over the years what I learned in the Peace Corps. Among so many things, one was learning from those months "on the road" about the resilience, ups, downs and growth of these young Americans (including myself) working and living in villages where the culture and conditions were so different from our own previous lives in the U.S.

Professionally, my overseas experiences helped prompt my interest and influenced my being offered my first post-Peace Corps job, at Lutheran Immigration and Refugee Service in New York City. That experience in turn lead to my next position as assistant director of the inter-Lutheran government relations office in Washington D.C., dealing with both domestic and international issues.

The last decades of my working life were spent in new congregational development for the Evangelical Lutheran Church in America, first as field staff in Wisconsin and later in the national offices in Chicago. One aspect of my work during the latter years was directly related to my Peace Corps experience. In the mid-1990s, we began thinking about specific ways to reach out to Filipino immigrants not already part of a religious community. We had no Filipino on staff, so I was asked to lead the needed explorations. Existing Lutheran pastors and lay leaders of Filipino heritage were gathered to help shape a strategy for outreach to Filipinos. Among the results of that strategy were: 1) development of a "Companion" network among the Filipino Lutherans in the US, 2) several Filipino-Americans began a process of discernment which led eventually to their ordination as Lutheran pastors, and 3) the initiation of a new Filipino congregation in San Diego. Our partner in this project was the Lutheran Church in the Philippines (LCP), which sent us a pastor for this still-continuing ministry. The LCP also invited me to speak at their seminary's 2001 graduation in La Union province. This gave me the opportunity for possibly my last trip to the Philippines, and for a "full circle" feeling about my life.

During the time of thinking about this essay, my mind has been full of many things that happened in those days, things which have stayed with me, shaped me, rewarded me. Among them, the Cuban missile crisis, when we lived each day in anticipation of hearing the latest VOA news that evening on our neighbors' radio, and during which we had conversations about what we would do if war broke out (as if there was anything we could do!); the Gonzagas, the large family in Iloilo City who provided a refuge for so many of us, sometimes Sunday dinners, Thanksgiving, joyous times around their piano, an occasional overnight in an air-conditioned bedroom, ice cream for the asking, and parental perspectives and wisdom as we, or at least as I, continued to grow up; *the chance to try something new.*

Though I had never taught, let alone directed a musical, I brought with me to the Philippines the scores for two middle-school level operettas. One was *Hansel and Gretel*, which students, some townspeople and we three volunteers put on one Alimodian evening. Joyce and Linda did the sets, I accompanied and did most of the directing, and Linda played the witch *(aswang)* when our friend Roselita had to withdraw. When many of us traveled to the Philippines on a Peace Corps 35th anniversary trip decades later, I was thrilled when a teacher at the Alimodian central school approached me with a smile and said "Susan, I'm Gloria." Gloria was Gretel in the operetta; I was pleased to see her again and pleased because she had addressed me by my first name, as I had always addressed her. Now we were both adults and I was "Susan."

Finally, high among the gifts to me of the Peace Corps experience was *each member of my group, Botch II,* my companions in that extraordinary situation and friends as we meet even now. *Salamat gid.*

After Peace Corps service, Susan Thompson worked at Lutheran Immigration and Refugee Service in New York City. Her next position was assistant director of the inter-Lutheran government relations office in Washington D.C., dealing with both domestic and international issues. Her subsequent working life was spent in new congregational development for the Evangelical Lutheran Church in America, first as field staff in Wisconsin and later in the national offices in Chicago. She is now retired and lives in Ottertail, Minnesota.

Patricia Toalson
Peace Corps Philippines: Important and Hard

Where I Was in the Summer of 1961

I graduated from the University of Chicago in 1960 and got to vote for John Kennedy. He proposed the Peace Corps and I knew immediately I wanted to try for that—something important and hard.

The job I took upon graduation was as a case worker for Cook County Public Assistance, an overwhelming experience. I felt chewed up and spit out before a year was up, and began a bit of a drifting around the country. I drifted with a broken heart, having said goodbye to my college lover. We were totally unable to imagine or create a future for ourselves—she was black and I was Missouri white. Connection with my parents and hers was tricky and distant—I had too much to hide. Somewhere during that summer I had gotten my application in to the Peace Corps, and I think I also sat for some kind of test.

After bouncing around from west coast to east coast I landed in Washington D.C. I ended up there because I wanted the challenge of arriving by bus in a city where I knew no one—to see if I could get a job and find a place to live—seems a bit nuts to me now. I was in D.C. when my folks called that I was to report to Penn State for training for the Philippines.

What would I have done if not the Peace Corps? I think I would have stayed in Washington D.C., worked and eventually gone to graduate school in history. The academic world would have felt like a good fit for me.

My Job in the Philippines

After training at Los Baños, I lived in the beautiful province of Iloilo, Island of Panay, the Visayas, town of Cabatuan. This was mango country, rice country, water buffalo with little boy asleep on its back country. My house was constructed of split bamboo walls, floors, nipa roof. And it remains the most beautiful structure I have ever lived in. My job as teaching aide in the barrio school was excruciating. I felt inept and at sea and I still cringe at the memory. But, my co-teachers were so kind and accepting, and life in my neighborhood was lovely. My best memories are of Iloilo—full moon strolls in the plaza, aroma of jasmine at night, neighbors, kids, *fiestas* and laughter. I lived there for eight months before being reassigned to Cebu City for my next job as a volunteer leader.

Compared to the barrio school role, the PCVL job was so much easier for me. I had 100 new volunteers on Cebu and Bohol to settle in, visit and deliver supplies. I liked setting up the regional office and working with the staff. I liked problem-solving for the new folks and planning for trainings and workshops; and always planning for the next batches of volunteers to arrive in-country.

Some Random Thoughts about the Philippines

The Japanese occupation of the Philippines was very harsh and cruel. To find my townspeople so welcoming and unflaggingly kind only 15 years after such suffering was amazing and says something important about their character I think.

I loved training at Penn State, and I got a great introduction to Philippine history. Then being in-country became a full graduate course in international power and the part the United States had played and was playing in Southeast Asia. It was the beginning of our Viet Nam buildup. I remember meeting a Filipino who had worked as a driver in Viet Nam. He had many stories to tell of U.S. covert military activity. I read Graham Greene's *The Quiet American*. Volunteers were worried. We were pretty clear we were about peace.

Cebu City became a major bombing airfield not long after my time there. I was selfishly glad to have missed the transformation of the places familiar to me.

My biggest failures: I couldn't do the twist; I couldn't eat nearly enough; I couldn't make a long enough speech.

Critical event

November 1963. President Kennedy was killed. The news came as I was preparing my last goodbye trip to friends in Iloilo. I had extended for a few months and was due to muster out in a few days. The awful news came in sporadically, rumors were flying and the need for concrete information, the need to know why, the need to not be alone, was overwhelming. I felt bereft, panicky. I was already fearful of returning to the unknown ahead for me in the States—no job, no plans, no destination. And I remember being so tired after months of on-the-road as a PCVL.

So, here is what I did next. A batch IV volunteer, a very nice guy, turns to me and says: "Let's get married". Me: "Oh, ok." Problem solved—someone to cling to. And so we married that December and stayed in-country until May 1964. Reentry into the U.S. was pretty rough, but for a short while my family was happy about me. He and I were together for a few years before I began my real life as my real lesbian self. I like to think that we took good care of one another, helped each other get on our feet back home.

Effects

I can't make a good assessment of our, the first batches', value to the Philippines, except to believe our face-to-face living together was genuine and countered images of movies, magazines, and walled-off government and military personnel.

I believe that joining the Peace Corps pulled us off of our narrow paths—right at a time our values could grow with the experience of service and life in another culture. This was an immense gift to us as individuals and to the country as a whole. Most of us kept on choosing service careers.

The role of volunteer was gender neutral—a radical environment for 1961. Once I got my bearings I became more able to push for equality, take risks, to act more on things that needed doing in my own country.

I learned I am not at ease in another country. I have little facility for language and I'm not comfortable in strange places. The possibility of finding a welcome mat out for a lesbian seemed pretty unlikely, so I have never considered serving abroad for any agency as have so many of Batch II folks. I like what I have accomplished here. Just once in a while I think about the new Peace Corps programs of short-term assignments. Maybe one day…

Pat Toalson has lived in Massachusetts since her return in 1964. Her work life focused primarily on counseling, first at Brandeis University, then on to private practice and some agency development and practice. She still keeps her license active although she is not currently doing counseling work. In addition to graduate work in counseling, she has an MA in Goddard's Social Change program. With her long-time partner, Kate Mitchell (and now spouse, thanks to Massachusetts), she owned and operated Island Women Construction on Nantucket Island for over 10 years. They hired and trained women in carpentry and built several interesting homes. While on Nantucket, Pat helped found a crisis center for domestic violence survivors and had a part-time counseling practice for women—the first counseling services focused on women on the island. Now on Cape Cod, she manages Kate's law office and occasionally dons tool belt to continue work on their 1770s' home. Pat's other volunteer activities have included serving as a training instructor for the American Red Cross, and as a Disaster Mental Health team member, including deployment to California wildfires. She has also helped with the construction of Habitat for Humanity homes.

(The second photo shows Pat with spouse Kate Mitchell.)

Robert Tyler
The "Nipa" People

Lila Gardner: Between 1988 and 1991, Bob and I shared stories about our lives on tapes and in letters. Here's what he had to say then of the Peace Corps days.

So many good memories connected to the Peace Corps especially Penn State. I just loved the people in our group; we were close. I remember some of the people who were rejected by the Peace Corps; they took it hard, especially Donna Monier. Pat Toalson pleaded for her. We were all upset about this—the little panel of shrinks, like so many, seemed really out of touch with reality….

When we got to the Philippines, had I known about myself what I know now, I would not have let them (administration) do to me what they did. They took three of us, they said we were really strong and could live by ourselves, and sent us out to visit Peace Corps volunteers and come back and report about the households.

I think this was a devious thing to do and I was hurt because I wanted to live with a household; instead, I bounced around Iloilo and the island next to it, a big sugar cane island where I stayed with Lone Castillo. That was … one of those experimental ideas we had many of in the Peace Corps in those days and it wasn't a good one….

Then the Peace Corps decided to put me in my own place; this town had built a Peace Corps house and someone up in 'Ma'NEEE'la' said they probably thought they were going to get a beautiful blonde and instead they got me. They were wonderful people and every night the little kids would come in the door, shy, and finally they would be around the table and I'd be eating my fish and rice. I loved that. Later I lived with Eliot and he was a good guy.

I went to Manila; (a staff member) had an idea that we should live with rich families so we'd get over our socialist tendencies—that was hysterical. I lived with the Ambassador to St. James (*sic*.) in a virtual palace on the Pasig River—that was wonderful! I had my own suite of rooms with lions' heads on it, a refrigerator, a courtyard front and back on the river.

His kids and wife were wonderful; she's a famous woman, Jesse La Chaco. During the day I worked in this giant prison called Welfareville for three months; then I was sent to Aklan.

That time in Manila, I was just starving because we were living on 212 pesos—$50—a month. In Manila I'd shoot through that in about three days. I'd take my last pesos to the *Jai Alai* Arena and try to win myself some money. I ended up at Larry (Fuchs)'s place a lot; he'd give me extra money to live on awhile, but not much. I felt bad not having a roommate cause at Penn State we were so close.

There were some strange things going on there (Manila) but overall I think they were very liberal with us and were criticized for it by subsequent Peace Corps administrators who couldn't wait to get us out of there. They had a special name for us, the 'nipa' people and they thought we were just whacked out, totally unproductive. I thought we had a wonderful creative group. Those were good times, living in a household like Dirk and Eric; there was a lot of support in that. The Corts (a Peace Corps staff member) were a vibrant family, full of love.

The hardest part was getting a piece of paper my last month there saying I was drafted into the army, the complete antithesis of what we were doing in the Peace Corps. I was on Panay, watching sunsets, thinking life was wonderful, finally in a place where I loved life and people around me, and a little kid walks up with a telegram which says 'Greetings, you are being drafted into the army—that was a real downer!

Having been sent to military school, which he hated, Bob Tyler managed to avoid Vietnam. After Peace Corps service, he studied at Columbia and Tulane Universities, taught cultural anthropology and worked in public health. He loved South America and worked in Colombia. By 1988 he was living in Denver, working on government social work and public health policies and volunteering nights in a homeless shelter. He later moved to Aurora, Colorado; he died in 2005 of a massive heart attack.

(The first photo shows Bob in 1961 at Penn State with fellow volunteer Eric Peterson on the right; the second photo shows him in Dillard Colorado in 1989.)

Carl Valentine

A Brief Reflection on My Time in the Philippines

Looking back after nearly 50 years—Carol and I are sitting on the small front porch of our beautiful home in Panay, Capiz, with its highly shined mahogany floors, *capiz* shell windows and a nipa roof. We see Mr. Hernandez, a small elderly man walking down the street in white pants, white shirt, straw hat and walking stick. He waves and comes up to sit with us, sip some lemonade and talk about old times. In the course of the conversation he tells us about his childhood over fifty years earlier when he attended an elementary school established by the Americans in Panay after the Spanish American War and about his dream that his daughter, a primary school graduate, attend high school.

Later that day Carol and I walked from our home over the Panay Bridge to the Hernandez home to meet Pilar, Mr. Hernandez's daughter, her mother who did not speak English, and her younger brother, Rosealeo. We arranged for Pilar to live with us, help with household chores and in return we would send her to high school in Roxas City. Pilar was joined by another young girl, Celeste, who became a working high school student, and our household was complete.

Celeste, after graduating from the local primary school, had been helping at home for two years waiting for her older brother to finish high school. Their family was very poor, and could only afford to send one child to high school at a time. Celeste's father was a *herbolario*, a medicine man, who helped the sick and was paid in chickens or other in-kind services. Neither of Celeste's parents could speak English, but we had little difficulty communicating as long a she was with us. The chores of bringing ice from Roxas City daily and killing the chicken for dinner fell to Pilar and Celeste as did the Saturday floor polishing task where they both would skate over the floors with coconut husks strapped to their feet.

Pilar and Celeste assisted us with our summer school for some 25 or so elementary children living in our neighborhood. The highlight was the weekly trip to the nearby seashore, a trip most of the kids had never taken. It required traveling about ten kilometers through Roxas City to Baybay beach. The summer school ended with a summer school production attended by family and friends featuring Carol and me dancing the *tinikling*.

I also remember the women patting Carol's stomach, "any good news yet," as we traveled to Roxas City to shop or attend the Baptist Church on Sunday to meet other Peace Corps volunteers and perhaps be invited to Dr. Curry's home for lunch. Dr. Curry ran the local Baptist hospital and his wife taught in the Baptist school. Or the day Carol rode her new bike down the street and upon her return the entire town turned out to watch. Women just didn't do that. Or, the way everything came to a stop at 6 pm each evening for the *Angelus* with the chiming of the church bells in the plaza. Immediately thereafter, the old World War II generator would kick in, lighting up the twenty five or so politically favored homes in town with neon lights (burning no more than 125 watts). If you missed the six o'clock start-up, your lights would flicker all night long.

As I think back to the two Peace Corps years in the Philippines and our trip home through Asia and Europe, long forgotten memories flood to the surface—a time of self discovery—a time that had a profound and wonderful influence on my life.

Carl Valentine and his wife Jane live on Riverside Drive in New York City. Working about half time, they spend two days a week in art school at the 92nd Street YMCA and one day a week at the Frederick Douglass High School in Harlem where they are teacher aides in the English Department, assisting students with their college essays. One of the students who became homeless over the past year is now their "foster child" and has recently graduated and will be going to college at Hobart on full scholarship in the fall. The rest of the time Carl tries to keep in touch with his four children, two step children and twelve grand children as well as maintaining a part time involvement in F.C. Valentine and Associates LLC, a consulting firm specializing in the design and financing of programs for at risk children and families, for states and communities across the country. After spending two years in the Peace Corps with his wife Carol, he completed his Master's Degree in Social Work at Columbia University and became first a Head Start Director and then Director of the Schenectady N.Y. Community Action Program. He worked for the State of New York for fifteen years in the design and development of programs for children and families and in 1984 joined a consulting group specializing in the design and financing of programs for children in foster care. In 1996 he formed F. C. Valentine and Associates that has specialized in the financing of programs designed to support families and prevent the need for foster care. After his wife's death five years ago, he married Jane. In addition to art school, they enjoy spending summer on Martha's Vineyard with their extended family and friends and their two dogs Lexi and Gus.

(The first photo shows Carl during Peace Corps training at Penn State in 1961; the second shows him on Sacandaga Lake in Mayfield, New York in 2010.)

David Ziegenhagen
David's Peace Corps Adventure

Most Important Memories and Critical Incidents

Soon after arriving in the Philippines for in-country training, I was asked to serve as a "volunteer leader." It was an undefined job for which there were no established criteria. Essentially, it meant helping the Peace Corps and the Philippine schools troubleshoot the first Peace Corps assignments of the earliest Peace Corps volunteers (PCVs), of whom I myself was one. That responsibility exposed me to what some other PCVs were doing as they worked with teachers and as they became immersed in family and community living. I also had contact with some of their friends and co-workers. I operated from one centrally located rural community, where I shared a home with three other PCVs. But this also meant that, other than my first few weeks in the Philippines, my personal experience included little of those community-based elements. Instead, I charted my own course in interactions with other PCVs, the Bureau of Public Schools (BPS) and Peace Corps staff, working simultaneously and mostly independently with the joys of being among the first PCVs on the ground while helping the program to get started, as well as laying the groundwork for what was yet to come.

This experience helped prepare me for later working as the sole Peace Corps presence in Northern Luzon, before communities and schools were selected as volunteer assignments. Working together with two BPS staff members, one of whom died and another who replaced him, we surveyed all communities and schools in seven provinces, considering potential assignments for the first two groups of PCVs to be assigned in Northern Luzon.

That experience, in turn, helped me to develop both skills and confidence to work with early Peace Corps programs in Thailand and Samoa, as well as later with startup emergency relief activities for the American Refugee Committee on the Cambodian-Thai border.

Because the Peace Corps was a new U.S. program, in the days before the first volunteers touched ground in any country, no one in Washington knew what a PCV would be, much less what one might do or be called upon to do. Oddly, only some male members of my group first went to Washington for a psychiatric interview and soon thereafter to Puerto Rico for four weeks of Outward Bound training. (I never understood why only the males were afforded that opportunity.) In itself this was a great personal experience for those who would be breaking Peace Corps ground. The biggest personal lesson I took away from Outward Bound was that of knowing and believing the most real obstacles are in one's head, not in whatever seems to be blocking the way. That was a valuable lesson!

Motivation

I was first excited about the Peace Corps when I heard John F. Kennedy's speech at the University of Michigan. I had a long-standing interest in international affairs, world peace, and being somehow involved. I was ready to get involved.

It was May 1961, and I was at the end of my second year of law school, starting to think about where I would be a year later after graduation. By that time I had already decided I wanted to go into public interest law, rather than a traditional practice.

By the end of May that year I wrote to the Peace Corps, saying I was close to graduating from law school, and asking to be placed on a list of those who might be interested in joining in a year or so.

Late that summer I received a message, asking whether I could be ready to begin training two weeks later for service in the Philippines. Looking back, I honestly don't believe I thought about all the implications for more than a few minutes before I said yes to the Peace Corps. Shortly thereafter I gave notice at my summertime job that involved outfitting and guiding wilderness canoe trips in Northern Minnesota and Ontario.

I had a journalism degree and during the school year was working in a TV newsroom 30 hours a week, dispatching photographers and reporters to cover news. When I told the News Director what I intended to do, he was not pleased. But the decision had been made, and I had already given thumbs up to the Peace Corps. Without my involvement, the station went on to win a Peabody award for the quality of its local news coverage.

I was like someone diving off a high board or jumping out of a plane wearing a parachute. It was too late to think about anything but becoming a Peace Corps volunteer.

The Peace Corps' Personal Effect

The Peace Corps' effect on me is ongoing. Now I am more sensitive to the images of America and Americans that are conveyed to the world by both our appearance and our deeds. I look for opportunities to cross paths with Filipinos and try to reach out with at least greetings and conversation about my interest in their country. In several places I have lived, there are active Filipino-American organizations and activities. Because my Peace Corps experience also includes living and working in Thailand and Samoa, I also reach out to Thai and Samoan people.

In 1979, when the Khmer Rouge genocide was taking place in Cambodia and thousands were fleeing to safety in neighboring Thailand, I volunteered to head a group of Minnesota physicians and nurses for the newly organized American Refugee Committee, which set up the first hospital on the border for Cambodian refugees. Because I could speak Thai and was familiar with Thailand, I was able to act independently to circumvent obstacles that commonly thwart good intentions of non-governmental organizations in an international crisis. I was especially pleased to be able to help reunite one Cambodian refugee I met with the rest of his family who had settled earlier in Minnesota through the help of a church in my hometown.

I was also a witness to history of what went on in other places. During the Cuban missile crisis, I was visiting communities and schools in the Cagayan Valley of Northern Luzon. I tracked the events as they were reported on shortwave radio.

When President Kennedy was assassinated, I was in a Thai village on the Burmese border. As I walked through the heat and dust that day, a shopkeeper ran out of his store and said, "You have to hear this!" Together with a group of Thais who were strangers to me, I listened and reeled as the news from Dallas was reported on the shortwave radio in his store.

My Peace Corps activities of course impacted my family in many ways. One sister became an early PCV in Peru. She married another early volunteer during her time in that country. My brother became an early PCV in Malawi.

Even after years since those experiences of the 1960s, the Peace Corps remains a subject of interest and conversation in our family. I am grateful beyond words for my personal experiences, as well as for the work the Peace Corps has done and is doing. And I know my siblings share the same kinds of gratitude and awe from their experiences in Latin America and Africa.

Since 2000, David and Mary Kinsella Ziegenhagen have lived in Cloverdale, a northern California city of 8600, ninety miles north of San Francisco, euphemistically said to be "where the vineyards meet the redwoods." Although both Minnesotans, they met in the Philippines, he with Peace Corps Group II and Mary on the country staff. In addition to the Philippines, their Peace Corps experience eventually included Thailand (1963-65), and Samoa (then Western Samoa) from 1967-70, where the first of their two sons was born. Returning to Minnesota after nine years with the Peace Corps, David and Mary found new challenges and opportunities. Mary was co-founder of the women's movement in that state and also started what became a successful community newspaper in the city where they lived. David headed two separate statewide non profit organizations, one in mental health and the second in health care quality improvement. He also used his journalism training and experience to join Mary at the weekly community newspaper. When the Khmer Rouge ransacked Cambodia, David went to Thailand as volunteer Field Director for the American Refugee Committee, which set up and operated the first hospital on the Thai-Cambodian border for survivors and refugees from "the killing fields." Now, in their "golden years," they are thriving in small town living, with community involvement and responsibilities in areas such as the brand new History Center (Mary), the Cloverdale Planning Commission (David), and community-based health care services (both).

Philippines III

December 1961—Departure for Puerto Rico to begin training

January 24, 1962—Arrival at Penn State for training

March 28, 1962—Arrival in the Philippines for training at UP/Diliman

May/June 1962—Arrival in Samar and Leyte

November 1963—Completion of Peace Corps service

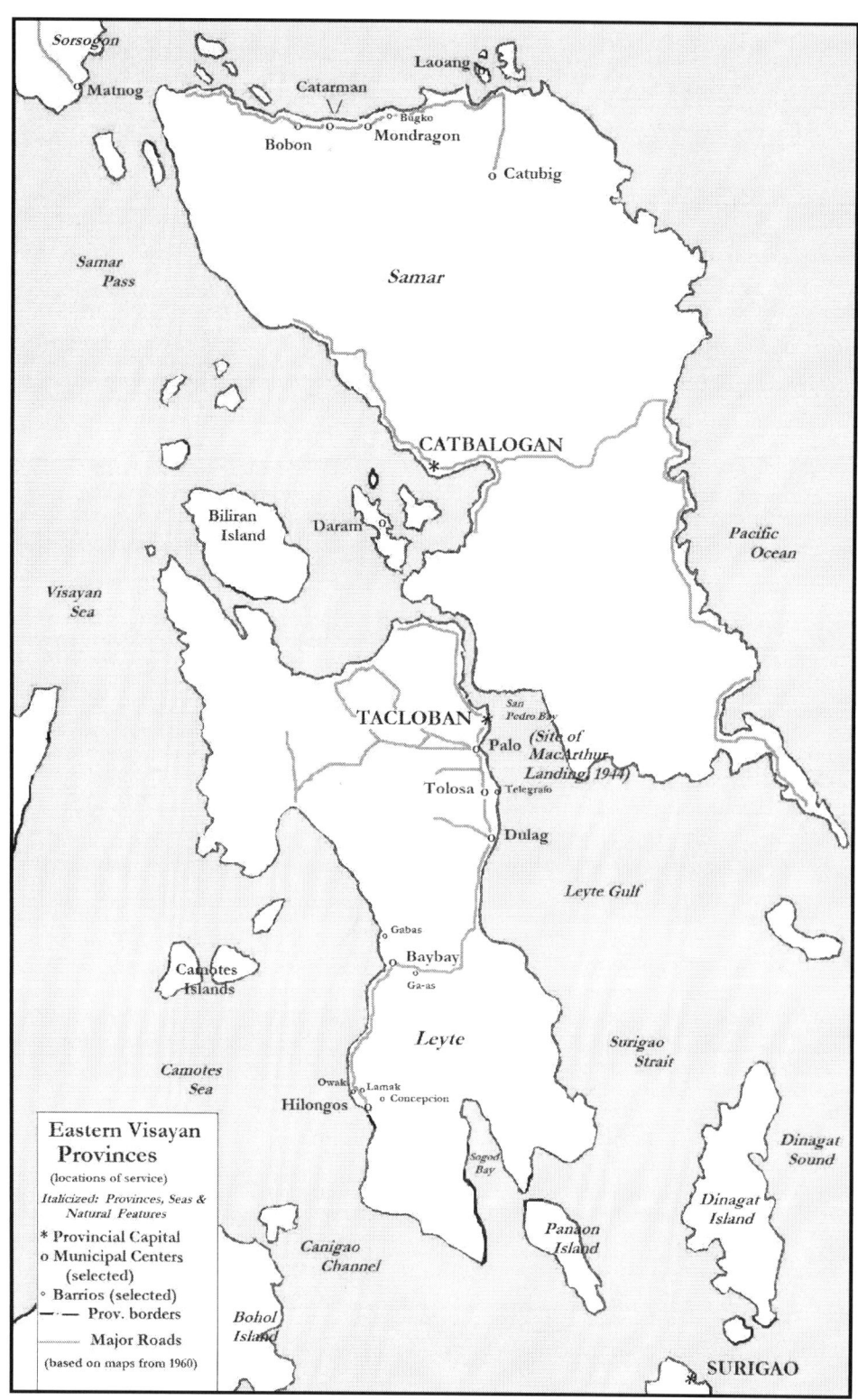

Steve Wells
Outward Bound*

Philippines Group III began its training in Puerto Rico where we all participated in the Outward Bound Program. The males in Group II had participated in an earlier version of this program, but we were the first group where all volunteers, male and female participated. The course lasted four weeks and consisted of the Outward Bound Program plus an overnight community development experience. This essay examines only the Outward Bound side of the program.

Drownproofing

It was December 1961 and we were part of John F. Kennedy's New Frontier, pioneers in this new idea called the Peace Corps. Few of us knew what to expect when we stumbled off a Pan Am flight from New York to San Juan and were trucked away to a rustic, hastily assembled jungle wilderness camp near Arecibo.

I watched as one by one the members of my Peace Corps training group attempted to swim 50 meters underwater without surfacing or taking a breath.

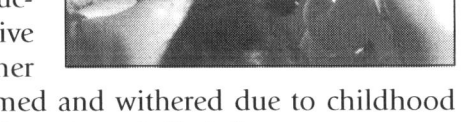

The idea was to jump off the edge and somersault in the air so we were going backward when we hit the water. Then we were to turn around in the water, swim the length of the pool, then back, the head below the water at all times. One slip, that's it—you failed this test.

My job was to pull them out of the water once they had lost consciousness. I had been assigned this job by Freddie Lanoue, our bombastic Drownproofing instructor, who knew I'd been an intercollegiate competitive swimmer at Iowa State University. Lanoue, the former swimming coach at Georgia Tech had one leg deformed and withered due to childhood polio. He referred to himself as "The Ramblin' Wreck from Georgia Tech."

It was Freddie's idea in this final week of our Outward Bound Peace Corps training in Puerto Rico, to escalate the challenges placed before us, the better to prepare us for unknown challenges.

Freddie was completely in character in the Outward Bound camp. He'd invented something called "Drownproofing," a simple method of staying afloat in the water without the usual thrashing or arms and legs, conserving energy and avoiding panic while awaiting rescue.

For those with a lifelong fear of water, learning Drownproofing was the very kind of self-achievement that Outward Bound was designed to impart. Along with rock climbing,

---

*This essay is being placed at the beginning of the Group III essays because it provides an overview description of the course taken by all Group III volunteers when they started their Peace Corps training. Since other essays comment on this training, the editors thought it would work best at the beginning of the section.

camping, trekking and the infamous obstacle course, the idea was to leave each of us with a heightened sense of self-confidence, prepared to take on any challenge that lie before us, just as the British U-boat crews felt in 1941 when they went through the very first Outward Bound training.

Before this underwater challenge, Freddie had tied the legs and arms of each of us, then pushed us into the water to see if we could stay afloat using the Drownproofing techniques he taught us. We all succeeded.

Now for the ultimate test: Freddie talked to all of us the day before about this fearsome underwater challenge. He taught the rest of the group members something he called the "keyhole" stroke for effective underwater swimming. Then he said we could practice, but were *not* to swim the length of the pool, just across the width and back.

You made it when you touched the end you started on. He reinforced the simple rule, come up for a breath for any reason and that's it. The big thing was—*no second chance.* If any of us failed this test, there will not be another chance, period.

Freddie then did some serious confidence building. He explained to us exactly what to do as we swam: look for the lane lines on the bottom of the pool, come in low at the other end so we would not mistakenly push our heads out of the water, and graze the bottom of the pool as we pushed off the other end.

More, he told us how we would feel at critical points: "Your stomach will start to throb," and so on. He said he had a lot of experience with watching people in this situation and when they got close to fainting he could tell and others would be right there to pull them out. So, don't worry about drowning.

Then he told us about hyperventilating and how to use it, pointing out that when your fingers start to tingle, it means you are ready to begin the underwater swim.

Chip Salmon was skeptical. He recalled, "I knew this was going to be near impossible. I was sure there was *no way* I could possibly make the length. I couldn't even do the *width*. Others were of the same mind. Freddie had us snookered."

We were still reeling from the Drownproofing lesson conducted in heavy surf on an isolated beach several days earlier. As waves broke, we were thrust violently into underwater currents that left us with sand burns, bruises and frightened from the disorienting effect of tumbling over and over underwater, wondering *which way is up?*

This morning we sat on the edge of the pool, our legs dangling in the water, as we listened disbelievingly at what Freddie wanted us to do.

Chip recalled, "I remember us all being quiet, uptight and concerned, but determined too."

Throughout our training, there was always individual pressure to go further, do more, push the envelope. Each of us was acutely aware that the Damocles sword of "deselection" constantly hung over us. If any one of us was judged to be somehow unfit, inept, unworthy of Peace Corps' high standards, the staff could simply wash us out and send us home on the next plane. It was that simple. No reasons, just here one day and gone the next—and along with it, one's dreams of serving overseas in the Peace Corps.

So we were all under tremendous self-imposed pressure to excel in anything we did, proving our worthiness, digging deep within ourselves to exhibit impressive levels of motivation attesting to our commitment to be part of John F. Kennedy's New Frontier.

It was a test none of us wanted to fail.

It was a test of endurance, swimming without breathing until you—drowned? Passed out? Came up and got a breath and then ended up hustled out on the next flight to the mainland?

It had finally come down to this one test of individual resolve and commitment. The group couldn't help you anymore. It was self-conflict in its purest form, battling instinct for survival against the will to go beyond endurance, to venture into the unknown.

To build the self-confidence of the group, Freddie planned it so the stronger swimmers, those most likely to succeed, went first. Chip recalled, "Finally, the last big boost: he picked *you* as the starting swimmer."

I dove in without even the slightest feeling of anxiety. And when my group saw me go the required two lengths of the pool underwater before I surfaced, it *did* serve as a confidence-builder for the others: *Look how easy it seems!*

Chip recalled, "I remember you underwater. Grace itself. I believe you completed the down and back in 37 seconds! Unbelievable, and you were not even breathing hard!"

Then four more went in. All of us completed the course in under a minute.

Then it was Chip's turn.

"I found Freddie's predictions exactly on and very comforting, so those disconcerting stomach throbs were OK," Chip recalled. "I made it! I was delighted!"

Then others went, with us all cheering each other on. The trouble with the underwater swim was that the people who most needed encouragement and strength from the others couldn't hear underwater. It was silent down there.

Finally we got down to those group members who would have a much harder time. Freddie nudged me to be ready to jump in and help anyone who appeared to be in distress.

"Watch their head and the back of their neck very carefully," he instructed me in a whisper, so the others wouldn't overhear, as I walked up and down the deck ready to spring to their aid. "Just before they pass out, you'll see this involuntary twitch. For a moment you'll see them raise their head slightly in a jerky way. That's the moment when they lose consciousness. *That's* your sign to jump in and get them."

I watched. Sure enough, for those who didn't decide to finally surface on their own there was a slight involuntary twitch just as Freddie said there would be. Then they would go limp, arms floating by their sides, head down in the water.

When I saw the twitch, I jumped in and grabbed their jaw and led their face to the surface. They emerged sputtering, blinking and choking, but conscious. And breathing.

And still alive.

What went through the minds of each of the underwater swimmers that morning as they fought instinct to surface and gasp to inhale air? I watched as their arm movements got slower and slower, as they meandered off-course while making their way underwater, becoming disoriented, slowing to impossible speeds, strokes becoming feeble and uncoordinated, then recumbent and finally that little twitch of the head indicating they'd passed out.

Chip recalled, "Charlie Terry was especially interesting. He was determined, but the last 10 feet were agony to watch. He was flailing, just barely moving forward. Freddie told you to watch and be ready but do nothing. Charlie finally luckily grazed the end with his hand. Freddie told you to grab him. You pulled him out. Charlie was not pleased. *Why did he do that?* He was just about ready to turn around and go back. He had no idea how much trouble he was in! Meanwhile, Don Smith went off on some unknown tangent and you had to grab him. A couple of others ended up flailing the water and going nowhere. You had to grab them as well. M.L. Corwin took 90 seconds, bobbing up and down on the surface. But she, too, made it!"

"As a group, as I remember it, we almost *all* made it," he recalled. "We did well as a group, and no one disgraced themselves. *Everyone tried hard.*"

And that, after all, was the whole idea: to muster the courage and wherewithal to *try*, to reach deep within and haul up heroic levels of performance.

It was a moment of accomplishment, a new sense of pride and capability, the very thing Outward Bound attempted to impart in each of us.

Still, for each of those who passed out underwater, it must have felt like experiencing a little death that day. Later there was grumbling that Freddie had gone too far, taken the challenge thing over the top. One who had passed out, inhaling water into her lungs, developed pneumonia. She dropped out to recover, later completing training with the next group.

Survival Training

I wrote a letter to my friends from Puerto Rico:

> The 50 volunteers, heading for jobs as teachers in the Philippines, will do much in their 28 days here. They will climb over the face of a 125-foot rock cliff, overlooking a large lake amid lush, green hills. They will do this after having practiced for weeks on smaller rocks, and when they attempt the big one they will sweat and scratch and grasp for handholds and footholds. They will think about backing down but instead hear the encouragement of their fellow Volunteers below to keep on going. They may slip and fall; but fall only a few feet until their safety belay rope stops their fall and then they will continue upward. Each one will make it to the top, rest, and look at the hills and the lake, and then attach himself to a special rope rigging and rappel down the sheer cliff, bounding with wide-spread legs as he slips easily through the rope, descending in 20 seconds the rock it took 20 minutes and two quarts of sweat to ascend. And he will feel proud of this small climb.
>
> Inevitably, the Volunteer will go around the much-publicized obstacle course, crawling like a snake along a 75-foot horizontal rope, swinging like Tarzan from each of six progressive ropes, balancing on a shaky three-rope "Burma Bridge" 40 feet up in the trees, taking the "commando swing" across a creek to a cargo net he will scale and then descend, and then hanging onto the pulley of the zip wire, race 100 feet back to earth again.
>
> Later, he will sleep overnight in the jungle with just himself, his hammock and a sandwich. Then he and four others will trek for four days and 40 miles through river valleys, jungles, over hills, along ridges and through swamps, accepting coffee from hospitable farmers, learning Spanish, sleeping in tobacco barns, sometimes with chickens and hogs—and living on half-rations so he will know how a hungry Filipino feels. He will meet and talk with Puertoriqueños, in their language, and learn to read a contour map, following a prescribed route. It is an experience hard to forget.

What kind of heart-stopping challenges did we encounter? For some, it was the shaky instability of the Burma Bridge, a three-rope arrangement on the obstacle course that bridged two trees 40 feet above the ground. The Burma Bridge never delivered on the promised stability it seemed to visually offer, one large rope for your feet and two smaller ropes on either side as hand-holds. The smaller ropes, positioned hip-high, were lashed at intervals to the larger base rope. But somehow as you stepped aboard and moved forward, the whole arrangement began to swing and steadily became looser with each advancing move. By the time you advanced to its midpoint, it transformed into a sort of ugly death swing, assuming lateral looping motions exacerbated by your legs that were now shaking uncontrollably. This in turn froze you in your tracks, certain you'd plunge to your death below, once again fighting instinct: *I can stay here motionless and not fall, but not make it to safety. Or I can risk everything on the slim hope I can make it to the other end. Which will it be?* Confident steps became timid mincing, pathetic motions toward the other end where the lines were anchored high on another tree.

The Burma Bridge did to each of us exactly what the underwater swim accomplished: it challenged us to move *beyond* the instinct for self-preservation and comfort, and to seek something of unknown dimensions even *more* challenging. And if the Burma Bridge failed to impart this, it was the rock climb on rocky ridges bordering Rio Abajo. We climbed straight up sheer vertical surfaces, a safety belay rope secured around us. Scrambling for handholds and footholds, we individually clawed our way up. Two footholds and one handhold was security, the remaining hand groping for the next fissure or surface. Then it was a choice: leave this known level of security and advance further, higher, leaving safety and security behind for something surely more perilous. And what then? Slowly we made our way up, sweating profusely, occasionally looking down to see how far we'd advanced, how little the people had become, then a darting glance upward to see how much *further* we had to go.

Before long the belay rope, although still attached, no longer provided any reassuring level of comfort. The whole ascent was an anxiety-ridden, sweaty trial beyond the point of no return. By remaining focused and treating it as a challenge, one could scale the rock with a minimum of terror and psychic damage. But others froze midway, paralyzed with conflict and fear, unable to make the death-defying choice of leaving what was tenuous security for the unknown. Then we'd sense it, just as I was looking for involuntary head twitches through the clear water of the pool, and we'd shout encouragement from below.

We were all humbled, not so much by malevolent do-or-die boot-camp schemes and challenges to test us, conjured up by demented Outward Bound staff members like Freddie Lanoue, Davey Borden and Al Ferraro. We were humbled instead by coming face-to-face with self-imposed limitations we had unwittingly placed upon *ourselves—the* result of years of comfortable living and predictable lives. Now, faced with adversity in what seemed to be authentic life-or-death situations, we suddenly became acquainted with our own flabby self-resolve and unflattering timidity.

Providing a good example of this was the initial day of a four-day trek we took in small, six-person teams. This was our culminating event, the penultimate challenge. Do this successfully and you could move on the stage two of the training.

The idea was simple. Carry everything you need on your back. Use the geological contour map provided. Stay off roadways and stick to trails, following the route marked on the map. Sleep wherever you can. Eat sparingly, as only half-rations are provided. On the fourth and final day, be at the finish line.

We were literally on our own to read and interpret the maps, follow the trails, stop and sleep when we needed to, and make our final destination on time. We were warned not to solicit nor accept local hospitality of Puerto Rican farmers and others we might come across, though we were to seek their permission, if, for instance, we wanted to sleep in their tobacco barn or use water from their well. As one last touch the staff provided us enough food (Army rations) for normal meals for two and a half days, even though we were to be gone four or more days. The idea, they explained, was that since most of the world goes hungry most of the time, we should know from firsthand experience what it's *like* to really be hungry.

We conserved our rations, quickly learning how to track elevations indicated on the map and relate them to the hilly terrain we trekked. Always looking for navigational confirmation and aware that other teams were stumbling through the Puerto Rican backwoods like us, we quickly learned a few Spanish phrases to try out on farmers we'd come across:

"*¿Donde estan los otros Americanos?*" Where are the other Americans? Occasionally they would point and chatter in rapid Spanish, and instantly we knew we were on the right track.

We managed to survive. The only "cheating" occurred when, sleeping on a meadow near a farmhouse one night, the local farmer sent his small daughter out to us with a Thermos of hot Puerto Rican coffee, which is really a mostly-milk mix. He urged us to at least move into his barn under shelter. We refused, but we thought we'd create an international incident by refusing the simple act of kindness and hospitality represented by the coffee, so we accepted the coffee and shared it among ourselves, savoring it ceremoniously almost like taking the sacrament at communion service in church.

The farmer is still probably still shaking his head, wondering why these five strange Americans ended up sleeping on the meadow on his farm.

At the end of the fourth day we crossed the finish line, joyous and proud, dirty and sweaty, hungry and thirsty. The staff was there to cheer and greet us.

There were many other experiences and surprises in store for us those first 28 days of 1962.

The first came on our very first morning, awakening from our bunks in large platform tents only hours after crawling into bed. It was January 1, 1962. We had all been guests of the Mayor of Arecibo at New Year's Eve party he hosted the night before. Most of us had partaken generously of the bottles or Puerto Rican rum that sat invitingly on each table.

It was 6 a.m. and Davey Borden was yelling at us that the first of what would be daily one-mile runs was about to take place.

Woozy and sleepy, we grumbled to the road and began a breathless run up and down the inclines of this hilly region of Puerto Rico.

It was the longest mile any of us ever experienced. But we made it, though some ended up walking the last portion.

Bill Delano and the Meaning of It All

The director of our camp at Arecibo was the late Bill Delano, newly-appointed General Counsel of the Peace Corps. He'd arrived at the same time we did. A big-city lawyer and Washington policy maker, this was a far cry from his tony Georgetown townhouse, located in the same neighborhood as another townhouse once occupied by Senator Kennedy. Bill was hopelessly out of place in this rustic paramilitary setting where emphasis was on physical achievements. He was obviously ill at ease. Just how or why he ended up as director of this remote outpost was beyond any of us.

Yet somehow we clicked. Bill's ineptness became *our* ineptness. We identified with him. Bill was game to try anything thrown at him. He was with us on rock climbing and rappelling. He struggled with basic Spanish as we did. He learned alongside us. He laughed at himself, finding humor in his own predicament, unafraid to lose all pretense and artificial dignity to come down to our level and identify with us.

We were in this together. It was at that moment a quiet bonding occurred between Bill and us and through Bill, with the entire Kennedy government.

This is what it was all about!

It was all about self-challenging moments of truth, about being self-effacing enough to admit fear and overcome it, about digging deeper into yourself to come up with the solution in a way that provided growth for you and everyone else around you.

And it was being unafraid of personal challenges, willingness to leave the comfort of the known for the challenge of the unknown. We were all restless people unhappy with the *status quo*, seeking something better, striving to achieve our manifest destiny. Outward Bound was the perfect metaphor for what was surely to follow when we left for our assignments in the Philippines. Who knew what lay in store for us there?

Bill embodied the very spirit of adventure, self-discovery and humility that the Peace Corps was all about. Bill proved to all of us that nobody among us was too gifted, too proud, too privileged to be immune. It was a fresh start for everyone. Even Bill.

In our minds, Bill began as a misplaced, privileged despot and before our very eyes transformed into the sort of soldier for peace that we saw ourselves becoming.

He became *one of us!*

And he knew it and enjoyed every minute of his gloriously transforming journey.

Before long Bill found himself transferred back to Washington to do what he was supposed to be doing in the first place.

Clearly, his Outward Bound experience had the same transforming effect on him as it did on us. He clearly sensed this special bond with us. On our departure to the Philippines, he flew to Seattle to see us off, gathering us in a special lounge at SeaTac airport for some final words.

He was genuinely regretful that somehow he missed the opportunity now being provided us to make a difference in the world as Peace Corps Volunteers, that he would be chained to matters of legality and policy and litigation while we were in the barrios building schools, teaching kids, doing what really counted. He said he wished he were going with us. It was an expression of envy, sadness and longing. He made us feel special and gifted. Not bad, coming from a guy who was special and gifted. He said he'd fly to the Philippines to visit us in our assignments, a promise he kept a year later.

Afterward

Later, after Penn State and in-country training, I had a chance to reflect on what—if anything—Outward Bound contributed to our preparedness for Peace Corps service and the quality of that service. The immediate effect was to anneal our group into a closely knit "band of brothers" bound for unknown adventure. Additionally, it seemed to prove to each of us that it was OK to move *beyond* the instinct for self-preservation and comfort, and to seek something of unknown dimensions even *more* challenging. After all, if we could survive a test to will ourselves to push beyond limits and actually pass out while underwater, how could we possibly fail in our Peace Corps assignments? That was, after all, the oblique concept of Outward Bound—namely, to help one discover an inner reserve of strength that could be channeled to any unknown challenge. Our Outward Bound experience seemed to have toughened us sufficiently to endure and enjoy life in the rural Philippines to the maximum. It provided us the inner strength to overcome self-doubts, confident that each of us possessed the inner strength and resolve to prevail over any challenge. As evidence of this, there were no early terminations of Group III members, as there had been in previous groups.

As a group, Outward Bound left us strong-willed, determined to strike out against the establishment and have things our way. We were cocky, self-assured, outspoken and impatient. If we didn't like something, we said so. We took risks, both individually and collectively. We were, after all, the pioneers, the chosen ones, members of the Peace Corps in its very first year of its existence. This cocky self-assuredness first appeared at a speech at Penn State by the ever-skeptical CBS commentator Eric Sevareid which most of us attended. When Sevareid used the term "Kiddie Korps" in his remarks that night in disparaging reference to the concept of the Peace Corps, we stood as a group and staged a mass walk-out. Later, upon completion of in-country training we insisted (again as a group) that we travel by interisland ship to our assignments in Samar and Leyte, not by air as the Peace Corps had planned. After all, that's how our counterpart teachers would travel.

Sargent Shriver later wrote to William Sloan Coffin Jr., Yale's dynamic chaplain, who assisted in the establishment of Peace Corps' Outward Bound program in Arecibo, Puerto Rico. Shriver observed that "The Philippine Volunteers…began evaluating their program at Penn State in terms of your leadership and inspiration and found everything suffered by comparison…the [Puerto Rico Outward Bound] camp has proven to be one of the best examples of the what the Peace Corps has done to date."

Steve Wells was a volunteer in Dulag, Leyte, then served as a volunteer leader for Northern Mindanao. Later he returned to the Philippines as an Associate Peace Corps Director where he served for five years as Bicol Regional Director. Additional information about Steve appears after the essay about his Peace Corps experiences in a later section of this volume.

(The first photo shows Freddie Lanoue explaining his Drownproofing technique to Group III volunteers in Puerto Rico; the second shows Group III volunteers preparing for their rappelling session at the Outward Bound Camp in Arecibo, Puerto Rico.)

Jonathan Epstein
Ordinary Happiness

After six months teaching English in elementary schools on Leyte, I take a Peace Corps-sponsored course in Cebuano that reveals latent linguistic skills. I am asked to co-run the new Volunteer Language Program and immediately set to work with native informants to analyze Maranao, a language spoken by 800,000 Muslims living in the Lake Lanao area of Mindanao. This results in a grammar, two books of lessons and a four-week intensive language training course for volunteers in Mindanao. Afterward, with three months to go in my tour, I begin to long for the community I left behind and ask to return to my original assignment on Leyte.

When I get out of the *tartanilya* (two-wheeled horse-drawn carriage) that brings me to the small coastal town of Hilongos, Leyte, neighbors gather to welcome me. First to greet me is Lino, now a toddler. Ten months before, when I left Hilongos with its fine 18th century Spanish church, Lino was terrified of me. For six months, each time I got near him, he started howling to wake up the dead. Now 18 months old, Lino walks steadily toward me, all grin, and raises his arms to be picked up. I talk to him softly, as if we do this every day. With Lino aloft and his siblings in tow we walk the neighborhood and re-connect to old friends. Everyone is happy I'm back. I stop at a corner sari-sari store (still with my entourage of children) and drink a glass of tuba, which throws me for a loop.

The glow of this moment extends uniformly over the next three months. On the surface, it may seem like "nothing to write home about," yet the feeling of it—of each recalled moment—is lit as if from within. At six each morning when the sun streams into my face through the upstairs window I get up, take a cold shower and dress. Joe, my Filipino friend and cook, makes eggs and toast. I bicycle three miles down a dirt road, cross the plank bridge over the river to Lamak (mud), teach three classes, enjoy a *merienda* snack and chat with teachers. On alternate afternoons I cycle to Concepción (uphill and sweat, sweat, sweat) or down the road to Owak (crow). At each school I am treated to lunch and a nap before afternoon classes. As I cycle home, people wave and call me by my name (It's no longer "Hey, Joe!"). I am 24 years old, 6' 3", weigh 170 pounds and can't seem to gain weight.

At dinner, Lino and siblings, who live next door, lean across the open kitchen window to watch me eat. I never go to the market or seashore unaccompanied by children. Each day I alternate teaching and observing with co-teachers, then plan the next day's lesson. Weekends might be a visit to a rice farmer to help with harvest or a pre-dawn trip with fishermen followed by pancakes made of tiny ghost fish fried in batter. Or there might be a fiesta or a wedding or an outing to the beach. It is a continuum of quiet joy enhanced by speaking Cebuano, my second language. This "foreign tongue" is the glue that binds my happiness together. When I speak it and hear it, I float in a sea of tranquility.

The role I play as a co-teacher sharing teaching duties is enough for me to feel I am contributing. All duties, people, relationships and routines weave into the fabric of a day. Everything is part of a unity. Everything has a place in the scheme of things. On my last day as a volunteer, people flock to the town airport to say good-bye. As the plane lifts off, I begin to mourn this never-to-be-repeated sense of belonging.

After Jon's Peace Corps years, he moved on to teach English-as-a-Second Language for forty more years. "Languages remain my passion, and memories of this life of ordinary happiness remind me of what is important," he reflects.

Douglas Foley
The Good Old PC Days and a Life Well Spent

I was raised by my grandparents and went to a rural one-room school in Iowa. We were tenant farmers, and I was able to go to Northern Iowa University on a sports scholarship. When I applied for the Peace Corps, I was teaching high school social studies and coaching in Davenport, Iowa. Like many volunteers, President Kennedy's call to service inspired me, but to be honest, the Peace Corps also seemed like a good way to have an adventure and see the world. My family thought I was a little crazy, but my superintendent said it was a great opportunity. From teaching American history, I knew the Philippines was a former U.S. colony, and that we liberated it from the Japanese during World War II. I imagined the Philippines as a poor, dependent country compared to its more prominent neighbors, China, India, and Japan. I expected to teach rural Filipino teachers science and English for two years then travel for a year throughout Asia. I went into the Peace Corps feeling that my dedication to athletics had left me less than well educated. The game plan was to come back to America worldlier than when I left.

Meeting the group III trainees was initially a little intimidating. Many were from urban backgrounds and fancy East and West coast schools. During our Outward Bound training in Puerto Rico it became obvious, however, that we all had a variety of skills and abilities. The training presented many physical and psychological challenges that encouraged us to bond together. Thanks to Jonathan Epstein, I left Puerto Rico realizing it would be a long two years if I did not speak a Filipino language. We received additional training in a very cold, boring Penn State program and then more relevant training in Manila from Filipino teachers, one my future wife. After too many training programs, we boarded an inter-island vessel, the *General Lukban*, overflowing with people, pigs, and produce. We  slept on reed mats on the deck and woke up the next morning in Catbalogan, Samar. I will never forget peering over the railing at a band blaring and a gaggle of teachers, children, and local politicians. We walked down this rickety plank into the dusty streets, sweltering heat, and all those smiling brown faces. That was my first inkling of what the next two years were going to be like. It was scary yet exhilarating. When we left for Leyte's capital, Tacloban, I wondered when we would see the Samar volunteers again. We had heard all these stories about the wilds of Samar, so I imagined them disappearing into a tropical rain forest.

After a few days of fiestas and meetings in Tacloban City, we boarded a converted school bus stuffed with people and cargo and traveled via a gravel road to the municipality of Dulag. It was a small market town of about 5,000 people located on the ocean and included eight smaller, outlying villages. My roommates, Steve Wells, another Iowan and "Chip" Salmon from New Jersey, and I lived in a nice two-story wood frame house of the ex-superintendent of schools. The family had divided the house and put in a kitchen and water seal toilet in the downstairs, and they lived upstairs. Our household united around learning Waray-Waray, and each one did his thing in different elementary schools. Steve stayed in the town's central school, and Chip and I biked to small village schools outside the town center. We were all jock types, so we were always doing something active outside the house. Steve had been a swimmer for Iowa State University, I a college basketball player, and Chip never met a physical activity he did not do with abandon. We had a good and harmonious household, perhaps even a model one, because within a year Steve and Chip were tapped to be Volunteer Leaders. They went off to help Peace Corps Regional Directors cope with a rapidly expanding number of Philippine PCVs. Chip stayed in the Leyte/Samar region where he was able to roam the back roads in a Peace Corps Jeep delivering toilet paper and fighting the dreaded *bok bok* (termites) that ate the Peace Corps houses he built. Steve went to the Bicol Region in Southern Luzon where his innovative approaches became legendary, and no doubt, a pain-in-the ass to Peace Corps bean counters in Manila.

I stayed in Dulag the full two years and trained local teachers. At times it was a little lonely without my roomies, but there was always the challenge of getting teachers interested in science and English. I ground away, building board games for teaching English and a science room for doing experiments. There were the usual ups and downs. One of my principals was a drunk; the other was a dedicated saint. Some teachers were totally enthusiastic; others were just collecting their paycheck. I had experienced these things while teaching in Iowa, so it all seemed pretty "normal." I quickly concluded that a twenty-two-year-old, inexperienced American was not going to make major changes in the way Filipinos teachers did things. I found Filipinos to be much more into singing and dancing and socializing than dour Iowa farmers. So I did what I could in the schools and settled in to the constant round of fiestas and afternoon *meriendas*.

Being a tall (6'3") white guy, I was the object of much gossip and flirtations, and the kids often followed me around town yelling "Hey Joe, give me chocolate." Or they mocked my accent in Waray, which was annoying. I was the local exotic object, a minor celebrity of sorts, and because my name was Douglas, I played Douglas MacArthur in the local re-enactment of his Leyte landing. This led to endless "Douglas-landed-here-jokes" and stories about good-hearted American GI's. The twist was also all the dance rage, so I was obliged to demonstrate it at every party. I entertained people with reckless abandon, but that also got a little old. These were the small irritations, but the longer I lived in Dulag, the more it seemed like an Asian version of rural life in Iowa. The differences in customs and language narrowed as I learned to just go with the flow and enjoy life.

During the summers I created a town basketball league for elementary and high school students. We refurbished an old Army generator and lit a rundown court near the municipal building. The league involved about eighty kids with several teams from the outlying barrios. Eventually the peasant kids beat the town kids, and the Dulag high team eventually beat urban kids from the capital city. For me the basketball league was this great democratizing event that gave little kids, peasants, and small town kids an equal opportunity to play and be successful. I initially met with some resistance, but the townspeople eventually came to understand what I was doing. Lots of parents and friends of the players loved watching the games, which were often spirited. Some years later during my dissertation research in Central Luzon, I took a sentimental journey back to Dulag. To my surprise, the town had become THE basketball power of East Leyte. They had built a new, well-lit cement court in the town square, and several of my players had earned college scholarships. They threw a party for me to express their gratitude. They had forgotten all the times I screamed at and embarrassed them publicly. It was a touching, unforgettable moment and the highlight of my Peace Corps experience. The basketball league was what cemented my relationships with people and helped me enjoy Filipino culture and learn the language. It was what endured after I left.

Looking back, my main regret is that I never visited other volunteers in their villages. Not sharing our experience now seems like a missed opportunity. Once my roomies left, I just burrowed into my school projects and the basketball league. I also did not travel much during vacations, but I did visit my future wife in Manila, and during one trip a fellow volunteer invited me to visit Clark Air Base. That visit was a turning point, the moment I grew up politically. The base was like an American suburb, except for the shantytown of brothels that provided our troops R&R. After a year of living and working in a small fishing town, I was shocked at the racist, sexist comments that my fellow Americans made about Filipinos/Filipinas. I could also see that my country was using the Philippines to stage an unnecessary war in Vietnam. That visit was so sobering.

I never did take my grand tour of Asia. I was more interested in going back to graduate school. In the early days some universities and schools thought that returned volunteers might be special. Being in the first wave of RPCVs helped me get a couple teaching jobs and a scholarship for graduate studies. I started graduate school in history at Columbia University where I was a student counselor at the International House. I befriended a die-hard Russian "commie" who loved American culture and introduced me to poetry readings, Shakespeare-in-the-park, off-Broadway plays, and the Washington Square folksingers. Meanwhile, I was poring over the papers of the Philippine's first colonial governor, William Howard Taft. His papers were full of patronizing, racist views of our "little brown brother," and benevolent Americans, who were supposedly "democratizing" backward Filipinos.

After a glorious year in New York, I moved to Chicago and lived with ex-Philippine PCVs Dave Szanton and Nick Royal. I taught American history at the University of Chicago Lab School while Gloria finished her M.A. During the year in Chicago another miraculous event occurred. An anthropologist, Bob Textor, who was returning from Southeast Asia was visiting Dave, who was studying anthropology. When introduced to me, he recalled my name from Father Lynch's survey of Philippine PCVs. After a good conversation, Bob offered me a scholarship to be his first anthropology student at Stanford. I jumped at the chance, married Gloria, and headed west. The bay area of the mid-sixties was filled with street demonstrations, smoking pot, free love, and hailing the revolutions of Che, Mao, and the Black Panthers. As my sophisticated urban Group III buddy Tom Newman quipped, those were pretty heady times for a "rube from Iowa." I participated in the great American "cultural revolution" as much as possible for a married graduate student with two kids. Meanwhile, ex-Philippine PCVs Ron Herring, Roger and Ellen Watson and I designed and ran two Peace Corps training programs. That gig proved to be an interesting challenge, and we helped quite a few people avoid the Vietnam draft while serving in the Peace Corps. Our main innovation was to replace shrinks and psychological testing with an intense group dynamics and self-selection process. We were also big advocates of doing most of the training in country. We had high hopes that the Peace Corps would adopt our approach to training.

After finishing my graduate studies, we returned to the Philippines to do dissertation research. As I was completing the fieldwork, the Ford Foundation offered me a regional rep job. When my wife's family learned that we might stay, they were anxious for me to help them create a modern swine farming operation. I almost put writing the dissertation on hold to stay in the Philippines, but my advisor convinced me that if I started working for Ford I would never finish. I followed Textor's advice and returned to the U.S. and wrote a dissertation on American's colonial educational policy and its legacy, a politically corrupt education system. In the spring of 1970 I took a teaching job at the University of Texas in Austin. In the early years, I taught South East Asian courses and had hopes of returning to the Philippines to do more research. But when the Marcos dictatorship solidified, that became very difficult. Splitting up with my Filipina wife also soured me on returning. Instead, I studied Spanish and turned my attention to the Texas Chicano civil rights movement. After researching the movement for sixteen years and writing a couple books, I did a comparative study of Charles Evers, the first black mayor in Mississippi. Then I returned to my hometown, Tama, Iowa, and wrote a book about Indians and white racism. Reconnecting with my family and rediscovering the Meskwakis turned out to be the highlight of my academic career. Aside from writing books, I spent many enjoyable summers renovating houses and learning carpentry from Steve West, a buddy from Mississippi.

I have always been a little sad about not returning to the Philippines more, but I was able to use what I learned as a PCV in my own country. I am quite sure that Americans gained much more from my Peace Corps service than Filipinos did. And I definitely came away the big winner. The Peace Corps was the intellectual, emotional, and moral experience of my life. No one can ever be absolutely certain that the path taken was better than the path not. I would have had a good life as an Iowa high school teacher and coach, but living in a strange culture and learning its languages launched me into a new life as an anthropologist, writer, and university teacher. I am fairly certain I chose a richer, more challenging life. I developed whatever intellectual and ethical potential I had and passed on what I know about life to many students. My superintendent was right, and my family was wrong. Joining the Peace Corps helped me go through some new doors. What it did not do was teach me how to make peace with my personal demons. That required another large cast of loving characters and is another story. Now, as I head toward the final door, my language-learning mentor Jonathan Epstein has popped up again. A believer in reincarnation, he assures me that we can and will become one with this shining, powerful life force. I will hold onto that image when my little ego, that I worked so hard to perfect, becomes ancient history.

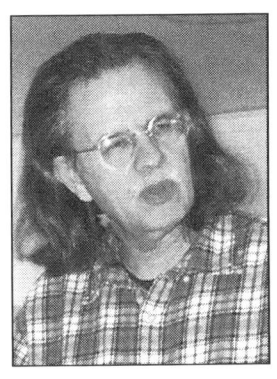
Douglas Foley lives in Austin, Texas, and has been a professor of Anthropology and Education at the University of Texas (UT) since 1970. He has two grown children. Kristina has an MBA from Columbia and lives in London with her Irish stockbroker husband and two boys, eight and ten. Greg has his BFA from the Rhode Island School of Design and lives in Greenwich Village. He is the art director for Visionaire Magazine *and writes children's books. Doug's Filipina ex-wife, Gloria Navarro, is a counselor at Austin Community College. In the spring of 2011, Doug is scheduled to retire from UT and move to Guanajuato (GTO), Mexico. He currently lives with Mariesther Arteaga, a GTO architect/urban planner, and they are building what the philosopher Ivan Illich calls a "convivial space" in the town center. Their Centro de Artes will be a place where people can eat, drink, and enjoy the music, art, artisania, films and cuisine of Mexico. Doug's new career will be running the Center and helping build a few houses for American retirees to Guanajuato.*

Sunshine Gibbs

The Human Connection

In the springtime of my life, in 1961, I was still a green and slippery tadpole following the 9 to 5 stream. I had graduated in the pod of silent generationers and was on a career path to be a building appraiser. Naturally I jumped at the opportunity to swim in the next pool with its visionary promise of a better world.

I packed up my new mantras which I had learned in training: I am a change agent, I am flexible, I am sensitive to others, and I love culture exchanges. I boarded the *M.V.Lukban* out of Manila, a vintage ship under repair, overcrowded, and hardly ready for us, the princes and princesses situated on improvised cots on the captain's deck. Catbalogan was even more of a shock; I saw a wharf and the encroaching green jungle. I was sure the Samar volunteers were goners.

Gamely, I went on to Baybay, Leyte venturing into a surprisingly unknown, exotic, and extraordinary beautiful world that I had little foreseen. The natural creatures were in my face, the mosquitoes, and the geckos chasing them, and the rats that came in for shelter from the rain pounding the tin roof. Then there was the invariable kindness and humanity of the Filipinos, my landlady, Parading, the principal, Mr.Pilapil, and the teachers at the barrio school. And Yolando, a bright student, helped with the chores. When I took the trail behind my two-story house on the road to Tacloban, through the jungle and over the creek, I could see cobras and water snakes, not a bad trade off to being stuck on the freeway to the L.A. County Assessor's Office.

Charles Terry and I seemed to be invited everywhere, and soon after we arrived we attended a prayer service that went on for nine nights for a man whom we had never met. This inclusion in family ritual, the hospitality, and the acceptance was staggering. "Just try," they would say to me. I have tried to maintain that attitude that we are all family—though the other lesson that I learned was that we are formed by very different cultural values, and those differences can be staggering.

The next gigantic wave was conscription which simply swept me up and shipped me to Danang, Vietnam. I learned some new mantras: I am a killer, I protect my loved ones, and I destroy what harms them. I was occasionally able to teach English to students at the Buddhist High School and at the Friendship Association. This war was certainly a wake up call, with its stupidity and cruelty. And I thought we would learn a better way. Better to throw books than bombs, and better to leave a country with schools and clinics instead of bases, unexploded devises and napalm.

At graduate school, I began to look at the streams that had brought me to Southeast Asia and then on a Fulbright I went back again. My Claremont girlfriend joined me in Cebu to meet the Filipinos I worked with and to travel home with me. We climbed Mt.Fuji, difficult but civilized compared to Mt. Mayon with its leeches and not very secure trail. Soon after I joined the protest marches against the war and next joined the war against poverty, working in collaboration with the poor in programs to enhance their ability to control their lives.

The next stream was the most radical; I moved to Santa Cruz from Bakersfield and began to follow spiritual and social values that were an alternative to the mainstream. I climbed my third volcano while on a nine month road trip and off road trip through Mexico and Guatemala. Vulcan Pacaya was heaving and belching lava as I watched the birthing of the earth. Not quite done with amazing adventures, I climbed the great pyramid of Tikal—below, howler monkeys and parrots in the tree canopy and the remains of the great Mayan civilization. The next mantra has been invaluable: go slow, and then slower, open your eyes, wider, everything before you is fragile and I will never see it again.

While camped at the Kit Carson campground in Taos, and recovering from hepatitis, I met my next love, Donna, who travelled with me to Santa Cruz. I joined a men's consciousness raising group. By 1976 I was not straight and not willing to live with duplicity. Harvey Milk's assassination and my fear of my teachers and friends and families' reaction scared me. I began to study painting at the community college and I began to join the gay pride parade and to fight for equal rights.

In the winter of my life, I am retired from teaching developmentally delayed young adults. I belong to a number of organizations which never existed before: a gay Sierra club, a gay veterans group, a gay returned Peace Corps organization, a gay community center, and I run in the gay games. Next is a trip to the Four Corners to visit the homeland of the ancestor people with my partner Ralph Alpert whom I hold in the highest esteem and with whom I share this great sea of emotional stability. I am a contented old frog in the increasingly warm and at the moment fouled ocean waters.

I am proud that after our rough start the Peace Corps has been continuously invited to participate in the Philippines, even as that country has searched for its national identity (a process which led to the termination of U.S. military bases). I feel a kinship with Filipinos who took to the streets and contributed to the departure of President Marcos. I admire *Ang Ladlad* for fighting its case before the Philippine Supreme Court, which allowed the gay party's participation in the 2010 elections. Moreover, Ralph and I established a university scholarship for a Visayan student, and Yolando, with help, graduated from college. That kinship with the Philippines and Filipinos is part of my life; and again I experienced their wonderful sense of humanity and compassion when Filipina healthcare workers lovingly attended to my mother during her last year.

Wayne Guise
Why Can't We Be More Like Them?

Our eyes met. He waved, and the motorcade continued. It was 1960, fifty years ago, and John Kennedy was campaigning in my city of York, Pennsylvania. My presidents up to that time had been Roosevelt, Truman, and Eisenhower, each for eight years of my life. They were respected by my family and many, because of their ages and experience. Now Kennedy, only 43, maintained that a new generation was ready to lead, at home and around the world.

I had just taken my first trip overseas, to Europe, and it included a full month in the Soviet Union. Fifteen of us, mostly in our twenties, traveled slowly by bus from Leningrad in the North, to Moscow, and then to Yalta and the Black Sea in the South.  Many Soviets we encountered had never seen an American before, and were curious and surprised, along with us, at how much we seemed to have in common. Only 15 years removed from World War II, when more than 20 million Soviets died, they wanted nothing more than peace, though our two governments, mired in a bitter cold war, were threatening just the opposite. We travelers began to take seriously our possible roles of little peace ambassadors, where honest discussion and friendliness dealt with our many misconceptions. We found the experience to be tremendously invigorating. The concept of "people-to-people" now had an urgent relevance to me.

Back home, during my third year of teaching, John Kennedy's admonition that America's younger generation could play a role in fighting poverty, and in promoting peace and understanding abroad, really spoke to me. I eagerly applied for his Peace Corps and in December of 1961 entered training to serve in the Philippines.

My assignment to a small farming village in Leyte, suited me fine, for I was born on a farm and grew up in a very small town near Gettysburg, Pennsylvania. My parents had very little education, but they were hard working, religious, and patriotic. I too loved my country and the ideals for which it stood. World War II, which took my father from us for 2 years, impacted my world view.

Armed with this background, along with a degree in education, and a share of Kennedy's idealism, I was motivated to have the experience of a lifetime, and that it was.

My two years in the Philippines included some teaching, but a lot of working with teachers. There were serious health and sanitation issues in my barrio needing extensive adult education and the construction of toilets for every house. Music and sports provided me with many connections and enjoyment. There was the traveling library, the organizing of youth groups, and helping to start a local newspaper. I experienced my first earthquake, the eye of a typhoon, and the climbing to the top of a volcano, Mt. Mayon. Once a snake that had curled up on my toothpaste gave me pause. I gave mouth-to-mouth resuscitation to a villager who had stopped breathing, only to learn later that the death was caused by infectious tuberculosis. Staff physicians assigned to Peace Corps Manila were not happy.

Christmas caroling was wonderful. The lush green expanse of rice fields, the coconut palm groves, the amazing tropical sunsets, and magical moonlight were always feasts for my eyes. There was no electricity, running water, or telephones of any kind; my vehicle was a bicycle, my road unpaved and very muddy in the rainy season.

I was boarding a bus on November 23, 1963 when I heard the shocking words, *Pinatay hi Kennedy*. My president was dead. I gathered with some other PCV's, and we sat in stunned silence for a time. Oddly, one of my grandmothers died at about the same time in a Pennsylvania highway accident.

Mr. Antoni, Mrs. Tan, Andres Yu, Lily Pedrera, and Mana Basiang were just a few of my adult friends whose faces and voices are still fresh in my memory, like it was yesterday. The same for so many of my students like Salvador and Maria.

I was in a position to assist financially a number of very poor high school and college students. That work still goes on today. After eight years of struggle and support, Mary Grace Jimenez graduated from college just a few months ago in April of 2010. She can now help her family and give back to her community. Jay Ann Capate will follow next year.

When my extended tour of duty was coming to an end, two busloads from my village accompanied me to the airport, an hour away, to say goodbye. Tears, including mine, were plentiful.

I look back and marvel at the genuine friendships that had been formed. What is it that happens when well-meaning hearts reach across a significant cultural divide to work together? This process, at the core of the Peace Corps ideal, is a gold mine for international harmony.

On the way home to the USA I traveled alone, for three months, visiting 34 countries in Asia, Africa, and South America—far too many experiences to share here. Once home, I completed a graduate degree at Northwestern University, and my ongoing career was ready for the choosing.

I was finished with the Peace Corps, but the Peace Corps was not finished with me. Propelled by my experience in the Philippines, I sought and received a teaching assignment in the inner city of Philadelphia. Promising myself to stay at least three years, I instead reached to 30 years, all the way to my retirement. During those years there came a number of additional undertakings that connected to the Peace Corps still in me. I volunteered extensively at the International House in Philadelphia, and for one summer was a North Carolina Volunteer, serving a rural community which needed to better access government services. In the 1980s, three different spring breaks saw my family, which included two teenagers, doing a full week of volunteer service, one in Haiti helping to staff a free medical clinic; another was in Mexico for construction and day care services, and then Montserrat to help rebuild after hurricane Hugo. In Calcutta, I met Mother Teresa and did volunteer work at her sites there as well as in Nairobi and Addis Ababa. 1994 saw me at a refugee camp in Tanzania, just across the border from crisis riddled Rwanda. My group helped to process those fleeing the carnage.

In recent years I have tutored Chinese students to help improve their English skills, and have used teaching materials dating back to my Peace Corps training. Ah, those minimal pairs. I even applied to fly in the Space Shuttle's "Teacher in Space" project. It seemed that Peace Corps in my resume would improve my chances. Maybe not. I have revisited my barrio in the Philippines six times over the years. Friendships there have withstood the test of time and live on.

Just now I am reminded again how much the Peace Corps was an event that forever changed me. At age 73, I am still influenced by it and thankful for the legacies of John Kennedy, Sargent Shriver, and all who have served.

To be sure I experienced plenty of moments and days that were very frustrating and discouraging. The cycle of poverty was a formidable adversary. Applying our special "American know-how" often did not work. Sometimes there was the feeling, "Why can't they…be more like us?"

Then came cultural immersion, a slower pace, more patience, and focus on family and personal relations.

Back home in the USA, where material possessions usually defined a person, my feelings now became…

Why can't we…be more like them?

John Halloran
Samar Memories

Witch Doctor

Personae: Doñing, their cook. Tony, his twelve-year-old son.

Doñing's mind was soon focused on another problem. His small daughter lay sick with fever, then chills. She had vomited up the Peace Corps pill. He said he had sent his son Tony out at midnight for some medicine from the doctor. I remembered that our public health doctor was out of town just then, so I asked what doctor he had consulted.

Doñing had sent Tony to a witch doctor who supplied some herbs for five pesos. The witch doctor said some secret words over the herbs, and then revealed the reason the little girl had gotten sick. At six o'clock one evening, she had wandered away from the yard to a seesaw in the schoolyard. In doing so, she had crossed the path of a group of *encantos* passing by on their way toward the ocean. They were angry with her interference, and had made her sick.

The girl seemed to improve with the herbs, but the witch doctor said there must be further appeasement. Doñing must cook a black chicken on a certain day, and have it ready at six o'clock, when the same procession of *encantos* would pass by again (they seemed to pass by quite often at six o'clock). The family could eat the chicken later, but it must be ready as an offering for the passing spirits. Doñing said the *encantos* come and go to the sea on a sort of "highway" that runs near his house. These are the people we cannot see, Doñing said.

Doñing cooked the black chicken, and the small girl continued to improve. However, this was not the end of the matter.

A few days later, Doñing asked if he could borrow seven of our Noritake china plates (included in a Peace Corps-provided kit awaiting each Group III household) and seven cigarettes. When I quizzed him, he said there would be an appeasement banquet for the people we cannot see. He further said the witch doctor did not want me to know about the arrangements, but that my American cigarettes would be better than Filipino cigarettes. The banquet would be at six o'clock that evening, when the *encantos* would pass by again.

I was greatly interested in the strange proceedings that were to take place. I wanted to go to Doñing's house to see everything up close, but Doñing said it was a secret affair. The witch doctor had said that John must "not know." I closed our shutters and pretended to be absent, but I watched as much as possible through a wide crack at the front of our house.

Doñing first had to buy a black pig. It cost him twenty pesos. A nephew of the witch doctor butchered it in the afternoon. Doñing made a fire in his yard and roasted the pig without salt. Shortly before six o'clock, the witch doctor himself arrived. From what I could tell, he was rather modern looking. He was dressed in a colorful flowered shirt that he wore loose over the top of his trousers. The men built a special fire in the yard and threw some incense into it, which caused a mystical haze in the air. They then placed a long table in the schoolyard near the seesaw, on which they placed seven plates of pork and other foods. They carefully arranged a cigarette at each plate.

The men returned to the house and waited. At the appointed time, the witch doctor went alone and stood at the head of the table. He began summoning the people we cannot see. He emitted three shrill shrieks, which was the invitation. He then talked in Waray to the *encantos,* who by that time were evidently seated at the table. He apologized for the wrong the little girl had done, and asked forgiveness on her behalf. There was a long silence at that point, which I assumed was the dining and response time of the *encantos.*

After this strange supper, the men took the food back to the house, added salt, and the people we can see—Doñing, the witch doctor and all—had a big supper with *tuba.* From my vantage next door, the affair sounded like a happy gathering.

Doñing related all these events to me next day. He also told me that the witchdoctor was disappointed there was not more *tuba.* Doñing had supplied only one gallon.

In the aftermath of this affair, Doñing's daughter was still sick. She was now partially paralyzed. I was afraid the witch doctor would prescribe more appeasement (and this time with more than one gallon of *tuba*), but after a few days, the little girl greatly improved. She could walk and talk and seemed to be recovering from her polio-like sickness. "Witch doctor very good," Doñing said.

Christmas

Personae: Fred, his Peace Corps housemate. Doñing. Tony.

On Christmas Eve day, I decided to make a quick trip to Catarman to buy a few things for Christmas. With the warm, sunny weather, it was difficult to acknowledge that Christmas was next day. I realized that I missed snow.

My shopping in Catarman involved little more than buying a hard-crusted loaf of bread at the Chinese bakery that I took home wrapped in newspaper. In wandering about, I happened upon a number of Bobon people searching the markets and stores to pick up last minute items before going home for the celebration of the Nativity. One man told me that chickens were hard to find, another that there was a scarcity of good fish. On the crowded bus that returned us home, a number of chickens and strange-looking fish rode along. I had earlier watched some shoppers load a pig into the baggage compartment under the floorboards. The pig squealed a great deal.

It was on this hot, crowded, smelly bus that I experienced the universal excitement and anticipation of Christmas. Everyone had sought out last-minute purchases of special little things for their families. Innumerable times I was asked (and asked in return), "What will be your viand for Christmas?" I was getting as nosey as anyone. Some passengers were from other towns, going home on the eve of the feast, when the most important place to be in the world is in the intimacy of your family. Halfway to Bobon, I found a place to sit in the rear section of the bus. I parked myself on the floor next to a stack of cargo. A woman I knew who had squeezed into a crowded seat nearby turned and said, "You will observe how we observe Christmas in the Philippines." Later, she turned again and said, "Christmas is our happiness."

That evening, Fred and I lit some candles and a kerosene lamp and listened to children carolers passing by on their rounds of serenading. Doñing was back and forth between our house and his, doing last-minute tasks. He asked if he could borrow a pair of my leather shoes for Tony to wear to Midnight Mass. The shoes fit Tony quite well, although they were a few inches too long. I had a feeling of anticipation that night, as if something tremendous was about to happen.

I asked Doñing if he would go to Mass and take communion. He said that was the custom in Bobon. "Jesus comes and the people are fond of taking Him," he explained. He talked about the birth of Christ as if we had never heard the story before. "Jesus will be born about twelve o'clock tonight," he said, adding "If not at 12, then maybe 12:30 or 1." He said that he and his daughter would take communion, but "Tony, no." Although older than his sister, Tony had not yet made his first communion. Nothing was said about Doñing's wife, Doling, and her religious habits.

At 11 that night, the church bells began to ring. Doñing came to our doorway dressed in a bright white suit that looked like a pair of pajamas not quite large enough to accommodate his short, stocky physique. I had never seen him dressed up before. He looked transfigured from his usual tattered T-shirt and shorts.

We joined people from all over to walk in the darkness to the church, which was soon packed for the midnight service. Images of Joseph in a felt hat and Mary beside him stood in the sanctuary, but the baby had not yet arrived. As the ritual began, the voice of the priest competed with the crying and rustle of children. All hell broke loose at the Gloria that holy night—bells clanged overhead, firecrackers sounded in the entryway, a huge sun and moon passed over our heads from the back of the church to the front, moved on ropes. Rushing their role in the activities, the *Tres Reyes* of cardboard descended into the sanctuary on ropes. And lo, there was suddenly a baby in the center of things, coming from where, I do not know. I looked at my watch: 12:25. The Incarnation had indeed taken place as scheduled.

I could think of no better place to be that noisy, mysterious night. The Word was made flesh and dwelt amongst us Filipinos and all the world. As the crowd filed out from the church, I noticed Tony walking cautiously in my long, narrow shoes. I thought he looked quite redeemed.

Reflections on the Peace Corps

Personae: Members of Group III

A wedding of two of our group members in Leyte was also a reunion of some thirty of our Group III assigned in Samar and Leyte. It was great to see many of the people again, contemporaries who had joined the Peace Corps in its first year of existence. How we were doing was in the minds of all. We brought each other up to date, swapped stories, and assessed our roles in the work of the Peace Corps. It seemed we were not at all effective as catalysts for change. However, as people adjusting to and fitting into Philippine communities, our record was better. I had the gut feeling that Fred and I were as well adjusted as anyone, but it was impossible to evaluate either our work or our adjusting with certainty. Clearly, there was much frustration (both expressed and unexpressed). Some were ready to go home.

About that same time, Groups I and II were actually preparing to go home. Their prevailing mood seemed to me to be frustration and resentment. Many felt like guinea pigs in a noble effort that might be based on a false premise.

After much reading and reflecting in later years, I concluded that we were a mild, harmless, modern-day form of colonialism in the Philippines. We were involved with a society that could smile and seem to approve our suggested changes, but did not really want the changes. Their priority of having smooth interpersonal relationships made them hospitable and smiling. It was okay if changes were introduced (and actually made), because once the innovators left the scene, the Filipinos could always go back to their old ways. Stanley Karnow's *In Our Image* was important in helping me to reach this conclusion.

Nonetheless, our wedding weekend in Tacloban made clear, whether we admitted it or not, that we all wanted to make our mark in the long run—certainly for ourselves, and possibly for America as well. I know now, many years later, that some Volunteers left their mark on my memory. By this time, I realized there was nothing more pleasing and endearing to Filipinos than an American who learned their language. I reached that conclusion after talking to a Filipino on a rural bus who told with tears of joy about meeting a Peace Corps man, Chip Salmon, who could speak Waray "like a native." Chip was a member of our Group III. Several others had become fluent in Waray. Several others had learned Cebuano, the language spoken on the west coast of Leyte. Still another Volunteer in our group, Steve Wells, stayed in the Philippines for ten years as Peace Corps staff, working on the assignment and support of Peace Corps Volunteers. And, of course, Kathy Mooney had left her mark on me as a real live presence of the Blessed Virgin at a barrio fiesta. Hers was no mean achievement, if not for religion, at least for sportsmanship. In the end, perhaps the best marks were made by those who realized they never made a mark at all.

Leaving Samar

Personae: Doñing. Fred. Margaret, my sister, who came from the States to travel home with me, Terry, the Filipina who became Fred's wife.

The night before our final departure I slept little. After midnight, the world outside our nipa house lay in total darkness. We had said goodnight earlier to some of the townspeople who remained after the party ended. They seemed not very aware that in a few short hours we were actually leaving for good. Doñing had been in and out with a sad air before retiring to his house. Fred had also gone to his rattan bed. All was quiet as we closed the front shutters. We left a kerosene lamp burning low in the front room as Margaret and I lay down in a nervous night watch. We rose about 3 am, sealed up our travel bags, and prepared to walk to the main road of town. The early bus from Catarman was scheduled to pass by about 4 am. As the town lay in sleep, we were slipping away in the darkness, unnoticed.

I had walked the path to the dirt street that led to town a thousand times, but in the pitch darkness we literally had to feel our way. The world was devoid of light as well as life. I knew the general direction, but I stepped cautiously, a hand outstretched. Margaret followed, holding onto the back end of my suitcase. It was so dark we could not even see ourselves.

I knew the terrain—a path, then a sharp turn down a side street. With each step, I cautiously tested what lay ahead. There were houses and buildings on both sides, but they were invisible. We crossed a stretch of cement where our neighbors dried rice in harvest season. We moved slowly. A light rain began to fall. This last, short walk to the main road was a long, awkward journey. Finally, I sensed that we had reached the main road. An interior light from a building affirmed my surmise. We stood close to the structure beneath an overhang to watch for the bus.

We could not see the soft rain, but we heard its sound and felt its wetness in the air. We waited in silence. At last, a light appeared in the distance. It became a double light as it grew larger, the headlights of a vehicle. We now saw the straight lines of rain illuminated by the headlights. Soon we heard the rattle of the bus. The dim light of its interior became visible. I stepped onto the road to signal our presence. The bus came to a halt where we stood. With a shout from the driver, we climbed aboard and took places on the hard wood seats of the half-empty bus.

I was leaving Bobon with a mixture of joy, relief, and regret. My role there, my story, seemed not yet complete. It was difficult simply to get on a bus and ride away from the lives of people who for so long had been of such interest and importance. I had heard many Filipinos express an aphorism that seemed trite: "We know not our fate." Now the idea seemed not so trite, and certainly apropos to my state of mind. I was as interested in knowing the fate of these people as I was my own future. The bus rattled through town, crossed the Bobon River, and moved west in the night....

My last view of Samar is deeply etched in memory. I looked back as the ferry moved out on the water. Through a mist, the green hills looked pristine, as if undiscovered. I thought I was leaving a place that would never change, while knowing that all things do change.

In the decades following, the Philippines saw an increase in dire poverty, caused in part by the plundering of the nation's treasury by President Ferdinand Marcos. In the 1980s, the Communist insurgency of the New People's Army, strong in northern and eastern Samar, created factions not unlike the fissures caused by the Japanese occupation. A confusion in loyalties made for mistrust and divided communities. Samar was a hotbed for the New Peoples Army. Two armies seemed to be operating on the island, one government, and one insurgent. With myriad political feuds and competitions already existing, this confusion created further unrest, uncertainty, and death. Robbers affiliated with the New Peoples Army killed Terry's uncle, Mr. Alvarez, at his fish farm.

I fancied that, if I returned to Samar some day, things would be much the same as when I left. I see now that my fancies were selfish and unfair. Samar needed and deserved change. Nonetheless, in the years ahead I became somewhat disconcerted, even astonished, when I learned of some of the changes. In photos that came decades later, Bobon looked less gray, as if it were a victim of some strange coloration process. Had they discovered paint? With whitewash and a bell tower I thought was folly, the church looked less Spanish. And why were so many streets paved? Why was the National Road through Bobon all concrete? I learned there was now a paved highway that connected Allen and Calbayog, with connections to other points south. I thought of Marcos—and of Hitler and his Autobahns.

Bobon was eventually electrified. Much later, it was also cable-ized. For those who could afford 200 pesos a month (as well as some who could not), the Cable News Network was now available. Beneath the cosmetics and new links with the world, I knew (or at least hoped) the Samar I left behind still existed—its fiestas and fireworks, its *encantos* and *wakwaks*, its pleased and displeased Santos Niños, its Sacred Hearts over dashboards, the passage of people we cannot see, bolos for cutting weeds, the *kuratsa* and new dance steps, strange ladies in white, 4 am butchering for viands to eat, subtrahends and minuends, the national anthem sung in schoolyards, carabao racing (but none riding buses), and sixth graders harmonizing *Whispering Hope*.

I never returned to the Philippines. In my memory, however, I really never left, for Samar and its people are often in my thoughts. Living in Bobon was a focal experience of my life.

This essay is taken from A Wedding in Samar, *a memoir by John Halloran, which will be published posthumously. John brought more worldly experience to his Peace Corps service than did most Volunteers. Born in Bismarck, North Dakota in 1930 to a long-resident Irish family, John was an Army veteran who served in Korea. He left a job teaching high school English to join the Peace Corps, and was the oldest of the Group III contingent. If John was not exactly one of "Kennedy's children," he wanted an opportunity to do some good in the world, hopefully amidst exotic surroundings. After his Peace Corps service, John returned to Bismarck and worked for several years as a writer/editor. Later, he opened and operated two gift shops that featured imported crafts, mostly from Third World countries. In 1978, he married Virginia Nelson, another gift shop operator. From their union was born a daughter, Katherine. John and Virginia combined their businesses into one store, which the couple operated until a few years before John died in 2000. John shared his Peace Corps assignment in Bobon, Samar with Fred Knoth.*

Fred Knoth
Peace Corps English Fluency Projects in the Philippines:

Then and Now

Imagine being in same Philippine town where you worked as a Volunteer almost fifty years ago and discovering that eight PCVs were in the throng of Santo Niño fiesta celebrants. That's exactly what happened to me this last January in Bobon, Northern Samar. Another surprise was to find that two of them had been assigned to work in educational settings, one at a high school in Bobon, the other at a university nearby. A large part of their efforts were to be devoted to improving English fluency. (They had arrived in the Philippines in November, 2009).

Another surprise was receiving an invitation to write up some recollections of my early '60s experience as a member of one of the "pioneer" Peace Corps groups to go to the Philippines. I decided I would accept by comparing (my experience of the) ways the Peace Corps planned our training and job duties then with what is going on now. The Peace Corps in today's Philippines is working in a variety of fields. However, there is one field of activity that connects past and present and that field is education, more specifically work in promoting English fluency.

Important Note:

Most of the early Volunteers in the Philippines were assigned to work in two elementary school subjects: English and Science. In order to make a feasible comparison between the sixties and now, I will limit my discussion to the PCs role in English fluency projects as science education is not an area of focus for today's Volunteers. Since I am focusing mainly on the Volunteers' "technical assistance" role, I won't be giving much attention to the roles of promoting better understanding of America on the part of Filipinos and a better understanding of Filipinos at home.

Let's take a look at some ways to compare the beginnings of the Peace Corps' English fluency program (1961-1963) with what's going on now. I am picking out these factors: length of service, training, plus coordination between host country institutions and the PC including work activity structure, and supervision.

Length of Service

Then, training and service totaled two years. Now, pre-service is normally three months plus two years of service.

Training

Training seems different not so much in content as in venue and process. The most important change is that now all training takes place in the Philippines and often in a provincial town in the language/dialect area where volunteers will be working. For instance, 20 volunteers currently assigned to the Leyte/Samar region received the formal part of their training in Tacloban/Palo area of Leyte. My group, Philippines III, was sent to a jungle mountain camp in Puerto Rico to undergo an "Outward Bound" program which was expected to help prepare us physically and psychologically to endure the culture shocks that assignment to remote areas overseas would entail. There was nothing in this training that was semi-relevant to the Philippines aside from the climate and Puerto Rico's Spanish colonial history. The classroom training that followed took place in the winter snows of Penn State University with all in-country training done in a Manila suburb. As part of their pre-service training, volunteers now live for three months with a host country family that lives in the area where they are assigned. This gives them a familiarization with the country's culture that was not a part of the Corps training plan for us in 1961-2. During this time, they also assess the status of English teaching activities at their school work sites; then they write up a project plan for their service period and submit it for review/approval by the school's principal or administrator.

Obviously, today's English fluency project volunteer is benefiting from a long history of Peace Corps involvement in Philippine and world-wide operations in the education sector. I will just cite one example: volunteers are given a well thought out manual on Teaching English as a Foreign or Second Language. The manual anticipates many of problems that the volunteer English teacher is going to face in a third world school and offers many apt solutions. We early educational aides would have loved to get our hands on this manual which includes ten different approaches to teaching English to non-native speakers. Our language training focused on one method.

Coordination with local officials

The Planning/Coordination of the PCVs Work Site Activities with Host Country School Representatives is another area where the past can hardly compare with the present. The Peace Corps representative who set up our work site in the town of Bobon had apparently been impressed with its young mayor's ideas and enthusiasm for community development. This was the main reason the rep said he had selected Bobon to be one of the two municipalities (out of 24 towns in the northern part of Samar province) to receive America's New Frontier messengers. Somehow advance word of the rationale for our assignment to the town did not trickle down with much clarity to my companion, PCV John Halloran (1930-2000), and me in terms of why we were there. We heard later that the central elementary school principal informed her teachers that a "Priest Corps" would soon be working with them. Naturally, the school staff were wondering just what the priests' classroom involvement would be.

During our training, we were told that one of our activities would be assisting the Philippine Bureau of Public Schools with a new method of teaching English as a second language. We concluded that this meant that that teaching staff had received some prior in-service orientation/training and perhaps even printed materials on the new method. Local and regional school personnel had not heard anything about it. It seemed as though we few PCVs were the only ones assisting in this new approach to teaching English.

In general, our roles and responsibilities as educational aides then were mostly unstructured. A fair number of PCVs in our group were able to take advantage of this situation to create and improvise. Some were successful. Whatever positive gains that were made in the area of helping the Filipinos meet their needs "for trained manpower" by volunteers in those days, I believe, can be attributed almost exclusively to their own individual efforts. The Peace Corps as an organization had little to do with Volunteer achievement aside from a monthly living allowance plus medical and psychological support. The wonder was the amazing work volunteers were able to do despite a seemingly impossible work environment.

Unfortunately, I was not one of those self-starting and creative people that many of my colleagues turned out to be. I had no academic background or experience in teaching. John Halloran, my partner in Bobon, who had been a high school teacher with five years' experience, after some noble attempts in local elementary classrooms (more prolonged attempts than mine) joined me in a fallback position as representatives of an America that projected goodwill, understanding and concern for "those living in the poorest areas" of the world. People mostly thought of us as friendly dignitaries that lent a kind of Kennedy aura to the town. They wanted us to enjoy life there and we were entertained as local celebrities at a seemingly endless round of parties.

What about the tasks of today's PCVs working in Philippine education? Their roles and responsibilities seem very structured compared with the near total freedom we had to develop our job duties. For instance, during training and before they go to their assigned work sites, they meet one or more times with their host country school administrator/principal to discuss mutual expectations and begin clarification of the PCVs role/s. The volunteer currently assigned to the Bobon School of Philippine Craftsmen (a vocational high school) is co-teaching two first-year English classes and two fourth-year English classes. She is also taking on a library improvement project there. During the School's summer vacation period (April and May), she is joining other PCVs who will gather in the Manila area. They then will serve as presenters and coaches at English fluency workshops for secondary school teachers being flown in from Mindanao. As civil unrest in Mindanao prevents Peace Corps operations there, these workshops will give teachers from that area some exposure to the English fluency project services being provided by volunteer instructors elsewhere in the country.

In contrast, if my memory serves me correctly, we Group III Volunteers were left mostly to our own devices during those languorous Philippine summer vacation months. One summer, we even had an extra free month, as the Bureau of Public Schools had decided to move the summer vacation months in increments so that the country's school year would eventually coincide with the school year in the United States. Heaven knows why!

Rationales for Peace Corps English Fluency Projects in the Philippines

What were we told about reasons why the Philippines needed volunteers to promote English fluency in the early sixties? The word most frequently heard on this subject was deterioration in the use of English by Filipinos. One of my PCV colleagues remembers that "the rationale for our program was that after the Americans left following WW II, the creeping influence of Filipino dialects into spoken English was rendering Filipino English less and less understandable to non-speakers of Filipino-English." I remember being told in training that studies had been done showing that deterioration over the years had definitely taken place. As far as I can remember, our trainee group asked no questions about the "studies." I believe we were so excited and enthusiastic about becoming volunteers in this New Frontier effort, that we had no interest in questioning why we were needed. I didn't have any trouble understanding the English spoken by host country teachers.

To help stem the deterioration, PCVs would serve as mother tongue models of English speech and assist the Philippine Bureau of Public Schools (BPS) in introducing the "aural-oral" method of teaching English as a second language. As I mentioned earlier, teachers in the area where I was stationed were unaware that the BPS had decided to begin implementation of this new approach. We discovered that that there had been a change in the language curriculum in grades one and two. In 1957 the medium of instruction in those grades was changed from English to the vernacular to promote literacy in the language students were using in everyday life. In that year as well, English began to be taught as separate subject in those grades. Children entering first grade then started learning to read and write in their vernacular language (Waray-Waray) plus English and Filipino (the national language) taught as separate subjects. This was setting for the Bobon Peace Corps when they entered a couple of the town's schools to introduce the new English teaching method and serve as mother tongue models of English speech.

As far as I can determine, our training program offered no official rationale for placing most of our group of volunteers in elementary schools in rural towns and barrios.

What is official rationale for today's Peace Corps involvement in Philippine English proficiency projects? Just as it was thought to be happening after WW II when the GIs left, the deterioration of English still seems to be going on, but the needs of foreign business now provide the incentive for the promotion in its proficiency:

> Over the past two decades declining knowledge of English has weakened the Philippines' once strong competitiveness among Asian countries vying for foreign business investment. In 2006 the Philippine president requested Peace Corps to assist in a national campaign aimed at restoring English fluency. (Quoted from: *A Welcome Book*, Peace Corps Philippines 2009, p. 10.)

Today's PCVs working in Philippine education are no longer assigned to elementary school classrooms. They work as co-teachers of English Language fluency in high schools, primary teacher education, and in government funded colleges/universities.

Concluding Remarks

Would it be an exaggeration to say that, in its pioneer years, the Peace Corps needed the Philippines more than the Philippines needed it? My musings over the years reinforced by recent reading of that era compel me to say "no." I believe that expediency played a more than lightweight role in the selection of the Philippines as one of the first countries to "invite" volunteers. President Kennedy had charged Sargent Shriver with a mandate to submit a plan for the Corps within one month of his inauguration. Against the advice of some who recommended a start-up on a limited pilot basis, Shriver was galvanized by a plan developed by two young Foreign Service officers, Warren Wiggins and William Josephson. To be truly distinctive agency that would demonstrate a serious commitment to helping with third world needs, it had to begin on a much larger scale than the small nongovernmental efforts than had preceded it. A month after the Executive Order creating the Peace Corps was signed, Shriver implemented plans to have volunteers for Tanganyika, Philippines, and Nigeria begin training within the next four weeks. The following year (1962) Kennedy wrote to Shriver:

> I note that you have plans of increasing the number of Peace Corps volunteers in various parts of the world, such as North Borneo. I would like for you to keep in mind the importance of Latin America, which I think should be the primary area. At the present time do we not have as many in the Philippines as we have in all the Latin American countries? Quoted from: Elizabeth C. Hoffman, *All You Need is Love* (Harvard University Press, Cambridge, 1998), pp. 65-66.

Because of the relatively large numbers of volunteers and the speed with which they were deployed, it doesn't seem surprising that there were problems in structuring the volunteers' job responsibilities and coordinating their efforts with host country agencies. This background explains much of the puzzlement (as described earlier) of the local teaching force in Bobon, Samar as to what they could expect from volunteers John Halloran and Fred Knoth. Another factor bearing on the loosely defined job structure for we early sixties educational aides, was the apparent belief of the Peace Corps planners and administrators at the time that at bottom line it was a people-to-people program. How else can the decision to send the overwhelming majority of volunteers to elementary schools in small rural towns and villages be explained other than the planners mind-set of who "the people" were? Their vision reflected the words of the Peace Corps Act to the effect that Volunteers would help "peoples of interested countries…in meeting their needs for trained manpower, particularly in meeting the basic needs of those living in the poorest areas of such countries." Their image of where "the poor" resided obviously was not the slums of Manila; "the poorest areas" were rural. (70% of Filipinos were rural dwellers at the time.) There was the need for the Corps to find placements for the large number of 'BA generalist' volunteers, the "trained manpower" that had been recruited and trained for service in the country. The small towns and villages of the Philippines, where "the people" were, thus began receiving PCV aides to help with English and Science teaching in their elementary schools, even though in retrospect it seems difficult to connect these work roles with "meeting the basic needs" of the poorest areas.

The first Director of Peace Corps Philippines, Dr. Laurence Fuchs, was well aware of the issues surrounding weakly defined volunteer job tasks and the problems of coordinating volunteer activities with host country education officials. When he wrote his *Ultima Adios* memo to volunteers in May, 1962, he not only recognized the troubling aspects of the Peace Corps Philippines organization but reaffirmed his belief in the supremacy of the Peace Corps people-to-people/mutual understanding goals:

> We have simply recognized that effective human relationships cannot be easily achieved unless Volunteers have worthwhile jobs to do. For me human understanding has been the over-riding and all-pervasive goal of the Peace Corps. The Peace Corps was founded on the belief in the essential community of man. It tests the proposition that truly emphatic and genuine relationships can develop across cultural barriers. That is why we continue to assign Volunteers to rural areas….

Among its early shakers and movers, like Shriver, Fuchs, and others, there was another ideal—that the Peace Corps should be as non-bureaucratic as possible and a corresponding faith in the spirit of American individual initiative and enterprise. This faith meant that given essential support, most volunteers could be trusted to perform well without a great deal of job structure. This is why Fuchs could write later that:

> "The single strongest motivation of volunteers appears to have been the desire to improve the world as individuals on their own."[1]

Many volunteers proved the point but others were confused and frustrated about how to work in the situation they found themselves.

In closing, I pose the question: Who are the pioneers of Peace Corps Philippines? Although it cannot be denied that we Groups I, II, and III are the historic pioneers, a good case can be made that volunteers in the country today face such daunting frontiers there that it makes our sixties era challenges seem like a golden age. Look at a simple statistic: in 1960 the Philippine population was about 27 million; in 2009 it was 97 million. Correspondingly, there has been an immense increase in students. Look at a micro example of this increase. In the 1962-63 school year, the Bobon Central School graduated a class of about forty; in the 2009-10 school year 192 graduated. The education system also has to contend with fewer resources as country's education budget is frozen in compliance with World Bank mandates. In this context, think of the volunteer currently assigned to promote English fluency at the Bobon School of Philippine Craftsmen. She has accepted the challenge of promoting English fluency among a population that outside of school normally speaks neither English nor the national language, Filipino. Partly due to earlier government policies, Filipino language media outlets (television and print) have overtaken the English media that prevailed in the sixties. Satellite television has reached most provincial areas and broadcasts mostly in Filipino/Tagalog. Another micro example: as my wife walked down a Bobon street this April, she noticed a group of children watching a Filipino language comedy through the counter window of a sari-sari store. Our contemporary colleagues surely are as worthy of the title of "pioneer" as we are.

When Fred returned to the United States as a newlywed after completing his Peace Corps service in Samar, he worked in social service for Los Angeles County for 30 years, mostly in training assignments. His last assignment before retiring was a program, "Independent Living Skills," helping older youth in their transition from foster care to independent life. Fred's wife was an elementary school teacher in Northern Samar. She went back to school at California State University in Los Angeles to become a cardiac nurse. They have two children.

---

[1](Lawrence H. Fuchs, *Those Peculiar Americans*, (Meredith Press, New York, 1967), p. 5.

Kathy Hannan Rohan
A Day in the Life of a Peace Corps Volunteer

The sun flashing through the leaves of the tall bamboo provided a sort of magical film strip of dappled light. The principal of my school had invited my roommate and me to a wedding in an interior barrio. To get there we had to walk some distance on a narrow path through a thick bamboo woods—at least I *think* it was bamboo. I felt like we were in an enchanted forest completely removed from the coastal area along the road where we lived.

The path ended at a house where the wedding celebration was in progress. The bride and groom, family, and other guests were gracious and welcoming but made no particular  fuss about our visit. Shortly, the bride and groom began a series of dances. Wow, I thought, I am seeing real folk doing real folk dances. This is a privilege. The young couple was not at all self-conscious. Everything about their demeanor expressed joy and ease with the occasion.

I had no camera or tape recorder or notebook nor did I record my impressions later. I don't remember talking to my principal about the experience and only hope I thanked him appropriately. I never returned to the path through the beautiful woods. But this exquisite experience is the highlight among the memories of my Peace Corps adventure in the Philippines.

OK, the wedding invitation was one of the gratifying opportunities the Philippines provided for me but what did I do for the Philippines? Others have written at length about the Peace Corps project there. I can't imagine that the teachers in Telegrafo were enthusiastic about an advocate of English instruction because at the time the policy of English and Tagalog introduced in first grade and English as the medium of instruction from third grade on was burdensome and unrealistic. But together we worked out some programs in arithmetic and English that went pretty well. And I'd gladly do it all over again.

Kathy Hannan Rohan lived in Tolosa, Leyte and worked at the barrio school in Telegrafo. She was later a volunteer leader in Mindanao assigned to Misamis Oriental, Lanao del Sur and Lanao del Norte. After the Peace Corps, Kathy worked in the first War on Poverty Headstart program in Chicago. She subsequently obtained a Master's in Social Work and was employed by the Utica Community Schools in Macomb County, Michigan for 24 years. Kathy is married to Barry Rohan, a retired newspaperman. They have two children, Elizabeth and Brendan.

Ruth Kesselring Royal
Two Peace Corps Vignettes

Hain it Imo Upod? or Where is Your Companion?

I was twenty-three, beginning my second year in Peace Corps, Philippines. My first year had not been easy. My roommate and I were assigned to a small town at the dead-end of a jog off the main road running through Samar. A pair of dreamers from a group of Volunteers who had been in the Philippines barely longer than us had chosen our barrio because of an American priest there fluent in *Waray*, the local dialect. But between the time this outpost was selected and our arrival, the priest had left. The new American priests didn't speak the language, and were ten-foot-pole-wary of the American girls across the fence.

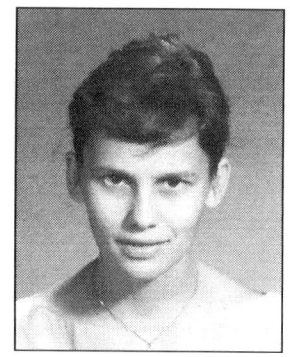

Though materials had been bought to build us a nipa and bamboo house, it still wasn't completely built after four months, and it turned out that the local principal spent the money drinking. When we finally moved in, bamboo for the walls had not been seawater cured and bamboo beetles nibbled away each day and excreted sawdust each night. The bamboo was replaced. The principal was replaced, but the new one had no idea of what to do with me. We were doing an ill-defined job at best—so early in the history of the Peace Corps that often our hosts didn't know what to do with us. I carved out a schedule to help with English as a Second Language and science, and tried to conduct classes for reluctant teachers with much more teaching experience than I had. Half the school had been destroyed by a typhoon ten years before, and it had never been rebuilt. The same was true of the bridge across the river to the nearest town and medical services. At the end of our first year my roommate married another volunteer and moved to his town, and Peace Corps decided that I should not be out there alone.

I was reluctant to move, but went to visit a possible new site near my friends, Tom and Anne who lived on Daram, a small island between Samar and Leyte. It was a delightful refreshing visit that helped me seriously consider moving to an even smaller nearby island of about five miles by seven miles. But now I needed to get back.

There were two ways to get to Samar from Daram. The motor launch, *Samareño* plied daily between Catbalogan, Samar, and Tacloban, Leyte, but did not stop at Daram. To catch the boat Tom could take me across the channel in his outrigger *banca* by 5 in the afternoon and I could ride into Catbalogan, and catch the next morning bus up the west coast of Samar. Or I could take the *Joevic*, a smaller boat which left directly at 2 am and would deposit me in Catbalogan just before the bus left. This would allow us another evening together. So we decided on that one.

We woke in the darkness-before-dawn to the deep-throated boat horn calling would be travelers. We threw on our clothes but could not get to the shore in time. People on the boat and shore laughed to see us run, and miss the boat, but it wouldn't turn back.

Despite the frustration of much of what I was doing, I was anxious to get back to my barrio. So, rather than waiting for the evening boat, or the next early morning one, Tom contacted Romeo, a teen-aged friend, Anne made a grocery list, and Tom and Romeo and I set off in his small boat from Daram to Catbalogan, about 15 miles away.

As long as we were in the shadow of Daram we could move along quite briskly. The phosphorescence you see at night in tropical waters dulled, then seemed to extinguish as pre-dawn greeted us. But as we moved out of the protection of the island and reached the main channel, the slap of the waves on the tiny boat increased and the wind blew against our faces. Tom steered for the sunrise. Romeo and I bailed water with cooking oil tins. Spray off the waves consistently hit me. At the point when the waves were the highest, the wind the strongest, we couldn't see land in any direction at all and I seriously wondered if we were going to make it. But the motor kept chugging away, and eventually the mass of Samar rose in the east. As we drew closer and were sheltered, the wind and waves diminished and we could make more headway.

When we arrived at the wharf, I said a hasty good bye. Tom and Romeo secured the boat and prepared to do grocery shopping, and I scuttled into a public bathroom and wrung seawater from my skirt. Almost immediately after boarding, the bus filled, pulled out and headed north. Though the trip was not more than eighty kilometers, only four were paved. The rest was gravel or dirt, and included one river crossing where the ferry was pulled across hand over hand on a rope.

I shared a seat with an older woman who pulled her clothes away from my damp ones. "*Hain it imo upod?*" she asked me. "Where is your companion?" Traditionally women did not travel alone, but that day I had no companion. She offered me a hard roll from her bag. My stomach was happy to have something, but the dry bread turned to cotton in my mouth.

When we were an hour or so into the trip I began to feel distinctly bad. Little clutches deep in my belly quickly progressed to menstrual cramps that grabbed hold and wouldn't let go. I bent over my knees, trying to alleviate the pain. Perhaps I groaned, turned pale. My seatmate began to shout that I was sick and, at her suggestion, a passenger vacated his seat beside the driver, and helpful hands in each row of seats guided me toward the front of the bus.

The bus was going along a stretch of road perched on a ridge with a few scattered nipa houses behind which fields or open land stretched down the hillsides. My clothes, which had dried, felt clammy and cold again. A passenger opened her bag and shook out a full skirt over me. I was barely conscious of anything except pain. I didn't know how I could hold out for the two or three more hours the trip would take.

Then the bus stopped in a tiny hill village where the driver shouted questions out the window. A young man gestured down the road, and we pulled ahead and stopped. Here the driver sent a child down the road with instructions, but to me he said carefully, "This is a teacher's house. You stay here and rest." His worried brow glistened with sweat.

I objected. I could only think of getting home, and didn't want to be stranded, but the woman who had covered me with a skirt urged me out of the bus and into the unlocked house. A crowd followed me in, gaping and staring until the bus driver and the skirt-woman pushed them out. I curled up on a wooden and rattan settee in the front room. A child brought my bag and set it on the floor beside me.

The bus driver squatted alongside me. "The other bus driver will get you next trip," he assured me. "You sleep now."

I did sleep. As far as I know, the teacher whose house I slept in never came back while I was there. A couple of hours later I was feeling much better. I heard the honks of the northbound bus, gathered my things, and came to the door.

This bus driver grinned at me. "Jorge, the other bus driver, told me to get you here."

I had not known the first bus driver's name, never found out the names of the helpful women on the bus, or ever met the teacher whose house I slept in. But I had encountered the kindness of strangers, the hospitality of the Philippines.

Letter to My Mother—Four Months after Termination Date

You asked me if my extended stay in the Philippines was for romantic reasons. Perhaps you might say so. I, myself, am reluctant to claim love, not being sure of all its complications and responsibilities. So I will tell you what I feel, and have felt, and you must judge if what I describe is love.

You asked me if "the south wind whispered sweet nothings." I don't know if that is what you would call it. On a nice day the sun and sea and sky make music of their own, and even on a gray day, the high tide fills up an echoing tension within me. The heavy rain shuts in the office like a tower above the smell of dampened street dust, and sight of the lights coming on across the street. The hills around have come to seem a part of me. How can those grass-covered slopes which I have never even climbed, seem to express a part of myself? A part of myself. Is that then love? An aching, going-out-from-me intensive feeling of oneness with something not me, but as though it is a part of myself?

In the evening the sun sets across the water, and the hills tinge pinkish. The *kaingin* (slash and burn) fires stand out starkly against the darkening sky. Venus gives bright promises. My feeling is one of estrangement, love that is close and possibly never complete. Communication not quite fulfilled.

Is it love when you can see faults but believe that there is also goodness that makes your belief worthwhile? Is it love that wants something so badly for the other that should staying hurt you, but be best for the other, then you would stay, but if staying creates more hurt, then you would go.

Generosity, hospitality, closeness despite lack of communication, the sweetness of children's faces and words, their laughing eyes. All balanced with jeers and embarrassment. How much does love encompass?

Concern, respect, enjoyment, beauty, empathy. All of these I find here and feel deeply. But also disgust and impatience at filth, greed, and corruptness, as well as my own loneliness. And they are not separate but entwined together, as some of my reasons for staying are also reasons for going, and vice versa.

Is my long stay in the Philippines a romantic attachment? It is an involvement that encompasses all of me with a people who are beautiful and do not acknowledge their own beauty, who sometimes seem to be unconsciously dishonest, yet simply and guilelessly generous, who have renounced most of their own cultural heritage during 400 years of Western imposition, yet subtly retain their own and vestiges of Asian subcultures in ways that they probably wouldn't even admit to themselves.

I am involved with a country that takes me unquestioningly in, yet holds me carefully away; whose languages, culture, manners, religion, foods, are all other than my own; which, with the greatest knowledge, I would still stand only on the threshold of understanding. And yet I am concerned, and feel in some ways responsible.

Is this love, or only infatuation?

Ruth Kesselring Royal was a member of Philippines III. She and her husband, Nick Royal (Philippines II) have lived in Santa Cruz, California since 1969. They have two adult children. Their daughter lives in Berlin, Germany with her husband, and their son lives an hour away from Santa Cruz with his wife and their only grandson. Ruth returned from Peace Corps to the Master of Arts of Teaching program at the University of Chicago that she had left to go to the Philippines. Her husband-to-be Nick was the only other returned Peace Corps Volunteer in that program, and they met there. They both worked a few years for Upward Bound in Milwaukee before coming to Santa Cruz. In Santa Cruz she taught English, science through gardening, and homebound students, and worked at a small library. Since retirement, Ruth tutors adult students working on high school diplomas and basic skills, gardens, and braids rugs. Currently she is editing letters exchanged by a college friend and her during her time in the Philippines and her friend's stint as a PCV in Afghanistan.

Charles Terry

Proud to Be a (Lower-Case) "Peace Corps Pioneer"

I don't actually really know why I applied to the Peace Corps. "Doing something for my country" was much more concrete than any other plan I had. This may sound flippant, but it is not much of an exaggeration.

After a brief stay at a New York hotel which I only dimly remember, training for the Philippines started with three weeks or so of an intense outward bound school type of experience in the Arecibo, Puerto Rico area. Our resiliency and cooperative nature were tested by placing novel demands on us. We learned Drownproofing techniques, rappelled off cliffs and dams, trekked in the rain forest, slept out in a hammock overnight in the rainforest by ourselves, went through Marine Corps type obstacle courses, learned some Spanish, and stayed with Puerto Rican families. It was very instructive to get help and to give help during these challenges, which I think, was one of the points. The staff was colorful and effective.

There were then several months of a more conventional and academic type of training at Penn State University, i.e. Filipino history and culture, as well as teaching techniques and strategies. We were to help train teachers to teach English as a second language and science.

We had little or no classroom work although we were scheduled to have a short observational period in classrooms later in the Philippines. I am astounded that I have no recollection of a vigorous protest from other Group III members about the lack of relevancy of our training. I must be much more of a conformist and a less-critical person than I thought.

In retrospect, at the time, we seemed to be operating with an appalling level of arrogance or at least an overconfidence of a sort which assumed that even admittedly bright and reasonably well balanced liberal arts college graduates could learn to train teachers in English as a second language—a relatively new discipline in the time.

We also received inoculation shots every Friday for prevention of exotic tropical maladies and it seemed as if we were sick every weekend from side effects of these immunizations. The song *Moon River* flooded the airwaves.

We flew west to the Philippines on a flight that went on forever and which was punctuated by a full breakfast including fresh strawberries, served apparently every time we entered a new time zone. If we were flying east, would we have fasted?

Eventually, four of us ended up in the town of Baybay on the west coast of the island of Leyte in the central Philippines, on a stage at night being greeted, it seemed, by the whole town. I was quite intimidated but the stress became much more subtle by the time I got to my own small village (barrio) of Ga-as and settled in.

During the day, I taught parts of classes and sometimes found myself teaching science in Cebuano (Visayan), a language of the central Philippines, instead of English because I cared more about learning than insisting on the approved language of instruction.

The best and the most useful thing I did, however, *way* late in my two-year tour, was to start a revolving loan system to allow families in the community to build water seal toilets. These were concrete emplacements designed in the shape of flush toilets but you had to manually pour water down them to flush them.

Townspeople built a house for me on the grounds of an elementary school. It was a wood frame house with a palm thatch roof, woven palm wall sections and wooden floors—the windows had no screens. I had a wooden bed with mosquito netting, a trunk full of books, a short wave radio and a kerosene pressure lantern. It was about 70-80 degrees year round, but it felt cool at night after your blood thinned out. I had a well until the kids broke it by playing on the handle. You could read easily by the moonlight.

A young Filipino was paid to help haul water for me, deliver breakfast makings and polish the floor by dancing on it with coconut husks, I had lunch with the family of the vice lieutenant of the barrio. Instead of the poor rice farmer's everyday meal of cold rice, tiny salty fish and a root crop, I was treated to plump fish, chicken and pork morsels with hot rice and elaborate salads. Dinner was even more upper middle class and companionably spent with Sunshine (Gene) Gibbs the nearest volunteer a few miles away. There I also got to take a cold shower after negotiating the entrance of a small structure separate from the house, which was shared by a pig tied up there.

Shame v. Guilt

On a perhaps loftier plane, I would become intensely intrigued by the differences between Filipino and American culture and language. Was shame vs. guilt culture a valid if oversimplified differentiation? How did they get by with having only one word for he and she? I think living in what seemed like a very different culture made me understand my own American culture more clearly.

To an American, newly in the country, Filipino culture seemed to be based on the group vs. the individual and on the external constraints of shame vs. internalized guilt. It seemed as if they assumed we were pretty much all alike, for example that we had never eaten rice before and that we were rich (which was true, relatively speaking). Our stipends while there placed us in the lower middle class—not poor but not that rich. They also assumed that a Filipina I courted, despite both of us playing by Filipino rules with the constant presence of a chaperone which I suppose came from 400 years of Spanish colonial culture, essentially rendered her a fallen woman. Their view of Americans came perhaps mostly from G.I.'s who were generous with both blankets and chocolates and also, I suspect, their desire for local women.

Generally, Filipino culture was a very welcoming culture, so that when the Superintendent of the school district and I went into the mountains for a visit, a feast was inevitable, for which a chicken was slaughtered in our honor.

Filipinos laughed and coped easily. They had a saying: *Bisan sagin basta labin*. (Even if we have only bananas as long as we have loving.) In fact, although the everyday rice farmer had little materially, the poverty was more benign than in many developing parts of the world because the climate and soil were good, there was clean water and serious diseases like malaria or cholera seemed not to threaten, at least not relentlessly.

I was fluid but not fluent in Cebuano. At a public meeting, the barrio Lieutenant said "Listen carefully to Charlie because he speaks *mao rag Insec* (like the Chinese) who were a somewhat insulated community in town. Local Chinese apparently distorted Cebuano from native Chinese about as much as I distorted Cebuano from native English.

At night I would often hang out outside the local store where I would drink palm wine, someone would play the guitar and stories were told.

Although I don't recall experiencing very much culture shock or homesickness, I did go through a very serious period of psychological paralysis because I didn't think I could do what we were there to do. I overcame this essentially with help and encouragement and by just "doing it." This might make a good ad slogan for some sportswear company like Nike.

I wrote a revealing letter to another PCV suggesting Sunshine and I put on a fairly sophisticated-sounding seminar for teachers that could have proved quite useful. In my letter I remarked how clearly and supremely irritated I was at how undisciplined (un-American?) the attendees were. Was this more evidence of some culture shock I was experiencing?

Support and communication for our work consisted of volunteer leaders showing up with various forms of encouragement and supplies. They were first-rate, without exception and their paths were not easy: their jeeps broke down on the crushed coral "roads" about every two hours. There was also the telegraph office in town three to four miles away, or you could send messages entrusted to bus drivers. There was no TV and no telephone. I don't remember any local radio. I think transistors were just about to arrive and I think mail had to be picked up in town. I really don't know how we did it.

Unusual events, perhaps fortunately in some cases, occurred infrequently as they are supposed to in life. In town one day I saw a horse-drawn cart run over and kill a dog. The driver, after checking at a nearby store, threw the dog into the back of the cart and drove off, presumably with dinner. Sunshine and I once had dog at a picnic but our companions didn't tell us until a few months later.

Another time I was delivering a bicycle to one of the women PCVs and while riding over a typical rural Filipino bridge of two planks per tire, railroad ties cross-ways and a lot of gaps with no railing, my front tire caught in a groove and over I went sideways and down onto a concrete abutment. The bicycle and I both sustained some damage.

Then there was the volcano adventure—not Mt. Mayon, the regional landmark which a larger group of us climbed or at least in my case assaulted, but in our case a more local version. We hiked up through sugar cane, an unusual crop for the region, and down through slash and burn forest into the crater of a dormant volcano, where you could lie in a cold stream and move near the volcanically heated stone until you reached sauna level. Later we cooked chickens in small bubbling natural pot holes in the stone and subsequently found that any skin rashes magically disappeared apparently because of the natural sulfur type minerals in the water.

I once accompanied a Filipino violinist to a concert in the next town. While riding on the fender of a jeep holding the arm of his impresario who was sitting on the opposite fender, the man's arm became dislocated. It turns out that the Japanese had hung him up by his arms during the war. WWII was only 17 years past and memories were still distinct. For example, easily identifiable foxholes were still discernable on the small hill behind my house and metal landing field strips were in wide use around public spaces such as plazas. The violinist tried to have me reset his arm but I was too timid. It would take a doctor and drugs to take care of his arm.

Near the end of our stay, my relatively meager stuff, including the bicycle and the radio, was shipped or packed. Sunshine's young helper showed up one afternoon and said to me that someone very important in my country was dead and that he didn't know whether it was our President or my father or who. After I walked a few miles to Sunshine's house, I found out it was Kennedy. We went to a friend's house and listened to the Voice of America until they kept repeating themselves and we knew, if we had doubted, that it was real. VOA broadcasts in special English using 800 words and a slow, regular, and authentic intonation pattern sounded normal to us by then.

The Long Way Home

I took six months traveling home, going west. I recall the plane taking an evasive anti-aircraft maneuver by corkscrewing in a tight spiral in its landing descent into Saigon even in early 1964; smelling the reddish brown dust and seeing the swarm of humanity in Calcutta; waking up in the cab of a truck driven by a Sikh to see the tops of the Himalayas; and seeing a funeral pyre on the banks of the Ganges. I continued through the Middle East and Europe and even now when I hear about something happening in the world anywhere near where I was, I feel that I can relate to the distances, the smells, the foods and somehow make much more sense out of it than I could from an atlas.

My Peace Corps experience may have influenced my so-called career. There's a thread but it's much clearer looking backward. After being entranced by such a different language and culture, I went into an academic program called Language and Behavior and almost received a PhD I left to help start a journalism company and eventually ended up designing and writing technical communications. So are teaching teachers and instructional publications related enough to be called a thread? I don't know—whatever.

I am sad and ashamed to say that a few years after leaving the Philippines, I stopped keeping in touch with any of the Filipinos that I was involved with, so that I don't know if I (we) had any real impact on them, but I know they had an impact on me (us) for sure. I still feel very proprietary about the Philippines and what I believe I know about them. Once, when I was newly back in this country, I wrote a bristling letter to a national newsweekly. In an article about election season in the Philippines, they said that most Filipinos prefer to go armed and that they wore sport shirts. Actually, most Filipinos couldn't afford to go armed if they wanted to, and the so called sport shirts were actually fancy embroidered special dress shirts worn for special occasions. I was outraged, but the editors were unimpressed by learning about their own ignorance.

When someone finds out that I was in the Peace Corps, I am invariably proud and I make sure that they know that I was there very early. But I realistically and modestly avoid grandiose words such as "pioneer." Well, okay, maybe not if it's in lower case).

What is the ultimate value of the Peace Corps in and of itself and/or as foreign policy?

Along with the obvious value of efforts such as disaster relief, even relatively untrained, naive young Americans living and trying to help in other countries is a valuable part of a foreign policy and infinitely superior to waging unilateral preemptive war and other sorts of serious misadventures.

Charles Terry and his wife Angel live outside Whitewater, Wisconsin in gracefully rolling dairy country. Part of their limestone house is 160 years old. They raised horses (and a few pigs), had a litter of Bouvier dogs, drive sports cars, and generally have a huge share of fun. Charles designs and writes technical publications. His wife was CEO of a high tech communications company until she suffered a severe head injury. The company's technology was eclipsed by the internet so that they eventually ended up wiser but not richer. Now they are active in various singing groups, read a lot, eat too well, are annoying scrabble players because they know absurdly obscure words, and are active in a church community, one as a believer and one as an agnostic. Charles adds, "This essay was written without reference to any journals recorded at the time which have long since been lost or misplaced. One can only hope that memory serves."

Steve Wells

"I Thought You Were One of Us!"

Achieving Fluency in the Language

From the time I was invited to Philippines Group III training in late 1961, I began to formulate an image of what my Peace Corps experience would bring—and what I would bring to it.

To me, being a Peace Corps Volunteer meant assimilating into the local culture. This was core to the entire concept—to break the mold of the Ugly American. What better way than becoming fluent in the local language?

In the daylong Peace Corps exams I took in Denver in 1961, the Peace Corps naively asked applicants to select from a small list their "country of preference" for consideration for assignment. Colombia was one of those listed. Assuming language fluency simply came with the job and aware that Colombians spoke Spanish, I checked it, thinking that I could at least come back fluent in a major language—the single bankable residual in Peace Corps' infancy when no one knew what value Volunteers would derive upon rejoining U.S. life after their service.

I ended up instead going to the Philippines where there was no operant national language other than Pilipino, the government's attempt to make Tagalog, spoken in the Manila and Central Luzon area, the national language. Pilipino was taught in all schools, but outside the classrooms and in everyday life, local dialects are the lingua franca. A nation of islands, some 87 languages are spoken. A few common words and some Malayo-Polynesian syntax prevail, but if one speaks one language, it is unlikely he or she will be understood by someone from another language area.

Our assignments were to be in the Eastern Visayas region. About half our group would be assigned to areas speaking Cebuano. The other half would live in areas in Samar and Leyte Islands speaking a language called Waray-Waray (literally: "nothing-nothing"). Waray-Waray is one of the ten officially recognized regional languages in the Philippines.

Since individual assignments would not be made until the end of training, the best Peace Corps could do was to teach us about linguistics and some broad-stroke commonalities of Philippine languages. The closest we came to speaking anything was when we memorized the Pilipino lyrics to the Philippine national anthem, *Lupang Hinirang*.

By the time our lengthy in-country training was completed and assignments were made, we arrived just as the school year ended. With no jobs to report to, we had plenty of time on our hands to learn the language.

That's just what my two roommates and I decided to do. We committed to spend as much time as humanly possible to become fluent in Waray-Waray in the two months before classes began. We'd do whatever it took to learn the language, understanding it and speaking it fluently.

It was a daunting task. Waray-Waray wasn't (and still isn't) a written language—only spoken. There are only three main vowels and 16 consonants in the language. Here are some example Waray phrases:
- Good morning (noon/afternoon/evening): *Maupay nga aga (udto/kulop/gab-i)*
- Can you understand Waray? *Nakakaintindi/Nasabut ka hin Winaray?*
- I don't care: *"Baga saho"* or *"Waray ko labot"* or *"baga la bot ko"*
- Where are you from? *Taga diin ka?*
- How much is this? *Tag pira ini?*
- I can't understand: *Diri ako nakakaintindi*

Like any language, Waray is a blend of many languages. Many nouns are Spanish in origin, especially household and clothing articles as well as all time references including months and days—all introduced by the Spanish in their 400-year reign ending in 1898. Other words are derived from Indonesian, something I learned by comparing language notes with a friend who came to visit me from his Peace Corps assignment in Indonesia. Many words are derived from English and some (especially food items) from Chinese. Waray is used for numbers one through ten. From eleven upwards, Spanish is used except for "one hundred" *(usa ka gatos)*.

We had to build vocabulary one word at a time. I kept a notepad with me at all times and built my own Waray-to-English dictionary, organizing words into categories like ("human body," "feelings," "around the house," and so on. Each day we would fan out and strike up conversations with whomever would talk to us—men, women, children. At the end of the day we would huddle around our Petromax kerosene lantern (we had no electricity in our town) to share what each of us had learned, exchanging notes on new discoveries and vocabulary.

Conjugating "Kuan"

Learning conjugation and structure was challenging. In Waray, as in all other Philippine languages, predicates precede subjects. There is no linking verb "to be." Tense and other conjugation is created by combinations of various prefixes, suffixes and/or infixes. Further, the colloquial language is full of contractions and slang. The proper noun "I," for instance—*ako*—became simply *'ak*. In other usages it was shortened to *'ko*. Helpfully, places were always preceded by the word *ha* and people by the word *hi*. Better yet, a conjugatable word, *kuan* could be substituted for anything (verb, noun, name, place) that you couldn't readily recall, like our "what's-his-name" or "whatchamacallit."

The stress of listening intensely to unfamiliar sounds and utterances was fatiguing. To maintain motivation, I asked people to tell me jokes in the Waray so I would be better motivated to concentrate on every word and nuance in order to understand the punch line—the "payoff." Not surprisingly, men favored telling lewd stories, an added bonus making it all the more motivating—not to mention opening the door to a whole new category of words and slang!

Since the only movie theaters were an hour's bus ride from our town, it was common for one person who'd been there to return home and "tell" the movie storyline to his or her friends so everyone could share the experience. Sometimes we'd join the group. With any luck, it was a movie plot we were already familiar with.

Local talk radio was also helpful. One morning show featured jokes and long folksy stories. We were apt listeners.

Practicing the language could get tedious, especially since we found ourselves mentally translating everything we heard into English, then composing a response in English and finally translating it as best we could into Waray. This was a time-consuming process, although I grew to appreciate that the greater one's English vocabulary and skills, the better one will become in a new language.

I would emulate tonal qualities and mannerisms of speakers I conversed with. This had its own pitfalls, because if I'd been conversing with young children, I'd start to sound childlike which was inevitably pointed out to me the next time I practiced on an adult. Likewise with gender—too much time with women and I'd start to sound feminine.

Over time I realized that gaining fluency was like an endless word-game, complex but fascinating, especially when cultural context elements emerged. Culturally, I now knew that language was only the beginning—I had much more to learn about the culture from my Filipino friends. For example, there was almost no way to express any time, other than the present, with any degree of precision. "Yesterday at four o'clock in the afternoon" became as nonsensical as "next Tuesday noon." While it was possible technically to string words together to say these things, they simply didn't make any sense to the listener. In this culture, one had no domain over time. What was past was past and the future bore nothing but uncertainty. The idea that you could speak of actions yet to take place and assign a precise time in the future to them was, well, simply absurd.

Similarly with simple greetings: in the Philippines the typical greeting is *nga-in ka?* meaning, "Where are you going?" We attempted to come up with a vague, noncommittal response, "just wandering around," *mapasi-ada ako*. This would always produce a puzzled response from the locals, who considered it nonresponsive. Eventually we figured out their invasive curiosity was actually a manifestation of the socio-cultural fabric in those pre cell phone days to keep tabs on everyone's whereabouts, a sort of *It Takes a Village* extended-family tracking system.

We weren't the first to display our gaffes when attempting to literally transfer idiomatic phrases from English to Waray *verbatim*. In 1944, General Douglas MacArthur led hundreds of thousands of American troops ashore near our town during the famous Leyte invasion to liberate the country from oppressive Japanese occupancy. Inevitably, certain military areas would be fenced off as secure zones. Since many locals couldn't read *Keep Out* signs, GIs helpfully translated to Waray instead: *Iwas did-to!* Literally, that means "Get off that spot where you're now standing!" achievable by a little hop in any direction. This was retold to us as a common joke among locals.

We struggled along, continuing our quest toward fluency when schools re-opened and our classroom work began. A new issue arose: should we mangle English words and phrases as Filipinos did in order to achieve rapid comprehension, or lapse into slurred-style American pronunciations? I favored deliberately mangling my English words.

I knew I was on my way when I could begin to carry on a decent conversation without have to painstakingly translate and retranslate every word. One drowsy Saturday morning in the house we shared with a family, I could overhear children and their parents right outside our open window conversing. In my half-sleep state of wakefulness, I understood everything they said—*without translating to English!* I half-dreamt I even responded in Waray.

To Assimilate or Not?

There was a fear, of course, that fluency would result in our "going native," surrendering one's own sovereign identity, the very asset that was core to effectiveness as a change agent and ambassador from the U.S. inherent in the Peace Corps concept. Happily, I gradually realized that by becoming fluent I would neither surrender my unique identity nor transform myself into someone else. My unique personality and intellect would survive intact. More importantly, I became a willing, eager student of my cultural environment, appreciating all that Filipinos had to teach me.

Sadly, one of my roommates saw fluency as a way to adopt a new personality. Curiously he chose that of an angry, garrulous and profane character. He went out of his way to learn profanity and insults that supported this identity. Maybe he was simply trying to appear streetwise, but the result drove people away from him.

Eventually I became so fluent in the local language that I completely lost my American accent. One day on a crowded bus, I conversed for an hour with my local companion speaking only the local language. People seated in front of us overheard me. When we finally got to our destination, the lady turned around to see me for the first time. She had a look of astonishment and shock on her face as soon as she saw who I was.

"You're *American*!' she exclaimed.

"That's right," I said. "'Why are you surprised?"

"Because you know our language," she explained. "I overheard you and I thought you were one of us."

One of us! I just smiled. It was a smile of victory, of a goal achieved. That's what I wanted to be, and at least from her perspective that's what I achieved. It was my goal and she'd just confirmed I attained it. I was grateful and proud.

But could I ever be "one of us" if my physical appearance made me stand out wherever I went? Happily, I realized now it went deeper than physical appearances. Now I was a citizen of *two* worlds, *two* cultures, *two* languages. But I was still one person, with a single personality and a single, though expanded, outlook.

At any rate, for just that moment on the bus, *I was one of them!* I had become not what I set out to become, but what I learned I *must* become.

Later as a volunteer leader in Mindanao and subsequently an Associate Peace Corps Director for the Philippines, I continued speaking only Waray in my household, which comprised my cook from Leyte and a helper also from Leyte. It was my language for nearly eight years, 1962-1969. Now, almost 50 years later, I still retain a good vocabulary, evidence of the retentive power of those long-term memory banks the brain reserves for human language.

Steve Wells was a Philippines Group III Volunteer assigned to Dulag, Leyte elementary school as a science class co-teacher. Later he was promoted to a PCVL and reassigned to Surigao del Norte Province in Mindanao where he supervised Group VII Volunteers. He completed his service in June 1964 and applied to become a Peace Corps staff member. He was hired by the Peace Corps as Associ-

ate Peace Corps Director/Philippines assigned to the Philippines in July 1964 and became Regional Director for Central Luzon. In 1965 he was reassigned to the Bicol Region as Regional Director, where he remained until his completion of service in July 1969. Upon his return to the United States, he directed activities in various Poverty Program Job Readiness Training Centers in southern states for U.S. Research and Development Corporation, a contract organization founded and directed by Peace Corps Pioneer Bill Haddad. Later Steve joined a private training, consulting and communicating firm in Detroit, spending nearly 30 years working with clients including GM, Ford, Harley-Davidson, IBM, McDonald's, Jaguar Cars and Sea Ray Boats. He led client benchmarking teams to a "who's-who" of world-class organizations that include Hallmark, Caterpillar, USAA, Steinway & Sons, Wal-Mart, L.L.  *Bean, Disney, 3M, GE and Harley-Davidson. His work took him throughout the United States and to Belgium, Germany, the UK, Mexico, Canada and seven Latin American nations. He married Kathryn Kerze, a Peace Corps/Philippines XIV Volunteer assigned to his region, in 1975. They have two children, now married adults, and two grandchildren.*

Alexandra York (*née* Barbara Simpson)
Little Charlie Joins the Peace Corps

This Peace Corps at 50 initiative asked writers to answer two important questions: who were you when you entered Peace Corps and what legacy did you leave? The experiences and legacies my fellow essayists describe possibly differ so much from mine they mark me as a clear failure. Perhaps, however, like "Little Charlie"—the little tramp character played by Charlie Chaplin in the 1936 silent film, *Modern Times*—I was destined to evolve into a late bloomer who would eventually bear fruit and please the Peace Corps visionaries who believed in us when they first sent us out as neophytes 50 years ago.

Outward Bound Training

Our Peace Corps training began with an Outward Bound Camp where we would run, climb, crawl, swing, swim and otherwise attempt to conquer various obstacles. I failed at the first one on our first day.

We were to swing over a small stream by holding an overhead rope. Apparently the 40-plus volunteers before me all did so; but when I tried to reach the overhead rope, it was too high. After several tries I finally ran off the pier and into nearby shrubbery, where I sat on the ground and sobbed. Within a few minutes, three men from our group sat down next to me. As I continued to cry and repeat I would leave that day to return to New York, the three of them kept repeating, "Don't let the bastards do this to you!" And they didn't. I slunk back to camp in shame, but we three would remain close friends for more than 30 years.

That incident perfectly demonstrated the true purpose of the Outward Bound program as originally designed in England in 1941 to give seamen the ability to survive harsh conditions at sea. The most important lesson of Outward Bound was to learn to help one's comrades survive.

Almost every day for three weeks, we trainees were also required to climb up a mountain and then descend quickly by leaping backward and bouncing down holding only a rope that ran under our backsides and up to the hands of a trainer who would hopefully remain holding it on the mountaintop (on belay). With the smallest hands and feet in our group, I was fast and nimble as a goat going up, but frightened of height and could only descend very slowly with timid tiny steps.

The Outward Bound idea aimed to work through your fears and try to conquer them in the three weeks before graduation. On "graduation day" we were taken to a dam where I watched these Indiana Joneses, one by one, stand atop the lip of a dam, then with one great leap backward fly out into space in the hope that one's rope would work and, a few huge jumps later, be congratulated by colleagues at the bottom of this (for me) monstrously intimidating dam. My recollection is that I was the only one never brave enough to leap.

On "graduation day," as with the obstacle course, I was ashamed, but this time refused to leave the dam even after all of our approximately 40 trainees had left, all except me and a single trainer.

My trainer assured me I could go to the Philippines even if I did not do the great leap. But it had become a fierce contest with my inner self. For nearly an hour after all others had left, the trainer and I remained there. Again and again I climbed up on the lip, stood on its top belay facing the trainer while clutching the rope tight, then inched back, out, down, and eventually under the lip with my feet pressed tight against it and my head hanging upside down nearly touching the dam inches away. Through all my repeats of this ridiculous posture, I insisted to myself that if I could somehow just straighten and stand upright on the dam I could then hop down more or less like everyone else.

As the sun sank and our camp *Jefe* Bill Delano [then General Counsel of the Peace Corps] arrived to find us. I eventually gave up defeated and again slunk sadly back to camp.

Our daily swim was the worst. I had been in a pool only three times before entering the Peace Corps and had once briefly walked on the shore of the ocean; but I had never seen a lake. Our tough trainer Frank Lanoue, on loan to Peace Corps from Georgia Tech, was hard as nails with those he thought could take it. His "drownproofing" technique required every trainee to eventually swim down and back an Olympic-sized pool underwater with no surfacing with hands tied behind their backs. If a swimmer passed out or began to pass out underwater, a fellow Group III trainee, Steve Wells, was charged with rescuing him or her. If instead he or she came up for air, that poor fish would supposedly be "deselected" out of the Peace Corps. But soon after the Georgia Tech instructor saw me enter the pool with no idea how to swim, turn blue and sink, he told me to get out and stay out of our swims. Once again "Little Charlie" was ashamed but grateful.

Four tiny successes slightly diluted these repeated ignominies. Early each morning, a trainer's loud yell awakened us to jump out of our cots in sleeping clothes, immediately hit a footpath, do a fast run to a designated point, then turn and race back to our cabins. I was later told I had a three-week unbroken record as the fastest lady runner.

Toward the end of our training, we were sent out in small groups of men or women to trek in the jungle for three days with only a small map to guide us, instructed to carry on our backs all the gear we would need or want—including sleeping bags and mosquito nets but deliberately insufficient food and water. When one member of our group, the largest of the women in training, unexpectedly collapsed and had to be removed for medical care, her gear was divided, and I was pleased to be one of the few who volunteered to carry it despite my small size. As we limped back into camp on our fourth and final day, I also suggested to my companions that we wrap some of our body parts in toilet paper to look like bandages and prepare three large signs respectively reading "Bataan or Bust" to be worn one each of the first three ladies entering Camp. I faked a small flute that made me look more like 1776 than Bataan, but the humor was appreciated. And every court needs a jester.

Another small pleasure came toward the end of our training when we were sent in groups of two to stay overnight with a local family. I had carried a small chessboard and enjoyed more or less teaching the family's teen-age boys how to play chess in Spanish.

Finally, despite failures with our Big Three (the obstacle course, climbing and swimming), I did well in our nightly camp discussions about Phil-Am history and politics and so was passed on to Pennsylvania State University for further "training."

Penn State Training

At least one member of our group has, I think unfairly, described Penn State as our "penitentiary." Perhaps this was true for the "adults" like him in our group who had previously known freedoms, but for me who had long been strictly regulated by nuns, parents and a college dormitory, Penn State University was a great freedom adventure in snow I had not seen for nearly 20 years. As for the art of listening to generally boring professors, I had already mastered that in college.

I was housed with two lively roommates with whom I do not remember ever having studied, although the anthropology, sociology and Philippine history reads were interesting. I did not have a camera, but thanks to others who later gave me copies of their photos I remember three other Penn State University events: first, a chalk drawing one morning high on our college classroom blackboard depicting a skull and crossbones and beneath it my name and those of several other ladies who had snuck into the rooms of male colleagues, removed their underwear from dresser drawers and left it in their freezers to be discovered the next icy January morning; second, a shot of a few of us doing the then-current dance craze, the twist, rather suggestively at an impromptu party; and third, our farewell dinner with Penn State teachers where we all looked very understandably happy to be leaving.

In-Country Training—University of the Philippines

I do not remember how many weeks we participated in in-country training at the University of the Philippines' main campus near Manila in Diliman, Quezon City. I do remember that at night we Peace Corps females were locked early into the college dormitory we shared with Filipina student housemates aged 15-19 while our male colleagues were free to cavort in Manila.

Ladies' treat Friday nights turned out to be a movie shown by a projector on a large screen in the center of our dorm patio. After a lecture one day on superstitious beliefs including Filipinos" fear of ghosts" called *aswang*, I suggested one evening to our tallest Peace Corps lady—a Swedish American nearly six feet tall—that she don a white sheet and pass in front of the movie screen. She did so to a large female audience who screamed with fear and scattered immediately but gradually melted back into the patio where they laughed a long time and said they had greatly enjoyed the *aswang* break. The next morning I was called to the Peace Corps office to explain myself.

The second time I was called in to explain myself was also while at the University of the Philippines (UP). I along with one of the three men who had rescued me the day of the obstacle course failure had, the night before—Saturday was ladies' night out from the dorm—unknowingly won a twist contest in a local bistro. The next morning our rather acrobatic picture appeared large on the front page of a Manila newspaper.

Most of our group survived UP and eventually went out to our assignments in the Eastern Visayan Islands.

My Assignment in Leyte

Fred Knoth's essay offers the carefully nuanced and sophisticated observation that when we entered, trained for and gave our services to Peace Corps from 1961 to 1963 to teach English as a Second Language, there had already occurred in the Philippines for nearly two decades—for several complicated and intertwined reasons—a general deterioration of English that not even our best efforts could significantly cure.

Many, or maybe most of our tadpole Peace Corps Volunteers, soon realized that the teaching methods we had been taught did not very well fit the educational needs we saw. But especially in those early and optimistic days of tadpole Peace Corps Grand Vision, it would not have been useful or wise to comment upon the wisdom of Peace Corps policy. Instead, some, or maybe many, Peace Corps Volunteers worked with their teachers to help design and implement creative and long-lasting educational alternatives. My failure was that I did all my teachers asked but little else.

I did look for some better ways to justify my classroom appearances and settled in part on the old American song *Bye Bye Blackbird*. It highlights one of the so-called Filipino language characteristics, namely the inability to distinguish between "f" and "p" consonant sounds, or likewise "b" and "v" sounds. These language characteristics are called "allophonic" by linguists. In translation, the resulting pronunciations can be hilarious. It was precisely one of the English fluency issues which we were supposed to resolve. Since our schoolhouse had no window panes, that song sung in one room would be heard throughout the building as students everywhere stopped whatever else they were doing and with their teachers' approval joined the singing. My entire schoolhouse rocked with blackbirds:

> *Pack up all your cares and woes,*
> *Cares and woes*
> *Bye bye blackbird!*

At Christmas Peace Corps brought all of its Leyte teachers to Cebu for a Visayan brush-up course. When I returned to my Leyte schoolhouse in Barrio Gabas, three weeks later it still rocked, but differently:

> *Fack up all your cares and woes,*
> *Cares and woes,*
> *Vye, vye vlacvird!*

Not only had I not improved English as a second language, I had arguably set it back.

During the summer vacation that followed our first school year I told our Peace Corps Director politely but clearly that I thought my assignment as an English teacher in a remote Visayan fishing village was essentially a waste of time and money for all concerned. He remained placid and noncommittal, but asked me if I was familiar with the Peace Corps policy that volunteers did not choose their own assignment but went where they were assigned. Of course, I answered, and then left for vacation. When I returned, he called me back to Cebu and asked me what I would do if Peace Corps denied my request for a transfer to Cebu. "Of course return to Gabas," I answered. Peace Corps then immediately transferred me to Cebu.

Transferred to Cebu

While my first teaching assignment in Leyte may have been of little long-lasting educational value to Filipinos, my second assignment was of even less. Since cars were few in Cebu City in 1963, I spent two hours each day riding to and from my outlying school in a taxi and a horse-drawn *calesa*. My teachers and I agreed I would stay every day in the library where I would be on call for them to schedule as they wished. I did so, but no one called, although they were always very friendly with me. Only much later would I understand the teachers were apparently too "ashamed" to implement our agreement and I too psychologically frozen (as partially described below in *Depression*) to suggest we do so.

Human Relations

Was I a success as a Peace Corps Volunteer English teacher? Of course not. Were I and my Peace Corps colleagues successful (to quote Fred Knoth again) "in a fallback position as representatives of an America that projected goodwill, understanding and concern for those living in the poorest areas of the world?" You bet.

But here again, I may have been one of the least successful Peace Corps Group III Volunteers. Most of the essays I have seen in this collection describe some lasting personal connection or connections made with Filipinos we knew and worked with in our barrios. I made none except for bringing my cherished housekeeper with me to Cebu and later Manila. There, before she married, she would work happily for several years for the Filipino employer I had introduced her to.

I never much cared much for the dinners, parties, fiestas, or small talk, although I always did my share of participating and crowning various queens. After my Peace Corps housemate and I moved to different schools, I discovered my greatest pleasure while in Peace Corps was the quiet time to read through the much-maligned footlocker of books about history, politics and economics that Peace Corps had given each one of us. When I moved to Manila after Peace Corps and worked there with members of the government, I did finally form several friendships with Filipinos that have now lasted nearly 50 years. But over the next decades I would discover I was essentially a recluse. And perhaps a recluse was not the best choice for interacting with friendly, caring, sensitive, fun-loving and gregarious Filipinos, at least in small barrios.

After the Peace Corps

Group III completed its Peace Corps service in Manila in November 1993, barely a week after President Kennedy was assassinated. I had already decided I wanted to remain at least a short time to learn more about the country than had been possible either in my Leyte *nipa* hut or then-small Cebu City.

Shortly after arriving, I received a call from the legislative assistant to the then Speaker of the Philippine House of Representatives. He invited me to join a newly formed six-member Economic and Legislative Advisory Group that would be traveling the country interviewing the Speaker's constituents and helping to formulate legislative proposals. That group would consist of three Filipinos including a journalist, an economist, a future Philippine ambassador to the UK and future father of well-known CNN and *Al Jazeera* reporter Veronica Pedrosa, a Dutch representative of the World Bank, and an American professor from the Stanford Research Institute. Of course I was delighted to accept.

For the next six months we Economic and Legislative Advisory Group members traveled in small groups throughout the Philippines including the far north and key cities in Mindanao, interviewing people of interest to the Speaker including farmers, bankers, journalists, teachers and others, especially local officials and politicians. For the first time I was meeting and listening to Muslim would-be secessionists. When some articles began to appear in the Manila press asking why Filipinos needed foreign political advisers, however, I decided it might be time to leave.

A small part of our formal Peace Corps training had been the one or two days and one overnight we had spent in trainee pairs with local Puerto Rico families. At the time, that training seemed inconsequential. But in writing this essay I now realize it was by far the most important "training" for me and the professional legacy I would leave, because it set me on the long and fairly arduous track that would eventually result in some colleagues calling me "a citizen of the world" and I winning high praise for original international legal projects I would propose and develop.

Before Peace Corps I had not been out of the U.S. After my Economic and Legislative Advisory Group experience I would travel overland through as much as I could of 16 countries including Hong Kong, Vietnam, Cambodia, Thailand, Burma, India, Nepal, Pakistan, Afghanistan, Iran, Jordan, Lebanon, Egypt, Greece, Italy and France, sanguine with only about $1,500 I had received as our $50 monthly Peace Corps stipend for two years, and no prospect of more anywhere.

Depression

Immediately after my extended trip back to the U.S. from the Peace Corps, I entered into what I now understand was for many years a deep and dangerous clinical depression.

My family situation was always difficult with ignorance, poverty, violence and racism.

For example, the night Martin Luther King died I sent a message of condolence to Mrs. King from New York, then called my parents in San Francisco to suggest they do the same, but my father said he and my mother were not sorry. After that call I sat quietly in my living room in Washington D.C. trying to understand what had happened, but I never did. My father had been a boxer, then became a merchant seaman, but always loved hitting people especially my mother and me, his only child. No friends or relatives ever visited us after we moved from the east coast to the west. Neighbors forbade me to play with their children after he hit my mother so hard that the police were called. He told her to go to work if she wanted a refrigerator and stove, then stole her money. Eventually he became a purser, then lost his bond and was demoted to a bellhop. We were several times evicted from apartments for non-payment of rent. At school the nuns for years reprimanded me for non-payment of my tuition. Twice I brought local priests home to help her. Both told her she must leave my father for the sake of her daughter. She then told me both times that I "need a father." He told me as a child he always lost our money at the racetrack because I did not love him. If I had not won a scholarship to a distant college and entered Peace Corps I cannot imagine what my life might have become.

Fifty years later I understand that the psychologically fragile and reclusive young woman who entered PC probably received from it much more than she was able to give at the time. But somewhere along the way Little Charlie vanished—maybe after my Peace Corps service.

Barbara Simpson legally changed her name to Alexandra York 25 years ago. She recognizes she largely lost 23 years from 1964 to 1987 when she mostly stayed home reading, watching TV, and walking alone on the streets of Washington, D.C., and New York for hours on end. She attended law school for four years at night during this period and became a lawyer, but never found either enjoyable work or a satisfying personal relationship.

In 1987 her life changed when she joined the environmental bureau of the New York State Attorney General and then prevailed in all her cases until she left the AG seven years later to become counsel for foreign affairs for the Congress of the Federated States of Micronesia (FSM). From 1989 until 1992, she also proposed, developed, and presented over hundreds of hours as a member of The Association of the Bar of the City of New York (ABCNY) several programs and projects that ABCNY, the U.S. EPA and other international environmental leaders around the world praised as "brilliant" and "seminal" contributions to that "brand new field of law she helped create." Her projects dealt with climate change, deforestation, mega-cities, new legal and new financing structures including NAFTA. ABCNY said that without her "pioneering" contributions regarding the first UN Conference on Environment and Development (UNCED) to be held in Rio De Janeiro in 1992, ABCNY would not have been able to participate in UNCED. The American Bar Association asked her to present similar programs for it around the U.S., and she represented the FSM at UN conferences including the Geneva Climate Change Negotiations. She is listed in Who's Who in American Law and Who's Who in the World for these contributions.

Alexandra believes that all of her professional successes since 1989 were at least indirectly attributable to the Peace Corps after a chance meeting with Bill Delano on a New York City street in 1978; he introduced her to the ABCNY greenhouse where those successes would bloom.

Peace Corps Staff in the Philippines

Larry Fuchs

The Peace Corps Philippines: Big Ideals and Big Adjustments

With the election of John F. Kennedy, I knew that I would take some part in the Kennedy administration. I had written a few speeches for Kennedy and campaigned for him vigorously among certain constituencies. Eleanor Roosevelt, with whom I was particularly close, suggested the position of Assistant Secretary of State for International Organization Affairs. I made an appointment with Dean Rusk, the newly appointed Secretary of State, who wasted little time telling me that he had already chosen—although not yet announced—Harlan Cleveland, who I thought was a better qualified candidate for the position. I really did not want the job.

It did not take long for me to head over to Sargent Shriver's office in the old State Department building where he and my old friend, Harris Wofford, were making plans for the Peace Corps, including a survey of potential staff leadership. My friendship with Wofford went back a long way, all the way to the United World Federalists in the 1940s. My knowledge of the Peace Corps was not extensive, but the ideals that it represented meant a great deal to me. Shriver made a marvelous representation of his and the President's plans for the Peace Corps. My job as Dean of Faculty at Brandeis University, while challenging, did not present the opportunities for excitement, growth and political activity that the Peace Corps did. So when they offered me the job of the first Peace Corps Director in the Philippines, I took it.

I was about to leave for the Philippines when Shriver invited me to the family compound in Hyannis Port, where I had the opportunity to sail a small boat with Bobby Kennedy's wife and two children. I departed from the dock, where President Kennedy was in his yacht, the *Honey Fitz*, smoking what probably was a Cuban cigar. His main business that weekend was to rescue the U.S. from a crisis over the danger of fighting in Berlin. As he worried about that important matter, our little boat capsized, and he roared with laughter, exclaiming, "There goes the Peace Corps."

If it were not for the near heroic behavior of staff members such as Bill Warren and Roger Flather in administering the Peace Corps day after day, we might have indeed sunk. The most troublesome time I faced had to do with the death of a young journalist, David Mulholland, from Fall River, MA. When volunteers organized a special program called Camp Brotherhood, he left his home barrio to become one of the leaders. Soon he became ill with an intestinal problem that was misdiagnosed by our Peace Corps doctor. I followed his deterioration closely and was at his side when he died at Clark Air Force Hospital. I was devastated.

Another difficult incident had to do with a marvelous volunteer from Indiana who came to me in Manila to resign from the Peace Corps. It was Peace Corps policy at that early stage to resist such resignations. Shriver and others in Washington tended to think of such volunteers as quitters. The idea was that volunteers did not leave their posts. But she was a courageous young woman whose reasons for resigning were entirely plausible. She felt much better equipped to teach in an inner-city school in Indiana than in a rural school in the Philippines, and she was right. In any case, I could not stop her, and she became the first Peace Corps volunteer to resign.

What was important about these incidents was that Peace Corps volunteers in the Philippines took exceptional risks and had exceptional autonomy. We had to be prepared for both. Both experiences exposed a weakness in our operations. We did not have enough staff to assure optimum health and programmatic effectiveness. One way of compensating for the inadequacy of the number of staff available was to hire Filipino staff. Bert Pumento of USAID was hired to become the head of financial affairs in the Peace Corps. Elena Borneo became my secretary, Annie Gison became our office manager, and we worked out a much closer relationship with the Philippines Bureau of Public Schools. But no improvements in administration could compensate for the intrinsic difficulties in the volunteers' assignments as educational aides. There was a kind of floundering characteristic to volunteer programming from their point of view, and there was an indifference on the part of many teachers and school administrators to the lack of specificity in their assignments. As long as the Americans seemed happy, Filipino hosts were satisfied. One major trouble was that volunteers often were not happy. My number one priority was to change that.

One time, at an evening soiree at the United States Embassy in Manila, I was told by a U.S. Senator from New Hampshire—a conservative one at that—how wonderful the Peace Corps was. "You're the Peace Corps man," he said. "How wonderful your program is." I replied, "It's probably not as wonderful as you think. We have plenty of problems." He responded, "Oh, you can't kid me, it's absolutely marvelous." Part of the strength of the Peace Corps was its celebrity. It had become an icon for American values. Meanwhile, there were many problems in the field, essentially revolving around the inability of volunteers to extract meaningful work from their assignments as educational aides.

It was understandable that there should be criticism of Peace Corps Philippines. Many volunteers experienced considerable cultural fatigue. Most volunteers had set high standards for themselves, reinforced by Peace Corps advertising and the pressures of training. They had expected to test their mettle and accomplish much. They also fervently wanted to show their love for mankind in practical, day-to-day ways. When frustration led to helplessness, volunteers felt guilty. Several volunteers started to sleep late in the mornings and spent only an hour or so in school for almost an entire month. One wrote to me, "My conscience bothered me constantly. I had guilt feelings because I knew I was sleeping late every day."

Advertised as self-sufficient supermen and women, some volunteers at first believed the propaganda. But when faced with unanticipated obstacles, they became needy. While never recanting their ideological commitment to self-sufficiency, a large number asked for more support. They complained of not being adequately trained. Sometimes, they asked for more equipment and supplies. They doubted if Shriver or the Washington office really cared about them and their frustrating work in the barrios. But many of them resented help when it was given because it betrayed just how difficult it was to fight against emotional and psychological isolation in a vague job in a strange and disorienting culture. They didn't want to need help, and they were uncomfortable about their dilemma.

As the volunteers settled into their barrios, newspaper and magazine articles at home and abroad continued to emphasize their alleged brilliant successes. Most volunteers felt it was impossible to be as sacrificial or as successful as publicity indicated.

The volunteers in the field did not appreciate the New Hampshire Senator's exaltation of the Peace Corps, and I was in a dilemma: I did not want to talk about the problems of the Peace Corps any more than the Senator from New Hampshire. Yet, I contributed to some of the rave reviews myself. Newspaper people would come through Manila worrying about whether the volunteers were trained adequately, and I had to give an answer that was less revealing than I would have liked. Part of my job was to represent the Peace Corps in its best light and where I could truthfully represent its exciting prospects, I also would tend to minimize problems. I worked with the Bureau of Public Schools to have us all be realistic about the limitations we experienced, yet those speeches tended to pick out anecdotes that reflected the strengths of the volunteers and their capacity to interact joyously with Filipinos in the barrios.

I recall one evening when I was in Washington on leave, Shriver played host to me and a congressman from Brooklyn, New York who wanted to learn more about the Peace Corps and how it was different from USAID programs. Shriver and I presented "ugly American" type stories to impress him. We talked into the night until our congressman guest became increasingly enthusiastic about the Peace Corps being a new kind of American program that embodied the best of American values. At a subsequent House Committee Appropriations Hearing, the chairman, Otto Passman from Louisiana, was critical of Shriver and me for hiring a new staff member whose trip to the Philippines would involve paying the travel costs for his nine children. Our congressional hero chastised Passman by exclaiming: "What's the matter, Otto? Don't you like children?" Later, we were happy to send him a Sunday copy of the leading Philippines newspaper with its feature story on the family of John Cort.

The Peace Corps did represent something new. Volunteers, for the most part, did live comfortably with Filipinos in the barrios and made close friends with them. Languages were learned and cultural adaptations made. Despite the problems of the job, these Americans—mostly youngsters—were helping teachers and students become more adept at learning science and English. But there was no mistaking that many resented being celebrated as heroes in the barrios. One volunteer wrote that he appreciated the thankfulness of Filipinos, "though it makes me feel guilty that I have not yet done anything to deserve their thanks." Another volunteer astutely saw that the Peace Corps was more than just another agency. It was a basic expression of national values and character, but it worried him. "There seems to be a tendency," he wrote, "to regard the volunteers as a kind of front line in the holy war of human development."

Many volunteers took solace in practical work such as Camp Brotherhood, which, one wrote, was "of a concrete nature—something that a volunteer could devote time and effort to just as he would in the States." But "I'm sick and tired of reading stateside papers my parents send me which contain nothing but positive comments about the work of the Peace

Corps." Another volunteer wrote: "We are embittered by facile self-congratulation and persisting inaccuracies in depicting our experiences . . . we know it is B.S., and we feel used."

Small triumphs were blown up out of all proportion by visitors from the Peace Corps in Washington. A Peace Corps official, who saw a volunteer making mats out of a fiber that had not been used for anything in particular, reported to Washington that a new weaving industry was on the way in the Philippines. That kind of exaggeration, often used by agencies to justify their existence, made volunteers angry.

Peace Corps volunteers often were seen as celebrities in the barrios and towns. Most of them were feted with extraordinary hospitality. Neighbors brought bananas and sometimes chickens, which they could not afford for themselves, to show hospitality. The volunteers were invited to weddings and baptisms. "It still amazes me," wrote one volunteer, "there is no limit to the sacrifices these people have made for us." Another volunteer wrote that it is "a tremendous feeling to have a place where the people make you feel so welcome."

Many of the problems issued from the conception of the job of volunteer aide to begin with. It was too vague. The head of the Bureau of Public Schools explained at a news conference that volunteers would have an easy job. When teachers asked them to explain simple words or science concepts, the aides would oblige them. It was a simplistic idea that would never satisfy most volunteers. There had to be more, and eventually, to the credit of volunteers, there was much more. But it took a while to work out the details.

Members of my staff and I were not the only ones to see the weakness in the educational aide idea. American newspaper editors travelling at Los Baños, our first domestic training camp, picked on the concept relentlessly, but we had no agreement with the Bureau of Public Schools that settled on its meaning in specific terms. The Bureau, in many conversations with me, preferred to keep it vague. Washington, wanting to get the program off on a large scale, had a stake in satisfying the program's flexibility, yet, Washington officials were increasingly disturbed by complaints about Peace Corps back in the capitol and in the Philippines.

My interest focused almost entirely on elevating the job satisfaction of volunteers. One of the best ways of doing that was to appoint terrific volunteers to be volunteer leaders and to give them the support they needed to do their job. But there were still major distractions in the job of director which kept me from doing that. For example, one day, I received a cable from Shriver telling me that I should represent him at a conference chaired by Averill Harriman and Chester Bowles in Baguio in the north of the Philippines where American ambassadors from Far Eastern countries would be in attendance to review American interests in Vietnam and China. This was 1963. In addition, I was asked by the chairpersons to make a speech about the beginnings of the Peace Corps—another pep rally. The conversation was extremely stimulating, but it had nothing to do with the problems I faced as Peace Corps director in the Philippines. Of course, I did what I knew Shriver would want me to do, which was to make the Peace Corps sound like the seventh wonder of the world. The results were as expected. Harriman and Bowles had much to argue about, but everyone agreed that the Peace Corps was wonderful.

Other distractions had to do with internal Peace Corps Philippines matters. One of my staff members had the reckless habit of making fun of USAID and state department agencies behind their backs. While he may have been right, and almost surely was in some instances, it was something that was bound to get him and even us in trouble. For example, when

Peace Corps overseas staff was offered free copies of *Time Magazine,* he rejected the offer, indeed rudely turned it down, without consulting me. Since I thought him to be the most skilled analyst of the problems of the Peace Corps program, I was particularly distressed to have him fired by Washington, but he deserved it. Despite my efforts to protect him, I lost an extremely smart, capable staff member.

Other staff problems emerged of a very different sort. One volunteer requested permission to return home via Japan. I knew from such circumstances as I could fathom that she wanted to have an abortion. I cleared the way by routing her as she suggested, and I had her come to the training center in Zamboanga where she could have an exit interview with me far from the office in Manila. One of my dearest staff friends in Manila wrote Shriver and me a memo protesting that he knew what I was doing. He was a devout Catholic, and I knew well what he was trying to do but could not accept his protest because I didn't think it was in the best interest of the Peace Corps, or the young woman. Understandably, Shriver and I never passed a word on the subject.

Another aspect of my job was to take Washington staff and/or visitors from the United States on important trips to Peace Corps programs in the field. The most memorable of these came when Shriver made his first visit to the Philippines. I had a big stake in one of these trips since I had arranged to change my field office from Manila to a barrio near Zamboanga in Mindanao as a way of getting closer to the volunteers who now came frequently to the Peace Corps training center there. It had been turned into a place where volunteers and Filipino teachers and other educators could work together in order to improve the program.

The center was built next to the Peace Corps residence in which my family and I lived. It was an unusual situation to have the Directors' home and office in a rural spot rather than a capital city, but it was a great advantage for me. I lived only a twenty-minute drive from the airport at Zamboanga and could easily arrange trips around the country. At the same time, I was free to be anchored at the Peace Corps training center and get important work done. Ironically it was also a place where important visitors such as Governor Meyner of New Jersey and the American Ambassador to the Philippines, William Stevenson, would come to learn more about the real life of the Peace Corps.

Not everybody in Washington approved of the move, but Shriver did. His taste for unorthodox decisions involving some risk made my life much easier. On one of my trips to Washington, he told me privately that I was free to report on my dissatisfaction with the support Peace Corps Philippines was getting from U.S.A.I.D. It was upsetting to some of the USAID personnel, but that was exactly the result I think Shriver wanted.

Shriver realized that a one-size fits all approach to volunteers' assignments could not work in the Philippines. Projects in piggery or anti-blight tomato growth were just as valid as those in new science if they worked. Volunteers were brilliant in their improvisation. A big project such as Camp Brotherhood had the advantage of encompassing many volunteers. There was a powerful incentive to work with one's hands as a volunteer from Camp Brotherhood said of his job at the camp, "it accounted for two months of the hardest work I have ever done, and I can say the most enjoyable time I have ever had."

The same could be said for me. Being a Peace Corps director was the hardest work I have ever done, and I loved it. Work was almost nonstop, and while it could be troubling, it was exceptionally satisfying. More difficult even, were the challenges of the volunteers, such as the creation of a whole new dictionary in one of the dialects. I had a lesser language challenge when I was given an honorary degree at Central Cebu University and tried my best to accept the degree with a short speech in Cebuano.

Most of my work dealing with Filipinos was deeply pleasurable. The only part of my work that was unpleasant was dealing with a Peace Corps visitor from Washington who thought he knew more than everybody else. He was nasty and coarse, but my way of dealing with him was to virtually ignore him, which is what I thought I was supposed to do anyway, even though I had no discussion about him with Shriver. I had a simple rule for making decisions on which I was not instructed. It was to imagine what Shriver would do—assuming he would want me to act on my own—and do it, as in the case of the young woman who presumably had an abortion in Japan. I found the key to my own satisfaction was to trust my boss and members of my staff to do the right thing. The quality of volunteers generally and of volunteer leaders and staff justified that trust repeatedly. By the last quarter of my two-year posting in the Philippines most volunteers had worked out their own systems of trust with Filipinos, and the projects which they started (in and out of the schools) bore considerable success. It was the largest of the Peace Corps efforts to date—128 volunteers when we started, and 630 volunteers when I left for home.

When it came time to write about those successes in my book *Those Peculiar Americans*, I could list dozens of remarkable achievements that made me realize that the Peace Corps was indeed wonderful. One of the major rewards was to be supported by Shriver. In the nearly two years that I worked for him, I never heard a critical word. On many occasions, he went out of his way to be personally supportive. That meant visits before I left for the Philippines to the compound at Hyannis, or afterward to Timberlawn, his home in Maryland. Most important of all, it meant support for the flexible approach to the Peace Corps project, leaving myself—and the volunteers—much autonomy to be creative and truly responsive to the unique situations in which we found ourselves.

I learned a lot from Shriver, and I believe he would have been an outstanding president of the United States. He had a spacious and energetic mind that brought with it inspirational qualities. He was clear in what he believed and had the energy to carry through important ideas and programs. We made a flight around the country to look at volunteer sites—visiting several dozen housing units. He came to understand how big and complex the Philippines Peace Corps project was. On one trip we made alone, Shriver and I slept on the floor of Philippine Airlines. He was Peace Corps all the way.

By approving my key decision to move the Director's office from Manila to Zamboanga, he not only strengthened many aspects of the program, but he provided an unusual learning opportunity for me. Every time I drove my Jeep to the airport from the Peace Corps training center, I passed small barrios where houses were crammed together and often built on stilts over the water. The children, in rags, sometimes wore gold earrings, bracelets, and pearl rings. There were cockfights almost everywhere. Sometimes we attended a Sunday cockfight where men were squashed together, shouting and jumping up and down. Each rooster had a razor-like a blade attached to his leg and after a bell sounded, they would try to kill or badly wound each other, rushing at each other, heads down and neck feathers ruffled, until in a few seconds, the fight was over. At the cockfight and communities nearby, one could learn a vast amount of Mindanao's southern culture.

Here I was, running a major United States government project, where most volunteers were assigned by the Bureau of Public Schools to Christian barrios—but I had an opportunity for firsthand observation of the complexity of the country's mixed ethnic and cultural experience. I visited a Chinese Buddhist temple not too far from the Chung family. An old Chinese monk played the drum and gong as he said prayers. The family and friends chanted and prayed in front of a large golden Buddha as the smell of incense and jasmine filled the air.

I found out that Filipinos often hated Chinese merchants, who worked hard, and no matter what their legal disadvantages, they had managed to make a living and influence much of the business of the country. This type of intercultural dynamic was learned only by experience in the field, not in the meeting room.

Given the complexity of cultural life in the Philippines—Muslim, Spanish, Chinese, American, and dozens of other dialect cultures—I have thought often of my friend Carlos Romulo, a major leader at the United Nations conference in San Francisco and his dream of a world federal government. It was a dream. Was it worth pursuing? One had to begin somewhere. The Peace Corps was a good place to start.

After his work as the first Director of the Peace Corps program in the Philippines, Larry Fuchs returned to Brandeis University where he wrote several more books and taught about race, ethnicity and public policy until 2005, when he retired. He and his second wife now live in a long-term retirement community in Boston where they both receive skilled care.

Bill and Jay Warren
The Magical Years

It was in July of 1961 that Bill, employed at Polaroid's Education Department, met up with Larry Fuchs who was finding staff for Peace Corps/Philippines. We didn't even hesitate. Our experience with the newly forming project remains the most exciting, challenging, rewarding adventure of our lives. We thought then, and still do, that the idea of Americans living and working with people of other lands offers the best way to create mutual understanding and appreciation of each other—and we were lucky enough to share it all with our six children.

After arriving in Manila in September, we helped prepare for the arrival of Group I on October 12 and then took off for Legaspi, Albay, where Bill supervised about 60 volunteers in the Bicol region. Then, in May 1962 we moved to Zamboanga in Mindanao to welcome and supervise Group VII. We stayed there until the fall of 1963 when we went directly to Peace Corps Nepal for another Peace Corps assignment until the following spring.

So many memories! Where to begin? Volunteer leaders, best of friends, absolutely indispensable. Servants, best of friends, absolutely indispensable. The children, delightful, plentiful and best friends for our six. Romances, some followed by weddings, especially Celie and John' Bossany's at which we were sponsors and our daughter Jan a flower girl. Meriendas everywhere and for whatever reason. Swimming in Fuch's pool. Jack Harkness stitching up our son Chris's chin. Beautiful perfect-cone Mt. Mayon, Tiwi Hot Springs, Pasananca and, of course, Ayala. The graciousness of teachers and school personnel. Dancing and singing, everywhere and for whatever reason. Son Billy and Reggie Salara being rescued in their small motor boat by some Moslem fishermen. Visiting brass from DC—they seemed SO removed from us. Cort kids visiting and everyone doing the *tinikling*. Our kids schooling at the Albay and the Zamboanga Normal Teacher Training Schools. Keeping a bit removed from those "other" Americans until we found some "just like us". Imagine that! Larry and other staff dealing with some tragic and very sad happenings. Being entertained by Jerry Mullins and John Bossany in their tiny nipa shack at Caragasan. Visiting volunteers in their homes and welcoming them into ours, and sharing their frustrations and disappointments, and delighting in their successes.

The Volunteers wrote to us and we treasure yet their observations and comments:

"This district is very progressive and they are overwhelmingly confident we can perform miracles."

"Demonstrated science techniques before 238 teachers at the district meeting."

"I'm living with the principal, his wife, a teacher, his son (an agricultural worker about my age), five beautiful co-teachers of mine, the principal's daughter, son-in-law, three grandchildren and two maids. Together, we are a happy family."

"…and trying to get through the 50-60 kids that are outside our cottage from 7 a.m. to 6 p.m., weekends included."

"The bedbugs are on the run."

"Our public speaking is getting better, but our singing still has plenty of room for improvement."

"We have a regular schedule of classroom demonstrations, visitations and consultations…John has begun a Saturday morning science club."

"We answered questions about the role of the Peace Corps, American foreign policy, problems of integration in Mississippi, etc."

"…but most of all, I love the children."

"We tell each other our complaints and troubles. Talking about it really helps."

"We're studying the dialect constantly."

"We've had some funny experiences like riding on bakery trucks, gravel trucks, jeepneys full of wood and those god-awful buses originally meant to hold 50, but bulging with 100, not to mention the fish, bananas, pigs, sleeping mats and anything else you can think of."

"We feel like worn out celebrities as we have to attend parties and fiestas and consequently eat and eat and eat until we're blue in the face, sing "You are my Sunshine" until we're hoarse and serenade the female teachers to keep the elders of the community happy and amused."

"Beyond English and science we have many plans and dreams, but will begin with firsts first."

"The views are incomparably lovely—coral reefs, lagoons, fishing bancas, and rolling hills covered with banana trees."

"We had wild boar yesterday (scrumptious)."

"Slowly, but surely, we are learning to accept the fact that everything runs two hours behind schedule."

"Right now Barbie and I don't know whether to laugh at the funniness of the situation or cry at the seriousness of it all. Actually, Barbie is crying and I'm laughing, so it's a little of both."

"The sanitary conditions are deplorable."

Many of the letters contained requests for urgently needed educational supplies and refills of Aralen and other drugs. One of the most memorable was addressed, "Dear Santa, Please send a person who has heard of Aristotle, an American male—age 21 to 30, 6 feet tall or over, some snow, a letter from my parents—I haven't hear from them since I left home—my horse, mashed potatoes and gravy and green peas and carrots and turkey with celery dressing, 50 pounds of Plasticine, and my father's sculpture base and tools, and letters from my brothers—I haven't heard from them either."

After returning to the States in 1964, we settled in Sudbury, Massachusetts, had another baby, and prepared for a three-year stay in Kenya where Bill worked with the Education

Development Center. The program developed science materials and trained teachers for the elementary schools in several African countries. We then lived in Wayland, Southboro, and Harvard in Massachusetts and Rindge in New Hampshire while Bill was an elementary school principal in Lincoln, Massachusetts for 14 years. He then joined Jay working with an educational collaborative in Fitchburg until retirement. We then made yet another move to Spokane, Washington, where we're close to our two youngest children and four young grandchildren. While living in Southboro we shared our lives with another family with three kids and were foster parents to some 17 over the four years—.almost as exciting as the Peace Corps years.

Our seven children continue to be a source of excitement, companionship and great joy as do 12 wonderful grandkids. We travel to Norway every couple of years to visit daughter Jan and her family, and we've had several grand family reunions here in the States. We frequent our local Y and enjoy several activities of the local Parkinson's group (Bill has Parkinson's) including a dance program and singing with the Tremble Clefs. Life is good.

Love and wishes that all those dreams we had fifty long years ago may yet come true. The world at times seems so troubled, but the hopes of those magical Kennedy years live on with all of us.

Bill and Jay Warren have shared their life story in their essay. They are beloved staff members who have made it to every Group 1 reunion but one. We expect to see them for the big one in September 2011.

(The first photo shows the Warren family at their home in Zamboanga in 1962. In the rear from the left are Lee and Bill. In the front from the left are Jan, Jay (holding Chris), Bill (holding Lynn) and Carl on the far right. The second shows Bill and Jay more recently.)

Lawrence C. Howard
A Sense of Belonging

On September 22, 1961, Congress established the Peace Corps as a permanent, semi-autonomous agency within the State Department. During fiscal year 1962, the Congress approved an appropriation of $30 million and authorized a ceiling of $40 million. As early as October, 1961, approximately 400 Peace Corps were already in the field and several hundred more were in training. About 2,700 volunteers are expected to be in the Corps by June 1962. This rapid development of the Peace Corps from a little known idea scarcely a year before to a vigorous operation is the most dramatic testimonial to the unusual appeal of the underlying concept. As early as January 1962, the Gallup Poll reported that 71 percent of the American people favored the idea and only 18 percent opposed it.

At the time, my wife Betty and I and our two young children were deeply immersed in the busy life of Wellesley Hills, Massachusetts. I was teaching in the Politics Department at Brandeis University, and we had just bought a house. Then, an unexpected telephone call interrupted our July vacation on Martha's Vineyard and pointed us westward toward the Far East. Larry Fuchs, Dean at Brandeis University, told us he was heading to the Peace Corps in the Philippines, and asked me to consider joining him as an Associate Representative. It took some soul-searching to reach a decision, plus several trips to Washington, interviews, physicals, and more, but on September 2, 1961, three weeks before Congress had authorized the Peace Corps legislation, the whole family was aloft for  the Philippines. Fortuitously, I had been there before during a World War II tour in the U.S. Army serving as the editor of the Base X Newspaper and writing the column, *The General Speaks*. The Philippines was familiar and welcoming sixteen years later.

I spent the first month in Manila planning the six week orientation program for the first group of 128 volunteers, who arrived on October 12. They were to be followed in January by a second group. My family and I moved with the first group to Los Baños, 40 miles away from Manila, to the campus of the College of Agriculture of the University of the Philippines. The next weeks were full and busy as we came to know individuals in Group 1 and tried our best to deliver a training program to enable them to live with the range of cultures and language groups in the Philippines. Our basic task was to establish a people-to-people assistance program with one of the closest U.S. allies in the Pacific. That took the form of volunteers serving in these elementary schools as "assistants", rather than "advisers" to teachers in the schools, and being open to assisting community residents in community development projects. We enjoyed the many conversations in our home in the evenings over dessert, sometimes dinner, with small groups of thoughtful, idealistic young people who had signed up for this exciting brand new program for peace.

We enjoyed living in a faculty house and meeting Agricultural College faculty, experiencing universal warmth and welcome. My family was well occupied. Betty studied Tagalog with the volunteers. Jane, age 4, enrolled in a university pre-school. We all enjoyed the seasonal celebrations: All Soul's Day festivities in the cemetery, nine nights of pre Christmas caroling with the sight of colorful lanterns hanging from every porch. We learned much about Philippine culture during our five months in Los Baños and learned much about the interests and aspirations of the volunteers. When Group 2 arrived for in-country training, we felt very much at home. After their shorter training program, we moved back to Manila, where we continued to host volunteers who came to town for dinner or dessert and for conversations—or for just letting off steam.

The decision to have the Associate Representatives live in the various regions where volunteers were setting up households made it possible for staff and their families to experience in depth Filipino life and culture, and to some degree, experience the life of a volunteer. My family and I moved to Dumaguete, the capital of the province of Negro Oriental. It was an ideal spot from which I could travel to visit volunteers throughout the Visayan Region. These trips to see the volunteers in their habitats and in their schools demonstrated that in general they were indeed working hard toward accomplishing the goals of the Peace Corps.

My wife described Dumaguete as paradise. A long established American university, Silliman, added to the cultural richness of the area. We lived close to the sea in a community of faculty and townspeople, mainly Filipino families but also some American missionaries. Betty studied piano and sang in the university choir. The girls attended a pre-school and the university kindergarten. We participated actively at Sunday services at the local Aglipayan Church (Philippine Independent Church), which is in communion with the Episcopal Church. Betty spent six weeks volunteering in a school engaging children in choral reading, and coaching and judging declamations in English—a very popular school activity at the time.

The field visit to the Philippines by Peace Corps Director Sargent Shriver was a memorable experience. He affirmed that our focus on Americans learning deeply about Filipinos and Filipinos similarly about Americans was on target and of great value. I also remember hosting U.S. Ambassador Stevenson for dinner in our home in Dumaguete and sharing with him how Peace Corps volunteers were gaining at least as much as were the Filipinos they were serving. Together, we were promoting peace and friendship through an increasing respect and understanding of each other, and even more, we were putting into practice that we all should love God and our neighbor.

From Dumaguete, I continued to travel around the country, from Baguio to Zamboanga, exploring potential volunteer sites in response to a steady stream of requests for volunteers, which led to the rapid expansion of the Peace Corps program. These trips permitted establishing strong ties to local college programs and to churches. My Filipina secretary Annie Gison, one of the first Filipino employees, made all of the arrangements for these trips. She later married one of the Group 1 volunteers, Emery Bontrager, and we have remained close friends to this day. Their marriage was just one of numerous marriages that took place between Volunteers and Filipino men and women.

We completed our tour of service along with Group 1 in the summer of 1963. Our departure was bittersweet. Betty said she felt like a Filipina and indeed she was sometimes mistaken for one. We felt that we would forever have a sense of belonging to this place and its people. (When our third daughter was born two years after our return home, we asked Annie Gison to suggest a Filipino middle name. Annie suggested Ligaya, a Tagalog name that means "joy." Laura Ligaya Howard loves her name.

We took advantage of my status as a senior United States Foreign Service Officer, and sailed first class on an American vessel to Japan, and then after a brief visit there, returned by sea to San Francisco. Inspired by the Peace Corps experience I decided not to return to teaching, but to explore other possibilities for service.

From the beginning, Peace Corps seemed designed to achieve a purpose best described by historian Arnold Toynbee: "to overcome the disastrous barriers that have hitherto segregated the affluent Western minority of the Human Race from the majority of their fellow men and women." (Quoted in a speech by Theodore Vestal at the celebration of the 40th anniversary of Peace Corps in Tulsa, OK, April 28, 2001.) I believe the Peace Corps has succeeded admirably in that ideal, and the Howard family is proud to have been a part of building its foundation in the Philippines.

Once back in the States, Larry Howard accepted a position in the Office of Innovation with the New York State Department. of Education. During the 1960s he also directed the Institute for Human Relations at the University of Wisconsin and became vice president of the Danforth Foundation in St. Louis. From 1969 to 1993 he served the University of Pittsburgh, first as Dean of the Graduate School of Public and International Affairs and then as a professor at the school. During the '80s and '90s Larry was a consultant on retraining administrative personnel for the government of the Bahamas, and he was a Fulbright professor in public administration at the University of Mai-

duguri, Nigeria (1981-82). After retirement, he was a Distinguished Professor in the political science department at Chatham College. He has spent his retirement years organizing the papers of his father, Charles P. Howard LLD, who wrote copiously from the United Nations syndicated columns tracking the emergence of African nations as independent self-governing entities. Larry has also conducted Bible Study at Calvary Episcopal Church and at a church-related senior citizen home.

Betty Howard (former children's librarian) returned to homemaking and child-raising and ESCRU (Episcopal Society for Cultural and Racial Unity). Betty acquired an MLS and then a PhD and taught at West Virginia University in a school librarian certification program, specializing in literature for children and young adults. Active in the American Library Association, she was inspired to follow a latent bent toward writing for children. She has published 10 picture books and hopes to continue.

(The first photo shows Larry at a planning meeting with Philippine officials prior to the arrival of the first volunteers in 1961; the second shows him more recently with wife Betty.)

Harvey Pressman
Winging It for Peace?

Motivation

I didn't decide to apply for a Peace Corps staff position. I doubt the Peace Corps even had a staff application process set up in the summer of 1961. The opportunity just showed up on my doorstep, at a very inopportune moment, and I made the unrealistic decision to invite it in.

In 1961, I was in graduate school in Cambridge, Massachusetts, in the middle of writing a dissertation on U.S./East Asian relations at the turn of the 20th Century. I had a six-month old daughter, was deeply involved in civil rights activities, and had a fellowship that paid me enough so that I didn't have to work I was enjoying a cushy academic existence.

Then I got the call from Larry Fuchs, who had been named country director for the Philippines. My best guess is that he didn't have quite enough money in his budget to recruit an adult for the position of Associate Peace Corps Representative, or he thought that my public relations and organizational skills in mounting civil rights protests in Boston might come in handy—or both.

I decided to take the job not really for any advantages or attractions I saw in it, but out of fear. Fear of what I might miss if I turned down this once-in-a-lifetime opportunity. Fear that, if I turned him down, I might later look back and regret it. And, fear that I would miss out on learning something (I know not what) that would prove important to my future academic career.

My Role as A Staff Member

The initial definition of my role as Associate Peace Corps Representative had very little to do with what I ended up doing. At best, my initial role was ill-defined, inchoate and sketchy. (I didn't think this was a bad thing at the time, and I don't think so now.) As best I can recall, I was to be a kind of "add-on" to the staff, doing public relations in Manila, supervising a limited number of volunteers in the field, helping out with in-country training, and editing a volunteer newsletter *(Ang Boluntaryo)*.

What I ended up doing primarily was supervising a large number of volunteers in Negros Occidental and Negros Oriental, roaming around the countryside renting nipa huts for volunteers soon to arrive, dealing with the logistics of getting supplies into the field, and planning and running in-country training for Philippines II.

Most Important Memories/Experiences

• Staying overnight with volunteers in rural barrios—no electricity, no running water, chickens underfoot, nowhere to go, no hurry—and realizing that the majority of the earth's inhabitants lived in similar circumstances.

- The shocking death of volunteer David Mulholland from complications of untreated amoebic dysentery.
- Hot and heavy staff sessions at central headquarters, discussing a wide range of issues, most of which I assume must now be incorporated into some fat Peace Corps manual.
- The periodic visits to Manila of Peace Corps Washington—big wigs like Lee St. Lawrence, Bill Haddad (a.k.a. "The Inspector General"), Jay Rockefeller, Charley Peters, etc., which I would entitle "The Clueless Wonders from Washington Come To Call." These "authorities" who came to look over our shoulders from Washington were even less likely than us on the field staff to know what the hell we were doing. We were all flying blind, they were flying blinder, and the volunteers were the innocent "beneficiaries." Lee's rants were part of a pattern of substituting macho profanity for policy profundity, common to these guys since they didn't seem know what else to say. Jay was, of course, an exception, because he was too rich to have learned those words on the street, and too young to have learned them in WW II.
- How difficult it was to get so many "intelligent" PCV's to follow some simple health and dietary precautions, in the face of their insistence on going native or demonstrating their youthful sense of imperviousness to disease or danger.
- How "foreign" so many of the PCV's seemed to me—mountain men like Doug Watts, Southern belles, a guy packing a gun on arrival, and other varieties of Americana that I had had precious little contact with.
- Winning an official JFK "Presidential Censure" by signing an objection to a Florida draft board's failure to defer Charley Kamen, which I had nonchalantly just signed on to one day months earlier.
- Backlash from Washington to some of my most "sensible" initiatives: praising Leo Pastore's leadership style for going into debt and immediately erasing the rich Americano stereotype, and thus infuriating Shriver, who insisted that "we pay our way"; jousting with "Inspector General" Haddad (shades of Danny Kaye!) in the Bacolod airport (probably should NOT have threatened to punch him in the mouth), telling Henry Luce "no thanks" on his offer to send free *Time Magazine* subscriptions to all volunteers, etc.

Background

Like most Americans then and now, I knew very little about the Philippines before accepting the assignment. My first impressions, after I arrived and got out into the provinces for the first time, were of the stark contrasts between Manila, where I was to live, and the rest of the country. One could visit the Philippines for weeks, stay in Manila, and leave with no idea of what the country or people were like.

One thing I wished I had known more about before I arrived is how the public school system of the Philippines had evolved and, more generally, the nature of the relationship between post-colonial officials and their former imperialist mentors. At a number of points along the way I thought all of us staff members just didn't understand enough of the long-term context in which we were operating.

By the time I left the country, I had a vague sense of a nation that was somewhat paralyzed by its recent past, a country whose progress towards greater prosperity and more democratic practices would somehow be impeded unless and until it figured out how to break free from the legacy of its colonial past.

Today, I feel much the same about the Philippines. A country still too much a client state of its former colonial master, a country which has emerged from its Marcos-era nightmare with a still-corrupt power structure and an ever-diminishing likelihood of providing basic health, safety and sustenance to its growing masses of very poor people.

Immediate Effects of the Experience

What I most liked about my experience was getting a chance to think about effective teaching and how to get other people to think about it in different ways. I also really liked being able to go out into the field and get chauffeured around by the volunteer leaders in rickety old jeeps, because I got to see a nice cross-section of barrio existence in a relatively short period of time.

My major frustrations were not being able to get through to some of the volunteers around health and safety issues, and dealing with the job role for volunteers that I believe we had inherited from our friends in the USAID Mission who had cut the original deals with Filipino officials. In many ways, the volunteers were all dressed up with nowhere to go.

What was the most rewarding, for me, was the opportunity to help a lot of creative volunteers to re-think their roles with an eye to having a more significant impact than they could have had under the poorly defined "teacher's aide" role. Working with volunteer leaders like Leo Pastore, Joan Weiss, Duncan Yaggy and Marjorie Bakken (nee Pfankuch) gave me the chance to help "redefine" the mission, individual volunteer by individual volunteer.

Subsequent Effects of the Experience

My Peace Corps experience had a significant subsequent impact on my life professionally. When I got back to graduate school, I ditched my dissertation in-progress and started another on the colonial origins of the Philippines public education system. For the next few years, I slowly pieced together a story that was light years different from the "official story" I had gleamed from the popular literature. I learned a lot about the differences between policy and practice, and how and why those differences came about. That has served me in very good stead in the work I have done and the books I have written about the education of poor kids in America. The combination of what I learned from my experience in the Philippines and the study and reflection I did after I got back had a significant impact on some of the later career choices I made, and the way I comported myself in some of my jobs. (I suspect, for example, that I got fired as often as I did in part because of the things Fuchs let me get away with, and the lessons I learned from them.)

Another example of the Philippines experience that clearly influenced my thinking involves the origins of the National Upward Bound Program. A couple of years after I left the Philippines, I found myself by some fluke in the role of consultant to the newly formed Office of Economic Opportunity (the anti-poverty program), once again working for Shriver. My task was to design the original plan for the National Upward Bound Program that was to be proposed to Shriver and then, after its acceptance, to work on the guidelines for prospective grantees. Because of what I had learned by then about the "colonial" nature of education for poor kids, in both the Philippines and the United States, I fought vigorously and (ultimately) successfully to establish a policy that excluded the public high schools that were already so clearly failing poor and minority kids from eligibility as initiators of Upward

Bound Programs. Some forty-five years and tens of thousands of students later, the Upward Bound Program continues, its long-term success due in part, in my estimation, to some of those original restrictions we put in place.

On a more personal note, the contacts I made with a few volunteers who became lifelong friends and colleagues were also of great significance. For example, I think I must have hired Duncan Yaggy at least three times in the decade after his Peace Corps service (he was so obviously more competent than I.) Both Jerry Poznak and Marjorie Pfankuch-Bakken moved serially into the Cambridge apartment upstairs from us during their stints at Harvard Graduate School, and both worked with me in Upward Bound Programs at Brandeis and Tufts. Bakken and I even taught different sections of a college freshman International Relations course at a local Boston school.

Mostly through Larry Fuchs' initiative, we were also able to keep in regular touch with other staff families, in particular the Warrens and the Corts, as well as Larry's family. Together with the volunteers mentioned above, we enjoyed a post-Peace Corps network.

In Retrospect

In retrospect, looking through the long lens of history, I don't believe the Peace Corps provided much "added value" to either the Philippines or the United States, nor would it have been realistic to expect it to. The Peace Corps perhaps added a little "cement" to the already close post-colonial relationship between the two countries, which probably came in handy for the United States during the Vietnam War, when the Philippines was a major Asian staging base for American Air, Naval, and Intelligence forces.

The main value, of course, was to the many individual Peace Corps volunteers and the individual Filipinos with whom they interacted, whose lives were quite significantly altered as a result of their interactions. (Mike Forman who found and married his lifelong partner in the Philippines, leaps to mind.) Many of the early Peace Corps volunteers, who asked not what their country could do for them and joined when not much was known about what they were joining, had subsequent careers whose trajectories were significantly altered because of the experience. But, I can't for the life of me figure out how that aggregated much beyond their personal life experiences.

Harvey Pressman is currently President of the Central Coast Children's Foundation. Prior to becoming an eccentric philanthropist, he has, at various times, been (1) a writer of non-fiction books and articles on subjects relating to assistive technology, education, disability and the like, (2) the founder and director of a variety of demonstration programs in education and the human services, (3) a singer/actor, (4) an editor, (5) a college professor, (6) a teacher trainer, (7) a "senior leagues" baseball player, (8) a foundation executive,(9) a board member of a variety of non-profit organizations, (10) a Peace Corps bureaucrat, and (11) a "jack-of-all-trades" consultant in a number of totally unrelated areas. The variety of these experiences can be attributed to (1) a serious case of adult-onset attention deficit disorder, (2) his advanced age, and (3) the fact that he regularly got fired every five years or so. He resides in Monterey, California.

Charles F. Dey
An Unintended Consequence

In 1961, I had no thought of joining the Peace Corps. I was new to the Dartmouth administration as Assistant Dean of the College and had much to learn. With daughters aged 3 and 2, we were getting our bearings in Hanover, New Hampshire. Thanks to a college mortgage subsidy, we were moving into our first home.

No doubt influenced by Peace Corps media hype, at the second semester college registration, I inserted a brief questionnaire asking students to respond if they might be interested in Peace Corps service. Almost as an afterthought, I forwarded the results to Peace Corps Washington—some 850 of the 2500 students had responded positively.

The next thing I knew, I received a call asking if two Peace Corps representatives might visit this presumed recruiting goldmine and talk with prospective Dartmouth volunteers.

Two senior staff persons, Harris Wofford and Bill Delano, spent two days interviewing on campus. Before departing they asked if I would be willing to serve. Peace Corps Director Sargent Shriver believed that college deans, accustomed to the unexpected, were just what he needed to ride herd on volunteers in unfamiliar, challenging circumstances.

The lessons were many. The reality of being light skinned novelties in a dark skinned barrio was only the beginning. With two daughters and a pregnant wife, we soon moved into Legaspi, the capital of Albay province in Southern Luzon. From a reasonably modern house, we were able to provide a Peace Corps office and guest quarters for visiting volunteers.

Given that volunteers were scattered over some 200 square miles (or more), communication was ever difficult. On the other hand, when the need was medical assistance or evacuation, the Peace Corps doctor and Air Force evacuation team responded with reassuring alacrity.

At times, life seemed to be a never ending series of personal turmoil. When a volunteer told me she wanted to marry a Filipino professor, I used my counseling skills as a dean to persuade her to return home to Nebraska. If after 6 months she still wanted to marry him, she would have my full support.

Peace Corps Washington had other ideas. "To gain Congressional approval for a budget increase, we cannot have volunteers coming home." As surrogate father of the bride, with huge misgivings, I gave her in marriage. At our 50th Peace Corps Anniversary reunion in 2011, I anticipate seeing them again—he retired from a tenured position at Cal State, she an accomplished educator and entrepreneur, they parents of five high achieving young adults. So much for my dean-like omniscience!

Perhaps the greatest learning curve for this history teacher was the dispiriting legacy of colonialism—deference to lighter skinned people, wanting to please in responses to foreigners, Filipinos having to accommodate to institutions and cultural grafting that left a sometimes inauthentic mix of East and West. Through it all, however, they had quite remarkably preserved layers of enthusiastic hospitality and gentle decency.

Nonetheless, centuries of deference to westerners, whether Spanish or American, had institutionalized and prolonged Filipino dependence that inevitably undermined individual and national self confidence. I would never teach colonialism the same way again.

Closer to home, Phoebe and I will be ever grateful for relationships with so many volunteers of varied ages and backgrounds, caring and courageous countrymen giving of themselves to others. Had the pioneering PC groups not had the personal qualities necessary to surmount the frustrations and disappointments of their early service, we would not be celebrating a Peace Corps 50 years later.

Charley and Phoebe Dey returned home to Dartmouth College with daughters and their 5-month-old American brother born in the Philippines. Charley resumed his duties as Associate Dean of the College. Shortly thereafter, in the wake of President Kennedy's assassination and civil rights upheaval, he developed a transition program, A Better Chance, for talented, minority students to integrate private secondary schools. Throughout his career Charley has been preoccupied with how to harness the freedom of the private sector to public purpose. As Dean of Dartmouth's Tucker Foundation,

that included education for Native Americans, a Jersey City Learning Center, ABC Public School programs from coast to coast, and a bridge program for gang leaders from Chicago's Vice Lords. As Head of Choate Rosemary Hall, the search included ways to broaden access, increase diversity, and establish a full time office of public/private collaboration. International initiatives included a faculty-student exchange with an elite Soviet math/science boarding school, a Young Science Scholars program for 11th graders from around the globe, and assisting South African schools in their efforts to loosen the bonds of apartheid. More recently, with the National Organization on Disability, he founded and directed Start on Success, a coalition of school districts, universities, hospitals, businesses and special education teachers that has prepared over 3500 low income, mostly minority high school students with disabilities for competitive employment. Charley and Phoebe now live in Walpole, New Hampshire. They have 4 grandchildren. In 2006 Charley was honored as a recipient of The Purpose Prize for social innovators over 60; and in 2010, his 80th year, he received the Harvard Graduate School of Education Alumni Award for Outstanding Contribution to Education.

(The first photo shows Charley and Phoebe with their two daughters, Penny and Robin; the second shows Charley and Phoebe in recent years.)

Aniceto "Annie" Gison Bontrager
(As told to Maureen Carroll)

The Job of My Life

When the two airplanes carrying the first group of Peace Corps Volunteers landed within a short time of each other at the Manila International Airport on October 12, 1961, I was there. Although I was a mere secretary for Peace Corps, I was invited to stand in the reception line with high level Filipino and American officials. I remember feeling so glad that the volunteers had arrived safely, and I was thrilled to be meeting so many Americans for the first time in my life.

I had been on the job for just a few months, the first Filipino hire of the Peace Corps. I had graduated from Far Eastern University and had worked as a secretary for a British firm. I was also quite active in semi-professional basketball and volleyball leagues, having traveled to Hong Kong for a volley ball tournament.

I wound up at the Peace Corps through sheer serendipity. Having always wanted to travel to the U.S., perhaps to stay, I applied to the U.S. Embassy for a job in June or July of 1961. Sadly, I was told that there were no openings, BUT there was a new American organization coming to the Philippines that needed some help. I was referred to Dr. Larry Howard, Peace Corps Associate Director, and after a second interview with the Director, Dr. Larry Fuchs, I was hired. Dr. Howard and I worked in a home in Santa Ana before we were able to move to the Peace Corps office at 728 Herran Street. At the time I was hired, I knew nothing about the Peace Corps mission or philosophy.

What I recall about the volunteers in those first days after their arrival was how friendly they seemed and how wide-eyed and open-mouthed they were in taking in the reality of the Philippines. I think they were a bit surprised at some of what they saw, perhaps a bit shocked. They also seemed surprised to find that so many of us spoke good English, which I had studied since kindergarten, as most children did.

Soon after the arrival of the volunteers, I moved out to Los Baños to continue to work with Dr. Howard. I was housed in the same dormitory as the girls, but I had a private space instead of being in the large room with all the bunk beds. When a volunteer got sick, she would become a roommate of mine for a short time. I really enjoyed my time there and was appreciative of how helpful the volunteers and staff were in helping me to do my job well. One volunteer, in particular, would come to my office at the end of each day to turn in gas receipts. Dr. Howard had enlisted the volunteers to help in the administration of the program. He asked for "farm boys" to volunteer to run the car pool of U.S. Air Force jeeps that had been lent to Peace Corps. Emery Bontrager from Kansas was one of those who volunteered. An additional duty for Emery, assigned by Dr. Howard, was to be my driver when I needed to go up and down the hill from Mt. Makiling to Los Baños town to buy supplies or run other errands. It was clear that he really liked me but I was not attracted to him at that time—he was so skinny!

Several months later, after the first PCV conference in March of 1962, Emery invited me to go to a movie with him. I couldn't go without a chaperone, so PCV Sondra Williams volunteered to accompany us on our first date. In January of 2011, Emery and I will celebrate our 46th wedding anniversary.

The Filipino cultural practices around dating and my own very strict father did not make it easy for Emery to win my hand. The first time that Emery visited me at my home, my father stayed in the room with us, not engaging in the conversation, but listening to us while pretending to read. He would not allow us to go out. In fact, much later, when Emery asked for my father's permission to marry me, my father refused. He didn't like his second to youngest daughter, his favorite, marrying a foreigner and moving far away. He also believed that Americans got divorced too frequently.

My father was a wonderful provider for his family of nine children—six girls and three boys, but he was a very stern man who never smiled. He had two degrees, one in Veterinary Science and one in Agriculture from Kansas State University and was the first director of The National Government Bureau of Animal Husbandry. Early in the 20th century, the Americans had selected promising young Filipinos to go abroad to study, and my father was selected. His experience was challenging, as the only Filipino in the Kansas community, and he did not seem to have pleasant memories of that time—which probably also affected his view of Emery as a potential son-in-law. Love won out, however, and in October 1964, I left the Philippines to "visit" Emery and Tom Carlton in Los Angeles. In January 1965 Emery and I married. When we returned to the Philippines for a visit in 1967, my father treated Emery like a son.

I had learned a lot about adjusting to another culture by listening to the volunteers talk about their experiences in the barrios and observing them at their posts when I visited them. Nevertheless, that didn't prepare me for my own cultural adjustments when I first arrived in the States. Since I had come from a comfortable family, I had never cooked or cleaned house, and our house, built of solid mahogany in 1784, was spacious and well-furnished. Emery and I could afford only a very small apartment in south LA near Watts.

All of our furniture was handed down from Tom Carlton's family and friends. Faced with the housekeeping tasks, I often cried and accused Emery of marrying me to be a maid!

I was unable to work for nearly a year, since I had to wait for my permanent residency. Getting my first job felt like the happiest day of my life—getting out of the house at last!

Another major adjustment for me was being separated from my large family and friends. During my working years I was able to visit the Philippines only every three years for short periods of time. Now, Emery and I have bought a house there, and we spend several months each year. My niece and her family and two sisters live in the house so when I return I am back again in the large extended family circumstances that I value so much.

The scariest thing that happened to me in America was being so close to the 1965 Watts riots. A store near us was burned down, and the looters were stashing the goods they stole in our garbage cans. Emery's parents were visiting us, and his father inadvertently drove right into the heart of the riots. They were rescued by a group of good black people who directed them onto a route to safety.

Working for the Peace Corps was the most enjoyable job I ever had because it was so comprehensive—not just work but lots of interesting experiences, like the time I went with Group VII, accompanied by Jay Rockefeller, on the boat to Mindanao where they were to be assigned. I unfortunately got very seasick, which made it all the more memorable. Throughout my time with Peace Corps, the volunteers were so nice to me, showed me respect, and gave me love. I made many lifelong friends—not to mention finding a wonderful husband and achieving my dream of living in America. I am grateful that the volunteers came to my country and went to the provinces to help us develop. The most important thing they did was to establish relationships with Filipinos in a totally new way from anything we had known before from Americans.

Annie Bontrager had a long and successful career in the Los Angeles area, working as an executive secretary or assistant to high-level corporate executives. She spent 23 years at the Xerox Corporation, where she joined the Xerox Golf Club and became a skilled golf player. She has retained her athletic interest and abilities and has been a champion bowler for many years. She and Emery both retired in 1994 and enjoy a life blessed with good friends, travel, and pursuit of their passions for golf and bowling. Annie and Emery moved out of their tiny apartment years ago and live in a spacious home in Rancho Palos Verdes in Southern California. They still eat out a lot!

Editor's note: To this day, Annie retains the glamour (a wardrobe to dazzle!) and graciousness that made us all love her. She is the one true "sweetheart" of the Group I "kwans."

Bert Pumento
A Priceless Opportunity

In August 1961, I attended a staff meeting at USAID at which there was a lively discussion about Peace Corps. We learned that the Philippines had been chosen to host a Peace Corps program and members of an advance team were in consultation with the Bureau of Public Schools and the University of the Philippines to plan the program. USAID had been designated to provide interim administrative and logistics support. I was requested to assist the Peace Corps Director, Dr. Larry Fuchs. I met with him and we discussed Peace Corps objectives, volunteers, office space and support staff. In the course of the conversation, Larry asked if I would consider working full time. I replied, "When do I start?"

The imminent arrival of Group I intensified pressure to find an office, hire support staff and acquire a myriad of essential equipment, furniture, motor vehicles and supplies. I solicited help from the procurement specialists at USAID. We visited surplus depots in search of serviceable motor vehicles, office equipment and other goodies. Our collective efforts made it possible to finalize a rental agreement for an office, hire support staff and procure the essential supplies in a timely manner.

On October 12, 1961, Group I arrived on schedule. There was the customary welcome ceremony at the airport. I was impressed with the infectious enthusiasm of the volunteers. There was no sign of jet lag. I sensed a flood of energy. Their arrival validated the effectiveness of the support system. Immigration, customs and baggage handling were accomplished beyond expectation. Buses transported the volunteers to the training facility at the University of the Philippines at Los Baños.

Early on, there was a spirited discussion on how to deliver the monthly stipend to the volunteers once they were at their sites. The options were: open individual checking accounts with local banks; use the postal system; or, hand delivery. I thought I would experiment with hand delivery. An acquaintance at the Embassy offered to fly me to Legaspi City in the Bicol Region, free of charge, in his Piper Cub. When I consulted with Larry, he expressed concern for our safety, but I assured him that the prevailing weather was favorable. The following morning we took off flying slightly above the tree tops, hugging the coast line because the directional instrument was in an erratic mode. We landed about noon time, and I handed the checks to the Volunteer leader. After lunch we returned to Manila. I told my wife about the trip, and she went ballistic, accusing me of being juvenile and irresponsible. You know what? She was absolutely right.

In July of 1967 I went to visit Peace Corps/Washington (PC/W). I was assigned a "tour guide" in the person of Skip Conway, a contracts officer, and a frequent visitor to Peace Corps/Philippines. He introduced me to key officials. From Washington, I flew to Boston to visit with my former boss, Larry Fuchs.

I returned to Manila via Honolulu, and I met with the University of Hawaii Vice President in charge of the Peace Corps training center in Hilo, on the big island. He expressed his frustration in obtaining reimbursement from Peace Corps. PC/W refused to process requests for reimbursement because of insufficient information. He asked about my work experience and then offered me a position as a special assistant reporting directly to him. I told him that I needed time to consult with my family and the Peace Corps country director at the time, Art Purcell. I returned to my job and about a month later I approached Art with the idea. He was very gracious and suggested that I give it a try for a couple of months. I notified the University of Hawaii and flew to Honolulu to begin a new adventure. We were able to correct the training records within a few months and the University got reimbursed for its training costs. I was reassigned to the University Budget Office. In December of 1967, I tendered my resignation personally to the Philippines Peace Corps Director who was in Honolulu on official Peace Corps business. I wound up staying at the University for 26 years, 10 years as Controller.

My work experience with various U.S. agencies was wonderful and rewarding. It enriched my life as well my family's. However, if I am to select a *Numero Uno* of my professional experience, my seven years with Peace Corps/Philippines tops them all. Working for and with the volunteers was priceless, and I'm grateful for the opportunity.

Bert Pumento was born in Libagon, Southern Leyte—a small and friendly town. However, he was determined to get out of his village. He enlisted in the army and following his tour of duty he was honorably discharged in 1949. He worked as a night manager in a U.S. Army Officers Club. In his spare time, he earned a degree in business administration and a law degree. He then worked in the Finance Division of the U.S. Veterans Administration. He married Aurora, who also worked at the Veteran's Administration, and had one son, Joselito. In March of 1959 he accepted the position in USAID that led to his employment with Peace Corps.

(Editor's Note: Volunteers knew that Bert was always the man to go to if you wanted to get something done!) Bert subsequently spent 26 years at the University of Hawaii, ten as Controller. He retired in 1990.

Bert currently splits his time between Honolulu and San Francisco, where he lives with his grandson Gilbert, Gilbert's wife Charina, and his great-grandchildren, Gabrielle (9) and Cole (6).

(The first photo shows Bert and his now late wife Aurora on the left with Mary Kinsella, a Peace Corps staff member who later married David Ziegenhagen from Group II standing between them.)

Filipino school children at the door. Photo by Linda Cover Bigelow in San Joaquin, Iloilo. Linda also provided several of the photos on page 276.

Filipino Peace Corps Friends

Vladimir Velasco
Looking Back To a Life Changing Month

The month of October 1961 might have been a blur in the glorious and colorful history of University of the Philippines at Los Baños, but most assuredly it was the most influential month in my young life. I was a 17 year old high school senior when I was handed this unique and rare opportunity to get to know up close and personal some 128 young Americans who were the first group of Peace Corps volunteers to arrive in the Philippines. They were a group of fresh faced, enthusiastic, idealistic and seemingly invulnerable men and women ready and willing to unflinchingly face the challenges head-on whatever they may be. A modern day version of the "Thomasites," those first American teachers who had arrived in early 1900s that my professor father so aptly compared them to. They all seemed to have a *joie de vivre*. The genuine exuberance, naïveté, and camaraderie were infectious. The affection and regard they had for one another were remarkable. I marveled at and emulated their enthusiasm, positive outlook, and humor.

My father suggested that I could do my share in welcoming these Americans to the country by assisting in a month long program of Tagalog language familiarization. So, along with a few of the other Filipino "language informants," we divided the 128 Americans into groups of ten or so. This meant that for 8 hours a day, 5 days a week, basic Tagalog phrases and pronunciations were repeatedly "drummed" into their culture-shocked heads. Unfortunately, the program was destined to fail as almost all of the 128 Americans were assigned to non-Tagalog speaking areas.

From the program I made life long friendships with a few of the volunteers such as Phil Nicholas (and later also with his wife Donette), Jim Turner, Emery Bontrager (and later his wife, Annie), Hans Groot, Gerry Mullins, Maureen Carroll, and David Mulholland to name a few.

Crushes I had on a couple of the ladies—EV Dobbins, Arlene Pearson or Sue Johnson. On whom was my biggest crush? I could not decide.

I was fascinated and enthralled by Betty Jo McMakin's southern drawl and red hair. Her energy was scintillatingly refreshing.

No Exit by Jean Paul Sartre is a play that is forever etched in my memory. This was the play that was produced and mounted in three weeks by an ensemble of Peace Corps volunteer and Filipino actors. What a treat it was to watch Nancy Jeffers and Mary Baker act on stage. The production crew was a combination of PC volunteers such as Dave King, Don Cecchi, and Hans Groot and Filipinos such as Doming Castillo, Leo Rimando and several others. I was this "stage-struck" kid watching from the sidelines. I thought it was a great feat of concentration and determination to work on a role, rehearse and perform in a play while adjusting to jet lag and a new culture. The experience rekindled a passion for the theatre I had kept bottled in. I became very active in the college theatre community. I then moved to Manila and became an active member of the Manila Theatre Guild and other local theatre companies. My passion having been aroused, I left for New York City in 1967 to get better training.

Not until much later did I understand why most of the fellows clapped every time one of the male volunteers entered the dining room at Lancauan Hall. I thought then that it must have been because he was such an important and well respected person in the group. I did not realize that it was because of a particular medical situation he got into.

I remember John Lagomarsino packing an endless supply of toothbrushes. He would tell David Mulholland that it was healthy to regularly replace toothbrushes every six weeks. I listened and took heed. I have since always "packed" an endless supply of toothbrushes.

My pal through the first year of PCV service was David Mulholland. We corresponded regularly. He wrote of his aspirations, frustrations, fears, challenges and happiest times. I wrote of my goals and discussions with my father about my college plans. I wanted to study the arts and theatre abroad. My father thought I should become an agriculturist like him. David wrote of his family, his alma mater (Tufts University), his hometown (Boston), his barrio (Ilog). Indeed, writing was his passion. Through our correspondences, I came to know a very sensitive and reflective soul. As a result of having bonded so strongly in such a short time, I think that his unexpected death struck me harder than most of his Peace Corps colleagues. For a very long time, I felt a mixture of pain and guilt. Pain because I lost a kindred soul. Guilt because he hinted at a desire to be a martyr in a couple of his letters and I neither commented nor discouraged him.

I felt honored when Phil Nicholas asked me to be the proxy for his brother at his eldest daughter's baptism some five years later in Manila. We reconnected a couple of years later in New York and visited regularly before he moved his family to Canada.

Hans Groot is one volunteer who has remained a constant in my life. We are in fact brothers. We joined the same fraternity at the University of the Philippines in the same year. My family has welcomed him as a son and sibling. He has always been a part of every family event. Coincidentally, Hans retired and built a home a couple of towns away in the Cavite province. Although we never lived in the same U.S. city at the same time, we communicated regularly. I visited with him in NYC when I was at the University of Montana at Missoula and he visited with me in Honolulu. When I come to the Philippines to visit, a weekend at least at his home in Silang, Cavite is a must.

Hans was the catalyst in my attending the Group I reunions. I have attended two or three such reunions since. I had the pleasure of helping organize the LA (Pasadena) reunion in 2009 including a photo montage of Penn state, Los Baños, and reunions of the group taken over the years. A flood of long forgotten memories came when I was shifting through all those Group I photos. Choosing which ones to use was so difficult because those photos meant so much to so many people.

Early in the '70s, while in graduate school at the University of Hawaii, I was slumming at a piano bar somewhere in Honolulu when from a far corner, I heard this familiar booming basso voice that could be no one other than David Pierson. There he was larger than life singing in full gusto, full of life, and filling the room with his laughter. It was a joy to connect again with someone from Group I.

Return visits to the Philippines have involved stopping by Jim Turner's "Hobbit House" in Malate and Ermita of late. He seems to have made his establishment a regular "watering hole" for visiting former volunteers from all groups.

I am not in a position to assess the impact the Peace Corps program may have had on their Filipino communities as I went abroad in 1967. However, if any misconceptions on Americans were dispelled and lasting friendships fostered, the program would have been well worth it. Personally, my association with "The Kwans" (that strange name members in group I called themselves which in Tagalog was a filler word for anything unidentifiable or not remembered), in particular allowed me to look at things a little more differently, more positively and with a sense of humor. Laughter has sustained me through the hills and valleys of life and I have only "The Kwans" to thank.

Vladimir Velasco has made Los Angeles his home since 1975. For 26 years, he was the Marketing Director for Malaysia Airlines while pursuing a secondary career acting in theatre and films. He received his BFA in Theatre from the University of Montana at Missoula and his MFA in Theatre from the University of Hawaii in Honolulu. On television, he had guest roles in Hawaii 5-0, Hardy Boys, Tales of the Gold Monkey, Bring 'em Back Alive, Gallagher, Simon & Simon *and* Star Trek (the Next Generation) *to name a few. He has been involved with the East West Players in Los Angeles.*

Several of Vladimir's siblings live in the USA. A sister is retired from the World Bank and a brother is a veterinarian in the Los Angeles area. Coincidentally, another brother was a former Dean of the U.P College of Agriculture and is currently the Chancellor of the University of the Philippines at Los Baños.

In 2009, he was invited to become the first and only honorary member of the Peace Corps Philippines Group I (The Kwans).

Susan Heraldo Carlton
The Paracaleño Perspective

Almost 50 years ago, Paracale, my birth place, became host to four brave young men—Parker from Minnesota, Emery from Kansas, Don from New York and Tom from California. They lived together for two years as Peace Corps Volunteers, helping out in both elementary and high schools as teachers and completing several community projects. They built friendships that would last for years, even now.

I left for college when they arrived in Paracale so didn't get to socialize with them. Yet, because their activities were always top topics in the town, I felt like I knew them all. Many stories were told about them, some good, some funny and some meaningful because they touched so many aspects of the townspeople's lives, from community projects and youth theatre to elementary and high school education. The people loved and respected them for they adjusted very well to the Filipino way of life. They danced, sang, ate and drank (there were funny stories about this but they are better left untold). They cracked jokes, but, of course, when you translate Filipino and American jokes, they are mostly lost in translation. They tried most everything, including dancing the native dances, singing the native songs and proudly wearing the native formal and casual attire like the Barong Tagalog. Their stay in Paracale led to lasting friendships, transformed lives, and wonderful memories.

My life was changed forever when Emery and Annie Bontrager matched Tom and me right after I arrived in Los Angeles in 1968. We were married two years later, and our union produced three beautiful children: Rick, 38, married to Michelle, Christopher, 35, married to Elizabeth, and Elisabeth, 33, the youngest, who lives in Brooklyn. Tommy joined the clan, in 2008 in DC. I wish Tommy had met his grandfather, but he is getting to know him through stories and pictures and calls him Lolo.

My brother, Ricardo Heraldo Jr. (aka Junior) had the following to say about the Peace Corps in Paracale:

> Parker Borg, Thomas Carlton, Emery Bontrager and Donald Cecchi became my closest American friends in my life. My experiences having them as my mentors during their short stay in Paracale was all positive. They sacrificed and adopted the liv-

ing ways of the Filipinos during their stay in our remote small town. I experienced with them walking miles of rugged and jungled terrain just to reach school children waiting for their arrival in barrio schools, the children chanting "Amerikano, Amerikano!" They would hand books and other school supplies to the needy children and even spend their own money just to make sure they had the basic needs for the school. I remember Mr. Carlton (who later became my brother-In-law), teaching English in high school. He gave us all the tools to learn English in a more special way.

I remember that the students never gave them a break during their stay in Paracale. Even after hours, their residence in Paracale was always busy with students at night time just to give them extra attention. They accepted the daily situation with all their hearts until they left two years after.

To sum it up, it was a very positive and remarkable experience having them around in Paracale.

Our connection with the Peace Corps is so strong and we deeply appreciate the fact that we are invited to the Peace Corps functions. We will continue to be interested because we think highly of all of you as a very special group of people who had taught, inspired thousands and thousands of people of all ages, races, cultures in the world. Thank you all for all the good that you have done since 1961 and are still doing now. To Don, Emery, Parker and Tom, the four volunteers of Paracale—all of it was a positive experience for those you touched and will last for generations to come. *Mabuhay!*

Susan Heraldo Carlton is a native Filipina whose family had a close relationship with the Group 1 volunteers in Paracale. She has had careers in nursing, teaching, real estate rental management, and immigration administration. Susan is a beloved mother, grandmother and mother-in-law, and a long-time friend of the Peace Corps. She currently lives in Richmond, Virginia, and enjoys gardening, cooking, traveling, and spending time with her family and friends, especially babysitting her grandson, Tommy.

(Photo shows Tom and Susan after their marriage in 1970.)

Gloria Rada Chu
Memories from Camarines Sur — 1961-1963

While memories from fifty years ago fade with time, some remain vivid and enduring. Between 1961 and 1963, our family in Naga City, Camarines Sur was fortunate to host four fabulous members of the first batch of Peace Corps workers on a shared basis. In a city that is approximately 250 miles from Manila, it's not often that we saw foreigners, let alone Americans. But lucky us, we met Evelyn Mittman, Sondra Williams, Pat Joslyn, and Barbara Mitchell. They were assigned to some of the small towns adjacent to Naga. However, on weekends they came to Naga to experience the commercial center of the region.

My parents, Fidel and Emer Rada (the founders of Moderna Bakery), were one of several host families in Naga who enthusiastically welcomed them for rest and relaxation on weekends. Some of the other families were the Sisons (the family that founded the University of Neuva Caceres), the Bicharas (who owned several movies in town), and the Sarthous (he was the president of the local Coca Cola factory). Although I am uncertain of the direct connection between the Peace Corps and them, I am aware that these families were the movers and shakers of the local Naga Rotary Club. Back then, the club was very interested in community service, humanitarian projects, and exchange programs, so it is probable that these members volunteered to be host families.

When visiting us, the group would join us in our weekend activities, which included dinners, parties, and Rotary functions. I have three sisters of varying ages, Teresita, Linda, and Odette, and it was a chance for us to use whatever little English we knew on the group. One memorable time was Christmas 1962, when they joined my family for *Noche Buena* events, which included a midnight family dinner. Since we had a bakery, they would enjoy the treats and occasionally even try their hand at making some of the local cookies. I also recall that our cute Pekingese, named Pee Wee, was the source of great amusement for our guests.

After their tours of duty were completed, they departed for home. I also headed for America to sightsee at about the same time. This was a gift of my parents for graduating from college. In 1964, Evelyn organized a mini-reunion with some of the group in Chicago. Afterwards, Evelyn and I also got together for a French dinner in New York City.

For almost fifty years we have drifted in different directions, although I wondered about my Peace Corps friends from time to time. The opportunity to reconnect came recently, when I saw a notice in the *Filipino Reporter* (a NYC newspaper) seeking recollections for the Peace Corps' 50th Anniversary.. This set in motion an attempt to find them. I recalled Evelyn Mittman's name and searched for her on Google. Lo and behold, I found her in Washington D.C. and confirmed her identity in a photo showing her receiving an award. With the magic of searching in the computer's White Pages, I found a telephone number for Evelyn and her husband. We've had a few wonderful phone conversations, recalling events and people that came together fifty years ago to improve cross-cultural understanding. Recently, I send photos of our 1962 Christmas gathering to the group. I am hoping that our paths will cross again.

(In the photo: Seated from left to right are Evelyn Mittman Wrin, Gloria Rada, Sondra Williams, and Linda Rada; standing are an unidentified woman, Pat Jocelyn Johnson, Barbara Mitchell, Helen Sales, Evangeline Abella, Teresita Rada and Nelita Rada.)

Emma Perfecto
Letter to a Volunteer's Mother

San Jose, Camarines Sur
December 30, 1961

Dear Mrs. Campbell,

The above appeals more to me than the more correct form, "Dear Madam," which sounds so business-like, stilted, and formal. I can only hope and keep my fingers crossed that you will grant me the liberty of addressing you this way. Every since Bruce showed me a snap of you in a white dress sitting around a table at a send-off dinner for him, I have the strongest feeling that maybe after all, you will not be displeased with my greeting you this way.

Dear me! How I ramble on and on even minus the needed introductions. I am positive that by now you must be consumed with curiosity about this unfamiliar penmanship. Our school, Kinalansan Elementary, is one of the fortunate 28 schools in Camarines Sur assigned a Peace Corps Volunteer. We were doubly fortunate that we drew your son, Bruce. As one mother to another, may I say that you have every reason to be very proud of your only child? He is a perfect gentleman and a born diplomat. He is doing a very fine job of being a goodwill ambassador of the United States and a real credit to his parents. Orchids and congratulations to both of you!

I'm afraid that once again I have unwittingly strayed from making myself known to you. By a happy twist of fate I have been assigned as head teacher of Kinalansan Elementary School since 1957. Emma Imperial Perfecto is my full name. I also come from a family of teachers, which is one impelling reason which prompted me to write to another teacher, you. My father was a teacher—he lived as one and died as one. My mother still teaches—she also heads another complete barrio school. (But she isn't a recipient of the PCV project, and how she envies me.) My husband is also a teacher—he heads another barrio school in the opposite direction of my own school. He also grows green with envy every time the PCV project is mentioned. He alleges that the gods seem to smile upon me every time. It's because Kinalansan is a barrio school along the provincial road, just a mere 4 kilometers away from town and cars whiz by every twenty-minutes or so; while his station is in an out-of-the-way place and the only bus that goes there chugs along at the ungodly hour of five-thirty in the morning and fetches them of the twilight hours of 6 p.m. If he over-sleeps, he has to resign himself to the fate of using his own leg power for locomotion—for the whole length of 4 kilometers. Add to this the happy accident of having been allotted a Peace Corps Volunteer; while he was left out—its no wonder then that at times he grows a bit bitter. I have three children—Amy, 15 years and in third-year high; Marlene, 12 years, a sixth grader; and Edmundo Jr. (we call him "Boy"), 9 years and in the third grade. I have been teaching since 1942 when I was just in my teens (17) and was a mere high school graduate. At that time there was a dearth of teachers in the Philippines (it being the occupation period and the veteran teachers were deathly afraid that if they rendered service at that time their Filipino loyalties would be questioned. I was a fresh high school graduate and I had no such scruples. All I was after was a job to keep me busy.) and the position was practically offered to me on a silver platter. Down through the years, in the midst of raising a family and teaching and housekeeping, my husband and I managed to pick up an Elementary Teachers' Certificate and a Bachelor of Science in Education diploma. I am the oldest of five children and our youngest brother is as old as Bruce. So I practically look upon Bruce as my youngest brother, too. That about rounds up everything about my picture.

Now, for some more news about Bruce. I am sure that everything I can relate about him would just be perfect balm for that gnawing ache in a mother's heart for an only child. Dear Mrs. Campbell, I take my hat off to you! As I write this, I put my hand over my heart and try to feel how you must have felt when Bruce enplaned for this land of ours. I stand awed and admiring before such motherly display of courage and unselfishness. I don't think I can summon up enough courage to part with my only son in order to share him with another people. But you did it! Why? I know. Because, first of all—you are a teacher; then a mother. The Philippines, my mother, my husband, my sisters, my brothers, my children—all of us; thank you for your generosity! With your kind permission, I would like to express my thanks by letting you know all about Bruce every now and then.

Bruce and company made a lovely gesture when they gave an "open house" on December 28. The whole town was invited and needless to say that mother, husband and I made it a point to be there too. We all immensely enjoyed the eats and the company. The PCV's from another town, Tigaon, also came too. I noted that Bruce tackled the potato salad and the preparation of the sandwiches single-handed. And was the potato salad delicious! If ever I have a party, I think I'll be tempted to engage the services of Bruce to whip me up a potato salad. Bright and early on the morning of the 28th, Bruce was up to his ears peeling, and cubing potatoes; Ray, with his sleeves rolled up and one of his legs up on the table was also very busy slicing the ham for the sandwiches. Tim, who was already hale and hearty at that time, was very happily serving as errand boy buying more supplies from a nearby town. Warren? Well, he was out of town at that time and he was indeed very sorry that he missed out on that affair when he came back. At about 10 a.m. the girl PCVs from Tigaon arrived, and they, too, pitched in where they could best help. Gini Hopkins baked a tempting sweet potato pie with the help of Claire Horan, who shipped up the crust. At 2 p.m., the people started pouring in. All in all, the affair was a big success! We were especially impressed with the tasty eggnog that the boys mixed. Ray assured me that in the States it is the traditional Christmas drink and they were all keeping it up their sleeve as their ace-in-the-hole for the affair.

Bruce sent me a box of chocolate crunches for Christmas. The children had a field day dipping into it and before long it had vanished just like smoke. I thought I would also like to let you know and to thank you for having a thoughtful boy.

Before the Christmas vacation set in, I took Bruce and company to a round of parties given in their honor in the different barrio schools of this town and to other towns. Bruce has already been to the school of my mother and to the school where my husband is assigned. Speaking of schools, I keep on wondering what Bruce's reaction is to our schools over here where they are at best—makeshift affairs; where it also rains when it rains and golden shafts of sunlight come in through the roof-holes when the sun is shining. Bruce's introduction to our school was almost anti-climactic. Of course we were informed about his coming a month ahead and we—the entire school population—tried to spruce up for his coming. First impression and all that—you know. Painting the rooms, putting up new fences, new pictures, cleaning the grounds, planting & trimming the plants and all that. Bruce was scheduled to arrive on Dec. 11. But the best-laid plans of mice and men always seem to miss-carry. Dec. 9—along comes typhoon Ellen—lasting for the whole two days with pouring rain. Our school is located in a low place. By the time typhoon Ellen had passed over, our school was a shambles. The waters rushed in waist—deep bringing with it lots of mud and debris. Good-bye to the freshly pained fences, neat grounds, plants & all. We did the best we could under the circumstances but when Bruce finally arrived, he had to slosh though the miserable mud hole that our school grounds had been transformed to.

I guess the whole town of San Jose is deeply concerned that Bruce and company is well taken care of; that they will be comfortable and not so very lonely. Judging from the looks of it, the town and the PCV's are really clicking. Don't worry, ma'am, in our own humble way we are trying all we can to smooth over the rough edges of trying to adopt to a foreign land and to make Bruce's stay most enjoyable and satisfying.

By the way, Bruce fathered the unique idea of exchanging cards with our school children here at Kinalansan. How did the idea go through with your children? Our children are counting the days until the Xmas cards from your school arrive.

Whoo! My, oh my! How I have chattered on and on and on. I think it's time I say goodbye. Regards to Mr. Campbell and here's a belated wish for a joyous Christmas season.

Very sincerely,
Emma I. Perfecto

P.S. When is Bruce's birthday? Please tell us.

(Photo shows Mrs. Perfecto with her family.)

Remedios Sierra

(Excerpts from letters to Maureen Carroll from her former head teacher)

The Significance of Peace Corps…January 1964

Your stay in the Philippines had its effect on your life and habit. Would I be right if I say, attitude also? I feel and believe that most if not all of the PCVs who came here had gone home to the Western world with a greater and broader understanding of our life and way of living. I am glad that the late president had that deep insight into world problems and sent intelligent young Americans who could learn from us and understand why we are what we are. You know I was happier with your coming because then we Filipinos do not have to toe up to the level of foreigners and just be natural and sincere.

The Death of John F. Kennedy…March 1964

We in the Philippines have been deeply grieved over the untimely demise of your beloved president. Aside from his being a Catholic like us, his ideals and principles were identical with our own. As a very promising young statesman, his place in world affairs, his very human family and his simple, sincere and exemplary conduct had been greatly admired and respected. A magazine published here runs a serial on the Kennedys now as it did before the tragedy. To read them one cannot but feel the loss of a great man. Fortunately for her, Mrs. Kennedy has such a strong character that helps to keep her sanity. I can understand and feel for her because I lost my husband when I was only 31 and except for the times and the work of rearing five small children I might have gone mad when the Japanese killed my husband. The after effects of such a tragedy will last throughout one's lifetime.

(Photo shows head teacher Mrs. Remedios Sierra with volunteer Maureen Carroll outside Milagrosa Elementary School in Castilla, Sorsogon.)

Alfredo Hernandez

(Posted as a "Letter from Port Moresby" on July 8, 2008)

Tribute to an American Peace Corps Volunteer

As a grade six student in 1961, my first encounter ever with a foreigner was with Parker W. Borg. He was a 22-year-old American Peace Corps volunteer from Minneapolis, Minnesota, USA, who, as an English teacher, was assigned at our school, apparently to help improve the teaching of English and to boost our curriculum.

Parker, who was among the first batch of PCVs who came to the Philippines in 1961, taught in my school, the Jose Panganiban Elementary School (JPES), in Jose Panganiban, Camarines Norte, Philippines.

Being a foreigner, he became an instant celebrity among the townspeople, particularly with the students and teachers. Likewise, he became a curiosity, which was not surprising—not because he was tall, good looking and friendly, but because he was the first foreigner with whom young students had a field day interacting.

However, as far as I was concerned, Parker's first year in our town was uneventful.

The next year, he moved to the community high school, the Jose Panganiban High School (JPHS), where I was a first year student.

It was at this time that I had worked closely with Parker. As part of his job to teach English and literature, he was also the adviser to the school's campus newspaper, *The Waves*.

Incidentally, I had just been recruited to join its staff and showing up at the campus paper's office for the first time where he was at work with some English teachers. I knew I did not surprise him.

Parker knew me very well from his stint at the elementary school the previous year. He was the one who helped me work my speech which I delivered during our graduation just three months ago. For Parker, my joining the campus paper's editorial staff was just a matter of course and he expected it.

When we were preparing the paper's edition for the first grading period, I submitted a poem—my first—which I titled "The sky has a million eyes".

Taking an interest in what I had written, Parker sat down with me to point out what was wrong with my stuff. Of course he was aware that it was my first attempt at writing poetry. He told me that many poets started in the same way as I did. It was a big consolation for me simply because I had no idea how a poem looked like or how it was supposed to be written.

A literary critic that he was, Parker minced my masterpiece—word for word, line by line and verse by verse—taking notes of the inconsistencies in my rhythm, beat and meter—all basic ingredients that should strictly play harmoniously in poems with such a style.

Finally, he was satisfied with the changes and ultimately, with the finished product, while I felt some numbness in my face due to embarrassment over my rubbish creation. He explained that poetry submitted for publication should not be edited—it is either accepted or rejected by the editor. That's why when it is returned to the contributor, the editor would usually attach his comments on how he believed the poem could be improved.

In my case, however, or in the case of my submitted work, my "masterpiece" had to undergo such intense processing to extract the gem from the raw materials which actually were the words that I heaped all over the poem's four verses.

He told me: If you want to write poetry, you should start reading the works of great masters like English poet Shakespeare or Spanish poet Lorca.

However, as a teenager and first-year student at that, my interest did not swerve toward reading the works of the masters but onto something else like playing the guitar and listening to the music of the Beatles who were then taking the world by storm.

My poetry "The sky has a million eyes" finally saw print when The Waves was published at the end of the first grading period. It was also my first time to see the byline "By Alfredo P Hernandez".

When Parker returned to the United States in 1963 after finishing his two-year tour of duty at our school, he left with me all his pocketbooks and several other reading materials. He told me: Get the habit of reading ... it will help you later when you decide to write or become a journalist.

Twenty-two years later in 1984, I suddenly had an urge to find out about my friend Parker Borg. That time, I was the deputy chief of the Japanese newspaper *Yomiuri Shimbun* at its bureau in Manila, headed by a Japanese journalist. Yomiuri was then and still today's biggest newspaper in the world with a daily circulation of over 15 million—both in Japan and in Japanese communities across the U.S.

The truth is that I had just been sacked along with 24 other journalists at the daily newspaper *Times Journal*, where I previously worked for eight years when the management learned of the labor union that we organized. TJ was owned by Benjamin "Kokoy" Romualdez, brother of the former First Lady Imelda Romualdez Marcos. Losing my job at the *Times Journal*, I found a fresh start with *Yomiuri*, where I worked for the next eight years.

While having an after-hour drink at my favorite watering hole in Ermita, Manila, I happened to meet an American who turned out to be a former PCV holidaying in the Philippines.

I told him about my old friend Parker Borg. He suggested that I wrote the U.S. Embassy in Manila for a trace on Parker. Surprisingly, just three weeks after I requested our contacts at the embassy for his whereabouts, I received a surprise letter from no-one else but Parker Borg, who was now 46 years old.

Alfredo Hernandez began a career as a working journalist while he was still a student. Seeing the streets teeming with military vehicles and troops on September 21, 1972 and suspecting that martial law would soon be declared, he grabbed all the incriminating material about his political views from the office of his university newspaper UE Dawn, *dumped them in the sewer, and thus avoided arrest and detention. Freddy subsequently took a job as a reporter with the* Times Journal of Manila, *but was told he needed to get a security clearance. Though he postponed action for a year, he eventually met a security officer who confronted him with the dossier about his student activities. Freddy got the necessary passes after he explained that he was now married and a family man.*

While covering social issues in 1977, the Secretary of Social Services provided exclusively to Freddie an internal report, commissioned by her Ministry, about the sad state of the delivery of social services in the Philippines. This was a big story because the Ministry was under the patronage of the President's wife. The Minister had leaked the report to Freddy because she believed that only the Times Journal *would have the guts to print it. Freddy's work yielded a front page headline with his bi-line, applause from the Secretary and her staff, a tough conversation with President Marcos, and once again almost detention. The Secretary was forced to resign within two weeks. Freddie remained at the* Times Journal *until 1983, when he was fired for organizing a company union. He continued his journalism career as a correspondent for Japanese newspapers in Manila.*

In 1992 he worked for a public relations organization that assigned him to set up a clandestine press bureau to write favorable stories about Gloria Macapagal Arroyo during her first political campaign as a candidate for the Philippine Senate. He spent two days with her and then the next four months churning out stories, which may have helped get her elected.

While doing free lance work in 1993, Freddy was offered a position to move to Port Moresby, Papua New Guinea to help launch a new daily newspaper, the National, *which has become the country's largest. For many years he also maintained a weekly blog called "Letters from Port Moresby." His current primary outside interest is the promotion of Tembari Children's Care, an orphanage dedicated to providing support for children whose parents have died because of HIV/AIDS. Information is available at http://tembari.blogspot.com.*

(The Photo shows journalist Freddy Hernandez seated in front of two rebel soldiers at the Manila Intercon Hotel during a December 1989 coup attempt against the government of Corazon Aquino.)

Ravelo V. Argamaso, M.D.
Lipoma of the Hand—A Story of Candelaria

From *The International Journal for Plastic and Reconstructive Surgery*, 1984

After a seven year stint of postgraduate training in the United States, I returned to the Philippines. I was unable to find a teaching position in Manila, so proceeded to Iloilo. At the Iloilo Mission Hospital, I was appointed consultant in plastic surgery. In those days, being a consultant did not make a difference in such a small community. Any United States trained doctor worth his salt was good enough to treat the sick regardless of their illnesses. As it was customary for a hospital-based doctor to care for all patients seeking treatment, I was also cast into the role of a generalist. Between the years 1961 and 1963, I was tracking down all sorts of intestinal parasites, draining amoebic abscesses of the liver, extirpating goiters, assisting mothers deliver their babies, etc. Now and then I would be the specialist to whom burn victims, patients with cleft lips or palates, and those with skin tumors and facial trauma would be referred.

An experience with one remarkable patient stays vivid in my mind.

Candelaria was discovered by a member of the Peace Corps in a seemingly forsaken barrio in the province of Capiz. She was not different from other children who were scrawny, shabby and shy. What attracted attention to her was this enormous-sized tumor which was attached to her right hand like a bowling ball. There were times when she would carry this hand in a sling suspended around her neck.

In spite of her functional handicap, she looked upon it with a certain degree of humor. It was her good luck charm, although it was hideous looking. Her family believed this unsightly lump issued talismanic influences. To simple folk whose minds were steeped in superstition, whatever good fortune came upon them, whether it be a good harvest or to win in a gambling spree, it was attributed to Candelaria's mysterious tumor which had grown in the past nine years.

About the same year my practice started in Iloilo, Richard Holzman, a new member of the United States Peace Corps came to Mambusao in the province of Capiz. Capiz is known for the beautiful lamp shades fashioned from shells that bear its name. This young man easily captivated the natives by his extremely good looks and above all by his gentle ways. At 6'4" he was a tower of brawn compared with the diminutive Filipinos. He succeeded where others failed, in convincing Candelaria's parents to let him bring their daughter from Capiz to Iloilo for the operation. This would mean a day's trip for the child who had never been away from home. In Iloilo he heard there was a plastic surgeon. Our meeting could not have happened under a more auspicious circumstance.

The lipoma or fat tumor is not very common in the hand. I have seen only a few within the last 30 years. These are usually benign and symptomless. Symptoms appear only when they extend to compressed nerves or blood vessels. When they involve tendons or intrinsic muscles of the hand, functional disturbances may occur. Candelaria's tumor was the largest lipoma I have removed from the hand. Surgery was performed at the Iloilo Mission Hospital. Historically, this hospital holds the distinction of being the first school of nursing in the Philippines. This institution was under the auspices of the American Baptist Foreign Mission.

Richard Holzman was a spectator during the operation. The skin flaps outlined before the incision and the manner they were made to fit together at closing time was commonplace of course with plastic surgeons because they always think "flaps." To him, however, it was something short of a miracle. What Richard did not begin to realize was that his involvement in the welfare of the patient would result in a greater miracle.

Candelaria regained the full use of her hand. Just before returning home to the United States, Richard gave Candelaria a piglet. The life of this poverty stricken provincial girl gradually transformed from this point on. I remember on her first night at the hospital she refused to sleep in a bed, mattress and all. Throughout her life she always slept on floors. The miracle unfolds in the following 22 years. Influenced by the members of the Peace Corps, particularly by her benefactor, Candelaria worked hard and studied well. Through hard endeavor and good management, she became an entrepreneur in pig farming. She is also an outstanding member of the community. Her business has diversified. More importantly, her lifestyle has changed. She has become a caring and grateful person. Recently, Richard returned to the Philippines and visited Mambusao. To his great surprise and joy, he was welcomed by Candelaria, the successful *provinciana*. God only knows what would have happened to that poor girl with the ugly tumor on her had if it were not for the Peace Corps handsome American.

Dr. Ravelo Argamaso was born in the Philippines in 1926 and received his M.D. degree at the University of Santo-Tomas in Manila in 1953. After general surgery training in Portland, Oregon, he went to Montefiore Hospital in the Bronx section of New York as the first resident in Plastic Surgery from 1959-1961. He returned to the full-time faculty at Montefiore in 1966 and achieved the rank of full professor in Plastic Surgery in 1982 and in Neurosurgery in 1989 at the Albert Einstein College of Medicine. He was considered an extremely innovative surgeon—artistic and skilled. His main interests were in the area of cleft lip and palate surgery and congenital ear reconstruction. His surgical talents created major improvements in the quality of life for these children. He was recognized by his peers with membership in many scientific organizations, among which were the Association of Plastic Surgeons and the American Society of Plastic and Reconstructive Surgeons. He passed away in New York City at the age of 81 in April 2007, leaving his wife Carol and three daughters Charlene, Susanne, and Stephanie and their families.

(Photo shows Dr. Argamaso with Richard Holzman.)

Glossary

Throughout the essays in this book, writers use words or expressions that were in use in the Philippines during their service that may not be familiar to readers, even to other volunteers who served in a different province or region. Spelling, and sometimes definition, for the same terms may differ across essays, reflecting the variety of Philippine languages, the influence of Spanish on the languages, and variations in local usage. In some cases, the writers may never have seen the word written, thus they spell it phonetically. Also, some terms refer to objects, people, activities, foods or drinks that are peculiar to the Philippines. This Glossary is an attempt to provide the reader with a guide to fully understanding the essays.

Word/Expression Definition

Adobo: A popular dish, usually chicken or pork, stewed in vinegar and other spices

Aguinaldo: Emilio Aguinaldo, first president of the Philippines, former general, politician, and independence leader at the turn of the 20th century

Angelus: A Christian devotion in honor of the Incarnation, observed three times a day, and usually accompanied by the ringing of church bells at set hours of 6 am, noon, and 6 p.m.

Ang Boluntario: *The Volunteer*, a newsletter for and by Peace Corps volunteers

Aswang: Mythical creature, often a combination of vampire and witch, always female; ghost

Ay naku/Ay nako: Expression of surprise, like "uh-oh, " or "oh, my gosh"

Bahala na: Resignation to one's fate; Never mind! What will be will be

Bahay kubo: An indigenous house, on stilts, constructed out of bamboo tied together, with a thatched roof using nipa leaves; also known as nipa hut; a popular children's song

Balikbayan: Return to one's homeland

Balut: A fertilized duck egg that is cooked several days before full maturation; eaten as a delicacy in some parts of the Philippines—feathers and all!

Banca/Bangka: Dug out boat, often with outriggers, commonly used for fishing

Barong Tagalog: An embroidered formal garment worn by Filipino men, untucked and over undershirt

Barrio: A subdivision of a municipality—a village; originally a Spanish term that has been converted to barangay in recent years

Bayanihan: Working together cooperatively; the origin of the term is a common tradition in Philippine towns where community members volunteer to help a family move to a new place, literally carrying the house to its new location; also the name of the national dance company

Betel nut: The seed of the areca palm, which grows in much of the tropical Pacific; commonly referred to as "betel nut" as it is often chewed wrapped in betel leaves; chewed for its effects as a mild stimulant that could be compared to drinking a cup of coffee

Bibingka: Sweet rice or rice flour cake

Bicol/Bikol: The southeastern peninsula of Luzon comprising six provinces; also the language of the region; spelling interchangeable

Bolo: Machete

Borrachos: Drunks

Calamansi/kalamansi: A small citrus fruit used in many Filipino recipes and as a juice

Calesa/kalesa/karatela/tartanilya: Two-wheeled horse-drawn carriage used for transport in the '60s

Camote/kamote: Sweet potato; important food crop in poor areas

Cano, cana (m, f): American (sometimes spelled with a "k")

Capiz: Capiz is both the name of a province and the name of a shell that is used largely in interior decorating and for decorative gifts and accessories

Carabao/kalabaw: Domesticated water buffalo used in Southeast Asia for plowing rice fields and pulling carts

Cassava/casaba/kasaba: Tuberous root crop used as carbohydrate source either sun dried or made into flour; tapioca or manioc

Compadre/comadre: Godfather/godmother, sponsors at a child's baptism; a mutually supportive relationship with both the child and the child's parents

Despedida: A farewell or going-away party

Diang suerte: No luck (possibly Bicol expression)

El Tor: Cholera

Encantas: Enchanted spirits

Haciendero: Owner of a large plot of land or big home, usually associated with sugar plantations in Negros

Halo-halo: Cold drink of shaved ice and milk mixed with various fruits and beans

Harana: Serenade

Herbolario: Medicine man, native healer

Hiya: Shame; *Walang hiya* is commonly used to describe a person "without shame"—an insult in Filipino culture

Iglesia ni Cristo: Protestant church indigenous to the Philippines

Jai Alai: Basque ball game played in a *fronton* (court) in Manila

Jeepney: The most popular means of public transportation in the Philippines; Jeepneys were originally made from U.S. military jeeps left over from WWII and are known for their flamboyant decoration and crowded seating; passengers enter from the rear to sit on padded benches along either side of the vehicle

Kanding: Goat stew with Filipino spices

Kaingin: The method of burning portions of lands in the forest to convert it to farmland

Kaingiñeros: Slash-and-burn farmers

Kimona: Native-dress blouse

Kusina: Kitchen

Kuan/Kwan: A noun, verb, proper name or modifier without meaning, meant to substitute for a forgotten word—like "whatchamacallit"

Lavandera/labandera: Laundress

Leche flan: Philippine version of crème caramel, often cooked with more egg yolks than Spanish flan

Lechon/litson: Suckling pig roasted on a spit, usually for fiestas or other special occasions

Lolo, lola (m, f): Grandfather; grandmother

Luminaria: Lights or lanterns enclosed in star-shaped holders of bamboo and tissue paper used during Christmas season

Lumpia: Egg roll-like Filipino food

Lupang Hinirang: Philippine National Anthem, *Chosen Land*

Mabuhay: Long live! Used in greetings, as toasts, or congratulations

Macapuno: Young coconut

MahJongg: A game of skill, strategy and calculation that originated in China, in which four players use a set of 152 tiles based on Chinese characters and symbols

Malate: A neighborhood or section in Manila

Manok: Chicken

Mapa oli: Very dear, expensive

Merienda: A light meal or snack, especially in the afternoon

Misa de Gallo: Christmas Day in the Philippines is ushered in by the nine-day dawn masses that start on December 16; known as the *Misa de Gallo* ("Rooster's Mass") this novena of masses is the most important Filipino Christmas tradition

Modista: Dressmaker

Nanay: Mother

Nga-in 'ka: Where are you going? (Waray)

Nipa: Southeast Asian palm that grows in tidal waters and rivers; fronds are most commonly used for roof thatching and basketry

Nipa Hut: See *Bahay kubo* above

PACD: Presidential Assistant for Community Development, the national community development program in the Philippines at that time; PACD workers often were "partners" for volunteers in community projects

Padi/paddy: A rice paddy; alternatively, the shoots of young rice growing in a rice paddy

Pan de sal/pandesal: Bread rolls very popular in the Philippines

Pancit: Filipino dish of rice noodles, fish, meat, and vegetables

Parada: A town square; place where parades and ceremonies take place, often around a flagpole

Patadyong: Wrap-around tube or barrel skirt, part of native dress; different spellings found in difference parts of the Philippines

Patis: Fish sauce

Peso: Philippine currency, worth about 25 cents in the early 1960s.

Pilipino: During the Marcos years an attempt was made to develop a national language based on Tagalog but including new words to replace Tagalog words of foreign origin; has since been replaced by "Filipino" as the national language

Pinatay: Killed

Pinoy, pinay (m, f): A Filipino; used for self-identification by the first wave of Filipinos in the United States. Both a term of endearment and a pejorative, but is now a slang term used in the Philippines as well to refer to all people of Filipino descent

Poblacion/publasiyon: Literally "town" or "population" in Spanish, the name commonly used for the central *barangay* or *barangays* of a Philippine city or municipality; common features of the *poblacion* include a town plaza, church, market, school, and town hall

Pomelo: Fruit similar to a grapefruit

Portero: Porter; someone who carries things; often used to refer to people in cemeteries who dig graves and do burials

Provinciano/probinsiyano: A person from the provinces; a term akin to hick or hayseed

Sala: Living room or main sitting room in a Filipino home

Salamat gid: "Thank you very much" in Hiligaynon

San Miguel: Filipino beer

Sayang: Popular expression: "Such a waste," a pity

Sari-sari store: A very small convenience store selling basic items like candles, salt, matches, canned meat, etc.; popular small-business or entrepreneurial venture run by Filipinos in barrios and towns

Sinigang: Beef or chicken soup, flavored with tamarind

Sitio: A section of a barrio or *barangay* that is often located some distance from the center of the barrio

Tahong: Green mussels

Tapos na: Done; finished (often used at the end of a meal)

Tinikling: The national dance of the Philippines—performed by jumping through rhythmic beating and sliding bamboo poles

Thomasites: American teachers who came to the Philippines in 1901 aboard the *SS Thomas*

Tuba: Palm wine or toddy made from the fermented sap of several species of palms

Utang na loob: Reciprocal debt—an important cultural value in the Philippines. A sense of obligation or indebtedness to another based on assistance given

Wak-wak: Spirits

Waray: Language spoken in Samar; literally, the word means "nothing"

Volunteer Name Lists: Philippines Groups I-III

Alphabetical by surname at time of entering Peace Corps; married names in parentheses; asterisk indicates deceased. These lists comprise all volunteers who served in the three groups entered Peace Corps Philippines in 1961.

Philippines I

Name	Home State
Waldo M. Allen	Illinois
Martha A. Allshouse (Hull)	California
Mary L. Baker (Johnson)	Ohio
Barbara A. Bassett (McIver)	Michigan
Emery M. Bontrager	Kansas
Parker W. Borg	Minnesota
John M. Bossany*	Illinois
Frances D. Boylston	South Carolina
Patrick M. Brennan*	Michigan
Ellen F. Brindle (Jeronimo)	Michigan
Brenda A. Brown (Schoonover)	Maryland
Joanne V. Bryan (Mallory)*	New York
Carol A. Byrnes (Alexander)*	Pennsylvania
Bruce C. Campbell	Oregon
Thomas O. Carlton*	California
Maureen J. Carroll	New Jersey
Leonel J. Castillo	Texas
Ralph B. Cauthen	Virginia
Donald J. Cecchi	New Jersey
Virginia F. Cochran (Rusch)	New York
Karen R. Cole (De La Fuente)	Ohio
Kathryn J. Conway	Iowa
Judith K. Cridler (Claire)	Michigan
Pera P. Daniels	California
Douglas Darling	Oklahoma
Richard N. Dertadian	California
Elinor V. Dobbins (Capehart)	Illinois
Marjorie A. Donnelly (Clarke)	New York
Dolores Ducommun	California
Judith A. Edwards (Delmendo)	California

Carolyn J. Ekdahl (Wylie)* . . . . Kansas
Susan M. Feller (Siegel) . . . . New York
Phyllis Flattery . . . . Ohio
Michael L. Forman . . . . Ohio
Francis T. Froschle . . . . Pennsylvania
Ethel J. Gardner (Sapico) . . . . Maryland
Leonard F. Giesecke, Jr.* . . . . Texas
Richard J. Gilbert . . . . New York
James M. Gilbreth . . . . Missouri
Elaine E. Gilvear . . . . Pennsylvania
Barbara J. Gladysiewicz (Soohoo) . . . . New York
Hope Gould . . . . New Jersey
Marianne Gould . . . . Massachusetts
Jenifer Grant (Marx) . . . . New York
Marcel H. Gregoire . . . . New Hampshire
Hans C. Groot . . . . California
Anne C. Hankins (Bing) . . . . New Jersey
Edmee F. Hawkes (Pastore) . . . . California
Dolores D. Hawraney (Forge) . . . . Ohio
Margaret M. Heineman (Daniels) . . . . Indiana
Virginia L. Hopkins (Hayes) . . . . Oregon
Claire P. Horan (Smith) . . . . Rhode Island
Patricia Horne (Maravilla) . . . . Tennessee
Clarinda "Britt" Horner . . . . New York
Charlotte J. Hough (Stocek) . . . . Vermont
Martin A. Hurwitz . . . . New York
Nancy R. Jeffers (Schmidt) . . . . Nevada
Paul D. Jett . . . . Kentucky
Lee E. Johnson* . . . . California
Susan M. Johnson (Johnson)* . . . . Ohio
Brian D. Johnston . . . . California
Patricia Joslyn (Johnson) . . . . Illinois
Lee A. Justice (Pelea) . . . . Ohio
Edward T. Kelley, II . . . . Massachusetts
John C. Kennedy* . . . . Ohio
Miriam P. Kennedy* . . . . Ohio
David E. King* . . . . Indiana
Charles A. Kingsland . . . . Oregon
Max Klass . . . . Pennsylvania
Bernice P. Koffler (Roy) . . . . New Jersey
Frank R. Krajewski . . . . Rhode Island

John M. Lagomarsino	California
Blaine G. Larson-Crowther	Arizona
Rayna P. Larson-Crowther	Arizona
Karen J. Long (Santos)	Nebraska
Patricia A. Lutz	Pennsylvania
Luther C. McCormack	Florida
Raymond T. McEachern	Florida
Betty Jo McMakin (Brooks)	South Carolina
Warren L. McNeely	Wisconsin
Stanley G. Mazaroff	Maryland
Jacqueline A. Melvin	California
Melinda L. Meyer (Hunter)	Iowa
Ray F. Meyer	Missouri
Martha J. Miller (Abaya)	Missouri
Barbara A. Mitchell	New Jersey
Evelyn M. Mittman (Wrin)	Illinois
David A. Mulholland*	Massachusetts
Gerald W. Mullins	Wisconsin
Patricia A. Nash	Montana
Philip G. Nicholas	New York
Leo A. Pastore*	Massachusetts
Gloria M. Paulik (Sampson)	Illinois
Arlene A. Pearson (Gilbert)	Illinois
Ronald J. Peters	New York
A. Timothy Peterson*	Hawaii
Marjorie B. Pfankuch (Bakken)	Wisconsin
Sally H. Pierce (McCandless)	Vermont
David J. Pierson	Massachusetts
Michael F. Rosenthal	Connecticut
William P. Rowe	Idaho
Charles D. Schmidt	Maryland
John B. Seidensticker	Texas
Thomas W. Sharpless	Florida
Elizabeth A. Sherriffs (Anderson)	California
Jack R. Simnick	Indiana
Joan L. Smith (Lindgren)	Maryland
M. Ann Snuggs	Alabama
Elizabeth S. Sorenson (Plummer)	Massachusetts
James G. Sousane	Maryland
Marilyn L. Struble (Daniels)	Missouri
Barbara Swanekamp*	New York

Stuart R. Taylor . . . . California
Mary K. Teasler (Giesecke) . . . . Tennessee
Ralph B. Thomas . . . . Indiana
James P. Turner . . . . Iowa
Lynne A. Walker . . . . California
Douglas R. Watts* . . . . New Hampshire
Joan E. Weiss (Landsfield) . . . . Indiana
Clair A. Whiting (Sharpless) . . . . Ohio
Eleanor L. Whitlach . . . . Pennsylvania
Wiggins, Edmond F.* . . . . Rhode Island
Sondra G. Williams (Klein) . . . . Texas
Anne H. Wilson . . . . Vermont
Janet L. Wright (O'Connor) . . . . Nebraska
M. Deane Wylie . . . . California
Duncan Yaggy . . . . Maryland
Donald D. Zelinski* . . . . Pennsylvania

Philippines II

Joan Aragone . . . . California
William R. Austin . . . . Kansas
Dirk A. Ballendorf . . . . Pennsylvania
Marthlu Bledsoe . . . . Missouri
Philip H. Bloom . . . . New York
Sylvia J. Boecker . . . . Illinois
Albert G. Bradford . . . . South Carolina
David W. Christenson* . . . . Wisconsin
Phyllis C. Clemensen (Halton) . . . . New Jersey
Linda A. Cover (Bigelow) . . . . Indiana
Nancy Dunetz . . . . New York
Joyce E. Edwards (Pendleton) . . . . California
Linda K. Egan (Saltz) . . . . Massachusetts
Janet G. Everett (Putnam) . . . . Missouri
Lila Gardner . . . . Arkansas
Charles R. Gostlin* . . . . Ohio
Linda J. Henry (Perron) . . . . Pennsylvania
Richard J. Holzman . . . . New York
Robert J. Hoyle . . . . Minnesota
Becky Johnston . . . . California
Janet S. Karon . . . . Minnesota
Thomas J. Kincaid . . . . Delaware

Annette L. LaBarre (O'Connor)............Connecticut
Hazel Mae Land........................Florida
Richard G. Lewis......................Alabama
Barbara Litrop........................Connecticut
Mark Magee............................Texas
Owen C. Maher.........................New York
Patricia MacDermot (Kasdan)............New York
Frances McDonald (Santos de Dios).......California
William L. Mehlhoff...................Oregon
Michael E. Menster....................Ohio
Robert A. Miller......................California
Leonard Mirin.........................New York
Harvey L. November....................New York
Eric Niels Peterson...................Washington D.C.
Jerry Poznak..........................New Jersey
Eliot T. Putnam, Jr...................Massachusetts
Kenneth R. Rashid.....................Kansas
Norman L. Ridker......................California
Nicholas N. Royal.....................Maryland
John H. Schweitzer....................New York
Phyllis B. Smith (Baer)...............New York
Martha Spencer........................Virginia
David Szanton.........................New York
Donna H. Thatcher.....................Colorado
Susan A. Thompson.....................Minnesota
Patricia G. Toalson...................Missouri
Robert B. Tyler*......................Virginia
Carol S. M. Valentine*................New York
Carl F. Valentine.....................New York
Alice E. Waters*......................California
Sandra Phillips. (Yaggy)..............Texas
David M. Ziegenhagen..................Minnesota

Philippines III

Joy Aspinwall.........................Washington
Edith J. Barksdale....................New York
Phyllis Brunkau*......................Oklahoma
Merry Lee "ML" Corwin.................Massachusetts
Charles E. Downing....................Missouri
Janice B. Durand......................Wisconsin

John C. Durand	Wisconsin
Jonathan Epstein	California
William Finister	Louisiana
Douglas E. Foley	Iowa
Eugene (Sunshine) Gibbs	California
Philip Ginsburg	New York
Wayne K. Guise	Pennsylvania
Theresa Gurzynski (Pearre)	New York
John F. Halloran*	North Dakota
Kathryn L. Hannan (Rohan)	Illinois
Gary A. James	Ohio
Ruth M. Kesselring (Royal)	Illinois
Frederick R. Knoth	California
Joyce K. Miller	North Dakota
Kathleen M. Mooney	Pennsylvania
Thomas W. Newman	New Jersey
Bethel I. Oestman	Colorado
Allan J. Pastryk	Illinois
Neill Payne	Pennsylvania
William P. Pearre	Illinois
Kenneth C. Platt	Wyoming
Ivan K. Probst	Illinois
Thomas C. Robinson*	New Jersey
Dana B. Rodgers, Jr.	New York
Herbert "Chip" Salmon III	New Jersey
Donald R. Smith	Illinois
Barbara R. Simpson (Alexandra York)	California
Marian L. Solheim*	Minnesota
Charles E. Terry	Massachusetts
Stephen W. Wells	Iowa
Anne I. Wilson (Irving)	Maryland
Carl M. Wilson*	California
Thomas A. Wilson	Rhode Island
J. Gordon Zaloom*	New Jersey
Robert F. Zimmerman*	Ohio

Made in the USA
Charleston, SC
10 August 2011